Python for MATLAB Development

Extend MATLAB with 300,000+ Modules from the Python Package Index

Albert Danial

Apress®

Python for MATLAB Development: Extend MATLAB with 300,000+ Modules from the Python Package Index

Albert Danial
Redondo Beach, CA, USA

ISBN-13 (pbk): 978-1-4842-7222-0   ISBN-13 (electronic): 978-1-4842-7223-7
https://doi.org/10.1007/978-1-4842-7223-7

Managing Director, Apress Media LLC: Welmoed Spahr
Acquisitions Editor: Steve Anglin
Development Editor: James Markham
Coordinating Editor: Mark Powers

Cover designed by eStudioCalamar

Cover image by Shutterstock (www.shutterstock.com)

Distributed to the book trade worldwide by Apress Media, LLC, 1 New York Plaza, New York, NY 10004, U.S.A. Phone 1-800-SPRINGER, fax (201) 348-4505, e-mail orders-ny@springer-sbm.com, or visit www.springeronline.com. Apress Media, LLC is a California LLC and the sole member (owner) is Springer Science + Business Media Finance Inc (SSBM Finance Inc). SSBM Finance Inc is a **Delaware** corporation.

For information on translations, please e-mail booktranslations@springernature.com; for reprint, paperback, or audio rights, please e-mail bookpermissions@springernature.com.

Apress titles may be purchased in bulk for academic, corporate, or promotional use. eBook versions and licenses are also available for most titles. For more information, reference our Print and eBook Bulk Sales web page at http://www.apress.com/bulk-sales.

Any source code or other supplementary material referenced by the author in this book is available to readers on GitHub at https://github.com/Apress/python-for-matlab-development. For more detailed information, please visit http://www.apress.com/source-code.

Printed on acid-free paper

To Ashley, Theodore, Mimi

Table of Contents

About the Author

Logan Delancey Studio

Albert Danial is an aerospace engineer with 30 years of experience, currently working for Northrop Grumman near Los Angeles. Before Northrop Grumman, he was a member of the NASTRAN Numerical Methods team at MSC Software and a systems analyst at SPARTA. He has a Bachelor of Aerospace Engineering degree from the Georgia Institute of Technology and master's and Ph.D. degrees in Aeronautics and Astronautics from Purdue University. He is the author of cloc, the open source code counter.

Al has used MATLAB since 1990 and Python since 2006 for algorithm prototyping, earth science data processing, spacecraft mission planning, optimization, visualization, and countless utilities that simplify daily engineering work.

About the Technical Reviewers

Darrell Yocom earned a master's degree in Computer Science from USC and has over 40 years of experience programming in the aerospace industry. Through the years, he's seen programming change from the monolithic spaghetti-Fortran programs of the 1970s to today's object-oriented approaches. Darrell is an avid sailor and sails the Pacific weekly on his sailboat, Stargazer.

Dr. Phillip Feldman, after receiving a PhD in Electrical Engineering from the University of Southern California in 1987, spent six years as a technology policy analyst with the RAND Corporation in Santa Monica, CA. Since then, he's worked in the aerospace industry for over 20 years.

Much of this work involves communications satellites and related technology. Outside of work, Dr. Feldman has a broad range of interests, many of which are showcased on his website at `http://phillipmfeldman.org`.

Preface

In 2018, I was chatting with a young engineer who had recently earned an engineering master's degree. MATLAB came up and she spoke of her frustration with license shortages when projects came due at school. I had the same frustrations—25 years earlier. Had nothing changed?

Of course, a lot had changed.

By then, we had already found our separate ways to Python to do the kind of work we used to do in MATLAB. Why were so few MATLAB users aware of the power and freedom Python could bring them?

I began assembling notes comparing Python solutions to their MATLAB equivalents and shortly afterward learned of MATLAB's py module. A binary API to Python?! Too good to be true. It *was* too good to be true, in a sense; early versions couldn't use critical modules such as NumPy.

The MathWorks improved py with each MATLAB release, though, and today MATLAB can run code from NumPy, SciPy, Pandas, matplotlib, statsmodels, dask, even modules compiled with Cython, Numba, Pythran, and f2py. The MATLAB + Python combination offers astounding possibilities to both languages, yet few MATLAB developers know of this capability or how to take advantage of it. Fertile ground for a new book, I thought.

Acknowledgments

Rachel Rybarczyk's comments about MATLAB and Python inspired me to start the journey that led to this book.

Alain Sei, although bowing out as my coauthor after realizing the magnitude of the work ahead, nonetheless stayed on as my first reader. At our weekly meetings in building R2, Alain put thought-provoking spin on things to keep my perspective fresh.

Rocco Samuele helped elevate the literary quality of the text. While I don't have Rocco's chops for the written word, his edit suggestions clarified my writing.

Ravi Narasimhan's critique of an early draft felt more like a mugging than a review. After the bruises faded, it was clear he'd given me a goldmine of improvement suggestions. Implementing them led to a more balanced tone and more convincing assertions. Ravi also provided the MATLAB examples for the point and line plots on maps shown in Section 12.4.

When Curtis Webb first told me about Numba four years ago, I dismissed his claims that it could make Python functions run 10 ×, even 30 × faster—without using a C/C++/Fortran compiler. Impossible! Yet somehow, like a magical alien technology, Numba does just that. Best tip ever, thanks, Curtis!

Parker Hudnut gave valuable "big picture" suggestions on the book's overall structure. Thanks! The beer's on me the next time we're at building H.

Thank you Steven Millett, Petra Poschmann, Drew Swalley, and Mark Vaughn for tips on missing or incomplete topics.

Thanks to Professor John Hedengren for letting me copy his `predband()` function in my section on prediction intervals (Section 11.7.3). His website[1] has excellent videos on statistical computations in Python.

Thanks to Professor James Doyle for advice on, and a technical review of, the frequency response section, Section 14.13.7. His classic "red book" on structural wave propagation [1] remains one of my favorite technical reads.

---

[1] https://apmonitor.com/che263/index.php/Main/PythonRegressionStatistics

ACKNOWLEDGMENTS

Dale Williamson's insights on structural dynamics were inspiring and educational, and for that I'm grateful; thanks Dale. Errors with the formulation of equations and procedures are entirely mine.

My technical reviewers, Phillip Feldman and Darrell Yocom, are the unsung heroes behind the operational aspects of the code and examples. Both found numerous code errors and saved me from embarrassingly wrong explanations. Phillip guided me through the confidence and prediction intervals in the regression section, Section Section 11.7.3. Darrell was the original "observant reader" mentioned at the end of the TCP Recipe, Section 7.18, and first altered me to MATLAB's type downcast behavior for mixed-type math, Section 15.2.

To the Apress team, thank you: Steve Anglin for taking a chance on me; Mark Powers for shepherding the book from early draft to production; Sherly Nandha for the extensive copy editing and typesetting work needed to turn my draft into a book.

Finally, and most importantly, thanks to Ashley, Theodore, and Mimi for believing in me and giving me time and space to write.

A.N.D.

November 2021

CHAPTER 1

Introduction

MATLAB is amazing—but you already know this. With a few lines of code, you can load data, manipulate it countless ways, view it, and extract its deeper meaning. MATLAB is also a terrific sandbox for prototyping algorithms and exploring numerical experiments, for simulating phenomena, for churning through test results, and for generating reports.

Additionally, MATLAB's documentation and tutorials—either built-in, hosted at The MathWorks' website, or available on YouTube—are thorough and high quality.

The underdocumented and underappreciated MATLAB py module, however, motivated the creation of this book. The py module provides a binary interface between MATLAB and Python. That's huge—it opens a door from MATLAB to hundreds of thousands of open source Python packages for machine learning, artificial intelligence, data mining, database access, astronometric computation, geographic information services, web services, high performance computing, and countless others.

Better still, the power of Python via MATLAB's py is available for free to individuals and at low cost to corporations (see Section 1.2). There is a caveat though: to use py, you must also know Python. This book aims to be your guide to learning Python and taking full advantage of MATLAB's ability to interact with it. When viewed as a MATLAB extension, it can be said without exaggeration that

---

Python is the most powerful of all MATLAB toolboxes.

A. Danial, *Python for MATLAB Development*, https://doi.org/10.1007/978-1-4842-7223-7_1

1.1 Learn Python Through MATLAB Equivalents

As a MATLAB developer, you have a head start on learning Python because the two languages have much in common. This book takes a Rosetta Stone–like approach by presenting MATLAB and Python code side by side. MATLAB appears on the left, and Python, usually in the form of an ipython interactive session, is on the right:

MATLAB:	Python:
`>> format long e`	`In : import numpy as np`
`>> x = [2.3 3.3];`	`In : x = np.array([2.3, 3.3])`
`>> y = [-4 5.0];`	`In : y = np.array([-4, 5.0])`
`>> x*y'`	`In : x.dot(y)`
`    7.300000000000001e+00`	`Out: 7.300000000000001`
`>> whos`	`In : whos`
`Name Size Bytes Class`	`Var Type      Data/Info`
`x    1x2  16    double`	`x    ndarray  2: float64, 16 bytes`
`y    1x2  16    double`	`y    ndarray  2: float64, 16 bytes`

To keep the examples tight, I've edited them for brevity; the actual result from both whos commands has more columns than are shown. MATLAB's ans = line is also stripped throughout.

Helpful too are the many function names Python's numeric and scientific modules share with their MATLAB counterparts. Table 1-1 shows a small subset of these. The Python function prefixes np, npr, plt, and sci are defined with Python statements `import numpy as np`, `import numpy.random as npr`, `import matplotlib.pyplot as plt`, and `import scipy.interpolate as sci`.

Table 1-1. *Some function names common to MATLAB and Python*

Category	MATLAB	Python	Notes
Creation	meshgrid()	np.meshgrid()	Create a pair of coordinate arrays
	logspace()	np.logspace()	Exponentially distributed terms
	linspace()	np.linspace()	Evenly distributed terms
	ones()	np.ones()	Create a ones-filled array
	zeros()	np.zeros()	Create a zero-filled array
	rand()	npr.rand()	Create a random array
Operations	all()	np.all()	True if all terms evaluate as true
	angle()	np.angle()	Angle of complex terms
	any()	np.any()	True if any term evaluates as true
	ceil()	np.ceil()	Ceiling function
	cross()	np.cross()	Cross product
	cumprod()	np.cumprod()	Cumulative product
	cumsum()	np.cumsum()	Cumulative sum
	diag()	np.diag()	Create a diagonal matrix or extract diagonal terms
	tril()	np.tril()	Extract lower triangular terms
	triu()	np.triu()	Extract upper triangular terms
	floor()	np.floor()	Floor function
	histogram()	np.histogram()	Create histogram matrices from coordinate vectors
Interpolation	polyfit()	np.polyfit()	Fit a polynomial to data
	griddata()	sci.griddata()	2D interpolation
Plotting	plot()	plt.plot()	Create line plots
	imshow()	plt.imshow()	Display an array graphically
	contourf()	plt.contourf()	Display filled contours
	spy()	plt.spy()	Display sparsity pattern

While the similarities are encouraging, the two languages have fundamental differences that will be most noticeable in Chapter 4.

1.2 Is Python Really Free?

The source code for Python and its most important modules is freely available under open source licenses. However, there's a world of difference between millions of lines of free source code and a robust Python installation with secure package management on your organization's Windows, Linux, and macOS computers.

At least two companies, Anaconda and ActiveState, offer licensed Python distributions which solve complex installation, bundling, deployment, package management, and security-vetting issues. Both companies permit free use of their distributions for individuals, but charge for commercial deployments.

Large organizations can bypass licensed distributions from Anaconda or ActiveState by building their own distributions—but this requires considerable expertise and adds commensurate labor costs. In addition to the challenges of compiling Python and the hundreds of library dependencies needed by popular modules on multiple architectures, a skilled team would be needed to maintain the organization's private module repository and continuously update and scan modules for security.

In this sense, a Python deployment for anything beyond a small organization is decidedly *not* free. This situation is not unique to Python. Any popular open source software package deployed widely in an organization should be managed with installation tracking, security vetting, version management, and so on. This applies to node and its package manager, npm, Ruby and its Gems, Rust and crates, Perl and CPAN, R and CRAN, and so on.

If Python has a substantial cost, why not just stick with MATLAB? There are four main reasons: (1) Python is so popular that large organizations may have Anaconda or ActiveState licenses anyway, independently of MATLAB and its users' needs; (2) Python licenses from Anaconda and ActiveState are far less expensive than MATLAB licenses; (3) unlike MATLAB toolboxes, extra Python modules do not add costs; and (4) Python instances are not bound to license servers or license files—once a corporation purchases licenses from Anaconda or ActiveState, subsequent Python use by the covered number of developers is unrestricted. This last point greatly reduces logistical hassles for deployment on stand-alone networks and use at home or on the road.

1.3 What About Toolboxes?

MATLAB's full power is realized through a large collection of domain-specific—and separately sold—toolboxes. The examples in this book, however, use only the core MATLAB product.

Nonetheless, many solutions that are otherwise only available from many toolboxes, namely, Mapping, Curve Fitting, Database, Parallel Computing, Symbolic, Statistics, Optimization, Controls, and Signal Processing, are available to MATLAB by calling Python functions. As a simple example, a weighted least squares function exists in MATLAB's Curve Fitting Toolbox. If you don't have the Curve Fitting Toolbox, though, you can compute weighted least squares in MATLAB by calling Python's `WLS()` function in the `statsmodels` module (demonstrated in Section 11.7.1).

1.4 Why Python Won't Replace MATLAB

I'm occasionally asked if Python will replace MATLAB. For certain tasks, yes, it absolutely can. As problems become more specialized, however, you'll find that MATLAB toolboxes made to solve those problems have no credible competition. Controls engineers will rightly insist on one or more of the Controls Toolboxes; engineers that work with embedded hardware will need Coder and the Fixed-Point Designer; aircraft designers will be able to explore large tradespaces with the Aerospace Blockset.

Even in cases where Python alternatives exist, it is much easier and cleaner to call a toolbox function than maintain a hybrid Python/MATLAB code base, keep Python installations synchronized with MATLAB updates, and write harder-to-read code with awkward-looking function calls and type conversions. In the long run, it may even cost less to use toolboxes by avoiding the complexity of adding Python to your MATLAB work flow. The balance of benefits against drawbacks will vary between use cases, individuals, projects, and organizations.

No further mention of Simulink will appear in this book because it stands in a league of its own; there are no Python projects with remotely similar capabilities.[1]

---

[1] Development on SimuPy at `https://github.com/simupy/simupy`, the closest Python project to Simulink, has stagnated.

The MathWorks products are invaluable when you're using them to solve the most niche and technically specialized problems conveniently, thoroughly, and quickly. Python can play a supporting role alongside MATLAB and Simulink but won't be their replacement.

Having said that, once you're proficient with Python you'll find you need MATLAB less. That's not so much an indictment against MATLAB as it is an endorsement of Python. Python, being a general-purpose language, excels at many things MATLAB is less suited for. Let Python take care of the "low-hanging fruit" tasks such as aggregating data from a collection of NetCDF4 files, scanning a directory for Excel files having tabs named "2017 inventory," and reformatting plain text data into a set of JSON records.

Oddly, Python may also be the better choice at the other end of the spectrum for the biggest and most computationally challenging jobs. Unlike MATLAB, Python's parallel processing modules such as Dask are not restricted by licenses, so you can run on as many processors as you can access.

Knowing Python alongside MATLAB expands your problem-solving options. Whether that means solving new problems with just Python or with MATLAB/Python hybrids, you'll have considerably more power at your command than you have with MATLAB alone.

1.5 Contents at a Glance

This book aims to be several things: a Python tutorial; a collection of MATLAB/Python equivalent expressions, functions, and programs; a reference manual for solving computational problems in Python; and a cookbook of MATLAB-calling-Python examples. Where should you start?

All readers, even Python experts, should begin with Chapter 2, "Installation." It describes how to create a MATLAB-friendly virtual environment needed to run the examples in this book.

MATLAB developers unfamiliar with Python can get up to speed by reading—and practicing examples in—Chapters 3 and 4, "Language Basics" and "Data Containers." Once you're comfortable with the basics of Python, skip around to sections that interest you.

Chapter 5, "Dates and Times," covers the details of measuring, reading, writing, and shifting date and time objects.

Chapter 6, "Call Python Functions from MATLAB," begins the heart of this book. It covers the basics of MATLAB's py module, shows how to extend the Python search path within MATLAB, describes the nuances of Python-native variables in MATLAB and how to convert them to MATLAB-native variables, and shows other mechanisms for the two languages to interact.

"Input and Output," Chapter 7, covers reading and writing text and binary files common to numeric work: plain text, JSON, YAML, XML, CSV, Excel, raw binary, HDF5, netCDF. The section on network I/O shows how to write TCP/IP clients and servers in both Python and MATLAB. The first simple MATLAB-calling-Python recipes (to let MATLAB read YAML and .ini files) appear in this chapter.

In addition to reading and writing files, programs must sometimes read directory contents, search for files, get file metadata like size and modification time, and remove directories. These actions are covered in Chapter 8, "Interacting with the File System."

Python and MATLAB occasionally need to run external executables, check environment variables, and monitor the computer's load. Chapter 9, "Interacting with the Operating System and External Executables," shows how this is done in the two languages.

Chapter 10, "Object-Oriented Programming," shows how classes are defined and instantiated in MATLAB and Python.

Chapter 11, "NumPy and SciPy," spans nearly a quarter of this book. It covers NumPy's *ndarray*, the Python object closest to MATLAB's matrix, as well as the many functions that perform array operations, linear algebra, and interpolation. SciPy, a scientific computing package built on NumPy, brings additional capability such as sparse matrices, optimization, curve fitting, and differential equation solvers.

Data visualization is covered in Chapter 12, "Plotting." In addition to the basics of point, line, and contour plots, overlaying data on maps is also described.

The Pandas module for Python appeared five years before The MathWorks added tables to MATLAB. Chapter 13, "Tables and Dataframes," shows the basics of Pandas dataframes and how equivalent operations are done with MATLAB tables.

Chapter 14, "High Performance Computing," explores ways to make Python run faster—and faster Python can mean faster MATLAB programs if you're willing to implement slow MATLAB functions in Python. The chapter has examples of using Cython, Pythran, f2py, and Numba to make Python run faster on a single computer, and dask to run Python on clusters. You'll see that wherever a Python program is accelerated, the analogous MATLAB program can also be accelerated the same amount just by having MATLAB call faster Python functions.

MATLAB and Python both have sharp edges that can bring grief to new developers. Chapter 15, "Language Pitfalls," covers aspects of the two languages to watch out for.

Appendix A lists all MATLAB-calling-Python recipes in this book while appendices B-E contain source listings that are too long for the body of the book. All source code from the book can be found at the book's Github repository at `https://github.com/Apress/python-for-matlab-development`.

1.6 I Already Know Python. How Do I Call Python Functions in MATLAB?

First, create a MATLAB-friendly virtual environment, `matpy`, as described in Section 2.5.1. Then jump straight to Chapter 6, "Call Python Functions from MATLAB." Refer to Appendix A for the list of MATLAB-calling-Python recipes; these examples can help guide your own code development.

1.7 The Recipes Don't Work! MATLAB Crashes! (and What to Do About It)

MATLAB and Python, specifically the Anaconda distribution, occupy a large footprint on your computer. Among other files, each comes with more than a thousand shared libraries. Some libraries are common to both (e.g., ARPACK, BLAS, HDF5, Intel Math Kernel Library, JPEG, LAPACK, Qt, Xerces-C), but these common libraries are often at different—and incompatible—versions.

This is a problem. If you're in MATLAB and you use its py module to access a Python function which loads a shared library common to both Python and MATLAB, which version is loaded, MATLAB's or Python's? The answer depends on several factors including your environment variables. If your environment is not set up properly, the function call may invoke an incompatible library routine causing the function call to fail, or MATLAB to crash.

The best MATLAB-friendly environment I've been able to devise is the `matpy` virtual environment described in Section 2.5.1. `matpy` cannot prevent all MATLAB crashes. An example is loading Python's `matplotlib` module into MATLAB, then making a plot using `matplotlib`'s default Qt backend. MATLAB crashes as soon as the plot command is called:

MATLAB 2020b:

```
>> plt = py.importlib.import_module('matplotlib.pyplot');
>> plt.plot()
```

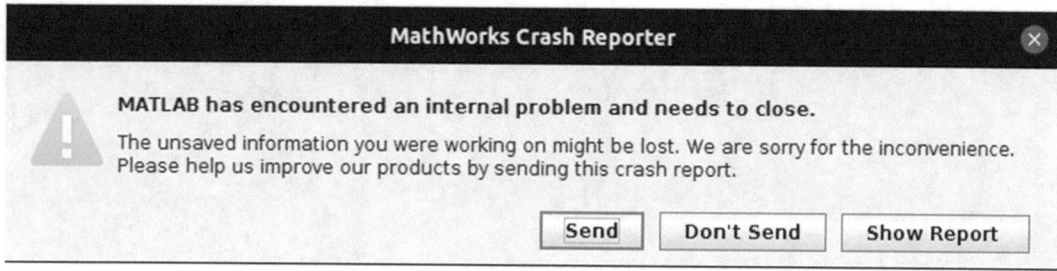

The workaround is to configure a different `matplotlib` backend: TkAgg on Linux and macOS and WXAgg on Windows; details are in Section 12.4.5.

Software on a computer is in constant flux. Operating system updates, security patches, MATLAB version changes, and Python module updates can all affect how hybrid MATLAB/Python programs work from a `matpy` environment.

If an example from this book doesn't work or causes MATLAB to crash, describe your setup in an issue at the book's GitHub page, `https://github.com/Apress/python-for-matlab-development`.

Ideally, I'll be able to post a working solution. That won't always be possible since I might not be able to duplicate your problem or match your combination of OS and MATLAB versions. If nothing else, the problem you hit will get wider exposure—and possibly a crowd-sourced solution.

CHAPTER 2

Installation

Installing MATLAB is pretty straightforward: download the installation package from the MathWorks' website, run the installer, then either authenticate with your MathWorks credentials or provide licensing information. Installing Python is equally easy on Windows and Linux, but installing the recommended Anaconda distribution on macOS is more involved because it requires one to also install the Xcode development environment. Finally, configuring a Python installation that MATLAB can use seamlessly is harder still. In this chapter, I'll cover installation steps, explain why Python configuration is more problematic than MATLAB, then show how to create an installation that can run the examples in this book.

2.1 Downloads

Python installers for macOS and Windows are freely available from python.org. Linux and macOS distributions generally come with Python preinstalled.

It is best to avoid using a Python installation that comes with your operating system, however. If you install new modules or upgrade existing ones, you might break functionality your OS relies on. You are best off leaving the OS-provided Python version alone.

Regardless of your computer's operating system, my recommendation is to download and install the Anaconda Python distribution from anaconda.com. Unless you are making one installation for multiple people, install it into a directory or folder that you own. Unlike the "vanilla" Python installer from python.org, Anaconda comes with NumPy, SciPy, matplotlib, Pandas, and many other modules of interest to scientists and engineers. Anaconda also includes the Spyder IDE, which, while not as capable as the MATLAB IDE, has useful editing, debugging, and profiling options. Spyder even includes a MATLAB theme.

© Albert Danial 2022
A. Danial, *Python for MATLAB Development*, https://doi.org/10.1007/978-1-4842-7223-7_2

2.1.1 Match Your Python and MATLAB Versions!

If you plan to call Python from MATLAB (explained in Chapter 6), you'll need to take care to install a version of Python supported by your version of MATLAB. Visit the MathWorks' website[1] to see which Python versions your release of MATLAB supports. You may need to go to Anaconda's archive[2] area to get an older distribution if the current one is too new for your MATLAB version.

This book uses MATLAB 2020b and Python 3.8.8.

2.1.2 Verify That Python Runs

After you've installed Python, open a terminal window on Linux or macOS or an Anaconda terminal on Windows and type

```
> python --version
```

The result should show Python 3.8.8—or higher, if your MATLAB version supports newer releases.

2.2 Post-Install Configuration and Checkout

The following instructions assume you're using the Anaconda Python distribution.

The first step after installing the downloaded bundle from anaconda.org is to update the installation with the latest security updates and packages. The easiest way to do that is to issue the command conda update in a terminal (pick an "Anaconda Terminal" on Windows). The command will print an error message containing the command that will actually work. It looks like this on Linux:

```
(base) > conda update

CondaValueError: no package names supplied
# If you want to update to a newer version of Anaconda, type:
#
# $ conda update --prefix /usr/local/anaconda3/2020.07 anaconda
```

---

[1] www.mathworks.com/help/matlab/matlab_external/install-supported-python-implementation.html

[2] https://repo.anaconda.com/archive/

and this on Windows:

```
(base) C:\>conda update

CondaValueError: no package names supplied
# If you want to update to a newer version of Anaconda, type:
#
# $ conda update --prefix C:\ProgramData\Anaconda3 anaconda
```

The correct update commands for these particular installations are therefore Linux:

```
conda update --prefix /usr/local/anaconda3/2020.07 anaconda
```

and
Windows:

```
conda update --prefix C:\ProgramData\Anaconda3 anaconda
```

After the update, run `ipython` either from the command line on Linux and macOS or an Anaconda Prompt terminal on Windows to start a read-evaluate-print-loop (REPL) similar to MATLAB's console-like interactive environment.

Our first step will be to make a simple variable assignment and then invoke the `whos` command to see what's in your environment:

MATLAB:	Python:

`>> a = 1;`
`>> whos`
`  Name Size Bytes Class`
`  a    1x1  8     double`
	`In : a = 1`
	`In : whos`
	`Variable Type Data/Info`
	`----------------------------`
	`a          int  1`

Already we see a difference—the Python a is an integer scalar, while the MATLAB a is a two-dimensional array, sized 1 x 1, with a type of double.

This highlights a conceptual difference between the two languages: MATLAB's default data container is a double-precision matrix, while Python's is a scalar whose type is inferred from the value on the right-hand side. Chapter 4 covers MATLAB and Python data containers in depth.

2.3 Creating and Running a Python Program

A Python program consists of Python source code in a text file. The file name does not have to have a `.py` extension, but this is the most common practice. There are several ways to run a Python program:

- On all operating systems, open a terminal which has the Python executable on the path, then type python (or python3) followed by the name of the source file.

- On Windows, create an association between the `.py` file extension and the full path to the Python executable. (In general, this is not a good idea since it will complicate your life when you try to switch virtual environments which will be discussed later.)

- On Linux and macOS, add a *pound-bang* line pointing to your preferred Python executable and then make the file itself executable with the chmod command:

  ```
  > chmod a+rx my_program.py
  ```

When they are invoked as commands, Unix-like operating systems examine the first line of executable text files for the characters #!—the pound-bang, or shebang. If these exist, the operating system invokes the rest of the first line to interpret the remaining lines in the file. Examples are

```
#!/usr/bin/env python3
#!/usr/bin/python3
#!/apps/python/3.8.8/bin/python
```

The first of these runs the env command to select the first python3 executable in your $PATH. Doing so is considered a best practice.

Pound-bang lines are ignored on Windows.

Interestingly, the path to the MATLAB executable can also be used on the pound-bang line to run MATLAB code as a stand-alone batch script:

```
#!/apps/matlab/2018a/bin/matlab -nojvm -nodisplay -nosplash -nodesktop
a = rand(3);
b = rand(3);
fprintf('Random eigenvalues:');
eig(a,b)
```

2.4 The Curse of Choice

MATLAB enjoys a fundamental advantage over Python with its hegemony of toolboxes. The fact that there is only one Optimization Toolbox means you don't have to decide which to use.

Freedom of choice is great, but in the world of open source software, choice adds configuration and installation complexity often summarized as "dependency hell." As a trivial example, consider a software package M that depends on Z version 2.4. You download M and Z 2.4 and install them. Later, you also need package N which depends on an older version of Z, version 2.1. All is well if your software configuration system allows multiple versions of the same package; you just need to install both versions of Z and make sure M uses Z v2.4 while N uses Z v2.1. If you simply replace Z v2.4 with Z v2.1, N will continue working, but you'll break M.

Scale this small scenario by two or three orders of magnitude, include forced package and operating system updates for security reasons, and you'll have a sense of the difficulty involved in maintaining large software packages.

MATLAB's seamless updates and toolbox installations look especially appealing in light of Python's module installation and update challenges.

2.5 Virtual Environments

To simplify package and plug-in installation, many open source languages—Python, Perl, Ruby, Node, R, and Rust, to name a few—come with package managers that determine which dependencies are needed to install a requested package, then recursively download and install those dependencies. The challenge for Python's package managers, pip, or conda if you're using the recommended Anaconda distribution, is that a Python installation permits only one version of a package or module. *This means Python modules with conflicting dependencies cannot coexist in the same installation!* Well, technically they *can* coexist on the file system, but modules lacking compatible dependencies will fail, leading to a broken Python installation.

Python's solution to the problem of module dependency conflicts is to support the creation of, and easy switch between, multiple shared installations known as *virtual environments*. A virtual environment looks and acts like an independent Python installation even though under the hood common libraries and modules are shared with other environments. Each virtual environment has its own copy of modules that could conflict with those in other environments.

2.5.1 matpy, the Virtual Environment Used in This Book

For the most part, MATLAB works well with any Python version supported for that release. In my case, the successful pairing is MATLAB 2020b and Python 3.8. There are two problematic cases though. First, the Python GeoPandas module depends on a prodigious list of shared libraries which have MATLAB counterparts. On Linux, this can be overcome by matching GLIBC libraries in the virtual environment with that used by MATLAB. Success on Windows and macOS can be a hit-or-miss proposition. I was able to use GeoPandas from MATLAB on a Windows laptop successfully for several months until I applied security updates, after which importing GeoPandas failed with a DLL load error.

The second case involves loading compiled Python modules into MATLAB, as done in Section 14.12, to boost MATLAB's performance. On Linux, MATLAB can only import such modules if they are compiled in an environment with a compatible version of GLIBC.

It is a credit to the conda developers that such a fundamental dependency challenge can be overcome. I was able to create a virtual environment with an older version of GLIBC to match MATLAB's simply by "pinning" versions of the needed libraries. With this change, MATLAB can use GeoPandas without issues. This command creates the virtual environment matpy which allows one to run all Python and MATLAB+Python examples in this book:

Linux (Ubuntu 20.04):

```
conda create --name matpy python=3.8.8 libgcc-devel_linux-64=8.4.0 \
    libgcc-ng=8.4.0 geopandas matplotlib pulp cartopy austin faker \
    pint poliastro psycopg2 pymongo pythran redis redis-py simanneal \
    netCDF4 descartes h5py statsmodels pyyaml psutil lxml dask \
    distributed paramiko sympy requests pyflakes uncertainties seaborn \
    cython pytest scikit-umfpack ipython -c conda-forge
conda activate matpy
pip3 install scalene
```

Windows 10:

```
conda create --name matpy python=3.8.8 geopandas matplotlib pulp ^
    cartopy faker pint poliastro psycopg2 pymongo pythran redis ^
    redis-py statsmodels simanneal netCDF4 descartes h5py pyyaml ^
```

```
    psutil lxml dask distributed paramiko sympy requests pyflakes ^
    cython uncertainties seaborn pytest ipython -c conda-forge
conda activate matpy
pip3 install wxPython scalene
```

macOS (Catalina, Big Sur):

```
conda create --name matpy python=3.8.8 geopandas matplotlib pulp \
    cartopy austin faker intel-openmp=2021.2.0 llvm-openmp=10.0.0 \
    libllvm10=10.0.1 llvmlite=0.36.0 \
    pint poliastro psycopg2 pymongo pythran redis redis-py simanneal \
    netCDF4 descartes h5py statsmodels pyyaml psutil lxml dask \
    distributed paramiko sympy requests pyflakes uncertainties seaborn \
    cython pytest ipython -c conda-forge
conda activate matpy
pip3 install scalene
```

The MATLAB command must be started from a terminal session which has matpy activated, for example:

console:

```
conda activate matpy
matlab
```

2.5.2 Commands to Manage Virtual Environments

The following conda commands[3] use the matpy virtual environment as an example:

List existing virtual environments

```
conda env list
```

Create a virtual environment

```
conda create --name matpy
```

Create a virtual environment using a YAML file

```
conda env create -f environment.yml
```

---

[3] https://conda.io/projects/conda/en/latest/user-guide/tasks/
manage-environments.html

Create a virtual environment with pinned versions

```
conda create --name matpy python=3.8.8 libgcc-devel_linux-64=8.4.0
libgcc-ng=8.4.0
```

Create a virtual environment in a specified directory

```
conda create --prefix /path/to/env/name matplotlib=3.1 numpy=1.16
```

Show where virtual environments are installed

```
conda info --envs
```

Activate a virtual environment

```
conda activate matpy
```

Deactivate the current virtual environment

```
conda deactivate
```

Search for a package

```
conda search libgcc-devel_linux-64
```

List packages in a virtual environment

```
conda list -n matpy
```

Delete a virtual environment

```
conda remove --name matpy --all
```

2.5.3 Keeping Your Virtual Environment Current

Anaconda updates their packages frequently. To stay current with security updates and bug fixes, run conda update periodically. The conventional way to do this is with console:

```
(matpy) $ conda update --all
```

However, don't do this yet! Our matpy conda environment was created with pinned versions of modules whose shared libraries need to be consistent with their MATLAB counterparts. Without taking precautions, update --all may install newer versions of shared libraries that cause MATLAB to fail when it runs Python code.

The necessary precaution requires adding a file called pinned in the relevant conda environment's conda-meta directory. Where is this directory? Output from conda info will tell you the location. conda-meta is in the directory shown for active env location. For example:

console:

```
(matpy) $ conda info

       active environment  :  matpy
      active env location  :  /usr/local/anaconda3/2020.07/envs/matpy
              shell level  :  2
         user config file  :  /home/al/.condarc
             ..lines deleted..
```

Therefore, for this particular environment, the necessary file is /usr/local/anaconda3/2020.07/envs/matpy/conda-meta/pinned. Create this file with a text editor and add lines to match pinned entries that were used when creating the matpy environment (see Section 2.5.1). On macOS, pinned would contain

macOS:

```
python=3.8.*
intel-openmp=2021.2.*
llvm-openmp=10.0.*
libllvm10=10.0.*
llvmlite=0.36.*
```

The asterisks in the third numeric position means any value may be used. It's safe to run conda update --all after this file is in place.

Note   conda environments like matpy are easy to create, modify, experiment with, and destroy. Once you have an environment you want to keep for a while, remember to add a pinned file before you update it.

2.6 ipython, IDEs

MATLAB is more than a language; its IDE is an integral part of the overall MATLAB experience. MATLAB developers learning Python may be disappointed that an equally capable IDE does not exist for Python.While several powerful Python IDEs do exist-- PyCharm, Visual Studio Code with Microsoft's excellent Python extension, and Spyder-- only Spyder provides an experience resembling MATLAB's IDE. Rather than explaining Spyder's use in this book, please see the book's Github repository, `https://github.com/Apress/python-for-matlab-development`, for links to videos showing how MATLAB IDE interactions such as editing, debugging, and plotting are done with Spyder. For the text in this book, I will use the ipython REPL which comes with each of the three distributions mentioned in the previous section. While the `python` command itself is a REPL, its user interface is primitive compared to ipython's.

After verifying that you have a suitably recent version of Python (Section 2.1.2), start an ipython session either by typing `ipython` at the command line (Linux, macOS) or selecting an iPython session through the application navigator (on Windows: Start/Programs/).

```
> ipython
In : import numpy
In : import matplotlib.pyplot
In : import scipy.interpolate
In : import pandas
In : import statsmodels
In : import h5py
In : import dask
```

We'll use many additional modules, but if these import without errors, your installation will be sufficient for rigorous numerical analysis.

2.6.1 Autoload Modules When ipython Starts

MATLAB will automatically run commands in `startup.m` in the directory identified by the command `userpath`. This is useful for adding directories to your MATLAB search path, setting `format` to something other than the default and so on.

ipython has a similar mechanism to run commands at the start of each session. This is even more necessary in Python than MATLAB because most Python sessions begin with module imports that should be done every time; importing these automatically is a terrific convenience. First identify the ipython "profile" directory:

```
In : import IPython
In : IPython.paths.locate_profile()
Out: '/home/al/.ipython/profile_default'
```

ipython start-up commands can be added to any file ending with .py in the startup directory below the profile directory. If multiple .py files exist there, they are executed in alphabetical order. I've customized my ipython start-up with the file

```
/home/al/.ipython/profile_default/startup/00-start.py
```

which contains

```
import os
import sys
import numpy as np
import matplotlib.pyplot as plt
from matplotlib.pyplot import plot, show, scatter, imshow, figure, savefig
```

2.7 Python and MATLAB Versions Used in This Book

All Python code in this book used 3.8.8 from Anaconda 2020.07.

All MATLAB code used Release 2020b. This version of MATLAB predates Python 3.9 which was released in October 2020 and therefore does not support 3.9.

CHAPTER 3

Language Basics

The fundamental elements of the Python language—variable assignment, indentation, array indexing, for and while loops, if statements, functions, comments, exceptions, modules—are covered in this chapter. Although classes and object-oriented programming are also fundamental aspects of Python, these will be covered in Chapter 10.

3.1 Assignment

Python supports four forms of variable assignment: conventional, conditional, in-place, and the recently added "walrus operator."

3.1.1 Assignment with =

Variable assignment in both languages looks similar:

MATLAB:	Python:
`>> a = 1.2;`	`In : a = 1.2`
`>> b = [1 2 .3];`	`In : b = [1, 2, .3]`
`>> c = "this is MATLAB";`	`In : c = "this is Python"`

The semicolon at the end of each MATLAB line is optional. Without it, MATLAB prints the contents of the variable to STDOUT—helpful for observing values during development but distracting for working code.

© Albert Danial 2022
A. Danial, *Python for MATLAB Development*, https://doi.org/10.1007/978-1-4842-7223-7_3

Both languages allow multiple expressions on the same line separated by semicolons, but Python additionally supports assigning multiple values with a single =. MATLAB can assign multiple left-hand side values only from function calls, not static assignments.

MATLAB:	Python:
>> d = 4; e = 2.71	In : d = 4; e = 2.71
	# or
	In : d, e = 4, 2.71

Python also supports chained assignment where all variables are set to the same value:

Python:

```
In : f = g = 5.5
In : f
Out: 5.5

In : g
Out: 5.5
```

Unlike MATLAB, Python supports a conditional assignment statement that works like the ternary operator (e.g., x = (y < z) ? y : z) in C, Perl, and Java, among others. It allows assignment of either one or another value depending on a condition:

Python:

```
In : g = 7
In : h = 'bigger than 5' if g > 5 else 'smaller'
In : h
Out: 'bigger than 5'

In : g = -7
In : h = 'bigger than 5' if g > 5 else 'smaller'
In : h
Out: 'smaller'
```

3.1.2 In-Place Updates with +=, -=, and Others

A clumsy aspect of MATLAB is its lack of increment and decrement operators. Python does not have ++ or -- operators but supports in-place updates with +=, -=, and many additional operators.

MATLAB:	Python:
>> a = 0;	In : a = 0
>> a = a + 1	In : a += 1
a = 1	In : a
	Out: 1

MATLAB's a = a + 1 looks harmless enough, but replace a with an element of a nested class or structure, for example, `catalog.volume(j).on_loan.count`, and the text duplication becomes unwieldy.

Table 3-1 summarizes Python's in-place update operators.

Table 3-1. *Python in-place update operators*

Operator	Effect on Left-Hand Side
+= x	Increment by x
-= x	Decrement by x
*= x	Multiply by x
/= x	Divide by x
**= x	Raise to the x power
|= x	Bitwise OR with x
&= x	Bitwise AND with x
^= x	Bitwise exclusive OR with x
<<= x	Bit shift left x times
>>= x	Bit shift right x times

Of course, MATLAB can perform these operations too, just not in-place.

3.1.3 Walrus Operator, :=

The last of the four Python assignment expressions, the walrus operator, or :=, was introduced in Python 3.8. It works like a conventional assignment statement with the side effect that the entire expression, both left-hand side and right-hand side, has the value of the right-hand side. The walrus operator has no MATLAB equivalent.

Here's a simple example:

Python:

```
In : x := 100
In : x
Out: 100
```

Nothing surprising here; x was set to 100. What's not obvious is that the entire statement x := 100 *also* has the value of 100. We can see that if we capture the full expression with another variable:

Python:

```
In : y = (x := 100)
In : x
Out: 100
In : y
Out: 100
```

One practical use of this behavior is inserting intermediate variables in the middle of a computation for use later. Here's the Pythagorean theorem equation with additional variables inserted to store intermediate values of Δ_x and Δ_y:

Python:

```
In : from math import sqrt
In : x1, x2 = 1.73, 9.31
In : y1, y2 = 24.6, -6.77
In : d = sqrt( (dx := (x2-x1))**2 + (dy := (y2-y1))**2 )
In d
Out 32.272795044743184
```

```
In : dx
Out: 7.58

In : dy
Out: -31.37
```

Inserting dx := and dy := lets us save these intermediate values without disrupting the larger computation for d.

The walrus operator is also convenient when working with regular expressions (to be covered in Section 4.2.6) as it allows one to populate a match object and test whether or not it was successful in a single step:

Python, Without Walrus:	Python, with Walrus:
```import re L = "n= Bob" m = re.search(r"n=\s*(\w+)", L) if m is not None: print('name is ',m.group(1))```	```import re L = "n= Bob" if m := re.search(r"n=\s*(\w+)", L): print('name is ',m.group(1))```

3.2 Printing

In the MATLAB IDE and .m files, the results of an expression are printed immediately unless the line ends with a semicolon. A Python REPL such as ipython will also print expressions that have no assignment, that is, without an equals sign:

MATLAB:	Python:
```>> i = 1 i = 1 >> i, length('abc') i = 1 ans = 3```	```In : i = 1 In : i Out: 1 In : i, len('abc') Out: (1, 3)```

Similarly, within a MATLAB .m file, the result of every assignment is printed unless the line ends with a semicolon. Python follows more typical programming conventions and requires a call to its print() function to display output from a running .py file. MATLAB's fprintf() function is a close analog to Python's print() and provides similar capability to displaying formatted text. There are a few notable difference between the two, though.

Python's print():

- By default automatically appends a newline (this can be suppressed by adding the optional argument end='')

- Supports an optional argument to flush its output stream immediately (flush=True).

- Supports an optional argument to write to a given output stream, including STDERR (file=sys.stderr). MATLAB does not support writing to STDERR which complicates error handling.

String formatting in Python is covered in detail in Section 4.2.3; these few lines give a quick preview of equivalent string and floating-point output formatting:

MATLAB:	Python:
fprintf('abc\n ')	print('abc')
x = 1.23;	x = 1.23
e = 'easy';	e = 'easy'
fprintf('x = %8.3f\n', x)	print(f'x = x:8.3f')
fprintf('e = %-10s\n', e)	print(f'e = e:<10s')

3.3 Indentation

A Python hallmark is its use of indentation to define the scope of classes, functions, loops, if statements, exception handlers, and so on. Interestingly, code written in other computer languages that ignore leading whitespace generally end up with similar indentation because this makes code easier to understand and is considered good coding style.

Here are equivalent functions in MATLAB and Python. (Details about Python functions appear in Section 3.8.) The MATLAB code is deliberately not indented.

MATLAB:	Python:
| ```
function [a] = ramp(m)
fprintf('got %d\n', m)
n = 5*m;
a = 1;
if mod(m,2)
for i=1:n
a = a + i;
end % for
end % if
end % function
``` | ```
def ramp(m):
    print(f'got {m:d}')
    n = 5*m
    a = 1
    if m % 2:
        for i in range(1,n+1):
            a += i
    return a
``` |

(Despite the apparent loop size difference, `for i=1:n` in MATLAB vs. `for i in range(1,n+1):` in Python, both perform n iterations. The difference is explained in Section 3.4.) A cleaner layout of the MATLAB code is

```
function [a] = ramp(m)
    fprintf('got %d\n', m)
    n = 5*m;
    a = 1;
    if mod(m,2)
        for i=1:n
            a = a + i;
        end % for
    end % if
end % function
```

Clearly, indentation helps readers understand the code.

How many spaces to indent Python code? It doesn't matter; the number need only be consistent within a given indent block. Most Python programmers use four spaces. The MATLAB IDE editor—specifically its "Smart Indent" feature—by default also indents loops, if statements, and so on by four spaces.

3.3.1 Tabs

Tabs are problematic and are not permitted in Python source code. They are problematic because tab widths are not standard; one person's editor may be configured for eight spaces per tab, while another person's editor is set up to use four. If tabs were allowed, a Python file with a mix of tabs and spaces could give completely different results for the two people—if it even passes a syntax check.

3.4 Indexing

As you'll see in the next five sections, MATLAB and Python indexing methods and capabilities vary considerably.

3.4.1 Brackets vs. Parentheses

Python uses brackets, [ ], to index lists and arrays, while MATLAB uses parentheses, ( ), for matrices and a combination of parentheses and braces, { }, for cells and tables. This difference is notable because MATLAB also uses parentheses around function arguments. Consequently, one cannot distinguish variables from functions by reading MATLAB source code. As an example, consider these assignments to the variable u:

MATLAB:	Python:
`u = G(ind(case_N(i)));`	`u = G[ind(case_N[i])]`

In the MATLAB version, one cannot tell if `G, ind`, or `case_N` are variables or functions. The distinctions are readily apparent in Python—`G` and `case_N` are variables, while `ind` is a function.

3.4.2 Zero-Based Indexing and Index Ranges

Perhaps the most notable indexing difference between MATLAB and Python is that Python indices begin with zero, while MATLAB indices begin with one. Python matches most other programming languages in this regard, but, interestingly, languages with a strong mathematical bias such as MATLAB, Mathematica, Fortran, and Julia use one-based indexing.

Additionally, index *ranges* in the two languages also differ by one. In MATLAB, one can extract a subset of a matrix with start and end indices separated by a colon. Python uses the same notation, but the value indexed by the end range term is not returned:

MATLAB:	Python:
>> z = [21 22 23 24 25]; >> z(2:4) 22 23 24	In : z = [21, 22, 23, 24, 25] In : z[1:3] Out: [22, 23]

Python's z[1:3] returns only z[1] and z[2]; to also get z[3], our range notation would need to be z[1:4]. More generally, for the range J:K, MATLAB returns K-J+1 terms beginning at index K, while Python returns K-J terms beginning at index K.

3.4.3 Start, End, and Negative Indices

The end keyword in MATLAB, among other things, represents the last term in an array. Python streamlines this concept by treating an absent end range marker as the end of an array or list.

MATLAB:	Python:
>> z = [21 22 23 24 25]; >> z(4:end) 24 25	In : z = [21, 22, 23, 24, 25] In : z[3:] Out: [24, 25]

Similarly, an absent start of range marker denotes the beginning of an array or list:

MATLAB:	Python:
>> z = [21 22 23 24 25]; >> z(1:3) 21 22 23	In : z = [21, 22, 23, 24, 25] In : z[:3] Out: [21, 22, 23]

Unlike MATLAB, Python allows negative indices; these count array locations from the end of the array going backward.

MATLAB:	Python:
`>> z = [ 21 22 23 24 25 ];`	`In : z = [ 21, 22, 23, 24, 25 ]`
`>> z(end)`	`In : z[-1]`
`   25`	`Out: 25`
`>> z(end-1:end)`	`In : z[-2:]`
`   24 25`	`Out: [24, 25]`
`>> z(1:end-3)`	`In : z[:-3]`
`   21 22`	`Out: [21, 22]`

3.4.4 Index Strides

MATLAB and Python use two colons to denote an index range with a stride, but the position of the stride differs—in MATLAB, the stride appears in the middle, and in Python the stride is at the end.

MATLAB:	Python:
`>> z = [ 21 22 23 24 25 ];`	`In : z = [ 21, 22, 23, 24, 25 ]`
`>> z(1:2:end)`	`In : z[::2]`
`   21 23 25`	`Out: [21, 23, 25]`
`>> z(2:3:end)`	`In : z[1::3]`
`   22 25`	`Out: [22, 25]`

3.4.5 Index Chaining

An advantage Python enjoys over MATLAB is its ability to index any multivalued object merely by subscripting the object. For example, say you have a function that returns three items:

MATLAB:	Python:

``
function [a,b,c] = Fn3()
    a = 1;
    b = -2;
    c = 33;
end
``
	``
	def Fn3():
	    a = 1
	    b = -2
	    c = 33
	    return a,b,c
	``

If you only want the third return value, in Python you merely need to append a subscript to the end of the function call:

MATLAB:	Python:
``` >> Fn3()(3) Error: Indexing with parentheses '()' must appear as the last operation of a valid indexing expression. ```	``` In : Fn3()[2] Out: 33 ```

3.5 for loops

For loops have a similar structure in MATLAB and Python, but Python's have additional capabilities. A collection of examples follow.

Print the numbers 1 through 5:

MATLAB:	Python:

``
for i = 1:5
    fprintf('i=%d\n', i);
end
``
	``
	for i in range(1,6)
	    print(f'i={i}')
	``

Print items in a cell or list: (Python lists: Section 4.3)

MATLAB:	Python:

`for i = { 7, 'parts' }`
`    fprintf(i);`
`end`
	`for i in [ 7, 'parts']:`
	`    print(i)`

Print items in a struct[1] or dictionary: (Python dictionaries: Section 4.6)

MATLAB:	Python:

`S = struct('one',1,'two',2);`
`fields = fieldnames(S);`
`for i = 1:numel(fields)`
`  fprintf('%s = %d\n',...`
`      fields{i}, S.(fields{i}))`
`end`
	`Dict = { 'one' : 1, 'two' : 2 }`
	`for Key in Dict:`
	`   print(f'{Key} = {Dict[Key]}')`

Multiple iterands

Python for loops allow an arbitrary number of iterands, useful when the iterator has multiple values:

```
temp_data = [ ['Miami', 'FL', 104.1], ['Seattle', 'WA', 83.8],
              ['Chicago', 'IL', 94.0], ['Boston', 'MA', 74.6],]
for city, state, deg_F in temp_data:
    print(f'{city}, {state} temperature is {deg_F:.2f} F')
```

At each iteration, all three variables city, state, deg_F are set to the values of the three entries of the inner list items. The output of the preceding for loop is

```
Miami, FL temperature is 104.10 F
Seattle, WA temperature is 83.80 F
Chicago, IL temperature is 94.00 F
Boston, MA temperature is 74.60 F
```

[1] MATLAB's containers.Map is a close analog to a Python dictionary. In practice though, MATLAB developers use structs much more frequently than containers.Map. Even MATLAB's py module translates Python dictionaries to and from structs rather than containers.Maps.

The equivalent in MATLAB is less elegant:

```matlab
temp_data = { {'Miami', 'FL', 104.1}, {'Seattle', 'WA', 83.8}, ...
             {'Chicago', 'IL', 94.0}, {'Boston', 'MA', 74.6}};
for i = 1:length(temp_data)
    fprintf('%s, %s temperature is %.2f F\n', ...
        temp_data{i}{1}, temp_data{i}{2}, temp_data{i}{3})
end
```

The variable `city` from the Python code has a more meaningful name than `temp_data{i}{1}` in the MATLAB code; to achieve the same clarity, a MATLAB developer would need to define the three extra variables at the top of the loop.

Enumeration

A frequent task when iterating over items is tracking an iteration counter. Python's `enumerate()` function returns a pair of objects, the iteration counter (starting with zero), and the next item from the iterator. Achieving the same functionality in MATLAB requires manually defining and incrementing a counting variable.

MATLAB:	**Python:**

``matlab
i = 1;
for L = {'a','b','c' }
    fprintf('L %d is %s\n', i, L{1});
    i = i + 1;
end
``
	``python
	for i,L in enumerate(['a','b','c']):
	    print(f'L {i+1} is {L}')
	``

Both produce this output:

```
L 1 is a
L 2 is b
L 3 is c
```

Parallel for loops are covered in Chapter 14. If the body of the loop contains relatively simple expressions, the easiest way to implement these is with Numba's `prange()`, Section 14.10.1. The more generic method that works with arbitrarily complex code is to use Python's `multiprocessing` module, covered in Section 14.6.

3.5.1 Early Loop Exits

MATLAB and Python both use `continue` and `break` to, respectively, skip to the next iteration and to exit the loop.

These loops print the numbers 2, 4, 6, 8, 10:

MATLAB:	Python:
| ```
for i = 1:10
  if mod(i,2)
    % skip odd numbers
    continue
  end
  disp(i)
end
``` | ```
for i in range(1,11):
  if i % 2:
    # skip odd numbers
    continue
  print(i)
``` |

while these print 1, 2, 3:

MATLAB:	Python:
| ```
for i = 1:10
  if i > 3
    break
  end
  disp(i)
end
``` | ```
for i in range(1,11):
  if i > 3:
    break
  print(i)
``` |

3.5.2 Exit from Nested Loops

An irritant with both MATLAB and Python is that neither has an elegant way to leave nested loops from an inner loop because `break` only works for its immediately-enclosing `for` loop. One must employ an extra variable to let the outer loop know that the inner loop wants to break out. Some Python programmers advocate the use of exceptions to achieve this goal, but exceptions are just as clunky to code as using an extra variable.

This example iterates over terms in a matrix and uses the Boolean variable done to let the outer loop know that the inner loop wants it to exit. The condition is triggered when it encounters a term in the matrix with a value greater than 0.95:

MATLAB:	Python:
| ```
nR = 10;
nC = 12;
X = rand(nR,nC);
done = 0;
for r = 1:nR
  for c = 1:nC
    if X(r,c) > 0.95
      done = 1;
      break
    end
  end
  if done
    break
  end
end
``` | ```
import numpy as np
nR, nC = 10, 12
X = np.random.rand(nR,nC);
done = False
for r in range(nR):
  for c in range(nC):
    if X[r,c] > 0.95:
      done = True
      break
  if done:
    break
``` |

3.6 while Loops

While loops, like for loops, have a similar structure in MATLAB and Python; both also use continue to skip to the next iteration and break to exit the loop.

The following example uses the Newton-Raphson iteration to compute the square root of 117. If the solution has not already converged, the while loop exits after five iterations.

MATLAB:	Python:
| ```matlab
N = 117; tol = 1.0e-8;
x = N/2;
i = 1;
while abs(N - x.^2) > tol
   y = N/x;
   x = (x+y)/2;
   if i >= 5
     fprintf('hit 5 iter\n')
     break
   end
   i = i + 1;
end
fprintf('sqrt(%f)=%f\n',N,x)
``` | ```python
N, tol = 117, 1.0e-8
x = N/2
i = 1
while abs(N - x**2) > tol:
   y = N/x
   x = (x+y)/2
   if i >= 5:
     print('hit 5 iter')
     break
   i += 1
print(f'sqrt({N})={x}')
``` |

3.7 `if` Statements

If statements look like this in the two languages:

MATLAB:	Python:
| ```matlab
if condition_1
    result = 'in 1';
else if condition_2
    result = 'in 2';
else
    result = 'in else';
end
``` | ```python
if condition_1:
    result = 'in 1'
elif condition_2:
    result = 'in 2'
else:
    result = 'in else'
``` |

The variables `condition_1` and `condition_2` represent Boolean expressions and can take many forms.

3.7.1 Boolean Expressions and Operators

MATLAB's "logical" constants true and false have equivalents in Python's Boolean constants True and False. In MATLAB, one generally represents these with 1 and 0, although any non-zero value evaluates as true. Like MATLAB, Python interprets numeric zero (either integer or floating point) and empty strings, lists, sets, dictionaries, or tuples as false. Python additionally has a special constant, None, which represents uninitialized or nonexistent data (similar to NULL in C-type languages and SQL, or undef in Perl) also evaluates to false.

Common comparison operators for scalar numbers and strings (in MATLAB, these must strictly be strings and not character vectors) in both languages are shown in Table 3-2.

Table 3-2. *Comparison operators for scalar and array values*

	MATLAB	Python Scalars	NumPy Arrays
Equality	$a == b$	$a == b$	$a == b$
Inequality	$a \sim= b$	$a != b$	$a != b$
Less than	$a < b$	$a < b$	$a < b$
Range[2]	*unavailable*	$a < b < c$	*unavailable*
NOT	$\sim a$	not a	$\sim a$
AND	$a \&\& b$	a and b	$a * b$
OR	$a \mid\mid b$	a or b	$a + b$
XOR	$xor(a, b)$	bool(a) ^ bool(b)	a ^ b

3.7.2 Range Tests

The numeric range expression $a < b < c$ is a valid notation in MATLAB. However, MATLAB evaluates such expressions in a strict left-to-right manner so the result may not match expectations. For example, the first two expressions in the following evaluate to the correct answer, but MATLAB gives the wrong result for the third:

---

[2] Any combination of <, <=, >, >= may be used.

MATLAB:	Python:
`>> 1 < 2 < 3`	`In : 1 < 2 < 3`
`ans = 1`	`Out: True`
`>> 1 < 2 < 1`	`In : 1 < 2 < 1`
`ans = 0`	`Out: False`
`>> 1 < -1 < 3`	`In : 1 < -1 < 3`
`ans = 1`	`Out: False`

MATLAB evaluates these expressions as $(a < b) < c$, so the third one gives an unexpected result because $(1 < -1)$ evaluates to 0 which carries into the next expression of $0 < 3$. The expression then evaluates to true in MATLAB which is of course incorrect because $1 < -1 < 3$ is false.

Python expands the range evaluation to $(a < b)$ and $(b < c)$ and therefore gives the expected result for all scalar values of a, b, and c.

3.8 Functions

As in MATLAB, functions are easily defined in Python. MATLAB uses the `function` keyword, while Python uses `def`. A MATLAB function's return arguments appear on the function definition line itself, but Python's are embedded within the function at the `return` keyword. Both languages allow one to return multiple values and to specify optional arguments—although Python allows this more elegantly. Here's a simple example to start. The "np." prefix to atan2 and sqrt in the Python function refers to the NumPy numerics module which will be covered briefly in Section 4.1 and extensively in Chapter 11.

MATLAB:	Python:

`[r, theta] = function cyl(x,y)`
`  theta = atan2(y,x);`
`  r = sqrt(x^2 + y^2);`
`end`
	`def cyl(x,y):`
	`  theta = np.atan2(y,x)`
	`  r = np.sqrt(x**2 + y**2)`
	`  return r, theta`

The sections that follow cover the details of argument references, variable numbers of inputs, keyword and default arguments, and argument validation.

3.8.1 Pass by Value and Pass by Reference

MATLAB and Python have complex answers to "are function arguments passed by value or passed by reference?" An argument passed by value is copied to a new local variable inside the function, so modifications to the argument in the function do not propagate back to the calling environment. The data copy exacts a performance penalty though—a costly one if the data is large. Functions that work with argument references are much faster, but modifications to these arguments in the function appear in the calling environment too. Sometimes, that's desired, other times not.

MATLAB functions behave as though they are passed by value. Under the hood, MATLAB actually passes arguments by reference to get the performance benefit. However, if an argument is updated inside the function, MATLAB will first make a local copy of it—this technique is known as "copy on write." The argument update then remains local to the function. One technique that can bypass the copy on write logic is to define the same variable in a function's input and output sections, for example, `function [M] = update(M, x)`. If the right conditions are met,[3] MATLAB skips the copy and works directly with the contents of the variable.

Python also has a mixed story here. Scalars are passed by value, but iterables (lists, dictionaries, tuples, NumPy arrays, sets) are passed by reference—mostly. Wholesale replacement of an iterable does not work, but reassignment of every item within an iterable is possible for lists, dictionaries, and arrays. The following examples illustrate these points.

3.8.1.1 Scalars Are Passed by Value

The increment function `f()` updates the input argument, but that update is only seen within the body of `f()` itself. Values in the calling environment remain unchanged:

---

[3] `www.mathworks.com/help/matlab/matlab_prog/avoid-unnecessary-copies-of-data.html`

Python:

```
In : def f(a):
 ...:      a += 1

In : b = 6
In : f(b)
In : b
Out: 6
```

3.8.1.2 Lists, Dicts, and Arrays Are Passed by Reference

Changes to list, dictionary, and array arguments are seen in the calling environment. After defining the functions on the left, the function calls on the right show how the arguments are updated:

Python:	Python:

`# list`
`def f_L(a):`
`    a.append(999)`
	`In : L = [6]`
	`In : f_L(L)`
	`In : L`
	`Out: [6, 999]`

`# dict`
`def f_D(a):`
`    a['z'] = 999`
	`In : D = {'x' : 1}`
	`In : f_D(D)`
	`In : D`
	`Out: {'x': 1, 'z': 999}`

`# NumPy Array`
`def f_A(a):`
`    a[1] = 999`
	`In : A =`
	`np.array([2,-3,4])`
	`In : f_A(A)`
	`In : A`
	`Out: array([ 2, 999, 4])`

3.8.1.3 List, Dict, and Array Contents Can Be Replaced in Their Entirety

List, dictionary, and array arguments can be replaced completely if one uses container-specific code constructs:

Python:	Python:
```# list```	```In : b = [6]```
```def f_L(a):```	```In : f(b)```
``` a[:] = [7,8,9]```	```In : b```
	```Out: [7, 8, 9]```
```# dict```	```In : D = {'x' : 1}```
```def f_D(a):```	```In : f_D(D)```
``` a.clear()```	```In : D```
``` a.update({'a':7, 'b':2})```	```Out: {'a': 7, 'b': 2}```
```# array```	```In : A = np.array([2,-3,4])```
```def f_A(a):```	```In : f_A(A)```
``` a[:] = 12, 14, 20```	```In : A```
	```Out: array([12, 14, 20])```

3.8.2 Variable Arguments

Both languages can accept a variable number of function arguments. MATLAB has several mechanisms to do this; the oldest of these stores the variables in the 1 x N cell array varargin, while Python stores them in a list whose name is prefixed by an asterisk in the argument list. The following example shows a function with one required argument followed by an arbitrary number of arguments:

MATLAB:	Python:

<pre>function F(x, varargin)
  N = size(varargin,2);
  fprintf("x=%f N=%d\n", x, N)
  for i = 1:N
    fprintf("v[%d]: ", i);
    disp(varargin{i})
  end
end</pre>
	<pre>def F(x, *args):
	  N = len(args)
	  print(f'x={x:f} N={N:d}')
	  for i,V in enumerate(args):
	    print(f'v[{i}]=',end='')
	    print(V)</pre>

The output for different invocations looks like this:

MATLAB:	Python:

<pre>>> F(7)
x=7.000000 N=0</pre>
	<pre>In : F(7)
	x=7.000000 N=0</pre>

<pre>>> F(8,"hi",[2 3])
x=8.000000 N=2
v[1]: hi
v[2]: 2 3</pre>
	<pre>In: F(8,"hi",[2,3])
	x=8.000000 N=2
	v[0]=hi
	v[1]=[2, 3]</pre>

3.8.3 Keyword Arguments

Both languages also have mechanisms to pass in optional arguments defined by keywords with default values. This capability in MATLAB requires the argument definition block which was introduced with R2019b.

MATLAB:	**Python:**

```function F(x,A,B)```
```arguments```
``` x```
``` A (1,1) int64 = 0```
``` B (1,1) double = -6.5```
```end```
```fprintf('x=%f A=%d B=%f\n',x,A,B)```
```end```
	```def F(x, A=0, B=-6.5):```
	``` print(f'{x:f} A={A:d} B={B:f}')```

Representative output:

MATLAB:	**Python:**
```>> F(9)``` ```9.000000 A=0 B=-6.500000```	```In : F(9)``` ```9.000000 A=0 B=-6.500000```
```>> F(10, B=23.4, A=-5)``` ```10.000000 A=-5 B=23.400000```	```In : F(10, B=23.4, A=-5)``` ```10.000000 A=-5 B=23.400000```
```>> F(11, A=700)``` ```11.000000 A=700 B=-6.500000```	```In : F(11, A=700)``` ```11.000000 A=700 B=-6.500000```

Python supports an even more flexible version of keyword arguments that accepts *any* keyword and value pair. This is done by prefixing a variable in the calling arguments with two asterisks to define it as a dictionary:

Python:

```
def F(x, **kwarg):
    print(f'x={x:f}')
    N = len(kwarg)
    for key in kwarg:
        print(f'{key}  value={kwarg[key]}')
```

A pair of calls passing in whatever comes to mind:

Python:

```
In : F(12)
x=12.000000

In : F(13, y=25.6, z=[True, -19])
x=13.000000
y value=25.6
z value=[True, -19]
```

3.8.4 Decorators

Python supports a concept known as a function decorator which has no counterpart in MATLAB. A decorator is essentially a function which wraps another function. Decorators are useful for adding functionality, for example, collect timing information or add debug statements, to existing functions without modifying those functions. Decorators are applied to functions by preceding the function definition with a line starting with the @ symbol and followed immediately by the decorator's name.

This simple example applies the timer decorator to functions sleeper() and add_numbers(). Each time either of these functions runs, the decorator reports how long the call takes. (The if __name__ == "__main__": main() line is explained in Section 3.14.2.)

Python:

```
#!/usr/bin/env python3
# code/basics/timer_decorator.py
import time

def timer(Fn):
    def inner(*args, **kwargs):
        Ts = time.time()
        Fn(*args, **kwargs)
        Te = time.time()
        print(f'dT = {Te-Ts:.3f} seconds')
    return inner
```

```python
@timer
def sleeper(sec):
    time.sleep(sec)

@timer
def add_numbers(N):
    return sum(range(N))

def main():
    sleeper(2)
    S = add_numbers(100000000)
    sleeper(3)

if __name__ == "__main__": main()
```

Output:
Python:

```
dT = 2.002 seconds
dT = 1.651 seconds
dT = 3.002 seconds
```

3.8.5 Type Annotation and Argument Validation

MATLAB's argument block shown earlier enforces argument types and sizes if these are provided; pass a variable with the wrong type or size and MATLAB will stop with an error. Python supports type annotations for function arguments and function return types, but as of Python 3.8, these are merely hints for code editors such as PyCharm and Visual Studio Code to enable features like code completion and type mismatch warnings. Type violations are not enforced by Python at runtime.

The next example shows what type annotation and argument validation look like in Python alongside the equivalent in MATLAB. Both functions F() take one required argument x of unspecified type, an optional integer argument A with default value 0, and a 1 x 2 array of doubles (MATLAB) or a list with two items (Python) with default values of 1 and 9. Both functions return the value A plus x multiplied by the sum of terms in B. The Python function's return type is additionally defined as a float (note: a Python "float" is 64 bits and therefore equivalent to MATLAB's "double").

MATLAB:	Python:

```
[z] = function F(x,opt)          def F(x, A: int=0,
  arguments                              B: list=[1,9]) -> (float):
    x                             return A + x*sum(B)
    opt.A (1,1) int = 0
    opt.B (2,1) double = [1 9]
  end
  fprintf('x=%f A=%d B=%f',...
          x,A,B)
  z = opt.A + x*sum(opt.B)
end
```

The MATLAB function is considerably longer than the one in Python, but it also does more work; the MATLAB version validates input, while the Python version accepts anything—and fails accordingly when inputs are invalid.

The equivalent input validation in Python takes considerably more code:

MATLAB:	Python:

```
[z] = function F(x,opt)          def F(x, A: int=0,
  arguments                              B: list=[1,9]) -> (float):
    opt.A (1,1) int = 0            if not isinstance(A,int):
    opt.B (2,1) double = [1 9]       print('Error: A is not an int')
  end                               return 0
  fprintf('x=%f A=%d B=%f',...    if not isinstance(B,list):
          x,A,B)                     print('Error: B is not a list')
  z = opt.Z + x*sum(opt.B)          return 0
end                               if len(B) != 2:
                                    print('Error: len B is not 2')
                                    return 0
                                  return A + x*sum(B)
```

Note   A more robust way to deal with the error cases is to raise exceptions (ref. Section 10.1.3).

3.8.6 Left-Hand Side Argument Count

Another advantage MATLAB has over Python is that a MATLAB function can know how many arguments it is expected to return—this count is stored in the variable nargout— and therefore can perform different actions depending on what the caller asks for. An example is the eig() eigenvalue function. If the left-hand side has one variable, eig() returns only the eigenvalues. If the left-hand side has two variables, eig() returns eigenvectors and eigenvalues.

MATLAB:

```
>> [a] = eig(diag([1,2,3]))
a =

   1
   2
   3

>> [v, a] = eig(diag([1,2,3]))
v =

   1   0   0
   0   1   0
   0   0   1

a =
Diagonal Matrix

   1   0   0
   0   2   0
   0   0   3
```

Python functions have no mechanism that tells them how many items appear to the left of an equal sign. To achieve the same functionality, a Python function would need to take an additional argument that indicates the number of return values desired.

3.9 Generators

A Python generator is a function that returns one item from a sequence each time it is called. It maintains the state, so the first call returns the first item in the sequence; the second time it is called, it returns the second item; and so on. When the sequence ends, calling the generator raises the StopIteration exception. This makes generators ideal targets of for or while loops since StopIteration causes loops to end cleanly.

Generators can help reduce a program's memory footprint because only one iteration's worth of data needs to be stored. Section 8.6, shows generators in action when walking a directory tree.

MATLAB has no equivalent to Python's generators.

3.9.1 yield, next()

Generators are regular Python functions that return a value with the yield keyword instead of return. Each successive call returns the next item in the sequence:

Python:

```python
def letters():
    for w in ['a', 'bb', 'ccc']:
        yield w
```

Python:

```python
In : for x in letters():
...:     print(x)
a
bb
ccc

In : L = letters()
In : print(next(L))
a
In : print(next(L))
bb
In : print(next(L))
ccc
```

```
In : print(next(L))
---------------------------------
StopIteration          Traceback
```

Generators are often the target of for loops or appear in a while statement where each successive value is retrieved by calling next() on the generator object.

3.9.2 range()

The range() function returns a sequence of consecutive integers and is one of the most used functions in Python. Its output is comparable to MATLAB's range expression of *a:b*. The difference is that range() is lazily evaluated and must be explicitly iterated over, while MATLAB's range creates a one-dimensional array of terms.

MATLAB:	Python:
`>> 5:8` `    5  6  7  8`	`In : range(5,9)` `Out: range(5, 9)`

	`In : for i in range(5,9):`
	`...:     print(i)`
	`5`
	`6`
	`7`
	`8`

Most of the time, the distinction between an explicit array of numbers and the output of a lazily evaluated function is not important. It begins to matter if the array is large and memory is at a premium. As an example, 1:10000000 in MATLAB uses 80 MB of memory, while range(10000000) uses only 48 bytes:

MATLAB:	Python:

`>> a = 1:10000000;`
`>> whos`
`  Name  Size        Bytes    Class`
`    a 1x10000000 80000000 double`
	`In : import sys`
	`In : a = range(10000000)`
	`In : sys.getsizeof(a)`
	`Out: 48`

If an explicit array is needed in Python, one can call `list()` on the iterator to expand every term. Better still, one can use NumPy's `arange()` function to create a NumPy array which permits vector operations.

Python:

```
In : list(range(5,9))
Out: [5, 6, 7, 8]

In : np.arange(5,9)
Out: array([5, 6, 7, 8])
```

A brief overview of NumPy appears in Section 4.1, while Chapter 11 covers NumPy in depth.

3.10 Scoping Rules and Global Variables

MATLAB is unusual among programming languages in that its functions have strictly local scope—computations within a function may only refer to variables defined as input arguments or left-hand side outputs unless global variables are explicitly cited.

Python follows more traditional scoping rules with highest priority given to local variables, then enclosing, global, and built-in (LEGB). These are defined as follows:

- **local** scope includes variables defined within the same function.

- **enclosing** scope applies to nested functions; an inner function can see variables defined in the function that encloses it.

- **global** scope covers variables defined at the outermost level of the enclosing file (a.k.a. module).

- **built-in** scope refers to objects from the core Python language itself, including keywords and imported modules.

Like MATLAB, Python has a `global` keyword, but `global` means different things in the two languages. In MATLAB, `global` can be used inside a function to make a global variable visible.

Python functions have read-only access to all global variables. There, the `global` keyword allows a function to change the value of the global variable.

MATLAB and Python allow one to nest functions which raises another scoping complexity: how do inner functions distinguish between their local variables and variables of their parent function? MATLAB does not allow inner functions to have local variables with the same name as variables in the parent function; the parent's variables are used. Python, with its `nonlocal` keyword, offers a degree of flexibility when both inner and outer functions use the same variable names; `nonlocal` lets the inner function know to use the parent's variable.

In the following example, calls to `nested()` return 1, 3 in both languages. If the `nonlocal` line in Python were removed though, Python's `nested()` would return 1, -2 since assigning to b has no effect on b in `nested()`.

MATLAB:	Python:
`function [a,b] = nested()`	`def nested():`
`  a = 1;`	`    a = 1`
`  b = -2;`	`    b = -2`
`  new_b();`	`    def new_b():`
`  function new_b()`	`        nonlocal b`
`    b = 3;`	`        b = 3`
`  end`	`    new_b()`
`end`	`    return a, b`

Output is

MATLAB:	Python:
`>> [a,b] = nested()`	`In : a, b = nested()`
`a =`	`In : a`
`        1`	`Out:   1`
`b =`	`In : b`
`        3`	`Out:   3`

`nonlocal` is also needed to implement a closure in Python. An example of this can be found in the function `iterrows()` in the bridge module for Recipe 13.13, for creating maps in MATLAB with GeoPandas.

3.11 Comments

Comments can be added to Python code in two ways. First, any text to the right of a pound symbol, #, is a comment. Second, text on multiple lines between triple single or double quotes is a block comment. Block comments cannot be nested. Both the pound sign and triple quote comment styles appear in this example:

Python

```
def ramp(m):
  print(f'got {m:d}')
  n = 5*m
  # this is a comment
  a = 1 # another comment
  if m % 2:
    for i in range(1,n+1):
      """
      A block comment.
      """
      a += i
  return a
```

3.11.1 Docstrings

Triple quotes actually serve three purposes:

1. As noted earlier, they delimit block comments.

2. They delimit multiline strings and can therefore appear to the right of an equals sign, as a function argument, or any place where a string is valid.

3. When they appear at the start of a file or a function, they are known as *docstrings*. These are parsed by documentation tools such as Sphinx, Doxygen, and the ipython REPL. In this case, they correspond to % comments at the top of MATLAB functions.

Here's an example of a docstring and the equivalent MATLAB help string:

MATLAB:	Python:
| ```
function [a] = ramp(m)
  % Prints a series of
  % increasing numbers
  % based on the input.
  fprintf('got %d\n', m)
  n = 5*m;
  a = 1;
  if mod(m,2)
    for i=1:n
      a = a + i;
    end % for
  end % if
end % function
``` | ```
def ramp(m):
    """

    Prints a series of
    increasing numbers
    based on the input.
    """
    print(f'got {m:d}')
    n = 5*m
    a = 1
    if m % 2:
        for i in range(1,n+1):
            a += i
    return a
``` |

We can get the help information with help ramp in MATLAB and either help(ramp) or ramp? in ipython:

MATLAB:	Python:
| ```
>> help ramp
  Prints a series of
  increasing numbers
  based on the input.
``` | ```
In : ramp?
Signature: ramp(m)
Docstring:
Prints a series of
increasing numbers
based on the input.
Type:    function
``` |

3.12 Line Continuation

Long expressions in MATLAB can be split across multiple lines by adding ellipses, ..., to the end of lines which continue on the following line. The selection of a three-character-long continuation marker is curious. After all, the most common reason to continue one line to the next is because there's not enough space on the line. If space is tight, why use three characters on the continuation marker itself? I'm unaware of any other programming language that uses more than one character to denote a continuation.

Incidentally, ellipses are valid Python code as well. When used on a line by themselves, they act as a no-operation placeholder for future code.

Python lines may be spread across multiple lines by adding the backslash, \, to the end of a line which is to be continued. Note that the backslash must be the last character in the line; otherwise, it is ignored.

There's a useful exception to this rule, though: expressions within an unclosed parenthesis, bracket, or brace pair do not need the trailing \:

```
# open parentheses: no backslash needed
    A = (- x1y3 - x2y1 - x3y2
        + x1y2 + x2y3 + x3y1)/2

# multiline statement: need backslash
T = '<a href=https://www.python.org>' + link_text + \
    '</a>'
```

3.13 Exceptions

MATLAB and Python take different approaches to handling exceptions. MATLAB catches all exceptions into an exception object, while Python lets one differentiate between exception types, similar to C++ or Java.

As an example, we'll create an error by invoking an undefined function, zyx():

MATLAB:	Python:

`>> zyx(7)`
`error: 'zyx' undefined`
`    near line 1 column 1`
	`In : zyx(7)`
	`---------------------`
	`NameError Traceback`
	`----> 1 zyx(7)`

MATLAB prints a generic error message, but Python identifies the error type, in our case NameError, which we can subsequently use in our error handling code. Trapping the preceding code with exception handlers looks like this in both languages:

MATLAB:	Python:
| ```
try
    zyx(7)
catch EO
    fprintf('error: %s', ...
            EO.message)
end
``` | ```
try
    zyx(7)
except NameError as err:
    print(f'Name Err: err')
except:
    errmsg = sys.exc_info()[1]
    print(f'Other Err: {errmsg}')
``` |

The MATLAB line catch EO creates a new variable, the exception object EO, which has attributes such as the formal message name, EO.identifier; a text string explaining the error, EO.message; and the location where the error was triggered, EO.stack.

The Python line except NameError on the other hand specifies that the lines in the exception block apply only to errors of type NameError—any other type of error cascades to the next except block (if one exists). In our case, the second except is not bound to any type of error class and therefore will catch everything else. The error message can be found in the second return value from a call to the less-than-obvious sys.exc_info() function.

Python try/except blocks support two optional keywords, else and finally. else begins a code block that is executed only if no exceptions are caught, while finally begins a code block that is always executed, regardless of exception status. A common use for finally is to run clean-up code, for example, removing temporary files, created by the code in the try block.

Python:

```
try:
    code_that_might_fail()
except IOError as err:
    print(f'File I/O error: err')
```

```
else:
    print(f'ran successfully!')
finally:
    remove_temp_files()
```

3.14 Modules and Packages

A Python module is a single source `.py` file or binary shared object typically containing one or more functions and/or classes. A Python package is a collection of modules organized in a specific directory structure. Conceptually, Python modules and packages resemble MATLAB toolboxes in that they usually contain functions to solve specific classes of problems. Python's Cartopy module and MATLAB's Mapping Toolbox, for example, display data on maps. Code in Python modules and packages, however, remain in the module's namespace, while MATLAB toolbox functions immediately inhabit the global namespace. As an example, if I have only the core MATLAB product, there would be no issue if I have a program that uses `batch` as a variable name. However, if I were to purchase and install the Parallel Computing Toolbox, my variable would conflict with the `batch` function added by the toolbox.

3.14.1 Namespace

A namespace is the set of all the variable and function names that are in scope in a program. For example, the NumPy module has a cosine function that works on both scalars and arrays. To use this function, we first have to load, or *import*, the NumPy module with `import numpy` and then refer to the cosine function by its full name, `numpy.cos()`. This extra step of importing modules strikes many MATLAB programmers as cumbersome. In contrast, when one installs a MATLAB toolbox, all functions in that toolbox are immediately available. While this may seem convenient, it can also introduce problems because common function names, such as `open()`, can come from the core MATLAB library or from any toolbox that defines the same function. Python's use of namespaces removes ambiguity about a function's origin.

Modules, or functions from within modules, may be loaded into a Python session in three different ways.

3.14.1.1 import X, or import X as Y

The most common way to load a module is to simply import the entire module as is. These import statements appear at the top of many Python programs:

```
import sys
import os
import re
```

In order, these are the systems module which includes things like the command-line arguments (sys.argv) and the module search path, Section 3.14.3 (sys.path); the operating system module which has environment variable settings (os.environ) and commands to rename (os.rename()) and delete (os.delete()) files; and the regular expression module useful for finding text patterns in strings (re.search()). All three are standard modules that are included in every Python installation.

A variation of import is to invoke it with an alias, usually an abbreviation, to reduce the amount of text around function names. The most common example of this is probably importing the NumPy module so its functions can be referenced with just np:

```
import numpy as np
```

NumPy is not a standard module, but it is included with the Anaconda and Enthought distributions. It is the foundational engine for nearly all scientific and numeric capabilities currently available in Python. NumPy has over 600 functions for all types of numerical analysis: linear algebra, statistics, curve fitting, trigonometry, interpolation, random number generation, and extended numeric types like quad-precision real and complex numbers.

A substantial portion of this book will cover NumPy and its capabilities.

3.14.1.2 from X import Y

Sometimes, you need access to just a single function from a module. One can cherry-pick functions using the from module import function notation. A common use of this is to pull the glob() function (which captures file and/or directory names using a pattern) from the similarly named module or the datetime() and timedelta() functions from the datetime() module:

```
from glob import glob
from datetime import datetime, timedelta
```

The imported functions can then be called directly without their parent module names.

3.14.1.3 `from X import Y as Z`

The least commonly seen import method uses both selective function imports and abbreviations:

```
from numpy.random import multivariate_normal as mnorm
```

3.14.1.4 An Antipattern: `from X import *`

Avoid this! The wildcard * means everything should be imported from module X without the need for a module prefix. This is especially problematic if done with NumPy, that is, writing `from numpy import *`, because NumPy functions that share names with functions in the standard library such as abs(), max(), min(), and so on will fail to load, leaving you with a handful of basic functions that do not work with numeric arrays.

In addition to hiding functions you may need, the `import *` also leads to the same namespace inflation (or pollution) that plagues MATLAB.

3.14.2 `def main()`

When a Python program imports a module, even if it just cherry-picks individual functions using the `from X import Y` notation, Python will run the entire module file before proceeding to the next line of the program. This can be problematic if you want to reuse functions from an older program because as soon as you import from that older program, Python will run it.

There's a simple solution to protect yourself from inadvertent code execution: just wrap the main part of your program—the entry point and code after it—in a function (typically called `main()`). That way, when the file is imported by another program, the main part won't do anything.

This raises the next issue of how do you get `main()` to run when you invoke the file as a program, that is, not as an import from another program, but as an executable unto itself? The solution to that is to end your program file with the lines

Python:

```
if __name__ == "__main__":
    main()
```

This tells the Python interpreter that if the file itself is being run (rather than imported), it should call `main()`. Flouting convention, I generally combine the lines so my programs end with

Python:

```
if __name__ == "__main__": main()
```

3.14.3 Module Search Path

Like MATLAB, Python can use functions and classes defined in files located in arbitrary directories, so long as one tells a program which directories to search. The languages are similar in the way search directories are handled: both can return the list of directories (MATLAB uses a function, `path`, which returns a colon-separated character array, while Python stores directories in a list, `sys.path`); both have a function to extend the list; and both recognize an environment variable that can optionally be set to include additional directories. Table 3-3 shows analogous constructs in MATLAB and Python for extending the search path.

Table 3-3. *Controlling the module search path*

	MATLAB	Python
Function showing search directories (MATLAB) and variable containing search directories (Python)	path	sys.path
Add a directory	addpath	sys.path.append()
Environment variable	MATLABPATH	PYTHONPATH

MATLAB:	Python:
addpath '../mfiles' addpath '/path/to/proj'	import sys sys.path.append('../pyfiles') sys.path.append('/path/to/proj')

A sample session looks like this.

Python modules have an attribute, .__path__, that contains the name of the directory from where the module was loaded:

Python:

```
In : import numpy as np
In : np.__path__
Out: ['/usr/local/anaconda3/2020.07/lib/python3.8/site-packages/']
```

This can be a useful troubleshooting aid on large projects if developers simultaneously work on multiple versions of the same module. The which command in MATLAB will only resolve to a file path when the function name is unique in the search path.

3.14.4 Installing New Modules

As of October 2021, more than 333,000 freely available Python modules can be found at the Python Package Index (PyPI) website, https://pypi.org. Think of the PyPI as Python's analog to MATLAB's File Exchange, but without the File Exchange's necessity for authenticating with a MATLAB account. As with the File Exchange, code on the PyPI will vary widely in quality. Any PyPI package can be installed easily on computers attached to the Internet with the command pip install X, where X is the name of the desired module.

If you are using the recommended Anaconda distribution of Python though, the better choice is to install using the conda package manager which searches for modules and packages in Anaconda's curated repository:

Python:

```
conda install X
```

conda has a more sophisticated dependency resolver than pip, and its packages are more rigorously examined for security issues. Once a consistent set of dependencies is computed, conda will offer to downgrade and/or upgrade existing modules—even Python itself—to accommodate your request.

A downside to conda is the Anaconda repository is much smaller than PyPI so it is possible the module you want to install can't be found. There's a second tier of the Anaconda repository known as "conda-forge," a github.com hosted collection of community-provided contributions that augment the official Anaconda collection. You can configure conda to also look at conda-forge with

Python:

```
conda config --add channels conda-forge
conda config --set channel_priority strict
```

3.14.5 Module Dependency Conflicts and Virtual Environments

Dependency resolution over hundreds of interdependent modules and packages is a surprisingly complex task that conda sometimes can't solve. Making matters worse, users sometimes manually install or use pip in addition to conda to install modules, leaving an installation with incompatible dependencies. As a result, the entire Python installation could be corrupted, forcing a complete reinstall.

The cleanest solution is to install a collection of modules related for a specific task into a conda environment as described in Section 2.5.

CHAPTER 4

Data Containers

MATLAB and Python have many powerful data containers. MATLAB's primary containers are the matrix, cell array, and struct, while Python mainstays are lists, dictionaries, and, for the intended audience of this book, NumPy arrays. A fourth key container in the Python landscape is the Pandas dataframe which corresponds most closely to a MATLAB table. Tables and dataframes are covered in Chapter 13. Approximate equivalences of MATLAB and Python containers appear in Table 4-1.

Similarities and differences between MATLAB and Python data containers are worth studying because knowledge of how the containers work is essential for the design and implementation of efficient algorithms. The next sections cover the most important containers in both languages.

Table 4-1. *Data containers in MATLAB and Python*

MATLAB	Python Equivalent	Section
Matrices	NumPy ndarrays (or just "arrays")	4.1, 11
Cell arrays	Lists	4.3
Structs	Dictionaries; attributes; data classes	4.6 4.7
Tables	Pandas dataframes	13

NumPy arrays are covered thoroughly in Chapter 11 and appear frequently in most other chapters. Here, we merely give a cursory introduction to the NumPy module and its primary container, the n-dimensional array, also known as the ndarray.

© Albert Danial 2022
A. Danial, *Python for MATLAB Development*, https://doi.org/10.1007/978-1-4842-7223-7_4

4.1 NumPy Arrays

Python, accompanied by the core modules in the standard distribution, has little to offer for numeric computation. For this, we need NumPy, the numerics module at the heart of nearly every Python-powered scientific and numeric capability. NumPy arrays are covered thoroughly in Section 11.1; here, we just introduce them with a sneak preview.

The standard way to import NumPy is with

```
import numpy as np
```

Subsequently, all NumPy-related functions can be invoked by prefixing them with np. One may be tempted to use the "import everything" option with

```
from numpy import   *
```

but, as mentioned in Section 3.14.1.4, this could break your code in subtle ways.

Here's a basic example to give an indication of how a simple linear algebra problem looks in NumPy compared to MATLAB:

MATLAB:	Python:
`>> A = [1 2; 3 4]`	`In : A = np.array([[1,2],[3,4]])`
`A =`	`In : A`
`    1 2`	`array([[1,2],`
`    3 4`	`        [3,4]])`
`>> b = ones(2,1)`	`In : b = np.ones((2,))`
`b =`	`In : b`
`    1`	`Out: array([1.,1.])`
`    1`	
`>> x = A\b`	`In : x = np.linalg.solve(A,b)`
`x =`	`In : x`
`    -1`	`Out: array([-1.,1.])`
`     1`	

Both MATLAB and ipython have a whos command that lists the names, types, and sizes of variables:

MATLAB

```
>> whos
Variables in the current scope:

Attr Name     Size                            Bytes    Class
==== ====     ====                            =====    =====
     A        2x2                                32    double
     B        2x1                                16    double
     x        2x1                                16    double

Total is 8 elements using 64 bytes
```

Python

```
In : whos
Variable      Type       Data/Info
-------------------------------
A             ndarray    2x2: 4 elems, type `int64`, 32 bytes
b             ndarray    2: 2 elems, type `float64`, 16 bytes
x             ndarray    2: 2 elems, type `float64`, 16 bytes
```

Note that A in Python is an integer array. The np.array() function infers a data type from the values passed in, all of which are integers. The np.ones() function on the other hand defaults to creating double-precision floats. If instead we want floating-point values, we'll need to change at least one of them to look like a floating-point value:

```
In : a = np.array([[1.,2],[3,4]])
In : whos
Variable  Type     Data/Info
--------------------------
a         ndarray  2x2: 4 elems, type `float64`, 32 bytes
In : a
Out:
array([[1., 2.],
       [3., 4.]])
```

67

Alternatively, we can explicitly tell array() what the data type should be with the optional dtype argument. This example creates a quadruple-precision complex[1] array:

```
In : a = np.array([[1,2],[3,4]], dtype=np.complex256)
```

```
In : a
Out:
array([[1.+0.j, 2.+0.j],
       [3.+0.j, 4.+0.j]], dtype=complex256)
```

The bulk of this book will be about NumPy arrays and operations on them. For now, though, we'll turn our attention to other data containers.

4.2 Strings

Both Python and MATLAB have extensive support for creating, modifying, and testing strings. Both also have a different data type for a *byte array* which is often considered the same as a string. They differ though: a byte array (or character vector in MATLAB) is a sequence of bytes, while a string is a sequence of text characters— and a text character may require several bytes to represent it. An ASCII string maps one to one with a byte array, but a Unicode string storing, say, Vietnamese characters, will not.

4.2.1 Strings, Character Arrays, and Byte Arrays

While both languages have similar concepts of strings, they differ in how and what their more simpler forms, character arrays (MATLAB) and byte arrays (Python), contain. MATLAB char arrays are essentially primitive strings where each character is stored in two bytes. Python byte arrays are a collection of uint8 values that can look like strings if the byte values fall in the range of printable ASCII characters. A MATLAB string is actually a 1x1 cell array containing a 1xN array of chars. You'll occasionally see MATLAB strings indexed by {1} since this construct returns the underlying char array---handy for numeric indexing of substrings.

---

[1] Available on Linux and macOS but not Windows.

The following examples show how strings, char, and byte arrays are created. MATLAB uses single quotes to denote a character array and double quotes to denote a string. In Python, single and double quotes are interchangeable (but of course must be paired properly). It uses the special notation of b" to denote a byte array.

MATLAB:	Python:
>> x = 'byte array'; >> y = "a string";	In : x = b'byte array' In : y = 'a string'
>> class(x) 'char'	In : type(x) Out: bytes
>> class(y) 'string'	In : type(y) Out: str

Both languages have functions or methods to convert between the types:

MATLAB:	Python:
>> x = 'byte array'; >> y = "a string";	In : x = b'byte array' In : y = 'a string'
>> x_str = string(x); >> b_arr = char(y);	In : x_str = x.decode() In : b_arr = y.encode()

Numeric values of the individual characters can be found by casting to a numeric type, say uint16 or double in MATLAB, or iterating through the bytes in Python:

MATLAB:	Python:

>> x = 'byte array';
>> uint16(x)
  98 121 116 101 32
    97 114 114 97 121
	In : x = b'byte array'
	In : [_ for _ in x]
	Out: [98, 121, 116, 101, 32,
	      97, 114, 114, 97, 121]

A commonly seen error in Python is `TypeError: a bytes-like object is required, not 'str'`. This happens when attempting to perform a string operation, covered in the next section, using a byte array. The simple fix is to apply the `.decode()` method on the byte array to turn it into a string.

4.2.2 String Operations

Python strings, like all data containers and functions in Python, are objects. Their attributes and methods can be queried interactively in ipython by adding a period after a string variable, then hitting the <TAB> key:

Python:

```
In : a = 'abc'
In : a.<TAB>
In : a.
capitalize()   isalpha()       ljust()        split()
casefold()     isascii()       lower()        splitlines()
center()       isdecimal()     lstrip()       startswith()
count()        isdigit()       maketrans()    strip()
encode()       isidentifier()  partition()    swapcase()
endswith()     islower()       replace()      title()
expandtabs()   isnumeric()     rfind()        translate()
find()         isprintable()   rindex()       upper()
format()       isspace()       rjust()        zfill()
format_map()   istitle()       rpartition()
index()        isupper()       rsplit()
isalnum()      join()          rstrip()
```

MATLAB has a similar capability with its `methods` and `methodsview` commands, but these are applied to the data type (or "class" in MATLAB terminology) rather than to a variable:

MATLAB:

```
>> a = "abc";
>> class(a)
    'string'
```

```
>> methods string
```

Methods for class string:

append	endsWith	extractBetween	join	pad	splitlines
cellstr	eq	ge	le	plus	startsWith
char	erase	gt	lower	replace	strip
compose	eraseBetween	insertAfter	lt	replaceBetween	strlength
contains	extract	insertBefore	matches	reverse	upper
count	extractAfter	ismissing	ne	sort	
double	extractBefore	issorted	or	split	

Common string operations are described in greater detail in the following sections.

4.2.2.1 String Length

As mentioned above, a MATLAB string is a 1x1 cell array containing a 1xN array of char. Applying length() on a string just returns the number of columns of the cell array---which is always 1. To get the string length one must use the special string function strlength() or call length() on the underlying char array obtained by indexing the string with {1}:

MATLAB:	Python:
`>> str = "string length";`	`In : str = "string length"`
`>> length(str{1})`	`In : len(str)`
`    ans = 13`	`Out: 13`

4.2.2.2 Append to a String

Use the addition operator, +, to append strings together in MATLAB and Python:

MATLAB:	Python:
`>> A = "cats";`	`In : A = "cats"`
`>> B = "dogs";`	`In : B = "dogs"`
`>> C = A +" "+ B;`	`In : C = A +" "+ B`
`>> C`	`In : C`
`    "cats dogs"`	`Out: 'cats dogs'`

Remember to use double quotes for string literals in MATLAB. Character arrays (single quoted strings) will not give the expected result:

MATLAB:	Python:
`>> 'a'+'b'`	`In : 'a'+'b'`
`195`	`Out: 'ab'`

4.2.2.3 Repeat a String

The multiplication operator, *, allows one to make multiple copies of a string in Python. Only nonnegative integer values may be used as multipliers.

MATLAB:	Python:
`>> A = "#.";`	`In : A = "#."`
`>> repmat(A,1,5)`	`In : A * 5`
`ans = '#.#.#.#.#.'`	`Out: '#.#.#.#.#.'`

4.2.2.4 Convert to Upper- or Lowercase

Case conversion uses the identically named functions in both languages. Both also return new strings without modifying the original.

MATLAB:	Python:
`>> A = "The String";`	`In : A = "The String"`
`>> upper(A)`	`In : A.upper()`
`ans = 'THE STRING'`	`Out: 'THE STRING'`
`>> lower(A)`	`In : A.lower()`
`ans = 'the string'`	`Out: 'the string'`

4.2.2.5 Replace Characters

As with `.upper()` and `.lower()`, the `.replace()` method in Python and `replace()` function in MATLAB return a new string; they do not alter the contents of variable being worked on. To modify A, this variable must be explicitly assigned to the return value from the replace function call:

MATLAB:	Python:

`>> A = "the fox box";`
`>> replace(A,'ox','it') "`
`   "the fit bit"`
	`In : A = "the fox box"`
	`In : A.replace('ox', 'it')`
	`Out: 'the fit bit'`

`>> A` `   "the fox box"`	`In : A` `Out: 'the fox box'`

`>> A = replace(A,'ox', 'it')`
`   "the fit bit"`
	`In : A = A.replace('ox', 'it')`
	`In : A`
	`Out: 'the fit bit'`

4.2.2.6 Method Chaining

Parsing text often requires multiple clean-up operations: remove commas, replace unwanted text with spaces, convert everything to lowercase, and so on. Multiple operations can be *chained* in Python where one method call is immediately followed by another.

Say we want to extract time and x,y coordinates from a log file containing other text we're not interested in. A line of input might look like this:

```
1588350589.176445772 x: 36.67, y: -67.3
```

There are several ways to extract the numbers (notably with regular expressions which will be covered in Section 4.2.6); one way is to simply replace "x:", "y:", and "," with spaces or empty strings. The equivalent of Python's method chaining is a cumbersome collection of nested function calls in MATLAB:

MATLAB:

```
>> line = "1588350589.176445772 x: 36.67, y: -67.3";
>> line = split(replace(replace(replace(line,'x:',''),'y:',''),',',' '))
  3x1 string array
    "1588350589.176445772"
    "36.67"
    "-67.3"
```

Python:

```
In : line = '1588350589.176445772 x: 36.67, y: -67.3'
In : line = line.replace('x:','').replace('y:','').replace(',',' ').split()
Out: ['1588350589.176445772','36.67','-67.3']
```

The .split() method is described in Section 4.2.4.

4.2.3 Formatting

Both MATLAB and Python can use C language–style formatting for strings:

MATLAB:

```
>> str = sprintf('[%-5s] [%6.3f] [%02d]','hi',pi,4);
>> str
   '[hi] [3.142] [04]'
```

Python:

```
In : str = '[%-5s] [%6.3f] [%02d]'%('hi', np.pi,4)
In : str
Out: '[hi] [3.142] [04]'
```

Python additionally supports a convenient feature known as *f-strings* that allow variables and expressions to be embedded within the format string instead of appearing afterward as arguments. Note the f" prefix on the format string:

Python:

```
In : h, q = 'hi', 4
In : str = f'[{h:<5s}] [{np.pi:6.3f}] [{q:02d}]'
In : str
Out: '[hi] [3.142] [04]'
```

The < symbol on the string format <5s means "left justify." The formatting designations are optional. Without them, the output is

Python:

```
In : h, q = 'hi', 4
In : str = f'[{h}] [{np.pi}] [{q}]'
In : str
Out: '[hi] [3.141592653589793] [4]'
```

4.2.4 Separate a String into Words

A frequently performed operation for reading input data is splitting a string into an array of words delimited by whitespace, commas, or other characters. Python's .split() method, like MATLAB's strsplit() function, will default to splitting the string on whitespace; passing an argument will split on that character or substring.

Outputs from split operations are a cell array in MATLAB and a list in Python. These containers will be described in detail in Section 4.3.

MATLAB:

```
>> str = "Nature's first green is gold";
>> strsplit(str)
  1×5 string array
    "Nature's"  "first"  "green"  "is"  "gold"

>> strsplit(str, 'e')
  1×3 string array
    "Natur"  "'s first gr"  "n is gold"
```

Python:

```
In : str = "Nature's first green is gold"
In : str.split()
Out: ["Nature's", 'first', 'green', 'is', 'gold']

In : str.split('e')
Out: ['Natur', "'s first gr", '', 'n is gold']
```

Splitting comma-separated value (.csv) files is such a ubiquitous task that both MATLAB and Python have special methods for this. Chapter 7 has an extensive section on working with .csv files.

4.2.5 Tests on Strings

When working with numeric data, MATLAB's notation is generally terser than Python's. The reverse is true for strings.

4.2.5.1 Testing for Equality

MATLAB:	Python:
>> str = "string equality";	In : str = "string equality"
>> strcmp(str{1}(1:6), "string")	In : str[:6] == "string"
ans = 1	Out: True
>> str{1}(end-1:end)	In : str[-2:]
ans = ty	Out: 'ty'
>> strcmp(str{1}(end-1:end),"tY")	In : str[-2:] == "tY"
ans = 0	Out: False

4.2.5.2 Check Trailing Characters

Say you want to grab the names of the .csv files in a directory (covered in Section 8.1). Simple, all you need to do is check that the last four characters in each file name are ".csv", right? That's true—so long as the string has four characters to check. Conveniently, both languages support methods to check if strings start and end with a given string:

MATLAB:	Python:
>> fname = "a.csv";	In : fname = "a.csv";
>> endsWith(fname,".csv")	In : fname.endswith('.csv')
1	Out: True

4.2.5.3 Check Starting Characters

MATLAB:	Python:
>> fname = "a.csv";	In : fname = "a.csv"
>> startsWith(fname,"a")	In : fname.startswith('a.')
1	Out: True

4.2.5.4 Do Given Characters Appear in a String?

Python's in operator lets us test for the presence of a substring within a string, similar to contains() in MATLAB:

MATLAB:	Python:
>> str = 'cat or dog or bird';	In : str = 'cat or dog or bird'
>> contains(str,'or')	In : 'or' in str
ans = 1	Out: True
>> contains(str,'and')	In : 'and' in str
ans = 0	Out: False

4.2.6 String Searching, Replacing with Regular Expressions

A regular expression, or regex, works with string patterns and is used for three purposes:

1. Check whether or not text has the desired pattern

2. Extract text patterns from a string (if they exist) for subsequent use

3. Replace text that matches a pattern with new text

Python has a complete Perl-compatible regex engine, while MATLAB implements only a subset of the Perl regex metacharacters. The underlying mechanisms of invoking the pattern search and extracting results also differ.

4.2.6.1 Does a String Match a Regex?

In the first example, we use a regex to see whether or not a string contains two integers separated by spaces, then either "dog" or "cat":

MATLAB:

```
>> Y = "7x U 12 14 cat?";
>> out = regexp(Y,"\s(\d+\s+){2}(cat|dog)");

>> if out ; fprintf('matched\n'); end matched

>> N = "7x U 12 14 mouse!";
>> out = regexp(N,"\s(\d+\s+){2}(cat|dog)");
>> if out ; fprintf('matched\n'); end
>>
```

Python:

```
In : import re
In : Y = "7x U 12 14 cat?"
In : out = re.search(r"\s(\d+\s+) {2}(cat|dog)", Y)
In : if out: print("matched!")
matched!

In : N = "7x U 12 14 mouse!";
In : out = re.search(r"\s(\d+\s+) {2}(cat|dog)", N)
In : if out: print("matched!")
In :
```

4.2.6.2 Match a Regex and Capture Substrings

Portions of a regular expression can be captured for subsequent use by wrapping the portion of interest with parentheses. The 'token' argument to MATLAB's regexp() function returns the matched portions as a cell array of strings. In Python, the object returned by re.search() has a .group() method which returns the matched portions and a .groups() method which returns a tuple of all of these matches.

A significant difference between MATLAB and Python is that Python can return results from nested captures—that is, from nested parenthetical expressions—but MATLAB can't. In the following example, we'll look for numeric year-month-day patterns in an input:

MATLAB:

```
>> str = "1door 1. 2019-03-04 14.55 L22-";
>> m = regexp(str,'(\d{4}(\-\d\d){2})','tokens')
  1×1 cell array
    {["2019-03-04"]}
```

Python:

```
In : import re
In : str = "1door 1. 2019-03-04 14.55 L22-"
In : m = re.search(r'(\d {4}(\-\d\d){2})',str)
In : m.group(1)
2019-03-04

In : m.group(2)
-04
```

The inner parentheses, qualified by a "2x" multiplier, hold the last match of the multiplied pattern, therefore just -04 instead of -03-04.

4.2.6.3 Replace Text Matching a Regex with Different Text

In this example, we'll replace either "cat" or "dog" with "fish" followed by a copy of the integer preceding it. The notation \g<1> in the Python regular expression is a backreference to the first grouped pattern, that is, the contents of the regular expression caught in the first pair of parentheses.

Backreferences are not supported in MATLAB 2020b, so an additional step is needed to first capture the integer before "cat" or "dog":

MATLAB:

```
>> Y = "7x U 12 14 cat?";
>> m = regexp(Y,"(\d+)\s+(cat|dog)",'tokens'); % m{1}{1} = '14'
>> regexprep(Y,"\d+\s+(cat|dog)",sprintf('%s fish %s', m{1}{1}, m{1}{1}))
    "7x U 12 fish 14?"
```

Python:

```
In : import re
In : Y = "7x U 12 14 cat?"
In : re.sub(r"(\d+)\s+(cat|dog)", 'fish \g<1>', Y)
Out: '7x U 12 14 fish 14?'
```

4.2.7 String Templates

String templates are useful for stamping out copies of text that is mostly boilerplate. Examples include simple HTML documents (we'll see an example of this in Section 7.17.2) and input files for other programs when performing a parameter sweep where just one value changes in each file.

The Python `strings` module from the standard library has a function, `Template()`, that returns a template object whose entries can be replaced by calling the object's `_substitute()` method. Here's an example:

Python:

```
In : import string
In : T = string.Template("""alpha = ${Alpha}
...: thickness = ${layer_mm}
...: E = 10.0e6
...: nu = 0.33
...: """)
In : t_new = T.substitute(Alpha=.125, layer_mm=0.11)
In : print(t_new)
alpha = 0.125
thickness = 0.11
E = 10.0e6
nu = 0.33
```

I'm unaware of a text templating mechanism for MATLAB.

The Jinja2[2] template engine offers much more power than the Python standard library's `string.Template()`. It offers text generation with loops, conditional expressions, template hierarchies with inheritance, macros, filters, Python code execution, and supports include files.

4.3 Python Lists and MATLAB Cell Arrays

A Python list contains a sequence of arbitrary scalar values and/or containers. A list is created with open and close brackets, [*item₁*, *item₂*, ...], so it superficially resembles a MATLAB array. However, unlike a MATLAB array, lists may contain different data types. Therefore, Python lists most closely resemble MATLAB cell arrays.

All Python variables (as well as functions and classes) are objects that have functions, or methods, associated with them. We can see the methods available for lists by using ipython's interactive help:

Python:

```
In : a.<TAB>
a.append    a.copy    a.extend    a.insert    a.remove    a.sort
a.clear     a.count   a.index     a.pop       a.reverse
```

Further help on any of these methods can be found by adding a question mark after the method's name:

Python:

```
In : a.append?
Signature: a.append(object, /)
Docstring: Append object to the end of the list.
Type:      builtin_function_or_method
```

---

[2]https://palletsprojects.com/p/jinja/

For completeness, here are the methods that work with MATLAB cell arrays:
MATLAB:

```
>> methods cell
```

```
Methods for class cell:
```

cellismemberlegacy	ismatrix	issortedrows	reshape	transpose
ctranspose	ismember	isvector	setdiff	union
display	isrow	maxk	setxor	unique
intersect	isscalar	mink	sort	
iscolumn	issorted	permute	strcat	

The following sections show how to manipulate Python lists and the MATLAB equivalent with cell arrays.

4.3.1 Initialize an Empty List

An empty cell array of a given size can be allocated in MATLAB with the cell() function. If given only one numeric argument, *N*, it will return an *N* x *N* collection of empty cells—not always the desired outcome. To simply make *N* empty cells, we'll need to supply a second dimension of 1.

In Python, we can preallocate a list of None values by multiplying a single item list by the desired count:

MATLAB:	Python:

`>> a = cell(1,3)`
`  {0x0 double} {0x0 double} {0x0 double}`
	`In : a = [ None] * 3`
	`In : a`
	`Out: [None, None, None]`

4.3.2 Create a List with Given Values

MATLAB:	Python:

`>> a = {1,2.2,'a string'}`
`a =`
  `1×3 cell array`
    `{[1]} {[2.2000]}`
    `{'a string'}`
	`In : a= [1,2.2,'a string']`
	
	`In : a`
	`Out: [1,2.2,'a string']`

Additional methods exist in both languages to convert other containers into lists. MATLAB has cell(), mat2cell(), and num2cell(), while in Python one can use the list() function or write a list comprehension (described in Section 4.3.14).

4.3.3 Get the Length of a List

MATLAB:	Python:
`>> size(a)` `1    3`	`In : len(a)` `Out: 3`

`>> n_items = size(a,2)`
    `3`
	`In : n_items = len(a)`
	`In : n_items`
	`Out: 3`

4.3.4 Index a List Item

Python list indexing (as with NumPy arrays as we'll see later) uses brackets, while MATLAB allows parentheses and braces. A MATLAB cell array indexed with parentheses returns the indexed container (recall that MATLAB insists that even scalar variables are matrices), while braces give the item within the indexed container. The difference between indexing with ( ) and {} is best illustrated with an example:

```
MATLAB:                    Python:

>> a(3)                    In : a[2]
   1x1 cell array          Out: 'a string'
      {'a string'}

>> a{3}
      'a string'
```

As with string indexing demonstrated in Section 4.2.5.1, Python makes it easy to reference list items from the end of the list by using negative indices; index -1 means "the last item in the list," index -2 means "the second to last item," and so on. MATLAB does not allow negative indices, but its end keyword refers to the last item:

```
MATLAB:              Python:

>> a{ end}           In : a[-1]
      'a string'     Out: 'a string'
```

Negative indexing has a drawback in that it can mask latent bugs. Say you write code that only accesses list items with zero or positive indices. If the code has a logic error which permits an index to become negative, instead of crashing with an index error like MATLAB, your code will continue to run—and yield bad results.

Attempting to access a positive or negative index that exceeds the size of the list will raise an error:

MATLAB:	Python:
| ```
>> a = {1, 2.2, 'a string'};
>> a{4}
Index exceeds the number of
    array elements (3).

>> a{-4}
Array indices must be positive
    integers or logical values.
``` | ```
In : a = [1, 2.2, 'a string']
In : a[3]
IndexError Traceback
----> 1 a[3]
IndexError: list index out of range

In : a[-3]
Out: 1

In : a[-4]
IndexError Traceback
----> 1 a[-4]
IndexError: list index out of range
``` |

4.3.5 Extract a Range of Items

Both MATLAB and Python allow one to extract a range of items, either continuously or by steps, using a colon, :, to denote a continuous range of indices or two colons to denote a range with a stride. We'll need a longer list to demonstrate this:

MATLAB:	Python:
| ```
>> a = num2cell(100:106)
a =
  1×7 cell array
  Columns 1 through 7
    {[100]} {[101]} {[102]}
    {[103]} {[104]} {[105]}
    {[106]}
``` | ```
In : a = list(range(100,107))

In : a
Out: [100, 101, 102, 103,
      104, 105, 106]
``` |

Note that in MATLAB, a = {100:106} produces a cell array with a single item (a matrix of seven values), which is not what we're after:

MATLAB:

```
>> a = {100:106}
a =
  1×1 cell array
    {1×7 double}
>> a{1}
    100 101 102 103 104
      105 106
```

To emphasize that MATLAB cell arrays and Python lists can hold disparate data types, we'll change one item to a float and one item to a string:

MATLAB:	Python:

`>> a{2} = -0.1;`
`>> a{7} = 'cell'`
`a =`
  `1×7 cell array`
  `Columns 1 through 7`
   `{[100]} {[-0.1000]} {[102]}`
   `{[103]} {[104]} {[105]}`
   `{'cell'}`
	`In : a[1] = -0.1`
	`In : a[6] = 'list'`
	
	`In : a`
	`Out: [100, -0.1, 102, 103,`
	     `104, 105, 'list']`

Cell arrays and list slices are accessed similarly as the following examples illustrate.

Extract the first three items

Python's range operator differs a bit from MATLAB's. In Python, the start index may be omitted if it is 0, and the value for the end index is not part of the returned list. In other words, [:3] returns list items 0, 1, and 2.

Here, we show the MATLAB cell array subscripted with both braces and parentheses.

MATLAB:	Python:
>> a{1:3}	In : a[:3]
100	Out: [100, -0.1, 102]
-0.1000	
102	
>> a(1:3)	
1×3 cell array	
{[100]} {[-0.100]} {[102]}	

Extract the last four items:

MATLAB:	Python:
>> a{end-3:end}	In : a[-4:]
103	Out: [103, 104, 105, 'list']
104	
105	
'cell'	

Extract every third item, beginning with the second one:

MATLAB:	Python:
>> a(2:3:end)	In : a[1::3]
1×2 cell array	Out: [-0.1, 104]
{[-0.100]} {[104]}	

4.3.6 Warning—Python Index Ranges Are Not Checked!

Although a single list index raises an IndexError if it exceeds the bounds of the list, index *ranges* have no such checks.

In Python, out-of-bounds index ranges merely return an empty list; they will not raise an error.

Consider this example:

```
In : a = [1, 2.2, 'a string']
Out: a[27636]
IndexError Traceback
----> 1 a[27636]
IndexError: list index out of range
```

Not surprising: indexing item 27,636 in a list having only three items gives an error. Here's an unpleasant surprise though:

```
In : a[27636:-524385732]
Out: []
```

There's no error! What is going on? Python will raise an error when a list is indexed by a single value outside the index bounds, but silently accepts index *ranges* which are out of bounds. Unchecked index ranges offer rich opportunities for code errors to pass undetected. They place the responsibility for checking start and end index values on the developer.

Allowing range bound violations does have convenient applications though. A simple example is truncating strings to a given length. In MATLAB, one must make sure the truncation length is less than or equal to the string length. Python doesn't care if the string is shorter than the truncation length:

MATLAB:	Python:
`>> S = "abcdefghijklm";`	`In : S = "abcdefghijklm"`
`>> n_chop = 6;`	`In : n_chop = 6`
`>> extractBetween(S,1,n_chop)`	`In : S[:n_chop]`
`    "abcdef"`	`Out: 'abcdef'`
`>> S = "abc";`	`In : S = "abc"`
`>> extractBetween(S,1,n_chop)`	`In : S[:n_chop]`
`Error using extractBetween`	`Out: 'abc'`
`Numeric value exceeds the number`	
`    of characters in element 1.`	

Another example is splitting a collection into evenly sized sets and not having to bother with leftovers on uneven splits. Here, we group the numbers 1 through 20 into three evenly sized sets:

Python:

```
n_items = 20
n_groups = 3
set_size = int(np.ceil(n_items/n_groups))
L = list(range(1,n_items+1))
for i in range(n_groups):
    print(L[i*set_size:(i+1)*set_size])
```

Obviously, 20 is not evenly divisible by 3, but we don't have to bother with that detail; the output sets have the desired counts of 7, 7, and 6 members:

Python:

```
[ 1,  2,  3,  4,  5,  6,  7]
[ 8,  9, 10, 11, 12, 13, 14]
[15, 16, 17, 18, 19, 20]
```

Had array bounds been checked, the last iteration would have raised an error since the print statement attempts to access a nonexistent 21st element. Instead, Python just returns nothing for the missing item.

The equivalent output can be produced with MATLAB code that caps the ending index at each iteration:

MATLAB:

```
n_items = 20;
n_groups = 3;
set_size = ceil(n_items/n_groups);
L = 1:n_items;
for i = 1:n_groups
    end_index = min(n_items, i*set_size); % prevent array bounds violation
    L((i-1)*set_size+1:end_index)
end
```

4.3.7 Append an Item

Items can be added to MATLAB cell arrays simply by introducing a new index. The new index can be any integer value; it need not be an increment of the last index in the cell array. If there is a gap of indices, the skipped terms are created and populated with an empty matrix.

In Python, items are added to a list via the list's .append() or .extend() methods, where .append() adds on a single item while .extend() can be used to join a second list to the first. New list entries cannot be added with subscripts.

MATLAB:	Python:

>> a{8} = 3.14
% equivalent to
>> a(8) = {3.14}
a =
  1×8 cell array
  Columns 1 through 8
    {[100]} {[101]} {[102]}
    {[103]} {[104]} {[105]}
    {[106]} {[3.1400]}
	In : a.append(3.14)
	
	In : a
	Out: [100, -0.1, 102, 103,
	      104, 105, 'list', 3.14]

The following example adds an entry directly into the MATLAB cell array's tenth position, even though it currently has only eight items. The ninth position is automatically populated by an empty matrix. The same manipulation cannot be done in Python. To put an entry into the tenth position, we first have to fill the ninth position with something. Here, we use None, the Python expression for null:

MATLAB:	Python:

`>> a{10} = 2.71`
`a =`
  `1×10 cell array`
  `Columns 1 through 10`
    `{[100]} {[101]} {[102]}`
    `{[103]} {[104]} {[105]}`
    `{[106]} {[3.1400]}`
    `{0x0 double} {[2.7100]}`
	`In : a.append(None)`
	`In : a`
	`Out: [100, -0.1, 102, 103,`
	    `104, 105, 'list', 3.14,`
	    `None]`
	
	`In : a.append(2.71)`
	`In : a`
	`Out: [100, -0.1, 102, 103,`
	    `104, 105, 'list', 3.14,`
	    `None, 2.71]`

4.3.8 Append Another List

The Python `.extend()` method for lists appends the contents of one list to another. MATLAB has a `horzcat()` function that achieves the same thing:

MATLAB:	Python:

`>> a = {1, 'two'};`
`>> b = {3, 4.4, 5};`
`>> c = horzcat(a,b)`
`c =`
  `1x5 cell array`
  `Columns 1 through 5`
    `{[1]} {'two'} {[3]}`
    `{[4.4000]} {[5]}`
	`In : a = [1, 'two']`
	`In : b = [3, 4.4, 5]`
	`In : a.extend(b)`
	`In : a`
	`Out: [1, 'two', 3, 4.4, 5]`

Alternatively, Python lists can be extended with the + operator:

```
In : a = [1, 'two']
In : b = [3, 4.4, 5]
In : a + b
Out: [1, 'two', 3, 4.4, 5]
```

and list entries can be replicated with the * operator:

```
In : a = [1, 'two']
In : a*3
Out: [1, 'two', 1, 'two', 1, 'two']
```

4.3.9 Preallocate an Empty List

Occasionally, it is convenient to create a list not by appending items but by inserting items nonsequentially into a predefined (but empty) list of known size. In MATLAB, one can achieve this by calling cell() with the desired dimensions. In Python, the desired initial value is put in a single item list, and then this list is multiplied by the desired size. The Python example shows two such initializations, once with None's and once with empty lists:

MATLAB:	Python:
`>> a = cell(4,1)`	`In : a = 4*[None]`
`a =`	`In : a`
`{`	`Out: [None, None, None, None]`
`  [1,1] = [](0x0)`	
`  [2,1] = [](0x0)`	`In : a[2] = -7.2`
`  [3,1] = [](0x0)`	`In : a`
`  [4,1] = [](0x0)`	`Out: [None, None, -7.2, None]`
`}`	
`>> a{3} = -7.2`	`In : a = 4*[[]]`
`a =`	`In : a`
`{`	`Out: [[], [], [], []]`
`  [1,1] = [](0x0)`	
`  [2,1] = [](0x0)`	`In : a[2] = -7.2`
`  [3,1] = -7.2000`	`In : a`
`  [4,1] = [](0x0)`	`Out: [[], [], -7.2, []]`
`}`	

Note that two dimensions were passed to MATLAB's cell(). If we were to call cell(4) instead of cell(4,1), the result would be a 4 × 4 cell array.

4.3.10 Insert to the Beginning (or Any Other Position) of a List

Python lists have an .insert() method that allows a new item to be inserted at any desired index. The method takes two arguments: the index which the object should occupy after the insertion and the object to be inserted. All other existing list items are shifted to the right by one position. Inserting an item to the beginning of a list is then done with .insert(0, item). Note, however, that adding list items anywhere other than at the end becomes expensive as the list becomes large.

MATLAB:	Python:
| ```
>> a
{[100]} {[-0.100]} {[102]} {[103]}
    {[104]} {[105]} {'list'}
>> a = horzcat('new',a)
 {'new'} {[100]} {[-0.100]} {[102]}
    {[103]} {[104]} {[105]} {'list'}
``` | ```
In : a
Out: [100, -0.1, 102, 103,
        104, 105, 'list']
In : a.insert(0, 'new')
In : a
Out: ['new', 100, -0.1, 102,
        103, 104, 105, 'list']
``` |

4.3.11 Indexing Nested Containers

Entries within nested cell arrays are indexed in MATLAB with both braces and parentheses; the braces index into the cell array, and parentheses index into the item within the cell.

Python's indexing is more straightforward as brackets are used ubiquitously:

MATLAB:	Python:

`>> a = {1, {'inner', 'cell'}, -3.3}`
`a =`
`  1x3 cell array`
`    {[1]} {1x2 cell} {[-3.3000]}`
`>> a{2}`
`  1x2 cell array`
`    {'inner'}  {'cell'}`
`>> a{2}(1)`
`  1x1 cell array`
`    {'inner'}`
	`In : a = [1, ['inner', 'list'], -3.3]`
	`In : a`
	`Out: [1, ['inner', 'list'], -3.3]`
	`In : a[1]`
	`Out: ['inner', 'list']`
	`In : a[1][0]`
	`Out: 'inner'`

4.3.12 Membership Test: Does an Item Exist in a List?

We saw at the beginning of this section that the `ismember()` function works for MATLAB cell arrays. I've not had luck using `ismember()` with mixed-type data in MATLAB 2020b though. (If all entries are numeric, the cell array can be converted to a matrix after which the `find()` function can be used.) Instead, I use this small function to check if an item exists in a cell array:

MATLAB:

```
function [found_it] = cell_has(C, value)
  found_it = 0;
  for i = 1:length(C)
    if C{i} == value
      found_it = 1;
      break
    end
  end
end
```

Python, in contrast, makes list, set, and dictionary key membership tests easy with the in operator:

MATLAB:	Python:
>> a = {'hi', 102, 3.3}; >> cell_has(a, 102) 1	In : a = ['hi', 102, 3.3] In : 102 in a Out: True
>> cell_has(a, 27) 0	In : 27 in a Out: False

Returning briefly to ismember() in MATLAB, the six attempts at checking if 102 is in a all yield the same error:

MATLAB:

```
>> a = {'hi', 102, 3.3};
>> ismember(a, 102)
>> ismember(a, '102')
>> ismember(a, {102})
>> ismember(a, {'102'})
>> ismember(a, {[102]})
>> ismember(a, {['102']})
```

```
Error using cell/ismember
Input A of class cell and input B of class cell must be
cell arrays of character vectors, unless one is a
character vector.
```

4.3.13 Find the Index of an Item

MATLAB employs the find() function to locate a value in a cell array of numeric values. Python's equivalent is the .index() method—which has the additional benefit of working with mixed data types, not just numeric values. Here, we identify the index of the value 102:

MATLAB:	**Python:**
>> a = num2cell(100:106)	In : a = list(range(100,107))

a =
 	
  1x7 cell array
  Columns 1 through 7
    {[100]} {[101]} {[102]}
    {[103]} {[104]} {[105]}
    {[106]}
	In : a
	Out: [100, 101, 102, 103,
	        104, 105, 106]

>> find([a{:}] == 102) 3	In : a.index(102) Out: 2

If we look for an item that doesn't exist, Python raises the `ValueError` exception:

MATLAB:	**Python:**
>> find([a{:}] == 27)	In : a.index(27) ValueError: 27 is not in list

Curiously, MATLAB's find() fails if the cell array has disparate data types *and* one attempts to find a nonnumeric term. Python has no such issue:

MATLAB:	Python:

``matlab
>> a{7} = 'string';
>> a
a =
  1×7 cell array
  Columns 1 through 7
    {[100]} {[101]} {[102]}
    {[103]} {[104]} {[105]}
    {'string'}
``
	``python
	In : a[6] = 'string'
	
	In : a
	Out: [100, 101, 102, 103,
	        104, 105, 'string']
	``

``matlab
>> find([a{:}] == 102)
     3
``
	``python
	In : a.index(102)
	Out: 2
	``

``matlab
>> find([a{:}] == 'string')
Matrix dimensions must agree.
``
	``python
	In : a.index('string')
	Out: 6
	``

4.3.14 Apply an Operation to All Items (List Comprehension)

Python *list comprehensions* closely resemble MATLAB's cellfun() and arrayfun() functions to apply an operation to each element in the array. This example returns the cube of each entry:

MATLAB:	Python:

``matlab
>> a = {0.3, 0.4, 0.5};
>> cellfun(@(x)(x.^3),a)
0.0270 0.0640 0.1250
``
	``python
	In : a = [0.3, 0.4, 0.5]
	In : [x**3 for x in a]
	Out: [0.027, 0.064, 0.125]
	``

The generic notation is

```python
LHS = [ operator(x) for x in List ]
```

where x is an arbitrary variable name, and List is the name of the list you want to operate on. The left-hand side variable LHS will contain a new list containing the result of the operator applied to terms of the original list. Expanded to a for loop, the preceding comprehension would look like this:

```
LHS = []
for x in List:
    LHS.append( operator(x) )
```

The list comprehension runs more quickly than the for loop though. This example creates a string showing each element of the list prefixed by "0x":

MATLAB:	Python:

`>> a = {100, 101, 102,...`
`        103, 'string'};`
`>> cellfun(@(y) "0x" +...`
`        string(y), a)`
`  1×5 string array`
`  "0x100" "0x101" "0x102"`
`    "0x103" "0xstring"`
	`In : a = [100, 101, 102,`
	`            103, 'string']`
	`In : [f'0x{str(y)}' for y in a]`
	`Out: ['0x100', '0x101', '0x102',`
	`        '0x103', '0xstring']`

4.3.15 Select a Subset of Items Based on a Condition

List comprehensions can be paired with Boolean expressions to create filters. The notation is

```
[ operator(x) for x in List if condition(x) ]
```

Here, we extract entries whose first letter is uppercase. Python strings, like MATLAB strings, may be indexed numerically to access individual characters or substrings. In this way, we can get the first character with x[0] and test if it is uppercase by applying the string method .isupper() to it. Thus, the following x[0].isupper() returns True if the first character of the iterator string, x, is uppercase and False otherwise. There are several possible solutions in MATLAB, but each requires multiple steps. The following solution creates an index array that identifies terms which satisfy the condition:

MATLAB:	Python:
| ```
>> a = {'Select','a','Subset',...
    'of','Items','Based',...
    'on','a','Condition'}
>> i = isstrprop(cellfun(@(x)...
    x(1), a), 'upper');
>> a(i)
    {'Select'} {'Subset'} {'Items'}
    {'Based'} {'Condition'}
``` | ```
In : a = ['Select', 'a', 'Subset',
            'of', 'Items', 'Based',
            'on', 'a', 'Condition']
In : [x for x in a if x[0].isupper()]
Out: ['Select', 'Subset', 'Items',
        'Based', 'Condition']
``` |

4.3.16 How Many Times Does an Item Occur?

Python lists have a .count() method which returns the number of times the given argument appears.

MATLAB:	Python:
| ```
>> a = {'To',2,'To','To','u'};
>> sum(cellfun(@(x) string(x)...
    == 'To', a))
        3
>> sum(cellfun(@(x) string(x)...
    == 'From', a))
        0
``` | ```
In : a = ['To',2,'To','To','u']
In : a.count('To')
Out: 3

In : a.count('From')
Out: 0
``` |

4.3.17 Remove the First or Last (or Any Intermediate) List Item

Python lists support a .pop() method which returns the last item in the array and removes that term from the list. If .pop() is given an index *n*, it returns—and removes—the *n*th item; .pop(0) therefore removes the first item in the list. The same result can be achieved in MATLAB with index slices.

MATLAB:	Python:
`>> a = {21, 22, 23, 24, 25};`	`In : a = [21, 22, 23, 24, 25]`
`>> b = a(end);`	`In : b = a.pop()`
`>> a = a(1:end-1)`	`In : a`
`  {[21]} {[22]} {[23]} {[24]}`	`Out: [21, 22, 23, 24]`
`>> b`	`In : b`
`  {[25]}`	`Out: 25`
`>> a = {21, 22, 23, 24, 25};`	`In : a = [21, 22, 23, 24, 25]`
`>> a(1)`	`In : a.pop(0)`
`  {[21]}`	`Out: 21`
`>> a = a(2:end)`	`In : a`
`  {[22]} {[23]} {[24]} {[25]}`	`Out: [22, 23, 24, 25]`

The slicing method for MATLAB gets clumsy when removing an item from the middle though:

MATLAB:	Python:
`>> a = {21,22,23,24,25};`	`In : a = [21,22,23,24,25]`
`>> i = 3;`	`In : i = 2`
`>> a(1)`	`In : a.pop(i)`
`  {[23]}`	`Out: 23`
`>> a = horzcat(a(1:i-1),a(i+1:end))`	`In : a`
`  {[21]} {[22]} {[24]} {[25]}`	`Out: [21, 22, 24, 25]`

4.3.18 Remove an Item by Value

If one knows the index of an item to remove from a list, the `.pop(index)` method described earlier works nicely. But what if you only know the value of the item to remove? In this case, the `.remove()` method is useful. Note that only the first occurrence of the matched value is removed. A `ValueError` exception is raised if the requested value doesn't appear.

The MATLAB solution uses an index array that stores locations of matching values. The negation of the index array, i, corresponds to locations of nonmatching values. Unlike Python's .remove() method, MATLAB doesn't care if a value is not found. In this case, it merely returns an index array with no hits.

MATLAB:	Python:
| ```
>> a = {22,21,'a',22,21};
>> i = cellfun(@(x) x == 22, a);
>> a = a(~i)
   {[21]} {'a'} {[21]}

>> i = cellfun(@(x) x == -4, a);
>> a = a(~i)
   {[21]} {'a'} {[21]}
``` | ```
In : a = [22,21,'a',22,21]
In : a.remove(22)
In : a
Out: [21, 'a', 22, 21]

In : a.remove(22)
Out: [21, 'a', 21]

In : a.remove(-4)
-------------------------------
ValueError
----> 1 a.remove(-4)
ValueError: list.remove(x):
         x not in list
``` |

4.3.19 Merging Multiple Lists

Related data items in separate lists must sometimes be grouped into individual pairwise (or, more generally, *n*-wise) items. For example, say you have a list of letters, 'A,' 'B,' 'C,' ..., and a corresponding list of those letters' ASCII values, 65, 66, 67, ..., and you want to merge these two lists into a single new list of letter and ASCII value pairs, [('A,' 65), ('B, 66), ...]. MATLAB allows one to create a new cell array by stacking existing cells, while Python has a function, zip(), which combines the lists. (Imagine a zipper joining two sections of fabric.)

zip() returns a generator to the combined list, rather than the combined list itself. Generators (Section 3.9) are great for iterating over, but they do not permit random indexing, as demonstrated with the following TypeError. If you need the fully populated list rather than a generator, invoke list() on the generator:

MATLAB:	Python:

```
>> Letter = {'A','B','C'}
Letter =
{
  [1,1] = A
  [1,2] = B
  [1,3] = C
}
>> ASCII = {65,66,67}
ASCII =
{
  [1,1] = 65
  [1,2] = 66
  [1,3] = 67
}
>> both={Letter;ASCII}
both =
{
  [1,1] =
  {
    [1,1] = A
    [1,2] = B
    [1,3] = C
  }
  [2,1] =
  {
    [1,1] = 65
    [1,2] = 66
    [1,3] = 67
  }
}
>> both{2}{3}
ans = 67
```

```
In : Letter = ['A','B','C']
In : Letter
Out: ['A', 'B', 'C']

In : ASCII = [65, 66, 67]
In : ASCII
Out: [65, 66, 67]

In : both = zip(Letter,ASCII)
In : both
Out: <zip at 0x7fc4500c4050>

In : list(both)
Out: [('A', 65), ('B', 66),
      ('C', 67)]

In : both[2][1]
-----------------------------
TypeError Traceback
----> 1 both[2][1]
TypeError: 'zip' object is
              not subscriptable

In : both = list(both)
In : both[2][1]
Out: 67
```

zip() is frequently seen in for loops that need to step through multiple lists in lockstep:

Python:

```
In : X = [0.21, 0.96, 0.26, 0.34, 0.90, 0.82]
In : Y = [-1.36, -1.88, -1.20, -1.10, -1.16, -1.27]
In : Z = [4.89, 4.08, 4.82, 4.62, 4.43, 4.93]

In : for x,y,z in zip(X,Y,Z):
...:      print(f'{x:6.3f} {y:6.3f} {z:6.3f}')

 0.210    -1.360    4.890
 0.960    -1.880    4.080
 0.260    -1.200    4.820
 0.340    -1.100    4.620
 0.900    -1.160    4.430
 0.820    -1.270    4.930
```

4.3.20 Unmerging Combined Lists

The previous section showed how to combine like-sized lists. Surprisingly, the opposite operation of unmerging a combined list into multiple individual lists is also done with zip(). The difference is that to unmerge, the argument to zip() is prefixed by an asterisk. In MATLAB, one must use slice operations to extract out subcell arrays one at a time. Using the same variable both from the previous section

MATLAB:	Python:
>> a = both{1,:}	In : a, b = zip(*both)
a =	In : a
{	Out: ['A', 'B', 'C']
[1,1] = A	
[1,2] = B	In : b
[1,3] = C	Out: [65, 66, 67]
}	
>> b = both{2,:}	
b =	
{	
[1,1] = 65	
[1,2] = 66	
[1,3] = 67	
}	

Prefixing a list or numeric array with an asterisk, as with *both earlier, means "expand the terms." In other words, if x = [9, 'b'], then x is a single item, a list. *x, however, means two separate terms, 9 and 'b'. The asterisk can be thought of as removing the outer container.

4.3.21 Sort a List

One can obtain a sorted list with the sorted() function, or one can sort a list in-place with the list's .sort() method. Sorting only makes sense for like types, so the MATLAB equivalent is straightforward as we would convert the cell array to a matrix and sort the matrix items:

MATLAB:	Python:
a = {31, -127, 28, 45} {[31]} {[-127]} {[28]} {[45]} >> sort(cell2mat(a)) -127 28 31 45	In : a = [31, -127, 28, 45] In : sorted(a) Out: [-127, 28, 31, 45] In : a Out: [31, -127, 28, 45] In : a.sort() In : a Out: [-127, 28, 31, 45]

Python's sorted() and .sort() both take two optional arguments: key, which allows one to customize the sort operation, and reverse, a Boolean which can reverse the sense of the sort. Here, we sort on the absolute value of each item, then also reverse the sort:

```
In : sorted(a, key=lambda x : abs(x))
Out: [28, 31, 45, -127]

In : sorted(a, reverse=True)
Out: [45, 31, 28, -127]

In : sorted(a, key=lambda x : abs(x), reverse=True)
Out: [-127, 45, 31, 28]
```

4.3.22 Reverse a List

Finally, the sequence of a Python list can be flipped with either the reversed() function or with the list's .reverse() method; using the .reverse() method alters the list in-place. MATLAB can reverse terms of vector or cell array x with fliplr(x) or flip(x,2).

Unlike sorted(), reversed() returns an *iterator*—a function which returns one value at a time—so to see the actual reversed items in the REPL, we'll also need to invoke list():

MATLAB:	Python:
>> a	In : a
{[31]} {[-127]} {[28]} {[45]}	Out: [31, -127, 28, 45]
>> fliplr(a)	In : reversed(a)
{[45]} {[28]} {[-127]} {[31]}	Out: <list_reverseiterator>
	In : list(reversed(a))
	Out: [45, 28, -127, 31]
	In : a
	Out: [31, -127, 28, 45]
	In : a.reverse()
	In : a
	Out: [45, 28, -127, 31]

4.4 Python Tuples

Python tuples closely resemble Python lists—both can contain a collection of items and can be indexed numerically. The primary difference is that a tuple of scalar variables is unchangeable[3] after it has been created; think of a tuple as a constant with multiple

---

[3] Not entirely true because tuples may contain lists, dictionaries, or numeric arrays, all of which are stored as references. The contents of these collections may change even if the references stored in the tuple do not.

values. This immutable property gives tuples a critical advantage over lists and sets as it lets tuples act as keys to dictionaries. The use of tuples as dictionary keys is explored in Section 4.6.5.

Not all tuples are "hashable" (meaning they can be dictionary keys), though. Tuples made with variables that are lists, dictionaries, or NumPy arrays can change since the tuple only stores references to these variables; the values in the underlying list/dict/array can still change. A tuple is hashable only if all its member items are hashable—and that rules out tuples that contain references to containers whose contents may change.

MATLAB has no comparable "frozen collection" data container.

Tuples are created by assigning a variable to comma-separated items or by calling the tuple() function with an iterable. Even a single item followed by a comma qualifies as a tuple:

Python:

```
In : S = 3,
In : type(S)
Out: tuple

In : len(S)
Out: 1

In : T = 3, -8.5, 'cat'
In : type(T)
Out: tuple

In : len(T)
Out: 3

In : T[1]
Out: -8.5

In : U = tuple(range(10,14))
In : U
Out: (10, 11, 12, 13)
```

Note   Stray commas create tuples! This can lead to mysterious errors far downstream from where the tuple was mistakenly created. As an example, say you write a function that computes a numeric value but the function ends with `return X,` instead of the intended `return X`. Later, another function scales this returned value by 4. If X were 1.1, the first function returns the tuple `(1.1,)`. The second function multiplies this by 4, producing `(1.1, 1.1, 1.1, 1.1)` instead of `4.4`. The bad value continues to propagate until an illegal operation, division, for instance, is attempted with the tuple.

Tuples are often seen wrapped in parentheses. This is in fact mandatory when passing a tuple as an argument to a function or assigning multiple tuples on one line:

Python:

```
In : T, V = (3, -8.5, 'cat'), ('grey', 'dog')
In : T
Out: (3, -8.5, 'cat')

In : V
Out: ('grey', 'dog')
```

Many NumPy array creation functions—for example, np.ones(), shown earlier in Section 4.1 where it is invoked as np.ones((2,))—expect the first argument to be a tuple defining the array's dimensions. The double set of parentheses often puzzles new Python programmers. The parentheses are needed to separate the dimension, which is a single variable, from subsequent arguments:

Python:

```
In : import numpy as np
In : np.ones((3,5), np.uint16)
Out:
array([[1, 1, 1, 1, 1],
       [1, 1, 1, 1, 1],
       [1, 1, 1, 1, 1]], dtype=uint16)
```

4.5 Python Sets and MATLAB Set Operations

MATLAB and Python can both perform set operations—unions, intersections, and so on—but only Python has a data container specifically for storing sets. Sets are created with braces or by calling the set() function on an iterable:

Python:

```
In : x = { 'CA', 'IL' }
In : type(x)
Out: set

In : y = set([44, 55, 'sixty'])
In : type(y)
Out: set
```

Set members are unique. Calling set() on a list with duplicate elements and then converting the set back to a list is a common way to remove the duplicates. MATLAB's unique() function behaves similarly:

MATLAB:	Python:

`>> Fib = [ 0 1 1 2 3 5];`
`>> unique(Fib)`
`   0   1   2   3   5`
	`In : Fib = [ 0, 1, 1, 2, 3, 5]`
	`In : set(Fib)`
	`Out: {0, 1, 2, 3, 5}`

Set members can be iterated over, but cannot be indexed numerically. Cast the set to a list if you need to index terms. Beware, though, that sets do not maintain sequence; iteration over a set and casting a set to a list puts the items in any order.

Python:

```
In : a = {54, 43, 32, 23}
In : a[1]
TypeError: 'set' object is not subscriptable

In : for x in a:
...:     print(x)
```

```
32
43
54
23

In : L = list(a)
In : L[2]
Out: 54
```

Membership tests look different in MATLAB and Python. MATLAB's ismember() function takes two arrays[4] as inputs and returns an array of zeros and ones equal to the size of the first array indicating whether or not the corresponding term appears in the second array. An additional call to all() would be needed to check that every item of the first variable exists in the second. Python uses the in operator to check for the presence of individual members. (Although in can also be used to test for membership in a list, performance there has complexity O(N); with sets it is only O(1).) For group membership checks, one can call the .issuperset() method:

MATLAB:	Python:
>> a = [54 43 32 23];	In : a = {54, 43, 32, 23}
>> ismember(43, a)	In : 43 in a
1	Out: True
>> ismember(44, a)	In : 44 in a
0	Out: False
>> all(ismember([32, 43], a))	In : a.issuperset({32, 43})
1	Out: True

---

[4] Even scalar values are 1 × 1 arrays in MATLAB.

Table 4-2 summarizes set operations in MATLAB and Python.

Table 4-2. *Set operations*

Operation	MATLAB	Python	Explanation
Union	`union(A,B)`	`A	B`	All members of A and B
Intersection	`intersect(A,B)`	`A & B`	Members that are in both A and B
Difference	`setdiff(A,B)`	`A - B`	Members of A after members of B have been removed from A
Symmetric difference	`setxor(A,B)`	`A ^ B`	Members which are only in A or only in B
Subset test	`all(ismember(A,B))`	`A.issubset(B)`	True if all members of A are in B
Superset test	`all(ismember(B,A))`	`A.issuperset(B)`	True if all members of B are in A
Disjointed test	`~any(ismember(A,B))`	`A.isdisjoint(B)`	True if A and B have no members in common

4.6 Python Dictionaries and MATLAB Maps

Dictionaries (also known as associative arrays or hashes in Perl; hashes or maps in JavaScript; and maps in C++, Java, and MATLAB) allow one to create a relationship between two datasets known as *keys* and *values*. Notationally, dictionaries look like lists that can be indexed by arbitrary scalars—strings, for example—instead of just integers. In addition to the convenience they provide developers, dictionaries are also performant. Both inserting new key-value pairs into and retrieving values from dictionaries are O(1) operations on average.

Oddly, despite its power, MATLAB programmers rarely use its Map data container.

Dictionaries are best explained by example. Say we need to look up a country's capital city. We could store the country-to-capital city relationship in a dictionary like this:

Python:

```
capital = {}  # define capital as an empty dictionary
capital['USA']      = 'Washington D.C.'
capital['Germany']  = 'Berlin'
capital['Japan']    = 'Tokyo'
capital['France']   = 'Paris'
```

Retrieving a country's capital is then just a matter of using the country's name as the subscript to the dictionary:

Python:

```
In : country = 'Japan'
In : print(f'The capital of {country} is {capital[country]}.')
The capital of Japan is Tokyo.
```

Dictionaries beat lists for storing relationships not only because of the key/value binding but because they permit much faster data lookup. Imagine storing the country/city data in a list and having to return a city given a country. Even if the list were sorted by country name, the fastest search would be $O(\log_2(N))$, no match for the $O(1)$ average speed of dictionary lookups.

4.6.1 Iterating over Keys

Iterating over keys of a dictionary is done with the `for key in dict:` looping construct:

```
In : for country in capital:
...:    city = capital[country]
...:    print(f'{country:10s} -> {city}')
...:
USA        -> Washington D.C.
Germany    -> Berlin
Japan      -> Tokyo
France     -> Paris
```

Python (as of version 3.6) iterates over dictionary keys in the order they were inserted, same as Map in JavaScript. In contrast, std::map in C++ iterates over keys in sorted order. (Before v3.6, Python dictionaries behaved more like Perl and JavaScript hashes which can return keys in any order.)

4.6.2 Testing for Key Existence

The for ... in construct iterates over all keys in a dictionary in the order they were inserted. If you get a key from another source, you can test whether or not the key exists in the dictionary with the construct *test_key* in *dict_name*:

```
In : 'USA' in capital
Out: True

In : 'America' in capital
Out: False
```

Indexing a dictionary by a nonexistent key raises a KeyError:

```
In [26]: print(capital['America'])
---------------------------------------------------------
KeyError                  Traceback (most recent call last)
----> 1 print(capital['America'])

KeyError: 'America'
Out: False
```

As dictionaries are heavily used in Python, KeyError tends to be among the more frequent error messages Python programmers see.

4.6.2.1 get() and .setdefault()

Most algorithms that populate dictionaries need separate logic to deal with the cases of the key being absent and the key being present. Thus, to avoid KeyError, we frequently end up with code that looks like this:

```
if key in Dict:
    perform_a_task(Dict[key])
else:
    Dict[key] = 'new data'
```

Python has two options to simplify dictionary lookups. The first is the .get() method which returns a dict's value if the given key exists and None if it doesn't—without throwing a KeyError. Returning to our capital cities dictionary:

```
In : capital['USA']
Out: 'Washington D.C.'

In : capital.get('USA')
Out: 'Washington D.C.'

In : capital.get('America')

In : capital.get('America') is None
Out: True
```

Now our four lines are reduced to just

```
perform_a_task(Dict.get(key))
```

but the perform_a_task() function has the additional burden to check for a None input and act accordingly.

.setdefault() is similar to .get() in that it returns a dictionary's value given a key. If the key is missing though, .setdefault() creates that key with a given default value. This is handy for creating counters.[5] For example, say you want to count the frequency of each character in the string 'Use setdefault to initialize a new dict keys.' We'll use the list() method to split the string into individual characters and the dict Count to store the number of occurrences of each letter:

```
In : sentence = 'Use setdefault to initialize a new dict keys.'
In : Counter = {}
In : for character in list(sentence):
...:     Counter.setdefault(character, 0) # no op if character exists
...:     Counter[character] += 1
In : Counter
```

---

[5] Python has a special Counter data container for such applications in the collections module.

```
Out:
  {'U': 1, 's': 3, 'e': 6, ' ': 7, 't': 5,
   'd': 2, 'f': 1, 'a': 3, 'u': 1, 'l': 2,
   'o': 1, 'i': 5, 'n': 2, 'z': 1, 'w': 1,
   'c': 1, 'k': 1, 'y': 1, '.': 1}
```

4.6.2.2 Key Collision

A key *collision* refers to the insertion of a key-value pair into a dictionary which already has an entry for that key. If this occurs, the second value replaces the original:

```
In : D = { 'a' : 10, 'b' : 11, 'c' : 12 }
In : D['a'] = -5  # collision with existing key 'a'
In : D
Out: {'a': -5, 'b': 11, 'c': 12}
```

Some applications, for example, vote counting, have strict requirements that an entry only appear once. In this case, one must test for the absence of a key before allowing an insert:

```
In : voted = {}
In : for name in ['George W', 'John A', 'Tom J', 'James M', 'John A']:
...:    if name not in voted: # then OK to insert
...:        voted[name] = True
...:        print(f'OK: {name}')
...:    else:
...:        print(f'Error: {name} already voted!')
OK: George W
OK: John A
OK: Tom J
OK: James M
Error: John A already voted!
```

4.6.3 Iterating over Keys, Sorting by Key

Insert order is not always the desired order to iterate through a dictionary. Frequently, one may wish to traverse a dictionary based on ascending or descending sort order of its keys or values. In this case, we have to employ the sorted() function (and optionally pass it the desired comparison operator).

In this example, we sort our country-to-capital city dictionary by the alphabetical order of the keys (i.e., the country names):

```
In : for country in sorted(capital):
...:         city = capital[country]
...:         print(f'{country:10s} -> {city}')
...:
France      -> Paris
Germany     -> Berlin
Japan       -> Tokyo
USA         -> Washington D.C.
```

As explained in Section 4.3.21, sorted() takes two optional keyword arguments, reverse, a Boolean, and key, which is assigned to an in-line function known as a *lambda*. The lambda takes the dictionary's key as its argument and returns a value that will be used to determine sort order. First, we'll use reverse to invert the alphabetical sort order:

```
In : for country in sorted(capital, reverse=True):
...:         city = capital[country]
...:         print(f'{country:10s} -> {city}')
...:
USA         -> Washington D.C.
Japan       -> Tokyo
Germany     -> Berlin
France      -> Paris
```

Next, we'll use key to provide an in-line function that determines sort order by the length of the country name from shortest to longest:

```
In : for country in sorted(capital, key=lambda X: len(X)):
...:         city = capital[country]
...:         print(f'{country:10s} -> {city}')
...:
USA         -> Washington D.C.
Japan       -> Tokyo
France      -> Paris
Germany     -> Berlin
```

The expression key=lambda X: len(X) bears additional clarification. The letter X is an arbitrary variable that represents the function's argument, which will be the dictionary keys, for example, 'France'. The lambda's return value, len(X), is the length of the dictionary key, or the number 5 when X is 'France'. Our case lambda function will cause sorted() to return the dictionary keys from the shortest length, 3 for 'USA', to the longest, 7 for 'Germany'.

4.6.4 Iterating over Keys, Sorting by Value

Lambda functions can just as easily control sorting based on the dictionary values, that is, the city names, instead of just keys. If we wanted to iterate based on the alphabetical order of city names, we simply use a lambda function that returns the string of the city name:

```
In : for country in sorted(capital, key=lambda X: capital[X]):
...:         city = capital[country]
...:         print(f'{country:10s} -> {city}')
...:
Germany    -> Berlin
France     -> Paris
Japan      -> Tokyo
USA        -> Washington D.C.
```

And if we want to sort on the reverse order of the length of the city names, we would do

```
In : for country in sorted(capital, key=lambda X: len(capital[X]), reverse=True):
...:         city = capital[country]
...:         print(f'{country:10s} -> {city}')
...:
USA        -> Washington D.C.
Germany    -> Berlin
Japan      -> Tokyo
France     -> Paris
```

4.6.4.1 Secondary Sorts

In the preceding result, both `'Tokyo'` and `'Paris'` have five characters. How should we handle tie breakers? If we want to perform additional sorts in cases where the primary sort has equal values, we'll need a secondary sort.

Secondary sorts take advantage of the fact that Python's sorts are *stable*. This means if there are two records R and S with the same key and R appears before S in the original list, R will appear before S in the sorted list. In other words, the city sort earlier will always show `'Tokyo'` before `'Paris'` regardless of how many new entries are added to, or removed from, the dictionary. To implement a secondary sort, we work backward by first sorting the dictionary by the secondary condition, then sort that result by the primary condition. Wherever the primary condition has ties, the equally valued items remain in the order they entered the sort, in other words, already sorted by the secondary condition.

Here's how it looks like in practice. First, we'll make a list of keys (i.e., country names) sorted by alphabetical value of the city names:

```
In : countries_sorted_by_capital = sorted(capital, key=lambda X: capital[X])
In : countries_sorted_by_capital
Out: ['Germany', 'France', 'Japan', 'USA']
```

The only significant property of `countries_sorted_by_capital` is that `'France'` appears before `'Japan'` because these countries have capital cities with the same number of characters and that the capital of `'France'`, `'Paris'`, appears alphabetically before the capital of `'Japan'`, `'Tokyo'`. The positions of the other countries are irrelevant.

Now we sort the secondary sort results, `countries_sorted_by_capital`, by our primary criterion—the length of the city name:

```
In : countries_sorted_by_capital = sorted(capital, key=lambda X:
capital[X])
In : for country in sorted(countries_sorted_by_capital,
...:             key=lambda X: len(capital[X]), reverse=True):
...:     city = capital[country]
...:     print(f'{country:10s} -> {city}')
...:
```

```
USA         -> Washington D.C.
Germany     -> Berlin
France      -> Paris
Japan       -> Tokyo
```

Finally, we have the result in the sequence we wanted: inverse order of city name length and alphabetical order where city names are equally long.

Tertiary and higher-level sorts work the same way: sort by the least significant factor, then work your way backward to the primary factor.

4.6.5 Tuples As Keys

All dictionary examples so far have used scalar keys. Tuples are, in a sense, multivalued scalars and can also be used as dictionary keys. This enables simple solutions to data relationships that involve multiple inputs.

As an example, if you wanted to keep track of defective pixels on a sensor, you could make a tuple from the *i, j* coordinates and index your dictionary with the coordinate tuple:

```
bad_pixel_coords = [ (432,66), (553,17), (846,295) ]
defective_pixel = {}
for ij in bad_pixels: # eg, ij = 553,17
    defective_pixel[ ij ] = True
```

to define

```
defective_pixel[ 432, 66 ] = True
defective_pixel[ 553, 17 ] = True
defective_pixel[ 846,295 ] = True
```

You could store the same information in a double-level dictionary, but it would be messier to code and slower to traverse.

4.6.6 List Values

Dictionary values are not limited to scalars; they may be any Python container, including other dictionaries. Dictionaries of lists are a popular combination. Among other things, these can store tree structures—the parent node is the dictionary key, and its list items are child nodes. This tree, for example

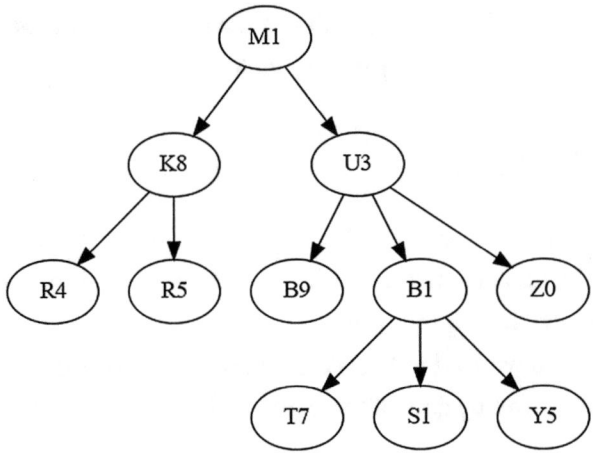

can be represented by this dictionary of lists:

```
tree = {}
tree['M1'] = ['K8', 'U3']
tree['U3'] = ['B9', 'B1', 'Z0']
tree['K8'] = ['R4', 'R5']
tree['B1'] = ['T7', 'S1', 'Y5']
```

4.7 Structured Data

MATLAB allows one to create structured variables on the fly. Python has several ways to do the same, albeit without MATLAB's simplicity. The more casual methods use the namedtuple class, imported from the collections module, and the SimpleNamespace class, imported from the types module. The most powerful method uses data classes. These can contain custom methods that operate on the data and contain relationships similar to joined tables in an SQL database.

4.7.1 Method 1: `namedtuple`

As its name implies, a `namedtuple` is a type of tuple, meaning its values cannot be changed after their initial assignment. They are ideal for read-only structured variables. While the MATLAB and Python structures contain the same data in the following example, the MATLAB values may be changed:

MATLAB:	Python:
`>> Pos.x = 354.8;`	`In : from collections import namedtuple`
`>> Pos.y = -28.7;`	`In : Pt = namedtuple('Coord',`
`>> Pos.z = 1.4572e+5;`	`                ['x', 'y', 'z'])`
`>> Pos`	`In : a = Pt(354.8, -28.7, 14570.0)`
`Pos =`	`In : a`
`  struct with fields:`	`Out: Coord(x=354.8, y=-28.7, z=14570.0)`
`    x: 354.8000`	`In : a.y = 0`
`    y: -28.7000`	`AttributeError          Traceback`
`    z: 1.4572e+05`	`----> 1 a.y = 0`
	`AttributeError: can't set attribute`

4.7.2 Method 2: `SimpleNamespace`

A `SimpleNamespace` is a more versatile structured data container than a `namedtuple` because its values can be changed. The MATLAB code fragment here is identical to the one earlier.

MATLAB:	Python:
`>> Pos.x = 354.8;`	`In : from types import SimpleNamespace`
`>> Pos.y = -28.7;`	`In : Pos = SimpleNamespace()`
`>> Pos.z = 1.4572e+5;`	`In : Pos.x = 354.8`
	`In : Pos.y = -28.7`
	`In : Pos.z = 1.457e+4`
	`In : Pos`
	`Out: namespace(x=354.8, y=-28.7, z=14570.0)`

One can check whether or not a field name exists in the structured variable with the `hasattr()` function, directly analogous to MATLAB's `isfield()` function.

To iterate over the fields in MATLAB, one can use the `fieldnames()` function. The same is possible in Python, but with less obvious notation. There, one must access the structured variable's underlying dictionary:

MATLAB:	Python:
| ```
>> isfield(Pos, 'x')
1
>> isfield(Pos, 'w')
0
fields = fieldnames(Pos);
for i = 1:length(fields)
F = fields{i};
val = Pos.(F);
fprintf(' Pos.%s = %.1f\n', F, val);
end
Pos.x = 354.8
Pos.y = -28.7
Pos.z = 145720.0
``` | ```
In : hasattr(Pos, 'x')
Out: True

In : hasattr(Pos, 'w')
Out : False

In : for F in Pos.__dict__:
...:     val = Pos.__dict__[F]
...:     print(f' Pos.{F} = {val}')
...:
Pos.x = 354.8
Pos.y = -28.7
Pos.z = 14570.0
``` |

4.7.3 Method 3: Classes

Conventional Python classes, to be covered in greater detail in Chapter 10, can also serve as data containers although they require a bit more code to set up. For completeness, here is how one would define a regular class to store structured data:

MATLAB:	Python:
```classdef Position```	```In : class Position:```
```properties```	```...: def __init__(self, X, Y, Z)```
```x {double}```	```...: self.x = X```
```y {double}```	```...: self.y = Y```
```z {double}```	```...: self.z = Z```
```end```	```In : Pos = Position(354.8, -28.7,```
```methods```	``` 1.457e+4)```
```function obj = Position(x,y,z)```	```In : Pos.x, Pos.y, Pos.z```
```obj.x = x;```	```Out: (354.8, -28.7, 14570.0)```
```obj.y = y;```	
```obj.z = z;```	
```end```	
```end```	
```end```	
```>> Pos = Position(354.8,```	
``` -28.7, 1.457e+4)```	
```Pos = Position with properties:```	
```x = 354.8000```	
```y = -28.7000```	
```z = 14570```	

As with `SimpleNamespace`—and any Python object for that matter—the existence of attributes can be checked with `hasattr()` and iterated over by accessing the object's underlying `.__dict__` dictionary. See Section 4.7.2 for an example.

The power of using classes as data containers is the ability to add methods that perform value-added computations with the data values. As we'll see in the next section though, data classes give us a fusion of concise notation to define the data structures and the ability to define methods that operate on the values. Data classes are therefore better choices for storing structured data than conventional classes.

4.7.4 Method 4: Data Classes

Data classes, introduced in Python 3.7, allow one to create structured variables that can include custom methods. In essence, they are a convenience mechanism that defines a class with automatically generated underlying code for the __init__() constructor, __str__() to produce a string representation of the data, and several other methods. Items within data classes have associated types, but, as with type annotations (Section 3.8.5), by default Python will not enforce a type violation.

Type enforcement can be added with the Pydantic module, though (Section 4.7.4.5), to achieve a capability similar to optional variable properties defined in MATLAB classes (Section 10.1). Another difference between MATLAB classes and Python classes, including its data classes, is that MATLAB can explicitly define private methods, while Python cannot (this is covered in greater detail in Section 10.1.1).

We'll begin with the data class version of our previous example. The MATLAB Position class is the same as defined above.

MATLAB:	Python:

`>> Pos = Position`
`   (354.8, -28.7,`
`   1.457e+4)`
	`In : from dataclasses import dataclass`
	`In : @dataclass`
	`In : class Position:`
	`...:     x: float`
	`...:     y: float`
	`...:     z: float`
	`In : Pos = Position(354.8, -28.7,`
	`                         1.457e+4)`
	`In : Pos.x, Pos.y, Pos.z`
	`Out: (354.8, -28.7, 14570.0)`

Nothing exciting here; the real fun begins when we add methods to the data class. We'll begin by adding a function that computes the distance of the point from the origin:

Python:

```
from dataclasses import dataclass
import numpy as np
@dataclass
```

```
class Position:
    x: float
    y: float
    z: float
    def mag(self):
        return np.sqrt(self.x**2 + self.y**2 + self.z**2)
```

Now after we define a point, we can compute its distance by calling mag():

Python:

```
In : Pos = Position(354.8, -28.7, 1.457e+4)
In : Pos.mag()
Out: 14574.347557609568
```

4.7.4.1 Field Values

Alternatively, we can make the data class compute the magnitude and save it as another internal variable when the point is first created. This is done by defining the method _post_init_() and an additional attribute whose value is not supplied when the class is created:

Python:

```
from dataclasses import dataclass, field
import numpy as np
@dataclass
class Position:
    x: float
    y: float
    z: float
    R: float = field(init=False)
    def __post_init__(self):
        self.R = self.mag()
    def mag(self):
        return np.sqrt(self.x**2 + self.y**2 + self.z**2)
```

A point object's attribute R, formally referred to as a *field value* because it depends on other values, is then defined when we create the point:

Python:

```
In : Pos = Position(354.8, -28.7, 1.457e+4)
In : Pos.R
Out: 14574.347557609568
```

Field values are not automatically recomputed when the initial values change. For example, changing the value of Pos.z will not result in an updated Pos.R without explicitly calling Pos.mag(). To achieve such a change, the class variables would need to include a *setter* method which updates the variables and then calls .mag():

Python:

```
from dataclasses import dataclass, field
import numpy as np
@dataclass
class Position:
    x: float
    y: float
    z: float
    R: float = field(init=False)
    def __post_init__(self):
      self.R = self.mag()
    def mag(self):
      return np.sqrt(self.x**2 + self.y**2 + self.z**2)
    def set(self, x=None, y=None, z=None):
      if x is not None:
        self.x = x
      if y is not None:
        self.y = y
      if z is not None:
        self.z = z
      self.R = self.mag()
```

By calling .set() instead of modifying the variables directly, we'll get the behavior we want:

Python:

```
In : Pos = Position(354.8, -28.7, 1.457e+4)
In : Pos.R
Out: 14574.347557609568
In : Pos.set(x=-1, z=0)
In : Pos.R
Out: 28.717416318325018
```

4.7.4.2 Relationships Between Dependent Data Classes

The utility of data classes becomes more apparent when data classes are nested, that is, they include variables whose types are also data classes. To explore nested data classes more fully, we'll use the Python faker[6] module, explained in more detail in Appendix B, to generate names of people, phone numbers, and names of companies. These will be stored in data classes Person, Phone, and Company, respectively.

Each person can have one or more phones and work at one company, and a company can have one or more employees. If the data were stored in an SQL database, the entity relationship would resemble this diagram:

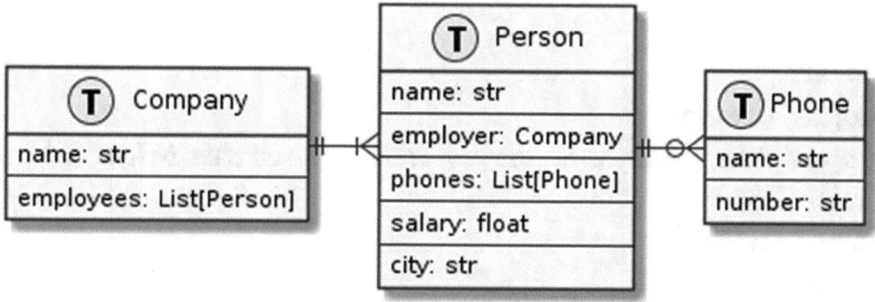

Before we generate data, we'll need to explore two more important data class properties: (1) the ability to modify data class properties dynamically and (2) that data class assignments as those for any mutable object[7] are by reference (ref. Section 4.8).

---

[6] https://github.com/joke2k/faker

[7] Examples: lists, dictionaries, NumPy arrays.

4.7.4.3 Dynamic Modification of Data Classes

The entity relationship diagram in Section 4.7.4.2 shows that a Company contains a list of Person as its employees, and a Person has a Company as their employer. Python does not permit forward declaration of data classes, so this presents a chicken-and-egg problem: which do we define first, a Person or a Company? Either way, we'll get an undefined data class error.

Fortunately, Python's mutability offers an easy solution to this dilemma: we can define either data class first and simply use a placeholder for the forward definition. The placeholder can be replaced later.

Python:

```
from dataclasses import dataclass, field
from typing import List
@dataclass
class Phone:
    type: str
    number: str

@dataclass
class Person:
    name: str
#   employer: Company
    employer: None #  place-holder, will be overwritten below
    salary: float
    phones: List[Phone]
    city: str

@dataclass
class Company:
    name: str
#   employees: List[Person] = field(init=False) # throws AttributeError
    employees: list = field(default_factory=list)
```

We'll use the faker module to populate names, cities, and companies with realistic strings. Here's a brief demo:

Python:

```
In : from faker import Faker
In : fake = Faker()
In : fake.name()
Out: 'Tammy Bennett'

In : fake.city()
Out: 'East Jacobchester'

In : fake.company()
Out: 'Lopez-Baker'
```

We can then make a person entry, make a corporation, and add that person as an employee of the corporation:

Python:

```
from faker import Faker
from random import random
fake = Faker()
company = None # forward reference; not known yet
salary  = 10 + 100*random()
phones  = [ Phone( 'mobile', fake.phone_number()),
            Phone( 'office', fake.phone_number()), ]
p_1 = Person(fake.name(), company, salary, phones, fake.city())
employees = []
c_1 = Company(fake.company(), employees)
# make person p_1 an employee of company c_1
p_1.employer = c_1 # resolve earlier forward reference
c_1.employees.append(p_1)
```

Sample values look like this:

Python:

```
In : p_1
Out: Person(name='Chuck Brown',
            employer=Company(name='Williams, Munoz and Green',
                    employees=[...]),
            salary=103.28236642597916,
            phones=[Phone(type='mobile', number='533.476.6020'),
                    Phone(type='office', number='629-596-5652x63457')],
                    city='Lauramouth')
In : c_1
Out: Company(name='Williams, Munoz and Green',
             employees=[Person(name='Chuck Brown', employer=...,
                    salary=103.28236642597916,
                    phones=[Phone(type='mobile', number='533.476.6020'),
                            Phone(type='office', number='629-596-
                            5652x63457')],
                    city='Lauramouth')])
```

Note the circular references of the person's employer details and the company's employees.

4.7.4.4 Traversing Linked Data Classes

The p_1 and c_1 objects created in Section 4.7.4.3 are linked together: the person is an employee of the company, and the company's employee list contains the person. As mentioned earlier, the objects only store memory references to each other, not copies of the data. In addition to being memory efficient, changes to either object are reflected immediately in all linked objects—an employee's office phone number change is seen by the employer as well.

Interlinked data class objects can be viewed as in-memory relational databases, where each data class is a table, each object a row entry, and interlinked references are foreign keys. As with SQL, information across linked data classes can be correlated rapidly. A company phone book could be prepared easily:

Python:

```
for person in c_1.employees:
    for phone in person.phones:
        if phone.type == 'office':
            print(f'{person.name} {phone.number}
```

4.7.4.5 Type Validation with Pydantic

The Position data class defined at the beginning of Section 4.7.4 says the three coordinates x, y, and z have type float (a 64-bit floating-point number). What happens if we create a Position with a string for one of these values?

Python:

```
In : a = Position("banana", 3.4, -5.1)
In :
```

It is accepted without complaint! This is bad news. Problems arise only when the bogus value appears in a computation:

Python:

```
In : a.mag()
------------------------------------------------
TypeError                          Traceback (most recent call last)
<ipython-input-7-e63ba7f2d72b> in <module>
----> 1 a.mag()

<ipython-input-3-0994e6029018> in mag(self)
      7     z: float
      8     def mag(self):
----> 9         return np.sqrt(self.x**2 + self.y**2 + self.z**2)

TypeError: unsupported operand type(s) for ** or pow() : 'str' and 'int'
```

Generally, you want to know there's a problem as soon as bad data is entered, not at some unknowable time in the future when the data is used.

The Pydantic module defines a data class that enforces types. Our `Position` class looks like this when created with Pydantic:

Python:

```
from pydantic import BaseModel
class Position(BaseModel):
    x: float
    y: float
    z: float
    def mag(self):
        return np.sqrt(self.x**2 + self.y**2 + self.z**2)
```

Now the error is raised when the object is created rather than when the improperly typed data is used:

Python:

```
In : good = Position(x=22.1, y=3.4, z=-5.1)
In : bad = Position(x = "banana", y=3.4, z=-5.1)

---> bad = Position(x = "banana", y=3.4, z=-5.1)

in pydantic.main.BaseModel.__init__()
ValidationError: 1 validation error for Position
x
   value is not a valid float (type=type_error.float)
```

4.7.5 Enumerations

Enumerations, or enums, are collections of related constants with descriptive names meant to clarify code. For example, a program that solves various types of partial differential equations might classify them as elliptic, hyperbolic, or parabolic. Rather than assigning numeric or string constants to these equation types, we can create an enumeration with these exact names:

MATLAB:	Python:
| ```
classdef EqType
    enumeration
        Elliptic, ...
        Hyperbolic, ...
        Parabolic
    end
end
``` | ```
import enum
class EqType(enum.Enum):
    Elliptic = 1
    Hyperbolic = 2
    Parabolic = 3
``` |

and subsequently use to the enumerated items like this:

MATLAB:	Python:
| ```
if b*b == a*c
  eType = EqType.Elliptic;
else if b*b > a*c
  eType = EqType.Hyperbolic;
else
  eType = EqType.Parabolic;
end

if (eType == EqType.Parabolic)
  parsolv(coeff, ...)
``` | ```
if b*b == a*c:
  eType = EqType.Elliptic
else if b*b > a*c:
  eType = EqType.Hyperbolic
else:
  eType = EqType.Parabolic

if eType == EqType.Parabolic:
  parsolv(coeff, ...)
``` |

Python enumerations are iterables, meaning we can loop over them. Additionally, the string and integer representations of each enumerated item can be found with the item's .name and .value attributes.

MATLAB does not provide a way to iterate over enumerated items.

Python:

```
In : for x in EqType:
...: print(x, x.name, x.value)

EqType.Elliptic Elliptic 1
EqType.Hyperbolic Hyperbolic 2
EqType.Parabolic Parabolic 3
```

4.8 Caveat: "=" Copies a Reference for Nonscalars!

A critical difference between MATLAB's data containers and Python's is that the assignment b = a in MATLAB makes a complete copy of a's contents and puts them in the new variable b. In Python, this is true only for scalars. If a is a list, dictionary, NumPy array, or any other higher-level data container, Python will only copy a *reference* to a into b. In other words, a and b will point to the same memory address; a and b become two names that refer to the same underlying data. Another way of putting it is that b = a makes b an *alias* of b. Conversely, changes made to a appear as changes to b as well.

Needless to say, copies of references rather than the entire data structure cause immense frustration for the unaware. Ostensibly simple computations report erroneous results, data appears to have been corrupted, results are not repeatable, and so on.

To duplicate MATLAB's = behavior and create a new variable b which contains a duplicate copy of everything in a, one must import the copy module and explicitly call one of its specialized methods, either copy.copy() or copy.deepcopy().

Here's a brief demonstration of the issue. The id() function reports an object's memory address:

```
In : a = [1, 2]
In : b = a
In : id(a), id(b)
Out: (139806965581896, 139806965581896)

In : b[0] = 999999
In : b
Out: [999999, 2]

In : a
Out: [999999, 2]
```

Creating b as a variable with duplicate contents as a would be done like so:

```
In : from copy import copy
In : a = [1, 2]
In : b = copy(a)
In : id(a), id(b)
Out: (139806060352840, 139806059562504)
```

```
In : b[0] = 999999
In : b
Out: [999999, 2]

In : a
Out: [1, 2]
```

The deepcopy() function from the copy module is needed for data containers that contain other data containers.

CHAPTER 5

Dates and Times

Temporal data appears frequently in computational work. Measurements recorded from sensors, economic results, stock prices, time-stepping numeric simulations, and so on are useless without accompanying time values. In this chapter, we'll cover Python's `datetime` module which offers capabilities similar to MATLAB's data type of the same name.

5.1 Time

Python's `time` module has functions to return the current time, either in the local timezone or UTC; measure CPU or elapsed time; and sleep for a desired amount of time.

5.1.1 Current Time

The Python `time.time()` function returns the same value as `posixtime(datetime())` in MATLAB, a double-precision representation of current time in Unix epoch seconds, a continuous increment of seconds since midnight, January 1, 1970, ignoring leap seconds, to a resolution of a microsecond. Among other things, it is useful in Python for computing elapsed time of code segments.

The `time.strftime()` function returns the current time according to a desired format:

© Albert Danial 2022
A. Danial, *Python for MATLAB Development*, https://doi.org/10.1007/978-1-4842-7223-7_5

MATLAB:	Python:
>> format long e	In : import time
>> posixtime(datetime())	In : time.time()
1.572210959845713e+09	Out: 1572210959.845713
>> t = datetime;	In : time.strftime('%Y-%m-%d %H:%M:%S')
>> datestr(t,'yyyy-mm-dd HH:MM:ss')	Out: '2019-10-27 14:25:26'
'2019-10-27 14:25:26'	

5.1.2 Time String Formats

Format arguments for strftime() include all arguments accepted by the 1989 C
standard library function of the same name plus a few others. In some cases, the output
depends on the computer's locale setting. This can be revealed by with the command
locale in a terminal on Linux and macOS and with systeminfo in a command prompt
on Windows (look for "System Locale" in the output). Examples in Table 5-1 use locale
settings of en_US and de_DE, as taken from the Python project's documentation.

MATLAB equivalent format strings for the datestr() function are given if the format
is supported.

Table 5-1. strftime() and strptime() format codes

Python Directive	Meaning	Examples	MATLAB Equivalent in datestr()
%a	Abbreviated weekday	Sun, Mon (en_US) So, Mo (de_DE)	ddd
%A	Abbreviated weekday	Sunday (en_US) Sonntag (de_DE)	dddd
%w	Weekday as integer	Python: 0 (*Sunday*) … 6 MATLAB: 1 (*Sunday*) … 7	e
%d	Two-digit day of month	01, …, 31	dd
%b	Abbreviated month	Jan, Dec (en_US) Jan, Dez (de_DE)	MMM
%B	Month	January (en_US) Januar (de_DE)	MMMM
%m	Two-digit month	01, …, 12	MM
%y	Two-digit year	99, 00, …, 19	yy
%Y	Four-digit year	1999, 2000, …, 2019	yyyy *or* u
%H	Two-digit hour, 0–23	00, …, 23	HH
%I	Two-digit hour, 0–11	00, …, 11	HH PM (output includes "PM")
%p	AM or PM	AM, PM (en_US) am, pm (de_DE)	AM *or* PM
%M	Two-digit minute	00, …, 59	mm
%S	Two-digit seconds	00, …, 59	ss
%f	Six-digit microseconds	000000, …, 999999	S .. SSSSSSSSS (tenth second to nanoseconds)
%z	UTC offset ±HHMM[SS[.ffffff]]	+0000, −0900015	Z

(continued)

Table 5-1. (*continued*)

Python Directive	Meaning	Examples	MATLAB Equivalent in `datestr()`
%j	Three-digit day of year	001, …, 366	DDD
%U	Two-digit week of year (week starts on Sunday)	00, …, 53	*Not available*
%W	Two-digit week of year (week starts on Monday)	00, …, 53	*Not available*
%c	Locale-specific date and time	Sun Oct 27 16:57:47 2019 (en US)	`datetime()` *default*
%x	Locale-specific date	10/27/19 (en_US) 27.10.2019 (de_DE)	*Not available*
%X	Locale-specific time	17:00:53 (en_US) 17:00:53 (de_DE)	*Not available*
%%	Literal %	%	%

5.1.3 tic, toc; %timeit

MATLAB's `tic` and `toc` compute elapsed CPU time of commands nested between them. `time.time()` in Python can do the same thing, but with more typing:

MATLAB:	Python:
>> N = 1000; >> tic >> a = eig(rand(N)) >> toc Elapsed time: 1.57437 seconds.	In : import time; import numpy as np In : N = 1000 In : tic = time.time() In : a = np.linalg.eig(np.random.rand(N,N)) In : time.time() - tic Out: 1.2564113140106201

The difference of calls to `time.time()` is useful in a Python program, but when working interactively in ipython, it is easier to use its "magic" command `%timeit` to measure how long a command takes:

Python:

```
In : %timeit np.linalg.eig(np.random.rand(1000,1000))
1.2 s ± 18.5 ms per loop (mean ± std. dev. of 7 runs, 1 loop each)
```

`%timeit` will run the command several times (seven in the preceding example) and return the mean time over all runs.

5.2 Dates

Python has three standard modules for working with dates, each with different capabilities:

- `datetime` is the most wide-ranging and will be the focus of discussion in this section. It has many functions to simplify computations with dates and perform conversions.

- `date` is more or less a subset of `datetime` and is useful when working purely with dates, without associated time within a day.

- `calendar` has functions to determine if a year is a leap year, the day of the week for a given date, and the number of days in a month.

5.2.1 datetime Objects to and from Strings

The `datetime` module, like the `time` module, uses the `strftime()` function to print a date in a desired format:

MATLAB:	Python:
`>> now = datetime()`	`In : from datetime import datetime`
	`In : datetime.now()`
`  28-Oct-2019 21:16:36`	`Out: datetime(2019, 10, 28, 21,`
	`               16, 36, 225635)`
`>> datetime(now,'Format',...`	
`        'u-MM-dd hh:mm')`	`In : datetime.now().strftime(`
	`             '%Y-%m-%d %H:%M')`
`  2019-10-28 21:16`	`Out: '2019-10-28 21:16'`

Both `datetime` and `time` have a similarly named function, `strptime()`, that does the opposite: it takes a string containing a date and a second string describing the format, then returns a Python variable which can subsequently be used to perform date computations.

Conveniently, `strptime()` uses the same format directives (Table 5-1) to parse dates from strings as `strftime()` uses to print dates in a desired format. Creating a `datetime` object from the string "Aug 12 04:05:51 2006" would be done like this:

MATLAB:	Python:
`>> S ='Aug 12 04:05:51 2006';`	`In : from datetime import datetime`
`>> dt=datetime(S,'InputFormat',...`	`In : S = 'Aug 12 04:05:51 2006'`
`        'MMM dd HH:mm:SS yyyy')`	`In : dt = datetime.strptime(S,`
`dt =`	`...:        '%b %d %H:%M:%S %Y')`
`  datetime`	`In : dt`
`  12-Aug-2006 04:05:00`	`Out: datetime.datetime(`
	`        2006, 8, 12, 4, 5, 51)`

5.2.2 Time Deltas

The `datetime` module function `timedelta()` creates time offsets that work like `duration` objects in MATLAB. This example prints a week's worth of Martian solar days (which last 24 hours, 39 minutes, and 35.244 seconds), starting at noon on June 28, 1986:

MATLAB:	Python:
| ```
Mars_day = duration(...
          24,39,35.244)
Start = datetime(...
      1986,6,28,12,0,0)
for i = 0:6
    Start + i*Mars_day
end
``` | ```
from datetime import datetime, timedelta
Mars_day = timedelta(hours=24,
    minutes=39, seconds=35.244)
Start = datetime(1986,6,28,12)
for i in range(7):
    print(Start + i*Mars_day)
``` |
| ```
28-Jun-1986 12:00:00
29-Jun-1986 12:39:35
30-Jun-1986 13:19:10
01-Jul-1986 13:58:45
02-Jul-1986 14:38:20
03-Jul-1986 15:17:56
04-Jul-1986 15:57:31
``` | ```
1986-06-28 12:00:00
1986-06-29 12:39:35.244000
1986-06-30 13:19:10.488000
1986-07-01 13:58:45.732000
1986-07-02 14:38:20.976000
1986-07-03 15:17:56.220000
1986-07-04 15:57:31.464000
``` |

timedelta objects have a method, .total_seconds(), that returns the number of seconds represented by the delta. The difference of two datetime objects is a timedelta, so we can easily determine how much time has elapsed between two dates:

MATLAB:	Python:
| ```
Jul4 = '1976-07-04 12:00';
Aug1 = '1976-08-01 18:00';
J=datetime(Jul4,'InputFormat',...
        'yyyy-MM-dd HH:mm')
A=datetime(Aug1,'InputFormat',...
        'yyyy-MM-dd HH:mm')
duration(A-J,'Format','s')
    2.4408e+06 sec
``` | ```
from datetime import datetime as DT
Jul4 = '1976-07-04 12:00'
Aug1 = '1976-08-01 18:00'
J = DT.strptime(Jul4, '%Y-%m-%d %H:%M')
A = DT.strptime(Aug1, '%Y-%m-%d %H:%M')
(A - J).total_seconds()

Out: 2440800.0
``` |

143

MATLAB and Python also allow one to compute ratios of time deltas. This example prints the number of Martian days in an Earth year:

MATLAB:	Python:
| ```
>> Mars_day = duration(...
            24,39,35.244);
>> duration(years(1))/Mars_day
    355.47
``` | ```
In : Mars_day = timedelta(hours=24,
...:     minutes=39, seconds=35.244)
In : timedelta(days=365.24)/Mars_day
Out: 355.4677472922519
``` |

5.3 Timezones

Datetime objects in both Python and MATLAB, by default, lack timezone information; they merely reflect the date and time of the host computer.

Python `datetime` objects can be made timezone-aware by populating the optional `tzinfo` or `tz` keywords in calls to `datetime()`, `datetime.now()`, or `datetime.fromtimestamp()` functions. Two Python modules that can create `tzinfo` objects are `pytz` and `dateutil.tz`. (Python 3.9 introduced the `zoneinfo` module which is discussed in Section 5.5. MATLAB 2020b, the version used in this book, predates Python 3.9 and therefore does not support it.) Although `pytz` has more features, the timezones from `dateutil.tz` yield more accurate results for corner cases, such as computing time deltas that span daytime/standard time transitions [1].

In this section, our only use of `pytz` will be to list all known timezone strings—like MATLAB's `timezones` command—something `dateutil.tz` can't do:

MATLAB:

Python:

>> timezones

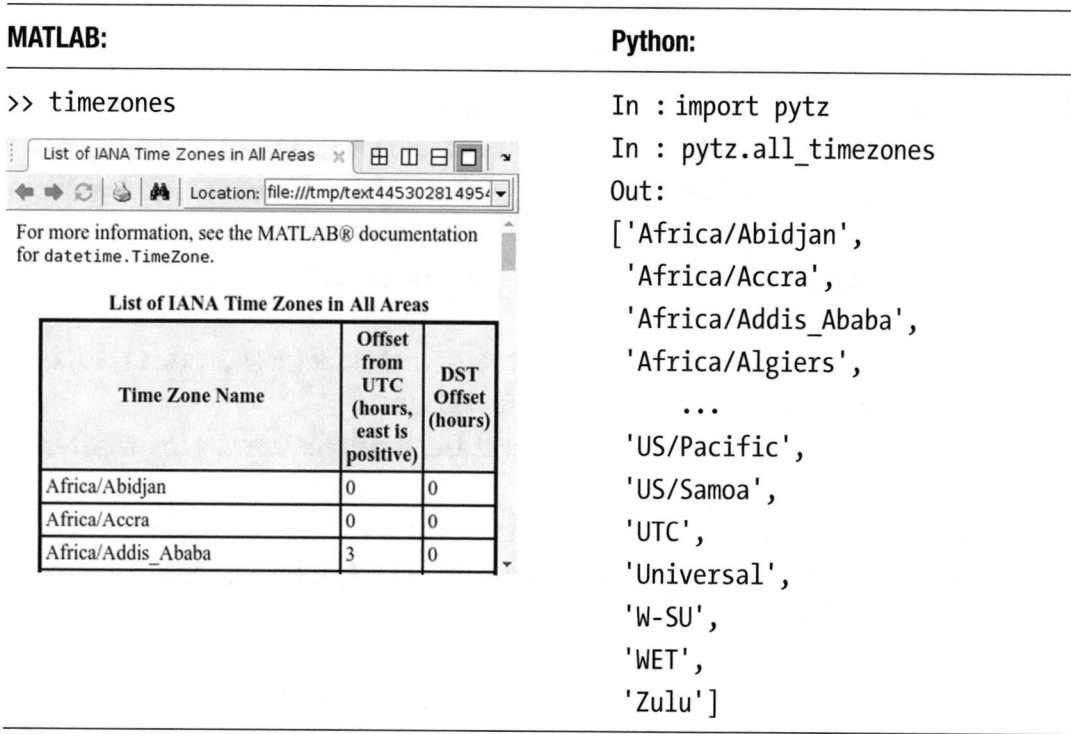

```
In : import pytz
In : pytz.all_timezones
Out:
['Africa/Abidjan',
 'Africa/Accra',
 'Africa/Addis_Ababa',
 'Africa/Algiers',
    ...
 'US/Pacific',
 'US/Samoa',
 'UTC',
 'Universal',
 'W-SU',
 'WET',
 'Zulu']
```

Timezone names in MATLAB's table match the names returned by pytz.all_timezones.

With a valid timezone name pulled from the preceding list, we're ready to create a timezone-aware datetime object. Note that datetime's output identifies the operating system's file from which timezone information was taken ('/usr/share/zoneinfo/America/Los_Angeles' in this example):

MATLAB:	Python:

`>> T = datetime(2020,2,14,...`
`        13,30,25,'TimeZone',...`
`        'America/Los_Angeles')`
`T =`
`    14-Feb-2020 13:30:25`
	`In : from datetime import datetime`
	`In : from dateutil import tz`
	`In : LA_tz = tz.gettz('America/Los_Angeles')`
	`In : T = datetime(2020,2,14,13,30,25,`
	`...:      tzinfo=LA_tz)`
	`In : T`

`>> T.TimeZone`
`    'America/Los_Angeles'`
	`Out: datetime.datetime(2020,2,14,13,30,25,`
	`        tzinfo=tzfile(`
	`        '/usr/share/zoneinfo/America/Los_Angeles'))`

`>> datetime(T,'Format',...`
`    'yyyy-MM-dd''T'...`
`    'HH:mm:ss''.''SSSSSS')`
`    2020-02-14T13:30:25.000000`
	`In : T.isoformat()`
	`Out: '2020-02-14T13:30:25-08:00'`

`>> datetime(T,'Format','Z')`
`    -0800`
	`In : T.utcoffset()`
	`Out: datetime.timedelta(days=-1,`
	`    seconds=57600)`

Displaying a timezone-aware `datetime` object in any other desired timezone is easily done:

MATLAB:	Python:

`>> datetime(T,'TimeZone',...`
`        'Asia/Tokyo')`
 	
`    15-Feb-2020 06:30:25`
	`In : Tokyo_tz = tz.gettz('Asia/Tokyo')`
	`In : T.astimezone(Tokyo_tz)`
	`Out: datetime.datetime(2020,2,15,6,30,25,`
	`        tzinfo=tzfile(`
	`        '/usr/share/zoneinfo/Asia/Tokyo'))`

5.3.1 UTC vs. Local Time

UTC, also called Zulu or Greenwich Mean Time, is the preferred timezone for recording events that span wide geographic areas. MATLAB and Python have several functions that explicitly work with UTC time as opposed to the local time on an individual computer.

Paradoxically, the datetime functions that return UTC time, datetime.utcnow() and datetime.utcfromtimestamp(), do not set tzinfo, and so they return timezone-unaware objects. In other words, the numeric values for day, hour, minute, and so on are correct, but there is no underlying metadata stating that this is the UTC timezone. If computational accuracy for subsequent date computations is important, the proper way to define UTC time is to use the functions without utc in their names and explicitly pass in tz=dateutil.tz.UTC [2]:

Python:

```
In : import time
In : from datetime import datetime
In : from dateutil import tz

In : datetime.now()  # local time (Los Angeles)
Out: datetime.datetime(2019, 11, 9, 18, 20, 57, 118448)

#    create UTC time from current time -- but without an associated
timezone!
In : datetime.utcnow()
Out: datetime.datetime(2019, 11, 10, 2, 20, 57, 118448)

#    the better way to create UTC time from current time
In : datetime.now(tz=tz.UTC)
Out: datetime.datetime(2019, 11, 10, 2, 20, 57, 118448, tzinfo=tzutc())

In : epoch_sec = time.time()
In : epoch_sec
Out: 1573352547.984918

In : datetime.fromtimestamp(epoch_sec)
Out: datetime.datetime(2019, 11, 9, 18, 22, 27, 984918)

#    the wrong way to create UTC time from epoch seconds
In : datetime.utcfromtimestamp(epoch_sec)
Out: datetime.datetime(2019, 11, 10, 2, 22, 27, 984918)

#    the right way to create UTC time from epoch seconds
In : datetime.fromtimestamp(epoch_sec, tz=tz.UTC)
Out: datetime.datetime(2019, 11, 10, 2, 22, 27, 984918, tzinfo=tzutc()))
```

Similar conversions in MATLAB look like this:

MATLAB:

```
>> a = datetime('now')  % computer is in Los Angeles timezone
   21-Nov-2023 11:28:52

>> a = datetime('now','TimeZone','America/Los_Angeles')
   21-Nov-2023 11:28:52

>> a = datetime('now','TimeZone','UTC')
   21-Nov-2023 18:28:52

>> epoch_sec = convertTo(a,'posixtime')
      1.700591332042366e+09

>> datetime(epoch_sec,'convertfrom','posixtime')
   21-Nov-2023 18:28:52
```

5.4 Time Conversions to and from `datetime` Objects

Section 5.2.1 showed how a `datetime` object can be converted to a string and how a string can be parsed into a `datetime` object. In this section, we explore additional format conversions to and from `datetime` objects using local time and UTC. The examples employ the following imports:

Python:

```
In : from datetime import datetime
In : import pytz
In : import time
```

5.4.1 Unix Epoch Seconds

Unix epoch seconds are independent of timezone, so the conversion from a timezone-enabled datetime object can be misleading:

Python:

```
In : epoch_sec = time.time()
In : epoch_sec
Out: 1572630202.1339452

In : dtZ = datetime.datetime.utcfromtimestamp( epoch_sec )
In : dtL = datetime.datetime.fromtimestamp(    epoch_sec )

In : dtZ
Out: datetime.datetime(2019, 11, 1, 17, 43, 22, 133945)

In : dtL
Out: datetime.datetime(2019, 11, 1, 10, 43, 22, 133945)

In : recovered_epoch_secZ = dtZ.timestamp()
In : recovered_epoch_secL = dtL.timestamp()

In : recovered_epoch_secZ
Out: 1572655402.133945

In : recovered_epoch_secL
Out: 1572630202.133945
```

For circular consistency, the Unix epoch value must be converted to the timezone where it was initially measured.

5.4.2 ISO 8601 Time String

Time strings in the ISO 8601 standard can have one of these forms:

- 2019-11-01T15:54:04

- 2019-11-01T15:54:04Z

- 2019-11-01T15:54:04+00:00

Although the datetime module includes a .fromisoformat() function, curiously the function does not accept the trailing "Z" (for "Zulu," also known as UTC); one must either omit the timezone designator or specify it as a numeric offset.

Also, since the ISO format function with a timezone offset explicitly sets the timezone, the local time variable is explicitly computed from the timezone-aware datetime object using the .astimezone() method:

Python:

```
In : dtZ = datetime.fromisoformat('2019-11-01T15:54:04+00:00')

In : TZ_LA = pytz.timezone("America/Los_Angeles")
In : dtL = dtZ.astimezone(TZ_LA)

In : dtZ
Out: datetime.datetime(2019, 11, 1, 15, 54, 4,
        tzinfo=datetime.timezone.utc)

In : dtL
Out: datetime.datetime(2019, 11, 1, 8, 54, 4,
        tzinfo=<DstTzInfo 'America/Los_Angeles' PDT-1 day, 17:00:00 DST>)

In : recovered_isoZ = dtZ.isoformat()
In : recovered_isoZ
Out: '2019-11-01T15:54:04+00:00'

In : recovered_isoL = dtL.isoformat()
In : recovered_isoL
Out: '2019-11-01T08:54:04-07:00'
```

5.4.3 Julian Date; Modified Julian Date; GPS Time

Anaconda comes with a module, astropy, which has powerful time conversion capabilities related to astronomy. These include Julian, Modified Julian, FITS, UT1, TAI, and GPS references.

The following examples use the US/Pacific timezone:

Python:

```
In : from astropy.time import Time
In : dt = datetime.fromisoformat('2019-11-03T05:29:04-07:00')
In : dt
```

```
Out: datetime.datetime(2019, 11, 3, 5, 29, 4,
            tzinfo=datetime.timezone(
                    datetime.timedelta(days=-1, seconds=61200)))
```

```
# from datetime to MJD, JD, GPS:

In : astropy_t = Time( dt )
In : astropy_t
Out: <Time object: scale='utc' format='datetime' value=2019-11-03 12:29:04>

In : astropy_t.mjd
Out: 58790.52018518518

In : astropy_t.jd
Out: 2458791.020185185

In : astropy_t.gps
Out: 1256819362.0
```

```
# MJD, JD, GPS to datetime:

In : Time( 58790.52018518518, format='mjd').datetime
Out: datetime.datetime(2019, 11, 3, 12, 29, 4)

In : Time( 2458791.020185185 , format='jd').datetime
Out: datetime.datetime(2019, 11, 3, 12, 29, 3, 999995)

In : Time( 1256819362.0, format='gps').datetime
Out: datetime.datetime(2019, 11, 3, 12, 29, 41)
```

5.5   zoneinfo in Python >= 3.9

Python 3.9 (not supported by MATLAB 2020b, Section 2.7) introduced the module
zoneinfo to improve timezone support. zoneinfo's primary benefit is its rigorous
treatment of time computations across daylight savings transitions. In addition, like
pytz, zoneinfo includes a mechanism to list all known timezone names, making it
unnecessary to import pytz merely to access its list of timezones, pytz.all_timezones.

5.5.1 List Available Timezones

Python 3.9:

```
In : import zoneinfo
In : zoneinfo.available_timezones()
Out:
{'Africa/Abidjan',
 'Africa/Accra',
 'Africa/Addis_Ababa',
 'Africa/Algiers',
 'Africa/Asmara',
 'Africa/Asmera',
   [...]
 'UTC',
 'Universal',
 'W-SU',
 'WET',
 'Zulu',
 'build/etc/localtime'}
```

5.5.2 Date Increments Across Daylight Savings Transition

This example demonstrates correct handling of standard time to daylight savings time transition using rules for the Los Angeles entry in the timezone database:

Python 3.9:

```
import zoneinfo
from datetime import datetime, timedelta
LA_tz = zoneinfo.ZoneInfo("America/Los_Angeles")
Start = datetime(2022, 3, 9, 10, tzinfo=LA_tz)
for i in range(7):
    day = Start + timedelta(days=i)
    print(day, day.tzname())
```

```
# output:
2022-03-09 10:00:00-08:00 PST
2022-03-10 10:00:00-08:00 PST
2022-03-11 10:00:00-08:00 PST
2022-03-12 10:00:00-08:00 PST
2022-03-13 10:00:00-07:00 PDT
2022-03-14 10:00:00-07:00 PDT
2022-03-15 10:00:00-07:00 PDT
```

5.6 References

[1]   Paul Ganssle. "pytz: The Fastest Footgun in the West." In: (Mar. 2018). URL: `https://blog.ganssle.io/articles/2018/03/ pytz-fastest-footgun.html`

[2]   Paul Ganssle. "Stop using utcnow and utcfromtimestamp." In: (Nov. 2019). URL: `https://blog.ganssle.io/articles/2019/11/ utcnow.html`

## CHAPTER 6

Call Python Functions from MATLAB

The MathWorks introduced the py module for MATLAB in 2014. This module provides a direct binary interface between MATLAB and Python, opening vast new possibilities for both languages. In addition to making it possible to call any Python function, MATLAB's py module allows one to create native Python objects within MATLAB. Such variables retain their full complement of Python methods—for example, a native Python string created in MATLAB can call all its 40 methods, from `.capitalize()` to `.zfill()`.

The py module has improved with each new release of MATLAB. MATLAB code examples in this book use MATLAB 2020b, so if you're working with an older version of MATLAB, some of the examples may not work.

This chapter just introduces the basic mechanics of using the py within MATLAB. Appendix A contains a list of "recipes" that show complete MATLAB programs that call Python to solve problems the core MATLAB product can't solve on its own.

6.1 Configure MATLAB to Recognize Python

The first step to using py in MATLAB is setting up a Python virtual environment with shared libraries that are compatible with MATLAB. The matpy environment described in Section 2.5.1 has been verified to work on Linux Ubuntu 20.04, Windows 10, and macOS 11.6, all with MATLAB 2020b.

Next, activate this environment, and invoke the matlab command from it: console:

```
> conda activate matpy
> matlab
```

© Albert Danial 2022
A. Danial, *Python for MATLAB Development*, https://doi.org/10.1007/978-1-4842-7223-7_6

Within MATLAB, check if it already recognizes Python, and if it doesn't, update the configuration to point to your Python installation. The pyenv command will tell if MATLAB is already configured for interaction with Python.

MATLAB (2020b):

```
>> pyenv

ans =

  PythonEnvironment with properties:

          Version: "3.8"
       Executable: "/usr/local/anaconda3/2020.07/bin/python"
          Library: "/usr/local/anaconda3/2020.07/lib/libpython3.8.so"
             Home: "/usr/local/anaconda3/2020.07"
           Status: NotLoaded
    ExecutionMode: InProcess
```

Note in particular the last entry, "ExecutionMode: InProcess." A troubleshooting option we'll see in the next section is to change this to "OutOfProcess."

If the pyenv command comes up empty, invoke it a second time telling it the path to your Python executable, for example:

MATLAB (2020b):

```
>> pyenv('Version','/usr/local/anaconda3/2020.07/bin/python')
```

On Windows, find the path to the Python interpreter by opening an Anaconda Prompt and entering where python.exe:

Windows:

```
(base) C:\Users\al> where python.exe
C:\ProgramData\Anaconda3\python.exe
C:\Users\al\AppData\Local\Microsoft\WindowsApps\python3.exe
```

Specify the path to the Anaconda version rather than Microsoft's! Microsoft's version doesn't come with NumPy, SciPy, or many of the additional modules you installed into your matpy virtual environment, so if you use it, most of the examples will fail.

> **Tip**   MATLAB on Windows may complain with
>
> `Error using pyversion`
>
> `Path argument does not specify a valid executable.`
>
> when setting the Python executable path with `pyenv` or `pyversion`. One solution to this error is to reinstall Anaconda, this time selecting "Install for all users."

On Linux and macOS, the comparable command is `which python3`, done from a terminal which is configured for Anaconda Python.

Your MATLAB version will support a subset of available Python versions; 2020b supports Python 2.7, 3.6, 3.7, and 3.8. Both MATLAB and Python must be on compatible architectures, that is, both 64 bits or both 32 bits.

6.2 Does It Work?

There are many ways a MATLAB/Python hybrid environment can fail, most of which trace back to conflicting shared libraries (or DLLs in the Windows world). Both MATLAB and Anaconda's Python distribution use the Intel Math Kernel Library (MKL), Intel's OpenMP library, and Qt 5 libraries, among others—but the library versions aren't necessarily at the same level. It is entirely possible for MATLAB or Python to crash because one called an incompatible library function from the other's installation. The MathWorks' ability to get these two large, complex applications to coexist peacefully most of the time is a considerable feat of software engineering.

Before proceeding, verify that MATLAB can load Python modules without difficulty. Let's jump straight to a challenging command:

MATLAB (2020b):

```
>> py.importlib.import_module('numpy')
```

At least four different things can happen:

- The successful case shows a long list of NumPy module attributes. If you see this, continue to the next section.

- Python Error: ImportError.

- Unable to resolve the name numpy.

- Segmentation violation detected.

The last three errors can be caused by a Python installation that is not version consistent with, or not visible to, MATLAB; the Python installation does not have NumPy installed; or you are not in the matpy conda environment and are hitting shared library conflicts between MATLAB and Python.

Possible workarounds:

1) Change "ExecutionMode" reported by pyenv from the default "InProcess" to "OutOfProcess" with

MATLAB (2020b):

```
>> pyenv("ExecutionMode","OutOfProcess")
```

2) [Linux only] Set the Python dynamic library load flag to 10:

MATLAB (2020b):

```
>> py.sys.setdlopenflags(int32(10));
```

I set this in my startup.m file on my Linux computer.

3) [Linux or macOS] If the terminal from which you configured matpy and then launched MATLAB shows an error about OpenMP library conflicts, try setting the environment variable KMP_DUPLICATE_LIB_OK to TRUE. This can be done in Python's view of the environment variables within MATLAB with

MATLAB (2020b):

```
>> os = py.importlib.import_module('os');
>> os.environ.update(pyargs('KMP_DUPLICATE_LIB_OK','TRUE'))
```

I include the preceding two lines in my startup.m file on my macOS computer.

See Section 6.4 for details on creating and modifying startup.m.

If the module import still fails, it is likely lower-level libraries installed to your matpy environment won't work with your version of MATLAB. There's no clear method to determining the right versions though.

6.3 Importing (and Reloading) Python Modules

As mentioned in Section 3.14, any Python source file may be imported as a Python module. Functions and classes in a module file can only be accessed if the file is in the Python search path, `sys.path` (see Section 6.6 on how to add directories to the Python search path within MATLAB), or exists in the current directory. Once on the search path, functions and classes in the Python module can be accessed in MATLAB in two ways: directly through py or as an alias created with `py.importlib.import_module()`.

As an example, say we have a Python file (a.k.a. a module), `integrate.py`, containing three functions that perform numeric integration: `rectangle()`, `trapezoid()`, and `simpsons()`. We can call the `trapezoid()` function using either of these methods:

- **Directly through py**

  ```
  >> area = py.integrate.trapezoid(Fn, a, b, delta)
  ```

- **Through a module import**

  ```
  >> Int = py.importlib.import_module('integrate')
  >> area = Int.trapezoid(Fn, a, b, delta)
  ```

Code changes to `integrate.py` are not seen in MATLAB if the changes are made after the module has already been imported. We need to explicitly reload the module for code updates to be seen:

```
>> py.importlib.reload(Int);
```

The reload method only works for modules brought in with `py.importlib.import_module()`. Functions accessed through `py.modulename.functionname()` cannot be reloaded; the only option there is to restart MATLAB.

6.4 Configure `startup.m` for Python Work

MATLAB will run the commands in `startup.m` at the start of each session if it finds such a file in the `userpath` directory. On my Linux computer, this is

MATLAB:

```
>> userpath
```

```
'/home/al/Documents/MATLAB'
```

The location can be changed by calling `userpath` with the desired location, for example, `userpath('/home/al/mfiles')`.

`userpath` is also the first directory in `path`, the collection of directories MATLAB searches to find m-files and compiled extensions. This directory is a perfect location for m-files containing utilities you use often.

To optimize your Python-within-MATLAB experience, make these customizations:

- Linux: Add to your `startup.m` file the line `py.sys.setdlopenflags(int32(10));`

  This will help deconflict shared library loads common to MATLAB and Python and reduce occurrences of MATLAB crashes.

- Windows: Figure out the location of the Python executable associated with the `matpy` virtual environment and then add to your `startup.m` file a line that calls `pyversion()` with this path. This can be done in two steps. First, open an Anaconda Prompt, then

  ```
  (base) C:> conda activate matpy
  (matpy) C:> where python.exe
  ```

  You may see multiple paths; choose the one containing `matpy`. Then, in `startup.m`, add, for example

  ```
  matpy_ path = 'C:/ProgramData/Anaconda3/envs/matpy/python.exe';
  pyversion(matpy_path);
  fprintf('Configured Python to %s\n', matpy_ path);
  ```

- Add to your `userpath` directory a copy of, or a symbolic link to, `py2mat.m`, mentioned in Section 6.5.7 and listed in Appendix D. You will call this function frequently from MATLAB code that calls Python functions.

Tip   A platform-independent way to edit your `startup.m` file is with this MATLAB command:

```
>> edit(fullfile(userpath,'startup.m'))
```

(If the file does not exist, you'll be prompted on whether or not to create it; click Yes.)

My Linux-based `startup.m` looks like this:

MATLAB 2020b:

```
pyenv('Version','/usr/local/anaconda3/2020.07/envs/matpy/bin/python');
py.sys.setdlopenflags(int32(10)); % prevents crashes w/numpy
addpath '/home/al/book/code/matlab_py'
fprintf('Ran code in /home/al/Documents/MATLAB/startup.m\n')
```

On macOS, my `startup.m` is

MATLAB 2020b:

```
fprintf('Running /Users/albert/Documents/MATLAB/startup.m'\n)
os = py.importlib.import_module('os');
os.environ.update(pyargs('KMP_DUPLICATE_LIB_OK','TRUE'))
```

6.5 Create Python Variables and Call Python Functions in MATLAB

We saw in Chapter 4 that Python and MATLAB data containers—lists, cell arrays, structs, dictionaries, numeric arrays—are similar but do not have a direct one-to-one mapping. Here, we'll give explicit examples that show how to create native Python data containers within MATLAB, how to pass MATLAB data to Python functions, and how to convert native Python variables back to native MATLAB variables.

For now, all Python files mentioned in the following should be in the MATLAB working directory. Later in Section 6.6, we'll show how to update the Python search path within MATLAB to allow MATLAB to find your Python code in other locations.

6.5.1 Scalars

Native Python doubles, integers, and strings can be created in MATLAB with the functions `py.float()`, `py.int()`, and `py.str()`. Despite their names, `py.float()` and `py.int()` create a 64-bit Python floating point value and a 64-bit Python integer.

MATLAB 2020b:

```
>> x = py.float(4.5)
x =
  Python float with properties:
    imag: 0
    real: 4.5000
    4.5

>> i = py.int(-22)
i =
  Python int with properties:
    denominator: [1x1 py.int]
          imag: [1x1 py.int]
      numerator: [1x1 py.int]
          real: [1x1 py.int]

    -22

>> s = py.str("native Python string")
s =
  Python str with no properties.
    native Python string
```

py.complex() is not implemented in MATLAB 2020b, but Section 6.5.4 shows py.numpy.complex() can be used. In either case, this is superfluous as complex numbers—and doubles—transfer natively between MATLAB and Python.

Explicit conversion to Python scalars is unnecessary when calling Python functions in MATLAB; these conversions happen automatically. In the following, we create a 32-bit integer, a double, a complex number, and a string in MATLAB and pass them directly to a Python function. The Python function returns modified values back to MATLAB. Within Python, return n, x, c, s means "return a tuple with four values." On the receiving end, MATLAB sees this tuple as a cell array—variable RV, for "return value"—having four items.

Note that while a 32-bit integer came in, default Python integers are 64 bits, so we retrieve the value back on the MATLAB side through the variable's .64bit attribute. Other integer types such as unsigned 16 bits are covered in Section 6.5.4. Of the other three return values, only strings have to be converted back to native MATLAB types; doubles and complex scalars pass seamlessly through the MATLAB/Python divide.

MATLAB 2020b:	Python:
`>> n = int32(10);`	`# file: xfer.py`
`>> x = 3.1415;`	`def modify_scalars(n,x,c,s):`
`>> c = 5.5 - 6.6i;`	`    n += 5`
`>> s = "in matlab";`	`    x *= 5`
`>> RV = py.xfer.modify_scalars(n,x,c,s);`	`    c *= 5`
`>> pn = RV{1}.int64;`	`    s = s.upper()`
`>> px = RV{2}; % double: 1-to-1`	`    return n,x,c,s`
`>> pc = RV{3}; % complex: 1-to-1`	
`>> ps = string(RV{4});`	
`>> pn,px,pc,ps`	
`pn =`	
`  int64`	
`    15`	
`px =`	
`    15.7075`	
`pc =`	
`  27.5000 -33.0000i`	
`ps =`	
`    "IN MATLAB"`	

6.5.2 Lists and Cell Arrays

In Section 4.3, we showed that Python lists are analogous to MATLAB cell arrays.
A native Python list is created by passing a cell array to py.list(). The list can be
modified with any of the Python list methods:

MATLAB 2020b:

```
>> L = py.list({42, "alpha", 2j})
L =
  Python list with no properties.
    [42.0, 'alpha', 2j]
```

```
>> L.pop()
ans =
   0.0000 + 2.0000i

>> L
L =
  Python list with no properties.
    [42.0, 'alpha']

>> L.append(6.022e+23)
>> L
L =
  Python list with no properties.
    [42.0, 'alpha', 6.022e+23]
```

As with scalars, MATLAB will automatically convert a cell array to a native Python variable when calling a Python function. The Python function, however, receives the MATLAB cell array as a Python tuple (Section 4.4). The tuple must be converted to a list (or dictionary, or array if possible) if its elements are to be modified. Finally, when a Python function returns a list to MATLAB, the underlying cell array can be accessed through the returned object's .cell attribute:

MATLAB 2020b:	Python:
| ```
>> ca = {'a', int32(20), -9.8}
>> ca =
  1x3 cell array
    {'a'}   {[20]}   {[-9.8000]}

>> RV = py.xfer.modify_list(ca);
>> CA = RV.cell
CA =
  1x4 cell array
  {1x7 py.str} {[-9.8000]}
    {1x1 py.int} {1x1 py.str}
``` | ```
# from file xfer.py
def modify_list(ca):
    # ca comes in as a tuple
    L = list(ca)
    L.append('flipped')
    L.reverse()
    return L
``` |

Aside from –9.8, all elements of the CA cell array are native Python objects—not useful at all for MATLAB work; further conversion is needed. We present a generic Python-to-MATLAB data converter function, py2mat(), in Section 6.5.7. There, we'll revisit this example and show how all elements of CA can be made MATLAB native.

6.5.3 Tuples

Python tuples (Section 4.4) can be created in MATLAB by passing a MATLAB array to the py.tuple() function. These are only needed when calling Python functions that explicitly expect a tuple argument—and in many cases, that requirement may be satisfied by a MATLAB array. As an example, recall NumPy's function np.ones() takes a tuple describing the matrix dimensions as its first argument:

Python:

```
In : np.ones( (3,5) )
Out:
array([[1., 1., 1., 1., 1.],
       [1., 1., 1., 1., 1.],
       [1., 1., 1., 1., 1.]])
```

To make the same matrix in MATLAB, we can explicitly pass in a tuple like so:
MATLAB:

```
>> py.numpy.ones(py.tuple([int64(3),int64(5)]))
  Python ndarray:
     1     1     1     1     1
     1     1     1     1     1
     1     1     1     1     1
```

(Recall also that NumPy only accepts integer arguments for matrix dimensions. Since MATLAB's default numeric constant is a double, we have to first explicitly cast 3 and 5 to be 64-bit integers.)

The interface to `np.ones()` is rather forgiving though, and an array instead of an explicit tuple also works:

MATLAB:

```
>> py.numpy.ones( [int64(3),int64(5)] )
  Python ndarray:
      1    1    1    1    1
      1    1    1    1    1
      1    1    1    1    1
```

6.5.4 Numeric Arrays

Unlike scalars and cell arrays, MATLAB numeric arrays cannot be passed to Python functions directly. They must first be converted to NumPy arrays (Section 11.1) within MATLAB with `py.numpy.array()`.

Similarly, NumPy arrays ("ndarrays") returned by Python also require conversion to native MATLAB variables before they can be used for computation. While the `py2mat()` mentioned in the previous section can perform this conversion, here we cover the details of how such conversions are done.

Python ndarray-to-MATLAB array conversion depends on the array type: Python double-precision arrays are converted to MATLAB with `double()`, unsigned 8-bit integers are converted with `uint8()`, and so on. The following example uses single-precision floats. The first MATLAB command creates a 2 x 2 matrix; the second creates an equivalent NumPy array from the MATLAB array and then passes it to the Python `modify_arr()` function in the third command; the final command converts the NumPy array returned by `modify_arr()` back to a MATLAB array:

MATLAB 2020b:	Python:
| ```
>> A = single([2.2 3.3; 4.4 -1])
A =
  2x2 single matrix
    2.2000    3.3000
    4.4000   -1.0000

>> py_A = py.numpy.array(A)
py_A =
  Python ndarray:
    2.2000    3.3000
    4.4000   -1.0000

>> RV = py.xfer.modify_arr(py_A)
RV =
  Python ndarray:
    2.4200    3.6300
    4.8400   -1.1000

>> result = single(RV)
result =
  2x2 single matrix
    2.4200    3.6300
    4.8400   -1.1000
``` | ```
# from file xfer.py
def modify_arr(A):
    return A * 1.1
``` |

MATLAB has ten type functions which accept NumPy arrays: `single`, `double`, `int8`, `int16`, `int32`, `int64`, `uint8`, `uint16`, `uint32`, `uint64`. Absent are single- and double-precision complex conversion functions; as of MATLAB 2020b, the `py.numpy.array()` function does not accept complex arrays. Complex arrays must be split into their real and imaginary parts to cross the language divide.

Python-native scalar constants with explicit numeric types can also be created in MATLAB using NumPy functions described in Section 11.1.3, for example:

MATLAB 2020b:

```
>> a = py.numpy.uint32(4)
  Python uint32:
   4

>> b = py.numpy.float16(44.55)
  Python float16 with properties:
       base: [1x1 py.NoneType]
       data: [1x1 py.memoryview]
      dtype: [1x1 py.numpy.dtype]
      flags: [1x1 py.numpy.flagsobj]
       flat: [1x1 py.numpy.flatiter]
       imag: [1x1 py.numpy.float16]
   itemsize: [1x1 py.int]
     nbytes: [1x1 py.int]
       ndim: [1x1 py.int]
       real: [1x1 py.numpy.float16]
      shape: [1x0 py.tuple]
       size: [1x1 py.int]
    strides: [1x0 py.tuple]
   44.56

>> c = py.numpy.complex(-3,4)
   -3.0000 + 4.0000i
```

6.5.5 Dictionaries and Structs

MATLAB's native key/value data type, container.Map, seems like the ideal counterpart to Python dictionaries, but maps are not supported:

MATLAB 2020b:

```
>> m = containers.Map({'x','y'},[3.4 5])
m =
  Map with properties:
        Count: 2
      KeyType: char
    ValueType: double
```

```
>> py.dict(m)
Error using py.dict
Conversion of MATLAB 'containers.Map' to Python is not supported.
```

Instead, Python a dictionary is associated with a MATLAB `struct`. A MATLAB `struct` passed to a Python function is seen by Python as a dictionary. Changes done to the dict in Python are seen by MATLAB as changes to the struct.

The other direction is less flexible. A dictionary returned by a Python function can only be converted to a MATLAB structured variable (with MATLAB's `struct()` function) if the dictionary keys are valid MATLAB variable names. This means the keys must be strings that begin with a letter followed by one or more letters, digits, and/or underscores.

MATLAB 2020b:	Python:

`>> x.a = 1;`
`>> x.b = -1;`
`>> x.c = 0.5;`
`>> x`
`x =`
`  struct with fields:`
`    a: 1`
`    b: -1`
`    c: 0.5000`
 	
`>> pyx = py.xfer.modify_dict(x)`
`pyx =`
`  Python dict with no properties.`
`    {'a': 1.0, 'b': -1.0,`
`     'c': 0.5, 'new': 6.1}`
 	
`>> xnew = struct(pyx)`
`xnew =`
`  struct with fields:`
`      a: 1`
`      b: -1`
`      c: 0.5000`
`    new: 6.1000`
	`# from file xfer.py`
	`def modify_dict(d):`
	`    d['new'] = 6.1`
	`    return d`

Methods to create, inspect, and update Python dictionaries within MATLAB are demonstrated as follows:

Create an empty dictionary:

MATLAB 2020b:

```
>> a = py.dict()
a =
  Python dict with no properties.
    {}
```

Create a dictionary with initial values:

MATLAB 2020b:

```
>> a = py.dict(pyargs('x', 3.4, 'y', 5))
a =
  Python dict with no properties.
    {'x': 3.4, 'y': 5.0}
```

A limitation is that the odd numbered arguments to pyargs(), meaning the dictionary keys, may only be strings. Python dictionaries can, of course, have integer keys, among many other types, but adding such keys to a Python dictionary within MATLAB violates the rule that keys be valid MATLAB variables. The integer 7 may be a dictionary key in Python, but is clearly not an allowable variable name in MATLAB.

Show all keys:

MATLAB 2020b:

```
>> py.list(a.keys())
ans =
  Python list with no properties.
    ['x', 'z']
```

Iterate over keys:

MATLAB 2020b:

```
>> for x = cell(py.list(a.keys()))
      string(x)
    end
```

```
ans =
    "x"

ans =
    "y"
```

Retrieve a value with a key:

MATLAB 2020b:

```
>> value = a.get('x')
value =
    3.4000
```

Add or change a key/value pair:

MATLAB 2020b:

```
>> a.update(pyargs('z', -10))
>> a
a =
  Python dict with no properties.
    {'x': 3.4, 'y': 5.0, 'z': -10.0}
```

Remove a key/value pair:

MATLAB 2020b:

```
>> a.pop('y')
ans =
    5

>> a
a =
  Python dict with no properties.
    {'x': 3.4, 'z': -10.0}
```

6.5.6 Keyword Arguments

Keyword arguments (Section 3.8.3) can be passed to Python functions in MATLAB with pyargs(). A function call that looks like this

```
Fn(a, B="blue", C=1.0)
```

in Python, would look like this in MATLAB:

```
Fn(a, pyargs('B', "blue", 'C', 1.0))
```

The following example calls the NumPy np.linspace() function with keyword arguments specifying the number of values and data type to return. Both Python and MATLAB versions are shown:

Python:

```
In : np.linspace(4, 5, num=6, dtype=np.float32)
Out: array([4. , 4.2, 4.4, 4.6, 4.8, 5. ], dtype=float32)
```

MATLAB:

```
>> py.numpy.linspace(4, 5, pyargs('num', int64(6), 'dtype', py.numpy.float32))
  Python ndarray:
    4.0000    4.2000    4.4000    4.6000    4.8000    5.0000
```

6.5.7 Python-to-MATLAB and MATLAB-to-Python Variable Converters

Appendix D has listings for py2mat() and mat2py(), MATLAB functions which convert, where possible, a Python variable within MATLAB into a native MATLAB variable and vice versa. Such conversions may be necessary to pass MATLAB data to Python functions and then convert data returned from Python functions back to native MATLAB variables. These functions can also be found in this book's Github repository, https://github.com/Apress/python-for-matlab-development .

6.5.8 Traversing Generators

MATLAB cannot traverse generators using a simple for loop. Instead, they have to explicitly call Python's next() function in a while loop. This Python generator, for example

Python:

```
#!/usr/bin/env python3
# file: code/matlab_py/gen_demo.py
def gen():
```

```python
    for i in [10, 20, 30, 40, 50]:
        yield i
```

can be traversed in MATLAB with

MATLAB:

```matlab
% code/matlab_py/traverse_gen.m
G = py.importlib.import_module('gen_demo');
fn = G.gen();
while true
    try
        i = py.next(fn);
        fprintf('got i=%d\n', i);
    catch EO
        if strcmp(EO.message, "Python Error: StopIteration")
            break
        else
            fprintf(EO.message)
        end
    end
end
```

Python's next() raises a StopIteration exception if it is called after the last item has been returned. The MATLAB code checks for this exception to leave the while loop cleanly. If any other error is caught, its message is printed.

A side note: Python's range() function is not a generator. Instead, it is a "lazily evaluated" function and, as such, *can* be traversed with a for loop in MATLAB. The catch is that range() has list-like behavior which translates to cell-like behavior in MATLAB. This means the iteration variable i's value must be dereferenced as i{1}:

MATLAB:

```matlab
for i = py.range(int64(5))
    fprintf('i = %d\n', int64(i{1}))
end

% output:
i = 0
i = 1
```

```
i = 2
i = 3
i = 4
```

6.5.9 Traversing `zip()`

A zipped Python list can be traversed in MATLAB with a conventional for loop if the call
to py.zip() is explicitly expanded with py.list(). Using x as the iteration variable, the
iteration item pairs are indexed as x{1}{1} and x{1}{2}:

MATLAB 2020b:

```
>> for x = py.list(py.zip({1,2,3},{'a','b','c'}))
        fprintf('i=%2d S=%s\n', x{1}{1}, x{1}{2})
    end
i= 1   S=a
i= 2   S=b
i= 3   S=c
```

6.6 Modifying the Python Search Path Within MATLAB

We saw in Section 3.14.3 that the Python list sys.path contains the module search
path, the collection of directories Python scans to find code. The Python search path
can be augmented in Python code with sys.path.append() just as MATLAB's path
can be expanded with addpath. Extending Python's search path within MATLAB is less
obvious. Although Python lists in MATLAB can use the .append() method, lists accessed
as module parameters such as sys.path cannot. In other words, the sys module has
among its many member functions and parameters the list sys.path, but one cannot use
sys.path.append() from MATLAB.

MATLAB (2020b):

```
>> a = py.list([1,2])
a =
  Python list with no properties.
    [1.0, 2.0]
```

```
>> a.append(3)
>> a
a =
  Python list with no properties.
    [1.0, 2.0, 3.0]

>> import py.sys.path
>> py.sys.path.append('/my/new/directory')
Unable to resolve the name py.sys.path.append.
```

6.6.1 Extending `sys.path` with an Alias

An interesting twist on `.append()`'s inability to update lists accessed as module parameters is that `.append()` works fine on aliases to such lists. Recall from Section 4.8 that a list assignment in Python such as `newlist = oldlist` merely creates an alias to `oldlist`; both `newlist` and `oldlist` point to the same data, and a change to either of them is reflected in both.

We can take advantage of this behavior to expand `sys.path` by using `.append()` on an alias to `sys.path`:

MATLAB (2020b):

```
>> py.sys.path
>> py.sys.path
  Python list with no properties.
    ['/path/dir/one', '/path/dir/two', '']
>> sys_path_alias = py.sys.path
>> sys_path_alias.append('/another/directory')
>> py.sys.path
    ['/path/dir/one', '/path/dir/two', '', '/another/directory']
```

6.6.2 Extending `sys.path` with `insert()`

MATLAB's `insert()` function can also modify Python lists. (Aside: `insert()` is a curious function. It has no built-in help, at least in MATLAB 2020b, and online documentation shows it as a function for adding data to SQLite, MongoDB, and other databases.)

More revealing is that its signature matches the Python .insert() method for lists—including requiring an explicit integer as the index argument. The obvious conclusion is that insert() is a direct interface to Python's list .insert() method.)

The following examples show how to add a directory to the beginning of Python's sys.path list and append a directory to the end of it:

MATLAB (2020b):

```
>> insert(py.sys.path, int64(0), '/new/directory/start/of/sys/path')
>> nDirs = length(py.sys.path);
>> insert(py.sys.path, int64(nDirs), '/new/directory/end/of/sys/path')
```

6.6.3 Extending sys.path with append()

There's an alternate way to achieve the same result by using Python's append() function from the Python list module. Unfortunately, MATLAB does not offer the ability to cherry-pick individual functions from a module like Python's from list import append, so we import *everything* from list. Afterward, we'll have access to append() which we call to update py.sys.path:

MATLAB (2020b):

```
>> py.sys.path
   Python list with no properties.
        ['', '/usr/local/anaconda3/2020.07/lib/python38.zip',
        '/usr/local/anaconda3/2020.07/lib/python3.8',
        '/usr/local/anaconda3/2020.07/lib/python3.8/lib-dynload',
        '/usr/local/anaconda3/2020.07/lib/python3.8/site-packages']

>> import py.list.*
>> import py.sys.path
>> append(py.sys.path, '/my/new/directory')
>> py.sys.path
   Python list with no properties.
        ['', '/usr/local/anaconda3/2020.07/lib/python38.zip',
        '/usr/local/anaconda3/2020.07/lib/python3.8',
        '/usr/local/anaconda3/2020.07/lib/python3.8/lib-dynload',
        '/usr/local/anaconda3/2020.07/lib/python3.8/site-packages',
        '/my/new/directory']
```

One might think the `append()` function can be called directly from `py.list`, but that, too, fails:

MATLAB (2020b):

```
>> py.list.append(py.sys.path, '/my/new/directory')
The class py.list has no Constant property or Static method named 'append'.
```

Something to be aware of is that the `import py.list.*` command in MATLAB brought 12 new functions into our namespace:

Python:

```
In :list.<tab>
append()  copy()   extend()  insert()  pop()     reverse()
clear()   count()  index()   mro()     remove()  sort()
```

Of the 12, all but `mro()` and `pop()` are existing MATLAB commands. Fortunately, MATLAB handles function overloading well. When given MATLAB-native variables, MATLAB invokes its own `sort()`, `append()`, and other functions. When these functions are given Python variables, MATLAB calls the Python versions instead.

6.7 Python Bridge Modules

Calls to Python functions from MATLAB can fail for a couple of reasons: there could be dynamic library load collisions that cause MATLAB to crash, or the Python objects visible from MATLAB have attributes or methods that cannot be seen in MATLAB.

The workaround for both cases is to write *bridge modules* that wrap problematic interfaces with ones MATLAB can handle. An example is the object returned by the weighted least squares function `WLS()` from the Python `statsmodels` module; MATLAB cannot access this object's `.predict()` method (Section 11.8). To get around this, we need a small Python module with a function that takes inputs from MATLAB, calls `WLS()` and the solution's `.predict()` method, then returns the answer in a dictionary that MATLAB can access.

Many examples of bridge modules appear in the recipes.

6.8 Debugging Python Code Called by MATLAB

Troubleshooting hybrid MATLAB/Python code can be a challenge because the MATLAB debugger won't step into Python code. The only recourse to see what's going on inside Python code is to instrument the code with print statements. Even that doesn't always work though; sometimes, prints in Python do not appear in MATLAB's console. If that happens with your code, you'll need to write debug statements to a file instead. Here's an example of that:

Python:

```python
with open('/path/to/log_file.txt', 'a') as LOG:
    LOG.write(f'in function abc(), XYZ = {XYZ}\n')
```

The file is opened in append mode with `'a'` to accumulate repeated writes. Note also that we have to use the file handle's `.write()` method rather than the `print()` function.

Logging can be automated somewhat with decorators or Python's own `trace` module, but both of these methods have drawbacks over tailored print statements. Decorators wrap entire functions and so cannot provide details on the inner workings of functions they act on. The `trace` module has the opposite problem in that it reports on every line that runs—which can be a prodigious amount of output to wade through—but has no mechanism to show values of variables along the way.

Nonetheless, `trace` can provide useful insight when a Python function called from MATLAB goes completely off the rails. The following code shows how `trace` is used to follow execution of functions that compute terms of the Mandelbrot sequence (we'll see this example again in Chapter 14):

Python:

```python
1   # code/matlab_py/trace_MB.py
2   import trace
3   import numpy as np
4
5   tracer = trace.Trace(count=0)
6
7   def nIter(c, imax):
8       z = complex(0, 0)
```

```
9      for i in range(imax):
10        z = z*z + c
11        if abs(z) > 2:
12            break
13      return np.uint8(i)
14
15  def MB(Re, Im, imax):
16      nR = len(Im)
17      nC = len(Re)
18      img = np.zeros((nR, nC),
19              dtype=np.uint8)
20      for i in range(nR):
21        for j in range(nC):
22          c = complex(Re[j],Im[i])
23          img[i,j] = nIter(c,imax)
24      return img
25
26  def do_work(N, imax):
27      nR, nC = N, N
28      Re = np.linspace(-0.7440, -0.7433, nC)
29      Im = np.linspace( 0.1315, 0.1322, nR)
30      img = MB(Re, Im, imax)
31      return img
32
33  def trace_do_work(N, imax):
34      img = tracer.runfunc(do_work, N, imax)
35      return img
```

Lines 7–31 are the unmodified functions. Tracing is enabled by importing the trace module (line 2) and calling the trace_do_work() function (lines 33–35) which is a wrapper to the regular entry point function, do_work(). First, we'll do a regular, untraced run by calling do_work() directly:

MATLAB:

```
>> Im = @py.importlib.import_module;
>> MB = Im('trace_MB')
>> MB.do_work(int64(5), int64(255))
    65    60    60    61    64
    83   203   158    64    65
   254   131   156   205    89
    37    41    42    69   129
    35    37    38    39    40
```

Now we'll call the wrapped function, trace_do_work(). It produces a huge amount of output, so before invoking it, enable MATLAB's diary mode to save STDOUT to a file. Only a small portion of the thousands of lines of output is shown here:

MATLAB:

```
>> diary
>> MB.trace_do_work(int64(5), int64(255))
MB.trace_do_work(int64(5), int64(255))
 --- modulename: pyio, funcname: do_work
MB.py(28): nR, nC = N, N
MB.py(29): Re = np.linspace(-0.7440, -0.7433, nC)
 --- modulename: function_base, funcname: _linspace_dispatcher
function_base.py(20):     return (start, stop)
 --- modulename: function_base, funcname: linspace
function_base.py(113):     num = operator.index(num)
            :
MB.py(10): for i in range(imax):
MB.py(11):    z = z*z + c
MB.py(12):    if abs(z) > 2:
MB.py(10): for i in range(imax):
MB.py(11):    z = z*z + c
MB.py(12):    if abs(z) > 2:
            :
MB.py(10): for i in range(imax):
MB.py(11):    z = z*z + c
MB.py(12):    if abs(z) > 2:
```

```
MB.py(13):      break
MB.py(14): return np.uint8(i)
MB.py(22):   for j in range(nC):
MB.py(21): for i in range(nR):
MB.py(25): return img
MB.py(32):   return img
               :
     65    60    60    61    64
     83   203   158    64    65
    254   131   156   205    89
     37    41    42    69   129
     35    37    38    39    40
>> diary off
```

6.9 Summary of Steps to Calling Python Code from MATLAB

Calling Python functions from MATLAB takes more effort than calling native MATLAB functions. These steps summarize the process:

1. Implement a pure Python testbed of the code fragment you want to call from MATLAB if you're calling many functions or manipulating several native Python variables within MATLAB. The pure Python solution will serve as a reference that can provide intermediate values and greatly simplify troubleshooting.

2. Start MATLAB from the command line in a virtual environment configured properly for your versions of MATLAB and Python (Section 2.5.1).

3. Augment the Python search path to include the directory containing your code (Section 6.6) if it isn't visible from your work directory.

4. Import the Python modules you want to call (Section 6.3).

5. Convert, where necessary, input arguments to the Python function from MATLAB-native variables to Python-native variables (Section 6.5). Scalars and strings are usually exempt from this, except for cases where the Python function expects an integer. Numeric scalars in MATLAB default to being double-precision floating-point type, so these need to be converted to integers with `int32()` or `int64()`. The `mat2py()` function (Appendix D) can simplify such conversions.

6. Call the desired Python function(s).

7. Convert objects returned from Python functions to MATLAB-native variables, either by calling built-in MATLAB functions such as `struct()` or by using the generic `py2mat()` function (Appendix D).

8. If the returned object does not include methods or attributes you need, write a bridge module with functions that explicitly call methods or fetch attributes that aren't exposed to MATLAB.

The call-Python-from-MATLAB recipes that appear in subsequent chapters employ either a subset of these steps for simple cases or use all for the harder ones.

6.10 Call MATLAB from Python

The MathWorks also makes it possible to call MATLAB from Python. This is done with a Python module, `matlab.engine`, that users can optionally add to a given Python installation.

6.10.1 Install `matlab.engine`

To install the MATLAB Engine API for Python, first determine the Python environment where you want to add this module by listing your available environments. On Windows, using an Anaconda Prompt, it might look like this:

Windows:

```
(base) C:\Users\al> conda env list
# conda environments:
#
base           * C:\ProgramData\Anaconda3
matpy            C:\ProgramData\Anaconda3\envs\matpy
```

Next, start MATLAB and explicitly tell it the environment where you want to install the module by giving `pyversion()` the path to the Python executable for the desired environment. For the example of the `matpy` virtual environment listed earlier, that would be

MATLAB:

```
>> pyversion('C:\ProgramData\Anaconda3\envs\matpy\python.exe')
```

Then install the module from MATLAB with
MATLAB:

```
>> cd (fullfile(matlabroot,'extern','engines','python'))
>> system('python setup.py install')
```

The two MATLAB commands earlier are operating system independent and work on Windows, macOS, and Linux.

6.10.2 Call Functions in a New MATLAB Session

The Python interface to MATLAB through its Engine API differs from MATLAB's `py` module because `matlab.engine` needs to either start a MATLAB session or connect to an existing one. In contrast, the `py` interface from MATLAB to Python works by calling Python library functions; no running Python session is needed. Here, I'll cover starting a new MATLAB session; connecting to an existing session will come in the following section.

A new MATLAB session can be created by calling `start_matlab()`. This function returns a handle to an engine instance from which all other MATLAB functions may be called:

Python:

```
In : import numpy as np
In : import matlab.engine
In : eng = matlab.engine.start_matlab()
In : eng.magic(3)
Out: matlab.double([[8.0,1.0,6.0],[3.0,5.0,7.0],[4.0,9.0,2.0]])
In : np.array(eng.magic(3))
Out:
array([[8., 1., 6.],
       [3., 5., 7.],
       [4., 9., 2.]])
```

Just as Python functions called from MATLAB return native Python variables, MATLAB functions called from Python return native MATLAB variables. Containers such as numeric arrays are easily converted to NumPy arrays simply by calling np.array() as done earlier.

6.10.3 Call Functions in an Existing MATLAB Session

If you already have a running MATLAB session on the same computer, you can save yourself the considerable session start overhead by connecting directly to the existing session. To do so, you'll first need to make your existing session shareable: MATLAB:

```
>> matlab.engine.shareEngine
```

Next, in Python, check if the engine can see any MATLAB sessions with find_matlab(). If exactly one engine is found, Python can attach to it by calling connect_matlab() without arguments. If multiple sessions are found, supply the name of the session of interest as an argument to connect_matlab():

Python:

```
In : import matlab.engine
In : matlab.engine.find_matlab()
Out: ('MATLAB_3000634',)
In : eng = matlab.engine.connect_matlab()
In : np.array(eng.magic(6)).astype(np.int)
Out:
```

```
array([[35,  1,  6, 26, 19, 24],
       [ 3, 32,  7, 21, 23, 25],
       [31,  9,  2, 22, 27, 20],
       [ 8, 28, 33, 17, 10, 15],
       [30,  5, 34, 12, 14, 16],
       [ 4, 36, 29, 13, 18, 11]])
```

Variables in the MATLAB session can be seen in a connected Python session through the dictionary eng.workspace:

MATLAB:	Python:
>> z = [pi exp(1)];	In : import matlab.engine
	In : eng = matlab.engine.connect_matlab()
	In : eng.workspace['z']
	Out: matlab.double([[3.141592653589793,
	2.7182818284590455]])

Unfortunately, env.workspace lacks true dictionary functionality. As of MATLAB 2020b, one cannot call len(env.workspace) to count the number of known variables, iterate through variables with for var in env.workspace:, or access variable names through env.workspace.keys().

The env.workspace interface is bidirectional. Values created in Python will appear in the MATLAB workspace:

Python:

```
In : import matlab.engine
In : eng = matlab.engine.connect_matlab()
In : eng.workspace['a_dict'] = { 'Mo' : 'Monday', 'Tu' : 'Tuesday' }
```

MATLAB:

```
>> a_dict
  struct with fields:
    Mo: 'Monday'
    Tu: 'Tuesday'
```

6.11 Other Mechanisms for MATLAB/Python Interaction

Older versions of MATLAB without the py module have less convenient vehicles for data exchange with Python. These include reading and writing .mat, JSON, XML, or plain text files or sending and receiving data over a network connection. MATLAB invocations of Python functions have to be done through system calls (Section 9.2) to stand-alone Python programs that implement the functions.

6.11.1 System Calls and File I/O

Calling Python functions directly from MATLAB is convenient and efficient, but is not the only way for the two languages to interact. Older versions of MATLAB without the py module obviously can't use this method, and even newer versions of MATLAB may crash on calling Python functions that load conflicting shared libraries.

In these cases, the more primitive method of employing system calls and exchanging data via files can be employed. In Section 9.2, we'll run other executables from MATLAB with its `system()` function. This simple example shows how MATLAB would run the Python program `compute_stuff.py` that exists in the MATLAB working directory:

MATLAB:

```
>> [status,result] = system('./compute_stuff.py');
```

`result` contains the combined lines of STDOUT and STDERR generated by `compute_stuff.py`, while the integer `status` has the program's exit code—zero indicates success, while any non-zero value means the program either was unable to run or ended with an error.

Small amounts of data may be passed from MATLAB to Python via the command line, or environment variables, or the returned `result`. As the data volume or parsing complexity grows, file or network-based data exchange becomes more attractive. The most MATLAB-friendly file format is, of course, the .mat file; reading and writing these from Python is covered in Section 7.14.

6.11.1.1 JSON

The .mat file is just one of several formats that MATLAB and Python have in common. Others include HDF5, NetCDF4, XML, and JSON. The first two were covered in Sections 7.9 and 7.10. XML, while infinitely flexible, is commensurately tedious because one must laboriously define all entries. In contrast, JSON—JavaScript Object Notation—functions in MATLAB and Python automatically serialize and deserialize complex data structures to and from text strings. These strings can then either be written to and read from text files or sent and received over a network connection. Still, both XML and JSON are text formats and therefore become unwieldy for large numeric arrays.

6.11.1.2 MATLAB to Python via JSON

The MATLAB function jsonencode() serializes a variable into a character array. We'll use it to write b to a file, then read the file in Python and use the load() function from Python's json module to convert the text back into a structured variable:

MATLAB (step 1):	Python (step 2):
| ```
>> b{1}.pos = [.5; -.3];
>> b{1}.vel = [2.7,3.8];
>> b{2}{1}.u = [0; 3];
>> b{2}{1}.v = { 'a '; 'bc' };
>> b{2}{2} = 22;
>> jsonencode(b)

    '[{"pos":[0.5,-0.3],
    "vel":[2.7,3.8]},[{"u"
    :[0,3],"v":["a ","bc"
    ]},22]]'

>> fh = fopen('b.json', 'w');
>> fprintf(fh, jsonencode(b));
>> fclose(fh);
``` | ```
In : import json
In : fh = open('b.json')
In : b = json.load(fh)
In : fh.close()
In : b
Out:
[ {'pos': [0.5, -0.3],
   'vel': [2.7, 3.8]},
  [{'u': [0, 3],
    'v': ['a ', 'bc']},
   22]]
``` |

6.11.1.3 Python to MATLAB via JSON

Going in the reverse direction works equally well: in Python, we can either first create a string serialization of a Python variable with json.dumps() and then write that string to a file or combine both steps with a call to json.dump(). On the MATLAB side, we'll read the file into a string and then pass the string to jsondecode() to deserialize the string into a variable:

Python (step 1):	MATLAB (step 2):

In : b
Out:
[{'pos': [0.5, -0.3],
   'vel': [2.7, 3.8]},
[{'u': [0, 3],
   'v': ['a ', 'bc']},
   22]]
 	
In : import json
In : json.dump('b.json', b)
	>> fh = fopen('b.json');
	>> L = fgetl(fh);
	>> fclose(fh);
	>> b{1}.pos
	    0.5000
	   -0.3000
	
	>> b{1}.vel
	    2.7000
	    3.8000
	
	>> b{2}{1}.u
	    0
	    3
	
	>> b{2}{1}.v
	   {'a '}
	   {'bc'}
	
	>> b{2}{2}
	    22

6.11.2 TCP/IP Exchange

MATLAB/Python network communication is described in Section 7.17.3. Data exchange over a network takes more coding effort than file-based exchange but offers higher I/O performance and does not consume file storage space. Also, the communicating programs must run simultaneously which complicates start-up and shutdown.

The code examples in Sections 7.17.3.1 through 7.17.3.4 sent integers and arrays of double-precision floats in native binary formats. Packing and unpacking each variable to and from binary buffers is tedious though. Another option is to serialize one or more variables into a commonly understood format—JSON, for example—and exchange that.

CHAPTER 7

Input and Output

The first step to solving many computational problems is reading data from the command line, interactive input, text or binary files, a network, a serial port, or a combination of these. The final step often involves writing data to text or binary files. In this chapter, we'll cover input and output methods in detail, including reading and writing file formats important to scientific and numerical analyses—plain text files; binary files; the ubiquitous Excel formats .csv, .xls, and .xlsx; HDF5; NetCDF4; XML; JSON; YAML; .ini; SQLite; and HTML.

We close this chapter with a discussion of methods to send data to, and receive data from, MATLAB itself. The methods include reading and writing .mat files, and using MATLAB's py module (Chapter 6), to communicate with MATLAB over a network.

Direct binary access of Python data from MATLAB code is described in Section 6.5.

7.1 Text Files

The most generic way to read text files in Python is to get a handle to the file by calling the open() function with the name of the file to read, iterate over the file handle with a for loop, then close the file handle. MATLAB and Python equivalents to print to STDOUT the contents of the file data.txt are

MATLAB:	Python:

```
fh = fopen('data.txt')           fh = open('data.txt')
while ~feof(fh)                   for line in fh:
    line = fgetl(fh);                print(line, end='')
    fprintf('%s\n', line);        fh.close()
end
fclose(fh)
```

A. Danial, *Python for MATLAB Development*, https://doi.org/10.1007/978-1-4842-7223-7_7

One difference between MATLAB's `fgetl()` and the implicit read in Python's `for line in fh:` is that `fgetl()` strips the line's trailing newline character. For this reason, we add the `\n` in the `fprintf()` format string; otherwise, the output appears as one long line. Python has the opposite issue—it keeps all characters in the line, but Python's `print()` function automatically adds a new line at the end. We suppress this with the optional `end="` argument; otherwise, the output is doublespaced.

Alternatively, in Python we could add the `.rstrip()` method to `line` to remove trailing whitespace and newlines on the right of the string before printing it. Then we'd use `print(line.rstrip())` instead of `print(line, end=")`.

The more Pythonic way of reading text files is to use a "context manager," in other words, a `with` statement:

Python:

```python
with open('data.txt') as fh:
    for line in fh:
        print(line, end='')
```

Note the absence of a file close statement. Context managers automatically release resources opened within the context—in our case, a handle to an open file—when the `with` block ends.

Another way to read text files in Python is with the `pathlib` module which we'll see again in Chapter 8. `pathlib.Path` objects have a method, `read_text()`, which returns a string containing the entire file. You can create a list of lines from a text file like this (the `split()` method is described in Section 4.2.4 and will be discussed later in Section 7.1.4.2):

Python:

```python
import pathlib
P = pathlib.Path('data.txt')
all_lines = P.read_text().split('\n')
```

Writing text files follows a similar pattern: obtain a file handle to the name of a file to write, this time passing in the `'w'` flag to denote *write* mode, use the file handle's `.write()` method to write a string, then close the file handle. The following example shows how to make a copy of a file where each line of the copy will be prefixed by a pound symbol and a space. Note that the `with` allows multiple expressions, in our case two file handle assignments, one for reading and one for writing:

MATLAB:	Python:

```
fin  = fopen('data.txt')
fout = fopen('copy.txt', 'w')
while ~feof(fin)
    L = fgetl(fin);
    fprintf(fout, '# %s\n', L);
end
fclose(fin)
fclose(fout)
```

```
with open('data.txt')      as fin,
     open('copy.txt', 'w') as fout:
    for L in fin:
        fout.write(f'#{L}')
```

7.1.1 Reading Corrupted Text Files with `pathlib`

I prefer to read text files with `pathlib` because it is so convenient—just call the `.read_text()` method on the `pathlib.Path()` object. Occasionally, this fails with some of the massive text files I deal with because the files have garbage binary characters, causing `pathlib` to raise a `UnicodeDecodeError`. Typical sources of undesired binary characters are malformed string output from buggy executables and network glitches.

   `pathlib` can handle corrupted text files, but they have to be ingested in binary mode and then explicitly converted to a string. The following example creates a text file with embedded binary characters, tries to read it back with `.read_text()`, and, on failing that, reads it with `.read_bytes()`:

   Python:

```
# file: code/IO/pathlib_bin.txt
import pathlib
import sys
File = 'text_w_binary.txt'
P = pathlib.Path(File)
chars = [ord(_) for _ in 'this is line 1\n' +
                         'this is line 2\n' +
                         'the end\n']
chars[8:12] = [0xFA, 0xFB, 0xFC, 0xFD] # insert non-text
P.write_bytes(bytes(chars))
try:
    lines = P.read_text()
```

```
except UnicodeDecodeError:
    print(f'failed reading {File} as text, trying binary')
    lines = str(P.read_bytes()).split(r'\n')
except:
    print(f'giving up on {File}')
    sys.exit(1)
print('\n'.join(lines))
```

Output looks like this:

```
failed reading text_w_binary.txt as text, trying binary
b'this is \xfa\xfb\xfc\xfd 1
this is line 2
the end
```

7.1.2 Reading and Writing Numeric Data

Chapter 11 has a detailed section in reading and writing numeric arrays to and from text files; see Section 11.1.9.

7.1.3 I/O Exceptions

Reading from and writing to a file system are frequent sources of runtime errors. Common problems are nonexistent input files, insufficient privilege to write files, file system is full, and file system is not responding due to a networking problem. To have your code fail gracefully in the presence of such conditions, at a minimum, file open statements should be protected with exception handlers as described in Section 10.1.3.

MATLAB and Python equivalents using exception handlers on our file copy example are

MATLAB:	Python:

```
try                                   try:
  fin  = fopen('data.txt')              with open('data.txt')      as fin,
  fout = fopen('copy.txt', 'w')              open('copy.txt', 'w') as fout:
  while ~feof(fin)                          for L in fin:
    L = fgetl(fin);                             fout.write(f'# {L}')
    fprintf(fout, '# %s\n', L);       except IOError as err:
  end                                     print(f'I/O error: {err}')
  fclose(fin)                         except:
  fclose(fout)                          err = sys.exc_info()[1]
catch EO                                print('other error: {err}')
  fprintf('error: %s', ...
          EO.message)
end
```

7.1.4 Parsing Text

Now that we can read text files, we'll want to do something useful with the files' contents like extract values of interest. Common operations to parse data from text include (1) stripping leading and trailing whitespace, (2) separating a string into words or phrases, and (3) searching a string for patterns. While strings were covered extensively in Section 4.2, the subset of string operations most commonly used to parse text are repeated here.

7.1.4.1 Stripping Whitespace

Whitespace at the start and end of a string can be removed with these string methods: .lstrip() (for left), .rstrip() (right), and .strip() for both left and right. They match MATLAB's strip() function with optional 'left', 'right', or 'both' (the default) arguments. The methods do not modify the contents of the string but instead return a new string without the whitespace. .rstrip() also removes a string's trailing newline character if it exists:

MATLAB:	Python:
| ```
>> L = " abc "
   " abc "
>> strip(L,'left')
   "abc "
>> strip(L,'right')
   " abc"
>> strip(L)
   "abc"
>> L
   " abc "
``` | ```
In : L = ' abc '
In : L
Out: ' abc '
In : L.lstrip()
Out: 'abc '
In : L.rstrip()
Out: ' abc'
In : L.strip()
Out: 'abc'
In : L
Out: ' abc '
``` |

7.1.4.2 Splitting a String with a Substring

A string can be subdivided by a substring using a string's .split() method. Without arguments, .split() returns a list of substrings separated by whitespace. If .split() is given an argument, the method will separate the string by that argument. A second optional argument, also definable with the maxsplit keyword, is the maximum number of separations to make (in other words, maxsplit=1 yields a list with two items):

```
In : L = "abc 123.4 def; 5; 6 7 "
In : L.split()
Out: ['abc', '123.4', 'def;', '5;', '6', '7']

In : L.split(";")
Out: ['abc 123.4 def', ' 5', ' 6 7 ']

In : L.split(maxsplit=1)
Out: ['abc', '123.4 def; 5; 6 7 ']
```

To split a string into individual characters, pass the string to the list() function:

```
In : list(L)
Out: [ 'a', 'b', 'c', ' ', '1', '2', '3',
       '.', '4', ' ', 'd', 'e', 'f', ';',
       ' ', ' ', '5', ';', ' ', '6', ' ',
       '7', ' ']
```

7.1.4.3 Regular Expressions

Regular expressions are an enormous topic that fill entire books so the discussion here is necessarily limited. For the most part, MATLAB and Python employ the same regular expression metacharacters and pattern matching rules. Rather than list these, the following sections show examples in both languages.

As mentioned in Section 4.2.6, Python's regular expression library is in a module called re, so the code examples include

```
import re
```

Tip   The interactive website https://regex101.com/ is a great resource for experimenting with and testing regular expressions.

7.1.4.4 Splitting a String with a Regex

A string can be subdivided by a regex with re.split(). This example uses the same line of text used in the constant string .split() method of Section 7.1.4.2. Instead of splitting on whitespace, here we'll craft a regex that gives us back only the numeric values. The pattern [^\ .\ d]+ means "one or more characters that are not digits or the decimal point":

```
In : import re
In : L = "abc 123.4 def; 5; 6 7 "
In : re.split(r'[^\d\.]+', L)
Out: ['', '123.4', '5', '6', '7', '']
```

The split isn't perfect since it returns null strings that we'll have to filter out manually. One way to do that is with a conditional list comprehension, where the trailing condition, if _, uses the "truthiness" of a string to decide whether or not to include the term in the output. A null string evaluates as False and is therefore excluded.

```
In : [_ for _ in re.split(r'[^\d\.]+', L) if _]
Out: ['123.4', '5', '6', '7']
```

7.1.4.5 Searching a String for Patterns

A string can be checked to see if it contains a text pattern with one of the following functions: re.search(), re.match(), and re.fullmatch(). Their arguments are a regular expression, a string to search, and optional flags which define whether or not to treat uppercase and lowercase letters the same.

Say we have a data file containing timestamps, latitude, longitude, and city name. Sometimes, the data is incomplete and is missing one or more legitimate values as in this sample:

```
1983-08-09 unknown Riverbank US America/Los_Angeles
2012-05-06 NaN -88.3162 Crystal Lake US America/Chicago
2016-12-09 unknown Evergreen Park US America/Chicago
2006-12-08 NaN -93.75018 Shreveport US America/Chicago
1999-02-15
1998-05-02 unknown Brenham US America/Chicago
2009-06-18 40.72371 -73.95097 Greenpoint US America/New_York
1992-11-25 NaN -76.72803 Woodlawn US America/New_York
1979-04-30 29.84576 -90.10674 Estelle US America/Chicago
1983-01-05 38.06084 -97.92977 Hutchinson US America/Chicago
2013-07-09 39.32288 -76.72803 Woodlawn US America/New_York
2005-08-31 NaN -102.36764 Odessa US America/Chicago
2014-02-05 unknown Fairview Heights US America/Chicago
2010-03-23
1990-09-04
```

Our goal is to extract numerical values for latitude and longitude wherever these are defined. Several approaches are possible, but here we'll craft a solution by matching a regular expression and saving the matched patterns. The characters representing latitude or longitude follow this sequence:

- Whitespace

- An optional minus sign

- One or more digits

- A period

- One or more digits

- Whitespace

Translated into the language of regular expressions, these become

- \s+

- [-]?

- \d+

- \.

- \d+

- \s+

Therefore, our regex to match either a latitude or longitude looks like this: \s+[-]?
\d+\.\d+\s+. To capture the matched text, we have to surround the pattern of interest with parentheses; thus, we get \s+([-]?\d+\.\d+)\s+ repeated twice, once for latitude and once for longitude. Experienced regular expression users may be tempted to use the pattern only once followed by a {2} quantifier to tell the regex engine "match the previous pattern twice." Doing so however complicates the capture of the numeric values for subsequent use. Instead, we'll explicitly copy the pattern twice.

The final regex we pass to re.search() is then \s+([-]?\d+\.\d+)\s+([-]?
\d+\.\d+)\s+. Regular expressions tend to be loaded with backslash characters. This poses a complication as the backslash also serves the purpose of defining nonprintable characters; control-c in a Python string, for example, would be '\c'. Regular expressions need the literal backslash which would ordinarily be expressed in a string as '\\'.
Fortunately, Python has a *raw string* mode, defined with a leading r before the string,

197

telling the interpreter to take every character within the string at face value. In this case, r'\c' represents two characters—backslash and the lowercase letter C—instead of control-c. For this reason, strings containing regular expressions are nearly always defined as raw strings.

re.search() returns an object of type re.Match which has a value of None if the desired pattern was not found. If there was a match with the provided string, the captured text is in m.group(1) for the first parenthetical group, m.group(2) for the second, and so on.

Let's test it:

```
In : import re
In : L = '1983-01-05 38.06084 -97.92977 Hutchinson US America/Chicago'
In : pattern = re.compile(r'\s+([-]?\d+\.\d+)\s+([-]?\d+\.\d+)\s')
In : m = re.search(pattern, L)
In : m
Out: <re.Match object; span=(10, 30), match=' 38.06084 -97.92977 '>

In : m is None
Out: False

In : m.group(1)
Out: '38.06084'

In : m.group(2)
Out: '-97.92977'

In : L = '1983-01-05 NaN -97.92977 Hutchinson US America/Chicago'
In : m = re.search(pattern, L)
In : m is None
Out: True
```

Note that the second line we tested against, containing NaN in place of a real latitude, reports the match failed as our regex insists on having two numbers.

We can now write a complete program that reads a data file and prints latitude and longitude values. Recall that regex matches are strings, so we need to typecast the matches to floats if we expect to use them numerically:

```python
#!/usr/bin/env python3
import sys
import re
if len(sys.argv) < 2:
    print("Usage: %s <file(s)>" % sys.argv[0])
    raise SystemExit

File = sys.argv[1]

pattern = re.compile(r'\s+([-]?\d+\.\d+)\s+([-]?\d+\.\d+)\s')
try:
    with open(File) as fh:
        for line in fh:
            m = re.search(pattern, line)
            if m is None:
                continue
            lat = float( m.group(1) )
            lon = float( m.group(2) )
            print(f'lat={lat: 8.3f} lon={lon: 8.3f}')
except IOError as err:
    print(f'Failed to read {File}: {err}')
```

Running the program on our data sample gives

```
lat=   40.724  lon= -73.951
lat=   29.846  lon= -90.107
lat=   38.061  lon= -97.930
lat=   39.323  lon= -76.728
```

7.1.5 csv

The comma-separated value (CSV) file format is, for better or worse (the general consensus seems to be "worse"), among the most prevalent of all data formats. While CSV is effective for purely numerical data, textual data introduces complications because the comma character itself may be part of a text entry. In this case, the CSV format dictates that a text string with embedded commas must be quoted—which raises the issue of how one would save quotes and so on. Embedded newline characters further complicate matters.

It goes without saying that we'd rather work with existing csv reading libraries than parse data ourselves. Fortunately, both MATLAB and Python have sophisticated csv readers.

MATLAB's `readmatrix()` function takes a CSV file name as an input and returns a structure which contains the columns of data.

Python has several options for loading data from CSV files:

1. The standard `csv` module which returns a list of lists

2. Pandas module's `read_csv()` function which returns a Pandas dataframe

3. NumPy module's `genfromtxt()` function which returns a NumPy array

4. Manually reading and parsing the data (not recommended!)

Pandas, covered in Chapter 13, has by far the most powerful CSV reader. The NumPy option is attractive if you plan to perform array computations with the loaded data.

This small CSV file will be used to demonstrate the first three read options:

file: `industry_data.csv`

```
lon, lat, name, industry, revenue ($M)
-106.52,35.079,"Acme, Inc.",cosmetics, 12.3
-86.17,41.717,FlexMex,restaurant,0.5
-80.75,41.214,"Titan Hercules, LLP",sporting goods, 45.3
-95.54,29.783,"The Chicken Palace", restaurant, 22.3
-98.48,29.355,"Joe's Diner", restaurant, 0.0045
-78.99,33.784,Amalgamated Powders,cosmetics, 1.9
-122.68,45.525,Pie and Cake,restaurant,2.2
```

7.1.5.1 Python's `csv` Module

```
In : import csv
In : fh = open('industry_data.csv')
In : for row in csv.reader(fh):
...:     print(row)

['lon', ' lat', ' name', ' industry', ' revenue ($M)']
['-106.52', '35.079', 'Acme, Inc.', 'cosmetics', ' 12.3']
```

```
['-86.17', '41.717', 'FlexMex', 'restaurant', '0.5']
['-80.75', '41.214', 'Titan Hercules, LLP', 'sporting goods', ' 45.3']
['-95.54', '29.783', 'The Chicken Palace', ' restaurant', ' 22.3']
['-98.48', '29.355', "Joe's Diner", ' restaurant', ' 0.0045']
['-78.99', '33.784', 'Amalgamated Powders', 'cosmetics', ' 1.9']
['-122.68', '45.525', 'Pie and Cake', 'restaurant', '2.2']
```

7.1.5.2 Pandas's `read csv()` Function

```
In : import pandas as pd
In : data = pd.read_csv('industry_data.csv')
In : data
Out:
```

	lon	lat	name	industry	revenue ($M)
0	-106.52	35.079	Acme, Inc.	cosmetics	12.3000
1	-86.17	41.717	FlexMex	restaurant	0.5000
2	-80.75	41.214	Titan Hercules, LLP	sporting goods	45.3000
3	-95.54	29.783	The Chicken Palace	restaurant	22.3000
4	-98.48	29.355	Joe's Diner	restaurant	0.0045
5	-78.99	33.784	Amalgamated Powders	cosmetics	1.9000
6	-122.68	45.525	Pie and Cake	restaurant	2.2000

The new variable data is a Pandas *dataframe,* an object with many powerful features. For starters, individual columns of data can be accessed in either dictionary or attribute styles:

```
In : data['lon']
Out:

0   -106.52
1    -86.17
2    -80.75
3    -95.54
4    -98.48
5    -78.99
6   -122.68
```

Name: lon, dtype: float64

```
In : data.lon
Out:
0     -106.52
1      -86.17
2      -80.75
3      -95.54
4      -98.48
5      -78.99
6     -122.68
Name: lon, dtype: float64
```

Note also that, unlike the standard `csv` module, Pandas automatically converts strings representing numerical values to numbers.

The conversion of column names to dataframe attributes works when the string in the first row has no leading or trailing whitespace or unusual characters. Our fifth column, `revenue ($M)`, is problematic because of the dollar sign; if we don't rename it, Pandas will rename it for us `_5` (as it is the fifth column). Renaming a column is easy though:

```
In : data.rename(columns={'revenue ($M)' : 'revenue'}, inplace=True)
In : data.revenue
0      12.3000
1       0.5000
2      45.3000
3      22.3000
4       0.0045
5       1.9000
6       2.2000
Name: revenue, dtype: float64
```

Details and examples of accessing, filtering, and modifying data loaded with Pandas can be found in Chapter 13.

7.1.5.3 NumPy's genfromtxt() Function

It is a general-purpose text file reader that works best with purely numeric data and simple strings. Quoted strings with embedded commas, handled easily by Pandas's load_csv(), will defeat genfromtxt():

```
In : data=np.genfromtxt('industry_data.csv', delimiter=',')
ValueError: Some errors were detected !
    Line #2 (got 6 columns instead of 5)
    Line #4 (got 6 columns instead of 5)
```

7.1.6 XML

Python has a standard XML module, unsurprisingly named xml, for reading and writing XML files. The lxml module, included with Anaconda, is a more powerful option though as it allows one to locate items with XPath[1] expressions.

Reading XML in MATLAB on the other hand is tedious at best. Retrieving data of interest often takes a half dozen or more chained calls to .getChildNodes, .getElementsByTagName(), and .item(0). In addition, data items are returned as java.lang.String, not MATLAB strings. These variables must be converted with string() before they can be passed to MATLAB string handling functions (like strip() in the following code to remove extraneous leading and trailing whitespace).

XML reading techniques differ slightly if the XML file in question uses namespaces. Such files can be identified by xmlns: entries at the top of the file and by tag names containing colons such as <gmd:language>. We'll begin with the easier case of no namespaces.

7.1.6.1 XML Without Namespaces

The MATLAB and Python XML-reading code examples read the file mondial-3.0.xml[2] that contains socioeconomic data on many countries and cities. A portion of the file looks like this:

---

[1] www.w3.org/TR/1999/REC-xpath-19991116/

[2] http://aiweb.cs.washington.edu/research/projects/xmltk/xmldata/data/mondial/mondial-3.0.xml

203

file: mondial-3.0.xml

```
<?xml version="1.0" encoding="UTF-8"?>
  <mondial >
    <continent id='f0_119' name='Europe'/>
      <city id='f0_1461' country='f0_136' longitude='10.7' latitude='46.2'>
        <name >Tirane</name>
        <population year='87'> 192000</population>
      </city>
    <country id='f0_162'
      name='Belgium'
      capital='f0_1477'
      population='10170241'
      datacode='BE'
      total_area='30510'
      population_growth='0.33'
      infant_mortality='6.4'
      gdp_total='197000'
      inflation='1.6'
      indep_date='04 10 1830'
      government='constitutional monarchy'>
      <name >
        Belgium
      </name>
      <province id='f0_17457'
        name='Antwerp'
        country='f0_162'
        capital='f0_2311'
        population='1610695'
        area='2867'>
        <city id='f0_2311'
          country='f0_162'
          province='f0_17457'
          longitude='4.23'
          latitude='51.1'>
```

```
        <name >
           Antwerp
        </name>
        <population year='95'>
           459072
        </population>
      </city>
    </province>
  </country>

  <lake id='f0_39145' name='Lake Nasser'>
    <located country='f0_1241' province='f0_19885'/>
    <located country='f0_1241' province='f0_19893'/>
    <located country='f0_1241' province='f0_19910'/>
    <located country='f0_1398' province='f0_20023'/>
  </lake>
</mondial>
```

The following code prints the name of each city which has latitude and longitude entries:

MATLAB:

```
xDoc = xmlread('data/mondial-3.0.xml');
countries = xDoc.getElementsByTagName('country');
cities = xDoc.getElementsByTagName('city');
fprintf('%d countries, %d cities\n',...
   countries.getLength, cities.getLength)
for i = 1:cities.getLength
   c = cities.item(i-1);
   nodes = c.getChildNodes;
   name = nodes.getElementsByTagName('name').item(0);
   name_txt = name.getChildNodes.item(0).getData;
   name_txt = strip(string(name_txt));
   lat = nodes.getAttribute('latitude');
   lon = nodes.getAttribute('longitude');
```

```
    if strip(string(lat)) == "" || ...
       strip(string(lon)) == ""
         continue
    end
    fprintf('%-20s %s %s\n', name_txt, lat, lon)
end
```

Python:

```
#!/usr/bin/env python3
import lxml.etree
dom = lxml.etree.parse('data/mondial-3.0.xml')
countries = dom.xpath('//country')
cities = dom.xpath('//city')
print(f'{len(countries)} countries, '
      f'{len(cities)} cities')
for c in cities:
    name = c.find('name').text.strip()
    if 'latitude' not in c.attrib or \
       'longitude' not in c.attrib:
          continue
    lat = c.attrib['latitude']
    lon = c.attrib['longitude']
    print(f'{name:20s} {lat} {lon}')
```

The output from both programs is the same. The first few lines are

```
231 countries, 3152 cities
Tirane               46.2 10.7
Shkoder              42.2 19.2
Durres               41.2 19.3
Vlore                40.3 19.3
Elbasan              41.1 20.1
Korce                40.4 20.5
Andorra la Vella     42.3 1.3
Eisenstadt           48 16
Klagenfurt           46.38 14.21
```

7.1.6.2 XML with Namespaces

XML containing namespaces requires more effort to parse. Only the Python solution is shown.

An example of such a file is bermuda_forecastgrids 2015.xml,[3] a water level forecast file produced by the National Environmental Satellite, Data, and Information Service (NESDIS). The first few lines of this file are

```
<?xml version="1.0" encoding="UTF-8"?>
<gmi:MI_Metadata xmlns:gmi="http://www.isotc211.org/2005/gmi"
xmlns:gco="http://www.isotc211.org/2005/gco"
xmlns:gmd="http://www.isotc211.org/2005/gmd"
xmlns:gmx="http://www.isotc211.org/2005/gmx"
xmlns:gsr="http://www.isotc211.org/2005/gsr"
xmlns:gss="http://www.isotc211.org/2005/gss"
xmlns:gts="http://www.isotc211.org/2005/gts"
xmlns:gml="http://www.opengis.net/gml/3.2"
xmlns:xlink="http://www.w3.org/1999/xlink"
xmlns:xsi="http://www.w3.org/2001/XMLSchema-instance"
xsi:schemaLocation="http://www.isotc211.org/2005/gmi
https://www.ngdc.noaa.gov/metadata/published/xsd/schema.xsd"
uuid="7fa9f1fe-6ef6-4e38-a57c-87bb2c56e825">
  <gmd:fileIdentifier>
    <gco:CharacterString>gov.noaa.ngdc.mgg.dem:bermuda_forecastgrids_2015
    </gco:CharacterString>
      </gmd:fileIdentifier>
      <gmd:language>
        <gco:CharacterString>eng; USA</gco:CharacterString>
      </gmd:language>
      <gmd:characterSet>
        <gmd:MD_CharacterSetCode codeList="http://www.isotc211.org/2005/
resources/Codelist/gmxCodelists.xml#MD_CharacterSetCode" codeListValue=
"utf8">utf8</gmd:MD_CharacterSetCode>
      </gmd:characterSet>
```

---

[3] https://data.noaa.gov/waf/NOAA/NESDIS/NGDC/MGG/DEM/iso/xml/bermuda_forecastgrids_2015.xml

To read such a file, an additional argument providing the namespace map must be supplied to each lxml call that extracts data. The namespace map itself is merely a dictionary of the xmlns: entries defined at the top of the XML file.

Here's another portion of the same XML file that defines geographic bounding boxes: file: bermuda_forecastgrids_2015.xml

```
<gmd:extent>
  <gmd:EX_Extent id="boundingExtent">
    <gmd:description>
      <gco:CharacterString>ISO valid extents for A Grid
        </gco:CharacterString>
    </gmd:description>
    <gmd:geographicElement>
      <gmd:EX_GeographicBoundingBox
          id="boundingGeographicBoundingBox">
        <gmd:westBoundLongitude>
          <gco:Decimal>-65.400</gco:Decimal>
        </gmd:westBoundLongitude>
        <gmd:eastBoundLongitude>
          <gco:Decimal>-64.200</gco:Decimal>
        </gmd:eastBoundLongitude>
        <gmd:southBoundLatitude>
          <gco:Decimal>31.700</gco:Decimal>
        </gmd:southBoundLatitude>
        <gmd:northBoundLatitude>
          <gco:Decimal>32.900</gco:Decimal>
        </gmd:northBoundLatitude>
```

Namespace-aware code to read the latitude and longitude values looks like this:

```
#!/usr/bin/env python3
import lxml.etree
F = 'data/bermuda_forecastgrids_2015.xml'
NSMAP = {
    "gmi"   : "http://www.isotc211.org/2005/gmi",
    "gco"   : "http://www.isotc211.org/2005/gco",
    "gmd"   : "http://www.isotc211.org/2005/gmd",
```

```
    "gmx"   : "http://www.isotc211.org/2005/gmx",
    "gsr"   : "http://www.isotc211.org/2005/gsr",
    "gss"   : "http://www.isotc211.org/2005/gss",
    "gts"   : "http://www.isotc211.org/2005/gts",
    "gml"   : "http://www.opengis.net/gml/3.2",
    "xsi"   : "http://www.w3.org/2001/XMLSchema-instance",
    "xlink" : "http://www.w3.org/1999/xlink",
}
xlink = NSMAP['xlink']
dom = lxml.etree.parse(F)
for SysInfo in dom.xpath('//gmd:referenceSystemInfo',
                         namespaces=NSMAP):
    title = SysInfo.attrib[f'{{{xlink}}}title']
    print(f'title = {title}')
for extent in dom.xpath('//gmd:EX_GeographicBoundingBox',
                        namespaces=NSMAP):
  for Dir in [ 'westBoundLongitude',
               'eastBoundLongitude',
               'southBoundLatitude',
               'northBoundLatitude']:
      Letter = Dir[0].upper() # N S E or W
      block = extent.find(f'gmd:{Dir}', namespaces=NSMAP)
      value = block.findtext('gco:Decimal', namespaces=NSMAP)
      print(f'{Letter}: {value} ', end='')
  print('')
```

The unusual expression f'{{{xlink}}}title' is a consequence of needing to print braces around an f-string expansion of the variable xlink. To print just the value, the f-string would be f'{xlink}'. However, we want the output to also include braces, { and }. The rule for printing braces in f-strings is to double them, hence the triple set.

The output is

```
title = WGS84
title = Mean High Water height
W:  -65.400  E: -64.200  S: 31.700  N: 32.900
W:  -65.060  E: -64.541  S: 32.175  N: 32.540
W:  -64.900  E: -64.630  S: 32.240  N: 32.425
```

7.1.6.3 Writing XML

If reading XML seems tedious, writing XML with the lxml or xml modules is doubly so. Rather than manually creating and populating XML "nodes," a shortcut is to use a module such as dicttoxml, installable via conda, to create a byte array of XML from a Python dictionary of other data containers. Here's an example:

Python:

```
In : from dicttoxml import dicttoxml
In : import numpy as np
In : a = { 'list' : [ 5, 3.3, 'fish',],
...: 'dict' : { 'golf' : 'ball', 'swim' : 'pool'},
...: 'array' : np.array([[4.4, 5.5],[6, 7]]),
...: 'scalar' : 42 }

In : a
Out:
{'list': [5, 3.3, 'fish'],
 'dict': {'golf': 'ball', 'swim': 'pool'},
 'array': array([[4.4, 5.5],
                 [6. , 7. ]]),
 'scalar': 42}

In : my_xml = dicttoxml(a)
In : my_xml
Out: b'<?xml version="1.0" encoding="UTF-8" ?><root><list
type="list"><item type="int">5</item><item type="float">
3.3</item><item type="str">fish</item></list><dict type=
"dict"><golf type="str">ball</golf><swim type="str">pool
</swim></dict><array type="list"><item type="list"><item
type="number">4.4</item><item type="number">5.5</item></
item><item type="list"><item type="number">6.0</item><item
type="number">7.0</item></item></array><scalar type="int"
>42</scalar></root>'
```

The byte array my_xml can then be written to a text file using one of the methods described in Section 7.1.

7.1.6.4 Pretty-Printing XML

The my_xml string created in the previous section is hard to understand.
The xml module has a function that prints XML data in a more attractive and
comprehensible form:

Python:

```
In : import xml.dom.minidom
In : dom = xml.dom.minidom.parseString(my_xml)
In : print(dom.toprettyxml())
<?xml version="1.0" ?>
<root>
        <list type="list">
                <item type="int">5</item>
                <item type="float">3.3</item>
                <item type="str">fish</item>
        </list>
        <dict type="dict">
                <golf type="str">ball</golf>
                <swim type="str">pool</swim>
        </dict>
        <array type="list">
                <item type="list">
                        <item type="number">4.4</item>
                        <item type="number">5.5</item>
                </item>
                <item type="list">
                        <item type="number">6.0</item>
                        <item type="number">7.0</item>
                </item>
        </array>
        <scalar type="int">42</scalar>
</root>
```

7.1.7 YAML

The YAML file format has many advantages, most notably the ease of reading and writing by humans, and makes an excellent format for storing small datasets like program configuration data. Like Python, the hierarchy of data items in YAML files is denoted by indentation. YAML data is easily loaded into Python, but the same is not true for MATLAB. There, partial support exists through some third-party tools or through a Java-based YAML reader tied to the Java-to-MATLAB interface. Alternatively, one can use Python from MATLAB to read and write YAML files; these operations are demonstrated in Sections 7.2 and 7.3.

Here's an example file:

file: `simple.yaml`

```
tolerance : 1.0E-7
max_iter : 100
cases :
    - { lat: -106.52, lon : 35.079, revenue : 12.3 }
    # a comment
    - { lat:  -86.17, lon : 41.717, revenue : 0.5 }
    - { lat:  -80.75, lon : 41.214, revenue : 45.3 }
    - { lat:  -95.54, lon : 29.783, revenue : 22.3 }
```

It can be loaded into a Python program with the yaml module's `safe_load()` function:

```
import yaml
with open('simple.yaml') as fh:
    data = yaml.safe_load(fh)
```

The variable data is then populated as a dictionary with keys tolerance, max_iter, and cases which itself is a list with four items, each of which is a dictionary with keys lat, lon, and revenue:

```
In : data
Out:
{'tolerance': 1e-07,
 'max_iter': 100,
 'cases': [{'lat': -106.52, 'lon': 35.079, 'revenue': 12.3},
```

```
{'lat': -86.17, 'lon': 41.717, 'revenue': 0.5},
{'lat': -80.75, 'lon': 41.214, 'revenue': 45.3},
{'lat': -95.54, 'lon': 29.783, 'revenue': 22.3}]}
```

> **Warning**   The yaml.load() function should never be used as it will execute Python code found in a specially crafted YAML file—clearly a security risk. Only the yaml.safe_load() function, which merely loads code into a string, should be used.

7.1.8 JSON

JSON, the JavaScript Object Notation format, has become nearly synonymous with web-based data transfers. Both MATLAB and Python support JSON natively. JSON closely resembles YAML, except braces are used to define a hierarchy rather than indentation; in fact, whitespace is ignored entirely in JSON.

The JSON representation of the data shown in the previous section on YAML might look like this:

file: simple.json

```
{"tolerance": 1e-07, "max_iter": 100, "cases": [{"lat": -106.52,
"lon": 35.079, "revenue": 12.3}, {"lat": -86.17, "lon": 41.717,
"revenue": 0.5}, {"lat": -80.75, "lon": 41.214, "revenue":
45.3}, {"lat": -95.54, "lon": 29.783, "revenue": 22.3}]}
```

Code to load the file simple.json and dereference the first two latitudes in both languages

MATLAB:	Python:

```
>> fh = fopen('simple.json', 'r');
>> str = fread(fh, '*char').';
>> fclose(fh);
>> J = jsondecode(str)
    tolerance: 1.0000e-07
    max_iter: 100
        cases: [4x1 struct]

>> J.cases
  4x1 struct array with fields:
    lat
    lon
    revenue
>> [J.cases(1:2).lat]
 -106.5200 -86.1700
```

```
In : import json
In : J = json.load(open('simple.json'))
In : J
Out:
{'tolerance': 1e-07,
 'max_iter': 100,
 'cases': [
 {'lat': -106.52, 'lon': 35.079,
  'revenue': 12.3},
 {'lat': -86.17, 'lon': 41.717,
  'revenue': 0.5},
 {'lat': -80.75, 'lon': 41.214,
  'revenue': 45.3},
 {'lat': -95.54, 'lon': 29.783,
  'revenue': 22.3}]}

In : [J['cases'][_]['lat'] for _ in [0,1]]
Out: [-106.52, -86.17]
```

7.1.9 ini

.ini files originated as a format for storing program configuration data in MS-DOS but are now ubiquitous. As with YAML, Python supports these natively, but MATLAB does not. Again, as with YAML, MATLAB can leverage Python's ability to read and write these files; examples are in Sections 7.4 and 7.5.

Here's a simple file, sample.ini:

ini:

```
[Main]
tolerance = 1e-07
max_iter = 100

[case_A]
lat = -106.52
lon = 35.079
revenue = 12.3
```

```
[case_B]
lat = -86.17
lon = 41.717
revenue = 0.5
```

It can be read with
Python:

```python
# file: code/IO/read_ini.py
import configparser
D = configparser.ConfigParser()
D.read('sample.ini')

for S in D.sections():
    print(f'Section {S}:')
    for k in D[S]:
        print(f'  {k} = {D[S][k]}')
```

to produce this output:

```
Section Main:
  tolerance = 1e-07
  max_iter = 100
Section case_A:
  lat = -106.52
  lon = 35.079
  revenue = 12.3
Section case_B:
  lat = -86.17
  lon = 41.717
  revenue = 0.5
```

Note   configparser's `.read()` method will not raise an error if the file does not exist or cannot be read for other reasons such as insufficient permission. Instead, it merely returns an empty object.

This example shows how the sample.ini file used earlier was written:

Python:

```
# file: code/IO/write_ini.py
import configparser
D = configparser.ConfigParser()
D['Main'] = {"tolerance": 1e-07, "max_iter": 100 }
D['case_A'] = {"lat": -106.52, "lon": 35.079, "revenue": 12.3}
D['case_B'] = {"lat": -86.17, "lon": 41.717, "revenue": 0.5}
with open('sample.ini', 'w') as configfile:
    D.write(configfile)
```

7.2 Recipe 7-1: Read YAML Files

As of MATLAB release 2020b, there is no official support for reading or writing YAML files. Several open source solutions exist such as yamlmatlab[4] and ReadYAML.[5] Alternatively, you can read YAML files directly with Python.

Here's a sample file:

YAML:

```
data :
    values : [2, 3, 4, 5.0]
    dict : { pet : fish, food : flakes }
    date : 2020-12-11 03:25:00
    items:
        -

            titles :
                - A Tale of Two Cities
                - Wuthering Heights
        - green
        - orange
```

YAML files can be read in MATLAB with just two lines of code, one to read the file with Python and one to convert the result to a MATLAB-native variable:

MATLAB 2020b:

---

[4] https://github.com/ewiger/yamlmatlab
[5] https://github.com/llerussell/ReadYAML

```
>> x = py.yaml.safe_load(py.open('demo.yaml'));
>> mat_x = py2mat(x);
>> mat_x.data
    values: {[2] [3] [4] [5]}
      dict: [1×1 struct]
      date: 11-Dec-2020 03:25:00
     items: {[1×1 struct] ["green"] ["orange"]}

>> mat_x.data.dict
      pet: "fish"
     food: "flakes"

>> mat_x.data.items{1}
    titles: {["A Tale of Two Cities"] ["Wuthering Heights"]}

>> mat_x.data.items{1}.titles{2}
    "Wuthering Heights"
```

7.3 Recipe 7-2: Write YAML Files

Writing a YAML file is as easy as reading it, so long as the MATLAB variable consists of simple numeric and string data types. As the following example shows, MATLAB datetime variables aren't understood by the Python YAML dump() serializer and must be converted to strings first. Here, we'll use the same mat_x structure from the previous example to first serialize the mat_x to a Python string, convert that into a MATLAB string, then write the MATLAB string to a file.

MATLAB 2020b:

```
>> py_str = py.yaml.dump(mat_x);
Error using py.yaml.dump
Conversion of MATLAB 'datetime' to Python is not supported.

>> mat_x.data.date = sprintf('%s', mat_x.data.date);
>> py_str = py.yaml.dump(mat_x);
>> py_str
```

Python str with no properties.

```
  data:
    date: 11-Dec-2020 03:25:00
    dict:
      food: flakes
      pet: fish
    items: !!python/tuple
    - titles: !!python/tuple
      - A Tale of Two Cities
      - Wuthering Heights
    - green
    - orange
    values: !!python/tuple
    - 2
    - 3
    - 4
    - 5.0
```

```
>> mat_str = string(py_str);
>> fh = fopen('new_demo.yaml', 'w');
>> fwrite(fh, mat_str);
>> fclose(fh);
```

7.4 Recipe 7-3: Read an ini File

As shown in Section 7.1.9, reading .ini files with the configparser module is easy.
Unfortunately, the object returned by configparser does not lend itself to traversal
in MATLAB; we'll need a bridge module to supply functions that provide otherwise
inaccessible key listing and indexing capabilities. This small module will serve
our needs:

Python:

```
# file: code/matlab_py/bridge_ini.py
import configparser
def read(File):
```

```
    D = configparser.ConfigParser()
    D.read(File)
    return D
def keys(D):
    return list(D.keys())
def get(D, key):
    return D[key]
```

We'll read the same .ini file as in Section 7.1.9:
ini:

[Main]
```
tolerance = 1e-07
max_iter = 100
```

[case_A]
```
lat = -106.52
lon = 35.079
revenue = 12.3
```

[case_B]
```
lat = -86.17
lon = 41.717
revenue = 0.5
```

It can be read in MATLAB with
MATLAB 2020b:

```
% file: code/matlab_py/read_ini.m
ini = py.importlib.import_module('bridge_ini');
in_file = 'sample.ini';
D = ini.read(in_file);
if ~length(D.sections())
    fprintf('Unable to read %s\n', in_file);
end
for S = py2mat(D.sections())
    fprintf('Section %s\n', S{1});
    sect = ini.get(D,S{1});
```

```
    for k = py2mat(ini.keys(sect))
        value = py2mat(ini.get(sect,k{1}));
        fprintf(' %s = %s\n', k{1}, value);
    end
end
```

The output is
MATLAB 2020b:

```
>> read_ini
Section Main
   tolerance = 1e-07
   max_iter = 100
Section case_A
   lat = -106.52
   lon = 35.079
   revenue = 12.3
Section case_B
   lat = -86.17
   lon = 41.717
   revenue = 0.5
```

7.5 Recipe 7-4: Write an ini File

Writing .ini files also requires a bridge module because the object returned by
configparser does not permit dictionary assignment with .update(). In addition, the
object's .write() method expects a Python file handle, so we'll make our lives easier by
implementing our own write() wrapper too:
   Python:

```
# file: code/matlab_py/bridge_ini_w.py
import configparser
def config():
    return configparser.ConfigParser()
def add_section(config, section, data):
    config[section] = data
    return config
```

```
def write(config, ini_file):
    with open(ini_file, 'w') as fh:
        config.write(fh)
```

Here's MATLAB code to populate a variable and then send it to our bridge module for writing:

MATLAB:

```
% file: code/matlab_py/write_ini.m
ini_w = py.importlib.import_module('bridge_ini_w');
d.pos  = [0.5 -0.3];
d.vel  = [2.7  3.8];
d.name = "point B";
a.CA.county = "LA";
a.CA.zip = 91234;
a.population = 1e7;
config = ini_w.config();
config = ini_w.add_section(config, 'DEFAULT', d);
config = ini_w.add_section(config, 'States', a);
ini_w.write(config, 'out.ini');
```

writes this file:

ini:

```
[DEFAULT]
pos = array('d', [0.5, -0.3])
vel = array('d', [2.7, 3.8])
name = point B

[States]
ca = {'county': 'LA', 'zip': 91234.0}
population = 10000000.0
```

7.6 Binary Files

Text-based data works well for small datasets or datasets intended to read by humans. As the volume of data grows though, the size and extra time required to read and write them become burdensome. In these cases, we can save storage space and speed input/output operations by using binary files.

As with text files, we'll begin with examples showing how to read and write general-purpose binary files, then switch to popular predefined binary formats such as Excel, HDF5, NetCDF4, SQLite, and MATLAB's own .mat.

A subsequent section, Section 11.1.9, in Chapter 11, deals solely with reading and writing NumPy arrays.

Files are opened for binary read in Python by passing 'rb', for "read binary," as a second argument to the open() function. The same is true in MATLAB except with fopen() instead of open(). Once a file is opened, we can read a desired number of bytes—or the contents of the entire file—into a byte array with the .read() method on the file handle; move to a desired offset within the file with .seek(); determine where we are within the file with .tell().

Most of the time, reading bytes is just half of the story. The other half involves converting blocks of bytes into the higher-level data types like integers, floats, strings, and so on.

The standard Python module struct has two functions, unpack() and pack(), that convert bytes into other data types and vice versa. unpack() and pack() take as an input argument a format string that describes the quantity and type of data expected. We'll first write a binary file of integers with values from 1 to 1,000,000 and then read the file back.

MATLAB:

```
x = 1:1000000; % double
fh = fopen('data.bin', 'wb');
fwrite(fh,x,'uint32');
fclose(fh);
```

Python:

```
import numpy as np
from struct import pack
n = 1_000_000
x = np.arange(1,n+1) # int64
raw = pack(f'{n}I', *x)
with open('data.bin', 'wb') as fh:
    fh.write(raw)
```

A few remarks about the Python version:

1. Underscores in numeric constants (n = 1_000_000) are ignored. They can be used as "syntactic sugar" to make large values easier to read.

2. The *x argument to pack() means the terms of the array are expanded; pack() wants to see individual scalar values, that is, 1, 2, 3, ..., rather than an array x (the "star" notation is discussed in Section 4.3.20).

3. struct.pack() is not needed to write a binary file of purely numeric values; NumPy arrays have a .tofile() method that can do this automatically. These lines yield the same file as the code using pack() earlier:

Python:

```python
import numpy as np
n = 1_000_000
x = np.arange(1,n+1) # int64
x.astype(np.uint32).tofile('data.bin')
```

In the following example, we'll read a large file into a tuple of bytes called raw, then from this tuple make a new array called Ints containing four-byte unsigned integers. The file's size should therefore be a multiple of four bytes.

MATLAB:	Python:

``matlab
fh = fopen('data.bin', 'rb');
raw = uint8(fread(fh));
fclose(fh);
Ints = typecast(raw(:),'uint32');
``
	``python
	from struct import unpack
	with open('data.bin', 'rb') as fh:
	    raw = fh.read()
	    n_ints = len(raw) // 4
	    Ints = unpack(f'<{n_ints}I', raw)
	``

Note   Binary files of single data-typed numeric data can be loaded with a call to NumPy's fromfile() function (ref. Section 11.1.10.5).

The format string passed to unpack() has three parts: < denotes little-endian data (this is optional; if omitted, the data will be loaded according to the endianness of the operating system running the code), a count of the number of unsigned integers to return, and the desired format—I means "unsigned four-byte integer." Table 7-1 shows the struct letter codes and their meanings.

Table 7-1. *struct format characters*

Format	C Type	Python Type	n Bytes
x	pad byte	no value	1
c	char	bytes	1
b	signed char	integer	1
B	unsigned char	integer	1
?	_Bool	bool	1
h	short	integer	2
H	unsigned short	integer	2
i	int	integer	4
I	unsigned int	integer	4
l	long	integer	4
L	unsigned long	integer	4
q	long long	integer	8
Q	unsigned long long	integer	8
n	ssize_t	native integer	*Varies*
N	Size_t	unsigned native integer	*Varies*
e	short float	float	2
f	float	float	4
d	double	float	8
s	char[]	bytes	1
p	char[]	bytes	1

Writing binary files in Python involves opening the file in "write binary" mode, `'wb'`, then passing the file handle's `.write()` method one or more bytes. We can create bytes from simple Python data types with struct's `pack()` function. The following code writes a binary file containing a short header followed by an array of double-precision numbers. The header contains the count of double-precision numbers as a signed 32-bit integer, followed by 20 characters describing the data, followed by the doubles themselves.

MATLAB:	Python:
| ```matlab
fh = fopen('data2.bin', 'wb');
N = 50;
info = "test data";
padded = sprintf('%-20s',info);
x = 0:N-1;
fh = fopen('data2.bin', 'wb');
fwrite(fh,N,'integer*4');
fwrite(fh,padded,'char');
fwrite(fh,x,'double');
fclose(fh);
``` | ```python
import numpy as np
from struct import pack
N = 50
info = "test data"
x = np.arange(N, dtype=np.double)
with open('data2.bin', 'wb') as fh:
    fh.write(pack('1i', N))
    fh.write(pack('20s', info.encode()))
    fh.write(pack(f'{N}d', *x))
``` |

The numerical portions of the `data2.bin` binary file produced by the two implementations will be the same. The string portion, however, differs because Python zero-pads the empty portions, while `sprintf()` in MATLAB uses space padding.

The Python notation `*x` (from `fh.write(pack(f'Nd', *x))`) may seem unintuitive. Recall from Section 4.3.20 that an asterisk before a list or array basically means "all the items in this container"; x is a single term, but *x is all 50 separate terms of x, as needed by `pack()`.

7.7 Excel `.xls`, `.xlsx`

The native Excel file formats `.xls` (Excel versions before 2007) and `.xlsx` are perhaps second in popularity only to `.csv` files. While they are most easily viewed and manipulated with the Excel application itself, file readers and writers are available for many languages including MATLAB and Python.

MATLAB's `sheetnames()` and `readtable()` functions are most closely matched by `ExcelFile()` and `read_excel()` from the Pandas module. Pandas itself is a substantial topic that will be covered more fully in Chapter 13. Here, I'll only use portions related to reading and writing Excel files. The Pandas Excel functions are wrappers around two lower-level Python modules, `xlrd` for `.xls` files and `openpyxl` for `.xlsx` files. All are included with Anaconda.

7.7.1 Reading `.xls` and `.xlsx` Files

Excel file reading is demonstrated with two files. `subprime_2006_distributed.xls`[6] contains names of financial institutions in the United States that provided subprime loans between 1993 and 2006, where each year's data is in a worksheet (a tab) named after that year. It looks like this in Google Sheets:

---

[6]www.huduser.org/portal/datasets/manu/subprime_2006_distributed.xls

`LiuXiaoyu A-wdcf_Data_Tables_Dictionary-20170804.xlsx` is more complex than the `.xls` file since it has multiple tables in a single worksheet. This spreadsheet accompanies a journal paper, "Measuring and modeling surface sorption dynamics of organophosphate flame retardants on impervious surfaces," and comes from the US Environmental Protection Agency website.[7] It looks like this:

Common read operations on spreadsheets are shown next.

7.7.1.1 Get Worksheet Names

In addition to getting the worksheet names, we'll also identify the index of the worksheet titled "1994." This index is needed in MATLAB to pull data from a specific sheet. It isn't needed in Python because there individual sheets can be selected by their titles.

---

[7] https://pasteur.epa.gov/uploads/10.23719/1373881/LiuXiaoyu_A-wdcf_Data%20 Tables%26Dictionary- 20170804.xlsx

MATLAB:	Python:
| ```
>> F = 'subprime_2006_distributed.xls';
>> tabs = sheetnames(F)
   13×1 string array
      "1993"
      "1994"
        :
      "2005"


>> find(tabs == "1994")
      2
``` | ```
In : import pandas as pd
In : F = 'subprime_2006_
distributed.xls';
In : tabs = pd.ExcelFile(F)
In : tabs.sheet_names
Out[16]:
['1993',
 '1994',
   :
 '2005']
``` |

7.7.1.2 Get a Worksheet's Size

MATLAB:	Python:
| ```
>> [nRows, nCols] = size(T)
nRows =
    85
nCols =
    5
``` | ```
In : nRows, nCols = T.shape
In : nRows, nCols
(85, 5)
``` |

7.7.1.3 Extract Rows

Here, we extract the ninth row from the "1994" tab of the `.xls` file. Row indexing can be tricky because both MATLAB and Pandas try to figure out reasonable column names and the proper offset to the actual beginning of data. MATLAB is able to make sense of the staggered titles in this file and begins loading data at row 4; therefore, the ninth row appears at row index 6. Pandas isn't able to figure this out on its own, so we pass an optional argument, `header=2`, to tell it to take column names from the third row (indexing starts at zero).

MATLAB:	Python:

``
>> F = 'subprime_2006_distributed.xls';
>> tabs = sheetnames(F);
>> i = find(tabs == "1994");
>> T = readtable(F,'Sheet',i);
>> Tc = table2cell(T);
>> Tc(6,:)
  1×5 cell array
 {'20000943518'} {'2'} {[943518]} {[1]}
    {'PROVIDENT BK OF KY'}
``
	``
	In : import pandas as pd
	In : F = 'subprime_2006_
	distributed.xls';
	In : T = pd.read_excel(F, \
	         sheet_name='1994',header=2)
	In : T.values[5,:]
	Out:
	array(['20000943518', 2.0, 943518, 1.0,
	       'PROVIDENT BK OF KY '],
	      dtype=object)
	``

Additional rows can be selected by replacing the 5 (in Python) or 6 (in MATLAB) with a range (e.g., 5:8).

The variable T is a table in MATLAB and a dataframe in Python. Tables and dataframes have powerful capabilities that are explored in Chapter 13, but they are overkill when you just want values from a spreadsheet without filtering, sorting, joining, and so on. For this reason, we'll convert the table to a simpler container in MATLAB and access the dataframe through its .values attribute in Python. MATLAB tables can be converted to matrices, cell arrays, or structured variables with one of the table2* functions. table2cell() is a reasonable choice for the mix of strings and numbers in the preceding data.

7.7.1.4 Extract Columns

Column subsetting works similarly to row subsetting; all that's needed is different indexing to the table variable. Here, we'll pull out values from columns C and D. The following session continues from the preceding row example.

MATLAB:	Python:
`>> table2array(T(:,3:4))`	`In : T.values[:,2:4]`
1.503300000e+04 1.000000000e+00	`array([[15033, 1.0],`
2.255900000e+04 1.000000000e+00	`       [22559, 1.0],`
6.126180000e+05 1.000000000e+00	`       [612618, 1.0],`
7.655780000e+05 1.000000000e+00	`       [765578, 1.0],`
8.567750000e+05 1.000000000e+00	`       [856775, 1.0]],`
:	:

7.7.1.5 Extract a Rectangular Block

The `.xlsx` file is more challenging to work with because several tables appear in each worksheet. We can't rely on either MATLAB or Pandas to figure out what's going on; instead, the burden is on us to identify a specific region of rows and columns to extract. The file's name in the examples is abbreviated to `LiuXiaoyu_A.xlsx` to accommodate the narrow format. We'll pull all numeric values from columns D, E, and F from worksheet "`Data Table (Figs 2a&b&c&d)`". First, we'll get a sense of what the autoloaders would pull in without row or column bounds:

MATLAB:	Python:
`>> F = 'LiuXiaoyu_A.xlsx';`	`In : import pandas as pd`
`>> tabs = sheetnames(F);`	`In : F = 'LiuXiaoyu_A.xlsx';`
`>> sheet = 'Data Table`	`In : sheet = 'Data Table`
`(Figs 2a&b&c&d)';`	`(Figs 2a&b&c&d)'`
`>> i = find(tabs == sheet);`	`In : T = pd.read_excel(F, \`
`>> T = readtable(F,'Sheet',i);`	`        sheet_name=sheet,header=2)`
`>> size(T)`	`In : T.shape`
`     301   19`	`Out: (301, 19)`

Unsurprisingly, neither recognizes the multiple tables here; both just return a single table bounded by the last row and column among all smaller tables. To select a block, MATLAB uses the `'Range'` optional argument to limit both rows and columns. Pandas uses keyword arguments `usecols` to select columns and a combination of `skiprows` and `nrows` to select a row range.

MATLAB:	Python:
| ```
>> F = 'LiuXiaoyu_A.xlsx';
>> tabs = sheetnames(F);
>> sheet = 'Data Table
(Figs 2a&b&c&d)';
>> i = find(tabs == sheet);
>> T = readtable(F,'Sheet',i,...
                'Range','D4:F304');
>> Tc = table2array(T);
>> Tc(300:end,1:2)
   1.4950e+03    3.9029e-02
   1.5000e+03    3.5008e-02
``` | ```
In : import pandas as pd
In : F = 'LiuXiaoyu_A.xlsx';
In : sheet = 'Data Table (Figs 2a&b&c&d)'
In : T = pd.read_excel(F, sheet_
                    name=sheet,\
usecols='D:F',skiprows=2)
In : T.values[299:,:2]
Out:
array([[1.49500000e+03,  3.90288541e-02],
       [1.50000000e+03,  3.50079764e-02]])
``` |

Note that we didn't need to tell Pandas how many rows to read—it just stops when there's no more data. MATLAB's rectangular block selection is less convenient since we have to know the end row number.

7.7.2 Writing .xlsx Files

Pandas can create .xlsx files as easily as it can read them—so long as your data exists in a Pandas dataframe. Similarly, MATLAB's writetable() can write tables directly to .xlsx files. The operations look like this for table T and dataframe df:

MATLAB:	Python:
| ```
writetable(T,'file.xlsx,
    'Sheet','tab name');
``` | ```
df.to_excel('file.xlsx',
        sheet_name='tab name')
``` |

If your workflow doesn't use Pandas, you'll have to insert your data into one or more dataframes before you can use the Pandas .to_excel() method. That can be more hassle than it's worth. If you don't already have a dataframe, an easier path is to use the openpyxl module directly. openpyxl's write capability is powerful as it gives access to font size, color, cell merging, and many other customizations that MATLAB by itself can only do on Windows and then only via COM.[8] (MATLAB can, of course, write a finely crafted .xlsx file with Python's help. Section 7.8 shows the following example implemented with MATLAB calling openpyxl.)

Here's an example showing openpyxl's ability to set font style and cell color, merge cells, and insert equations:

Python:

```python
# file: code/IO/demo_openpyxl.py
from openpyxl import Workbook
from openpyxl.styles import Font, Alignment, PatternFill
book = Workbook()
sheet = book.active
sheet.title = "Pets by weight"

# font styles, background color
ft_title = Font(name='Arial', size=14, bold=True)
ft_red = Font(color='00FF0000')
ft_italics = Font(bold=True, italic=True)
bg_green = PatternFill(fgColor='C5FD2F', fill_type = 'solid')

sheet.merge_cells('B2:D3')
sheet['B2'] = 'My Pets'
sheet['B2'].font = ft_title
sheet['B2'].alignment = Alignment(
    horizontal="center", vertical="center")

# column headings
category = ['Name', 'Animal', 'weight [kg]']
row, col = 4, 2
for i in range(len(category)):
    cell = sheet.cell(row,col+i,category[i])
    cell.fill = bg_green

pets = [['Nutmeg', 'Rabbit', 2.5],
        ['Annabel', 'Dog', 4.3],
        ['Sunny', 'Bird', 0.02],
        ['Harley', 'Dog', 17.1],
```

---

[8]www.mathworks.com/help/matlab/matlab_external/getting-started-with-com.html

```
        ['Toby', 'Dog', 24.0],
        ['Mr Socks', 'Cat', 3.9]]
for P in pets:
    row += 1
    for j in range(len(category)):
        cell = sheet.cell(row,col+j,P[j])
        if j == 2 and P[j] < 0.1:
            cell.font = ft_red

# equation to sum all weights
sheet[f'D{row+1}'] = f"=SUM(D4:D{row})"

row += 1
sheet.merge_cells(f'B{row}:C{row}')
sheet[f'B{row}'] = 'Total weight:'
sheet[f'B{row}'].font = ft_italics

book.save("pets.xlsx")
```

Figure 7-1 shows what pets.xlsx looks like in Google Sheets.

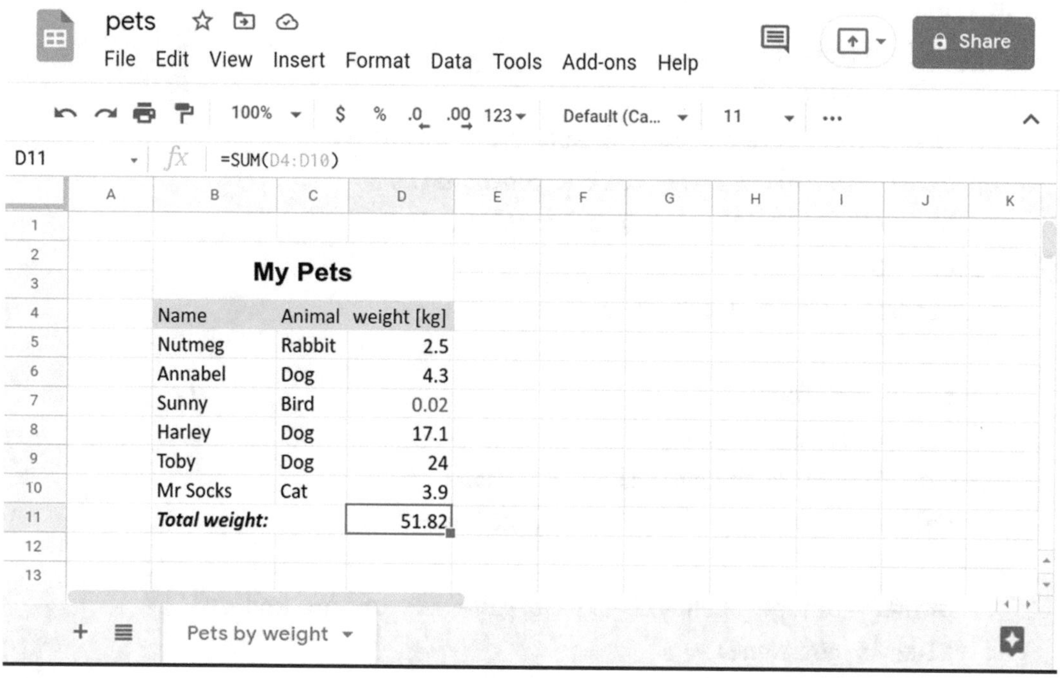

Figure 7-1. *Font styles, cell color, and cell merging with openpyxl*

7.8 Recipe 7-5: Write an .xlsx File

While MATLAB can write Excel .xlsx files by itself, fine control over cell elements can only be done on Windows through COM. The same degree of control can be done on any platform, without COM, by calling Python's openpyxl module from MATLAB. Here, we repeat the pure Python solution of Section 7.7.1.2 to create the pets.xlsx file.

A small bridge module with a function to permit cell assignments is needed.

Python:

```python
# file: code/matlab_py/bridge_openpyxl.py
def set(worksheet,
        loc=None,
        row=None,
        col=None,
        value=None,
        font=None,
        align=None,
        fill=None):
    """
    Provide
      worksheet[cell] = value
            - and -
      worksheet[cell].attribute = attribute value
    capability to MATLAB. The cell's coordinates
    can be specified with either a location, ie
      loc = 'B2'
    or 1-indexed row and column values.
    """
    if loc is not None:
        cell = worksheet[loc]
    elif row is not None and col is not None:
        cell = worksheet.cell(row=row, column=col)
    else:
        print(f'bridge_openpyxl error: give loc or row and col')
    if value is not None:
        cell.value = value
```

```
        if font is not None:
        cell.font = font
        if align is not None:
        cell.alignment = align
        if fill is not None:
        cell.fill = fill
```

The Excel file shown in Figure 7-1 can be created in MATLAB with
MATLAB 2020b:

```
% file: code/IO/demo_openpxl.m
Im = @py.importlib.import_module;
OP = Im('openpyxl');
styles = Im('openpyxl.styles');
OP_bridge = Im('bridge_openpyxl');
Workbook = OP.Workbook;
Font        = styles.Font;
Alignment   = styles.Alignment;
PatternFill = styles.PatternFill;
book = Workbook();
sheet = book.active;
sheet.title = "Pets by weight";

% font styles, background color
ft_title = Font(pyargs('name','Arial','size',int64(14),'bold',py.True));
ft_red = Font(pyargs('color','00FF0000'));
ft_italics = Font(pyargs('bold',py.True,'italic',py.True));
bg_green = PatternFill(pyargs('fgColor','C5FD2F','fill_type','solid'));

sheet.merge_cells('B2:D3')
OP_bridge.set(sheet, pyargs('loc','B2','value','My Pets'));
OP_bridge.set(sheet, pyargs('loc','B2','font',ft_title));
alignment = Alignment(pyargs('horizontal','center',...
                            'vertical','center'));
OP_bridge.set(sheet, pyargs('loc','B2','align',alignment));
```

```
% column headings
category = {'Name', 'Animal', 'weight [kg]'};
row = int64(4); col = int64(1);
for i = 1:length(category)
    OP_bridge.set(sheet, pyargs('row',row,'col',col+i,'value',category{i}));
    OP_bridge.set(sheet, pyargs('row',row,'col',col+i,'fill',bg_green));
end

pets = {{'Nutmeg', 'Rabbit', 2.5}, ...
        {'Annabel', 'Dog', 4.3},    ...
        {'Sunny', 'Bird', 0.02},    ...
        {'Harley', 'Dog', 17.1},    ...
        {'Toby', 'Dog', 24.0},      ...
        {'Mr Socks', 'Cat', 3.9}}};
for P = pets
    row = row + 1;
    for j = 1:length(category)
        OP_bridge.set(sheet, pyargs('row',row,'col',col+j,...
                                    'value',P{1}{j}));
        if j == 3 && P{1}{j} < 0.1
          OP_bridge.set(sheet, pyargs('row',row,'col',col+j,...
                                    'font',ft_red));
        end
    end
end

% equation to sum all weights
eqn = sprintf("=SUM(D4:D%d)", row);
loc = sprintf("D%d", row + 1);
OP_bridge.set(sheet, pyargs('loc',loc,'value',eqn));

row = row + 1;
sheet.merge_cells(sprintf("B%d:C%d",row,row));
Brow = sprintf("B%d",row);
OP_bridge.set(sheet, pyargs('loc',Brow,'value','Total weight:'));
OP_bridge.set(sheet, pyargs('loc',Brow,'font',ft_italics));

book.save("pets.xlsx")
```

7.9 HDF5

The Hierarchical Data File (HDF) format, conceived at the National Center for Supercomputing Applications and now developed and maintained by nonprofit HDF Group (`www.hdfgroup.org/`), has become a standard for many applications used in science, engineering, and finance. Currently in its fifth major revision, HDF can store collections of multidimensional numeric and text data efficiently and in a platform-neutral manner. Both MATLAB and Python can read and write HDF5 files with ease. In addition, The MathWorks changed the underlying format of their `.mat` file to HDF5 in the latest version, 7.3.

7.9.1 Reading an HDF5 File

The following examples use a file,[9] abbreviated SVDNB.h5 in the following code, containing "day/night band" imagery collected by the Suomi NPP weather satellite on June 18, 2019, between 05:10:14 and 05:15:53 UTC.

Before attempting to load its data into either MATLAB or Python, it helps to have some familiarity with an `.h5` file's contents.

Tip   The Anaconda Python distribution comes with HDF5 command-line utilities helpful for many tasks related to these files. Among them are

h52gif	h5clear	h5diff	h5import	h5redeploy	h5stat
h5c++	h5copy	h5dump	h5jam	h5mkgrp	h5repack
h5cc	h5debug	h5fc	h5ls	h5repart	h5watch

The h5ls command-line utility can print the table of contents of our h5 file:

```
> h5ls -r SVDNB.h5
/                          Group
/All_Data                  Group
/All_Data/VIIRS-DNB-SDR_All Group
/All_Data/VIIRS-DNB-SDR_All/ModeGran Dataset {4/Inf}
```

---

[9] SVDNB_npp_d20190618_t0510148_e0515534_b39581_c20190618091554795950_noac_ops.h5, downloaded from NOAA's Comprehensive Large Array-Data Stewardship System.

/All_Data/VIIRS-DNB-SDR_All/ModeScan Dataset {192/Inf}

/All_Data/VIIRS-DNB-SDR_All/NumberOfBadChecksums Dataset {192/Inf}

/All_Data/VIIRS-DNB-SDR_All/NumberOfDiscardedPkts Dataset {192/Inf}

/All_Data/VIIRS-DNB-SDR_All/NumberOfMissingPkts Dataset {192/Inf}

/All_Data/VIIRS-DNB-SDR_All/NumberOfScans Dataset {4/Inf}

/All_Data/VIIRS-DNB-SDR_All/PadByte1 Dataset {12/Inf}

/All_Data/VIIRS-DNB-SDR_All/QF1_VIIRSDNBSDR Dataset {3072/Inf, 4064/Inf}

/All_Data/VIIRS-DNB-SDR_All/QF2_SCAN_SDR Dataset {192/Inf}

/All_Data/VIIRS-DNB-SDR_All/QF3_SCAN_RDR Dataset {192/Inf}

/All_Data/VIIRS-DNB-SDR_All/Radiance Dataset {3072/Inf, 4064/Inf}

/Data_Products   Group

/Data_Products/VIIRS-DNB-SDR Group

/Data_Products/VIIRS-DNB-SDR/VIIRS-DNB-SDR_Aggr Dataset {11/Inf}

/Data_Products/VIIRS-DNB-SDR/VIIRS-DNB-SDR_Gran_0 Dataset {11/Inf}

/Data_Products/VIIRS-DNB-SDR/VIIRS-DNB-SDR_Gran_1 Dataset {11/Inf}

/Data_Products/VIIRS-DNB-SDR/VIIRS-DNB-SDR_Gran_2 Dataset {11/Inf}

/Data_Products/VIIRS-DNB-SDR/VIIRS-DNB-SDR_Gran_3 Dataset {11/Inf}

Let's load the /All_Data/VIIRS-DNB-SDR_All/Radiance dataset in Python and see how it looks from there:

Python:

```
In : import h5py
In : F = 'SVDNB.h5'
In : h5 = h5py.File(F, 'r')
In : dataset = '/All_Data/VIIRS-DNB-SDR_All/Radiance'
In : radiance = h5[dataset]
In : radiance
Out: <HDF5 dataset "Radiance": shape (3072, 4064), type "<f4">

In : radiance[10:12,10:12]
Out:
array([[0.00425367, 0.00468846],
       [0.00457452, 0.00468481]], dtype=float32)
```

```
In : x = radiance[:]
In : whos
Variable   Type     Data/Info
--------------------------------
F          str      SVDNB_npp_d20190618_t0510<...>8091554795950_noac_ops.h5
h5         File     <HDF5 file "SVDNB_npp_d20<...>0_noac_ops.h5" (mode r+)>
h5py       module   <module 'h5py' from '/usr<...>ckages/h5py/__init__.py'>
dataset    str      /All_Data/VIIRS-DNB-SDR_All/Radiance
radiance   Dataset  <HDF5 dataset "Radiance":<...>(3072, 4064), type "<f4">
x          ndarray  3072x4064: 12484608 elems, type `float32`, 49938432 bytes
                    (47.625 Mb)

In : h5.close()
```

The variable radiance is a handle to the HDF5 dataset rather than to the values contained within it. Numeric values are extracted from the handle by indexing either a slice of it, such as radiance[10:12,10:12], or all elements as with radiance[:]. The returned object is a NumPy array (NumPy will be covered extensively in Chapter 11).

7.9.2 Writing an HDF5 File

HDF5 files are as easy to write with Python as they are to read. This example shows how to create an .h5 file containing a 2D array of short (16-bit) floats, a 1D array of 64-bit unsigned integers, and a custom data type table whose columns are a 12-character string, a 32-bit signed integer, and a complex double. The create_dataset() function supports many high-end HDF5 features such as compression, scale/offset filters, setting a fill value, and time and order tracking via keyword arguments.

Python:

```
import h5py
import numpy as np
F = 'new.h5'
h5 = h5py.File(F, 'w')
array_2D = np.array([[1.1, 1.2], [2.1, 2.2]], dtype=np.float16)
array_1D = np.arange(30,33, dtype=np.uint64) # 30, 31, 32
table_type = np.dtype([('name' , 'S12'),
```

239

```
                     ('ID' , np.uint32),
                     ('phase', np.complex128)])
table_data    = np.zeros((2,), dtype=table_type)
table_data[0] = 'abc', 25573, 5.5-8.5j
table_data[1] = 'def', 42651, 9.2+4.5j
h5.create_dataset('/data/A2d', data=array_2D)
h5.create_dataset('/data/A1d', data=array_1D)
h5.create_dataset('/Table'   , data=table_data)
h5.close()
```

After running the preceding commands, we'll have a new HDF5 file, new.h5. The h5ls command-line utility confirms the contents are as expected:

```
> h5ls -r data/new.h5
/                      Group
/Table                 Dataset {2}
/data                  Group
/data/A1d              Dataset {3}
/data/A2d              Dataset {2, 2}
```

7.9.2.1 Abbreviated Writing Notation

The create_dataset() function shown earlier isn't strictly necessary as h5py allows an even more convenient write notation if you don't need to use advanced options in create_dataset(). This example shows how to write a 3 × 2 array of 8-bit signed integers to the dataset /db/x.

MATLAB:	Python:

```x = int8([-1 2; 3 -5; -6 7]);```
 ```h5create('x_matlab.h5', ...```
 ```   '/db/x', [3 2]);```
 ```h5write('x_matlab.h5', ...```
 ```   '/db/x', x);```
	```import h5py```
	 ```import numpy as np```
	 ```x = np.array([[-1,2],[3,-5],[-6,7]],```
	 ``` dtype=np.int8)```
	 ```h5 = h5py.File('x_python.h5','w')```
	 ```h5['/db/x'] = x```
	 ```h5.close()```

MATLAB needs a pair of h5create/h5write calls for every dataset, but in Python we can create and populate the dataset with the simple assignment h5['/db/x'] = x.

7.9.2.2 Beware: MATLAB's h5read(), h5write() Transpose Matrices

The MathWorks made curious design decisions on implementing h5read() and h5write() because these functions read and write transposed matrices. Let's take a closer look at x defined earlier:

MATLAB:	Python:
>> x = int8([-1 2; 3 -5; -6 7])	In : import numpy as np
3×2 int8 matrix	In : x = np.array([[-1,2],[3,-5],[-6,7]], ...: dtype=np.int8)
-1 2	In : x
3 -5	array([[-1, 2],
-6 7	[3, -5],
	[-6, 7]], dtype=int8)

No surprises here; both languages create the same 3 x 2 matrix. One would expect the two HDF5 files written earlier, x_matlab.h5 and x_python.h5, to contain the same data, but one would be wrong. The h5dump command-line utility (delivered with Anaconda) shows MATLAB actually wrote x^T:

```
> h5dump x_matlab.h5
HDF5 "x_matlab.h5" {
GROUP "/" {
   GROUP "db" {
      DATASET "x" {
         DATATYPE H5T_IEEE_F64LE
         DATASPACE SIMPLE { ( 2, 3 ) / ( 2, 3 ) }
         DATA {
         (0,0): -1, 3, -6,
         (1,0): 2, -5, 7
         }
```

```
        }
    }
}
}

> h5dump x_python.h5
HDF5 "x_python.h5" {
GROUP "/" {
   GROUP "db" {
      DATASET "x" {
         DATATYPE H5T_STD_I8LE
         DATASPACE SIMPLE { ( 3, 2 ) / ( 3, 2 ) }
         DATA {
         (0,0): -1, 2,
         (1,0): 3, -5,
         (2,0): -6, 7
         }
      }
   }
}
}
```

Note that MATLAB wrote doubles ("F64LE" means floating point, 64-bit, little endian) instead of int8's; to preserve the type in the output file, we have to pass 'Datatype','int8' as additional arguments to h5create(). Explicit type definition is a consequence of separating dataset definition from dataset population—h5create() doesn't know the data type of the variable that will be added. h5write() does, but by then it is too late since the dataset must have already been defined. Python can preserve the data type because dataset creation and population happen in the same step.

Fortunately (or not), h5read() also transposes matrices on reading, so at least MATLAB is internally consistent:

MATLAB:	Python:
| ```
>> new_x = h5read(...
    'x_matlab.h5', '/db/x')

   -1    2
    3   -5
   -6    7

>> new_xpy = h5read(...
    'x_python.h5', '/db/x')
 2×3 int8 matrix

   -1    3   -6
    2   -5    7
``` | ```
In : import h5py
In : h5 = h5py.File('x_matlab.h5','r')
In : h5['/db/x'][:]
Out:
array([[-1., 3., -6.],
       [ 2., -5., 7.]])
In : h5.close()
In : h5 = h5py.File('x_python.h5','r')
In : h5['/db/x'][:]
Out:
array([[-1, 2],
       [ 3, -5],
       [-6, 7]], dtype=int8)
In : h5.close()
``` |

Keep in mind MATLAB's odd transposition behavior if you use HDF5 files to exchange multidimensional arrays between MATLAB and any other language (not just Python).

7.9.3 Reading and Writing HDF5 Dataset Attributes

Additional metadata, referred to as "attributes," may be added to new or existing datasets through the dataset handle's .attrs object which behaves like a dictionary. This example creates a new dataset, /data/Avector, then adds to it an attribute named units, with a value of meters per second. Also, it adds to the existing dataset /data/A2d created earlier an attribute called scale factor and assigns it the value 1.995×10^{-3}:

Python:

```
In : a = h5.create_dataset('/data/Avector', data=[2,3,4])
In : a.attrs['units'] = 'meters per second'
In : b =h5['/data/A2d']
In : b.attrs['scale factor'] = 1.995e-3
```

Attributes of the /Data_Products/VIIRS-DNB-SDR/VIIRS-DNB-SDR_Aggr dataset from SVDNB.h5 look like this:

Python:

```
In : import h5py
In : F = 'SVDNB.h5'
In : h5 = h5py.File(F, 'r')
In : dataset = '/Data_Products/VIIRS-DNB-SDR/VIIRS-DNB-SDR_Aggr'
In : for attr_name in h5[dataset].attrs:
...: print(f'{attr_name:30s}',aggr.attrs.get(attr_name))
...:
AggregateBeginningDate         [[b'20190618']]
AggregateBeginningGranuleID    [[b'NPP002415066160']]
AggregateBeginningOrbitNumber  [[39581]]
AggregateBeginningTime         [[b'051014.820804Z']]
AggregateEndingDate            [[b'20190618']]
AggregateEndingGranuleID       [[b'NPP002415068721']]
AggregateEndingOrbitNumber     [[39581]]
AggregateEndingTime            [[b'051553.431811Z']]
AggregateNumberGranules        [[4]]

In : h5.close()
```

Datasets and attributes are persisted to the file when the file is closed.

7.9.4 Iterating over All HDF5 Datasets

Utility programs that work with .h5 files often need to know the names of every dataset in a file. The command-line utility h5ls can give this information, but we want to do this programmatically. Conveniently, the h5py module has a recursive function, visititems(), that runs a user-supplied callback function each time it reaches a "node" (an HDF5 Group or Dataset). All we need to do is supply the callback function and harvest the results. Here's one possible solution:

Python:

```
import h5py
def all_datasets(h5) -> list:
    DS = []
```

```
  def Fn(name, node):
      if isinstance(node, h5py.Dataset):
          DS.append(name)
  h5.visititems(Fn)
  return DS
```

Here's what the results look like using the SVDNB.h5 file mentioned earlier:
Python:

```
In : import h5py
In : h5 = h5py.File('SVDNB.h5', 'r')
In : datasets = all_datasets(h5)
In : datasets
Out:
['All_Data/VIIRS-DNB-SDR_All/ModeGran',
 'All_Data/VIIRS-DNB-SDR_All/ModeScan',
 'All_Data/VIIRS-DNB-SDR_All/NumberOfBadChecksums',
 'All_Data/VIIRS-DNB-SDR_All/NumberOfDiscardedPkts',
 'All_Data/VIIRS-DNB-SDR_All/NumberOfMissingPkts',
 'All_Data/VIIRS-DNB-SDR_All/NumberOfScans',
 'All_Data/VIIRS-DNB-SDR_All/PadByte1',
 'All_Data/VIIRS-DNB-SDR_All/QF1_VIIRSDNBSDR',
 'All_Data/VIIRS-DNB-SDR_All/QF2_SCAN_SDR',
 'All_Data/VIIRS-DNB-SDR_All/QF3_SCAN_RDR',
 'All_Data/VIIRS-DNB-SDR_All/Radiance',
 'Data_Products/VIIRS-DNB-SDR/VIIRS-DNB-SDR_Aggr',
 'Data_Products/VIIRS-DNB-SDR/VIIRS-DNB-SDR_Gran_0',
 'Data_Products/VIIRS-DNB-SDR/VIIRS-DNB-SDR_Gran_1',
 'Data_Products/VIIRS-DNB-SDR/VIIRS-DNB-SDR_Gran_2',
 'Data_Products/VIIRS-DNB-SDR/VIIRS-DNB-SDR_Gran_3']
In : h5.close()
```

7.10 NetCDF4

NetCDF, version 4, is built upon HDF5 and provides similar levels of convenience and performance for reading and writing scientific datasets. The fields of climatology and meteorology in particular have embraced the netCDF format. Their "Climate and Forecast convention" for netCDF metadata simplifies interoperability across libraries and applications for tasks such as regridding. As for HDF5, Anaconda conveniently ships with NetCDF command-line tools including nc-config, nccopy, ncdump, ncgen, and ncinfo.

7.10.1 Reading a NetCDF4 File

Our sample .nc file, avhrr-only-v2.20190101.nc,[10] comes from NOAA/National Centers for Environmental Information (NCEI). It contains global sea surface temperatures determined primarily from measurements taken by the AVHRR instrument on a NOAA satellite. The ncinfo command-line tool gives a helpful overview of the file's contents:

```
> ncinfo avhrr-only-v2.20190101.nc
<class 'netCDF4._netCDF4.Dataset'>
root group (NETCDF4 data model, file format HDF5):
Conventions: CF-1.6
title: NCEI Daily-OISST-V2 based mainly on AVHRR, Final
history: Version 2.0
creation_date: 2019-01-16 11:16
source_data: NCEP GTS,AVHRR19,MetOpA,NCEP ICE
source: NOAA/National Centers for Environmental Information
contact: oisst-help, email: oisst-help@noaa.gov
dimensions(sizes): time(1), zlev(1), lat(720), lon(1440)
variables(dimensions): float32 time(time), float32 zlev(zlev),
    float32 lat(lat), float32 lon(lon),
  int16 sst(time, zlev, lat, lon), int16 anom(time, zlev, lat, lon),
  int16 err(time, zlev, lat, lon), int16 ice(time, zlev, lat, lon)
  groups:
```

---

[10]www.ncei.noaa.gov/data/sea-surface-temperature-optimum-interpolation/v2.1/
access/avhrr/2

Temperature values are mapped to an evenly spaced Cartesian grid of latitudes and longitudes. These, as well as the sea surface temperatures, are easily loaded in both MATLAB and Python:

MATLAB:	Python:

```File = 'avhrr-only-v2.20190101.nc';```
```lat = ncread(File,'lat');```
```lon = ncread(File,'lon');```
```sst = ncread(File,'sst');```
	```from netCDF4 import Dataset```
	```File = 'avhrr-only-v2.20190101.nc'```
	```nc = Dataset(File, 'r')```
	```lat = nc["lat"]```
	```lon = nc["lon"]```
	```sst = nc["sst"]```

The variables lat, lon, and sst are quite different in the two languages though. In MATLAB, they are simply numeric arrays. In Python though, they are objects with metadata in addition to the numeric values:

MATLAB:	Python:

```>> lat```
``` -89.8750```
``` -89.6250```
```   :```
```   89.6250```
```   89.8750```
 	
```>> sst```
 	
``` NaN .. -1.7800```
```   :   :```
``` NaN .. -1.7800```
	```In : lat```
	```Out:```
	```masked_array(data=[-89.875, -89.625,```
	``` :```
	``` 89.625, 89.875],```
	``` mask=False,```
	``` fill_value=1e+20,```
	``` dtype=float32)```
	
	```In : sst```
	```masked_array(```
	``` data=[[--, --, --, ...,],```
	``` ...,```
	``` [-1.7800, -1.7800, ...]]```
	``` mask=[[True, True, ...,],```
	``` ...,```
	``` [False, False, ...]],```
	``` fill_value=-999,```
	``` dtype=float32)```

MATLAB collapsed the four-dimensional `sst` array to two dimensions. While this may seem convenient, it complicates writing code that has to work for files with multiple times and multiple levels. MATLAB also applies the mask array and inserts NaNs where the mask is True.

7.10.1.1 Reading NetCDF4 Attributes

Many weather-related datasets contain "fill values" to represent unknown data. Examples include land or sea surface temperatures measured from a satellite over cloud-obscured terrain. Space-based radiometers will return the temperature of the clouds rather than the ground behind them, so the ground temperature at those pixels is assigned a fill value. Fill values are typically stored as attributes in a NetCDF4 file. To figure out what the `sst` dataset's fill value is, we'll need to see what name this attribute is saved as. Python makes this easy because its `sst` is an object with a method, `.ncattrs()`, that lists all attribute names. This is much harder in MATLAB because, as noted earlier, its `sst` is just a matrix of doubles. We'll use the Python output from `.ncattrs()` to get the fill value attribute name and then use that in MATLAB:

MATLAB:	Python:

`>> ncreadatt(File,'sst','_FillValue')`
 	
    `-999`
	`In : sst.ncattrs()`
	`Out:`
	`['long_name',`
	` 'units',`
	` '_FillValue',`
	` 'add_offset',`
	` 'scale_factor',`
	` 'valid_min',`
	` 'valid_max']`
	
	`In : sst.getncattr('_FillValue')`
	`Out: -999`

7.11 SQLite

The relational database engine SQLite may seem like an unusual entry in a section about binary I/O, especially since database interaction is covered later in Section 7.19. SQLite is unique among all other Structured Query Language (SQL) programs (among them: PostgreSQL, MySQL, Oracle, and Microsoft SQL) for two reasons. First, it is file based rather than client/server network based; in other words, adding data to or reading data from an SQLite database works like writing to or reading from a binary file instead of sending and receiving data to and from a database server over a network. Being file based also means only one process may write to the database at a time.

Second, the SQLite interface module, `sqlite3`, is in the standard library and therefore available with all Python distributions. A database file written with SQLite can therefore be viewed as a binary file that can be read by any Python 2 or Python 3 program on any platform.

SQL experience is helpful to make the most of SQLite, but it is not a requirement. Developers unfamiliar with SQL should consider an SQLite database as equivalent to an Excel spreadsheet with multiple tabs, each of which holds one table.

As an example, we'll revisit the data used in the comma-separated value discussion in Section 7.1.5 and show how to create the database file, define a table, then insert, extract, and delete values.

Python:

```
#!/usr/bin/env python3
# code/IO/sqlite_create.py
import sqlite3
import os
import os.path
# create the database file lat_lon_company.db
db_file = 'lat_lon_company.db'
if os.path.exists(db_file):
    os.remove(db_file)
connection = sqlite3.connect(db_file)
cursor     = connection.cursor()
# add a table called 'companies' with five fields
cursor.execute('''create table companies(
```

```
                              lon float,
                              lat float,
                              name text,
                              industry text,
                              revenue_mil float);''')
data = [
    [-106.52, 35.079, "Acme, Inc.", "cosmetics", 12.3],
    [-86.17, 41.717, "FlexMex", "restaurant", 0.5],
    [-80.75, 41.214, "Titan Hercules, LLP", "sporting goods", 45.3],
    [-95.54, 29.783, "The Chicken Palace", "restaurant", 22.3],
    [-98.48, 29.355, "Joe's Diner", "restaurant", 0.0045],
    [-78.99, 33.784, "Amalgamated Powders", "cosmetics", 1.9],
    [-122.68, 45.525, "Pie and Cake", "restaurant", 2.2],
    ]
# insert the first row
cursor.execute('insert into companies values (?,?,?,?,?)', data[0])
# insert a bunch of rows at once
cursor.executemany('insert into companies values (?,?,?,?,?)', data[1:])
# commit the pending transactions
connection.commit()
connection.close()
```

After running the preceding program, we'll have a database file lat_lon_company. db with some values. Here's a small program that demonstrates how the data can be read back and updated:

Python:

```
#!/usr/bin/env python3
# code/IO/sqlite_read.py
import sqlite3
connection = sqlite3.connect('lat_lon_company.db')
cursor     = connection.cursor()
# read the contents of each row in descending order of revenue
query = 'select lat,name,revenue_mil from companies ' \
        'order by revenue_mil desc'
```

```
for row in cursor.execute(query):
    lat, name, revenue_mil = row
print(f'lat={lat:9.2f} {name:20s} {revenue_mil:9.5f}')

# update the revenue of restaurants by 20%
cursor.execute("update companies set revenue_mil = "
               "revenue_mil * 1.2 where industry = 'restaurant'");
# print updated restaurant values
query = "select lat,name,revenue_mil from companies " \
        "where industry = 'restaurant' order by revenue_mil desc"
for row in cursor.execute(query):
    lat, name, revenue_mil = row
    print(f'Updated: {name:20s} {revenue_mil:9.5f}')
connection.commit() # necessary to preserve update
connection.close()
```

Running this program yields

```
lat=    41.21 Titan Hercules, LLP    45.30000
lat=    29.78 The Chicken Palace      26.76000
lat=    35.08 Acme, Inc.              12.30000
lat=    45.52 Pie and Cake             2.64000
lat=    33.78 Amalgamated Powders      1.90000
lat=    41.72 FlexMex                  0.60000
lat=    29.36 Joe's Diner             0.00540
Updated:  The Chicken Palace         32.11200
Updated:  Pie and Cake          3.16800
Updated:  FlexMex               0.72000
Updated:  Joe's Diner           0.00648
```

While the sqlite3 module loaded the float and string fields into Python variables of the correct types (doubles and strings), more specialized data types such as half floats or unsigned short integers that can be represented in NumPy would have to be cast manually.

As a final SQLite code example, we'll remove businesses earning less than $10M:
Python:

```
#!/usr/bin/env python3
# code/IO/sqlite_delete.py
import sqlite3
connection = sqlite3.connect('lat_lon_company.db')
cursor     = connection.cursor()
# remove underperforming companies
cursor.execute("delete from companies where revenue_mil < 10;");
# print all entries once more
query = 'select lat,name,revenue_mil from companies ' \
        'order by revenue_mil desc'
for row in cursor.execute(query):
    lat, name, revenue_mil = row
    print(f'lat={lat:9.2f} {name:20s} {revenue_mil:9.5f}')
connection.commit()
connection.close()
```

And now the output is just

```
lat=    41.21 Titan Hercules, LLP    45.30000
lat=    29.78 The Chicken Palace      26.76000
lat=    35.08 Acme, Inc.              12.30000
```

7.12 Recipe 7-6: CRUD with an SQLite Database

MATLAB's Database Toolbox has functions to work with SQLite files. If you don't have access to the Database Toolbox, you can use MATLAB's py module to import Python's sqlite3 module and perform CRUD (create, read, update, delete) operations with SQLite files.

The following code repeats the SQLite database creation example of Section 7.11, this time in MATLAB. It looks remarkably similar to the pure Python code except for the last argument to the executemany() function. The cell array of cell arrays has to be coerced to a Python list before the function knows what to do with it.

MATLAB 2020b:

```matlab
% code/IO/sqlite_create.m
Im = @py.importlib.import_module;
sqlite3 = Im('sqlite3');
db_file = 'lat_lon_company.db';
if exist(db_file, 'file')
    delete(db_file);
end
connection = sqlite3.connect(db_file);
cursor     = connection.cursor();
% add a table called 'companies' with five fields (fails
% if the database already has such a table)
cursor.execute(strcat('create table companies(',...
                          'lon float, ',        ...
                          'lat float, ',        ...
                          'name text, ',        ...
                          'industry text, ',    ...
                          'revenue_mil float);'));
data = {...
  {-106.52, 35.079, "Acme, Inc.", "cosmetics", 12.3},...
  {-86.17, 41.717, "FlexMex", "restaurant", 0.5},...
  {-80.75, 41.214, "Titan Hercules, LLP", "sporting goods", 45.3},...
  {-95.54, 29.783, "The Chicken Palace", "restaurant", 22.3},...
  {-98.48, 29.355, "Joe's Diner", "restaurant", 0.0045},...
  {-78.99, 33.784, "Amalgamated Powders", "cosmetics", 1.9},...
  {-122.68, 45.525, "Pie and Cake", "restaurant", 2.2},...
  };
% insert the first row
cursor.execute('insert into companies values (?,?,?,?,?)', data{1});
% insert rows 2 to the end in one step
cursor.executemany('insert into companies values (?,?,?,?,?)', ...
                  py.list(data(2:end)));
% commit the pending transactions
connection.commit()
connection.close()
```

Reading from the SQLite database in MATLAB gets a bit ugly because of the mix of parentheses and braces needed to dereference query results:

MATLAB 2020b:

```
% code/IO/sqlite_read.m
Im = @py.importlib.import_module;
sqlite3 = Im('sqlite3');
connection = sqlite3.connect('lat_lon_company.db');
cursor      = connection.cursor();
% read the contents of each row in descending order of revenue
query = strcat("select lat,name,revenue_mil from companies ", ...
                "order by revenue_mil desc");
for row = cursor.execute(query).fetchall
    lat_name_rev = py2mat(row{1});
    lat = lat_name_rev(1);
    name = lat_name_rev(2);
    revenue_mil = lat_name_rev(3);
    fprintf('lat=%9.2f %-20s %9.5f\n', lat{1}, name{1}, revenue_mil{1})
end
% update the revenue of restaurants by 20%
cursor.execute(strcat("update companies set revenue_mil = " , ...
                    "revenue_mil * 1.2 where industry = 'restaurant'"));
% print updated restaurant values
query = strcat("select lat,name,revenue_mil from companies where ",...
                "industry = 'restaurant' order by revenue_mil desc");
for row = cursor.execute(query).fetchall
    lat_name_rev = py2mat(row{1});
    name = lat_name_rev(2);
    revenue_mil = lat_name_rev(3);
    fprintf('Updated: %20s %9.5f\n', name{1}, revenue_mil{1})
end
connection.commit() % necessary to preserve update
connection.close()
```

Deleting rows is straightforward:

MATLAB 2020b:

```
% code/IO/sqlite_delete.m
Im = @py.importlib.import_module;
sqlite3 = Im('sqlite3');
connection = sqlite3.connect('lat_lon_company.db');
cursor     = connection.cursor();
% remove underperforming companies
cursor.execute("delete from companies where revenue_mil < 10;");
% print all entries once more
query = strcat("select lat,name,revenue_mil from companies ",...
               "order by revenue_mil desc");
for row = cursor.execute(query).fetchall
    lat_name_rev = py2mat(row{1});
    lat = lat_name_rev(1);
    name = lat_name_rev(2);
    revenue_mil = lat_name_rev(3);
    fprintf('lat=%9.2f %-20s %9.5f\n', lat{1}, name{1}, revenue_mil{1})
end
connection.commit()
connection.close()
```

7.13 Pickle Files

Python has a module, pickle, that can save Python variables to a file and afterward load them back. Superficially, this is the same as writing and reading .mat files in MATLAB with save and load, but there is one important difference: pickle files are sensitive to the version of Python used to write the file and are therefore less portable or version compatible than .mat files. Unless precautions are taken to explicitly state the pickle format, chances are a pickle file written with an older version of Python will be unreadable in a newer version.

Warning   The pickle module is not secure. In addition to loading data, pickle files can also contain code which will run when the file is loaded. Do not load pickle files unless you trust the files' origin.

Here are a pair of programs that write Python variables to a pickle file and read the data back:

Python:

```
#!/usr/bin/env python3
import pickle
import numpy as np

cm = np.array([[2., 3],[0, 1]]) - np.eye(2)*1j
a_list = ['this', 'is', 'a', 'complex', 'matrix', cm]
a_dict = { 1 : 1, 2 : 'two', 'three' : 3}
an_int = 42
some_bytes = b'1ee50ffe2fb5104144142f001a8ca94ae56b90cf'
X = np.arange(12,dtype=np.float16).reshape(3,4)

P = {
    'a_list' : a_list,
    'a_dict' : a_dict,
    'an_int' : an_int,
    'some_bytes' : some_bytes,
    'X' : X,
}

with open('data.pkl', 'wb') as fh:
    pickle.dump(P, fh, pickle.HIGHEST_PROTOCOL)
```

The next program reads the pickle file data.pkl prints each variable in it:

Python:

```
#!/usr/bin/env python3
import pickle
import numpy as np

with open('data.pkl', 'rb') as fh:
    P = pickle.load(fh)

print(f'Loaded {len(P)} variables:')
for v in P:
    print(f'  {v} ===========')
    print(P[v])
```

Its output is

```
Loaded 5 variables:
   a_list ===========
['this', 'is', 'a', 'complex', 'matrix', array([[2.-1.j, 3.+0.j],
      [0.+0.j, 1.-1.j]])]
   a_dict ===========
{1: 1, 2: 'two', 'three': 3}
   an_int ===========
42
   some_bytes ===========
b'1ee50ffe2fb5104144142f001a8ca94ae56b90cf'
   X ===========
[[ 0.  1.  2.  3.]
 [ 4.  5.  6.  7.]
 [ 8.  9. 10. 11.]]
```

MATLAB's save command, when invoked without arguments, saves everything in the current session to the file matlab.mat. This can't be done with the standard pickle module, but can with the pickle drop-in replacement dill [2].

7.14 MATLAB .mat Files

The SciPy module scipy.io has a pair of functions, loadmat() and savemat(), that can read and write MATLAB .mat files saved in version 7.0 or earlier. Version 7.3 .mat files use HDF5 which, as we've seen in Section 7.9, Python has no difficulty with. Sections 7.14.1 to 7.14.3 cover scipy.io's functions that work with .mat file formats up to v7, while Section 7.14.4 covers the newest format, v7.3.

scipy.io additionally has a function, whosmat(), that returns names, sizes, and data types of variables stored in a .mat file. To demonstrate their operation, we'll first create a .mat file that contains a variety of MATLAB data containers:

MATLAB:

```
>> a1 = uint16([ 5441 32207 ])
  1x2 uint16 row vector
    5441 32207
```

```
>> a2 = rand(2,3)
    0.2785 0.9575 0.1576
    0.5469 0.9649 0.9706

>> b = { 'this is a', "cell", 5+6i }
  1x3 cell array
    {'this is a'} {["cell"]} {[5.0000 + 6.0000i]}

>> c.x = -17.6;
>> c.y = 4.98;
>> c
  struct with fields:
    x: -17.6000
    y: 4.9800

>> save('by_matlab.mat', 'a1', 'a2', 'b', 'c')
```

In MATLAB 2020b, the preceding save() command writes a version 7 .mat file by default. HDF5-based .mat files can be created by passing '-v7.3' to save():

MATLAB:

```
>> save('by_matlab_7.3.mat', 'a1', 'a2', 'b', 'c', '-v7.3')
```

7.14.1 Inspecting the Contents of a .mat File

whosmat() returns a list of tuples containing each variable's name, dimensions, and type. Here, we scan the contents of the file created earlier:

Python:

```
In : import scipy.io as IO
In : IO.whosmat('by_matlab.mat')
Out[2]:
 [('a1', (1, 2), 'uint16'),
  ('a2', (2, 3), 'double'),
  ('b', (1, 3), 'cell'),
  ('c', (1, 1), 'struct'),
  ('__function_workspace__', (1, 928), 'uint8')]
```

The last entry, __function_workspace__, contains additional type information Python needs to perform data conversions.[11] It is an "under the hood" variable we can ignore.

We can scan whosmat()'s return value with a list comprehension (Section 4.3.14) to see if a given variable exists in the file. The first tuple item, _[0] in the following code, contains the name of each variable in the .mat file:

Python:

```
In : import scipy.io as IO
In : contents = IO.whosmat('by_matlab.mat')
In : 'a2' in [_[0] for _ in contents]
Out: True

In : 'd' in [_[0] for _ in contents]
Out: False
```

The whosmat() function makes it possible to write a useful tool—a stand-alone utility program that prints variable names, sizes, and data types for given .mat files. The program lsmat.py takes just a few lines of code:

Python:

```
#!/usr/bin/env python3
# code/IO/lsmat.py
import sys
import scipy.io
if len(sys.argv) < 2:
    print(f'Usage: {sys.argv[0]} <.mat file(s)>')
    sys.exit(1)
for F in sys.argv[1:]:
    print(f'{F}:')
    for name, size, type in scipy.io.whosmat(F):
        if name.startswith('__'):
            continue
        print(f' {name:20s} {type:12s} {size}')
```

---

[11] https://stackoverflow.com/questions/52393278/what-is-contained-in-the-function-workspace-field-in-mat-file#56943418

With it, we can get a listing of a .mat file's contents directly from our operating system's terminal without having to start a MATLAB or interactive Python session:

Python:

```
> lsmat.py by_matlab.mat
by_matlab.mat:
  a1          uint16     (1,  2)
  a2          double     (2,  3)
  b           cell       (1,  3)
  c           struct     (1,  1)
```

7.14.2 Reading a .mat File

loadmat() takes the name of the .mat file as an argument and returns a dictionary keyed by variable name. It has several optional arguments to handle aspects of the data container differences between MATLAB and Python. Limitations, as of SciPy 1.5.0, include

- loadmat() cannot read MATLAB strings. Strings should be converted to char arrays in MATLAB before saving if these variables need to be readable in Python.

- loadmat() cannot read some toolbox-specific data types such as embedded.fi variables from the Fixed-Point Designer.

- savemat() cannot write Python sets.

We'll begin with the default options:

Python:

```
In : import scipy.io as IO
In : p = IO.loadmat('by_matlab.mat')
In : p.keys()
Out: dict_keys(['__header__', '__version__', '__globals__',
                 'a1', 'a2', 'b', 'c', '__function_workspace__'])

In : p['a1']
Out: array([[ 5441, 32207]], dtype=uint16)

In : p['a2']
```

```
Out:
array([[0.27849822, 0.95750684, 0.15761308],
       [0.54688152, 0.96488854, 0.97059278]])

In : p['b']
Out:
array([[array(['this is a'], dtype='<U9'),
        MatlabOpaque([(b'', b'MCOS', b'string', array([[3707764736],
        [ 2], [ 1], [ 1], [ 1], [ 1]], dtype=uint32))],
          dtype=[('s0', 'O'), ('s1', 'O'), ('s2', 'O'), ('arr', 'O')]),
        array([[5.+6.j]])]], dtype=object)

In : p['c']
Out:
array([[[(array([[-17.6]]), array([[4.98]]))]],
      dtype=[('x', 'O'), ('y', 'O')])
```

The arrays a1 and a2 look reasonable, but the cell array b and struct c are a mess. Their values are only accessible with indexing grief:

Python:

```
In : p['b'][0][0][0], p['b'][0][2][0]
Out: ('this is a', array([5.+6.j]))

In : p['c'][0][0][0], p['c'][0][0][1]
Out: (array([[-17.6]]), array([[4.98]]))
```

We deliberately skip the second item in p['b'] which was saved as a MATLAB string ("cell") and is incomprehensible to loadmat().

The optional argument squeeze_me=True removes superfluous dimensions and greatly simplifies indexing. In my view, this option should be True by default; I enable it in all calls to loadmat().

Python:

```
In : import scipy.io as IO
In : p = IO.loadmat('by_matlab.mat', squeeze_me=True)

In : p['a1']
Out: array([ 5441, 32207], dtype=uint16)
```

```
In : p['a2']
Out:
array([[0.27849822, 0.95750684, 0.15761308],
       [0.54688152, 0.96488854, 0.97059278]])

In : p['b']
Out:
array(['this is a',
       MatlabOpaque([(b'', b'MCOS', b'string', array([3707764736,
                     2, 1, 1, 1, 1], dtype=uint32))],
          dtype=[('s0', 'O'), ('s1', 'O'), ('s2', 'O'), ('arr', 'O')]),
       (5+6j)], dtype=object)

In : p['c']
Out: array((-17.6, 4.98), dtype=[('x', 'O'), ('y', 'O')])
       dtype=[('x', 'O'), ('y', 'O')])
```

Although we can now get to terms of the cell array and struct more easily, the "array object" type of the struct items needs additional massaging with float() to give scalar values we can work with:

Python:

```
In : p['b'][0], p['b'][2]
Out: ('this is a', (5+6j))

In : p['c']['x'], p['c']['y']
Out: (array(-17.6, dtype=object), array(4.98, dtype=object))

In : float(p['c']['x']), float(p['c']['y'])
Out: (-17.6, 4.98)
```

7.14.3 Writing a .mat File

savemat() takes two required arguments: the name of the .mat file to create and a dictionary containing all the data we wish to write. We'll demonstrate this with two arrays, a list, and a dict in Python and then see how they appear to MATLAB.

The Python dictionary we'll pass to savemat() looks like the dictionary loadmat() returned on reading a .mat file—keys are the names of variables that MATLAB will see, and values are the contents of those variables:

Python:

```
In : import numpy as np
In : import scipy.io as IO
In : a1 = np.array([5441, 32207], dtype=np.uint16)
In : a2 = np.array([[0.2785, 0.9575, 0.1576],
...:                 [0.5469, 0.9649, 0.9706]])
In : b = [ 'this is a', "list", 5+6j ]
In : c = { 'x' : -17.6, 'y' : 4.98 }
In : M = {}
In : M['a1'] = a1
In : M['a2'] = a2
In : M['b'] = b
In : M['c'] = c
In : IO.savemat('by_python.mat', M)
```

MATLAB sees Python's data with less fuss than the other way around:

MATLAB:

```
>> clear all
>> load by_python
>> whos
  Name      Size         Bytes  Class    Attributes
  a1        1x2              4  uint16
  a2        2x3             48  double
  b         3x9             54  char
  c         1x1            352  struct

>> a1
  1x2 uint16 row vector
    5441   32207

>> a2
    0.2785     0.9575     0.1576
    0.5469     0.9649     0.9706
```

```
>> b
  3x9 char array
    'this is a'
    'list '
    '(5+6j) '
>> c
  struct with fields:
    x: -17.6000
    y: 4.9800
```

7.14.3.1 Writing Cell Arrays

The biggest flaw in the previous example is that the list b comes to MATLAB as a 3 x 9 character array rather than a cell array—not desirable at all. The solution is simple though; we merely have to define b as a generic object:

Python:

```
In : b = np.empty((3,), dtype=object)
In : b[:] = ['this is a', "list", 5+6j ]
In : M['b'] = b
In : IO.savemat('by_python.mat', M)
```

The notation b[:] on the left-hand side of the assignment is important. Without the bracket, b would simply have been redefined as a list, leaving us in MATLAB with the same useless char array as before. The [:] preserves b's type as an object and simply fills b's data slots with values from the right-hand side. MATLAB likes this b much more:

MATLAB:

```
>> load by_python
>> b
  1x3 cell array
    {'this is a'} {'list'} {[5.0000 + 6.0000i]}
```

The object trick is powerful as it permits arbitrarily complex data structures:

Python:

```
b = np.empty((2,), dtype=object)
b[0] = {}
b[0]['pos'] = np.array([0.5, -.3])
b[0]['vel'] = np.array([2.7, 3.8])
b[1] = [ { 'u' : [0, 3], 'v' : ['a', 'bc'] }, 22 ]
M['b'] = b
IO.savemat('by_python.mat', M)
```

MATLAB sees this rather complicated b like this:

MATLAB:

```
>> load by_python
>> b
  1x2 cell array
    {1x1 struct}    {1x2 cell}

>> b{1}
  struct with fields:
    pos: [0.5000 -0.3000]
    vel: [2.7000 3.8000]

>> b{2}
  1x2 cell array
    {1x1 struct}    {[22]}

>> b{2}{1}
  struct with fields:
    u: [0 3]
    v: [2x2 char]

>> b{2}{1}.v
  2x2 char array
    'a '
    'bc'
```

Here's a more concise illustration of how b's internals are indexed:

MATLAB	Python
b{1}.pos = [0.5000 -0.3000]	b[0]['pos'] = np.array([0.5, -0.3])
b{1}.vel = [2.7000 3.8000]	b[0]['vel'] = np.array([2.7, 3.8])
b{2}{1}.u = [0 3]	b[1][0]['u'] = [0, 3]
b{2}{1}.v = ['a ' 'bc']	b[1][0]['v'] = ['a', 'bc']
b{2}{2} = 22	b[1][1] = 22

7.14.3.2 Writing an Array of Structs

Arrays of structs are natural MATLAB containers that take extra (and non-obvious) effort to write in Python. We already saw that Python dictionaries written to .mat files become structs in MATLAB, so one might think that a NumPy array of dictionaries become an array of structs. Unfortunately, this isn't the case; rather than an array of structs, we'll end up with a cell array of structs. Sure, the cell array can be converted to a regular array in MATLAB, but that's extra hassle on the MATLAB side. We can get the array of structs by creating a custom NumPy data type and then saving variables with that type. The following example illustrates the process. First, we'll create an array of structs in MATLAB:

MATLAB

```
for i = 1:4
    a(i).s = -sin(.34*i);
    a(i).c =  cos(.34*i);
    a(i).z.uu = exp(.34*i);
    a(i).z.vv = sqrt(.34*i);
end
```

The components of a look like this:

MATLAB

```
>> [a(:).s]
   -0.3335    -0.6288    -0.8521    -0.9779

>> [a(:).c]
    0.9428    0.7776    0.5234    0.2092
```

266

```
>> arrayfun(@(x)(x.uu), [a(:).z])
    1.4049    1.9739    2.7732    3.8962

>> arrayfun(@(x)(x.vv), [a(:).z])
    0.5831    0.8246    1.0100    1.1662
```

Code to create and save a Python variable which loads back into MATLAB with the identical structure and content as before looks like this:

Python

```
import numpy as np
from scipy.io import savemat
a = np.zeros((4,),dtype=[('s','O'),('c','O'),
              ('z', [('uu','O'),('vv','O')]  )])
for i in range(len(a)):
    a[i]['s'] = -np.sin(.34*(i+1))
    a[i]['c'] =  np.cos(.34*(i+1))
    a[i]['z']['uu'] = np.exp(.34*(i+1))
    a[i]['z']['vv'] = np.sqrt(.34*(i+1))
savemat('arr_of_struct.mat', {'a':a})
```

The (i+1) offset in the body of the loop is needed since Python's i goes from 0 to 3. Also, you may have guessed that 'O' is NumPy's shorthand for object.

7.14.4 mat Version 7.3

The v7.3 .mat file has advantages and disadvantages over the earlier formats. The primary advantage is that C++, Fortran, and Java programs can read these files via their respective HDF5 libraries much more easily than older .mat formats. The disadvantages for Python developers are that modules to read and write this format (mat73,[12] hdf5storage[13]) are still in early stages. While reading a v7.3 .mat file in Python isn't hard with h5py, it is less convenient because, unlike scipy.io.loadmat(), one cannot populate an entire data structure.

At the beginning of this section, we wrote a v7.3 .mat file with MATLAB:

```
>> save('by_matlab_7.3.mat', 'a1', 'a2', 'b', 'c', '-v7.3')
```

---

[12] https://github.com/skjerns/mat7.3
[13] https://github.com/frejanordsiek/hdf5storage

The h5ls command-line utility shows how these variables are mapped to datasets. Excluding the dozen metadata entries, the output is

```
> h5ls -r by_matlab_7.3.mat
/a1                     Dataset {2, 1}
/a2                     Dataset {3, 2}
/b                      Dataset {3, 1}
/c                      Group
/c/x                    Dataset {1, 1}
/c/y                    Dataset {1, 1}
```

With that information, it is easy enough to write code to read the data:

Python:

```
#!/usr/bin/env python3
# code/IO/read_mat_73.py
import h5py
F = 'by_matlab_7.3.mat'
h5 = h5py.File(F, 'r')
a1 = h5['/a1'][:]
a2 = h5['/a2'][:]
c  = {}
c['x'] = h5['/c/x'][:]
c['y'] = h5['/c/y'][:]
h5.close()
```

Not a big deal except for c whose fields must be loaded individually. Clearly, reading a complicated data structure will take a lot more effort than calling scipy.io.loadmat() would have been.

7.15 Command-Line Input

The MATLAB user experience is primarily an interactive one where individual commands and/or user-developed programs are developed and invoked from within the IDE. Python, of course, is also used interactively from IDEs such as PyCharm, Spyder, VS Code, and Eclipse, via a Jupyter notebook or Jupyterlab, or from console REPLs such as ipython or bpython.

Python, however, is also well suited for batch use, where a Python program is saved to a text file and then invoked as a command from the console or from another program. While also possible with MATLAB, this is done there much less often.

Inputs to batch, or command line, programs can be taken from command-line arguments, environment variables, and configuration files. In the following sections, we'll see how both languages capture and process command-line arguments.

7.15.1 Python: `sys.argv`

The simplest way to grab command-line arguments from a Python program is with the sys module which stores a list, `sys.argv`, of everything the program sees on the command line:

```python
#!/usr/bin/env python3
# code/IO/sys_argv_demo.py
import sys
nArg = len(sys.argv)
print(f'You gave {nArg} arguments.  They are:')
for i,Arg in enumerate(sys.argv):
    print(f'  sys.argv[{i}] = "{sys.argv[i]}"')
```

The program can be invoked on the command line directly on all operating systems by first typing the name of the Python executable, then following with the program's file name and its arguments:

```
> python sys_argv_demo.py 2.71828 -1 'a string'
You gave 4 arguments.  They are:
  sys.argv[0] = "sys_argv_demo.py"
  sys.argv[1] = "2.71828"
  sys.argv[2] = "-1"
  sys.argv[3] = "a string"
```

A couple of points are worth mentioning:

- The name of the program itself is always the first entry in the sys.argv list.

- Arguments are stored as strings. If you want them as numeric values, you first have to cast them to the desired type. For example, if you write 5*sys.argv[2] you'll get back the string -1-1-1-1-1. To get the expected result of -5, you'll need to cast the second argument to an integer: 5*int(sys.argv[2]).

7.15.2 MATLAB: Function Arguments; varargin

MATLAB has two ways of getting command-line arguments into m-files. The first expresses the desired "main" program as a function whose arguments will be provided on the command line:

MATLAB:

```
% code/IO/command_line_demo.m
function command_line_demo(arg_1, arg_2)
    if ~exist(arg_1, 'var') || ~exist(arg_2, 'var')
        fprintf('Two arguments required:  arg_1 and arg_2\n');
        return
    end
    fprintf('arg_1 = "%s"\n', arg_1);
    fprintf('arg_2 = "%s"\n', arg_2);
end
```

The file command_line_demo.m can then be invoked as a stand-alone program from the command line with a series of switches to suppress MATLAB's IDE (-nojvm), to suppress the splash screen (-nosplash), and to run (-r) the m-file:

Linux or macOS:

```
> matlab -nojvm -nosplash -r command_line_demo.m -1 'a string'
```

Windows:

```
> matlab /nojvm /nosplash /r command_line_demo.m -1 'a string'
```

This method of passing command-line arguments in directly as function arguments has two limitations:

- The arguments must be passed in using the same order they appear in the function definition.

- The method does not support a variable number of arguments.

The more general method, and the one closest to the flexibility of sys.argv, uses variables nargin, which is a count of the number of arguments, and varargin, a cell array holding the arguments:

```
% code/IO/varargin_demo.m
function varargin_demo(varargin)
    fprintf('You gave %d arguments.  They are:\n', nargin);
    for i = 1:nargin
        fprintf('varargin{%d} = %s\n', i, varargin{i});
    end
end
```

Linux or macOS:

```
> matlab -nojvm -nosplash -r varargin_demo.m 2.71828 -1 'a string'
```

Windows:

```
> matlab /nojvm /nosplash /r varargin_demo.m 2.71828 -1 'a string'
```

7.15.3 Python: argparse

Parsing command-line arguments with sys.argv is suitable only for simple programs. As programs evolve with new capabilities, parsing optional switches and flags can become as much work as coding the program's main logic. Python has several popular argument parsing modules to simplify this chore, but here we'll cover just the argparse module from the standard library.

This example shows how to parse Boolean switches; switches with integer, floating-point, and string arguments; and a switch which can take one of only four prescribed values. The program itself also takes an arbitrary number of file names as arguments:

```
% code/IO/argparse_demo.m
#!/usr/bin/env python
import sys
import argparse

def parse_args():
    parser = argparse.ArgumentParser(description=
    """Demonstrate the basic options of argparse.
    Simply echoes back the values given on the
    command line.
    """)

    # the names of the input data files; need at least one
    parser.add_argument('datafiles', metavar='DF', type=str, nargs='+',
                        help='Files to process.')

    # a Boolean
    parser.add_argument('-n', '--dry-run', dest='dry_run',
                        action='store_true', default=False,
                        help='Print actions to be performed '
                        'without executing them.')

    # a counter
    parser.add_argument('-v', '--verbose', dest='verbose',
                        action='count', default=0,
                        help='Verbose mode (may be specified '
                        'multiple times for more output).')

    # an integer
    parser.add_argument('--num-cases', dest='n_cases',
                        action='store', type=int, default=10,
                        help='Number of data lines to create '
                        '[10].')
```

```python
    # a string
    parser.add_argument('-o', '--out', dest='csv_file',
                        action='store', type=str, default='sales_data.csv',
                        help='Name of CSV file to create ["sales_data.csv"].')

    # one of four choices
    parser.add_argument('--type', dest='interpolation_type', action='store',
                        choices=['nearest', 'linear', 'bilinear',
                        'cubic'], type=str, default='nearest',
                        help='Interpolation type ["nearest"].')

    if len(sys.argv) == 1:
        # No arguments; echo the help information and exit.
        parser.print_help()
        sys.exit(0)

    args = parser.parse_args()

    return args

def print_args(A):
    print(f'datafiles = {A.datafiles}')
    print(f'dry_run   = {A.dry_run}')
    print(f'verbose   = {A.verbose}')
    print(f'n_cases   = {A.n_cases}')
    print(f'csv_file  = {A.csv_file}')
    print(f'interpolation_type = {A.interpolation_type}')

def main():
    args = parse_args()
    print_args(args)

if __name__ == "__main__": main()
```

Running the program without arguments, or with -h or --help, produces this:

```
usage: argparse_demo.py [-h] [-n] [-v] [--num-cases N_CASES]
                        [-o CSV_FILE]
                        [--type {nearest,linear,bilinear,cubic}]
                        DF [DF ...]
```

273

Demonstrate the basic options of argparse. Simply echoes back the values given on the command line.

positional arguments:
  DF   Files to process.

optional arguments:
  -h, --help   show this help message and exit
  -n, --dry-run   Print actions to be performed without executing
                          them.
  -v, --verbose   Verbose mode (may be specified multiple times
                          for more output).
  --num-cases N_CASES   Number of data lines to create [10].
  -o CSV_FILE, --out CSV_FILE
                          Name of CSV file to create ["sales_data.csv"].
  --type {nearest,linear,bilinear,cubic}
                          Interpolation type ["nearest"].

A typical invocation might look like this:

```
> ./argparse_demo.py -v --num-cases 5 x.dat
datafiles = ['x.dat']
dry_run   = False
verbose   = 1
n_cases   = 5
csv_file  = sales_data.csv
interpolation_type = nearest
```

Providing incorrect arguments yields

```
> ./argparse_demo.py --fast-mode x.dat
usage: argparse_demo.py [-h] [-n] [-v] [--num-cases N_CASES]
                        [-o CSV_FILE]
                        [--type {nearest,linear,bilinear,cubic}]
                        DF [DF ...]
argparse_demo.py: error: unrecognized arguments: --fast-mode
```

Or, if one of the choices to --type is not valid:

```
> ./argparse_demo.py --type farthest x.dat
usage: argparse_demo.py [-h] [-n] [-v] [--num-cases N_CASES]
                        [-o CSV_FILE]
                        [--type {nearest,linear,bilinear,cubic}]
                        DF [DF ...]
argparse_demo.py: error: argument --type: invalid choice:
'farthest' (choose from 'nearest', 'linear', 'bilinear', 'cubic')
```

7.16 Interactive Input

Generally, people prefer to supply inputs to a program up front and then let the program do its thing until it has results. Asking a user for additional information in the middle of a run is a nuisance. However, in cases such as initial prototyping or handling critical errors, a developer may wish to prompt for input interactively.

Both MATLAB and Python prompt for and receive input from a user with the input() function; however, MATLAB defaults to expecting a numeric argument, while Python always captures a string. (MATLAB will accept a string if input() is given 's' as a second argument.)

MATLAB:	Python:
``n_cases = input('how many cases? ');
if n_cases: % a number
print(f'got {n_cases}')
else:
print('got nothing')```	```n_cases = input('how many cases? ')
if n_cases: # a string
print(f'got {n_cases}')
else:
print('got nothing')```

If the user just hits *Enter* at the prompt, n_cases becomes an empty matrix in MATLAB and an empty string in Python. Such entries evaluate to False in the if test, sending code execution to the "else" clause.

```
> ./input_demo.py
how many test cases to run?
got nothing
```

```
> ./input_demo.py
how many test cases to run? 5
got 5
```

7.17 Receiving and Sending over a Network

MATLAB and Python support several network communication protocols including TCP/IP, HTTP/HTTPS, FTP, and WebSockets. Network communication is in fact another mechanism for Python and MATLAB programs to exchange data.

7.17.1 HTTP, HTTPS

MATLAB and Python have many options for downloading and parsing data from websites. Both downloading and parsing steps can be hassles depending on the website's application program interface (API). The following example uses the popular Python requests module, comparable to MATLAB's urlread, to pull real-time earthquake data from a US Geological Survey website. This website is created for programmatic access; it represents the best possible scenario for data downloading and parsing. Conveniently, data returned by urlread and requests is a struct in MATLAB and a dictionary in Python.

MATLAB:

```
% file: code/IO/urlread_demo.m
url = 'https://earthquake.usgs.gov/earthquakes/feed/v1.0/summary/2.5_hour.geojson';
data = jsondecode(urlread(url));
for i = 1:length(data.features)
    prop = data.features(i).properties;
    T = prop.time/1000;
    Tstr = datetime(T,'convertFrom','epochtime');
    P = prop.place;
    M = prop.mag;
    fprintf('Magnitude %5.2f at %s in %s\n', M, Tstr, P)
end
```

Python:

```
# file: code/IO/requests_demo.py
import requests
from datetime import datetime
url = 'https://earthquake.usgs.gov/earthquakes/feed/v1.0/summary/2.5_hour.
geojson'
data = requests.get(url).json()
for F in data['features']:
    T = F['properties']['time']/1000
    Tstr = datetime.utcfromtimestamp(T)
    P = F['properties']['place']
    M = F['properties']['mag']
    print(f'Magnitude {M:5.2f} at {Tstr} in {P}')
```

The output looks like this:

MATLAB:

```
Magnitude  3.40 at 05-Jun-2021 22:10:47 in 105 km ENE of Chignik, Alaska
Magnitude  2.57 at 05-Jun-2021 22:10:19 in 9km WNW of Calipatria, CA
Magnitude  2.51 at 05-Jun-2021 22:09:59 in 10km W of Calipatria, CA
Magnitude  3.12 at 05-Jun-2021 21:49:40 in 12km WNW of Calipatria, CA
Magnitude  2.48 at 05-Jun-2021 21:33:17 in 10km N of Westmorland, CA
Magnitude  2.65 at 05-Jun-2021 21:30:13 in 12km N of Westmorland, CA
```

Python:

```
Magnitude  3.40 at 2021-06-05 22:10:47.998000 in 105 km ENE of
Chignik, Alaska
Magnitude  2.57 at 2021-06-05 22:10:19.990000 in 9km WNW of Calipatria, CA
Magnitude  2.51 at 2021-06-05 22:09:59.760000 in 10km W of Calipatria, CA
Magnitude  3.12 at 2021-06-05 21:49:40.230000 in 12km WNW of Calipatria, CA
Magnitude  2.48 at 2021-06-05 21:33:17.460000 in 10km N of Westmorland, CA
Magnitude  2.65 at 2021-06-05 21:30:13.570000 in 12km N of Westmorland, CA
```

The Python requests module works well for many websites. Not all HTML can be converted to JSON though. In Chapter 12, Section 12.4.2, a whale's path over several months is overlayed on a map of the North Atlantic. Data for the whale's coordinates over time can be found at http://www2.whalenet.org/whalenet-stuff/StopBm2016/data_2018.

Unfortunately, `requests` can't parse the HTML from this site; the `.json()` method fails with a `JSONDecodeError`. In this case, we have to resort to manual parsing of the raw underlying HTML, something that the `lxml.html` module can help with.

7.17.2 Python As a Web Server

Python's `http` module includes a web server. Simply entering

```
> python3 -m http.server
```

at your terminal's command line starts the web service at port 8000 on the local machine. The content in the directory where the command was issued can then be seen by directing a web browser to any of these URLs:

- `http://localhost:8000/`

- `http://127.0.0.1:8000/`

- `http://0.0.0.0:8000/`

from the local machine or at `http://w.x.y.z:8000/` from other machines on the local network where w.x.y.z is the server's IP address. Hostnames can be used in place of IP addresses if name resolution works on the destination computer.

Hitting *control*-c stops the server.

Python's built-in web server can greatly simplify data exchange between computers on a local network if they don't share a file server or if they span authentication domains. Just start a web server in the directory containing the data, then use `wget` or `curl` on the destination computer to download files from the server; `wget`'s recursive option can even fetch all subdirectories as well.

Alternatively, take advantage of MATLAB's `urlread()` function or Python's `requests` module to load content from the Python-hosted directory directly into a program.

Other applications include hosting documentation that's delivered as HTML files and serving custom dashboards. A simple example of a custom dashboard is a Python program that repeatedly captures machine load information every few seconds and then writes this to an HTML file that instructs browsers to reload the page frequently (the `content="5"` value in the `<meta>` section forces a reload every five seconds). Here, we're getting a sneak preview of Python's `psutil` module which will be covered more thoroughly in Section 9.3:

```python
#!/usr/bin/env python3
# code/IO/post_cpu_load.py
from datetime import datetime
import time
import psutil
from string import Template
import pathlib

page = Template("""<html>
        <meta http-equiv="refresh" content="5" />
    <head>
    </head>
    <body>
      <p>${time}</p>
      <p>1 minute load = ${load_1}</p>
      <p>memory use percentage = ${mem_fraction}</p>
    </body>
</html>
""")

P = pathlib.Path('index.html')
while True:
    now = datetime.now().strftime("%Y-%m-%d %H:%M:%S")
    L1, L5, L15 = psutil.getloadavg()
    mem = psutil.virtual_memory()
    mem_pct = f'{100*mem.used/mem.total:0.1f}%'
    P.write_text(page.substitute(time=now, load_1=L1,
    mem_fraction=mem_pct))
    time.sleep(3)
```

Open a pair of terminals on the machine whose load is to be shown and run the program in one terminal and then start the web service from the same directory in the second terminal. The machine's local time, CPU load, and percentage of memory used can then be viewed in a web browser by other machines on the network.

> **Warning**   This is not secure! Anyone who can reach your computer will be able to see the data being served. Additionally, since this uses HTTP instead of HTTPS, content traverses the network unencrypted.

7.17.3 TCP/IP

The following example shows client and server programs that exchange numeric arrays: the client sends random square matrices to the server which inverts the matrices and returns inverses back to the client. The client's outbound request has two messages: an integer defining the dimension of the following matrix, then the matrix itself. The server waits for the matrix dimension, then waits for a stream of bytes equal to the expected matrix size. It converts the bytes into a linear array of doubles, reshapes the values into a 2D array, computes the inverse, then sends the inverse to the client.

The MATLAB client and server equivalents are presented after the Python versions. Since the two languages communicate with a standard protocol, the Python client works with the MATLAB server and *vice versa*.

7.17.3.1 Python Client

Python:

```python
#!/usr/bin/env python3
# code/IO/tcp/client.py
import socket
import numpy as np
import struct

def wait_for_nBytes(n, Sock):
    Bytes = b''
    received = 0
    block_size = 2048
    while received < n:
        data = Sock.recv(min(n-received, block_size))
        if not data:
            break
```

```
        Bytes += data
        received += len(data)
        if len(Bytes) == n:
            break
    return Bytes

def main():
    Host, Port = '127.0.0.1', 5006
    s = socket.socket(socket.AF_INET, socket.SOCK_STREAM)
    s.connect((Host, Port))
    for i in range(10):
        N = np.random.randint(3,10) # 3 <= N < 10
        A = np.random.rand(N,N)
        s.send(struct.pack('q',N)) # send N
        print(f'sending A ({N:2d} x {N:2d}) ',end='')
        s.send(A.tobytes()) # send A
        Bytes = wait_for_nBytes(8*N*N, s)
        Ainv = np.frombuffer(Bytes, dtype=np.float64)
        # could also do
        # Ainv = np.array(struct.unpack(f'{N*N}d',Bytes))
        Ainv = Ainv.reshape(N,N)
        err = np.max(np.eye(N) - A@Ainv)
        print(f'err = {err:e}')
    s.close()
if __name__ == "__main__": main()
```

TCP socket .send() and .recv() functions work with raw byte sequences just like binary file reads and writes. This means outgoing data must first be converted from its native storage into bytes using either the struct module's pack() function as done in Section 7.6 or with a NumPy array's .tobytes() method.

Similarly, incoming TCP data arrives in a group of bytes up to the size of the declared buffer, 2048 in our example.[14] If the expected message is larger than the buffer size, we accumulate bytes until the expected size is reached. An empty message means the

---

[14] Larger buffer sizes allow higher network performance.

connection has been broken. After the entire message has been received, the bytes must be decoded into the desired type using either struct.unpack() or, if creating a NumPy array, with np.frombuffer().

7.17.3.2 Python Server

The Python server program reuses the wait_for_nBytes() function defined in the client program:

Python:

```python
#!/usr/bin/env python3
# code/IO/tcp/server.py
import struct
import numpy as np
import socket
from client import wait_for_nBytes

def main():
    Host, Port = 'localhost', 5006

    s = socket.socket(socket.AF_INET, socket.SOCK_STREAM)
    s.bind((Host, Port))
    s.listen(1)

    conn, addr = s.accept()
    while True:
        try:
            Bytes = wait_for_nBytes(8, conn) # get bytes of N
            if not Bytes:
                break
            N = struct.unpack(f'q', Bytes)[0] # bytes -> N
            print(f'got N={N}')
            Bytes = wait_for_nBytes(8*N*N, conn) # get bytes of A
            A = np.frombuffer(Bytes, dtype=np.float64)
            # could also do
            # A = np.array(struct.unpack(f'{N*N}d', Bytes))
```

```
        A = A.reshape(N,N)
        print(f'received {N} x {N} from client')
        inv = np.linalg.inv(A)
        conn.send(inv.tobytes()) # send inv(A)
        print(f'sent inverse to client')
    except KeyboardInterrupt:
        break
  conn.close()
if __name__ == "__main__": main()
```

7.17.3.3 MATLAB Client

The MATLAB client is relatively straightforward; the only catch is that the matrix
dimension N must be cast to the data type expected by the Python server, namely, a
64-bit integer. Without the typecast, N would have the default MATLAB type of "double"
which Python would receive as a fantastically large, and incorrect, integer:

MATLAB 2020b:

```
% file: code/IO/tcp/client.m
Host = 'localhost';
Port = 5006;
Socket = tcpclient(Host,Port);
for i = 1:10
    N = int64(randi([3,10])); % type cast is important!
    A = rand(N);
    write(Socket, N);
    fprintf('sending A (%2d x %2d) ', N,N)
    write(Socket, A(:) );
    Ainv = read(Socket, N*N, 'double');
    Ainv = reshape(Ainv, N,N);
    err = max(eye(N) - A*Ainv, [], 'all');
    fprintf('error = %e\n', err)
end
```

The output from a typical run involving the Python server and MATLAB client as seen in the MATLAB console is

MATLAB:

```
>> client
sending A ( 6 x  6)   error = 4.440892e-15
sending A ( 5 x  5)   error = 4.440892e-16
sending A ( 6 x  6)   error = 5.551115e-16
sending A ( 9 x  9)   error = 5.771870e-15
sending A (10 x 10)   error = 1.422013e-15
sending A (10 x 10)   error = 1.792961e-15
sending A ( 6 x  6)   error = 1.998401e-15
sending A ( 3 x  3)   error = 1.332268e-15
sending A ( 6 x  6)   error = 1.776357e-15
sending A ( 5 x  5)   error = 6.106227e-16
```

7.17.3.4 MATLAB Server

Creating a TCP service in MATLAB needs either the Instrument Control Toolbox or Python's socket module. The next recipe shows how we can leverage the py module in MATLAB to make socket's server capabilities available.

7.18 Recipe 7-7: TCP Server

The Instrument Control Toolbox function tcpip() can create a TCP service. Without this toolbox, pure MATLAB programs can only be configured as clients. We can, however, write a hybrid MATLAB/Python program that uses Python's socket module to create a TCP service in MATLAB.

In addition to socket, we'll also reuse the wait_for_nBytes() function we wrote for the Python client in Section 7.17.3.1. We'll do this by adding the current directory to the Python path and then importing client.py as the MATLAB variable pyclient. The server does the same thing as the Python matrix inversion server of Section 7.17.3.2 and works with either Python or MATLAB clients shown in Sections 7.17.3.1 and 7.17.3.3.

MATLAB 2020b:

```matlab
% code/IO/tcp/server.m
import py.list.*
import py.sys.path
append(py.sys.path, '.')
pyclient = py.importlib.import_module('client');

AF_INET = py.socket.AF_INET;
SOCK_STREAM = py.socket.SOCK_STREAM;
s = py.socket.socket(AF_INET,SOCK_STREAM);
addr = py.tuple([{"localhost"}, int64(5006)]); % host, port
s.bind(addr)
s.listen(int64(1))
conn_addr = s.accept();
conn = conn_addr{1};
while 1
    bytes = pyclient.wait_for_nBytes(int64(8), conn);
    N = typecast(uint8(bytes), 'int64');
    if isempty(N)
        break
    end
    bytes = pyclient.wait_for_nBytes(int64(8*N*N), conn);
    A = typecast(uint8(bytes), 'double');
    A = reshape(A, N,N);
    Ainv = inv(A);
    bytes = typecast(Ainv(:), 'uint8');
    conn.send(bytes);
end
conn.close()
```

Observant readers may wonder how the Python server can work correctly with both a Python client and a MATLAB client because these clients store—and send—the matrix terms differently: the Python client sends its terms row major, while the MATLAB client sends them column major. If both clients send the same matrix, the server would get the original matrix from the Python client and the transpose of this matrix from MATLAB.

However, transposition between the Python server and MATLAB client happens on the return journey as well. Python sends back the inverse matrix row major, but MATLAB takes these terms and populates its `Ainv` column major. MATLAB ultimately gets the correct inverse because of the identity

$$A^{-1} \equiv [A^{-T}]^T$$

In other words, MATLAB gets `inv(A')'` which is the same as `inv(A)`.

Obviously, not all cross-language client/server applications that work with multidimensional matrices will have such a fortuitous setup. Knowledge of the matrix storage sequence is important to writing correct client/server applications.

7.19 Interacting with Databases

Pretty much every database engine in existence seems to have a corresponding Python module. Here, we'll show examples with PostgreSQL and MongoDB. (SQLite is supported on all Python installations; the interaction with it is covered in Section 7.11.)

7.19.1 PostgreSQL

The Python module `psycopg2` enables interaction with PostgreSQL. It is available from the Anaconda repository:

```
> conda install psycopg2
```

Before we can run Python code to work with a PostgreSQL database, we'll need an account and a database on the PostgreSQL server.[15] If you have access to the PostgreSQL instance, log in to the database account, usually user `postgres`, start the client program, and create an account and a database with commands such as these:

```
> psql
postgres=# create user "Al" with login password "SuperSecret";
postgres=# create database pet_store;
postgres=# grant all privileges on database pet_store TO "Al";
postgres=# quit
```

---

[15] Fly.io (`https://fly.io/blog/free-postgres/`) offers free PostgreSQL instances for small projects.

Confirm that the database engine is running and the user and database are accessible with this small Python program:

```
#!/usr/bin/env python3
import psycopg2
conn = psycopg2.connect(host="localhost",
    user="Al", password="SuperSecret",
    database="pet_store")
conn.close()
```

All is well if the program runs without errors. If there are errors, they'll likely be one of these three:

1. psycopg2.OperationalError: could not connect to server: Connection refused

2. psycopg2.OperationalError: FATAL: password authentication failed for user Al

3. psycopg2.OperationalError: FATAL: database pet_store does not exist

The first means either the database service is down, or a network issue (such as a firewall) is preventing access. The second and third errors show the database service is reachable, but the account or database you want to use either does not exist or is not configured properly. You or your database administrator will need to reexamine the setup.

The following program demonstrates create, update, read, and delete operations in Python. In the create step, we use psycopg2's executemany() function to handle batch insertions efficiently. This code example inserts 10,000 records in batch sizes of 3000:

```
1   #!/usr/bin/env python3
2   # code/IO/postgres_crud.py
3   import psycopg2
4   import random
5   import time
6
7   def record():
8       """Return a random integer, float, and pet type."""
```

```
9          n = random.randint(1,15)
10         price = 10.0 + 30*random.random()
11         pet = random.choice(['dog', 'cat',
12                   'bunny', 'fish', 'horse'])
13         return (n, price, pet)
14
15     def populate_table(conn, cur):
16         T_start = time.time()
17         cur.execute("""create table myvalues (id serial primary key,
18                   n integer, price float, pet varchar)""")
19         batch_size = 3_000
20         n_records = 10_000
21         batch = []
22         insert = "insert into myvalues (n,price,pet) values(%s,%s,%s)"
23         for i in range(n_records):
24             n,price,pet = record()
25             batch.append((n, price, pet))
26             if len(batch) < batch_size:
27                 continue
28             cur.executemany(insert, batch)
29             conn.commit()
30             batch = []
31         if batch:
32             cur.executemany(insert, batch)
33             conn.commit()
34         print(f'inserted {n_records} rows in {time.time()-T_
           start:.3} sec')
35
36     def query_results(cursor):
37         query = "select sum(price), sum(n), pet from myvalues
           group by pet"
38         cursor.execute(query)
39         print(f'Result of {query}:')
40         for sum_price, sum_n, pet in cursor.fetchall():
41             print(f' {sum_price:.2f} {sum_n:6d} {pet:>7s}')
42         print('-' * 60)
```

```
43
44   def rename_pets(cursor, before, after):
45       update_cmd = f"update myvalues set pet='{after}' where
         pet='{before}'"
46       cursor.execute(update_cmd)
47       print(f'Did: {update_cmd}')
48
49   def remove_pets(cursor, pet):
50       delete_cmd = f"delete from myvalues where pet='{pet}'"
51       cursor.execute(delete_cmd)
52       print(f'Did: {delete_cmd}')
53
54   def main():
55       try:
56           conn = psycopg2.connect( host="413.198.155.245",
57               user="al", password="SuperSecret",
58               database="pet_store")
59       except psycopg2.OperationalError as e:
60           print(f'Failed to connect: {e}')
61           return
62       cur = conn.cursor()
63
64       # drop the table 'myvalues' if it already exists
65       try:
66           cur.execute('drop table myvalues')
67       except:
68           pass
69
70       populate_table(conn, cur)
71       query_results(cur)
72
73       rename_pets(cur, 'bunny', 'rabbit')
74       query_results(cur)
75
76       remove_pets(cur, 'cat')
77       query_results(cur)
```

```
78
79      cur.execute('drop table myvalues')
80
81      conn.close()
82   if __name__ == "__main__": main()
```

7.19.2 MongoDB

The Python module pymongo enables interaction with MongoDB. It, too, is available from the Anaconda repository:

```
> conda install pymongo
```

Our example populates a MongoDB database with 10,000 purchase orders of fake data helpfully created with the faker module described in Appendix B. Our fake purchase orders have an order ID, order date, customer name and phone number, a list of purchased items, and a total order price. Here's a typical entry:

```
{'customer_name': 'Paul Reynolds',
 'customer_phone': '418.583.4214x467',
 'order_number': 'ba9b18f5-301a-4f75-8d44-587c3efca6ba',
 'order': [{'item': 'glove', 'quantity': 3},
           {'item': 'bike', 'quantity': 6},
           {'item': 'golf club', 'quantity': 6},
           {'item': 'glove', 'quantity': 7}],
 'total_price': 1450.0,
 'order_date': datetime.datetime(2021, 4, 6, 6, 51, 7)}
```

The order creation logic is not perfect since a multi-item order may have repeated entries for the same item—as with gloves earlier.

An instance of a MongoDB server needs to be running; the code here expects it to be on the local machine using the default port 27017:

Python:

```
1   #!/usr/bin/env python
2   # code/fake_data/mongo_fake_PO.py
3   from pymongo import MongoClient
4   from urllib.parse import quote_plus
```

```
5    from faker import Faker
6    from datetime import datetime
7    import time
8
9    fake = Faker()
10   Faker.seed(123) # for reproducibility
11   start_date = datetime(1997, 1, 31, 12, 0, 0)
12   end_date = datetime(2025, 1, 31, 12, 0, 0)
13
14   def start_new_order():
15       PO = {}
16       PO['customer_name'] = fake.name()
17       PO['customer_phone'] = fake.phone_number()
18       PO['order_number'] = fake.uuid4()
19       PO['order_date'] = fake.date_time_between_dates(
20                              start_date, end_date)
21       return PO
22
23   def order_items(price):
24       n_items = fake.random_int(min=1,max=len(price))
25       order = []
26       total_price = 0
27       for i in range(n_items):
28           item = fake.random_element(price.keys())
29           quantity = fake.random_int(min=1,max=8)
30           order.append({'item' : item, 'quantity' : quantity})
31           total_price += price[item]*quantity
32       return order, total_price
33
34   def main():
35       T_start = time.time()
36       n_orders = 10_000
37       price = { 'bike' : 80.00, 'golf club' : 120.00,
38                   'ball' : 4.50, 'glove' : 25.00, 'hat' : 8.25}
39       local = True
```

```
40        if local:
41            client = MongoClient('localhost:27017')
42        else:
43            uri = "mongodb://%s:%s@%s/purchase_orders" % (
44                    quote_plus('al'),
45                    quote_plus('SuperSecret'),
46                    quote_plus('413.198.231.158:27027'))
47            client = MongoClient(uri)
48        db = client.purchase_orders
49        all_PO = []
50        for i in range(n_orders):
51            PO = start_new_order()
52            PO['order'], PO['total_price'] = order_items(price)
53            all_PO.append( PO )
54        db.purchase_orders.insert_many( all_PO )
55        print(f'added {n_orders} orders in {time.time()-T_start:.3f} s')
56
57   if __name__ == "__main__": main()
```

We can use the MongoDB client program to query the database for things like the most expensive order:

```
> mongo --port 27017 purchase_orders
> db.purchase_orders.aggregate([ { "$group": {
    "_id" : null, "Max1": { "$max": "$total_price"} } } ]);
{ "_id" : null, "Max" : 1698 }

> db.purchase_orders.find({"total_price" : {"$eq":1698} }).pretty();
{
        "_id" : ObjectId("607b78452c748f4aacbdc34a"),
        "customer_name" : "Jeffery Hampton",
        "customer_phone" : "640.474.9845x311",
        "order_number" : "3d5d8f38-c97f-4215-b425-ffda9234554b",
        "order" : [ { "item" : "ball", "quantity" : 4 },
                    { "item" : "golf club", "quantity" : 8 },
                    { "item" : "golf club", "quantity" : 6 }
                  ],
```

```
        "total_price" : 1698,
        "order_date" : ISODate("2021-01-21T13:10:02Z")
}
> exit
bye
```

7.20 Recipe 7-8: CRUD with a PostgreSQL Database

MATLAB's py module gives seamless access to psycopg2 for working with PostgreSQL.

The following MATLAB program repeats the pure Python program of Section 7.19.1. The only notable aspects are that (1) the batch variable holding a collection of rows to insert must be a Python container since that's what the Python module psycopg2 expects, and (2) the query operation returns a Python list of tuples which is converted to a nested MATLAB cell array with py2mat().

MATLAB:

```
% code/matlab_py/postgres_crud.m
Im = @py.importlib.import_module;
psycopg2 = Im('psycopg2');

conn = psycopg2.connect(pyargs('host','413.198.155.245', ...
               'user','al','password','SuperSecret', ...
               'database','pet_store'));
cur = conn.cursor();

% delete the table if already exists
try
   cur.execute('drop table myvalues');
   conn.commit();
catch EO
   fprintf('Table "myvalues" did not exist, skipping drop.\n')
end

populate_table(conn, cur);
query_results(cur);
```

```matlab
rename_pets(cur, 'bunny', 'rabbit');
query_results(cur);

remove_pets(cur, 'cat');
query_results(cur);

cur.execute('drop table myvalues');

conn.close();

function [n, price, pet] = record()
   n = int64(randi([1,15]));
   price = 10.0 + 30*rand();
   pets = {'dog', 'cat','bunny', 'fish', 'horse'};
   pet = pets{randi([1,5])};
end

function populate_table(conn, cur)
   tic;
   cur.execute(['create table myvalues (id serial primary key, ' ...
               'n integer, price float, pet varchar)']);
   batch_size = 300;
   n_records = 1000;
   batch = py.list();
   insert = 'insert into myvalues (n,price,pet) values(%s,%s,%s)';
   for i = 1:n_records
      [n,price,pet] = record();
      batch.append(py.list({n, price, pet}));
      if ~(mod(i,100))
          fprintf('i = %5d\r', i);
      end
      if length(batch) < batch_size
          continue
      end
      fprintf('i = %5d inserting batch\n', i);
      cur.executemany(insert, batch)
```

```matlab
        conn.commit()
        batch = py.list();
    end
    if ~isempty(batch)
        cur.executemany(insert, batch)
        conn.commit()
    end
    fprintf('inserted %d rows in %.3f sec\n', n_records, toc)
end

function query_results(cursor)
    query = 'select sum(price), sum(n), pet from myvalues group by pet';
    cursor.execute(query);
    fprintf('Result of %s:\n', query)
    all = py2mat(cursor.fetchall());
    for i = 1:length(all)
        sum_price = all{i}{1};
        sum_n     = all{i}{2};
        pet       = all{i}{3};
        fprintf(' %.2f %6d %7s\n', sum_price, sum_n, pet)
    end
    fprintf(repmat('-',1,60)); fprintf('\n')
end

function rename_pets(cursor, before, after)
    update_cmd = sprintf("update myvalues set pet='%s' where pet='%s'",...
                         after, before);
    cursor.execute(update_cmd);
    fprintf('Did: %s\n', update_cmd)
end

function remove_pets(cursor, pet)
    delete_cmd = sprintf("delete from myvalues where pet='%s'",pet);
    cursor.execute(delete_cmd)
    fprintf('Did: %s\n', delete_cmd)
end
```

7.21 Recipe 7-9: CRUD with a MongoDB Database

Unlike psycopg2, the Python MongoDB interface module's pymongo database objects do not expose all their methods within MATLAB. We'll need a small bridge module to get around this shortcoming:

Python:

```
# code/matlab_py/bridge_mongo.py
def insert_many(db, database, document):
    db[database].insert_many(document)

def aggregate(db, database, pipeline):
    result = []
    for x in db[database].aggregate(pipeline):
        result.append(x)
    return result

def find_one(db, database, kwargs):
    x = db[database].find_one(**kwargs)
    return x

def delete_many(db, database, kwargs):
    x = db[database].delete_many(**kwargs)
    return x

def drop(client, database):
    client.drop_database(database)

def update_one(client, database):
    client.update_one(database)
```

The following code repeats the Python purchase order example of Section 7.19.2. As with the Python version, this MATLAB program creates a database called purchase_orders and then populates it with 10,000 fake orders. In addition to bridge_mongo.py, this MATLAB program imports a Python program, mongo_fake_PO.py, so it can call its start_new_order() function.

MATLAB 2020b:

```matlab
1   % code/matlab_py/mongo_fake_PO.m
2   Im = @py.importlib.import_module;
3   pymongo = Im('pymongo');
4   fake_PO = Im('mongo_fake_PO');
5   bridge_mongo = Im('bridge_mongo');
6
7   tic;
8   price.bike       = 80.00;
9   price.golf_club  = 120.00;
10  price.ball       = 4.50;
11  price.glove      = 25.00;
12  price.hat        = 8.25;
13  price_items = fieldnames(price);
14
15  local = true;
16
17  if local
18      client = pymongo.MongoClient('localhost:27017');
19  else
20      db_user = 'al';
21      db_passwd = 'SuperSecret';
22      db_host = '413.198.231.158';
23      db_port = 27027;
24      uri = sprintf("mongodb://%s:%s@%s:%d/purchase_orders", ...
25              db_user, db_passwd, db_host, db_port);
26      client = pymongo.MongoClient(uri);
27  end
28  db = client.get_database('purchase_orders');
29  n_orders = 10000;
30  all_PO = py.list();
31  for i = 1:n_orders
32      PO = fake_PO.start_new_order();
33      [order, total_price] = order_items(price, price_items);
34      PO.update(pyargs('order', order));
```

```
35        PO.update(pyargs('total_price', total_price));
36        all_PO.append( PO );
37    end
38    bridge_mongo.insert_many( db, 'purchase_orders', all_PO );
39    fprintf('added %d orders in %.3f s\n', n_orders, toc)
40
41    function [order, total_price] = order_items(price, price_items)
42        n_prices = length(price_items);
43        n_items = randi(n_prices,1,1);
44        order = py.list();
45        total_price = 0;
46        for i = 1:n_items
47            i_item = randi(n_prices,1,1);
48            item = price_items{i_item};
49            quantity = randi(8,1,1);
50            this_order = py.dict(pyargs('item',item,'quantity',quantity));
51            order.append(this_order);
52            total_price = total_price + price.(item)*quantity;
53        end
54    end
```

Insert performance is about 2× slower than the pure Python solution:

```
>> mongo_fake_PO
added 10000 orders in 23.459 s
```

7.21.1 Read

Here, we fetch the document having the largest total cost. Instead of performing a $max aggregation, we'll simply return the first document when they are sorted in descending order of cost.

MATLAB 2020b:

```
>> total_price =  py.tuple({"total_price", pymongo.DESCENDING});
>> total_price =  py.list( { total_price } )
>> sort_on_price = py.dict(pyargs('sort',total_price))
>> x = bridge_mongo.find_one(db,'purchase_orders',sort_on_price)
x =
```

Python dict with no properties.

```
{'_id': ObjectId('607cb7fb705a307702b591a0'), 'customer_name':
 'John Ford', 'customer_phone': '971-016-8700x4084', 'order_number':
 '7bd40678-3d1c-4381-959c-d35f87f74e8a', 'order_date':
 datetime.datetime(2021, 3, 28, 20, 16, 4), 'order': [
     {'item': 'bike', 'quantity': 8.0},
     {'item': 'golf_club', 'quantity': 7.0},
     {'item': 'hat', 'quantity': 4.0},
     {'item': 'golf_club', 'quantity': 8.0},
     {'item': 'golf_club', 'quantity': 8.0}], 'total_price': 3433.0}
```

The variables total_price and sort_on_price are Python-native MATLAB variables used to build up an expression that would look like this in a Python program:

Python:

```
db.purchase_order.find_one({'sort': [('total_price', pymongo.DESCENDING)]})
```

The returned variable x is Python native and therefore not directly useful in MATLAB. If it were not for the _id key, we could convert x to a MATLAB struct using the struct() function. However, struct field names must be legal MATLAB variables, and the leading underscore violates that rule. We'll either need to delete this key or use the py2mat() function (Appendix D). Here, we'll do the latter:

MATLAB 2020b:

```
>> y = py2mat(x)
      K000001__id: [1×1 py.bson.objectid.ObjectId]
    customer_name: "John Ford"
   customer_phone: "971-016-8700x4084"
     order_number: "7bd40678-3d1c-4381-959c-d35f87f74e8a"
       order_date: 28-Mar-2021 20:16:04
            order: {[1×1 struct]  [1×1 struct]  [1×1 struct]
                    [1×1 struct]  [1×1 struct]}
      total_price: 3433

>> y.order{2}
        item: "golf_club"
    quantity: 7
```

7.21.2 Update

Let's say our big spender, John Ford, updates his account information with a new phone number. The database update would look like this in MongoDB:

MATLAB 2020b:

```
> mongo purchase_order
> do findOne based on name
> db.purchase_orders.updateOne({'customer_name':'John Ford'},
        {'$set': {"customer_phone":"abc"}})
{ "acknowledged" : true, "matchedCount" : 0, "modifiedCount" : 0 }
```

which is implemented like this in MATLAB:

MATLAB 2020b:

```
>> name = "John Ford";
>> new_phone = "971-255-9876";
>> phone_dict = py.dict(pyargs("customer_phone", new_phone));
>> pipeline = py.dict(pyargs("$set", phone_dict));
>> bridge_mongo.update_one(db,'purchase_orders',pipeline);
```

7.21.3 Delete

The entire purchase_orders database can be dropped with

MATLAB 2020b:

```
>> bridge_mongo.drop(client,'purchase_orders')
```

7.22 Recipe 7-10: Interact with Redis

Redis, the "remote dictionary server," is a fast network-based in-memory database for key/value pairs. In addition to high performance and ability to store structured values, Redis implements a publish/subscribe service so that applications can be notified of changes to keys they subscribe to. The MATLAB Production Server has a Redis interface. Python does too; the conda repository has both the full Redis application and the Python interface module. These can be installed with

```
conda install redis redis-py
```

Only install `redis-py` if you already have the Redis application installed.

The following example programs are equivalent MATLAB and Python programs that demonstrate the following features:

- Configuring a Redis connection using hostname and port values

- Checking whether or not a connection to the Redis server is possible via a Redis `ping`

- Calling the `mset` function to set multiple keys at once

- Retrieving key values with `get`

- Programmatically setting the Redis client connection for notification of keyspace events

- Subscribing to keyspace changes

- Printing values of keys that have changed

- Exiting cleanly if the connection to the server ends

To run either demo program, you'll need three terminal sessions to perform the following actions:

1. Run an instance of the Redis server.

2. Run an instance of the MATLAB or Python demo program.

3. Submit arbitrary `set` commands with the Redis command-line tool.

The three terminal sessions may be on the same computer or on different computers on the same network. If you run them on different computers, you'll need to explicitly supply the hostname where the server is running to the demo programs and command-line tool.

Begin by starting an instance of the Redis server:

```
redis-server
```

By default, the server will expect client connections on port 6379; add to the preceding command the switch `--port 12345` to change the port value to 12345, for example.

Next, run one of these programs:

MATLAB 2020b:

```
% code/matlab_py/redis_demo.m
main()

function [clean] = redis_str(x)
  % Input is a Python byte array returned by the Python Redis module.
  % Returns a MATLAB string.
  % example  x = py.bytes([uint8(56), uint8(46), uint8(57), uint8(53)])
  %      clean = "8.95"
  clean = char( x );
  clean = string(clean(3:end-1)); % strip leading 'b' and trailing '
end

function main()
  redis = py.importlib.import_module('redis');
  R = redis.Redis(pyargs('host','localhost','port',int64(6379)));
  try
    R.ping();
  catch EO
    fprintf('Is Redis running? Unable to connect: %s\n', EO.message)
    return
  end

  fprintf('Connected to server.')
  R.config_set('notify-keyspace-events', 'KEA');
  mapping = struct;
  mapping.X = 8.9655;
  mapping.month = 'Feb';
  R.mset(mapping)

  retrieved_X     = redis_str(R.get('X'));
  retrieved_month = redis_str(R.get('month'));

  fprintf('Got X = %s\n', retrieved_X);
  fprintf('Got month = %s\n', retrieved_month);

  Sub = R.pubsub();
```

```
  Sub.psubscribe('__keyspace@0__:*')
  i = 1;
  while 1
   try
      message = Sub.get_message();
   catch EO
      fprintf('lost connection to server: %s\n', EO.message)
      break
   end
   if message == py.None
      pause(0.01)
      continue
   end
   keyname = replace(redis_str(message{'channel'}), '__keyspace@0__:', '');
   if keyname == '*'
      % initial subscription value
      continue
   end
   value = redis_str(R.get(keyname));
   fprintf('%s = %s\n', keyname, value)
  end

end
```

Python:

```python
#!/usr/bin/env python
"""code/matlab_py/redis_demo.py
https://tech.webinterpret.com/redis-notifications-python/

# start server:
   redis-server [config file] [--port 12345]

# issue set/get from command line:
   redis-cli config set notify-keyspace-events KEA

# issue set/get from command line:
   redis-cli set price 3.21
```

```
    redis-cli get price
"""
import time
import sys
import redis
R = redis.Redis(host='localhost',port=6379) # defaults

try:
    R.ping()
except redis.exceptions.ConnectionError as e:
    print(f'Is Redis running? Unable to connect {e}')
    sys.exit(1)

print(f'Connected to server.')

# modify configuration to enable keyspace notification
R.config_set('notify-keyspace-events', 'KEA')

retrieved_X     = R.get('X')
retrieved_month = R.get('month')

print(f'Got X = {retrieved_X}')
print(f'Got month = {retrieved_month}')

print('waiting for subscription events')
Sub = R.pubsub()
Sub.psubscribe('__keyspace@0__:*')
while True:
    try:
        message = Sub.get_message()
    except redis.exceptions.ConnectionError:
        print('lost connection to server')
        sys.exit(1)
    if message is None:
        time.sleep(0.01)
        continue
    keyname = message['channel'].decode().replace('__keyspace@0__:','')
    if keyname == '*':
```

```
    # initial subscription value
    continue
value = R.get(keyname)
print(f'{keyname} = {value}')
```

Finally, to exercise the subscription, use the Redis command-line tool to set key values. Here's an example:

```
redis-cli set price 93.67
```

7.23 Reference

[1]. M.M. McKerns et al. "Building a framework for predictive science."
      In: *Proceedings of the 10th Python in Science Conference* (2011).
      URL: https://github.com/uqfoundation/dill

CHAPTER 8

Interacting with the File System

A program that reads or writes files must sometimes interact with the file system in other ways, for example, checking whether or not a file or directory exists, seeing if a file can be read or written to, getting file size or modification time, reading a directory's contents, and so on.

The primary modules for working with the file system in Python include os, os.path, and pathlib. My preference is pathlib, the newest of the three, because its Path() function returns file path objects that can read, write, query, move, copy, and delete files and directories with single commands. The basic invocation looks like this:

Python:

```python
from pathlib import Path
fp = '/path/to/file/or/directory'
P = Path(fp)
P.exists()  # true if the file/directory exists
```

Table 8-1 shows a few MATLAB and Python equivalents for working with files and directories. The MATLAB column uses the variable fd to represent the string containing the path to a file or directory. The Python column assumes the prior creation of object P using pathlib.Path(fd) to the same file or directory as MATLAB.

© Albert Danial 2022
A. Danial, *Python for MATLAB Development*, https://doi.org/10.1007/978-1-4842-7223-7_8

Table 8-1. *File system operations.* `fd` *is a string containing the name of a file or directory.* `P` *is the* `pathlib.Path` *object created with* `P = pathlib.Path(fd)`

	MATLAB	**Python**
Does a file exist?	`exists(fd, 'file')`	`P.exists()`
Does a directory exist?	`exists(fd, 'dir')`	`P.exists()`
Is it a file?	`isfile(fd)`	`P.is_file()`
Is it a directory?	`isdir(fd)`	`P.is_dir()`
File size (bytes)	`dir(fd).bytes`	`P.stat().st_size`
File modification time	`dir(fd).statinfo.mtime`	`P.stat().st_mtime`
File permissions	`dir(fd).statinfo.modestr`	`P.stat().st_mode`

8.1 Reading Directory Contents

Print the names of all files and subdirectories of /usr/bin:

MATLAB:	Python:

<pre>entries = dir('/usr/bin');
for i = 1:length(entries)
  disp(entries(i).name)
end</pre>
	<pre>import pathlib
	P = pathlib.Path('/usr/bin')
	for FD in P.iterdir():
	    print(FD.name)</pre>

File paths on Windows are case-insensitive and may use either forward or backslash separators. If backslashes are used, they must either be paired, or the entire string must be prefixed by the Python raw-string designator, r". These three expressions are equivalent:

- `P = pathlib.Path('c:/program files/internet explorer')`

- `P = pathlib.Path('C:\\Program Files\\internet explorer')`

- `P = pathlib.Path(r'c:\Program Files\Internet Explorer')`

8.2 Finding Files

The `.glob()` method limits a directory listing to the desired file name pattern. It accepts `*`, `?` and `[ ]` wildcards and character classes but does not support ~ expansion or alternation with `{}`. Here, we search for only those executables in `/usr/bin` which end with `sum` (e.g., `md5sum` and `sha512sum`):

MATLAB:	Python:

`entries=dir('/usr/bin/*sum');`
`for i = 1:length(entries)`
`  disp(entries(i).name)`
`end`
	`import pathlib`
	`P = pathlib.Path('/usr/bin')`
	`for FD in sorted(P.glob('*sum')):`
	`        print(FD.name)`

Note   `glob()` does not return file or directory names in sorted order. Wrap `glob()` with `sorted()` for repeatable results.

8.3 Deleting Files

Files can be deleted in several ways in Python: with a `pathlib` object's `.unlink()` method, with the `os` module's `remove()` function, or with a system call to the underlying operating system's file delete command. (System calls are covered in Section 9.2.) Attempts to remove nonexistent files raise the `FileNotFoundError`, and attempts to remove files the user lacks permission to raise `PermissionError`.

MATLAB uses the `delete` command for this operation.

One file: This removes the file `/tmp/abc.txt`.

MATLAB:	Python:
`delete /tmp/abc.txt`	`P = pathlib.Path('/tmp/abc.txt')` `P.unlink()`

Multiple files: This removes all files in /tmp/ that end with .txt.

MATLAB:	Python:
delete /tmp/*.txt	P = pathlib.Path('/tmp') [_.unlink() for _ in P.glob('*.txt')]

8.4 Creating Directories

Programmatically creating directories can help organize data from output-intensive code. There are two ways to create them: the os.mkdir() function and a pathlib object's .mkdir() method. I prefer the second since it supports a useful optional keyword, parents, that allows one to create parent directories as needed. Here, we use it to create /tmp/A/B/C/, beginning with an empty directory /tmp.

MATLAB's mkdir() function will make at most two subdirectories at a time.

MATLAB:	Python:
mkdir('/tmp/A', 'B') mkdir('/tmp/A/B', 'C')	import pathlib P = pathlib.Path('/tmp/A/B/C') P.mkdir(parents=True)

8.5 Deleting Directories

Programs that create temporary directories, especially nested ones, should clean up after themselves. As with deleting files, there are several ways to achieve this in Python. The two obvious ways however, with a pathlib object's .rmdir() method or with the os module's rmdir() function, only work if the directory in question is empty.

The shutil module has a function, rmtree(), which recursively deletes the contents of the directory it is given. This is the Python equivalent of rm -fr D on Linux or macOS or rmdir D /s /q on Windows where D is the name of the directory to remove.

Warning!   Be especially careful calling when building up the directory name from variables! A small mistake with arguments to `shutil.rmtree()` can easily ruin your day.

By default, MATLAB's `rmdir` command will also only remove empty folders. It has a subtle option to delete recursively, though; to enable this behavior, one must append s to the end of the `rmdir` command.

This example recursively removes everything below the directory /tmp/Job0325:

MATLAB:	**Python:**
`rmdir /tmp/Job0325 s`	`import shutil` `shutil.rmtree('/tmp/Job0325')`

8.6 Walking Directory Trees

Large projects inevitably have files spread across nested directories. Traversing a directory tree programmatically—"walking a directory tree"—is an essential task for finding files of interest, aggregating data from a collection, or just harvesting metadata on available files (how many there are, how much space they occupy, when the latest one was added).

Python's `os` module has a function, `os.walk()`, specifically made for this purpose. MATLAB's `dir()` function can do the same by adding a file path separator and ** to the directory to traverse. The cleanest way to do that is with `fullfile()` as in `dir(fullfile(rootdir, '**'))` to walk `rootdir`.

Say we have `.csv` and `.xlsx` files spread across directories like so:

```
data
|--archive
|   |--2016
|      |--collect-2016-01.csv
|      |--collect-2016-04.csv
|      |--collect-2016-04-fixed.csv
|      |--summary-2016.xlsx
```

```
|--2017
|   |--collect-2017-06.csv
|   |--collect-2017-12.csv
|   |--summary-2017.xlsx
|--2018
|   |--collect-2018-06.csv
|   |--collect-2018-12.csv
|   |--summary-2018.xlsx
|--2019
    |--collect-2019-06.csv
    |--active.csv
```

The following example shows how to print the fully qualified name of every file below top_dir:

MATLAB:	Python:
| ```
files = dir(fullfile(...
            top_dir,'**'));
files = files(~[files.isdir]);
for i = 1:size(files,1)
  fprintf('%s/%s\n', ...
    files(i).folder, ...
    files(i).name)
end
``` | ```
import os
def find(top_dir):
  for root, dirs, files in \
      os.walk(top_dir):
    for F in files:
      full_path = f'{root}{os.sep}{F}'
      print(f'{full_path}')
find('data')
``` |

The output on a Linux system looks like this:

```
data/summary-2017.xlsx
data/summary-2018.xlsx
data/2019/collect-2019-06.csv
data/2019/active.csv
data/archive/summary-2016.xlsx
data/archive/2016/collect-2016-04.csv
data/archive/2016/collect-2016-01.csv
data/archive/2016/collect-2016-04-fixed.csv
```

```
data/2017/collect-2017-06.csv
data/2017/collect-2017-12.csv
data/2018/collect-2018-06.csv
data/2018/collect-2018-12.csv
```

Such find() functions are easily modified to, for example, return names of files having a specific extension or other property.

Generators—available in Python but not MATLAB—pair well with directory tree traversals. They allow one to operate on a file as soon as it is found before returning to the file system search. This can be achieved in MATLAB by passing a callback function that performs the desired operations to the search function—but callbacks add a layer of complexity and make the code more difficult to read. Of course, one could also embed the additional operations inside the search function, but that would remove the function's generality.

The following Python find() function is a generator-based tree walker which returns either all files found or optionally only those files which have a specific file extension. We'll use it to recursively descend the data/ directory. Each time a .xlsx file is found, some data is taken from it (here, a hypothetical extract_revenue() function returns a value taken from the file; see Section 7.7 on reading data from .xlsx files).

Python:

```python
import os
def find(top_dir, extension=None):
for root, dirs, files in os.walk(top_dir):
    for F in files:
       if extension and not F.endswith(extension):
         continue
       yield f'{root}{os.sep}{F}' # <- yield makes find() a generator

total_revenue = 0
for F in find('data', extension=".xlsx"):
  total_revenue += extract_revenue(F)
```

CHAPTER 9

Interacting with the Operating System and External Executables

Complex workflows rarely involve just MATLAB or Python in isolation. Other applications, whether custom in-house tools, commercial simulation and modeling packages, or open source tools, play important roles in the grander scheme of things. In this chapter, we'll see how Python programs can interact with the underlying operating system and other executables. We'll read and change environment variables, call other programs and capture their output, monitor the host computer's memory and CPU use, and kill processes that exceed given resource thresholds.

9.1 Reading, Setting Environment Variables

Environment variables can be accessed through the os.environ object in Python and the getenv() function in MATLAB:

MATLAB:	Python:

```>> getenv('HOME')```
```ans = /home/al```
	```In : import os```
	```In : os.environ['HOME']```
	```Out: '/home/al'```

© Albert Danial 2022

A. Danial, *Python for MATLAB Development*, https://doi.org/10.1007/978-1-4842-7223-7_9

os.environ has an advantage over getenv() because it behaves like a dictionary. This allows you to iterate over all known environment variables (recall from Section 4.2.3 that the format option <10s means "a string, 10 characters wide, left justified"):

Python:

```
In : for V in sorted(os.environ):
...:     print(f'{V:<10s} = {os.environ[V]}')

AUTOJUMP_ERROR_PATH = /home/al/.local/share/autojump/errors.log
AUTOJUMP_SOURCED = 1
CLUTTER_IM_MODULE = xim
COMPIZ_BIN_PATH = /usr/bin/
COMPIZ_CONFIG_PROFILE = ubuntu
CONDA_DEFAULT_ENV = base
CONDA_EXE  = /usr/local/anaconda3/bin/conda
CONDA_PREFIX = /usr/local/anaconda3
           :
```

MATLAB makes this much harder. The most common approach suggested on Stack Overflow is to parse the output of a system call to env on Linux and macOS and set on Windows. This is done in Section 9.2 where system calls in both languages are described.

Environment variables can be set programmatically as well, although changes made by a program persist only for the life of the program's process. When the program ends, the environment variables in the session where the program was run remain unchanged.

In Python, one can assign an environment variable merely by setting os.environ as one would a dictionary key. MATLAB sets variables with its setenv() function.

MATLAB:	Python:
`>> setenv('N_CASES', '42')`	`In : import os`
`>> getenv('N_CASES')`	`In : os.environ['N_CASES'] = '42'`
`ans = 42`	`In : os.environ['N_CASES']`
	`Out: '42'`

One quirk with both languages is that only string values are allowed. MATLAB will accept an integer and automatically typecast it to a string, but the resulting string will likely be unintended; the integer 42 becomes its ASCII character equivalent of "*". Python throws a TypeError error:

MATLAB:	Python:

`>> setenv('A', 42)`
`warning: implicit conversion`
`    from scalar to sq_string`
`>> getenv('A')`
`ans = *`
	`In : import os`
	`In : os.environ['N_CASES'] = 42`
	`Out: TypeError: str expected, not int`

9.2 Calling External Executables

External system calls are made in MATLAB with the `system()` function and in Python with functions in the `subprocess` module: `subprocess.run()` or `subprocess.Popen()`. The `.run()` function most closely resembles MATLAB's `system()`, while `.Popen()` allows one to orchestrate the execution of an entire chain of applications, piping output from one program to the input of the next.

Although `subprocess.run()` resembles `system()`, their methods of operation differ starkly. MATLAB's `system()` has only 1 optional argument (`'-echo'`, to additionally show the command's output in the Command Window; useful for interacting with the external command), while Python's `subprocess.run()` has 14 optional arguments. The most commonly used of these—check, `capture output`, `shell`, `timeout`—are illustrated by the following example.

In Section 9.1, we saw that MATLAB would need to call the operating system's env (Linux, macOS) or `set` (Windows) command to get a list of all environment variables and their values. Although Python has direct access through these via the `os.environ` object, we'll perform the same task with a system call.

MATLAB:

```
>> [Status, Result] = system('env');
```

Python:

```
In : import subprocess
In : Result = subprocess.run(['env'], capture_output=True)
```

MATLAB's return variables, Status and Result, are a double (the value 0 means the command ran successfully; a non-zero value indicates an error) and a character array containing the command's entire STDOUT stream. Individual lines of output can be iterated over by splitting Result on newlines via strsplit(Result, '\n').

Python's Result is an object whose attributes include .returncode, equivalent to Status in MATLAB; .stdout, equivalent to Result in MATLAB; and .stderr which contains error messages the command generated, if any. Curiously, MATLAB's system() provides no mechanism to capture STDERR.

We'll continue the example by iterating over lines of output from the env system call and extracting the environment variable name and value.

MATLAB:

```
[Status, Result] = system('env');
lines = strsplit(Result, '\n');   % separate lines from Result
for i = 1:len(lines)
    X = strsplit(lines{i,1}, '=');
    var = X{1,1};
    val = X{1,2};
    fprintf('%-10s : %s\n', var, val);
end
```

Python:

```
import subprocess
Result = subprocess.run(['env'], capture_output=True)
lines = Result.stdout.decode() # turn character array to string
for L in lines.split('\n'):
    var, val = L.split('=')
    print(f'{var:<10s} : {val}')
```

9.2.1 Checking for Failures

External executables may fail for many reasons: command not found, illegal arguments, missing or malformed inputs, processing errors, insufficient privilege to write to the output location, and so on. These are not Python errors, so, by default, if the command given to `subprocess.run()` fails, the function returns and Python program continues to run. `Result.returncode` will be non-zero, so we'll know that the command failed, but we won't know the reason for the failure.

This behavior can be changed by setting the optional keyword variable `check` to `True`. This causes a failure by the external executable to propagate to the Python program as `CalledProcessError` exception.

To explore failure behavior, we'll use `ffmpeg`, a powerful audio and video manipulation program, to convert an MPEG4 video file into the more highly compressed WebM format. As an input file, we can use the MPEG4 file created by Jake VanderPlas showing the chaotic motion of a triple pendulum;[1] the file can be downloaded from `http://jakevdp.github.io/videos/triple-pendulum.mp4`.

The nominal `ffmpeg` command to convert the file is

```
ffmpeg -loglevel quiet -i triple-pendulum.mp4 triple-pendulum.webm
```

If the `ffmpeg` executable is in the environment's search path, and if the input file can be read, both Python and MATLAB should have no issue invoking the command and producing the WebM file.

What we want to study is not the successful case but the failure. To trigger the failure, we'll misspell the log level setting `quiet` as `quiett`.

In the following Python code, we'll enable the optional `check` option to the arguments of `subsystem.run()` in Python.

MATLAB:

```
>> command = "ffmpeg -loglevel quiett -i triple-pendulum.mp4
triple-pendulum.webm";
>> [Status, Result] = system(command);
```

---

[1] Jake's blog at `http://jakevdp.github.io/` has excellent articles on Python for scientific computing.

Python:

```
import subprocess
command = ['ffmpeg', '-loglevel', 'quiett', '-i',
           'triple-pendulum.mp4', 'triple-pendulum.webm']
Result = subprocess.run(command, check=True)
```

The errors from MATLAB and Python look like this:

MATLAB:

```
>> [Status, Result] = system(command);
>> Status
    1

>> Result
    '[4;31mInvalid loglevel "quiett". Possible levels are numbers or:
    [0m[4;31m"quiet"
    [0m[4;31m"panic"
    [0m[4;31m"fatal"
    [0m[4;31m"error"
    [0m[4;31m"warning"
    [0m[4;31m"info"
    [0m[4;31m"verbose"
    [0m[4;31m"debug"
    [0m[4;31m"trace"
    [0m'
```

Python:

```
In : Result = subprocess.run(command, check=True)
Invalid loglevel "quiett". Possible levels are numbers or:
"quiet"
"panic"
"fatal"
"error"
"warning"
"info"
"verbose"
```

```
"debug"
"trace"
Traceback (most recent call last):
  [...]

CalledProcessError: Command '['ffmpeg', '-loglevel', 'quiett',
    '-i', 'triple-pendulum.mp4', 'triple-pendulum.webm']'
    returned non-zero exit status 1.
```

Handling errors from system calls in MATLAB means checking for a non-zero error status and in Python calling subprocess.run() with check=True and catching subprocess.CalledProcessError errors:

MATLAB:

```
[Status, Result] = system(command);
if Status
    fprintf('Command failure with %s\n', command)
end
```

Python:

```
try:
    Result = subprocess.run(command, check=True)
except subprocess.CalledProcessError as err:
    print(f'Command failure with {command}: {err}')
```

9.2.2 A Bytes-Like Object Is Required

The stdout attribute from the return value Result is a byte array rather than a string. If you try to apply a string operation like .split(), Python will raise a TypeError:

Python:

```
In : import subprocess
In : x = subprocess.run('dir', capture_output=True)
In : x.stdout.split('\n')
---------------------------------------------------------------------------
TypeError                                 Traceback (most recent call last)
<ipython-input-24-f1228a95ce2f> in <module>
----> 1 x.stdout.split('\n')
```

```
TypeError: a bytes-like object is required, not 'str'
```

The solution is to cast the byte array to a string:

Python:

```
In : import subprocess
In : x = subprocess.run('dir', capture_output=True)
In : x.stdout.split('\n')
In : str(x.stdout).split('\n')
Out: ["b'data.h5\\t\\t\\file_1.txt\\n'"]
```

9.3 Inspecting the Process Table and Process Resources

Numerical analyses and simulations tend to be resource-hungry. It helps to keep an eye on CPU, memory, and file system use to characterize a program's needs before launching a multiday run. Some of this characterization can be done by profiling code (Section 14.5). However, profiling does not answer questions such as "how much memory/CPU/network am I using right now?", "are other users putting a significant load on my machine?", or "how much disk space is available in the test data directory?"

MATLAB falls short when it comes to querying a computer's processes and the resources they consume. Making such queries involves calls to external utilities provided by the underlying operating system—the Process Explorer on Windows, Activity Monitor on macOS, or ps and top on Linux or macOS.

Python, on the other hand, has a module, psutil,[2] which provides an operating system–independent method for examining processes and the resources they use, as well as the computer's hardware including CPU load, CPU temperature, memory, network interfaces, storage, battery level, fan speed, and so on. In addition to inspecting processes, psutil can suspend, resume, and terminate them (provided the process belongs to the user issuing these commands).

Occasionally, I underestimate the amount of memory a computation needs (easy to do when creating, then computing eigensolutions of large sparse matrices as with the finite element benchmarks in Section 14.2.2), and my computer grinds to a standstill as the operating system spends all its time swapping memory to disk. The power button is

---

[2] Included with Anaconda.

my only recourse—very annoying. This problem can happen with any memory-hungry application in any language; MATLAB and Python are not special in this regard.

psutil makes it easy to write a job shepherd that kills any process that stresses the computer excessively. I run the following job shepherd in a separate terminal when I'm working on computations that push the limits of my laptop's hardware. If a run goes off the rails by consuming excessive memory and CPU cycles, the shepherd kills it, sparing me from a time-wasting and possibly file system–damaging hard reboot.[3] Some notes on how it works:

- Line 7: max_L1 is the one-minute load average below which the program does nothing. A load of 1.0 means one core on the machine is fully loaded.

- Line 8: Similarly, if the machine has less than max_mem_fraction of its memory in use, the program does nothing.

- Line 17: The program runs in a continuous loop, sleeping refresh_ sec seconds after every iteration.

- Line 28: If the one-minute load average and memory fraction limits are exceeded, the program iterates over all processes:

  - Line 29: If the process name is the ignore set, it goes on to the next one.

  - Line 31: If the process does not belong to the person running the shepherd, it is skipped. psutil cannot kill processes owned by other users.

  - Line 36: The process's CPU load is measured over a 0.2-second interval. If the value is less than min_cpu_pct, the loop proceeds to the next process.

    Processes may end before the measurement interval elapses, so this step may fail; an exception handler prevents the program from ending with an error.

  - Line 44: The process's memory is measured. This may fail even if we own the process, so the measurement is wrapped in another exception catcher.

  - Line 50: Finally, if the process uses more than half of the memory on the machine or its memory is being swapped to disk, the process is killed.

---

[3] Linux users can avoid a power cycle with "'Magic SysRq" key combinations, https:// en.wikipedia.org/wiki/Magic_SysRq_key

Python:

```python
# file: code/os/job_shepherd.py
import os
import psutil
import time

refresh_sec = 1.0
max_L1  = 1.5  # 1 minute load average
max_mem_fraction = 0.5
min_cpu_pct = 50.0

ignore = {
    'chrome', 'dbus-daemon', 'dconf-service', 'firefox',
    'gnome-terminal-server', 'ssh-agent', 'systemd', 'vim',
    'Xorg', 'top'}

uid_me  = psutil.Process( os.getpid() ).uids().real  # my user ID #

while True:
    L1, L5, L15 = psutil.getloadavg()
    mem = psutil.virtual_memory()
    if L1 < max_L1:
        time.sleep(refresh_sec)
        continue
    # under heavy system load
    if mem.used/mem.total < max_mem_fraction:
        time.sleep(refresh_sec)
        continue
```

```
27        # under heavy system and memory load
28        for proc in psutil.process_iter(['pid', 'name', 'uids']):
29            if proc.name() in ignore:
30                continue
31            if uid_me != proc.uids().real:
32                # process doesn't belong to me, can't do anything about it
33                continue
34            info = psutil.Process(proc.pid)
35            try:
36                cpu_pct = info.cpu_percent(interval=0.2)
37            except:
38                # process ended before cpu measurement finished
39                continue
40            if cpu_pct < min_cpu_pct:
41                # not doing anything, ignore
42                continue
43            try:
44                pmem = info.memory_full_info()
45            except psutil.AccessDenied:
46                # parent must own it, can't control this
47                continue
48            print(f'pid={proc.pid} name={proc.name()} CPU={cpu_pct} '
49                  f'pmem={pmem.rss} swap={pmem.swap}')
50            if pmem.rss/mem.total > 0.5 or pmem.swap > 0:
51                print(f'-> kill {proc.pid} name={proc.name()}')
52                proc.kill()
53        time.sleep(refresh_sec)
```

If you're curious to try it out, here's a small program that will eventually bring your computer to its knees. It makes an increasingly larger square matrix of random numbers and then multiplies it by a random vector. Raise the increment on N if the memory consumption rate is too slow. Also, modify the job shepherd's constants—especially the program names in the ignore set—to find the right balance of measurements to kill runaway processes on your computer.

Python:

```
#!/usr/bin/env python3
# code/os/machine_buster.py
import numpy as np
N = 200
while True:
    print(f'N = {N}')
    a = np.random.rand(N,N)
    b = np.random.rand(N)
    a.dot(b)
    N += 200
```

Object-Oriented Programming

Python is object oriented to its core. Every item—variable, function, operator, exception, signal, even a string literal—is an object. MATLAB also supports object-oriented programming, in fact with greater rigor than Python, but with less fluidity as well.

Neither language forces one to define classes; conventional procedure–based programming is entirely possible and may even be the default for most scientists and engineers. The ease with which one can define and use classes in Python, however, simplifies the path for developers new to OO to try this programming paradigm.

For the uninitiated, an object is an instance of a class in the same way a variable is an instance of a data type. Before we can define j as an integer, for example, the concept of an integer type must exist. Of course, MATLAB and Python predefine many useful data types and containers. Classes can be thought of as a kind of user-defined container which can include functions, called *methods*, that operate on the data in that container. Before we can work with objects, we must define *classes* from which objects are made.

10.1 Classes

Here's an example of a simple class that defines a circle. It includes three variables, x, y, and r, that define the center and radius and one method, area(), that returns the circle's area. The variables x, y, and r are known as *instance* variables because each object created from this class (i.e., each class instance) will have its own values for the center and radius.

In addition to instance variables, we'll also define a *class* variable, MAX_R, which is shared by all objects made from our class.

© Albert Danial 2022
A. Danial, *Python for MATLAB Development*, https://doi.org/10.1007/978-1-4842-7223-7_10

Python classes require an explicit constructor function called __init__() whose first argument is always the placeholder self. One can then create arbitrarily named attributes in the class using dot notation. Most often, this involves assigning the constructor's calling arguments to class attributes with lines like self.x = x.

MATLAB:	Python:

```matlab
% code/OO/Circle.m
classdef Circle
  properties (Constant)
    MAX_R = 20;
  end
  properties
    x {mustBeNumeric}
    y {mustBeNumeric}
    r {mustBeNumeric}
  end
  methods
    function obj = Circle(x,y,r)
      obj.x = x;
      obj.y = y;
      obj.r = r;
      obj.perim = 2*r*pi;
    end
    function [A] = area(obj)
      A = pi*obj.r^2;
    end
  end
end
```

```python
import numpy as np
class Circle:
  MAX_R= 20
  def __init__(self, x,y,r):
    self.x = x
    self.y = y
    self.r = r
    if self.r > circle.MAX_R:
      print('too big')
      self.r = circle.MAX_R
    self.R = r
  def area(self):
    return np.pi*self.r**2
```

With our `Circle` class defined, we'll make objects a and b which are instances of `Circle`:

MATLAB:	Python:
>> a = Circle(0,0,10);	In : a = Circle(0,0,10)
>> b = Circle(1,2,4);	In : b = Circle(1,2,4)
>> b.y	In : b.y
2	Out: 2
>> a.area()	In : a.area()
314.1592	Out: 314.1592

The act of creating an object from a class, as with a = `Circle(0,0,10)`, causes the class's *constructor* method—a function with the same name as the class in MATLAB, and the function __init__() in Python—to be called with the provided arguments.

10.1.1 Private vs. Public

Most object-oriented languages allow tight control over access to a class's attributes and methods by designating these as public or private. The former can be accessed by other objects, while the latter can only be seen and updated by members of the object itself.

MATLAB has mechanisms to allow access control, but Python is much looser in this regard, relying on naming conventions to indicate the developer's intent. In a nutshell, Python class attributes prefixed by two underscores are *name mangled* to hide them as though they were private. Name mangling simply consists of internally prefixing the variable to include the name of the class so a determined user will still be able to reach the data. The following example shows a variation of the `Circle` class defining an additional attribute, `perim`, as a private variable storing the circle's perimeter.

MATLAB:	Python:

```matlab
% file: code/OO/Circle.m
classdef Circle
  properties (Constant)
    MAX_R = 20;
  end
  properties (Access = private)
    perim
  end
  properties
      x {mustBeNumeric}
      y {mustBeNumeric}
      r {mustBeNumeric}
  end
  methods
   function obj = Circle(x,y,r)
     obj.x = x;
     obj.y = y;
     obj.r = r;
     obj.perim = 2*r*pi;
   end
   function [A] = area(obj)
     A = pi*obj.r^2;
   end
  end
end
```

```python
# file: code/OO/circle.py
import numpy as np
class Circle:
  MAX_R= 20
  def __init__(self, x,y,r):
    self.x = x
    self.y = y
    self.R = r
    self.__perim = 2*r*np.pi;
  def area(self):
    return np.pi*self.r**2
```

10.1.2 Custom Printers

The printed representation of a class can be changed in MATLAB by overloading the disp() function and in Python by defining a custom __str__() method. The following functions can be added to the preceding Circle class to print the circle's properties in a tight format. Note that __str__() returns a string rather than calling a print function directly.

MATLAB:	Python:

```matlab
function disp(obj)
 fprintf('X: %5.2f Y: %5.2f ', ...
        obj.x, obj.y);
 fprintf('R: %5.2f\n', obj.r);
end
```

```python
def __str__(self):
    return f'X: {self.x:5.2f} ' \
           f'Y: {self.y:5.2f} ' \
           f'R: {self.R:5.2f}'
```

Our custom output then looks like this:

MATLAB:	Python:

```matlab
>> c = Circle(.4,6.6, 3.14);
>> disp(c)
X:  0.40 Y:  6.60 R:  3.14
```

```python
In : c = Circle(.4,6.6, 3.14)
In : print(c)
X:  0.40 Y:  6.60 R:  3.14
```

10.1.3 Custom Exceptions

As a code base grows, so does the number of ways it can fail. Exception handlers, helpful
for managing failure modes, can be enhanced with custom exceptions that yield more
revealing and application-specific error states than generic errors. Custom exceptions are
easily added to both MATLAB and Python. The following example implements a simple
electric car simulator that throws a BatteryEmptyError exception when the car's battery
is depleted. The exception is defined with lines 2–4 in MATLAB and 3–4 in Python.

   MATLAB:

```matlab
1   % code/OO/ecar_sim.m
2   errID = 'ecar_sim:NotNumeric';
3   msg = 'BatteryEmptyError';
4   BatteryEmptyError = MException(errID,msg);
5   charge = 80.0; % kWhr
6   d_rate = 0.002;
7   while true
8       km   =   50*rand();
9       kmph = 20 + 120*rand();
10      discharge = d_rate*km*(20 + abs(kmph - 80))^1.4;
```

```matlab
11        charge = charge - discharge;
12        if charge < 0
13            throw(BatteryEmptyError)  .
14        end
15        fprintf(' %4.1f km at %6.2f km/hr remaining: %5.2f kWhr\n',...
16            km, kmph, charge);
17    end
```

Python:

```python
1   # code/OO/ecar_sim.py
2   import numpy as np
3   class BatteryEmptyError(Exception):
4       pass
5   charge = 80.0 # kWhr
6   d_rate = 0.002
7   while True:
8       km   =  50*np.random.rand()
9       kmph = 20 + 120*np.random.rand()
10      discharge = d_rate*km*(20 + np.abs(kmph - 80))**1.4
11      charge -= discharge
12      if charge < 0:
13          raise BatteryEmptyError
14      print(f' {km:4.1f} km at {kmph:6.2f} km/hr '
15            f'remaining: {charge:5.2f} kWhr')
```

Output from both programs looks similar; Python's is

```
21.0 km at  98.29 km/hr remaining: 73.09 kWhr
 2.9 km at  20.97 km/hr remaining: 70.45 kWhr
21.8 km at  73.85 km/hr remaining: 66.25 kWhr
10.9 km at  76.34 km/hr remaining: 64.43 kWhr
 5.7 km at 124.71 km/hr remaining: 60.50 kWhr
40.9 km at  21.33 km/hr remaining: 23.66 kWhr
Traceback (most recent call last):
File "code/OO/ecar_sim.py", line 13, in <module> raise BatteryEmptyError

    BatteryEmptyError
```

Downstream code that uses the car simulator can use an error handler like this in Python:

Python:

```
try:
    run_ecar_sim()
except BatteryEmptyError:
    print(f'Ran out of juice, recharge')
    bring_service_truck()
```

10.2 Performance Implications

Object-oriented programming can inhibit computational performance because it ruins data locality; values are dispersed across objects rather than near each other in tight arrays. This defeats vectorization in both Python and MATLAB.

Before we can demonstrate this however, we'll first need to cover numerical arrays, vectorization, and computational performance in detail. Chapter 11 covers these in detail. Specifically, Section 11.1.17 gives an example of a computational problem solved with and without object-oriented methods. Spoiler: The object-oriented method is much slower.

CHAPTER 11

NumPy and SciPy

NumPy is the foundational module for numeric computation in Python. Its primary data structure, the NumPy n-dimensional array, can be considered the Python equivalent of a MATLAB matrix. SciPy is a collection of modules built upon NumPy to solve a wide range of computational problems in clustering, differential equations, image processing, interpolation, linear algebra, linear programming, optimization, sparse matrices, statistics, and symbolic mathematics, among others. NumPy and SciPy together span the capabilities of the core MATLAB product plus functions from many toolboxes.

In this chapter, I'll show how to create, manipulate, subset, aggregate, and serialize NumPy arrays, then survey the broad capabilities found in NumPy and SciPy. Comparisons to MATLAB equivalents are shown throughout.

11.1 NumPy Arrays

A NumPy array, or, more formally, a `numpy.ndarray`, meaning "n-dimensional array," is functionally equivalent to a MATLAB matrix. Both are containers for a single (usually numeric) data type, both allow vectorized operations on their values, and both are accompanied by a large library of high performance mathematical, scientific, and statistical functions.

The NumPy module must be explicitly imported before NumPy arrays and functions can be used in a program or interactive computing session. This is most commonly done with

```
import numpy as np
```

The prefix `np.` will therefore represent the NumPy module throughout this book.

© Albert Danial 2022

A. Danial, *Python for MATLAB Development*, https://doi.org/10.1007/978-1-4842-7223-7_11

11.1.1 Formatting NumPy Array Values

We'll see many numbers in the following sections, so it's helpful to have control over their appearance. MATLAB's `format` command has a collection of useful styles. NumPy offers that and more; it gives control not only of the numeric format but also the line width and summary options if the array exceeds a given size.

MATLAB:

```
>> a = reshape(1:6, 3,2)/pi/14326
    2.2219e-05    8.8876e-05
    4.4438e-05    1.1110e-04
    6.6657e-05    1.3331e-04
```

Python:

```
In : a = np.arange(1,7).reshape(2,3).T/np.pi/14326
In : a
Out:
array([[2.22190344e-05, 8.88761374e-05],
       [4.44380687e-05, 1.11095172e-04],
       [6.66571031e-05, 1.33314206e-04]])
```

MATLAB:

```
>> format long e
>> a
    2.221903435598148e-05    8.887613742392592e-05
    4.443806871196296e-05    1.110951717799074e-04
    6.665710306794443e-05    1.333142061358889e-04
```

Python:

```
In : np.set_printoptions(precision=20)
In : a
Out:
array([[2.2219034355981481e-05, 8.8876137423925925e-05],
       [4.4438068711962962e-05, 1.1109517177990740e-04],
       [6.6657103067944433e-05, 1.3331420613588887e-04]])
```

Occasionally, in MATLAB you'll accidentally type the name of a massive array or enter an expression that produces volumes of numbers without a trailing semicolon. The result is many screens full of numbers scrolling by. NumPy is more forgiving in that it will simply print leading and trailing terms:

MATLAB:

```
>> a = reshape(1:1000000, 1000, 1000)
    ... entire matrix printed ...
```

Python:

```
In : a = np.arange(1000000).reshape(1000,1000)
In : a
Out:
array([[     0,      1,      2, ...,     997,     998,     999],
       [  1000,   1001,   1002, ...,    1997,    1998,    1999],
       [  2000,   2001,   2002, ...,    2997,    2998,    2999],
       ...,
       [997000, 997001, 997002, ..., 997997, 997998, 997999],
       [998000, 998001, 998002, ..., 998997, 998998, 998999],
       [999000, 999001, 999002, ..., 999997, 999998, 999999]])
In : np.set_printoptions(linewidth=40,edgeitems=2)
In : a
Out:
array([[     0,      1, ...,     998,
           999],
       [  1000,   1001, ...,    1998,
          1999],
       ...,
       [998000, 998001, ..., 998998,
        998999],
       [999000, 999001, ..., 999998,
        999999]])
```

If you're fortunate to have a large monitor, setting linewidth=200 (or something similar) can be a big help when poring over data.

11.1.2 Differences Between NumPy Arrays and MATLAB Matrices

The next five sections explain the primary differences between NumPy arrays and MATLAB matrices.

11.1.2.1 MATLAB Matrices Made of Numeric Literals Default to Double Precision

In contrast, NumPy array types are inferred from the inputs. Unless one of the terms has a decimal point or exponent, NumPy will create an array of 64-bit integers:

MATLAB:	Python:
`>> a = [1 2 3];`	`In : a = np.array([1, 2, 3])`
`>> class(a)`	`In : a.dtype`
`    'double'`	`Out: dtype('int64')`
`>> a = [1 2. 3];`	`In : a = np.array([1, 2., 3])`
`>> class(a)`	`In : a.dtype`
`    'double'`	`Out: dtype('float64')`

11.1.2.2 MATLAB Matrices Have a Minimum of Two Dimensions

NumPy arrays, in contrast, may have just one dimension.

MATLAB:	Python:
`>> a = [1 2 3]`	`In : a = np.array([1, 2, 3])`
`>> size(a)`	`In : a.shape`
`   1   3`	`Out: (3,)`
`>> ndims(a)`	`In : a.ndim`
`   2`	`Out: 1`

In the preceding example, a in MATLAB is a 1 x 3 matrix, while Python's a just has three terms. MATLAB can therefore distinguish between row vectors and column vectors which is useful for some linear algebra expressions.

One-dimensional NumPy arrays have no concept of vertical or horizontal arrangement; thus, their row or column affinity becomes a matter of context. A second dimension can be added explicitly to convey the same row or column sense as a MATLAB vector; this process is explained in Section 11.1.12.

11.1.2.3 MATLAB Numeric Scalars Are 1 x 1 Matrices

NumPy scalars are distinct from NumPy arrays; scalars have just one value.

MATLAB:	Python:
`>> a = 2.7183;`	`In : a = 2.7183`
`>> size(a)`	`In : a.shape`
	`AttributeError Traceback`
`   1    1`	`----> 1 a.shape`
	`AttributeError: 'float' object`
`>> ndims(a)`	`has no attribute 'shape'`
`   2`	

11.1.2.4 NumPy Arrays Are Row Major

By default a NumPy array uses row major storage internally, while MATLAB arrays are stored column major. In other words, if the numbers 1 through 12 were stored as consecutive values in memory, they would look like this as 3 × 4 matrix:

MATLAB:	Python:
`>> a = 1:12`	`In : a = np.arange(1, 13)`
`a =`	`In : a`
` 1 2 3 4 5 6 7 8 9 10 11 12`	`Out: array([ 1, 2, 3,  4,  5,  6,`
	`                7, 8, 9, 10, 11, 12])`
`>> reshape(a, [3,4])`	`In : a.reshape(3,4)`
`    1    4    7    10`	`array([[ 1,  2,  3,  4],`
`    2    5    8    11`	`       [ 5,  6,  7,  8],`
`    3    6    9    12`	`       [ 9, 10, 11, 12]])`

NumPy is capable of creating column-major arrays using the order='F' (Fortran-order) optional argument to the numpy.array() function.

Python:

```
In : a = np.arange(1, 13)
In : a
Out: array([ 1, 2, 3,  4,  5,  6,
            7, 8, 9, 10, 11, 12])

In : a.reshape(3,4, order='F')
array([[ 1,  4,  7, 10],
       [ 2,  5,  8, 11],
       [ 3,  6,  9, 12]])
```

11.1.2.5 NumPy Arrays Must Be Explicitly Resized to Add Terms

MATLAB matrices can be expanded simply by referencing new indices, but NumPy array sizes are fixed once the array is created. One can create new NumPy arrays using the vertical or horizontal stack functions np.vstack() or np.hstack() to add rows or columns from existing arrays. Alternatively, one can call the np.resize() function to add the desired number of terms in any dimension. MATLAB, by comparison, allows rows or columns to be appended by merely referencing a new index on the left-hand side matrix. This example shows how one would append a row to an existing 2×2 matrix using the .resize() method:

MATLAB:	Python:
`>> a = [1 2; 3 4]`	`In : a = np.array([[1,2], [3,4]])`
`a =`	`In : a`
`    1  2`	`Out: array([[1, 2]`
`    3  4`	`            [3, 4]])`
	`In : a.resize( (3,2) )`
`>> a(3,:) = [5 6]`	
`a =`	`In : a[2,] = [5, 6]`
`    1  2`	
`    3  4`	`In : a`
`    5  6`	`Out: array([[1, 2],`
	`            [3, 4],`
	`            [5, 6]])`

While MATLAB's matrix growing capability is convenient, it comes with a performance penalty. It is much faster to preallocate a MATLAB matrix, for example, by first creating a matrix of zeros, then populating existing rows or columns with values rather than starting with an empty matrix and growing it in a loop. Preallocation is fine when the final size of a matrix is known up front, but this is not always the case. Reading values from a file may require either two passes through the file, once to learn what the final size will be and a second time to populate matrix entries, or reverting to growing the matrix.

11.1.3 NumPy Data Types

Table 11-1 lists the possible types for `np.ndarrays` along with their MATLAB counterparts.

Table 11-1. *NumPy data types*

MATLAB Type	NumPy Type	Notes
logical	np.bool	8-bit Boolean
uint8	np.ubyte	8-bit unsigned integer
uint8	np.uint8	8-bit unsigned integer
int8	np.int8	8-bit signed integer
uint16	np.uint16	16-bit unsigned integer
int16	np.int16	16-bit signed integer
uint32	np.uint32	32-bit unsigned integer
int32	np.int32	32-bit signed integer
uint64	np.uint64	64-bit unsigned integer
int64	np.int, np.int64	64-bit signed integer
uint64	np.uint	64-bit unsigned integer
not available	np.float16	16-bit (short) float
single	np.float32	32-bit float
double	np.float64	64-bit float
double	np.float	64-bit float
not available	np.float128	128-bit (quad precision) float[1]
complex	np.complex	pair of 64-bit floats
single[2]	np.complex64	Pair of 32-bit floats
double[2]	np.complex128	Pair of 64-bit floats
not available	np.complex256	Pair of 128-bit floats[3]
char	np.str	Fixed-length strings
datetime	datetime.datetime	Datetime object

---

[1] Linux and macOS only.

[2] MATLAB has no explicit complex data type.

[3] Linux and macOS only.

11.1.4 Typecasting Scalars and Arrays

MATLAB's typecasting mechanism is straightforward: if you have a scalar or array in one data type (values are double precision by default), you just need to prefix the variable with the type name.

While NumPy's typecasting notation for scalars matches MATLAB's, NumPy uses different notation to typecast arrays. One must write `X.astype(np.uint8)` to cast array X to `np.uint8`:

MATLAB:	Python:

`>> p = 4.32;`
`>> uint8(p)`
` 4`
	`In : p = 4.32`
	`In : np.uint8(p)`
	`Out: 4`

`>> p = [4.32 1.23];`
`>> uint8(p)`
`   4   1`
	`In : p = np.array([4.32, 1.23])`
	`In : p.astype(np.uint8)`
	`Out: array([4, 1], dtype=uint8)`

Both MATLAB and NumPy support versions of "like" casting, meaning creating a new array using the type of an existing array:

MATLAB:	Python:

`>> p = [4.32 1.23];`
`>> q = uint8([0 0]);`
`>> cast(p,'like',q)`
`  1×2 uint8 row vector`
`    4   1`
	`In : p = np.array([4.32, 1.23])`
	`In : q = np.zeros((1,2),dtype=np.uint8)`
	`In : p.astype(q.dtype)`
	`Out: array([4, 1], dtype=uint8)`

`np.zeros()` and `np.zeros_like()` are described in Section 11.1.6.

11.1.5 Hex, Binary, and Decimal Representations

The content of some numeric data, specifically integers, may have properties that become apparent when represented in different bases. Bit mask operations in particular are more easily understood when their values are shown in binary form.

11.1.5.1 Decimal to Binary

MATLAB:	Python:
>> dec = 1234; >> dec2bin(dec) 10011010010	In : dec = 1234 In : np.binary_repr(dec) Out: '10011010010'

11.1.5.2 Binary to Decimal

MATLAB:	Python:
>> bin2dec('10011010010') 1234	In : np.int('10011010010', 2) Out: 1234

11.1.5.3 Decimal to Hexadecimal

MATLAB's dec2hex() function returns a hexadecimal string representing the provided integer. NumPy lacks a dedicated function for this conversion; instead, one can use %x and %X format strings. These work the same way in MATLAB and Python: %x produces lowercase hexadecimal, while %X produces uppercase. Additionally, a leading zero before the field width will zero-pad the resulting string. This provides a bit more control over the output than dec2hex().

MATLAB:	Python:
>> dec2hex(8765)	In : '%x' % 8765
223D	Out: '223d'
>> sprintf('%x', 8765)	In : '%X' % 8765
223d	Out: '223D'
>> sprintf('%X', 8765)	In : '%06X' % 8765
223D	Out: '00223D'
>> sprintf('%06X', 8765)	
00223D	

11.1.5.4 Hexadecimal to Decimal

MATLAB:	Python:
>> hex2dec('223D')	In : np.int('223D', 16)
8765	Out: 8765

11.1.6 Creating Arrays

NumPy arrays can be created many ways. The canonical constructor is the np.array() function which takes a list and optional settings for the data type (default np.float64) and storage scheme (default row major). Here, we see how basic matrices are created in both languages:

MATLAB:	Python:
>> a = [9 8 7; 6 5 4]	In : a = np.array([[9, 8, 7],[6, 5, 4]])
a =	In : a
	array([[9, 8, 7],
9 8 7	[6, 5, 4]])
6 5 4	

11.1.6.1 Zeros

Array allocation or initialization is often done by creating a zero-filled array with the desired shape and type. NumPy has two functions, np.zeros() and np.zeros_like(), for this purpose. The np.zeros_like() function is interesting because rather than taking the array size as an argument, it takes an existing matrix, then returns a zero-filled array having the same size and type of the given array. Another array creation option is np.empty() which creates an array without initializing its contents.

MATLAB's zeros() function supports a 'like' option, but it doesn't return the correct result in 2020b:

MATLAB 2020b:	Python:

>> a = zeros(2,3)
 	
  0   0   0
  0   0   0
	In : a = np.zeros((2,3))
	In : a
	Out: array([[0, 0, 0],
	             [0, 0, 0]])

>> b = [2; 4]
 	
  2
  4
	In : b = np.array([[2], [4]])
	In : b
	Out: array([[2],
	             [4]])

>> c = zeros('like',b)
 	
  0
	In : c = np.zeros_like(b)
	In : c
	Out: array([[0],
	             [0]])

11.1.6.2 Ones

An array of ones is another useful initializer. Its result is sometimes scaled to produce arrays filled with the same value, although a special function, np.full(), exists just for that purpose; its use is illustrated in Section 11.1.6.3. As with np.zeros_like(), np.ones() has a np.ones_like() companion:

MATLAB:	Python:
`>> a = ones(3,1)`	`In : a = np.ones((3,1))`
	`In : a`
`1`	`Out: array([[1],`
`1`	`        [1],`
`1`	`        [1]])`

11.1.6.3 NaNs

MATLAB has a nan() function which creates a matrix of NaN—*not a number*—values. NumPy has a more generic matrix initializer, np.full(), that initializes an array with the given value:

MATLAB:	Python:
`>> nan(2,3)`	`In : np.full((2,3), np.NaN)`
	`array([[nan, nan, nan],`
`NaN   NaN   NaN`	`       [nan, nan, nan]])`
`NaN   NaN   NaN`	

11.1.6.4 Range

A range of consecutive numbers can be created two ways in Python. The first is with the standard range() function and the second is with NumPy's np.arange() function which is more useful for numeric work because the return value is a NumPy array. Both have the same calling arguments, but neither, perhaps confusingly to MATLAB programmers, include the stop value in the output. This can be especially vexing when stepping with non-unit values:

MATLAB:	Python:

`>> b = -8:-4`
`b =`
`  -8  -7  -6  -5  -4`
	`In : b = np.arange(-8,-3)`
	`In : b`
	`Out: array([-8, -7, -6, -5, -4])`

`>> b = -8:1.5:-4`
`b =`
`  -8.00 -6.50 -5.00`
	`In : b = np.arange(-8,-4,1.5)`
	`In : b`
	`Out: array([-8. , -6.5, -5. ])`

11.1.6.5 Identity

Identity matrices are created with eye() and np.eye(), respectively:

MATLAB:	Python:

`>> eye(3)`
`   1   0   0`
`   0   1   0`
`   0   0   1`
	`In : a = np.eye(3)`
	`array([[1., 0., 0.],`
	`       [0., 1., 0.],`
	`       [0., 0., 1.]])`

11.1.6.6 Diagonal Matrices

Diagonal matrices can be created by passing diag() and np.diag() a 1D vector.
Additionally, these functions return the diagonal of a matrix when given a 2D array:

MATLAB:	Python:

`>> diag([9 8 7])`
`   9   0   0`
`   0   8   0`
`   0   0   7`
	`In : np.diag([9,8,7])`
	`array([[9, 0, 0],`
	`       [0, 8, 0],`
	`       [0, 0, 7]])`

`>> diag(eye(2))`
`   1`
`   1`
	`In : np.diag(np.eye(2))`
	`Out: array([1., 1.])`

11.1.6.7 Upper and Lower Triangular Matrices

These are formed in MATLAB with `triu()` and `tril()` and in NumPy with `np.triu()` and `np.tril()`. All four functions support an optional offset from the diagonal.

We saw at the beginning of Section 11.1 that MATLAB matrices are column major, while NumPy arrays, by default, are row major. The MATLAB definition of A in the following example is therefore transposed to yield the same pattern of numbers as NumPy's A. We'll use A to explore upper and lower triangle extractions:

MATLAB:	Python:
```>> A = reshape(5:16, 4,3)'```	```In : A = np.arange(5,17).reshape(3,4)```

MATLAB:

```
>> A = reshape(5:16, 4,3)'

A =

    5    6    7    8
    9   10   11   12
   13   14   15   16

>> triu(A)
    5    6    7    8
    0   10   11   12
    0    0   15   16

>> triu(A,1)
    0    6    7    8
    0    0   11   12
    0    0    0   16

>> tril(A)
    5    0    0    0
    9   10    0    0
   13   14   15    0

>> tril(A,-1)
    0    0    0    0
    9    0    0    0
   13   14    0    0
```

Python:

```
In : A = np.arange(5,17).reshape(3,4)
In : A
array([[ 5,  6,  7,  8],
       [ 9, 10, 11, 12],
       [13, 14, 15, 16]])

In : np.triu(A)
array([[ 5,  6,  7,  8],
       [ 0, 10, 11, 12],
       [ 0,  0, 15, 16]])

In : np.triu(A,1)
array([[ 0,  6,  7,  8],
       [ 0,  0, 11, 12],
       [ 0,  0,  0, 16]])

In : np.tril(A)
array([[ 5,  0,  0,  0],
       [ 9, 10,  0,  0],
       [13, 14, 15,  0]])

In : np.tril(A,-1)
array([[ 0,  0,  0,  0],
       [ 9,  0,  0,  0],
       [13, 14,  0,  0]])
```

11.1.6.8 Random

Pseudorandom arrays can be created using a variety of distribution functions, as can be seen by doing tab completion on np.random in an ipython session:

```
In : np.random.<Tab>
absolute_import        mtrand                      RandomState
beta()                 multinomial()               ranf()
binomial()             multivariate_normal()       rayleigh()
bytes()                negative_binomial()         sample()
chisquare()            noncentral_chisquare()      seed()
choice()               noncentral_f()              set_state()
dirichlet()            normal()                    shuffle()
division               np                          standard_cauchy()
exponential()          operator                    standard_exponential()
f()                    pareto()                    standard_gamma()
gamma()                permutation()               standard_normal()
geometric()            poisson()                   standard_t()
get_state()            power()                     test
gumbel()               print_function              triangular()
hypergeometric()       rand()                      uniform()
laplace()              randint()                   vonmises()
Lock()                 randn()                     wald()
logistic()             random()                    warnings
lognormal()            random_integers()           weibull()
logseries()            random_sample()             zipf()
```

np.random.rand() produces a uniform random distribution, like MATLAB's rand() function:

MATLAB:	Python:
>> rand(2)	In : np.random.rand(2,2)
0.095692 0.232535	array([[0.59219917, 0.62549076],
0.813753 0.892878	[0.21467385, 0.70801235]])
>> rand(3,2)	In : np.random.rand(3,2)
0.456106 0.908961	array([[0.664537, 0.219990],
0.274357 0.755147	[0.974484, 0.251934],
0.113177 0.900217	[0.827411, 0.063566]])

11.1.6.9 Equally Spaced Distribution (linspace)

MATLAB:	Python:
>> linspace(21,23,5)	In : np.linspace(21,23,5)
21.0 21.5 22.0 22.5 23.0	Out: array([21., 21.5, 22., 22.5, 23.])

11.1.6.10 Logarithmically Spaced Distribution (logspace)

MATLAB:	Python:
>> logspace(0.1, 1, 3)	In : np.logspace(0.1, 1, 3)
1.2589 3.5481 10.0000	Out: array([1.25892541, 3.54813389, 10.])

11.1.6.11 Horizontal and Vertical Stacking

MATLAB has a convenience edge on NumPy when it comes to creating new matrices by stacking terms of existing matrices; MATLAB matrix names merely need to be placed side by side within brackets. NumPy, in contrast, requires calls to special functions np.hstack() and np.vstack(). The new arrays d and e are created by horizontally and vertically stacking a, b, and c:

MATLAB:	Python:
`>> a = [1; 2]`	`In : a = np.array([[1],[2]])`
`    1`	`In : a`
`    2`	`array([[1],`
	`        [2]])`
`>> b = [0; -3]`	`In : b = np.array([[0],[-3]])`
`    0`	`In : b`
`   -3`	`array([[ 0],`
	`        [-3]])`
`>> c = [-1; 0]`	`In : c = np.array([[-1],[0]])`
`   -1`	`In : c`
`    0`	`array([[-1],`
	`        [ 0]])`
`>> d = [a b c]`	
	`In : d = np.hstack([a,b,c])`
`    1    0   -1`	`In : d`
`    2   -3    0`	`array([[ 1,  0, -1],`
	`        [ 2, -3,  0]])`
`>> e = [a;b;c]`	
	`In : e = np.vstack([a,b,c])`
`    1`	`In : e`
`    2`	`array([[ 1],`
`    0`	`        [ 2],`
`   -3`	`        [ 0],`
`   -1`	`        [-3],`
`    0`	`        [-1],`
	`        [ 0],`

11.1.6.12 Meshgrid

meshgrid() in MATLAB and its NumPy namesake np.meshgrid() are useful for creating coordinate pairs on a regular mesh. These, in turn, are often used as substrates over which 2D data is mapped for visualization or interpolation.

MATLAB:	Python:

`>> [y,x] = meshgrid([1 2 3],`
`              [3.5 3.6])`
`y =`
`   1    2    3`
`   1    2    3`
 	
`x =`
`   3.5000   3.5000   3.5000`
`   3.6000   3.6000   3.6000`
	`In : y,x = np.meshgrid([1,2,3],`
	`                    [3.5,3.6])`
	`In : y`
	`array([[1, 2, 3],`
	`       [1, 2, 3]])`
	`In : x`
	`array([[3.5, 3.5, 3.5],`
	`       [3.6, 3.6, 3.6]])`

11.1.6.13 Inflating Matrices

The `scipy.ndimage` module has a function `zoom()` which can be used to inflate a matrix by interpolation. (Interpolation is covered in Section 11.4.) The same result can be achieved in MATLAB, of course, but with more operations. The following example increases the number of rows by 3× and the number of columns by 2×:

MATLAB:	Python:

`>> a = [4 -4; 4 0]`
`     4    -4`
`     4     0`
 	
`>> nY = 2*3; nX = 2*2;`
`>> Xs = linspace(0,1,nX);`
`>> Ys = linspace(0,1,nY);`
`>> [Xq,Yq] = meshgrid(Xs, Ys);`
`>> interp2(X,Y,a,Xq,Yq)`
`  4.0000   1.3333  -1.3333  -4.0000`
`  4.0000   1.6000  -0.8000  -3.2000`
`  4.0000   1.8667  -0.2667  -2.4000`
`  4.0000   2.1333   0.2667  -1.6000`
`  4.0000   2.4000   0.8000  -0.8000`
`  4.0000   2.6667   1.3333        0`
	`In : from scipy.ndimage import zoom`
	`In : a = np.array([[4.0, -4], [4, 0]])`
	`In : a`
	`array([[ 4., -4.],`
	`       [ 4.,  0.]])`
	
	`In : zoom(a, [3, 2], order=1)`
	
	`array([[ 4. , 1.3333, -1.3333, -4.  ],`
	`       [ 4. , 1.6  , -0.8  , -3.2 ],`
	`       [ 4. , 1.8667, -0.2667, -2.4 ],`
	`       [ 4. , 2.1333,  0.2667, -1.6 ],`
	`       [ 4. , 2.4  ,  0.8  , -0.8 ],`
	`       [ 4. , 2.6667,  1.3333,  0.  ]])`

11.1.6.14 Test Matrices

Algorithm development typically begins with test data, or in its absence, random data with prescribed properties. The array creation methods of this section can be combined in interesting ways to yield data having properties useful for exploring algorithm robustness, error handling, or exercising various logic branches. Here, we explore some of those methods.

Note   The MATLAB and Python matrices in this section are generated from random number generators and therefore will not match each other.

Integers between -5 and +5

MATLAB:	Python:
`>> floor(10*rand(4,4) - 5)`	`In : np.random.randint(-5,6,size=(4,4))`
-5 -3 4 -4	`array([[-3,  5,  4,  5],`
-4 4 1 4	`       [ 0, -1,  1,  3],`
-3 0 -1 3	`       [ 0,  3,  1, -2],`
3 -3 0 -4	`       [-1, -1,  5, -5]])`

4×3 array of integers in a linear sequence, column major

MATLAB:	Python:
`>> reshape(1:12, 4,3)`	`In : np.arange(1,13).reshape(3,4).T`
1 5 9	`array([[ 1,  5,  9],`
2 6 10	`       [ 2,  6, 10],`
3 7 11	`       [ 3,  7, 11],`
4 8 12	`       [ 4,  8, 12]])`

4×3 array of integers in a linear sequence, row major

MATLAB:	Python:
`>> reshape(1:12, 3,4)'`	`In : np.arange(1,13).reshape(4,3)`
1 2 3	`array([[ 1,  2,  3],`
4 5 6	`       [ 4,  5,  6],`
7 8 9	`       [ 7,  8,  9],`
10 11 12	`       [10, 11, 12]])`

4 × 3 array of floats, half are NaN

MATLAB:	Python:
`>> a = 100*rand(4,3);`	`In : a = 100*np.random.rand(4,3)`
`>> a(a < 50) = nan`	`In : a[a < 50] = np.NaN`
`a =`	`In : a`
	`array([[60.551, 99.574, 78.620],`
69.082 NaN NaN	`       [  nan, 66.137, 64.343],`
NaN 73.604 NaN	`       [52.505,   nan,   nan],`
NaN 63.711 NaN	`       [96.109, 56.539,   nan]])`
51.612 76.674 63.956	

Note   MATLAB and Python generate different random matrices. The two matrices earlier are not intended to match.

11.1.7 Complex Scalars and Arrays

MATLAB and NumPy take slightly different approaches to creating complex scalars and arrays. MATLAB treats both i and j as $\sqrt{-1}$, but NumPy only recognizes j. Both also support a complex() function that takes real and imaginary arguments:

MATLAB:	Python:

>> 1+2i
  1.0000 + 2.0000i
	In : 1+2i
	   1+2i
	SyntaxError: invalid syntax

>> 3 - 4j 3.0000 - 4.0000i	In : 3 - 4j Out: (3-4j)
>> complex(5,6) 5.0000 + 6.0000i	In : complex(5,6) Out: (5+6j)

Curiously, neither the default Python complex() nor the NumPy version np.complex() accept array arguments. Instead, to create a complex numeric array from real and imaginary arrays in NumPy, one must multiply the array containing the imaginary part by the complex unit value 1j:

MATLAB:	Python:
>> N = ones(2,3); >> complex(N, -5*N) 1.00-5.00i 1.00-5.00i 1.00-5.00i 1.00-5.00i 1.00-5.00i 1.00-5.00i	In : N = np.ones((2,3)) In : N - 5*N*(1j) array([[1.-5.j, 1.-5.j, 1.-5.j], [1.-5.j, 1.-5.j, 1.-5.j]])

Once we have a complex variable, we can extract its real and imaginary components similarly:

MATLAB:	Python:

`>> z = complex([2.2;3.3],...`
`            [-4.4;5.5])`
	`In : z=np.array([[2.2],[3.3]]) + (1j)*\`
	`...:     np.array([[-4.4],[5.5]])`
	`In : z`

`   2.2000 - 4.4000i` `   3.3000 + 5.5000i`	`array([[2.2-4.4j],` `        [3.3+5.5j]])`

`>> real(z)`
`   2.2000`
`   3.3000`
	`In : z.real`
	`array([[2.2],`
	`        [3.3]])`

`>> imag(z)`
`   -4.4000`
`    5.5000`
	`In : z.imag`
	`array([[-4.4],`
	`        [ 5.5]])`

11.1.8 Linear Indexing

MATLAB matrices allow *linear indexing* whereby a single scalar index can be used to access terms of a multidimensional array. The scalar index is the offset from the beginning of the array to the desired term, striding along columns (or, more generally, incrementing the index of leftmost dimension most rapidly).

The same is possible with NumPy arrays using either their `.take()` or `.item()` methods. Keep in mind, though, that (1) NumPy arrays are row major so a different offset is needed to arrive at the same term, and (2) the argument to `.take()` is zero index based.

In this example, we extract the 12th item from the same array—but get different results because MATLAB counts down columns, while Python counts across rows.

MATLAB:	Python:

`>> a = [11 14 17 20 23;`
    `12 15 18 21 24;`
    `13 16 19 22 25];`
	`In : a = np.array(`
	    `[[11, 14, 17, 20, 23],`
	     `[12, 15, 18, 21, 24],`
	     `[13, 16, 19, 22, 25]])`

`>> a(12)` `22`	`In : a.take(11)` `Out: 16`

Both languages have convenience functions that return row and column indices corresponding to a linear index given the shape of the original array:

MATLAB:	Python:

`>> [r,c]=ind2sub([3,5],12)`
 `r =   3`
 `c =   4`
	`In : np.unravel_index(11,(3,5))`
	 `Out: (2, 1)`

`>> sub2ind([3,5],3,4)` `12`	`In : np.ravel_multi_index((2,1),(3,5))` `Out: 11`

`sub2ind()` and `np.ravel_multi_index()` give the linear offset into a multidimensional array given the indices of the desired term.

The `.take()` method also accepts lists of indices and an optional argument specifying the dimension to extract terms from. This turns out to be useful when extracting rows or columns of NumPy arrays within MATLAB because MATLAB syntax precludes indexing NumPy arrays with brackets.

Here, we show how the first row and third column of a can be extracted with `.take()` and the `axis` keyword argument:

Python:

```
In : a
Out:
array([[11, 14, 17, 20, 23],
       [12, 15, 18, 21, 24],
       [13, 16, 19, 22, 25]])
```

```
In : a.take(0,axis=0)
Out: array([11, 14, 17, 20, 23])

In : a.take(2,axis=1)
Out: array([17, 18, 19])
```

A practical application of this technique appears in Section 12.7, where a 1D NumPy array of RGBA values is pulled from a 2D NumPy colormap array within MATLAB; the line is

```
color = colors.take(col_ind + int64(4)*color_row);
```

11.1.9 Reading/Writing Arrays to/from Text Files

Sections 7.1 and 7.6 covered text and binary I/O of generic data. Here, we'll examine I/O for the special case of numeric arrays to and from text files.

11.1.9.1 Reading an Array from a Text File

Numeric values can be read from a text file several ways in both languages, but the easiest is with the MATLAB load() function and NumPy's np.loadtxt(). This is demonstrated with the text file a.txt containing this 3×2 matrix:

```
-3.2   4.3
1.e-5 2.9
6.6   -9.2
```

Both MATLAB and Python load functions allow the file to be annotated by comments—any text following a pound sign—and both skip blank lines.

MATLAB:	Python:

`>> a = load('a.txt')`
`a =`
 	
`  -3.2000e+00    4.3000e+00`
`   1.0000e-05    2.9000e+00`
`   6.6000e+00   -9.2000e+00`
	`In : a = np.loadtxt('a.txt')`
	`In : a`
	`array([[-3.2e+00,  4.3e+00],`
	`       [ 1.0e-05,  2.9e+00],`
	`       [ 6.6e+00, -9.2e+00]])`

(See Section 7.1.5 for reading data from comma-separated value files.)

11.1.9.2 Writing an Array to a Text File

Writing numberic data to a text file can also be done multiple ways, but again the easy way is with single function calls—save() in MATLAB and np.savetxt() in Python. We'll use the same a matrix as loaded from the a.txt file in the previous section:

MATLAB:	Python:
>> save("aM.txt","a","-ascii")	In : np.savetxt('aP.txt', a)

It produces these files:

aM.txt from MATLAB:

```
-3.20000000e+00  4.30000000e+00
 1.00000000e-05  2.90000000e+00
 6.60000000e+00 -9.20000000e+00
```

aP.txt from Python:

```
-3.200000000000000178e+00  4.299999999999999822e+00
 1.000000000000000082e-05  2.899999999999999911e+00
 6.599999999999999645e+00 -9.199999999999999289e+00
```

np.savetxt()'s format can be configured with the optional fmt keyword argument:

```
In : np.savetxt('aP.txt', a, fmt='% 10.3f')
In : cat aP.txt
    -3.200      4.300
     0.000      2.900
     6.600     -9.200
```

11.1.10 Reading/Writing Arrays to/from Binary Files

Performing input and output with arrays to and from binary files is much faster, and nearly always more space efficient, than I/O with text files. Binary I/O can be done either with just the raw bytes of numeric data in an array or the raw bytes plus additional metadata storing the array dimensions and data types. Here, we'll cover the four combinations of reading and writing with and without metadata and describe how to manage little/big endian byte conversions.

11.1.10.1 Reading a Raw Array from a Binary File

This can be done by opening a file with read binary mode in MATLAB or with NumPy's `np.fromfile()` function. This example shows how to read a binary file containing 64,800 single-precision floating-point numbers (representing, e.g., sea surface temperature spaced at 1° interval of latitude and longitude), in native byte order.

MATLAB:	Python:

`>> fh = fopen('f64800.bin');`
`>> sst = fread(fh, [360 ...`
`        180], 'single');`
`>> fclose(fh);`
	`In : sst = np.fromfile('f64800.bin',`
	`                dtype=np.float32)`
	`In : sst = sst.reshape(360,180)`

Given the same binary file, Python and MATLAB will load the same 1D array of terms. However, if the terms are loaded into a 2D or higher-dimensional array, the row versus column-major ordering difference between the two languages means terms will be ordered differently. In the preceding example, MATLAB's `sst` would have to be loaded like this to have `sst(i+1,j+1)` in MATLAB equal `sst[i,j]` in Python:

MATLAB:

```
>> fh = fopen('f64800.bin');
>> sst = fread(fh, 360*180, 'single');
>> fclose(fh);
>> sst = reshape(sst,180,360)';
```

11.1.10.2 Writing a Raw Array to a Binary File

Numeric arrays are easily written to binary files. Here, we'll write the sample sea surface temperature file used in the previous example:

MATLAB:	Python:

`>> sst = single(rand(360,180))`
`>> fh = fopen('f64800.bin','w');`
`>> fwrite(fh,sst,'single');`
`>> fclose(fh);`
	`In : sst = np.random.rand(360,`
	`                180).astype(np.float32)`
	`In : sst.tofile('f64800.bin')`

11.1.10.3 Writing Arrays to a Binary File with Metadata

This creates files that are more convenient to use later because the data type and
dimensions are also stored. The disadvantage is such file formats are then harder
for other applications to deal with. MATLAB's save() without arguments writes a
binary file with one or more arrays (or other data structures). The saved file, in .mat
format, includes MATLAB-specific headers and thus has more than a pure numeric
representation of the array's bytes.

NumPy has a pair of analogous functions, np.save() and np.savez(), which save
one or multiple arrays to a file in ".npy" or ".npz" formats. Like .mat files, .npy/.npz
files contain additional metadata on the arrays' shapes and types. Sadly, the names of
the arrays themselves are not captured by default; to add this information to an .npz file,
one must call np.savez() with the unusual notation of "array=name"—in our case, X=X
and Y=Y. If we omit that, the function stores our arrays with the names "arr_0", "arr_1",
and so on.

MATLAB:	Python:
| ```
>> X=reshape([-4:4], 3,3)'
X =


   -4   -3   -2
   -1    0    1
    2    3    4




>> Y = [pi e]
Y =

   3.1416    2.7183


>> save 'XY.mat'  X Y
``` | ```
In : X = np.arange(-4,5).reshape(3,3)
In : X
array([[-4, -3, -2],
       [-1,  0,  1],
       [ 2,  3,  4]])

In : Y = np.array([np.pi, np.e])
In : Y
Out: array([3.14159265, 2.71828183])

In : np.savez('XY.npz', X=X, Y=Y)
``` |

Saving NumPy arrays with np.save() or np.savez() is more efficient and more
portable across Python versions than using the pickle module (Section 7.13).

In Section 11.1.10.4, we'll see that XY.mat and XY.npz can be loaded with MATLAB's
load() and NumPy's np.loadz() functions, respectively.

Before loading the arrays back in, we'll write another pair of binary files, this time saving only bytes of the numeric data. This is useful when writing data for subsequent ingest by code written in other languages—C, C++, Java, Fortran, and so on—that do not understand .mat or .npz formats. A pure binary representation of an array also makes it possible for MATLAB to read arrays written by Python to binary files (although the converse is unnecessary because Python, through the SciPy module, can read .mat files, ref. Section 7.14).

The native binary write in MATLAB requires the write technique shown in Section 7.6. NumPy arrays, though, have a method, .tofile(), just for this purpose. In both cases, we expect the resulting binary file for array X to have 9 terms x 8 bytes per term = 72 bytes.

MATLAB:	Python:
`>> fh = fopen('Xm.bin','wb');`	`In : X.tofile('Xp.bin')`
`>> fwrite(fh, X, 'double');`	
`>> fclose(fh);`	
`>> ls -l X?.bin`	
`-rw-rw-r-- 1 al al 72 Nov 15 15:27 Xm.bin`	
`-rw-rw-r-- 1 al al 72 Nov 15 15:28 Xp.bin`	

While both files are 72 bytes, as we'll see in the next section, their contents are quite different (spoilers: MATLAB's array is written column-wise, and Python's is row-wise; MATLAB's array is of type double, while Python's is 64-bit integers).

11.1.10.4 Reading Arrays from a Binary File

The complementary functions to save and np.save()/np.savez() are, as one might expect, load() and np.load() (which reads both /.npy and /.npz files). Both languages read their respective files with single function calls, but MATLAB conveniently returns them directly into the existing namespace, while Python returns the results in a dictionary which is keyed by the saved name. Had we omitted calling np.savez() with the 'X=X, Y=Y' arguments, the data dictionary would have to be keyed by the default names, that is, data['arr_0'] for X and data['arr_1'] for Y.

MATLAB:	Python:
`>> load XY  % .mat is implied`	`In : data = np.load('XY.npz')`
`>> X`	`In : data['X']`
`X =`	`array([[-4, -3, -2],`
`  -4  -3  -2`	`         [-1,  0,  1],`
`  -1   0   1`	`         [ 2,  3,  4]])`
`   2   3   4`	
	`In : data['Y']`
`>>Y`	`Out: array([3.14159265, 2.71828183])`
`Y =`	
`   3.1416   2.7183`	

Next, we'll look at the raw binary files Xm.bin and Xp.bin we wrote in the previous section. As these contain only bytes of numeric data, they can be read by any programming language capable of reading a binary file and mapping the data to a numeric array. However, the lack of metadata means we need *a priori* knowledge of the number of dimensions, the size along each dimension, and the data type.

As done in Section 7.6, we'll open the files with the generic read function using binary mode and then use the struct module to recast the bytes into our numeric data types. We'll also need to know that

- The Python-written file Xp.bin contains 64-bit (8-byte) signed integers (the default data type from np.arange() when start, end, and increments are integers).

- The MATLAB-written file Xm.bin contains 64-bit (8-byte) floats (the MATLAB default for all numbers).

- The struct format characters for 64-bit signed integers and 64-bit floats are "q" and "d", respectively (Table 7-1).

- Both files contain 2D arrays of size 3 × 3.

We'll read each file in Python and MATLAB:

Python:

```
In : import struct

#    Python-written file
In : with open('Xp.bin', 'rb') as fh:
...:     raw = fh.read() # load entire contents into raw
...:     n_terms  = len(raw) // 8 # integer division
...:     Ints = struct.unpack(f'{n_terms}q', raw)
In : Ints
Out: (-4, -3, -2, -1, 0, 1, 2, 3, 4)

In : X = np.array(Ints).reshape(3,3)
In : X
array([[-4, -3, -2],
       [-1,  0,  1],
       [ 2,  3,  4]])

#    MATLAB-written file
In : with open('Xm.bin', 'rb') as fh:
...:     raw = fh.read()
...:     n_terms  = len(raw) // 8
...:     Flts = struct.unpack(f'{n_terms}d', raw)
In : X = np.array(Flts).reshape(3,3)
array([[-4., -1.,  2.],
       [-3.,  0.,  3.],
       [-2.,  1.,  4.]])
```

There's our first surprise—Python loaded a transpose of the MATLAB data. This happens because MATLAB's arrays are stored internally in column-major order, while NumPy arrays, by default, are stored row-major.

The MATLAB code to read the files is shown as follows. The second surprise appears if we forget the Python values are integers rather than doubles:

MATLAB:

```
>> fh = fopen('Xm.bin', 'rb');
>> X = fread(fh, 'double');
>> fclose(fh);
>> reshape(X, 3,3)
     -4    -3    -2
     -1     0     1
      2     3     4

>> fh = fopen('Xp.bin', 'rb');
>> X = fread(fh, 'double');
>> fclose(fh);
>> reshape(X, 3,3)
   9.9e-323 *
        NaN       NaN    0.1000
        NaN         0    0.1500
        NaN    0.0500    0.2000

>> fh = fopen('Xp.bin', 'rb');
>> X = fread(fh, 'int64');
>> fclose(fh);
>> reshape(X, 3,3)
     -4    -1     2
     -3     0     3
     -2     1     4
```

11.1.10.5 Endian Conversions

Little-to-big and big-to-little endian conversions are sometimes necessary when transferring numeric data between computers with different architectures. NumPy allows easy determination and manipulation of word endian format. MATLAB allows one to change an array's endian order but not determine what its current order is.

NumPy arrays have an attribute, .dtype, which stores the data type such as np.float16 or np.complex256. The data type itself is a NumPy object with the interesting property that endianness can be determined from the .str representation of the data type—if it starts with >, it is big-endian; with < it is little-endian:

Python:

```
In : a = np.array([1234, 5678], dtype=np.int32)
In : a.dtype
Out: dtype('int32')

In : a.dtype.str
Out: '<i4'
```

Endian conversion on I/O can be done directly in NumPy simply by providing np.tofile() or np.fromfile() the explicit dtype to read or write. Revisiting the sea surface temperature example of Section 11.1.10.2, this time explicitly writing and reading a big-endian file looks like this:

Python:

```
In : sst = np.random.rand(360, 180).astype(np.float32)
In : sst.tofile('f64800.bin', dtype='>f4')
In : sst_copy = np.fromfile('f64800.bin', dtype='>f4')
```

MATLAB variables do not have metadata indicating their endianness. However, one can change the endianness with swapbytes(). NumPy's .byteswap() method does the same thing:

MATLAB:	Python:

>> a = int32([1234 5678]);
>> b = swapbytes(a)
  1×2 int32 row vector
   -771489792   773193728
 	
>> dec2hex(a)
  2×4 char array
    '04D2'
    '162E'
 	
>> dec2hex(b)
  2×8 char array
    'D2040000'
    '2E160000'
	In : a = np.array([1234, 5678],
	                    dtype=np.int32)
	In : b = a.byteswap()
	In : b
	Out: array([-771489792, 773193728],
	                    dtype=int32)
	
	In : hex(a[0]),hex(a[1])
	Out: ('0x4d2', '0x162e')
	
	In : hex(b[0]), hex(b[1])
	Out: ('-0x2dfc0000', '0x2e160000')

Python's hex() function treats signed numbers differently than MATLAB's dec2hex(), but we can at least tell from the integer representations that the same operation is being performed.

11.1.11 Primitive Array Operations

11.1.11.1 Addition, Subtraction

Array addition and subtraction work identically in MATLAB and NumPy: if the array dimensions match, the terms are added or subtracted term-wise. If the array dimensions differ, an attempt is made to *broadcast* or perform an outer-loop add or subtract by expanding the array sizes until they match (broadcasting is explained in more detail in Section 11.1.13):

MATLAB:	Python:
>> a = [2, -3]	In : a = np.array([[2,-3]])
a =	In : a
2 -3	Out: array([[2, -3]])
>> b = [7; 8; 9]	In : b = np.array([[7],[8],[9]])
b =	In : b
7	array([[7],
8	[8],
9	[9]])
>> a+b	In : a+b
9 4	array([[9, 4],
10 5	[10, 5],
11 6	[11, 6]])

11.1.11.2 Elementwise Operations

NumPy's array operations default to working elementwise. In other words, multiplication, division, and exponentiation with *, /, and ** yield elementwise results. The MATLAB equivalents have a **.** preceding elementwise operations (.*, ./, and .^).

MATLAB:	Python:
`>> a = [2  7;  3 8;  4 9];`	`In : a = np.array([[2,7],[3,8],[4,9]])`
`>> b = [5 -6; -1 2; -3 4];`	`In : a**2`
`>> a.^2`	`array([[ 4, 49],`
4 49	`[ 9, 64],`
9 64	`[16, 81]])`
16 81	
	`In : a*b`
`>> a.*b`	`array([[ 10, -42],`
10 -42	`[ -3,  16],`
-3 16	`[-12,  36]])`
-12 36	

11.1.11.3 Bitwise Operations

Operations that work on individual bits typically make sense only with unsigned integers—$np.uint n$ and $uint n$ in NumPy and MATLAB, for $n = 8, 16, 32,$ or 64. Table 11-2 shows the MATLAB and Python bit operations.

Table 11-2. *Bit operations*

Operation	MATLAB	Python
Left shift bits of x y times	`bitshift(x,y)`	`x << y`
Right shift bits of x y times	`bitshift(x,-y)`	`x >> y`
x AND y	`bitand(x,y)`	`x & y`
x OR y	`bitor(x,y)`	`x	y`
x XOR y	`bitxor(x,y)`	`x ^ y`
Flip bits of x	`bitcmp(x)`	`~ x`

11.1.11.4 Transpose and Hermitian Operations

Array transposition differs slightly between MATLAB and NumPy. In MATLAB, the apostrophe after a matrix returns the transpose if the matrix is real and the complex conjugate transpose, or Hermitian, if the matrix is complex. In Python, the .T method returns the (purely structural) transpose for both real and complex arrays. To obtain the Hermitian, one must first invoke the .conj() method to obtain the complex conjugate, then .T:

MATLAB:	Python:

```>> a = [1 2; 3 4]```
```>> a = [1 2 ; 3 4]```
```a =```
```   1   2```
```   3   4```
 	
```>> a'```
```   1   3```
```   2   4```
 	
```>> a = a + j*eye(2)```
```a =```
```   1 + 1i   2 + 0i```
```   3 + 0i   4 + 1i```
 	
```>> a'```
```   1 - 1i   3 - 0i```
```   2 - 0i   4 - 1i```
	```In : a = np.array([[1,2],[3,4]])```
	```In : a```
	```array([[1, 2],```
	``` [3, 4]])```
	
	```In : a.T```
	```array([[1, 3],```
	``` [2, 4]])```
	
	```In : a = a + 1j*np.eye(2)```
	```In : a```
	```array([[1.+1.j, 2.+0.j],```
	``` [3.+0.j, 4.+1.j]])```
	
	```In : a.T```
	```array([[1.+1.j, 3.+0.j],```
	``` [2.+0.j, 4.+1.j]])```
	
	```In : a.conj().T```
	```array([[1.-1.j, 3.-0.j],```
	``` [2.-0.j, 4.-1.j]])```

11.1.11.5 Array Multiplication

Array multiplication is done with the * operator in MATLAB and the less intuitive @ operator in Python. Alternatively, one can use np.dot() to perform the matrix multiplication:

MATLAB:	Python:

`>> a = [2 7; 3 8; 4 9]`
`a =`
`   2   7`
`   3   8`
`   4   9`
	`In : a = np.array([[2,7],[3,8],[4,9]])`
	`In : a`
	`array([[2, 7],`
	`       [3, 8],`
	`       [4, 9]])`

`>> b = [ 1 5]`
`b =`
`   1   5`
	`In : b = np.array([1,5])`
	`In : b`
	`Out: array([1, 5])`

`>> a*b`
`   37`
`   43`
`   49`
	`In : a@b`
	`Out: array([37, 43, 49])`
	
	`In : np.dot(a,b)`
	`Out: array([37, 43, 49])`

MATLAB views all numeric values, whether they are scalars, one-dimensional vectors, or multidimensional matrices, as having at least two dimensions; MATLAB considers the preceding vector as having three rows and one column. In NumPy, one-dimensional arrays have just one dimension; concepts of "row" and "column" do not apply.

Warning   The * operator in Python performs an elementwise array product, like .* in MATLAB. This can be a source of bugs when translating MATLAB expressions to Python.

11.1.12 Adding Dimensions

MATLAB's "all variables have at least two dimensions" property is useful when the distinction between a row and column vector is important. As a simple example, consider the vector products $v^T v$ and $v v^T$. The first produces a scalar, while the second gives a square matrix with v's dimension. MATLAB can express these products as v'*v and v*v'.

In contrast, a one-dimensional NumPy array has no knowledge of row or column orientation; v.T@v and v@v.T (or v.T.dot(v) and v.dot(v.T)) both return $v^T v$. We need an extra dimension to compute the outer product.

A one-dimensional NumPy array can get a second (or higher) dimension using one of three ways:

- By explicitly reshaping it

```
In : v = np.array([1, 2, 3])
In : v.reshape(1,3)         # row
Out: array([[1, 2, 3]])

In : v.reshape(3,1)         # column
array([[1],
       [2],
       [3]])
```

- By passing it to np.atleast 2d()[4]

```
In : v = np.array([1, 2, 3])
In : np.atleast_2d(v)       # row
Out: array([[1, 2, 3]])

In : np.atleast_2d(v).T  # column
array([[1],
       [2],
       [3]])
```

- By indexing it with np.newaxis or None as an additional subscript

```
In : v = np.array([1, 2, 3])
In : v[np.newaxis,:]        # row
Out: array([[1, 2, 3]])

In : v[:,None]              # column
array([[1],
       [2],
       [3]])
```

---

[4] There also exist companion routines np.atleast_1d() and np.atleast_3d().

The last method using `np.newaxis` as a new index appears frequently when broadcasting arrays, a topic covered in the next section. As its name implies, `np.newaxis` brings into existence a new dimension with size 1 at the designated location. Indexing the one-dimensional array v in the preceding example as `v[np.newaxis, :, np.newaxis]` yields a 3D array with dimensions $1 \times 3 \times 1$ array.

11.1.13 Array Broadcasting

Broadcasting in both MATLAB and Python refers to implicitly extending array dimensions by copying existing rows or columns (or submatrices) to satisfy rules for numeric operations. Specifically, an array can be broadcast to the needed shape if its trailing dimensions are one or match the trailing dimensions of the other arrays in the computation; the nonmatching dimensions are simply copied to inflate the array to the correct size. `np.newaxis` often plays a useful role as the last dimension since its size is 1 and therefore pairs with the last dimension of other arrays.

Broadcasting is best explained with examples. In the following, the vectors (11, 12) and (4, 5, 6) are added by broadcasting two different ways, first by inflating them to 2 x 3 matrices:

$$\begin{bmatrix} 11 & 11 & 11 \\ 12 & 12 & 12 \end{bmatrix} + \begin{bmatrix} 4 & 5 & 6 \\ 4 & 5 & 6 \end{bmatrix}$$

then by going to 3×2 matrices:

$$\begin{bmatrix} 11 & 12 \\ 11 & 12 \\ 11 & 12 \end{bmatrix} + \begin{bmatrix} 4 & 4 \\ 5 & 5 \\ 6 & 6 \end{bmatrix}$$

sum the unequally-sized arrays (11, 12) and (4, 5, 6) directly, then the successful. The following code shows the errors MATLAB and NumPy give when attempting to sum when the arrays are altered to satisfy broadcasting rules:

MATLAB:	Python:
`>> a = [11 12];`	`In : a = np.array([11,12])`
`>> b = [4 5 6];`	`In : b = np.array([4, 5, 6])`
`>> a + b`	`In : a + b`
`error: operator +: noncon-`	`ValueError: operands could`
`formant arguments (op1 is`	`not be broadcast together`
`1x2, op2 is 1x3)`	`with shapes (2,) (3,)`
`>> a' + b`	`In : a[:,np.newaxis] + b`
` 15   16   17`	`array([[15, 16, 17],`
` 16   17   18`	`        [16, 17, 18]])`
`>> a + b'`	`In : a + b[:,np.newaxis]`
` 15   16`	`array([[15, 16],`
` 16   17`	`        [16, 17],`
` 17   18`	`        [17, 18]])`

11.1.13.1 Broadcasting Requires More Memory

Broadcasting—in MATLAB as in Python—is generally computationally efficient as it eliminates the need to write explicit loops. However, as more dimensions are copied, broadcasting can become a substantial memory and CPU sink. Say you have 1000 frames captured by a 4k camera where each frame has 4096 x 2160 pixels of uint32 values, and you need to multiply each frame's pixels by a filter matrix. If you were to use broadcasting, a temporary array containing 1000 copies of the filter would be made first before the multiplication takes place.

Writing a loop to iterate over each frame may be slower but could save you from an out-of-memory error.

11.1.13.2 Broadcasting Example 1: Normalize Vectors

In this example, we have five 3D vectors stored in a 5 x 3 array. We want to divide each vector by its magnitude to make them all unit vectors. The computation could be done by writing a loop to iterate over each vector, but broadcasting lets us skip the loop and implement a more efficient solution. We'll start by computing the magnitude of the vectors:

MATLAB:	Python:

```>> V = [-7.72 -2.84 -7.55; ...```
```   0.79   4.42   6.10; ...```
```   -9.99   4.24   9.29; ...```
```   5.84   7.65   0.20; ...```
```   -6.85   3.73   7.56];```
```>> mag = vecnorm(V');```
	```In : V = np.array(```
	``` [[-7.72, -2.84, -7.55],```
	``` [0.79, 4.42, 6.10],```
	``` [-9.99, 4.24, 9.29],```
	``` [5.84, 7.65, 0.20],```
	``` [-6.85, 3.73, 7.56]])```
	```In : mag = np.linalg.norm(V,axis=1)```

MATLAB conveniently figures out the correct broadcast expansion, but NumPy must be told which dimension to add; simply doing V/mag raises an error saying "operands could not be broadcast together with shapes (5,3) (5,)."

MATLAB:	Python:

```>> V = V./mag';```
```>> V```
```   -0.6914   -0.2544   -0.6762```
```   0.1043   0.5835   0.8054```
```   -0.6993   0.2968   0.6503```
```   0.6067   0.7947   0.0208```
```   -0.6306   0.3434   0.6960```
	```In : V = V/mag[:,np.newaxis]```
	```In : V```
	```array([[-0.6914, -0.2544, -0.6762],```
	``` [0.1043, 0.5835, 0.8053],```
	``` [-0.6993, 0.2968, 0.6504],```
	``` [0.6067, 0.7947, 0.0208],```
	``` [-0.6306, 0.3434, 0.6960]])```

11.1.13.3 Broadcasting Example 2: The Distance Matrix

Section 11.12.2 shows how the Traveling Salesman Problem can be solved with the stochastic optimization technique of simulated annealing. The TSP cost function is the sum of distances between adjacent cities in the route. The cities' locations remain constant, so we can speed up the inner loops of the TSP solvers by precomputing all city-to-city distances up front.

Let's say our city locations can be described on a 2D grid using Cartesian coordinates (x, y). Table 11-3 shows locations of four cities that will be used in the following examples.

Table 11-3. *City locations on a Cartesian grid*

	city$_0$	city$_1$	city$_2$	city$_3$
x	56.2	27.7	96.1	51.7
y	9.7	71.0	51.9	65.1

We want to compute the 4 × 4 matrix of distances for all city pairs *i* and *j*:

$D_{ij} = \sqrt{\left(x_i - x_j\right)^2 + \left(y_i - y_j\right)^2}$. The matrix D_{ij} is symmetric and will have zeros on the diagonal. We'll begin by computing the 4 × 4 matrix of *x* coordinate differences, $x_i - x_j$, with broadcasting:

MATLAB:

```
>> x = [56.2 27.7 96.1 51.7]
x =
 56.200 27.700 96.100 51.700

>> x'
 56.200
 27.700
 96.100
 51.700

>> x' - x
   0.00  28.50 -39.90   4.50
 -28.50   0.00 -68.40 -24.00
  39.90  68.40   0.00  44.40
  -4.50  24.00 -44.40   0.00
```

Python:

```
In : x = np.array([56.2,27.7,96.1,51.7])
Out: x
array([56.2, 27.7, 96.1, 51.7])

In : x[:,np.newaxis]
array([[56.2],
       [27.7],
       [96.1],
       [51.7]])

In : x[:,np.newaxis] - x
array([[  0. ,  28.5, -39.9,   4.5],
       [-28.5,   0. , -68.4, -24. ],
       [ 39.9,  68.4,   0. ,  44.4],
       [ -4.5,  24. , -44.4,   0. ]])
```

Squaring the terms to get $(x_i - x_j)^2$ is straightforward:

MATLAB:	Python:
>> (x' - x).^2	In : (x[:,np.newaxis] - x)**2
0.00 812.25 1592.01 20.25	array([[0. , 812.25, 1592.01, 20.25],
812.25 0.00 4678.56 576.00	[812.25, 0. , 4678.56, 576.],
1592.01 4678.56 0.00 1971.36	[1592.01, 4678.56, 0. , 1971.36],
20.25 576.00 1971.36 0.00	[20.25, 576. , 1971.36, 0.]])

Applying broadcasting to the *y* differences as well lets us compute the distance matrix with a single line of code:

MATLAB:	Python:
>> y = [9.7 71.0 51.9 65.1];	In : y = np.array([9.7,71.0,51.9,65.1])
>> D = sqrt((x'-x).^2 + (y'-y).^2)	In : D = np.sqrt((x[:,np.newaxis]-x)**2 +
D =	...: (y[:,np.newaxis]-y)**2)
	[[0. , 67.6013, 58.0762, 55.5824],
0.0000 67.6013 58.0762 55.5824	[67.6013, 0. , 71.0166, 24.7145],
67.6013 0.0000 71.0166 24.7145	[58.0762, 71.0166, 0. , 46.3206],
58.0762 71.0166 0.0000 46.3206	[55.5824, 24.7145, 46.3206, 0.]])
55.5824 24.7145 46.3206 0.0000	

11.1.14 Index Masks

MATLAB and Python allow one to identify and operate on array terms according to the value of an index mask. In addition to working as filters, index masks help one write vectorizable code and therefore are powerful tools for achieving high performance.

The following example shows mathematical operations are only performed at indices where the mask is non-zero or logical true (MATLAB) or True (Python).

MATLAB:	Python:

``matlab
>> a = reshape(0:8, 3,3)'
a =
 	
    0   1   2
    3   4   5
    6   7   8
>> mask=false(3,3);
>> mask(2:end,2:end) = true;
>> mask
  3×3 logical array
  0 0 0
  0 1 1
  0 1 1
 	
>> a(mask)'
  4   7   5   8
 	
>> a(mask) = -a(mask)
    0   1   2
    3   -4   -5
    6   -7   -8
``
	``python
	In : a = np.arange(9).reshape(3,3)
	In : a
	array([[0, 1, 2],
	       [3, 4, 5],
	       [6, 7, 8]])
	
	In : mask = np.zeros((3,3), dtype=np.bool)
	In : mask[1:,1:] = True
	In : mask
	array([[False, False, False],
	       [False, True, True],
	       [False, True, True]])
	In : a[mask]
	Out: array([4, 5, 7, 8])
	
	In : a[mask] *= -1
	In : a
	array([[0, 1, 2],
	       [3, -4, -5],
	       [6, -7, -8]])
	``

11.1.14.1 Creating Index Masks

Index masks can be created by applying Boolean expressions to arrays. The primary distinction between MATLAB and Python in this regard is how AND and OR operators are implemented. MATLAB uses & and | while NumPy uses * and +:

MATLAB:	Python:
>> a = -2:2	In : a = np.arange(-2,3)
a =	In : a
-2 -1 0 1 2	Out: array([-2, -1, 0, 1, 2])
>> -1 < a	In : -1 < a
0 0 1 1 1	Out: array([False, False, True, True, True])
>> a < 2	In : a < 2
1 1 1 1 0	Out: array([True, True, True, True, False])
>> (-1 < a) & (a < 2)	In : (-1 < a) * (a < 2)
0 0 1 1 0	Out: array([False, False, True, True, False])
>> abs(a) > 1	In : np.abs(a) > 1
1 0 0 0 1	Out: array([True, False, False, False, True])
>> (-1 < a) | (abs(a) > 1)	In : (-1 < a) + (np.abs(a) > 1)
1 0 1 1 1	Out: array([True, False, True, True, True])

11.1.14.2 Using Index Masks

Once we have an index mask, we can perform operations on terms of similarly sized arrays wherever the mask has a value of True (Python) or 1 (MATLAB). As an example, consider an array of longitudes with values ranging from –180 to +180 degrees that needs to be passed to a function expecting longitudes between 0 to 360 degrees. Longitudes are cyclic in that a longitude of λ is identical to λ+ 360 degrees, or $\lambda + 2\pi$ radians. To satisfy the function's desired input range we merely need to degrees that needs to be passed to a function expecting longitudes between 0 and 360 add 360 degrees to any negative longitude, a task well suited to index arrays:

MATLAB:	Python:
>> Lon = [40 -40 60 -120]; >> mask = Lon < 0; >> Lon(mask)=Lon(mask)+360 Lon = 40 320 60 240	In : Lon = np.array([40, -40, 60, -120]) In : mask = Lon < 0 In : Lon[mask] += 360 In : Lon Out: array([40, 320, 60, 240])

The mask variable itself need not be explicitly saved; the Boolean expression defining the mask can be used as the array subscript directly:

MATLAB:	Python:
>> Lon = [40 -40 60 -120]; >> Lon(Lon<0)=Lon(Lon<0)+360 Lon = 40 320 60 240	In : Lon = np.array([40, -40, 60, -120]) In : Lon[Lon < 0] += 360 In : Lon Out: array([40, 320, 60, 240])

11.1.15 Extracting and Updating Submatrices

Submatrices of an array can be accessed and updated easily within MATLAB and Python using either row and column slices or index matrices. Here, we make a 6×4 matrix, extract the lower-right 2×3 terms, then subtract 20 from the lower-right 3×4 terms:

MATLAB:	Python:
`>> a = reshape([1:24], 4,6)'`	`In : a = np.arange(1,25).reshape(6,4)`
`a =`	`In : a`
	`array([[ 1,  2,  3,  4],`
`    1    2    3    4`	`       [ 5,  6,  7,  8],`
`    5    6    7    8`	`       [ 9, 10, 11, 12],`
`    9   10   11   12`	`       [13, 14, 15, 16],`
`   13   14   15   16`	`       [17, 18, 19, 20],`
`   17   18   19   20`	`       [21, 22, 23, 24]])`
`   21   22   23   24`	
`>> a(4:5,2:4)`	`In : a[3:5,1:4]`
`   14   15   16`	`array([[14, 15, 16],`
`   18   19   20`	`       [18, 19, 20]])`
`>> a(4:5,2:4)=a(4:5,2:4)-20`	
`a =`	`In : a[3:5,1:4] -= 20`
	`In : a`
`    1    2    3    4`	`array([[ 1,  2,  3,  4],`
`    5    6    7    8`	`       [ 5,  6,  7,  8],`
`    9   10   11   12`	`       [ 9, 10, 11, 12],`
`   13   -6   -5   -4`	`       [13, -6, -5, -4],`
`   17   -2   -1    0`	`       [17, -2, -1,  0],`
`   21   22   23   24`	`       [21, 22, 23, 24]])`

MATLAB can just as easily use arbitrary index arrays instead of index slices to define our submatrix. NumPy makes this harder than it should be, though, because it permits only one dimension to be indexed by an array at a time. Say we wish to extract the 3×2 submatrix made from the third, fifth, and sixth rows and the second and fourth columns:

1	2	3	4
5	6	7	8
9	10	11	12
13	14	15	16
17	18	19	20
21	22	23	24

MATLAB conveniently lets us define our submatrix with a(I,J), where I and J are arrays of our rows and columns. NumPy (as of v1.20.2) disappoints here though as a[I,J] raises an IndexError. To achieve the same extraction as MATLAB, the special accessor function np.ix_() is needed:

MATLAB:	Python:

`>> a = reshape([1:24], 4,6)'`
`a =`
`    1    2    3    4`
`    5    6    7    8`
`    9   10   11   12`
`   13   14   15   16`
`   17   18   19   20`
`   21   22   23   24`
	`In : a = np.arange(1,25).reshape(6,4)`
	`In : a`
	`array([[ 1,  2,  3,  4],`
	`       [ 5,  6,  7,  8],`
	`       [ 9, 10, 11, 12],`
	`       [13, 14, 15, 16],`
	`       [17, 18, 19, 20],`
	`       [21, 22, 23, 24]])`

`>> I = [3 5 6];`
`>> J = [2  4];`
`>> a(I,J)`
`   10   12`
`   18   20`
`   22   24`
	`In : I = [2, 4, 5]`
	`In : J = [1, 3]`
	`In : a[np.ix_(I,J)]`
	`array([[10, 12],`
	`       [18, 20],`
	`       [22, 24]])`

Alternatively, we can use index chaining (Section 3.4.5) with a pair of single-dimension index arrays:

Python:

```
In : a[I,J]
Traceback (most recent call last):
    a[I,J]
IndexError: shape mismatch: indexing arrays could not be broadcast
together with shapes (3,) (2,)

In : a[I,:]
Out:
array([[ 9, 10, 11, 12],
       [17, 18, 19, 20],
       [21, 22, 23, 24]])
```

```
In : a[:,J]
Out:
array([[ 2,  4],
       [ 6,  8],
       [10, 12],
       [14, 16],
       [18, 20],
       [22, 24]])

In : a[I][:,J]
Out:
array([[10, 12],
       [18, 20],
       [22, 24]])
```

The notation a[I][:,J] is unintuitive though and is not encouraged.

11.1.16 Finding Terms of Interest

Both NumPy and MATLAB have functions useful for locating terms within an array that satisfy desired properties. The following sections will use the following 2D arrays to demonstrate searching for terms in an array with and without NaNs. (NaNs are used in fields such as the atmospheric sciences to represent unknown values, e.g., a satellite image of terrain may use NaNs to represent ground pixels hidden by clouds.)

In each example, we seek both the values satisfying the properties and indices of those values.

MATLAB:	Python:

`>> X = [0.22, -.47; ...`
`    0.97, -.31; ...`
`    0.32, 0.05];`
	`In : X = np.array(`
	`        [[0.22, -.47,],`
	`         [0.97, -.31,],`
	`         [0.32, 0.05,]])`

`>> Z = [0.22, -.47; ...`
`    0.97, -.31; ...`
`    nan , 0.05];`
	`In : Z = np.array(`
	`        [[0.22 , -.47,],`
	`         [0.97 , -.31,],`
	`         [np.NaN, 0.05,]])`

11.1.16.1 Find the Smallest Term

MATLAB's and NumPy's min() and max() functions work similarly except when handling NaNs—in NumPy one must explicitly call a NaN-aware function if one anticipates working with arrays containing NaNs. This example uses X and Z from the previous section:

MATLAB:	Python:
`>> min(X,[],'all')`	`In : np.min(X)`
` -0.47000`	`Out: -0.47`
`>> min(Z,[],'all')`	`In : np.min(Z)`
` -0.47000`	`Out: nan`
	`In : np.nanmin(Z)`
	`Out: -0.47`

Python is also a bit awkward in that the index of the minimum value returned by np.argmin() is a *linear* index, which, unlike MATLAB, requires the use of the .take() method for arrays having two or more dimensions. Alternatively, the linear index and the array's dimensions can be passed to np.unravel_index() to give the row and column (and higher dimensions as needed) indices corresponding to the linear index.

MATLAB:	Python:
`>> [Rval, Rind] = min(X)`	`In : lin_i = np.argmin(X)`
`Rval =`	`In : lin_i`
`   0.22000   -0.47000`	`Out: 1`
`Rind =`	
`   1   1`	`In : X.take(lin_i)`
	`Out: -0.47`
`>> [Cval, Cind] = min(Rval)`	
`Cval = -0.47000`	`In : R, C = np.unravel_index(lin_i, X.shape)`
`Cind =   2`	`In : R, C`
	`Out: (0, 1)`
`>> R = Rind(Cind); C = Cind;`	
`>> R, C`	`In : X[R,C]`
`R =   1`	`Out: -0.47`
`C =   2`	
`>> X(R,C)`	
` -0.47000`	

The identical process works in MATLAB for the NaN-containing Z array. In Python, however, one must call `np.nanargmin(Z)` to arrive at –0.47. Calling `np.argmin(Z)` leads to the linear index of 4, corresponding to the NaN term, instead of 1.

One aspect of finding minimum values that MATLAB and Python share is that if the matrix has multiple copies of the minimum value, both languages return the location of the first occurrence.

11.1.16.2 Find the Largest Term

Unsurprisingly, the process for finding indices of the largest term is identical to finding the smallest term except all function calls have `max` switched for `min`:

MATLAB:	Python:
`>> [Rval, Rind] = max(X);`	`In : lin_i = np.argmax(X)`
`>> [Cval, Cind] = max(Rval);`	`In : X.take(lin_i)`
`>> R = Rind(Cind); C = Cind;`	`Out: 0.97`
`>> R, C`	
`R =  2`	`In : R, C = np.unravel_index(lin_i, X.shape)`
`C =  1`	`In : R, C`
	`Out: (1, 0)`
`>> X(R,C)`	
`ns =  0.97000`	`In : X[R,C]`
	`Out: 0.97`

The call to `argmax()` in Python can also be written as a method call on the X array; `lin_i = X.argmax()` is equivalent to `lin_i = np.argmax(X)`.

11.1.16.3 Find Term Nearest a Given Value

The location of the term closest to a given value can be found by getting the location of the smallest delta between all terms of the array and the desired value. Here, we find the indices of the term closest to –0.5:

MATLAB:	Python:
`>> delta = abs(X - (-0.5));`	`In : delta = np.abs(X - (-0.5))`
`>> [Rval, Rind] = min(delta);`	`In : lin_i = delta.argmin()`
`>> [Cval, Cind] = min(Rval);`	`In : R, C = np.unravel_index(lin_i, X.shape)`
`>> R = Rind(Cind); C = Cind;`	`In : R, C`
`>> R, C`	`Out: (0, 1)`
`R =  1`	
`C =  2`	`In : X[R, C]`
`>> X(R,C)`	`Out: -0.47`
` -0.47000`	

Once again, in Python the equivalent search over terms of the NaN-containing Z array requires `nanargmin()` instead of `argmin()`. The MATLAB code shown earlier works with both X and Z.

11.1.16.4 Find Term Nearest a Given Value in a Sorted 1D Array

A special case of finding the term closest to a given value is when the array to be searched is one-dimensional and already sorted. The sorted data permits bisection searches to locate the desired terms rapidly. A typical use case is working with data accumulated chronologically; subsequent analyses often need to know what data was recorded nearest to a given time T.

MATLAB has an undocumented (and not guaranteed to exist in future versions) bisection search capability oddly invoked as `builtin('_ismemberhelper',A,S)`.[5] However, it only works for exact, not nearest, matches. In this case, we're no better off than the $O(N)$ `min()` method of Section 11.1.16.3.

Python's solution is the `.searchsorted()` method available to all NumPy arrays. It does an $O(log_2(N))$ binary search for the locations where the sought elements should be inserted to maintain the sort order.

MATLAB:	Python:
`X = 1000:1700;`	`In : A = np.arange(1000.0, 1701.0)`
`for t = [1234.4, 1245.6]`	`In : t = [1234.5, 1245.6]`
`  delta = abs(X - t);`	`In : ind = A.searchsorted(t)`
`  [val, ind] = min(delta);`	`In : ind`
`  fprintf('%.2f\n', X(ind))`	`Out: array([235, 246])`
`end`	
`1234.00`	`In : A[ind]`
`1246.00`	`Out: array([1235., 1246.])`

11.1.16.5 Find Indices of Terms Satisfying a Condition

The locations of terms satisfying a condition can be found with NumPy's `argwhere()` function which returns an array of indices for those matching terms. MATLAB's `find()` function does the same thing, but it returns linear indexes into the array instead of index sets (e.g., (i,j) pairs for 2D arrays) as Python does.

This example shows how to get indices of terms whose magnitude is less than 0.3:

---

[5] https://www.mathworks.com/matlabcentral/answers/92533-how-do-i-perform-a-binary-search-of-a-presorted-array

MATLAB:	Python:

`>> ind = find(abs(X) < .3)`
 	
   1
   6
	`In : ind = np.argwhere(np.abs(X)<.3)`
	`In : ind`
	`array([[0, 0],`
	`        [2, 1]])`

The returned value from MATLAB's `find()` can directly subscript the array, but the same is not true from Python's `np.argwhere()`. There, one must call the `tuple()` function on each index pair first:

MATLAB:	Python:

`>> X(ind)`
 	
  0.220000
  0.050000
	`In : X[ind]`
	`array([[[ 0.22, -0.47],    # not`
	`        [ 0.22, -0.47]],   # what`
	`       [[ 0.32,  0.05],    # we`
	`        [ 0.97, -0.31]]])  # wanted!`
	
	`In : X[tuple(ind[0])]`
	`Out: 0.22`
	
	`In : X[tuple(ind[1])]`
	`Out: 0.05`

Section 11.1.14.1 shows more complex array conditions that include numeric AND and OR operators.

11.1.17 Object-Oriented Programming and Computational Performance

Section 10.2 in the previous chapter mentioned object-oriented programming can have a negative impact on computational performance. To demonstrate this, we'll create simulations of balls bouncing within a rectangular enclosure. One sim will use conventional procedure–based coding with all data stored in arrays, while the other uses object-oriented techniques. The simulation has two computationally intensive parts:

determining collisions between the balls and updating velocity vectors for colliding ball pairs. Here, we'll just implement the collision detection portion of the simulation.

If we store the ball's coordinates and radii in conventional arrays, we can take full advantage of vectorization and easily compute collisions between a thousand balls at a rate of 60 Hz with both MATLAB and Python. Both languages take full advantage of broadcasting to compute the collision matrix, an $N \times N$ symmetric Boolean matrix which has 1 (MATLAB) or True (Python) at indices (i, j) and (i, j) if balls i and j are in contact for a simulation with N balls.

MATLAB:

```matlab
% file: code/00/collision_matrix.m
function coll = collision_matrix(x,y,R)
  dx = x - x';
  dy = y - y';
  sep = sqrt( dx.^2 + dy.^2 );
  sum_r = R + R';
  coll = sep < sum_r;
end
```

```matlab
% file: code/00/run_sim.m
function res = run_sim(N, n_iter)
  fprintf('n balls=%d\n', N)
  for i = 1:n_iter
    box_x = 10.;
    box_y = 6.;
    r_min = 0.1;
    r_max = 0.3;
    x = r_max + (box_x-2*r_max)*rand(N,1);
    y = r_max + (box_y-2*r_max)*rand(N,1);
    R = 0.1 + 0.8*rand(N,1);
    tic
    coll = collision_matrix(x, y, R);
    n_coll = (sum(sum(coll)) - N)/2;
    fprintf('n coll=%d Hz = %.2f\n', n_coll, 1/toc)
  end
end
```

Python:

```python
#!/usr/bin/env python3
# file: code/00/collision_matrix.py
import numpy as np
from numpy.random import rand
import time

def collision_matrix(x, y, R):
    """
    Use broadcasting to return a square matrix of Boolean
    values with True at position [i,j] and [j,i] if
    circles i and j intersect.
    """
    dx = x[:,np.newaxis] - x[np.newaxis,:]
    dy = y[:,np.newaxis] - y[np.newaxis,:]
    sep = np.sqrt( dx**2 + dy**2 )
    sum_r = R[:,np.newaxis] + R[np.newaxis,:]
    return sep < sum_r

def run_sim(N, n_iter):
    box_x, box_y = 10., 6.
    r_min, r_max = 0.1, 0.3
    print(f'n balls={N}')
    for i in range(n_iter):
        x = r_max + (box_x-2*r_max)*rand(N)
        y = r_max + (box_y-2*r_max)*rand(N)
        R = 0.1 + 0.8*rand(N)
        T_s = time.time()
        coll = collision_matrix(x, y, R)
        n_coll = (np.sum(coll) - N)//2
        print(f'n coll={n_coll} Hz = '
              f'{1/(time.time()-T_s):.2f}')
```

MATLAB and Python perform equally well:

MATLAB:	Python:
>> run_sim(1000, 10)	In : run_sim(1000, 10)
n balls=1000	n balls=1000
n coll=29965 Hz = 59.29	n coll=28836 Hz = 32.22
n coll=28679 Hz = 47.92	n coll=28728 Hz = 43.19
n coll=29406 Hz = 45.44	n coll=29613 Hz = 45.33
n coll=30536 Hz = 62.94	n coll=28559 Hz = 65.21
n coll=28888 Hz = 62.21	n coll=30694 Hz = 56.81
n coll=29597 Hz = 62.99	n coll=29023 Hz = 64.17
n coll=29443 Hz = 62.64	n coll=29755 Hz = 58.66
n coll=29441 Hz = 63.83	n coll=28404 Hz = 64.25
n coll=30324 Hz = 65.24	n coll=29196 Hz = 60.42
n coll=29286 Hz = 63.38	n coll=29824 Hz = 64.44

We'll repeat the simulation, this time defining each ball as a Ball object (a variation of Circle that includes a collision detection function) and adding a class method to detect if the ball is in contact with another given ball.

MATLAB:

```
% file: code/OO/Ball.m
classdef Ball
  properties
      x {mustBeNumeric}
      y {mustBeNumeric}
      r {mustBeNumeric}
  end
  methods
   function obj = Ball(x,y,r)
     obj.x = x;
     obj.y = y;
     obj.r = r;
   end
   function coll = collides_with(obj, other)
       dx = obj.x - other.x;
       dy = obj.y - other.y;
```

```matlab
        sep = sqrt( dx^2 + dy^2 );
        sum_r = obj.r + other.r;
        coll = sep < sum_r;
    end
  end
end

% file: code/00/run_oo_sim.m
function res = run_oo_sim(N, n_iter)
  fprintf('n balls=%d\n', N)
  box_x = 10.;
  box_y =  6.;
  r_min = 0.1;
  r_max = 0.3;
  for i = 1:n_iter
    tic
    balls = {};
    for j = 1:N
      x = r_max + (box_x-2*r_max)*rand();
      y = r_max + (box_y-2*r_max)*rand();
      R = 0.1 + 0.8*rand();
      balls{j} = Ball(x,y,R);
    end
    coll = eye(N);
    for j = 1:N
      for k = j+1:N
        coll(j,k) = balls{j}.collides_with(balls{k});
        coll(k,j) = coll(j,k);
      end
    end
    n_coll = (sum(sum(coll)) - N)/2;
    fprintf('n coll=%d Hz = %.2f\n', n_coll, 1/toc)
  end
end
```

Python:

```python
#!/usr/bin/env python3
# file: code/OO/Ball.py
import numpy as np
from numpy.random import rand
import time

class Ball:
  def __init__(self, x,y,r):
    self.x = x
    self.y = y
    self.r = r
  def collides_with(self, other):
    dx = self.x - other.x
    dy = self.y - other.y
    sep = np.sqrt( dx**2 + dy**2 )
    sum_r = self.r + other.r
    return sep < sum_r

def run_oo_sim(N, n_iter):
  box_x, box_y = 10., 6.
  r_min, r_max = 0.1, 0.3
  print(f'n balls={N}')
  for i in range(n_iter):
    balls = []
    for j in range(N):
      x = r_max + (box_x-2*r_max)*rand()
      y = r_max + (box_y-2*r_max)*rand()
      R = 0.1 + 0.8*rand()
      balls.append( Ball(x,y,R) )

    coll = np.eye(N, dtype=np.bool)
    T_s = time.time()
    for j in range(N):
      for k in range(j+1,N):
        coll[j,k] = balls[j].collides_with(balls[k])
        coll[k,j] = coll[j,k]
```

```
    n_coll = (np.sum(coll) - N)//2
    print(f'n coll={n_coll} Hz = '
        f'{1/(time.time()-T_s):.2f}')

def main():
  run_oo_sim(1000, 10)
if __name__ == "__main__": main()
```

In addition to taking more code, the object-oriented solution is much slower than the vectorized solution; updates happen at a frequency of less than 1 Hz, compared to about 60 Hz in the vectorized solution.

MATLAB:	Python:
`>> run_oo_sim(1000, 10)`	`In : run_oo_sim(1000, 10)`
`n balls=1000`	`n balls=1000`
`n coll=29788 Hz = 0.77`	`n coll=28442 Hz = 0.96`
`n coll=29959 Hz = 0.84`	`n coll=28054 Hz = 0.97`
`n coll=29236 Hz = 0.85`	`n coll=29002 Hz = 0.96`
`n coll=29422 Hz = 0.85`	`n coll=29128 Hz = 0.97`
`n coll=30776 Hz = 0.85`	`n coll=28722 Hz = 0.91`
`n coll=29626 Hz = 0.86`	`n coll=30064 Hz = 0.93`
`n coll=30527 Hz = 0.83`	`n coll=29300 Hz = 0.94`
`n coll=28534 Hz = 0.85`	`n coll=28034 Hz = 0.93`
`n coll=29844 Hz = 0.85`	`n coll=28609 Hz = 0.93`
`n coll=30211 Hz = 0.85`	`n coll=30782 Hz = 0.94`

11.2 Linear Algebra

MATLAB and Python, via NumPy and SciPy, offer similar capabilities—and similar computational performance—for linear algebra. There are three primary differences:

- MATLAB's operators for linear algebra notation are more concise than NumPy's or SciPy's.

- MATLAB has a uniform collection of linear algebra functions, while Python's are spread across NumPy and SciPy, which have overlapping capabilities in identically named linear algebra

submodules, numpy.linalg and scipy.linalg. In general, SciPy's
linear algebra offerings are more extensive than NumPy's.

- MATLAB's functions apply to both dense and sparse matrices. In
  both NumPy and SciPy, one must use differently named functions
  to operate on sparse matrices. Python's sparse matrix capability is
  discussed in Section 11.3.

11.2.1 Linear Equations

11.2.1.1 *Ax = b*

Linear equations with a square matrix A can be solved like this in the two languages:

MATLAB:	Python:
| ```
>> A = [1,2,-3; ...
        4,-5,6; ...
        -7,8,9];
>> b = [-1,0; 0,1; 1,0];
>> x = A\b
x =


  -0.375000    0.175000
  -0.250000    0.050000
   0.041667    0.091667
``` | ```
In : import numpy as np
In : A = np.array([[1,2,-3],
                   [4,-5,6],
                   [-7,8,9]])
In : b = np.array([[-1,0], [ 0,1],
                   [ 1,0]])
In : x = np.linalg.solve(A,b)
In : x
array([[-0.375     ,  0.175     ],
       [-0.25      ,  0.05      ],
       [ 0.04166667,  0.09166667]])
``` |

To obtain just the *LU* factors of a full-rank matrix for subsequent use with forward- and back-substitution, one can use SciPy's version of the `linalg` module:

MATLAB:	Python:
| ```
>> A = [1,2,-3; ...
        4,-5,6; ...
        -7,8,9];
>> [L, U, P] = lu(A)
L =
  1.00000  0.00000  0.00000
 -0.14286  1.00000  0.00000
 -0.57143 -0.13636  1.00000

U =
 -7.00000  8.00000  9.00000
  0.00000  3.14286 -1.71429
  0.00000  0.00000 10.90909


P =
Permutation Matrix

  0   0   1
  1   0   0
  0   1   0
``` | ```
In : import scipy.linalg as spla
In : A = np.array([[1,2,-3],
                   [4,-5,6],
                   [-7,8,9]])
In : LU, P = spla.lu_factor(A)
In : LU, P
(array([[-7.         ,  8.         ,  9.         ],
        [-0.14285714,  3.14285714, -1.71428571],
        [-0.57142857, -0.13636364, 10.90909091]]),
 array([2, 2, 2], dtype=int32))
``` |

Other options include Cholesky (`scipy.linalg.cholesky`, `scipy.linalg.cholesky_banded()`) and LDL (`scipy.linalg.ldl()`) factorizations of symmetric matrices. Forward- and back-substitution are then done with `lu_solve()` (or `cho_solve()` for a Cholesky factor):

MATLAB:	Python:
| ```
>> b = [1; 3; 5];
>> x = U\(L\(P*b))
  9.750000000000000e-01
  8.500000000000000e-01
  5.583333333333333e-01
``` | ```
In : b = np.array([1,3,5])
In : x = spla.lu_solve( (LU, P), b )
In : x
Out: array([0.975 , 0.85 , 0.55833333])
``` |

11.2.2 Singular Value Decomposition

NumPy and SciPy have identically named SVD functions, numpy.linalg.svd() and scipy.linalg.svd(). The SciPy version offers slightly more functionality by optionally checking for Inf and NaN values (use check_finite=True) and offering a choice of the LAPACK routine to use (lapack_driver='gesdd' is the default, while lapack_driver='gesvd' selects the same routine used by MATLAB).

MATLAB:	Python:

<pre>>> A = [9 8 7; 5 4 3; ...
        -1 2 -1; -5 5 0];
>> [U,S,V] = svd(A,0)
U =
 -8.9152e-01 4.7790e-02
  2.0140e-01
 -4.5163e-01 -1.9355e-02
 -3.8250e-01
  2.1957e-03 2.9513e-01
 -8.6635e-01
  3.4816e-02 9.5407e-01
  2.5014e-01
S =
  1.5615e+01   0
      0   7.3818e+00
      0   0 1.2919e+00
V =
 -6.6973e-01 -6.4105e-01
 -3.7485e-01
 -5.6100e-01 7.6749e-01
 -3.1021e-01
 -4.8656e-01 -2.5282e-03
  8.7365e-01</pre>
	<pre>In : A = np.array([[9,8,7],[5,4,3],
	...: [-1,2,-1],[-5,5,0.]])
	In : U, S, V = np.linalg.svd(A,
	...: full_matrices=False)
	In : U
	array([[-0.89152435, 0.04778986, 0.20140207],
	       [-0.45162746, -0.01935495, -0.38250147],
	       [0.00219575, 0.29512661, -0.86634739],
	       [0.0348158 , 0.95406593, 0.25014403]])
	In : S
	array([15.61537691, 7.38180298, 1.29189342])
	
	In : V
	array([[-0.66973287, -0.56100049, -0.48655557],
	       [-0.64105237, 0.76749298, -0.00252817],
	       [-0.37484629, -0.3102144 , 0.87364597]])</pre>

MATLAB and Python results for U and S match, but V is transposed. Here, we compute the solution's error by subtracting the reconstructed A from the original:

MATLAB:		Python:
`>> A - U*S*V'`		`In : A - U@np.diag(S)@V`
7.1054e-15	1.7764e-15	`array(`
4.4409e-15		`[[ 7.10542736e-15, 1.77635684e-15,`
2.6645e-15	1.7764e-15	`   4.44089210e-15],`
1.3323e-15		` [ 2.66453526e-15, 1.77635684e-15,`
2.2204e-16	1.5543e-15	`   1.33226763e-15],`
-1.1102e-16		` [ 2.22044605e-16, 1.55431223e-15,`
8.8818e-16	6.2172e-15	`   -1.11022302e-16],`
1.1657e-15		` [ 8.88178420e-16, 6.21724894e-15,`
		`   1.12317600e-15]])`

11.2.3 Eigenvalue Problems

MATLAB's ability to overload functions is appealing for solving eigenvalue problems since only two functions, eig() and eigs(), handle everything—eigenvalues only, eigenvalues and eigenvectors, simple form, general form, symmetric or asymmetric inputs, full or partial solution. In contrast, NumPy and SciPy together have nearly a dozen functions (several of which are identically named) to cover these cases. Table 11-4 shows how eigensolving capability is fragmented in Python compared to MATLAB. The "asym." column refers to a function's ability to work with asymmetric matrices. A function without a mark in this column only works with real symmetric or complex Hermitian matrices. The specialized Python functions eigvals banded() and eigh tridiagonal() are not included.

Table 11-4. *Capabilities of MATLAB, NumPy, and SciPy eigensolvers*

	dense	sparse	$Ax = \lambda x$	$Ax = \lambda Bx$	asym.	full	partial
MATLAB							
eig	•	•	•	•	•	•	
eigs	•	•	•	•	•		•
numpy.linalg							
eig	•		•		•	•	
eigh	•		•			•	
eigvals	•		•		•	•	
eigvalsh	•		•			•	
scipy.linalg	•				•	•	
eig	•		•	•	•	•	
eigh	•		•	•		•	
eigvals	•		•	•	•	•	
eigvalsh	•		•	•		•	
scipy.sparse.linalg							
eig		•	•	•	•		•
eigsh		•	•	•			•

MATLAB:	Python:

```
>> n = 3;                           In : import numpy as np
>> ones = ones(n);                  In : n = 3
>> off  = 2*tril(ones,-2);          In : ones = np.ones((n,n))
>> A = (n+2)*eye(n) - ones + off    In : off  = 2*np.tril(ones,-2)
A =                                 In : A = (n+2)*np.eye(n) - ones + off
                                    In : A
     4    -1    -1                  Out:
    -1     4    -1                  array([[ 4., -1., -1.],
     1    -1     4                         [-1.,  4., -1.],
                                           [ 1., -1.,  4.]])
>> [v,d] = eig(A)
v =                                 In : [d,v] = np.linalg.eig(A)
                                    In : v
  -0.5774    0.0000    0.7071       Out: array(
  -0.5774    0.7071    0.7071         [[ 2.22045e-15,  5.77350e-01,  7.07107e-01],
   0.5774   -0.7071   -0.0000         [ 7.07107e-01,  5.77350e-01,  7.07107e-01],
                                      [-7.07107e-01, -5.77350e-01,  4.44089e-16]])
d =
   4.0000        0        0         In : d
        0   5.0000        0         Out: array([5., 4., 3.])
        0        0   3.0000
                                    
>> A*v - v*d
   1.0e-14 *                        In : A@v - v@np.diag(d)
  -0.0444    0.0020        0        Out: array(
  -0.2220    0.2665    0.1776         [[-5.55111e-16, -4.44089e-16,  4.44089e-16],
   0.2220   -0.2665   -0.1228         [ 4.88498e-15,  3.10862e-15,  2.22046e-15],
                                      [-1.77636e-15, -8.88178e-16, -4.44089e-16]])
```

Aside from Python's capability fragmentation, solutions, computational performance, and accuracy are comparable those in MATLAB.

11.3 Sparse Matrices

Sparse matrices are central to many areas of numerical analysis including computational fluid dynamics, finite element analysis, network theoretic computations, and neural network computations for machine learning and artificial intelligence. SciPy's `sparse` module provides sparse matrix capability to Python. Under the hood, `sparse` uses the C and Fortran libraries SuperLU and ARPACK to solve systems of equations and eigenproblems.

SciPy's sparse matrix capability is good but not as convenient as MATLAB's. MATLAB has two advantages: its sparse matrices are more fully integrated into the language, and there is a single sparse storage scheme which is both efficient and flexible. SciPy provides many sparse matrix operations, but its sparse matrices may be used in only a subset of NumPy functions. Also, before creating a sparse matrix in SciPy, one must decide which of the seven (!) storage formats to use. Each storage format has different indexing capabilities and computational performance. Conversion between formats is easy however.

11.3.1 Sparse Matrix Creation with COO, CSC, CSR

A sparse matrix can be created from a dense matrix by passing the dense matrix to any of the sparse creation functions. This example uses the compressed row storage function `csr_matrix()`:

MATLAB:	Python:

`>> x = [1 2 0; 0 3 0; 0 4 5]`
`x =`
 	
    1   2   0
    0   3   0
    0   4   5
	`import scipy.sparse as sp`
	`In : x = np.array([[1, 2, 0],`
	`...:     [0, 3, 0],[0, 4, 5]])`
	`In : x`
	`array([[1, 2, 0],`
	`       [0, 3, 0],`
	`       [0, 4, 5]])`

`>> y = sparse(x)`
`y =`
	`In : y = sp.csr_matrix(x)`
	`In : print(y)`
	`Out`

(1,1)   1
  (1,2)   2
  (2,2)   3
  (3,2)   4
  (3,3)   5
	(0, 0) 1
	  (0, 1) 2
	  (1, 1) 3
	  (2, 1) 4
	  (2, 2) 5

Conversion from a dense matrix is generally only useful for testing sparse algorithms because only relatively small sparse matrices can be created this way. More typically, one builds up a sparse matrix from scratch. The most straightforward way to do that is with SciPy's "coordinate" format, also known as "COO." Its creation method is efficient and closely matches MATLAB's—one provides the constructor function linear arrays of row, column, and values. For example, the code to define this matrix

$$\begin{pmatrix} 0 & 1 & 0 \\ 8 & 0 & 2 \\ 0 & 4 & -3 \\ 0 & 0 & 0 \end{pmatrix}$$

looks like this:

MATLAB:	Python:
	`import scipy.sparse as sp`
`>> I = [1 2 2 3 3];`	`In : I = [0, 1, 1, 2, 2]`
`>> J = [2 1 3 2 3];`	`In : J = [1, 2, 2, 1, 2]`
`>> V = [1 8 2 4 -3];`	`In : V = [1, 8, 2, 4, -3]`
`>> A = sparse(I,J,V,4,3)`	`In : A = sp.coo_matrix((V,(I,J)),(4,3))`
	`In : A`
`A =`	`<4x3 sparse matrix of type`
`Compressed Column Sparse`	`'<class 'numpy.int64'>'`
`(rows = 3, cols = 3,`	`with 5 stored elements in COOrdinate`
` nnz = 5 [56%])`	`format>`
`  (2, 1) ->  8`	`In : print(A)`
`  (1, 2) ->  1`	`  (0, 1)        1`
`  (3, 2) ->  4`	`  (1, 2)        8`
`  (2, 3) ->  2`	`  (1, 2)        2`
`  (3, 3) -> -3`	`  (2, 1)        4`
	`  (2, 2)       -3`

MATLAB's output is sorted by column, while Python's is sorted by row; the matrices actually contain the same values at the same indices. This can be seen by viewing the dense representation of each matrix:

MATLAB:	Python:
`>>  full(A)`	`In : A.todense()`
`  0   1   0`	`matrix([[ 0,  1,  0],`
`  8   0   2`	`        [ 8,  0,  2],`
`  0   4  -3`	`        [ 0,  4, -3],`
`  0   0   0`	`        [ 0,  0,  0]])`

11.3.1.1 Repeated COO Indices

MATLAB's sparse() function sums terms where indices are repeated. In other words, if the index entry (i, j) appears three times in the input index arrays with corresponding values V_1, V_2, and V_3 in the value array, MATLAB's matrix value at (i, j) will be $V_1 + V_2 + V_3$. The same behavior is true for all SciPy matrix creation functions although the summation may be implicit—the three duplicate terms are stored separately, but all mathematical operations on the sparse matrix yield the same result as if the terms were summed. To see this in action, we'll create the sparse matrix

$$\begin{pmatrix} 1 & 3 \\ 0 & 4 \end{pmatrix}$$

by repeating the last row and column's indices twice, once with value 10 and a second time with value –6. This example omits the trailing dimension argument because the largest row and column indices in the input arrays I and J are enough to define the dimension:

MATLAB:	Python:
.	`In : import scipy.sparse as sp`
`>> I = [1 1 2 2 ];`	`In : I = [0, 0, 1, 1]`
`>> J = [1 2 2 2 ];`	`In : J = [0, 1, 1, 1]`
`>> V = [1 3 10 -6 ];`	`In : V = [1, 3, 10, -6]`
`>> A = sparse(I,J,V)`	`In : A = sp.coo_matrix((V,(I,J)))`
	`In : A`
`A =`	`<2x2 sparse matrix of type`
	`  '<class 'numpy.int64'>'`
`Compressed Column Sparse`	`with 4 stored elements in`
`  (rows = 2, cols = 2,`	`COOrdinate format>`
`  nnz = 3 [75%])`	
	`In : print(A)`
`  (1, 1) -> 1`	`  (0, 0)        1`
`  (1, 2) -> 3`	`  (0, 1)        3`
`  (2, 2) -> 4`	`  (1, 1)        10`
	`  (1, 1)        -6`

Although Python stores the repeated index values separately, computation with the matrix shows it uses the summed value of 4 for the last term:

MATLAB:	Python:
`>> A * [1; 1]`	`In : A.dot([1,1])`
`   4`	`Out: array([4, 4], dtype=int64)`
`   4`	

The Python repeated index terms can be explicitly summed with the sparse matrix object's `.sum_duplicates()` method:

Python:

```
In : print(A)
  (0, 0)        1
  (0, 1)        3
  (1, 1)        10
  (1, 1)        -6

In : A.sum_duplicates()

In : print(A)
  (0, 0)        1
  (0, 1)        3
  (1, 1)        4
```

11.3.1.2 Extracting Indices and Values

Indices and values of a COO sparse matrix are stored as object attributes `.row`, `.col`, and `.data`. These correspond to the output of MATLAB's `find()` function on a sparse matrix. Using A from Section 11.3.1.1:

MATLAB:	Python:
>> [I J V] = find(A);	In : A.sum_duplicates()
>> I' 1 1 2	In : A.row Out: array([0, 0, 1], dtype=int32)
>> J' 1 2 2	In : A.col Out: array([0, 1, 1], dtype=int32)
> V' 1 3 4	In : A.data Out: array([1, 3, 4])

Without the call to .sum_duplicates(), the index and value attributes would have shown the repeated terms.

Only COO matrices have .row and .col attributes. However, conversion from other formats to COO via matrices' .tocoo() methods is inexpensive. See Section 11.3.5.2 for a complete list of components available in the other formats.

11.3.1.3 Compressed Row, Column Storage

The Compressed Sparse Row (CSR) and Compressed Sparse Column (CSC) storage schemes allow more rapid matrix operations such as factoring and multiplication. Although their creation functions csr_matrix() and csc_matrix() can take the same arguments as coo_matrix(), it is usually faster to create matrices with coo_matrix() and then convert them to CSR or CSC formats using the matrices' .tocsr() or .tocsc() methods. Duplicate indices are summed during these conversions.

While csr_matrix() and csc_matrix() can accept explicit row and column index arrays, one can directly supply the tighter index and index pointer arrays native to the CSR and CSC internal representations. For csr_matrix(), this means an array of column indices (J in the preceding example) and an array of pointers that contain counts of terms in each row. The array of pointers, indptr, are defined such that indices for row i are stored in J[indptr[i]:indptr[$i+1$]] and their corresponding values are stored in data[indptr[i]:indptr[$i+1$]]. These inputs repeat the earlier example:

Python:

```
In : J = np.array([1,0,2,1,2])  # column indices
In : V = np.array([1,8,2,4,-3]) # matrix data values
In : indptr = np.array([0, 1, 3, 5, 5])
In : A = sp.csr_matrix((V, J, indptr), shape=(4, 3))
In : A.todense()
```

The indptr array bears additional clarification—how did we arrive at [0, 1, 3, 5, 5]? One way to think of it is the difference indptr[$i+1$] - indptr[i] is the count of terms in row i, and each term in indptr includes the sum of terms before it. Table 11-5 shows the contents of the index array J needed to capture indices of the sparse matrix at (0, 1), (1, 0), (1,2), (2, 1), and (2, 2).

Table 11-5. *indptr values for each row*

Row			Column Indices
0	J[indptr[0]:indptr[1]]	J[0:1]	[1]
1	J[indptr[1]:indptr[2]]	J[1:3]	[0,2]
2	J[indptr[2]:indptr[3]]	J[3:5]	[1,2]
3	J[indptr[3]:indptr[4]]	J[5:5]	[]

To convert an array of row indices, I = [1,0,2,1,2] in our case, into index pointers, we can take advantage of a data container, Counter, from the collections module. A Counter takes an iterable such as a list or array and returns a dictionary whose keys are unique entries in the iterable and whose values are the number of times those entries appeared. If the dictionary is keyed by a nonexistent key, rather than raising a KeyError, it simply returns zero.

Python:

```
In : I
Out: array([0, 1, 1, 2, 2])

In : from collections import Counter
In : n_terms_this_row = Counter(I)
In : indptr = [0]
```

```
In : for i in range(nRows):
...:        indptr.append( indptr[-1] + n_terms_this_row[i])
In : indptr
Out: [0, 1, 3, 5, 5]
```

Index pointer inputs to csc_matrix() work the same way as for csc_matrix(), except one supplies explicit row indices and pointers to column indices instead of the other way around.

11.3.2 Sparse Matrix Creation with LIL, DOK

The three storage formats of the previous section, coordinate and compressed row and column, require explicit entries for each row index, column index, and value to be given up front. Rather than compute locations and values and then create the sparse matrix from these, sparse matrices can be built up incrementally. In addition, many engineering applications, notably finite element analysis, produce sparse matrices from many smaller submatrices. The resulting sparse matrix has small blocks of non-zero terms in adjacent rows and columns.

SciPy has three storage formats, list of lists (LIL), dictionary of keys (DOK), and block compressed row (BSR), that enable efficient incremental assembly, access, and manipulation of such structured sparse matrices.

Here, we'll recreate the matrix

$$\begin{pmatrix} 0 & 1 & 0 \\ 8 & 0 & 2 \\ 0 & 4 & -3 \\ 0 & 0 & 0 \end{pmatrix}$$

using scalar inserts for the 1 in the top row and the 8 in the left column, then a block insert to place the submatrix

$$\begin{pmatrix} 0 & 2 \\ 4 & -3 \end{pmatrix}$$

into the second and third rows and columns.

This example uses the LIL constructor:

MATLAB:	Python:
.	`import scipy.sparse as sp`
`>> A = sparse(4,3)`	`A = sp.lil_matrix( (4,3) )`
`>> A(1,2) = 1;`	`A[0,1] = 1`
`>> A(2,1) = 8;`	`A[1,0] = 8`
`>> A(2:3,2:3) = [0 2;4 -3];`	`A[1:3,1:3] = np.array([[0, 2],`
`>> A`	`                    [4,-3]])`
`A =`	`In : print(A)`
`Compressed Column Sparse`	`  (0, 1)        1.0`
`  (rows = 4, cols = 3,`	`  (1, 0)        8.0`
`   nnz = 5 [42%])`	`  (1, 2)        2.0`
	`  (2, 1)        4.0`
` (2, 1) -> 8`	`  (2, 2)        -3.0`
` (1, 2) -> 1`	
` (3, 2) -> 4`	
` (2, 3) -> 2`	
` (3, 3) -> -3`	

The dictionary of keys (DOK) constructor is functionally identical to the LIL constructor. The only difference in the following code is calling dok_matrix() instead of lil_matrix():

MATLAB:	Python:
.	`import scipy.sparse as sp`
`>> A = sparse(4,3)`	`A = sp.dok_matrix( (4,3) )`
`>> A(1,2) = 1;`	`A[0,1] = 1`
`>> A(2,1) = 8;`	`A[1,0] = 8`
`>> A(2:3,2:3) = [0 2;4 -3];`	`A[1:3,1:3] = np.array([[0, 2],`
`>> A`	`                       [4,-3]])`
`A =`	`In : print(A)`
`Compressed Column Sparse`	`  (0, 1)        1.0`
`  (rows = 4, cols = 3,`	`  (1, 0)        8.0`
`   nnz = 5 [42%])`	`  (1, 2)        2.0`
	`  (2, 1)        4.0`
`  (2, 1) -> 8`	`  (2, 2)        -3.0`
`  (1, 2) -> 1`	
`  (3, 2) -> 4`	
`  (2, 3) -> 2`	
`  (3, 3) -> -3`	

In addition to direct insertion of terms, MATLAB and SciPy LIL and DOK sparse matrices allow summation of blocks with updates to the sparse structure where necessary:

MATLAB:	Python:
`>> A(2:3,2:3) = ...`	`A = sp.dok_matrix( (4,3) )`
`   A(2:3,2:3) + [0 2;4 -3];`	`A[1:3,1:3] += np.array([[0, 2],`
	`                        [4,-3]])`

11.3.3 Sparse Matrix Creation with BSR, DIA

The two remaining sparse formats, block compressed row (BSR) and diagonal (DIA), are more specialized than the previous five and are therefore seen less frequently.

As its name suggests, the block compressed row format stores a collection of dense submatrices. It has drawbacks though: submatrices must be equally sized, and direct indexing is not supported. The BSR constructor function bsr_matrix() takes as input a 3D array of data blocks, and 1D arrays containing the block column indices, and pointers into the column indices for each row. This example creates an 8 x 6 sparse matrix from four 2 x 2 matrices—the sparse matrix then has four block rows and three block columns:

Python:

```
In : V = np.array([[[1,1],[1,1]],
...:                [[2,2],[2,2]],
...:                [[3,3],[3,3]],
...:                [[4,4],[4,4]]])
In : J = np.array([1, 2, 0, 2])  # column indices
In : indptr = np.array([0, 1, 2, 2, 4])
In : A = sp.bsr_matrix((V, J, indptr), shape=(8, 6))
In : A.todense()
matrix([[0, 0, 1, 1, 0, 0],
        [0, 0, 1, 1, 0, 0],
        [0, 0, 0, 0, 2, 2],
        [0, 0, 0, 0, 2, 2],
        [0, 0, 0, 0, 0, 0],
        [0, 0, 0, 0, 0, 0],
        [3, 3, 0, 0, 4, 4],
        [3, 3, 0, 0, 4, 4]])
```

The indptr array is computed from block row indices (which would be I = [0,1,3,3] in this example) the same way indptr are created for csr_matrix() (refer to Section 11.3.1).

The diagonal storage format, DIA, is well suited for computational fluid dynamics problems that employ iterative solutions on finite difference grids. The dia_matrix() constructor resembles MATLAB's spdiags() function:

MATLAB:

```
>> data = [-2 -4 -6 -8 -10 -12 -14;
           10 11 12 13  14  15  16;
           -1 -3 -5 -7  -9 -11 -13]' ;
>> offsets = [2 0 -1];
>> A = spdiags(data, offsets, 7,7);
>> full(A)

   10    0   -6    0    0    0    0
   -1   11    0   -8    0    0    0
    0   -3   12    0  -10    0    0
    0    0   -5   13    0  -12    0
    0    0    0   -7   14    0  -14
    0    0    0    0   -9   15    0
    0    0    0    0    0  -11   16
```

Python:

```
In : data = np.array([[-2,-4,-6,-8,-10,-12,-14],
...:                   [10,11,12,13, 14, 15, 16],
...:                   [-1,-3,-5,-7, -9,-11,-13]])
In : offsets = np.array([2,0,-1])
In : A = sp.dia_matrix((data, offsets), shape=(7,7))
In : A.todense()
matrix([[ 10,   0,  -6,   0,   0,   0,   0],
        [ -1,  11,   0,  -8,   0,   0,   0],
        [  0,  -3,  12,   0, -10,   0,   0],
        [  0,   0,  -5,  13,   0, -12,   0],
        [  0,   0,   0,  -7,  14,   0, -14],
        [  0,   0,   0,   0,  -9,  15,   0],
        [  0,   0,   0,   0,   0, -11,  16]])
```

Note that in both MATLAB and Python, terms of data are dropped to accommodate the size reduction as one moves away from the diagonal. In our case, –2 and –4 do not appear above the diagonal, and –13 does not appear below the diagonal.

As with BSR, DIA sparse matrices cannot be subscripted.

11.3.4 Test Matrices

A few examples of dense test matrices were presented in Section 11.1.6.14; here, we do the same for sparse matrices. As with the dense random matrices, the MATLAB sparse random matrices will not match the Python sparse matrices.

11.3.4.1 Random Sparse 4 × 3 Arrays with Density of 40%

MATLAB:	Python:
>> A = sprand(4,3,.4);	In : A = sp.rand(4, 3, density=0.4,
>> full(A)	format='dok')
0.000 0.000 0.000	In : A.todense()
0.617 0.000 0.349	matrix([[0.688, 0.401, 0.],
0.000 0.000 0.000	[0. , 0. , 0.],
0.881 0.165 0.335	[0.337, 0. , 0.],
	[0. , 0.023, 0.]])

11.3.4.2 Random Sparse via I,J,V

Here, we'll also use the spy() function in MATLAB and Python's matplotlib to view the sparse matrix topology:

MATLAB:	Python:

Python:

```python
import scipy.sparse as sp
import numpy as np
import matplotlib.pyplot as plt
```

MATLAB:

```matlab
nR = 50;
nC = 50;
nNZ = 10*nC;
I = ceil(nR*rand(nNZ,1));
J = ceil(nC*rand(nNZ,1));
V = ceil(nC*rand(nNZ,1));
A = sparse(I,J,V);
spy(A)
```

Python:

```python
nR = 50
nC = 50
nNZ = 10*nC# number of non-zeros
I = np.random.randint(0, nR, size=(nNZ,))
J = np.random.randint(0, nC, size=(nNZ,))
V = np.random.randint(0, nC, size=(nNZ,))
A = sp.coo_matrix((V,(I,J)),shape=(nR,nC))
plt.spy(A)
plt.show()
```

11.3.4.3 Arrow Matrix

MATLAB:	Python:
`>> A = speye(4);`	`In : A = sp.identity(4).todok()`
`>> A(1,:) = 1;`	`In : A[0,:] = 1`
`>> A(:,1) = 1;`	`In : A[:,0] = 1`
`>> full(A)`	`In : A.todense()`
`  1   1   1   1`	`matrix([[1., 1., 1., 1.],`
`  1   1   0   0`	`         [1., 1., 0., 0.],`
`  1   0   1   0`	`         [1., 0., 1., 0.],`
`  1   0   0   1`	`         [1., 0., 0., 1.]])`

11.3.5 Sparse Matrix I/O

MATLAB's save and load commands make it easy to write sparse matrices to .mat files and to read them back. Unlike their NumPy counterparts, SciPy sparse matrices lack built-in methods for file input and output. Ironically, SciPy's savemat() and loadmat() functions support reading and writing sparse matrices to and from MATLAB .mat files.

11.3.5.1 Write to MATLAB .mat Files

MATLAB:	Python:
`>> A = sprand(4,3,.4);`	`In : A = sp.rand(4, 3, 0.4)`
`>> save A  % to A.mat`	`In : A.todense()`
`>> clear A`	`matrix([[0.   , 0.   , 0.264],`
`>> whos A`	`          [0.   , 0.   , 0.   ],`
` Name Size Bytes Class  Attributes`	`          [0.334, 0.743, 0.   ],`
	`          [0.059, 0.   , 0.   ]])`
` A    4x3    112 double sparse`	`In : import scipy.io as io`
`>> clear A`	`In : io.savemat('A.mat',{'A':A})`
`>> load A  % from A.mat`	`In : A = None`
`>> whos A`	`In : data = io.loadmat('A.mat')`
` Name Size Bytes Class  Attributes`	`In : data['A'].todense()`
	`matrix([[0.   , 0.   , 0.264],`
` A    4x3    112 double sparse`	`          [0.   , 0.   , 0.   ],`
	`          [0.334, 0.743, 0.   ],`
	`          [0.059, 0.   , 0.   ]])`

This method is also useful for passing sparse matrices between MATLAB and Python.

11.3.5.2 Write Component Parts As NumPy Arrays

The component parts of a sparse matrix—the data values and row and column indices—are NumPy arrays, so we can use NumPy's savez() and loadz() functions to read and write them efficiently. The catch here is that the item names vary by storage format, so one must know the format of the sparse matrix (stored in its .format attribute) before accessing its components:

- COO: A.data, A.row, A.col

- CSR: A.data, A.indices, A.indptr

- CSC: A.data, A.indices, A.indptr

- LIL: A.data, A.rows (contains both row and column indices)

- BSR: `A.data, A.indices, A.indptr`

- DIA: `A.data, A.offsets`

DOK is unique in that its components are stored in a dictionary rather than NumPy arrays. Its entries can be retrieved with `A.keys()` and `A.values()`. DOK matrices can either be converted to other formats to save as NumPy arrays or written to pickle files as shown in the next section.

After loading the components, the matrix has to be regenerated by calling the appropriate constructor. The process looks like this for a COO matrix:

Python:

```
In : A = sp.rand(4, 3, 0.4, format='coo')
In : A.todense()
matrix([[0.44250527, 0.        , 0.        ],
        [0.61852124, 0.        , 0.49900225],
        [0.        , 0.        , 0.10741277],
        [0.        , 0.        , 0.        ]])
In : np.savez('A_coo.npz', V=A.data, I=A.row, J=A.col, dims=A.shape)
In : !ls -l A_coo.npz
-rw-rw-r-- 1 al al 788 May 29 13:36 A_coo.npz
In : A = None
In : fh = np.load('A_coo.npz')
In : V  = fh['V']
In : I  = fh['I']
In : J  = fh['J']
In : dm = fh['dims']
In : fh.close()
In : A = sp.coo_matrix((V, (I, J)), shape=dm)
In : A.todense()
matrix([[0.44250527, 0.        , 0.        ],
        [0.61852124, 0.        , 0.49900225],
        [0.        , 0.        , 0.10741277],
        [0.        , 0.        , 0.        ]])
```

11.3.5.3 Write a Python Pickle Object

SciPy sparse matrices are conventional Python variables and can therefore be written to pickle files (ref. Section 7.13):

Python:

```
In : import pickle
In : import scipy.sparse as sp
In : A = sp.rand(4, 3, 0.4, format='csr')
In : A.todense()
Out: matrix([[0.   , 0.   , 0.899],
             [0.   , 0.054, 0.   ],
             [0.   , 0.   , 0.   ],
             [0.   , 0.625, 0.603]])

In : with open('A.pkl', 'wb') as f:
In :     pickle.dump(A, f, 4) # protocol v 4
In : !ls -l A.pkl
In : -rw-rw-r-- 1 al al 457 May 29 14:15 A.pkl
In : A = None
In : with open('A.pkl', 'rb') as f:
In :     A = pickle.load(f)
In : A.todense()
Out: matrix([[0.   , 0.   , 0.899],
             [0.   , 0.054, 0.   ],
             [0.   , 0.   , 0.   ],
             [0.   , 0.625, 0.603]])
```

11.3.6 Linear Algebra

SciPy's sparse matrix linear algebra functions are in the `scipy.sparse.linalg` module which must be imported independently from `scipy.sparse` itself.

As a representative matrix, we'll use a finite element–based symmetric sparse matrix, fidap037,[6] from the National Institute of Standards and Technology's Matrix Market.[7] It

---

[6] https://math.nist.gov/MatrixMarket/data/SPARSKIT/fidap/fidap037.html
[7] https://math.nist.gov/MatrixMarket/

can be loaded into Python with `scipy.io`'s `mmread()` function and into MATLAB with `mmread.m`.[8] SciPy's `mmread()` returns a sparse matrix in coordinate form (COO). If the matrix is to be factored, it will need to be converted to a form such as CSC.

The following code loads the file into the sparse variable K and defines a matrix b with an equal number of rows and two columns, the first of which has all +1 values, while the other column has –1.

MATLAB:	Python:
`>> K = mmread('fidap037.mtx');`	`from scipy.io import mmread`
`>> [nR,nC] = size(K);`	`import scipy.sparse as sp`
`>> b = ones(nR,2);`	`import scipy.sparse.linalg as spla`
`>> b(:,2) = -1;`	`K = mmread('fidap037.mtx') # COO format`
	`K = K.tocsc() # for factorization later`
	`nR,nC = K.shape`
	`b = np.ones((nR,2))`
	`b[:,1] = -1`

Matrix summary

The following commands print the dimensions and number of non-zero terms and show the sparsity pattern. Other matrix summary capabilities vary between the two systems. MATLAB has a function to estimate the condition number but not the norm, while SciPy supports the reverse. The Matrix Market values for these are 2.26e+02 and 1.5e+03.

MATLAB:	Python:
`>> size(K)`	`In : K.shape`
`    3565    3565`	`Out: (3565, 3565)`
`>> nnz(K)`	`In : K.nnz`
`    67591`	`Out: 67591`
`>> spy(K)`	`In : import matplotlib.pyplot as plt`
`>> condest(K)`	`In : plt.spy(K,markersize=1)`
`  226.3745`	`In : plt.show()`
	`In : spla.norm(K)`
	`Out: 1472.080010077052`

---

[8] https://math.nist.gov/MatrixMarket/mmio/matlab/mmiomatlab.html

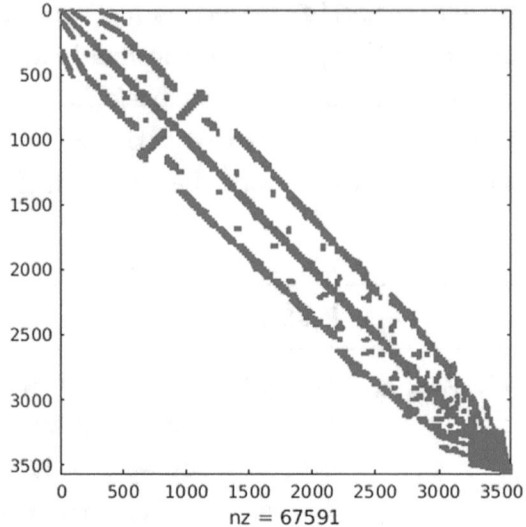

Figure 11-1. *MATLAB*

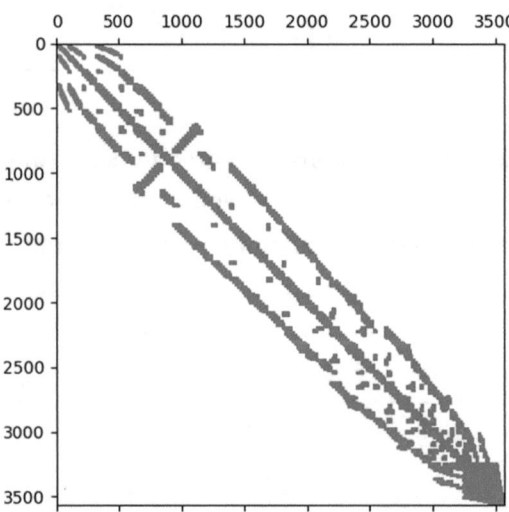

Figure 11-2. *Python*

Matrix-vector product

Unlike NumPy arrays which use @ for matrix multiplication, SciPy sparse matrices can use *. The .dot() method also works for sparse matrices. Only a portion of the 3565 rows of the product are shown:

MATLAB:	Python:
>> Kb = K*b;	In : Kb = K*b
>> Kb(191:195,:)	In : Kb[190:195,:]
	Out:
1.0000 -1.0000	array([[1. , -1.],
13.4848 -13.4848	[13.48478231, -13.48478231],
52.3418 -52.3418	[52.3417648 , -52.3417648],
1.0000 -1.0000	[1. , -1.],
27.2083 -27.2083	[27.20825099, -27.20825099]])

Solution to linear equations

MATLAB's backslash operator works with both dense and sparse matrices. SciPy uses spsolve() to solve for x in $Kx = b$ and splu() to factor K to lower and upper triangular matrices, stored together as LU, with subsequent solution with LU.solve(b):

MATLAB:	Python:
>> x = K\b;	In : x = spla.spsolve(K,b)
>> x(501:505,:)	In : x[500:505,:]
1.0000 -1.0000	Out:
0.0712 -0.0712	array([[1. , -1.],
0.0453 -0.0453	[0.07122914, -0.07122914],
1.0000 -1.0000	[0.04526046, -0.04526046],
0.0421 -0.0421	[1. , -1.],
>> [L,U,P,Q] = lu(K);	[0.04214178, -0.04214178]])
>> x = Q*(U\(L\(P*b)));	In : LU = spla.splu(K)
>> x(501:505,:)	In : x = LU.solve(b)
1.0000 -1.0000	In : x[500:505,:]
0.0712 -0.0712	Out:
0.0453 -0.0453	array([[1. , -1.],
1.0000 -1.0000	[0.07122914, -0.07122914],
0.0421 -0.0421	[0.04526046, -0.04526046],
	[1. , -1.],
	[0.04214178, -0.04214178]])

LU factorization performance is comparable between MATLAB and SciPy. Additionally, both have a collection of similarly named iterative solvers including conjugate gradient and minimum residual methods.

Solution to the standard eigenvalue problem

As indicated in Table 11-4, MATLAB's `eigs()` function handles all forms of sparse eigensolutions with options controlled by various arguments. SciPy has two functions, `eigs()` and `eigsh()`, to handle asymmetric and symmetric inputs. Both support a shift-and-invert argument, `sigma`, to search for solutions near a desired eigenvalue region, and both support extracting a given number of eigenpairs.

The following example solves $Kx = \lambda x$ for the ten eigenvalues and eigenvectors of our symmetric matrix K nearest a shift of $\sigma = -1$. This problem is especially challenging because it has 1651 repeated eigenvalues of 1.0, found by computing the Sturm number (explained later). Shifting near –1 does not guarantee the returned eigenvalues are complete in either MATLAB or Python. Although MATLAB returned seven eigenvalues of 1.0 compared to Python's six, ideally both should have returned ten values of 1.0.

MATLAB:	Python:
`>> [vec,val] = eigs(K,10,-1);`	`In : val,vec = spla.eigsh(K,k=10,sigma=-1)`
`> format long e`	`In : val`
`>> diag(val)`	`Out:`
`    9.999999999999947e-01`	`array([1.        ,`
`    9.999999999999947e-01`	`        1.        ,`
`    9.999999999999956e-01`	`        1.        ,`
`    9.999999999999969e-01`	`        1.        ,`
`    9.999999999999978e-01`	`        1.        ,`
`    1.000000000000000e+00`	`        1.        ,`
`    1.000000000000000e+00`	`        2.31912276,`
`    2.319122761249388e+00`	`        2.39076254,`
`    2.390762542515986e+00`	`        2.50070154,`
`    2.500701541757246e+00`	`        2.63542116])`

Sturm sequence number

Neither MATLAB nor Python sparse eigensolvers can tell if the requested number of solutions is comprehensive, that is, if n eigensolutions were requested near a shift of σ, are the returned n eigenvalues the closest to σ, or were some omitted? The Sturm sequence number for the general eigenvalue problem $Kx = \lambda Mx$, removes guesswork from this question. This number is the count of negative values on the diagonal of the LU factor of $K - \sigma M$, and it equals the number of eigenvalues below σ.

The following code computes the Sturm sequence number for our K at $\sigma_1 = 0.99$ and $\sigma_2 = 1.01$. Since we're solving the standard eigenvalue problem, $Kx = \lambda x$, M in this case is simply the identity matrix:

MATLAB:	Python:
`>> sigma = 0.99;`	`In : sigma = 0.99`
`>> [L,U] = lu(K-sigma*eye(nR));`	`In : LU = spla.splu(K - sigma*sp.eye(nR))`
`>> dU = diag(U);`	`In : dU = LU.U.diagonal()`
`>> sum(dU < 0)`	`In : np.sum(dU < 0)`
`        0`	`Out:    0`
`>> sigma = 1.01;`	`In : sigma = 1.01`
`>> [L,U] = lu(K - sigma*eye(nR));`	`In : LU = spla.splu(K - sigma*sp.eye(nR))`
`>> dU = diag(U);`	`In : dU = LU.U.diagonal()`
`>> sum(dU < 0)`	`In : np.sum(dU < 0)`
`        1651`	`Out: 1651`

Therefore, we know $Kx = \lambda x$ has 1651 eigenvalues between 0.99 and 1.01.

Solution to the general eigenvalue problem

The general eigenvalue problem, $Kx = \lambda Mx$, arises in structural vibration and buckling problems, among others. MATLAB's and SciPy's sparse eigensolvers both accept a second matrix to solve such problems. We'll manufacture a diagonal M matrix with values linearly spaced from 1 to 3565 to accompany our K.

Although SciPy's eigenvalues are returned in sorted order, neither it nor MATLAB's eigs() guarantees this order. MATLAB's output is explicitly sorted here to simplify the comparison.

MATLAB:	Python:

`>> M = spdiags([1:nR]', 0, nR, nR);`
`sigma = 1.8;`
`>> [vec,val] = eigs(K,M,10,sigma);`
`>> sort(diag(val))`
 	
1.097093867635186e+00
1.129980804603547e+00
1.362226236223728e+00
1.593598298009953e+00
1.743881417538397e+00
1.837195925535993e+00
2.042699252311738e+00
2.171083950484060e+00
2.236999096156634e+00
2.411152544918247e+00
	`M = sp.diags(np.arange(1,nR+1))`
	`sigma = 1.8`
	`val,vec = spla.eigsh(K,M=M,`
	`                k=10,sigma=sigma)`
	
	`array([1.09709389,`
	`       1.12998084,`
	`       1.36222621,`
	`       1.59359813,`
	`       1.74388143,`
	`       1.83719593,`
	`       2.04269926,`
	`       2.1710838 ,`
	`       2.23699914,`
	`       2.4111525 ])`

11.3.7 Summary of Sparse Formats and Capabilities; Recommendations

Table 11-6 summarizes SciPy's sparse matrix formats and capabilities.

Table 11-6. *Comparison of SciPy sparse storage schemes*

	Creation	Subscriptable	Change Sparse Structure	Matrix-Vector Product	Linear Algebra
MATLAB	fast	yes	yes	fast	yes
COO	fast	no	no	medium	no
CSC/CSR Indices	fast	yes	yes	fast	yes
CSC/CSR Subscripting	very slow	yes	yes	fast	yes
LIL	slow	yes	fast	fast	yes
DOK	very slow	yes	yes	fast	yes
BSR	medium	no	no	fast	yes
DIA	very fast	no	no	fast	yes

Performance measurements suggest two of the seven formats, DOK and BSR, could be dropped from SciPy with no impact on capability. LIL does everything DOK can do, only faster, and BSR, despite being tailored for block matrices, is both slow and inflexible.

The most effective way to work with sparse matrices in Python is to create them as COO, CSC, or CSR matrices using index arrays. COO matrices can be created marginally more quickly than CSC or CSR, but COO matrices cannot be subscripted or used for linear algebra operations beyond matrix multiplication. Converting COO matrices to CSC or CSR can be done quickly though.

Subscripted growth, that is, creation with A[i,j] += v, should be avoided if performance is a concern. Conversion between formats is cheap, usually less than 1% of the effort it took to create the matrix, so if many indexed updates are necessary, it may pay off to convert a matrix from COO/CSR/CSC to LIL (which can do subscripted updates the fastest), make the subscripted update, then convert back to CSC or CSR.

One wonders if these format switches could be abstracted away to give a single, seamless sparse matrix experience—like MATLAB's.

11.4 Interpolation

Numerical data must often be resampled at intervals different than originally recorded. This is especially true of observations taken from *in situ* measurements, test equipment, and so on.

While both NumPy and SciPy have interpolation functions, SciPy's offer more capability.

11.4.1 One-Dimensional Interpolation

The following figure shows five points on the interval 0 to 1. We'll demonstrate linear and spline interpolation methods to estimate values between known points. Extrapolation before the first and beyond the last points is best done with a curve fitting method such as linear regression (Section 11.5.1).

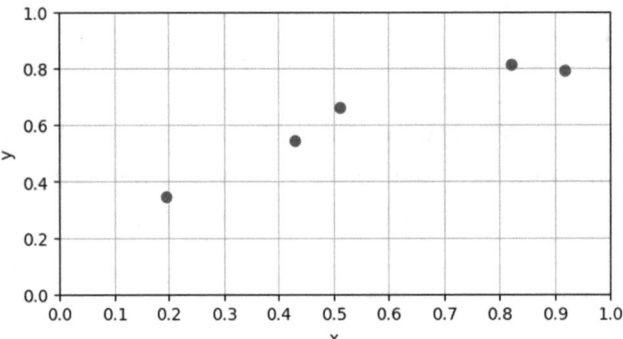

11.4.1.1 One-Dimensional Linear Interpolation

One dimensional linear interpolation can be done with NumPy's np.interp(). It takes three input arguments: an array of *x* values at which we want the corresponding *y* values, then the set of known *x* and *y*:

```
In : x_known = np.array([0.194, 0.429, 0.512, 0.821, 0.917])
In : y_known = np.array([0.347, 0.543, 0.661, 0.811, 0.793])
In : x_desired = np.linspace(0, 1, num=21)
In : x_desired
array([0.  , 0.05, 0.1 , 0.15, 0.2 ,
       0.25, 0.3 , 0.35, 0.4 , 0.45,
```

```
       0.5 , 0.55, 0.6 , 0.65, 0.7 ,
       0.75, 0.8 , 0.85, 0.9 , 0.95, 1.])
In : y_desired = np.interp(x_desired, x_known, y_known)
```

The interpolated points (x_desired, y_desired) are shown as blue plus signs:

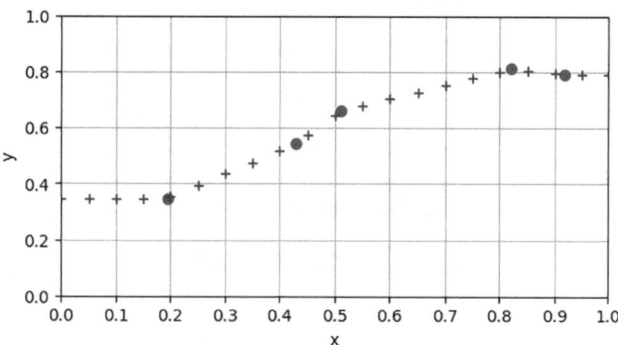

The extrapolated values are merely copies of the first and last known points. This can be changed to other values (such as np.NaN) with the optional keyword arguments left= and right= to np.interp().

11.4.1.2 One-Dimensional Spline Interpolation

Spline interpolation in one dimension requires the interp1d() function from the SciPy scipy.interpolate module. Instead of taking three arguments like np.interp(), interp1d() takes only the known *x* and *y* values as inputs, along with optional keywords kind which describes the interpolation method to use (options are listed in Table 11-7), bound_error, and fill_value. The bound_error and fill_value optional arguments are important because, unlike np.interp(), interp1d() will not extrapolate values before the first point or beyond the last point. By default, bound_error will be True which means an attempt to extrapolate will cause the code to raise a ValueError exception. We can avoid the exception by setting bound_error to False, but in this case we need to supply the value to use when x_desired is outside the range of x_known. That's what fill_value is for. A commonly used value for the out-of-bounds result is np.NaN, which can be used to inform downstream routines that the interpolator failed at the corresponding *x* value. Naturally, those downstream routines must be prepared to deal with np.NaN values. Conveniently, points with np.NaN values do not appear in plots.

Table 11-7. *Options for kind in* $scipy.interpolate.interp1d()$

kind	Description
`'linear'`	Linear; same as `np.interp()`
`'nearest'`	Nearest neighbor
`'zero'`	Zeroth-order spline
`'slinear'`	First-order spline
`'quadratic'`	Second-order spline
`'cubic'`	Third-order spline
`'previous'`	Value of the previous point
`'next'`	Value of the next point

interp1d()'s return value is a new function which takes the array of desired *x* values as its sole argument. The return value from this function is the *y* array for the given *x*'s. The code below uses the same x_known, y_known, and x_desired as in Section 11.4.1.1.

```
In : from scipy.interpolate import interp1d
In : new_fn = interp1d(x_known, y_known,
               kind='cubic', bounds_error=False,
               fill_value=np.NaN)
In : y_desired = new_fn(x_desired)
```

which yields

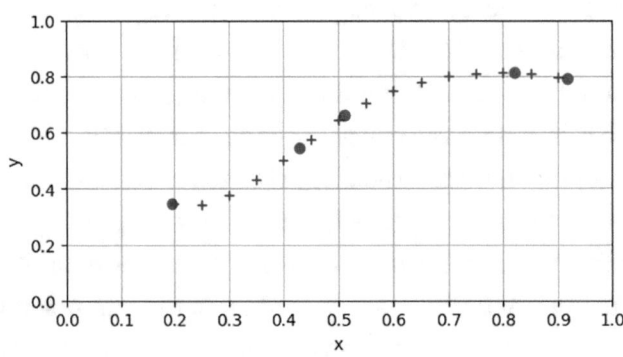

11.4.2 Two-Dimensional Interpolation

Two-dimensional interpolation is a common task in the fields of geographic information systems (GIS), mapping, and remote sensing. As with 1D interpolation, 2D interpolation takes values at known locations and returns estimated values at neighboring locations, typically a regularly spaced grid. Values on a regular grid are well suited for visualization as heat maps, contour plots, or map overlays.

As a simple example, let's look at the function $f(x, y) = x + 2(\cos 7x + \sin 5y) + 3y \sin 6x$ on the square bounded by $-0.6 < x < 1$ and $-1 < y < 0.4$. A contour plot of $f(x, y)$ looks like this:

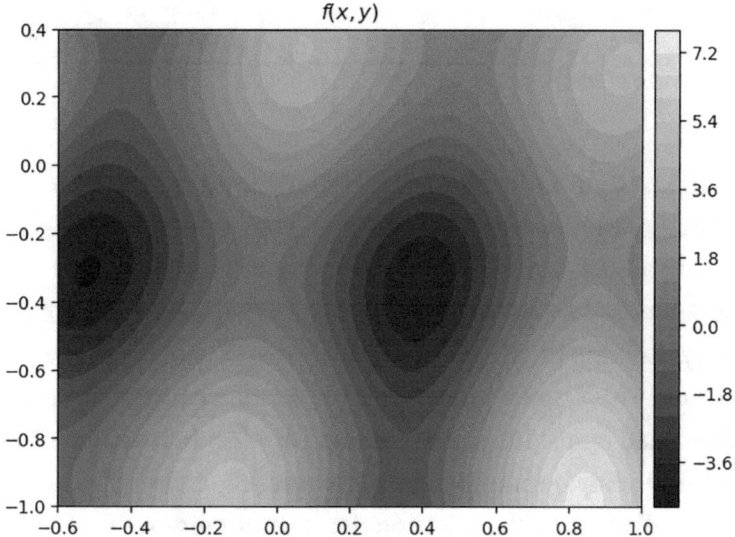

To test our 2D interpolation methods, we'll subsample $f(x, y)$ at 114 points taken from a region of a spiral and defined by these x and y values (Boolean index masks such as in_range are explained in Section 11.1.14):

```
K = 0.005
t = np.linspace(0,800,num=1100)
Spiral = np.array([K*t*np.cos(t)+1,
                   K*t*np.sin(t)-1])
in_range = (-0.6 < Spiral[0,:]) * (Spiral[0,:] < 1.0) * \
           (-1.0 < Spiral[1,:]) * (Spiral[1,:] < 0.4)
x = Spiral[0,in_range]
y = Spiral[1,in_range]
```

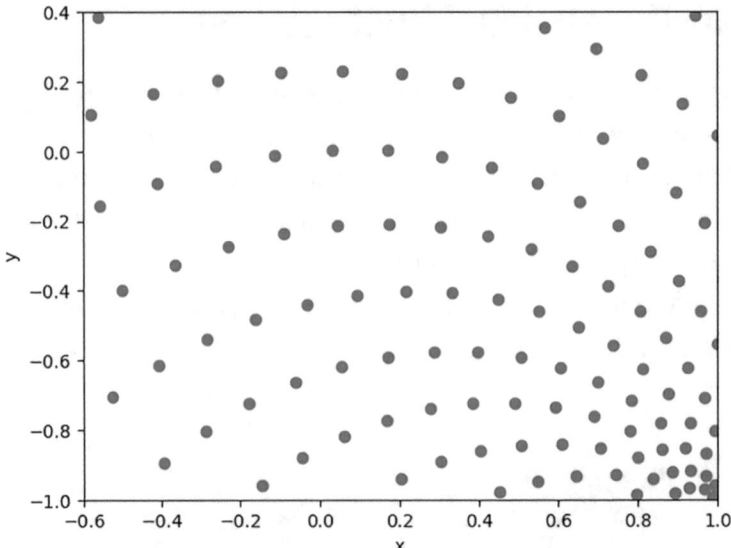

Both MATLAB and Python employ a function named griddata() to perform 2D interpolation of irregularly spaced data onto regular grids; Python's exists in SciPy's scipy.interpolate module. griddata()'s input arguments are the coordinates of the points at which we know data values, the data values themselves, then a pair of two-dimensional arrays holding the X and Y of coordinates at which we want the function to interpolate values. The X and Y arrays typically contain coordinates on a regularly spaced grid as returned by mgrid[] or np.meshgrid() (explained later); however, any arrangement of points may be employed. Points whose indices differ by one are assumed to be topologically adjacent for the interpolation computations.

We want results spaced over a regular grid, so we first have to create the coordinate values for that grid. This can be done two ways in Python. The first method uses NumPy's meshgrid() function:

MATLAB:	Python:
`>> nX = 3; nY = 4;`	`In : nX, nY = 3, 4`
`>> format short`	`In : X, Y = np.meshgrid(`
`>> [X, Y] = meshgrid(...`	`...:     np.linspace(-.6,  1,nX),`
`         linspace(-.6,  1,nX),...`	`...:     np.linspace(-1 ,-.4,nY))`
`         linspace(-1 ,-.4,nY))`	
`X =`	`In : X`
`    -0.6000     0.2000     1.0000`	`array([[-0.6,  0.2,  1. ],`
`    -0.6000     0.2000     1.0000`	`       [-0.6,  0.2,  1. ],`
`    -0.6000     0.2000     1.0000`	`       [-0.6,  0.2,  1. ],`
`    -0.6000     0.2000     1.0000`	`       [-0.6,  0.2,  1. ]])`
`Y =`	`In : Y`
`    -1.0000    -1.0000    -1.0000`	`array([[-1. , -1. , -1. ],`
`    -0.8000    -0.8000    -0.8000`	`       [-0.8, -0.8, -0.8],`
`    -0.6000    -0.6000    -0.6000`	`       [-0.6, -0.6, -0.6],`
`    -0.4000    -0.4000    -0.4000`	`       [-0.4, -0.4, -0.4]])`

The second method uses NumPy's `mgrid` object (not a function!) indexed by ranges with imaginary step sizes. Ordinary list and NumPy index ranges permit only integer values, but `mgrid` index ranges may have floating-point start, end, and increment values. Another quirk is that the x and y positions are reversed compared to `np.meshgrid()`:

MATLAB:	Python:
``` matlab code >> nX = 3; nY = 4; >> format short >> [X, Y] = meshgrid(... linspace(-.6, 1,nX),... linspace(-1 ,-.4,nY)) X = -0.6000 0.2000 1.0000 -0.6000 0.2000 1.0000 -0.6000 0.2000 1.0000 -0.6000 0.2000 1.0000 Y = -1.0000 -1.0000 -1.0000 -0.8000 -0.8000 -0.8000 -0.6000 -0.6000 -0.6000 -0.4000 -0.4000 -0.4000 ```	``` In : nX, nY = 3, 4 In : Y, X = np.mgrid[-1.0:-0.4:nY*1j, ...: -0.6: 1.0:nX*1j] In : X array([[-0.6, 0.2, 1.], [-0.6, 0.2, 1.], [-0.6, 0.2, 1.], [-0.6, 0.2, 1.]]) In : Y array([[-1. , -1. , -1.], [-0.8, -0.8, -0.8], [-0.6, -0.6, -0.6], [-0.4, -0.4, -0.4]]) ```

We now have all inputs needed for the 2D interpolation: coordinates of 114 locations where we know the function values and coordinates of a regular grid where we want interpolated values. By default, `griddata()` performs a linear interpolation but can also do cubic and nearest-neighbor interpolation. We'll evaluate all three on a 200 × 200 grid:

MATLAB:	Python:

```matlab
% code/griddata/spiral_interp.m
K = 0.005;
% subsample f(x,y) at 114 points
t = linspace(0,800,1100);
X = [K*t.*cos(t)+1; K*t.*sin(t)-1];
in_range = (-0.6 < X(1,:)) & ...
           (X(1,:) < 1.0) & ...
           (-1.0 < X(2,:)) & ...
           (X(2,:) < 0.4);
x_known = X(1,in_range);
y_known = X(2,in_range);

F_known = f(x_known, y_known);
% make a 200 x 200 regular grid
nX = 200; nY = 200;
[X, Y] = meshgrid(...
    linspace(-.6,  1,nX),...
    linspace(-1 ,-.4,nY));
% interpolate  to the regular grid
F_near   = griddata(...
        x_known, y_known, ...
        F_known, X,Y, 'nearest');
F_linear = griddata(...
        x_known, y_known,...
        F_known, X,Y, 'linear');
F_cubic  = griddata(...
        x_known, y_known,...
        F_known, X,Y, 'cubic');
function [S] = f(x,y)
   S = x + 2*(cos(7*x) + ...
      sin(5*y)) + 3*y.*sin(6*x);
end
```

```python
# code/griddata/spiral_interp.py
import numpy as np
from scipy.interpolate import griddata
def f(x,y):
    return x + 2*(np.cos(7*x)+
        np.sin(5*y)) + 3*y*np.sin(6*x)
K = 0.005
# subsample f(x,y) at 114 points
t = np.linspace(0,800,num=1100)
X = np.array([K*t*np.cos(t)+1,
                K*t*np.sin(t)-1])
in_range = (-0.6 < X[0,:]) * \
           (X[0,:] < 1.0) * \
           (-1.0 < X[1,:]) * \
           (X[1,:] < 0.4)
x_known = X[0,in_range]
y_known = X[1,in_range]

F_known = f(x_known, y_known)
# make a 200 x 200 regular grid
nX, nY = 200, 200
Y, X = np.mgrid[-1.0:-0.4:nY*1j,
                -0.6: 1.0:nX*1j]
# interpolate to the regular grid
F_near   = griddata(
        (x_known, y_known),
        F_known, (X,Y), method="nearest")
F_linear = griddata(
        (x_known, y_known),
        F_known, (X,Y),method='linear')
F_cubic  = griddata(
        (x_known, y_known),
        F_known, (X,Y),method='cubic')
```

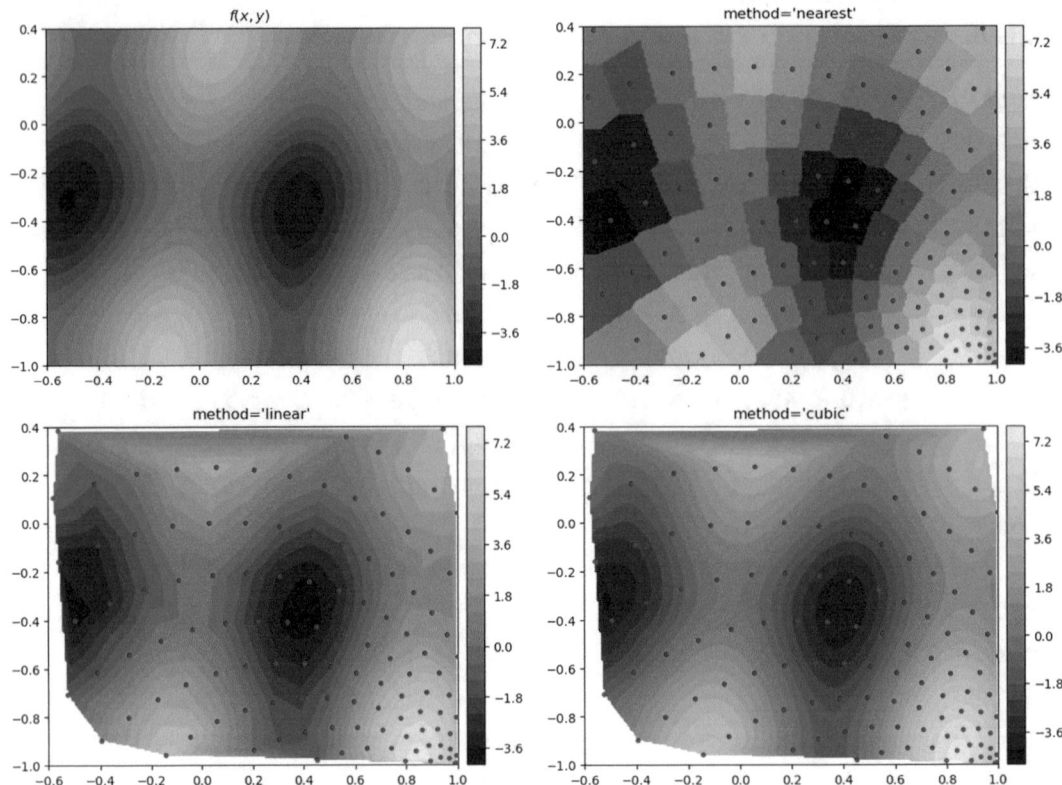

Which interpolation method is best? As with many problems, the answer is "it depends." The cubic method most faithfully captures the gradients of the original function, especially where there is a concentration of known data points. However, both the cubic and linear methods fail to capture the local peak at the top edge.

This failure is caused by `griddata()`'s linear and cubic methods' use of a Delaunay triangulation over the known data points. The triangulation fills a convex hull around the known points with elements, and any desired point inside the convex hull will receive an interpolated value from its bounding element. Points along the top and left edges are joined by thin slivers of elements that unhelpfully associate remotely spaced points.

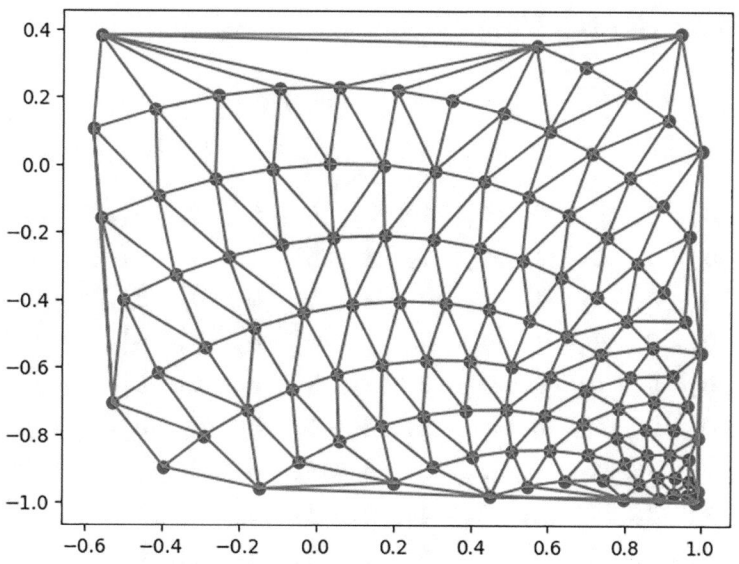

11.4.3 Two-Dimensional Interpolation on a Grid

A simplified, but still common, form of two-dimensional interpolation takes evenly spaced values on a coarse grid and interpolates the values to a finer grid. In image processing, this interpolation is referred to as image zoom since the finer grid has many more data points (or pixels) than the original grid.

Both `interp2` in MATLAB and `griddata` in Python, discussed in the previous section, can be used for this task. Both of those, however, require additional arguments that define the interpolation point positions. A simpler method is available in Python's `scipy.ndimage` module. Its `zoom()` function needs only two arguments: the input array and the amount to grow (or reduce it by). By default, `zoom()` performs a cubic spline interpolation, but the spline order can be set between 0 and 5. The following example interpolates values of a 3 x 5 matrix to fill a 10 x 12 matrix.

The second argument describes the amount by which each dimension should grow. We want 10 rows instead of 3 and 12 columns instead of 5, so the scaling argument is [10/3, 12/5]:

Python:

```
from scipy.ndimage import zoom
In : a = np.array([[0, 0, 0, 5, 6],
                   [0, 0, 0, 5, 6],
                   [4, 4, 5, 6, 8]])
```

```
In : b = zoom(a, [10/3, 12/5])
In : b.shape
Out: (10, 12)

In : b
array([[ 0,  0,  0,  0,  0,  0,  1,  3,  5,  6,  6,  6],
       [ 0,  0,  0,  0, -1, -1,  1,  3,  5,  6,  6,  6],
       [ 0,  0,  0,  0, -1, -1,  0,  2,  5,  6,  6,  6],
       [ 0,  0,  0, -1, -1, -1,  0,  2,  4,  6,  6,  6],
       [ 0,  0,  0,  0, -1, -1,  0,  2,  5,  6,  6,  6],
       [ 0,  0,  0,  0,  0,  0,  1,  3,  5,  6,  6,  6],
       [ 1,  2,  2,  1,  1,  2,  2,  4,  5,  6,  7,  7],
       [ 3,  3,  3,  3,  3,  3,  4,  4,  5,  6,  7,  7],
       [ 4,  4,  4,  4,  4,  4,  5,  5,  6,  7,  7,  8],
       [ 4,  4,  4,  4,  4,  5,  5,  5,  6,  7,  8,  8]])
```

If the scaling argument were a single value, both dimensions would be increased by the same factor.

The negative values are an artifact of the cubic spline that fits the step function across the 0/5 boundary. A bilinear interpolation can be done by setting (order=1):

Python:

```
from scipy.ndimage import zoom
In : a = np.array([[0, 0, 0, 5, 6],
                   [0, 0, 0, 5, 6],
                   [4, 4, 5, 6, 8]])

In : b = zoom(a, [10/3, 12/5], order=1)
In : b
array([[0, 0, 0, 0, 0, 0, 1, 3, 5, 5, 6, 6],
       [0, 0, 0, 0, 0, 0, 1, 3, 5, 5, 6, 6],
       [0, 0, 0, 0, 0, 0, 1, 3, 5, 5, 6, 6],
       [0, 0, 0, 0, 0, 0, 1, 3, 5, 5, 6, 6],
       [0, 0, 0, 0, 0, 0, 1, 3, 5, 5, 6, 6],
       [0, 0, 0, 0, 0, 1, 1, 3, 5, 5, 6, 6],
       [1, 1, 1, 1, 1, 2, 2, 4, 5, 6, 6, 7],
```

```
      [2, 2, 2, 2, 2, 3, 3, 4, 5, 6, 7, 7],
      [3, 3, 3, 3, 3, 4, 4, 5, 6, 6, 7, 8],
      [4, 4, 4, 4, 4, 5, 5, 6, 6, 7, 7, 8]])
```

11.5 Curve Fitting

11.5.1 Linear Regression

Linear regression finds the slope and vertical intercept of a line which best fits a collection of points. The "best fit" is defined as the line which minimizes the sum of the square of errors—the distances the points are away from the line. Motivations for solving linear regression problems generally fall into two categories: the need for just the slope and intercept of the best-fit line and the need for a comprehensive solution that returns error residuals, skew, kurtosis, and numerous other characteristic values.

In this section, we'll concern ourselves with the simple version of the problem. The comprehensive solution, including weighted least squares, appears in Section 11.7.

Both MATLAB and Python can solve the linear regression problem with their implementations of polyfit(), a general polynomial fit solver, by setting the degree of the polynomial to one. While the functions return the same solution, the Python function returns the vertical intercept and slope, while the MATLAB function returns them in the opposite order:

MATLAB:	Python:

```
>> Pts = [7.312 15.878;
          7.657 16.308;
          7.934 16.690;
          7.962 16.902;
          8.614 17.013;
          8.623 17.766];


>> polyfit(Pts(:,1),Pts(:,2),1)


   1.1346    7.6638
```

```
from numpy.polynomial.polynomial \
    import polyfit
In : Pts = np.array([
          [ 7.312, 15.878],
          [ 7.657, 16.308],
          [ 7.934, 16.690],
          [ 7.962, 16.902],
          [ 8.614, 17.013],
          [ 8.623, 17.766]])
In : b, m = polyfit(Pts[:,0],Pts[:,1],1)
In : m, b
Out: (1.134557, 7.663752)
```

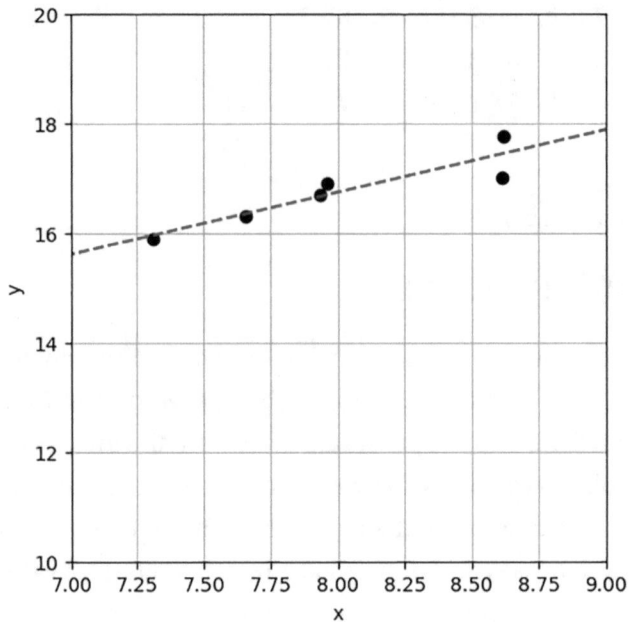

11.5.2 Fitting Higher-Order Polynomials

The polyfit() function shown in the previous section can of course be used to find coefficients of best-fit polynomials with a degree greater than one. Here, we compute the coefficients of a cubic which best fits another collection of points. Note that in this case the points are not sorted in ascending value of X coordinate—point order is irrelevant.

The solution has four values, a_3, a_2, a_1, and a_0, which are the coefficients to the cubic

$$a_3 x^3 + a_2 x^2 + a_1 x + a_0$$

that best fits the points. Aside from returning the coefficients in opposite order (MATLAB returns a_0, a_1, a_2, and a_3, while Python returns a_3, a_2, a_1, and a_0), the values match.

MATLAB:	Python:

```
Pts = [-0.938  16.875;
        0.326  21.290;
        1.787  22.317;
        2.968  28.767;
        4.038  10.210;
        5.358 -53.774];

>> polyfit(Pts(:,1),Pts(:,2),3)

-1.356 4.306 2.967 15.960
```

```
from numpy.polynomial.polynomial \
    import polyfit
In : Pts = np.array([
        [ -0.938,  16.875],
        [  0.326,  21.290],
        [  1.787,  22.317],
        [  2.968,  28.767],
        [  4.038,  10.210],
        [  5.358, -53.774]])

In : polyfit(Pts[:,0],Pts[:,1],3)
Out: array([15.960, 2.967,
                4.306, -1.356])
```

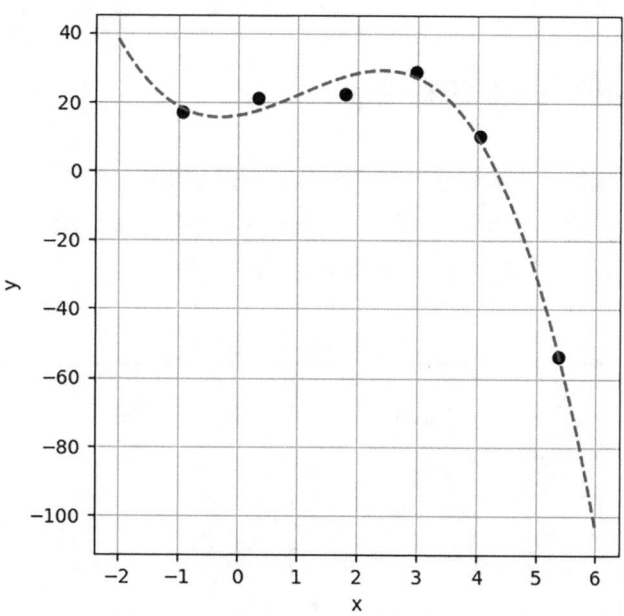

11.5.3 Fitting to Models

Few real-world datasets fit linear or polynomial models, at least not for wide ranges. More common distributions, at least among physical phenomena, are Gaussian, sinusoidal, and exponential or logarithmic decay or growth—or combinations of these.

The scipy.optimize module has a number of functions that can be used to fit models to data. Here, we'll examine two of them, curve_fit() and differential_ evolution(). MATLAB has a powerful Curve Fitting Toolbox, but for simpler curves the generic optimization function fminsearch() is often effective.

scipy.optimize.curve_fit() aims to find parameters of a continuously smooth model (e.g., the equation of a curve) that best fit a dataset. It works well when the model is monotonic, for example, the logarithmic growth seen in Figure 11-3.

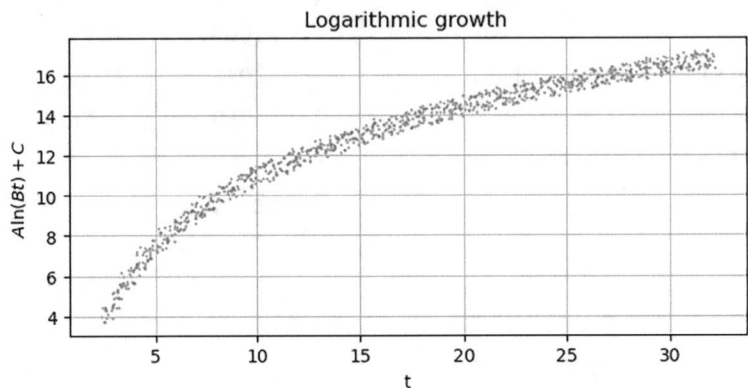

Figure 11-3. *Logarithmic growth data*

The scipy.optimize.curve_fit() function and MATLAB's fminsearch() fare poorly on more varying data such as sinusoidally decaying data from an underdamped system such as the point distribution shown in Figure 11-4.

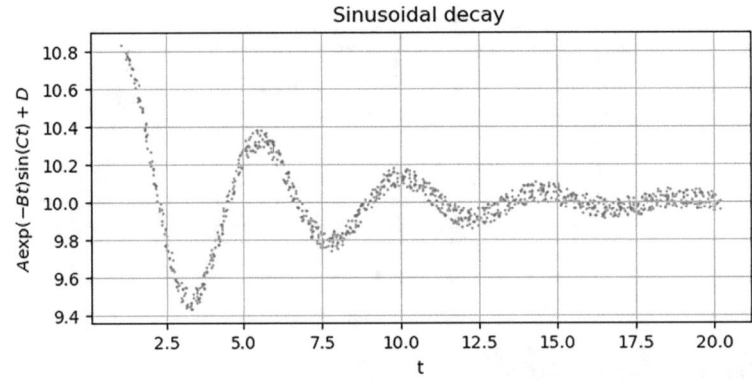

Figure 11-4. *Sinusoidally decaying data*

For such data we'll need a hardier method. One such option is the differential evolution algorithm [3], implemented in `scipy.optimize.differential_evolution()`. It is less sensitive to local minima in the objective function and often finds excellent solutions over wide input domains. A MATLAB implementation of this algorithm is available on the FileExchange.[9]

11.5.3.1 Case 1: Logarithmic Growth

The points of Figure 11-3 were created with the function

$$f(t) = A \ln Bt + C$$

using $A = 5$, $B = 14$, and $C = -13.7$ and then adding noise in the form of random values:

MATLAB:	Python:

`% code/optim/log_test_data.py`
`A = 5; B = 14; C = -13.7;`
`Fn = @(t,A,B,C)(A*log(B*t) + C);`
`rand('seed',234567);`
`n_pts = 1000;`
`t = 2 + linspace(.2,30,n_pts)+...`
`      .3*rand(1,n_pts);`
`y_true = Fn(t, A, B, C);`
`y_meas = y_true + 0.2*A*(0.5 -...`
`      rand(1,n_pts));`
`t_meas = t  + 0.1*A*(0.5 -...`
`      rand(1,n_pts));`
	`#!/usr/bin/env python3`
	`# code/optim/log_test_data.py`
	`import numpy as np`
	`A, B, C = 5, 14, -13.7`
	`def Fn(t, A, B, C):`
	`    return A*np.log(B*t) + C`
	`np.random.seed(234567)`
	`n_pts = 1000`
	`t = 2 + np.linspace(.2,30,n_pts)+\`
	`      .3*np.random.rand(n_pts)`
	`y_true = Fn(t, A, B, C)`
	`y_meas = y_true + 0.2*A*(0.5 -`
	`      np.random.rand(n_pts))`
	`t_meas = t  + 0.1*A*(0.5 -`
	`      np.random.rand(n_pts))`

---

[9]`www.mathworks.com/matlabcentral/fileexchange/18593-differential-evolution`

Our task is to determine values for A, B, and C using only the noisy data points and the model equation, $f(t) = A \ln Bt + C$. Before we begin we'll need a way to assess how well a given set of A, B, and C values fit our model. A reasonable choice is the R^2 coefficient of determination.

11.5.3.2 R^2 to Score the Solution

A plot overlaying the noisy data on a curve of the model equation with the solution parameters will give us a subjective idea on how good the solution is. While the plot is useful, a numeric estimate of the "goodness of fit" is also valuable. On the Python side, we'll use the r2_score() function from the sklearn.metrics (machine learning) module. It returns the R^2 coefficient of determination between known and estimated values; 1.0 represents excellent agreement, and 0.0 (or worse, a negative score) means terrible agreement. MATLAB's Statistics and Machine Learning Toolbox has functions to compute R^2. Implementations can also be found on the FileExchange.[10]

11.5.3.3   Fitting Logarithmic Growth with curve_fit()

The curve_fit() function has only three required arguments: the model function (Fn()), the independent variable (t_meas), and the dependent variable (y_meas). It returns two variables, popt, the optimal values of the parameters, and pcov, the estimated covariance of the optimal values.

Formulating the MATLAB solution takes a bit more work. In addition to the model function, we also have to define an error function in the form of a sum of squares of differences function which itself is invoked from another anonymous function. Adding to the difficulty is the need to estimate initial values for A, B, and C.

---

[10]www.mathworks.com/matlabcentral/fileexchange/34492-r-square-the-coefficient-of-determination

MATLAB:	Python:

```
% code/optim/log_test_data_full.py
A = 5; B = 14; C = -13.7;
Fn = @(t,A,B,C)(A*log(B*t) + C);
rand('seed',234567);
n_pts = 1000;
t = 2 + linspace(.2,30,n_pts)+...
       .3*rand(1,n_pts);
y_true = Fn(t, A, B, C);
y_meas = y_true + 0.2*A*(0.5 -...
       rand(1,n_pts));
t_meas = t  + 0.1*A*(0.5 -...
       rand(1,n_pts));
opt_Fn = @(x)sum_sq(x,t_meas,y_
meas);
popt = fminsearch(opt_Fn,[1 1 1])
function ss = sum_sq(x,t,ydata)
  A = x(1); B = x(2); C = x(3);
  ss = sum((ydata - A*log(B*t) +
  C).^2);
end
```

```
In : run log_test_data.py
In : from scipy.optimize import curve_fit
In : from sklearn.metrics import r2_score
In : popt, pcov = curve_fit(Fn,t_meas,
       y_meas)
In : popt
Out: array([  5.00663437,
             12.05087493,
            -12.99449958])
In : r2_score(y_meas, y_curve_fit)
Out: 0.9920846142243493
```

MATLAB's results aren't great. They are also sensitive to the initial guess:

MATLAB:

```
>> log_test_data_full
>> popt = fminsearch(opt_Fn,[1 1 1])
popt =
    4.9880    0.5889    -2.1631
>> popt = fminsearch(opt_Fn,[1 10 -10])
popt =
    4.9881   11.9819    12.8655
```

The Python R^2 score of 0.99 is excellent. Our estimates of $A = 5.007$, $B = 12.05$, and $C = -12.99$ are reasonably close to the true values of 5, 14, and -13.7; more impressively, the resulting curve matches the true curve so closely as to be indistinguishable from it:

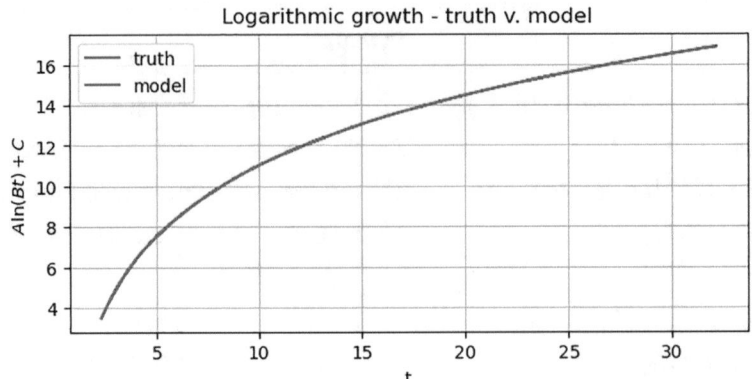

11.5.3.4 Case 2: Sinusoidal Decay

More complex models require increasingly more fiddling with `curve_fit()`'s options such as parameter bounds, initial values, uncertainty estimates, and Jacobian matrix. Instead we'll switch to the more robust (but more computationally expensive) `differential_evolution()` function.

We'll apply this model of an underdamped system:

$$f(t) = Ae^{-Bt} \sin Ct + D \qquad (11.1)$$

to estimate values of A, B, C, and D that best fit the points shown in Figure 11-4. The points in that figure are made with the following code. It begins with known values for A...D and then adds noise in the form of random values to the model function.

Python:

```
# code/optim/sin_decay_test_data.py
import numpy as np
A, B, C, D = 1, .2, 1.4, 10

def Fn(t, A, B, C, D):
return A*np.exp(-B*t)*\
        np.sin(C*t) + D

np.random.seed(234567)
n_pts = 1000
t = np.linspace(1,20,n_pts) + .3*np.random.rand(n_pts)
y_true = Fn(t, A, B, C, D)
y_meas = y_true + .11*(0.5 - np.random.rand(n_pts))
```

11.5.3.5 Fitting Sinusoidal Decay with `curve_fit()`

Sending our noisy data and model function to `curve_fit()` leads to an unsatisfactory result.

Python:

```
In : from scipy.optimize import curve_fit
In : from sklearn.metrics import r2_score
run sin_decay_test_data.py # set t, y_meas, y_true
In : popt, pcov = curve_fit(Fn,t,y_meas)
In : y_curve_fit = Fn(t, *popt)
In : popt
Out: [99.999 3.843 5.886 9.995]
In : r2_score(y_meas, y_curve_fit)
Out: 0.033069669065311835
```

The R^2 score of 0.03 means our solution is worthless. The green curve of Figure 11-5 in the next section shows exactly how bad it is.

11.5.3.6 Fitting Sinusoidal Decay with `differential_evolution()`

`scipy.optimize.differential_evolution()`, unlike `curve_fit()`, requires upper and lower bounds on the parameters. We'll give these wide ranges to illustrate the method's surprising robustness:

$$0.01 <= A <= 100$$
$$-10 <= B <= 10$$
$$0.01 <= C <= 10$$
$$-100 <= D <= 100$$

Python:

```
In : from scipy.optimize import differential_evolution
In : from sklearn.metrics import r2_score
In : def func(parameters, *data):
...:     A, B, C, D = parameters
...:     Fn, t, Y = data
```

```
...:         return np.linalg.norm(Fn(t,A,B,C,D)-Y)
In : bounds=([0.01, 100],
...:          [ -10,  10],
...:          [0.01,  10],
...:          [-100, 100])
run sin_decay_test_data.py # set t, y_meas, y_true
In : args = (Fn, t, y_meas)
In : DE_result = differential_evolution(func, bounds, args=args)
In : DE_result
    fun: 1.0028485230670718
    jac: array([ 1.15463195e-06, -2.70894418e-06,  9.99200722e-07,
    -3.79696274e-06])
 message: 'Optimization terminated successfully.'
    nfev: 3430
     nit: 55
 success: True
       x: array([1.00574221, 0.1992207 , 1.40038483, 9.99905623])
In : y_DE_fit = Fn(t, *DE_result.x)
In : r2_score(y_true, y_DE_fit)
Out: 0.9998993756587
```

This time the R^2 score is just about 1.0, indicating an excellent fit. Figure 11-5 shows the curve_fit() and differential_evolution() solutions to this problem.

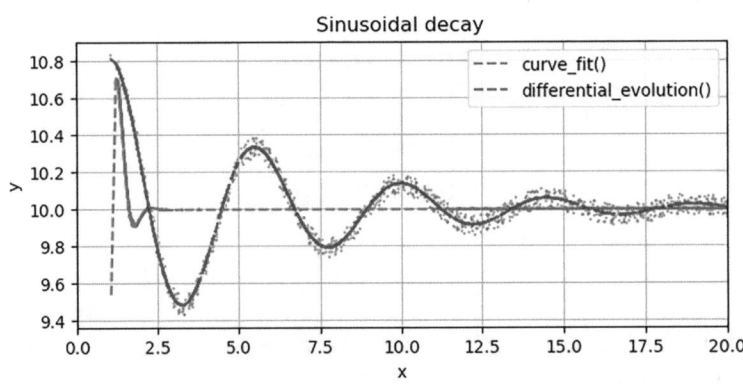

Figure 11-5. *Sinusoidal decay modeled with curve fit and differential evolution*

Rather than attempting to solve this more challenging problem with MATLAB's `fminsearch()`, the recipe in Section 11.6 shows how to solve the curve fit in MATLAB using SciPy's `differential_evolution()`. Of course, if the FileExchange implementation of `differential_evolution()` is available to you, it will be a more convenient alternative than using Python. It goes without saying that the Curve Fitting Toolbox is better still.

11.6 Recipe 11-1: Curve Fitting with `differential_evolution()`

The Curve Fitting Toolbox is the package of choice for determining equations of best-fit curves to data. In its absence, `differential_evolution()` from SciPy's `optimize` module is a more powerful alternative than `fminsearch` from the core MATLAB product. Here, we demonstrate using the Python implementation of `differential_evolution()` with MATLAB to find the coefficients A, B, C, and D of the decaying sinusoid function, as was done using only Python in Section 11.5.3.6.

This recipe reveals a limitation of MATLAB's py module: MATLAB functions passed as arguments to Python functions cannot be called from Python. This prevents us from calling optimizers such as `differential_evolution()` directly from MATLAB since their first argument is the function to be minimized or maximized.

There are at least two possible solutions: (1) write the cost function in Python and perform the optimization entirely in a Python bridge module or (2) call the MATLAB cost function from Python through the `matlab.engine` module (Section 6.10). The second method is much more powerful since it should be able to work with any MATLAB function. In practice, though, Python calls to `matlab.engine` objects frequently fail with the MATLAB error "failed to connect to matlab.engine: Unable to connect to MATLAB session." For this reason, only the first method is demonstrated.

When evaluating the cost function in Python, the MATLAB portion merely passes data points to a Python bridge module which contains both the cost function and the call to the optimizer. A function in the bridge module then returns the best-fit coefficients to MATLAB.

Python:

```
# code/optim/bridge_de.py
import numpy as np
from scipy.optimize import differential_evolution
def Fn(t, A, B, C, D):
    return A*np.exp(-B*t)*np.sin(C*t) + D
def func(parameters, *data):
    A, B, C, D = parameters
    Fn, t, Y = data
    return np.linalg.norm(Fn(t,A,B,C,D)-Y)
def compute_ABCD(bounds, t, y_meas):
    args = (Fn, t, y_meas)
    DE_result = differential_evolution(func, bounds, args=args)
    soln = { 'success' : DE_result.success,
             'message' : DE_result.message,
             'x' : DE_result.x,
           }
    if DE_result.success:
        y_DE_fit = Fn(t, *DE_result.x)
    else:
        y_DE_fit = []
    soln['y_fit'] = y_DE_fit
    return soln
```

The following MATLAB driver sends parameter bounds and test data to the Python compute_ABCD() function which returns a dictionary containing the solution—if one is found:

MATLAB:

```
% code/optim/fit_decaying_sine.m
Im = @py.importlib.import_module;
optim = Im('bridge_de');
np = Im('numpy');
sk = Im('sklearn.metrics');
A = 1; B = .2; C = 1.4; D = 10;
rng(234567);
```

448

```
n_pts = 1000;
t = linspace(1,20,n_pts) + .3*rand(1,n_pts);
y_true = Fn(t, A, B, C, D);
y_meas = y_true + .11*(0.5 - rand(1,n_pts));
bounds = py.tuple({[0.01, 100], ...
                   [ -10,  10], ...
                   [0.01,  10], ...
                   [-100, 100]});
solution = optim.compute_ABCD(bounds, np.array(t), np.array(y_meas));
if solution.get('success')
   R2 = sk.r2_score(np.array(y_true), np.array(solution.get('y_fit')));
   ABCD = py2mat(solution.get('x'));
   fprintf('A=%.6f, B=%.6f, C=%.6f, D=%.6f\n', ABCD)
   fprintf('score = %f\n', R2)
else
   fprintf('Failed: %s\n', solution.get('message'))
end

function [x] = Fn(t, A, B, C, D)
    x = A*exp(-B*t).*sin(C*t) + D;
end
```

The solution from MATLAB matches the Python solution of Section 11.5.3.6:
MATLAB:

```
>> fit_decaying_sine
A=1.005742, B=0.199221, C=1.400385, D=9.999056
score = 0.999899
```

11.7 Regression

11.7.1 Ordinary Least Squares

The Python module statsmodels has its own statistics-flavored linear regression, or least squares, solvers that return richer results than NumPy's polyfit() function described in Section 11.5.1. The primary functions are OLS(), for ordinary least squares, and WLS(), for weighted least squares.

The following examples generate points (x, y) that roughly approximate the line $y = mx + b$ for a given slope, m, and vertical intercept, b. We'll call OLS() and WLS() to see how well we can recover m and b.

MATLAB:	Python:

```matlab
% create random X,Y
m = 3.77;
b = -5.5;
nPts = 20;
X = -5 + 12*rand(nPts,1);
X = sort(X);
noise = 8*(rand(nPts,1)-.5);
Y = m*X + b + noise;
% recover m and b
mb = polyfit(X,Y,1);
m_ls = mb(1);
b_ls = mb(2);
fprintf("ML : %f %f\n", ...
        m_ls,b_ls)


Y_pred = m_ls*X + b_ls;
plot(X,Y,'g.')
hold on
plot(X,Y_pred,'r-')
grid
---------- Output:
ML : 3.558505 -4.843925
```

```python
import numpy as np
import statsmodels.api as stats
import matplotlib.pyplot as plt
# create random X,Y
m = 3.77 # true slope
b = -5.5 # true intercept
nPts = 20
X = -5 + 12*np.random.rand(nPts)
X.sort()
noise = 8*(np.random.rand(nPts)-.5)
Y = m*X + b + noise
% recover m and b
Xb = stats.add_constant(X,0)
ols = stats.OLS(Y, Xb).fit()
m_ls, b_ls = ols.params
print(f'OLS {m_ls} {b_ls}')

Y_pred = ols.predict(Xb)
plt.plot(X,Y,'g.')
plt.plot(X,Y_pred,'r-')
plt.grid(True)
plt.show()
---------- Output:
OLS 3.86476 -6.23757
```

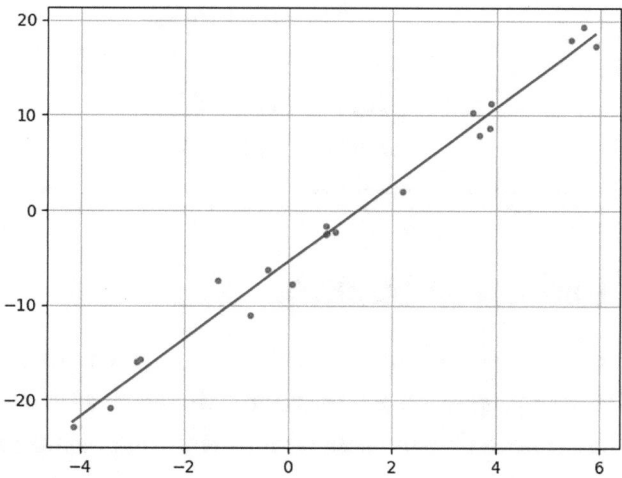

The MATLAB and Python implementations will see different point pairs, so we do not expect their respective solutions for *m* and *b* to match for small sample sizes. If we were to use 1000 points instead of 20, both Python and MATLAB will return values within 1% of the true values.

The ols object from the preceding Python example has numerous methods and properties. The following text is the output of print(ols.summary()):

```
                           OLS Regression Results
==============================================================================
Dep. Variable:                      y   R-squared:                       0.973
Model:                            OLS   Adj. R-squared:                  0.972
Method:                 Least Squares   F-statistic:                     653.9
Date:                Fri, 26 Jun 2020   Prob (F-statistic):           1.33e-15
Time:                        15:05:59   Log-Likelihood:                -42.682
No. Observations:                  20   AIC:                             89.36
Df Residuals:                      18   BIC:                             91.36
Df Model:                           1
Covariance Type:            nonrobust
==============================================================================
                 coef    std err          t      P>|t|      [0.025      0.975]
------------------------------------------------------------------------------
x1             3.8648      0.151     25.571      0.000       3.547       4.182
const         -6.2376      0.511    -12.214      0.000      -7.310      -5.165
==============================================================================
```

Omnibus:	0.521	Durbin-Watson:	2.171
Prob(Omnibus):	0.771	Jarque-Bera (JB):	0.578
Skew:	0.055	Prob(JB):	0.749
Kurtosis:	2.174	Cond. No.	3.62

===

11.7.2 Weighted Least Squares

Data points may have disproportionate importance—imagine a measurement campaign performed with different models of test equipment. Values observed with more accurate equipment should be accorded greater significance when aggregate properties of all points are computed.

MATLAB can perform weighted least squares fits with the `fittype()` and `fit()` functions from the Curve Fitting Toolbox or the `nlinfit()` function from the Statistics and Machine Learning Toolbox. Python's `statsmodule` solves such problems with `WLS()`, which takes the same inputs as `OLS()` shown in the previous section plus additional argument for weights.

The following example repeats the ordinary least squares example with weights assigned to the points linearly from left to right. Point size represents weight in the following plot:

Python:

```
#!/usr/bin/env python3
# code/statistics/wls.py
import numpy as np
import statsmodels.api as stats
import matplotlib.pyplot as plt
m = 3.77 # true slope
b = -5.5 # true intercept
nPts = 20
X = -5 + 12*np.random.rand(nPts)
X.sort()
W = X - np.min(X) + 1
noise = 8*(np.random.rand(nPts)-.5)
Y = m*X + b + noise
Xb = stats.add_constant(X,0)
```

```
wls = stats.WLS(Y, Xb, weight=W).fit()
m_ls, b_ls = wls.params
print(f'WLS {m_ls} {b_ls}')

Y_pred = wls.predict(Xb)
plt.scatter(X,Y, marker='o',s=5*W)
plt.plot(X,Y_pred,'r-')
plt.grid(True)
plt.title('Weighted Least Squares')
plt.show()
```

which produces

```
WLS 3.774306 -4.79019
```

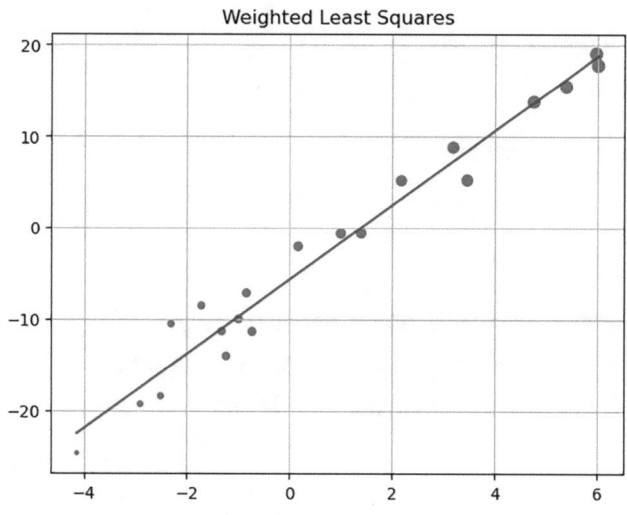

Solve the weighted least squares problem in MATLAB with the recipe in Section 11.8.

11.7.3 Confidence and Prediction Intervals

The coefCI() function from MATLAB's Statistics and Machine Learning Toolbox returns confidence intervals for coefficients of linear regression models. Plotting these takes a bit of extra effort though. In the absence of this toolbox, one can make confidence interval plots quite easily with the regplot() function from the Seaborn Python module.

This code repeats a portion of the ordinary least squares problem, increases the noise, and adds more points:

Python:

```python
#!/usr/bin/env python3
# code/statistics/conf_interval.py
import numpy as np
import matplotlib.pyplot as plt
import seaborn as sns
m = 3.77 # true slope
b = -5.5 # true intercept

nPts = 80
X = -5 + 12*np.random.rand(nPts)
X.sort()
noise = 30*(np.random.rand(nPts) - 0.5)
Y = m*X + b + noise

sns.regplot(x=X, y=Y, marker='.')
plt.xlabel('X')
plt.ylabel('Y')
plt.grid()
plt.title('Confidence interval with seaborn.regplot()')
plt.savefig('conf_interval.png', bbox_inches='tight',
            pad_inches=0.1, transparent=True)
plt.show()
```

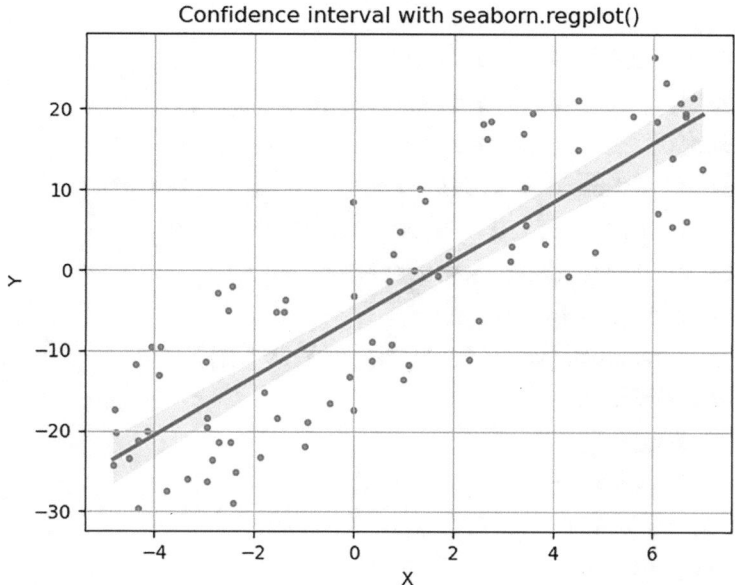

Prediction intervals are arguably more useful than confidence intervals. They can be computed with the predint() function in MATLAB's Curve Fitting Toolbox or with the predband() function [1] in Python, shown as follows:

Python:

```
#!/usr/bin/env python3
# code/statistics/predict_interval.py
import numpy as np
import matplotlib.pyplot as plt
import scipy.stats
import statsmodels.api as stats
import seaborn as sns

def predband(x, xd, yd, p, func, conf=0.95):
    """

    https://apmonitor.com/che263/index.php/Main/PythonRegressionStatistics
    x = requested points
    xd = x data
    yd = y data
    p = additional arguments to func, after xd
    func = function name
```

```
    """
    alpha = 1.0 - conf  # significance
    N = xd.size         # data sample size
    var_n = len(p)      # number of parameters
    # Quantile of Student's t distribution for p=(1-alpha/2)
    q = scipy.stats.t.ppf(1.0 - alpha / 2.0, N - var_n)
    # Stdev of an individual measurement
    se = np.sqrt(1. / (N - var_n) *
                 np.sum((yd - func(xd, *p)) ** 2))
    # Auxiliary definitions
    sx = (x - xd.mean()) ** 2
    sxd = np.sum((xd - xd.mean()) ** 2)
    # Predicted values (best-fit model)
    yp = func(x, *p)
    # Prediction band
    dy = q * se * np.sqrt(1.0+ (1.0/N) + (sx/sxd))
    # Upper & lower prediction bands.
    lpb, upb = yp - dy, yp + dy
    return lpb, upb

def model_function(x, m, b):
    return m*x + b

m = 3.77 # true slope
b = -5.5 # true intercept

nPts = 80
X_even = np.linspace(-5, 7)
X = -5 + 12*np.random.rand(nPts)
X.sort()
noise = 30*(np.random.rand(nPts) - 0.5)
Y = m*X + b + noise

Xb = stats.add_constant(X,0)
ols = stats.OLS(Y, Xb).fit()
m_ls, b_ls = ols.params # best fit slope, y-intercept

lpb, upb = predband(X_even, X, Y, [m_ls, b_ls], model_function, conf=0.95)
```

```
sns.regplot(x=X, y=Y, marker='.')
plt.plot(X_even, lpb, 'k--',label='95% Prediction Band')
plt.plot(X_even, upb, 'k--')
plt.xlabel('X')
plt.ylabel('Y')
plt.grid()
plt.title('Prediction and confidence intervals')
plt.legend(loc='best')
plt.savefig('pred_interval.png', bbox_inches='tight',
            pad_inches=0.1, transparent=True)
plt.show()
```

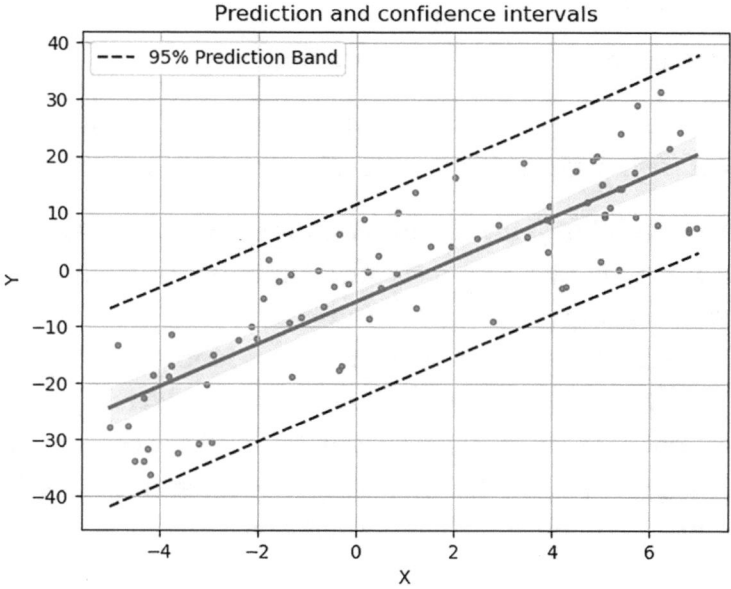

11.8 Recipe 11-2: Weighted Least Squares in MATLAB

A direct invocation of Python's weighted least squares function from MATLAB leads to a disappointing result. Here is such an attempt using the example problem of the previous section:

MATLAB:

```
m = 3.77; % true slope
b = -5.5; % true intercept
nPts = 20;
X = -5 + 12*rand(nPts,1);
X = sort(X);
W = X - min(X) + 1;
noise = 8*(rand(nPts,1)-.5);
Y  = py.numpy.array(m*X + b + noise);
Xb = py.statsmodels.api.add_constant(X,0);
wls = py.statsmodels.api.WLS(Y, Xb, pyargs('weight', W)).fit();
[m_ls, b_ls] = wls.params
```

The program fails on the last line with this error:

```
Unrecognized method, property, or field 'params' for class
'py.statsmodels.regression.linear_model.RegressionResultsWrapper'.
```

The reason for the failure is the wls object returned by py.statsmodels.api.WLS() lacks a .params attribute—as well as many other attributes and methods—so the attempt to access the nonexistent .params throws an error.

We'll need a small bridge module which contains a function that takes primitive MATLAB inputs, in this case the X, Y, and W arrays, calls statsmodels.api.WLS(), then returns desired portions of the solution in a form MATLAB understands. In other words, the call to WLS() happens entirely in Python without a traversal of the MATLAB/Python interface. The entire module defines only one function in ten lines:

Python:

```
# file bridge_WLS.py
import os
import sys
import statsmodels.api as stats
def slope_intercept(X, Y, W):
    if sys.platform == 'win32':
        os.environ['KMP_DUPLICATE_LIB_OK'] = 'TRUE'
    Xb = stats.add_constant(X,0)
```

```
        wls = stats.WLS(Y, Xb, weight=W).fit()
        m_ls, b_ls = wls.params
        Y_pred = wls.predict(Xb)
        if sys.platform == 'win32':
            del os.environ['KMP_DUPLICATE_LIB_OK']
        return { 'm' : m_ls,
                 'b' : b_ls,
                 'Y_predict' : Y_pred }
```

The returned dictionary is recast by py2mat() as a struct containing the slope (.m), intercept (.b), and array of predicted *y* values (.Y_predict). This MATLAB code calls Python's weighted least squares correctly:

MATLAB:

```
% code/matlab_py/weighted_LS.m
np  = py.importlib.import_module('numpy');
WLS = py.importlib.import_module('bridge_WLS');
m = 3.77; % true slope
b = -5.5; % true intercept
nPts = 20;
X = -5 + 12*rand(nPts,1);
X = sort(X);
W = X - min(X) + 1;
noise = 8*(rand(nPts,1)-.5);
Y  = np.array(m*X + b + noise);
X  = np.array(X);
W  = np.array(W);
mbY = WLS.slope_intercept(X,Y,W);
mbY = py2mat(mbY);
fprintf('slope= % .3f  intercept = % .3f\n', mbY.m, mbY.b)
scatter(X,Y,5*W,'b','filled')
hold on
plot(X,mbY.Y_predict,'r-')
grid on
saveas(gcf,'matlab_WLS.png')
```

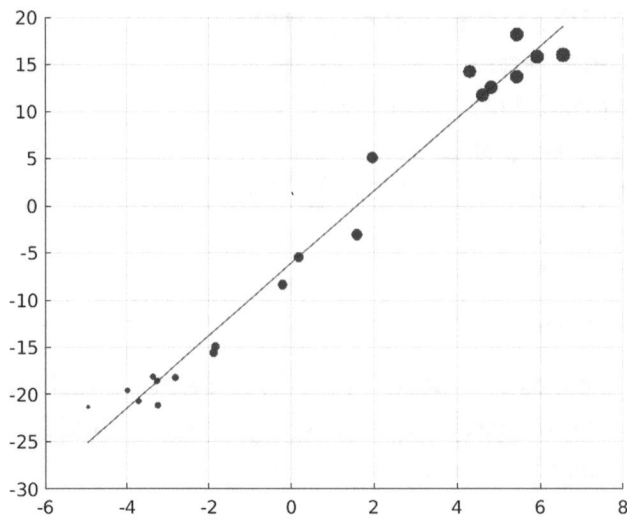

Note   The Python and MATLAB codes for this example create points randomly, so their locations on the two plots will differ.

11.9 Recipe 11-3: Confidence and Prediction Intervals in MATLAB

The following MATLAB programs replicate the confidence and prediction interval plots shown in Section 11.7.3. The only catch is Seaborn wants NumPy arrays, so X and Y are explicitly converted from MATLAB-native to Python-native variables with the mat2py() utility.

Confidence interval:

MATLAB:

```
% code/statistics/conf_interval.m
Im = @py.importlib.import_module;
plt   = Im('matplotlib.pyplot');
mpl   = Im('matplotlib');
sns   = Im('seaborn')
```

```
if ispc
    mpl.use('WXAgg')
else
    mpl.use('TkAgg')
end

m = 3.77; % true slope
b = -5.5; % true intercept

nPts = 80;
X = -5 + 12*rand(nPts,1);
X = sort(X);
noise = 30*rand(nPts,1) - 0.5;
Y = m*X + b + noise;

% seaborn wants Python-native arrays
X = mat2py(X);
Y = mat2py(Y);

sns.regplot(pyargs('x',X,'y',Y,'marker','.'))
plt.xlabel('X')
plt.ylabel('Y')
plt.grid()
plt.title('Confidence interval with seaborn.regplot()')
plt.show()
```

Prediction interval:

The following program imports both model_function() and predband() from the pure Python version of the prediction interval example:

MATLAB:

```
% code/statistics/predict_interval.m
Im = @py.importlib.import_module;
plt  = Im('matplotlib.pyplot');
mpl  = Im('matplotlib');
sns  = Im('seaborn');
np   = Im('numpy');
```

```
%scipy_stats = Im('scipy.stats')
stats = Im('statsmodels.api');
JH    = Im('predict_interval');
if ispc
    mpl.use('WXAgg');
else
    mpl.use('TkAgg');
end

m = 3.77; % true slope
b = -5.5; % true intercept

nPts = 80;
X_even = linspace(-5, 7);
X = -5 + 12*rand(nPts,1);
X = sort(X);
noise = 30*(rand(nPts,1) - 0.5);
Y = m*X + b + noise;

X = mat2py(X);
Y = mat2py(Y);

Xb = stats.add_constant(X,0);
ols = stats.OLS(Y, Xb).fit();
[m_ls, b_ls] = ols.params % best fit slope, y-intercept

[lpb, upb] = JH.predband(X_even, X, Y, [m_ls, b_ls], ...
                         JH.model_function, pyargs('conf',0.95));

sns.regplot(pyargs('x',X,'y',Y,'marker','.'))
plt.plot(X_even, lpb, 'k--',pyargs('label','95% Prediction Band'))
plt.plot(X_even, upb, 'k--')
plt.xlabel('X')
plt.ylabel('Y')
plt.grid()
plt.title('Prediction and confidence intervals')
plt.legend(pyargs('loc=','best'))
plt.show()
```

11.10 Finding Roots

11.10.1 Univariate

The root_scalar() function from SciPy's optimization module is the analog to MATLAB's fzero() function. root_scalar() offers eight algorithms for finding roots of a scalar equation: bisect, brentq, brenth, ridder, toms748, newton, secant, halley. The first five require limits on the independent variable, while the newton, secant, and halley methods work on unbounded domains. Additional information such as a starting guess or a slope function may be provided to accelerate convergence. If no method is specified, the solver chooses the best option for the given inputs (whether or not bounds were specified, slope function provided, and so on).

The following example finds x where $f(x) = 0$ on the interval $0 \le x \le 1$ where

$$f(x) = 2x^3 - 7x^2 + 12x - 4$$

without specifying a method. fzero() does not have an option to define boundaries; instead, we have to supply an initial guess to the solution. root_scalar() returns an object with the solution—if one was found—in its .root attribute:

MATLAB:	Python:

`>> F = @(x)(2*x.^3-7*x.^2+12*x-4);`
`>> fzero(F, 0)`
 	
    `4.265215061673047e-01`
	`In : import numpy as np`
	`In : import scipy.optimize as so`
	`In : def F(x):`
	`In :     return 2*x**3-7*x**2+12*x-4`
	`In : x  = np.linspace(-1,2, num=100)`
	`In : f_zero = so.root_scalar(F,`
	`...:               bracket=[0, 1])`
	`In : f_zero`
	`Out[14]:`
	`        converged: True`
	`            flag: 'converged'`
	`  function_calls: 9`
	`      iterations: 8`
	`            root: 0.42652150616730566`
	
	`In : f_zero.root`
	`Out: 0.42652150616730566`

The following invocation shows how a particular method is specified to solve the problem without bounds on x. The secant method does not require a slope function (newton and halley do), but needs two starting guesses, x_0 and x_1. Again, fzero() doesn't have comparable options, so instead we'll show its robustness by starting with a guess that is far from the true solution.

MATLAB:	Python:

`>> F = @(x)(2*x.^3-7*x.^2+12*x-4);`
`>> fzero(F, 100)`
 	
    `4.265215061673049e-01`
	`In : f_zero = so.root_scalar(F, x0=100,`
	`...:            x1=200, method="secant")`
	`Out[25]:`
	`        converged: True`
	`            flag: 'converged'`
	`  function_calls: 25`
	`      iterations: 24`
	`            root: 0.4265215061673047`

11.10.2 Multivariate

SciPy's more general multivariate root finder is `scipy.optimize.root()`. As with `scipy.optimize.root_scalar()`, one can select among several solution methods and optionally supply Jacobian functions. Its use is demonstrated by finding a point of intersection between a plane, a sphere, and an ellipsoid:

$$x + y + z = 1$$
$$x^2 + y^2 + z^2 = 1$$
$$x^2 + 4y^2 + z^2 = 2$$

MATLAB can solve this with `fsolve()` from the Optimization Toolkit. Alternatively, MATLAB can use `scipy.optimize.root()` to find the solution; this is demonstrated with the recipe in Section 11.11.

Python:

```
In : import scipy.optimize as so
In : def F(x):
...:    return x[0]+x[1]+ x[2]-1 - (x[0]**2+ x[1]**2+x[2]**2-1), \
...:        x[0]+x[1]+x[2]-1 - (x[0]**2+4*x[1]**2+x[2]**2-2), \
...:        (x[0]**2+x[1]**2+x[2]**2-1) - (x[0]**2+4*x[1]**2+x[2]**2-2)
In : so.root(F, [0,0,0])
    fjac: array([[-0.21557015,  0.57423188,  0.78980203],
                 [-0.78752535, -0.5804519 ,  0.20707345],
                 [ 0.57735027, -0.57735027,  0.57735027]])
     fun: array(
       [-1.08435e-12,  1.44386e-11,  1.55230e-11])
 message: 'The solution converged.'
    nfev: 37
     qtf: array(
       [ 7.84383e-09, -6.23725e-09, -4.21542e-22])
       r: array( [-2.19228e+00, -1.97436e+00,  8.33239e-01,
                   4.49321e-01, -2.26699e+00, -1.70549e-13])
  status: 1
 success: True
       x: array(
       [ 0.16314374,  0.57735027, -0.29406851])
```

Selecting a starting point far from the solution can make the method fail:

Python:

```
In : so.root(F, [0,10,10])
    fjac: array([[-7.06972124e-01, -7.07241361e-01, -2.69237135e-04],
                 [ 4.08481434e-01, -4.08015101e-01, -8.16496537e-01],
                 [-5.77350270e-01,  5.77350270e-01, -5.77350268e-01]])
     fun: array([-180., -479., -299.])
 message: 'The iteration is not making good progress, as measured by
          the \n  improvement from the last ten iterations.'
    nfev: 17
     qtf: array([ 4.66104096e+02,  3.66045040e+02, -5.80555266e-07])
       r: array([ 3.62141354e+01, -1.88545072e+04,  1.36198852e+03,
                  7.18371924e+01,  1.06466345e-01,  1.09677462e-07])
  status: 5
 success: False
       x: array([ 0., 10., 10.])
```

11.11 Recipe 11-4: Solving Simultaneous Nonlinear Equations

The plane/sphere/ellipsoid intersection problem of Section 11.10.2 can be solved in MATLAB with SciPy's multivariate root finder. As with the curve fitting recipe (Section 11.6), we will need to implement the function to be solved in Python because Python cannot evaluate MATLAB functions passed as arguments.

Here's the bridge module. The function that wraps the call to the solver, F_roots(), uses (0,0,0) as a default starting point if one isn't given:

Python:

```
# code/optim/bridge_nonlinear_roots.py
import scipy.optimize as so
def F(x):
  return x[0]+x[1]+ x[2]-1 - (x[0]**2+ x[1]**2+x[2]**2-1), \
         x[0]+x[1]+x[2]-1 - (x[0]**2+4*x[1]**2+x[2]**2-2),  \
         (x[0]**2+x[1]**2+x[2]**2-1) - (x[0]**2+4*x[1]**2+x[2]**2-2)
```

```
def F_roots(guess=[0,0,0]):
return so.root(F, guess)
```

Calling it from MATLAB is simple:

MATLAB:

```
>> soln = py.bridge_nonlinear_roots.F_roots();
>> soln.get('success')
  logical
      1
>> soln.get('message')
  Python str with no properties.
    The solution converged.

>> py2mat(soln.get('x'))

    1.631437374762493e-01   5.773502691851446e-01   -2.940685072817079e-01
```

Once more, this time supplying a bad starting location:

MATLAB:

```
>> soln = py.bridge_nonlinear_roots.F_roots(pyargs('guess',{0,10,10}));
>> soln.get('success')
v   logical
       0
v>> soln.get('message')
  Python str with no properties.
    The iteration is not making good progress, as measured by the
        improvement from the last ten iterations.
```

11.12 Optimization

SciPy's scipy.optimize module has many functions to solve optimization problems. We already saw one of its most powerful global optimizers, scipy.optimize.differential_ evolution(), in action Section 11.5.3. Here, we'll examine a wider scope of problems including local uni- and multivariate optimization with linear and nonlinear constraints, linear programming, and combinatorial optimization for problems such as route planning.

11.12.1 Linear Programming

Linear programming (LP) problems are ubiquitous in industrial engineering, operations research, logistics, and scheduling. MATLAB's Optimization Toolbox and SciPy have a function named linprog() that can solve real-valued LP problems. More difficult mixed-integer LP problems require modules not found in SciPy; for these we'll turn to PuLP, which can be added to Anaconda installations via conda install.

As a simple representative LP problem, say you've been tasked to assemble a computer server room to support your organization's various engineering and research departments. Some departmental needs are modest, while others require many powerful servers. The departments agree to a charge-back cost structure according to the resources they use; your goal is to figure out equitable parameters of the cost model. The server properties and negotiated charge-back rates are shown in Table 11-8.

Table 11-8. *Computer categories and properties*

	Cores	Power [kW]	Volume [ft³]	Charge Back [$/hr]
Small	4	50	10	0.10
Medium	8	105	20	0.60
Large	12	192	40	0.96
Huge	48	391	40	2.83

Your decision boils down to how many of each of Small, Medium, Large, and Huge servers to purchase such that

- The total power consumption is less than 30,000 kW.

- The total volume needed to house the servers is less than 80,000 ft³.

- The aggregate count of compute cores exceeds 1000.

- The number of cores in Large servers exceeds the count of cores in Huge servers.

The objective function is to maximize the charge-back

$$\text{maximize} \quad 0.1S + 0.6M + 0.96L + 2.83H$$

(the vision is that the more departments contribute, the greater the opportunity to grow the facility in the future) subject to

$$50S + 105M + 192L + 391H \leq 30000$$
$$10S + 20M + 40L + 40H \leq 80000$$
$$4S + 8M + 12L + 48H \geq 1000$$
$$12L \geq 48H$$

As the values for $S \dots H$ can only take on integer values, this is an integer-valued LP problem. Nonetheless, we'll see how close the real-valued solutions of SciPy's `linprog()` function match fully integer-based solutions from PuLP.

11.12.1.1 *SciPy* `linprog()`

Calling arguments to SciPy's `linprog()` are nearly identical to those for the Optimization Toolbox's version. Inputs are coefficients of the function to minimize, matrices of coefficients that describe the inequality relationships, equality relationships (if such exist), and upper and lower bounds. Inequality relationships must be expressed as less-than inequalities with independent variables on the left and constant values on the right. Greater-than relationships can be remapped to less-than by changing signs on both sides.

Our problem then becomes minimize -0.1S - 0.6M - 0.96L - 2.83H with constraints:

$$50S + 105M + 192L + 391H \leq 30000$$
$$10S + 20M + 40L + 40H \leq 80000$$
$$-4S - 8M - 12L - 48H \leq -1000$$
$$-12L + 48H \leq 0$$

The left-hand side coefficients define the matrix A, the right-hand side terms define b, and the coefficients of the cost function define f. A final constraint is that we seek only positive solutions so the first value in each of the four (lower, upper) bound tuples in variable UL_bounds is zero.

The Python solution looks like this:

Python:

```
from scipy.optimize import linprog
f = [ -0.1, -0.6, -0.96, -2.83])
A = [[ 50, 105, 192, 391],
     [ 10,  20,  40,  40],
     [ -4,  -8, -12, -48],
     [  0,   0, -12,  48]]
b  = [ 30000, 80000, -1000, 0]
UL_bounds = [ (0, None), (0, None),
              (0, None), (0, None) ]
sol = linprog(f,A,b,bounds=UL_bounds)
```

The function returns an object, sol in our example, with these attributes:

Python:

```
In : print(sol)
     con: array([], dtype=float64)
     fun: -172.64883520249523
 message: 'Optimization terminated successfully.'
     nit: 13
   slack: array([2.90929165e-08, 7.48231234e+04,
               1.48490078e+03, 1.47610990e-09])
  status: 0
 success: True
       x: array([1.15833172e-10, 1.37570134e-08,
               1.03537532e+02, 2.58843831e+01])

In : print(sol.status)
Out: 0

In : print(sol.x)
    array([1.15833172e-10, 1.37570134e-08,
          1.03537532e+02, 2.58843831e+01])
```

A solution status of 0 indicates a successful convergence, and the solution to our independent variables is in attribute .x. The closest integer values to our solution leaves us with $S = 0$, $M = 0$, $L = 104$, $H = 26$, which corresponds to an aggregate charge value of $172.42 per hour.

If you don't have the Optimization Toolbox, you can still solve the problem in MATLAB by calling SciPy's linprog():

MATLAB:

```
f = [ -0.1; -0.6; -0.96; -2.83];
A = [ 50 105 192 391; ...
      10  20  40  40; ...
      -4  -8 -12 -48; ...
       0   0 -12  48 ];
b = [ 30000; 80000; -1000; 0];
UL_bounds = { py.tuple({0, py.None}), py.tuple({0, py.None}), ...
              py.tuple({0, py.None}), py.tuple({0, py.None}) };

opt = py.importlib.import_module('scipy.optimize');
sol = opt.linprog(f,A,b,pyargs('bounds',py.list(UL_bounds)))
```

Running the preceding code gives the correct solution, but, frustratingly, the solution components are not accessible in MATLAB:

Python:

```
sol =

  Python OptimizeResult with no properties.

        con: array([], dtype=float64)
        fun: -172.64883520249523
    message: 'Optimization terminated successfully.'
        nit: 13
      slack: array([2.90929165e-08, 7.48231234e+04, 1.48490078e+03,
             1.47599621e-09])
     status: 0
    success: True
          x: array([1.15833172e-10, 1.37570134e-08, 1.03537532e+02,
             2.58843831e+01])

>> y = sol.x
Unrecognized method, property, or field 'x' for class
  'py.scipy.optimize.optimize.OptimizeResult'.
```

Once again, we'll need to write a small Python bridge module with a function that extracts and returns the components we want.

MATLAB:	Python:
| ```
LP = py.importlib.import_module(...
    'bridge_linprog');
py.importlib.reload(LP);
f = [ -0.1; -0.6; -0.96; -2.83];
A = [ 50 105 192 391; ...
      10  20  40  40; ...
      -4  -8 -12 -48; ...
       0   0 -12  48 ];
b = [ 30000; 80000; -1000; 0];
UL_bounds = { py.tuple({0, py.None}), ...
              py.tuple({0, py.None}), ...
              py.tuple({0, py.None}), ...
              py.tuple({0, py.None}) };
py_sol = LP.solver(f,A,b,pyargs(...
    'bounds',py.list(UL_bounds)));
m_sol = py2mat(py_sol);
``` | ```
# file bridge_linprog.py
from scipy.optimize import linprog
def solver(f,A,b,bounds=None):
    sol =
linprog(f,A,b,bounds=bounds)
    return { 'fun' : sol.fun,
             'message' : sol.message,
             'status' : sol.status,
             'success' : sol.success,
             'x' : sol.x}
``` |

Now the five components we captured in the bridge module can be used in MATLAB:
MATLAB:

```
>> m_sol

  struct with fields:

        fun: -172.6488
    message: "Optimization terminated successfully."
     status: 0
    success: 1
          x: [1.1583e-10 1.3757e-08 103.5375 25.8844]
```

11.12.1.2 PuLP

The Python PuLP module has two appealing aspects: one can define variables as being integer or real, and constraints can be expressed in a more natural form than other modules:

Python:

```python
import pulp
model = pulp.LpProblem("Server room", pulp.LpMaximize)

S = pulp.LpVariable('S', lowBound=0, cat='Integer')
M = pulp.LpVariable('M', lowBound=0, cat='Integer')
L = pulp.LpVariable('L', lowBound=0, cat='Integer')
H = pulp.LpVariable('H', lowBound=0, cat='Integer')

# constants
C_s, C_m, C_l, C_h = .10,  .60,  .96, 2.83  # cost
T_s, T_m, T_l, T_h = 50, 105, 192, 391      # thermal
O_s, O_m, O_l, O_h = 4,    8,   12, 48      # cores
V_s, V_m, V_l, V_h = 10,  20,   40, 40      # volume

# the function to maximize
model += C_s*S +  C_m*M +  C_l*L +  C_h*H, "Charge"

# subject to constraints
model += T_s*S +  T_m*M +  T_l*L +  T_h*H  <= 30000 # thermal
model += O_s*S +  O_m*M +  O_l*L +  O_h*H  >=  1000 # cores
model += O_l*L >= O_h*H # cores
model += V_s*S +  V_m*M +  V_l*L +  V_h*H  <= 80000 # volume

# compute the solution
model.solve()
print(pulp.LpStatus[model.status])
```

The result is Python:

```
  0 S,   30 M,   93 L,   23 H   charge = 172.37
Optimal
```

11.12.2 Simulated Annealing

Simulated annealing is a stochastic global optimization method based on the concept of crystal formation in metals as temperature drops. Briefly, the algorithm makes a random guess at a solution, then either uses a perturbation of that solution for the next iteration or makes a completely new guess. The decision as to whether to perturb the solution or make a new guess depends on the solution's cost and how far along the "annealing schedule" the algorithm has progressed. Early on, a guess that is worse than its predecessor will likely be accepted, but as iterations progress and the "temperature" drops, improvements to the solution are more likely to survive to the next round.

The Python module simanneal, available through conda-forge, provides a convenient framework to solve optimization problems with simulated annealing. simanneal requires the user to provide the following:

- A class which inherits from simanneal's `Annealer` class and provides a constructor (the `__init__()` function), a `move()` function which perturbs an existing solution, and an `energy()` function which evaluates the solution's cost function

- An initial guess to the solution

- An annealing schedule

To illustrate how these three items might be implemented, we'll solve the Traveling Salesman Problem (TSP) using a simplification of the TSP solution given in simanneal's documentation.[11]

The `Annealer`-derived class is defined with lines 12–22. Our problem's cost function is defined with the `energy()` method on line 20. The `.state` attribute is the collection of variables we wish to optimize—in our case, it is a list of city indices that defines the route. For us, the cost of a solution is the sum of distances between adjacent cities in the route. Here, we access the `.distance_matrix` attribute which is a look-up table of distances between cities; it is an N x N matrix where the term at index (i, j) is the distance between cities i and j. The distance matrix is populated in the class's constructor at line 13. Aside from adding `.distance_matrix` as an attribute, the constructor is entirely boilerplate. Finally, the `move()` method at line 16 defines how to apply a random perturbation to the current state, in other words, how to make a random change to our route.

---

[11] https://github.com/perrygeo/simanneal/blob/master/examples/salesman.py

The `compute_distances()` function at line 24 computes the distance matrix using the broadcasting technique mentioned in Section 11.1.13.

Lines 31–34 define 80 cities arranged on an 8 x 10 grid. The simplicity of this layout makes it easy to identify optimal solutions.

The annealing schedule is defined on line 42. The argument `tsp.auto(minutes=0.5)` tells the module to estimate schedule parameters so that a solution is returned in roughly 30 seconds of elapsed time. Alternatively, you can control the parameters yourself with

Python:

```
schedule = {
    'tmax' : 20000.0, # starting temperature
    'tmin' :     2.0, # ending temperature
    'steps' : 50000 , # n iterations
    'updates' : 100 , # n updates to stdout
}
tsp.set_schedule(schedule)
```

In practice, the automatic estimator provides an ideal balance between convenience, solution fitness, and knowledge of how long you'll need to wait for an answer. If your solution isn't sufficiently optimal, simply increase the amount of time you'll let the annealer to run (via the `minutes` parameter to `tsp.auto()`).

Python:

```
1   import numpy as np
2   import random
3   from simanneal import Annealer
4   import matplotlib.pyplot as plt
5
6   def plot_route(route, coordinates, fname):
7       circuit = [_ for _ in route] + [ route[0] ]
8       plt.plot(coordinates[circuit,0], coordinates[circuit,1])
9       plt.scatter(coordinates[:,0], coordinates[:,1], color='r')
10      plt.show()
11
12  class TravellingSalesmanProblem(Annealer):
13      def __init__(self, state, distance_matrix):
```

```
14          self.distance_matrix = distance_matrix # store distances in
            the object
15          super(TravellingSalesmanProblem, self).__init__(state)
16      def move(self): # swap two cities in the route; return that
        distance
17          a, b = random.sample(range(len(self.state)), k=2)
18          self.state[a], self.state[b] = self.state[b], self.state[a]
19          return self.energy()
20      def energy(self): # for this problem, energy = route distance
21          S = self.state
22          return sum([self.distance_matrix[S[i-1],S[i]]
            for i in range(len(S))])
23
24  def compute_distances( city_coord ): # uses broadcasting
25      X, Y = city_coord[:,0], city_coord[:,1]
26      dX = X[:,np.newaxis] - X[np.newaxis,:]
27      dY = Y[:,np.newaxis] - Y[np.newaxis,:]
28      return np.sqrt( dX**2 + dY**2 )
29
30  def main():
31      nR, nC = 8, 10
32      J, I = np.meshgrid(range(nR),range(nC))
33      city_coord = np.vstack( [I.ravel(), J.ravel()] ).T
34      distance_matrix = compute_distances( city_coord )
35
36      # initial state, a randomly-ordered itinerary
37      starting_sequence = list(range(nR*nC))
38      random.shuffle(starting_sequence) # modifies starting_sequence
        in-place
39      plot_route(starting_sequence, city_coord, 'tsp_start')
40
```

```
41        tsp = TravellingSalesmanProblem(starting_sequence,
          distance_matrix)
42        tsp.set_schedule(tsp.auto(minutes=0.5))
43        tsp.copy_strategy = "slice" # state is a list; slice method
          is fastest
44        state, e = tsp.anneal()      # start the optimization
45
46        print(f'Route distance = {e:.2f}, route = ',state)
47        plot_route(state, city_coord, 'tsp_solved')
48   if __name__ == '__main__': main()
```

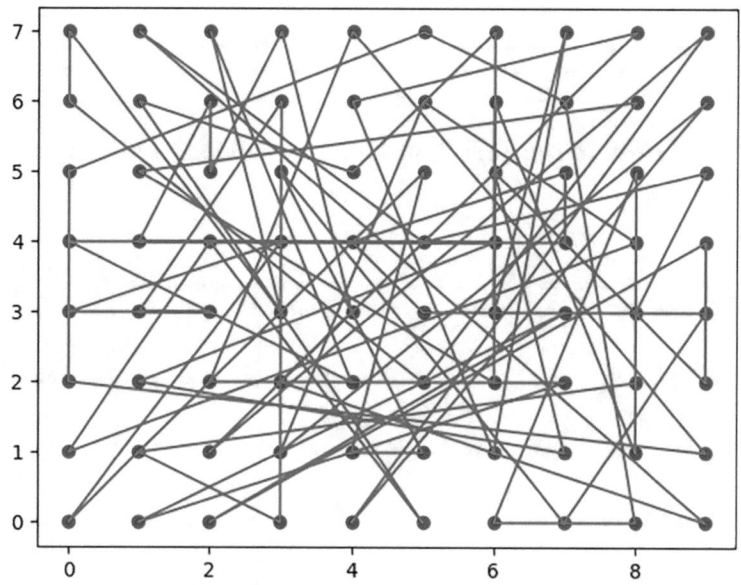

Figure 11-6. *Initial random guess to the TSP*

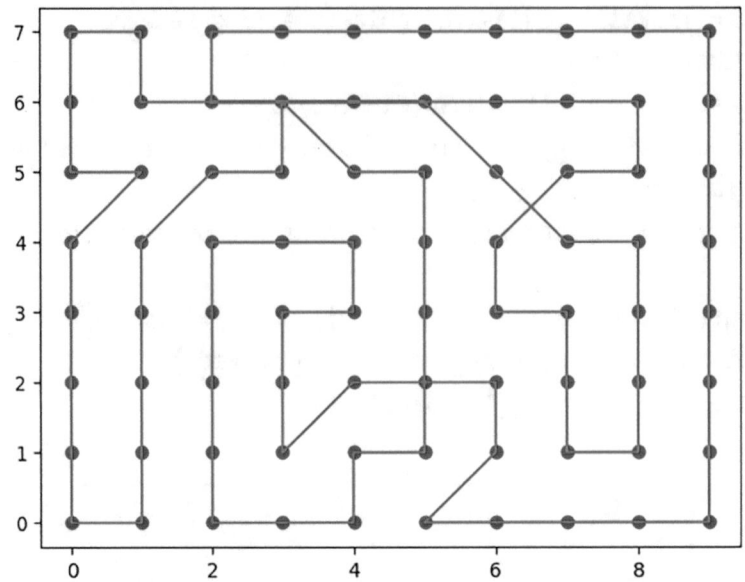

Figure 11-7. *A solution to the TSP found with* simanneal *with* tsp. auto(minutes=0.25)

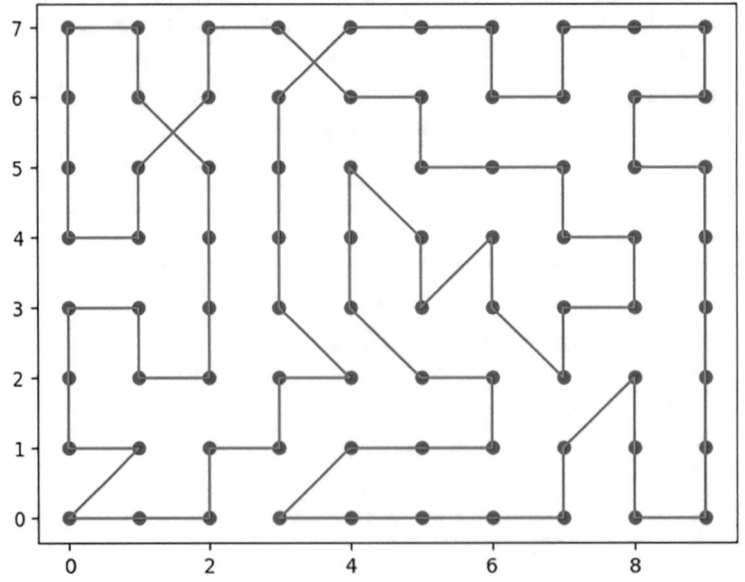

Figure 11-8. *A solution to the TSP found with* simanneal *with* tsp. auto(minutes=2.5)

11.13 Differential Equations

SciPy's collection of differential equation solvers is comparable to MATLAB's family of ode*() routines. The calling method is quite different though. MATLAB's routines return the full solution (if one can be found), while SciPy's return an iterator that must be called in a loop.

As a sample problem, we'll solve the Duffing oscillator equation:[12]

$$\frac{d^2 u}{dt^2} + c\frac{du}{dt} + ku + k_3 u^3 = A\sin(\omega t)$$

Since both MATLAB and Python solvers only work with first-order differential equations, this second-order equation must be linearized to a pair of first-order equations:

$$\frac{du_1}{dt} = u_2$$

$$\frac{du_2}{dt} = -ku_1 - cu_2 - k_3 u_1^3 + A\sin(\omega t)$$

The following MATLAB[13] and Python functions Duff() return a two-item array of values corresponding to the two right-hand sides of these equations:

---

[12] https://en.wikipedia.org/wiki/Duffing_equation

[13] Based on https://scicomp.stackexchange.com/questions/16190/nonlinear-ode-to-solve-duffings-equation

MATLAB:	Python:

```
% file: code/ode/duffing.m
Time = [0 40];
U_0  = [0; 0];
c = 0.1;
k = 0.7;
k3 = 1;
A = 44.5;
omega = 1.1;
options = odeset('RelTol',1e-7);
[t,u] = ode45(@(t,u)Duff(...
    t,u,k,c,k3,A,omega), ...
    Time,U_0,options);
figure
plot(u(:,1),u(:,2));
xlabel('Position');
ylabel('Velocity');
title('Duffing oscillator')
function u = Duff(t,u,k,c,k3,A,omega)
  u = [u(2); -k*u(1)-c*u(2)- ...
        k3*u(1)^3+A*sin(omega*t)];
end
```

```
# file: code/ode/duffing.py
import numpy as np
from scipy.integrate import RK45
import matplotlib.pyplot as plt
def Duff(t,u,k=0.7,c=0.1,k3=1,
            A=44.5,omega=1.1):
    return [u[1], -k*u[0]-c*u[1] -
            k3*u[0]**3+A*np.
sin(omega*t)]
T0, Tn = 0, 40
U_0 = [0, 0]
t, u = [], []
sol = RK45(Duff, T0, U_0, Tn,
            rtol=1e-7)
while sol.t < Tn:
    t.append(sol.t)
    u.append([sol.y[0], sol.y[1]])
    sol.step()
u = np.array(u)
plt.plot(u[:,0], u[:,1])
plt.xlabel('Position');
plt.ylabel('Velocity');
plt.title('Duffing oscillator');
plt.show()
```

The single line call to ode45() on the left corresponds to a call to RK45() followed by a while loop that successively calls the solver object's .step() method in Python. Both solvers are configured to return solutions with a relative accuracy of 10^{-7}, but MATLAB needs 5093 iterations, while Python only does 1002. A phase space plot of the solution shows good agreement:

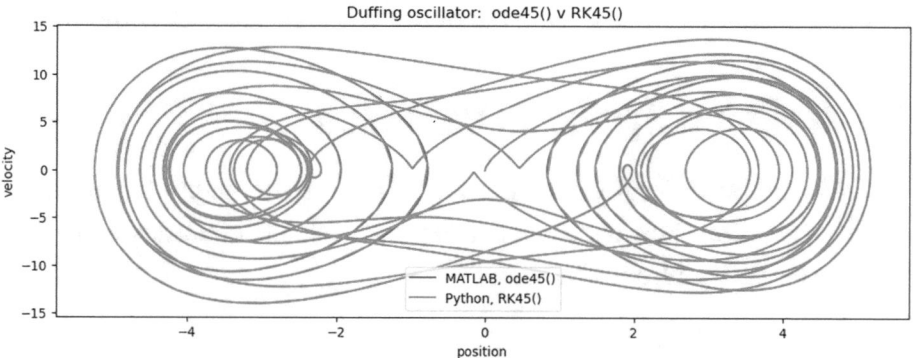

11.14 Symbolic Mathematics

The Python module SymPy is a Computer Algebra System (CAS) comparable
to MATLAB's Symbolic Toolkit. SymPy is an enormously capable CAS covering,
among other topics, calculus, differential geometry, combinatorics, number theory,
cryptography, series, and ordinary and partial differential equations. In addition to
computing results symbolically, it can also express the solutions in LaTeX or as computer
code in Python, MATLAB, and many other languages as shown in Table 11-9.

Table 11-9. *SymPy code generators*

Language	sympy.printing **Function**
C	ccode()
C++	cxxcode()
Fortran	fcode()
GLSL	glsl_code()
JavaScript	jscode()
Julia	julia_code()
Maple	maple_code()
Mathematica	mathematica_code()
MATLAB	octave_code()
Python	pycode()
R	rcode()
Rust	rust_code()

481

The examples shown in this section barely scratch the surface of SymPy's power.

11.14.1 Defining Symbolic Variables

Variables are identified in SymPy by importing them from the `sympy.abc` module. For example, the expression `from sympy.abc import x, y, phi` identifies `x`, `y`, and phi as variables to be treated symbolically.

11.14.2 Derivatives

Derivatives are obtained with the `sympy.diff()` function. This example shows how to compute the derivative of

$$f(\phi) = \frac{\phi}{\sin^2(\phi)} + \cos(\phi)$$

Python:

```
In : from sympy import cos, sin, diff
In : from sympy.abc import phi
In : from sympy.printing.latex import print_latex, octave_code
In : f = phi/sin(phi)**2 + cos(phi)
In : d = diff(f)
In : d.doit()

In : d.doit()
Out: -2*phi*cos(phi)/sin(phi)**3 - sin(phi) + sin(phi)**(-2)

In : print_latex(d)
- \frac{2 \phi \cos{\left(\phi \right)}}{\sin^{3}{\left(\phi \right)}} -
    \sin{\left(\phi \right)} + \frac{1}{\sin^{2}{\left(\phi \right)}}
```

The LaTeX output for the derivative renders like this:

$$-\frac{2\phi\cos(\phi)}{\sin^3(\phi)} - \sin(\phi) + \frac{1}{\sin^2(\phi)}$$

and MATLAB code for the input and output functions can be produced like so:

Python:

```
In : print(octave_code(f))
phi./sin(phi).^2 + cos(phi)
```

```
In : print(octave_code(d))
-2*phi.*cos(phi)./sin(phi).^3 - sin(phi) + sin(phi).^(-2)
```

11.14.3 Integrals

Integration is done with `sympy.integrate()`. For example, the integral

$$\int \frac{x}{1+x+3x^2}\,dx$$

is found with

Python:

```
In : from sympy import integrate
In : from sympy.abc import x
In : from sympy.printing.latex import print_latex
In : s = integrate(x/(1 + x + 3*x**2))
In : s.doit()
Out: log(x**2 + x/3 + 1/3)/6 - sqrt(11)*atan(6*sqrt(11)*x/11 +
sqrt(11)/11)/33
```

```
In : print_latex(s)
\frac{\log{\left(x^{2} + \frac{x}{3} + \frac{1}{3} \right)}}{6} -
\frac{\sqrt{11}
    \operatorname{atan}{\left(\frac{6 \sqrt{11} x}{11} +
    \frac{\sqrt{11}}{11}
    \right)}}{33}
```

which looks like this:

$$\frac{\log\left(x^2+\frac{x}{3}+\frac{1}{3}\right)}{6} - \frac{\sqrt{11}\operatorname{atan}\left(\frac{6\sqrt{11}x}{11}+\frac{\sqrt{11}}{11}\right)}{33}$$

11.14.4 Solving Equations

The equations

$$\left(x-1\right)^{2}+\left(y+3\right)^{2}=R^{2}$$
$$y=mx+b$$

describe a circle and a line. The following code solves for the points of intersection (x, y) in terms of R, m, and b:

Python:

```
In : from sympy import Eq
In : from sympy.solvers import solve
In : from sympy.abc import x,y,R,m,b
In : circle = (x-1)**2 + (y+3)**2 - R**2
In : line = m*x + b
In : solve(Eq(circle,line), (x,y))
Out: [(m/2 - sqrt(4*R**2 + 4*b + m**2 +
       4*m - 4*y**2 - 24*y - 36)/2 + 1, y),
      (m/2 + sqrt(4*R**2 + 4*b + m**2 +
       4*m - 4*y**2 - 24*y - 36)/2 + 1, y)]
```

11.14.5 Linear Algebra

11.14.5.1 Perform a Symbolic LU Factorization of

The matrix

$$\begin{bmatrix} 1 & 2 & -3 \\ 4 & -5 & 6 \\ -7 & 8 & 9 \end{bmatrix}$$

is factored to lower and upper triangular matrices using exact arithmetic with the following code:

Python:

```
In : from sympy import Matrix
In : A = Matrix([[1,2,-3],
```

```
                  [4,-5,6],
                  [-7,8,9]])
In : L, U, perm = \
...:     A.LUdecomposition()

In : L
Matrix([
[ 1,       0, 0],
[ 4,       1, 0],
[-7, -22/13, 1]])

In : U
Matrix([
[1,   2,      -3],
[0, -13,      18],
[0,   0, 240/13]])

In : perm
Out: []

In : L*U - A
Matrix([
[0, 0, 0],
[0, 0, 0],
[0, 0, 0]])
```

11.14.5.2 Symbolically Solve A*x* = b

This series of three equations and three unknowns

$$\begin{bmatrix} 1 & 2 & -3 \\ 4 & -5 & 6 \\ -7 & 8 & 9 \end{bmatrix} x = \begin{Bmatrix} 1 \\ -2 \\ 1 \end{Bmatrix}$$

is solved symbolically for x with Gauss-Jordan elimination using this code:

Python:

```
In : b = Matrix([1, -2, 1])
In : x, params = A.gauss_jordan_solve(b)
In : x
```

```
Matrix([
[ 1/20],
[ 3/10],
[-7/60]])

In : params
Out: Matrix(0, 1, [])
```

11.14.6 Series

SymPy has support for Fourier series, power series, series summation, and series expansion. This example shows how the closed-form summation

$$\sum_{k=1}^{N+1} \frac{e^{ik\pi}}{N^2}$$

can be found:

   Python:

```
In : from sympy import I, Sum, exp, pi
In : from sympy.abc import k, N
In : s = Sum( exp(I*k*pi)/N**2, (k, 1, N+1))
In : s.doit()
Out: (-(-1)**(N + 2)/2 - 1/2)/N**2
```

11.15 Recipe 11-5: Using SymPy in MATLAB

The series summation from Section 11.14.6 can be done from MATLAB after defining symbolic variables and SymPy-specific constants for i and π. We'll prefix all Python variables with "p" to avoid name collisions with built-in MATLAB variables even though in this case only pi would have caused a collision.

   MATLAB:

```
>> pI = py.sympy.I;
>> pPi = py.sympy.pi;
>> pk = py.sympy.abc.k;
```

```
>> pN = py.sympy.abc.N;
>> s = py.sympy.Sum( py.sympy.exp(pI*pk*pPi)/pN^2, py.tuple({pk,1,pN+1}));
>> s.doit()
   Python Mul with properties:

                       args: [1×2 py.tuple]
               assumptions0: [1×1 py.dict]
         canonical_variables: [1×1 py.dict]
           expr_free_symbols: [1×1 py.set]
              free_symbols: [1×1 py.set]
                       func: [1×1 py.sympy.core.assumptions.ManagedProperties]
               is_algebraic: [1×1 py.NoneType]
                              :
               is_rational: [1×1 py.NoneType]
                  is_real: [1×1 py.NoneType]
          is_transcendental: [1×1 py.NoneType]
                  is_zero: [1×1 py.NoneType]

   N**(-2.0)*(-(-1)**(N + 2.0)/2 - 0.5)
```

The output from s.doit() is a Python variable within MATLAB; to get a MATLAB character string containing the solution, we merely need to access the Python solution's .char attribute:

MATLAB:

```
>> s_soln = s.doit();
>> m_soln = s_soln.char;
>> m_soln
   'N**(-2.0)*(-(-1)**(N + 2.0)/2 - 0.5)'
```

11.16 Recipe 11-6: Compute Laplace Transforms

The laplace() function in MATLAB's Symbolic Toolbox can compute Laplace transforms. The laplace_transform() function in SymPy can do these too. The following example computes the transform of

$$f(t) = e^{-at} \cos \omega t$$

MATLAB 2020b:

```
>> sympy = py.importlib.import_module('sympy');
>> s = sympy.symbols('s');
>> t = sympy.symbols('t');
>> a = sympy.symbols('a', pyargs('real','True', 'positive','True'));
>> omega = sympy.symbols('omega', pyargs('real','True'));
>> f = sympy.exp(-a*t)*sympy.cos(omega*t);
>> L = sympy.laplace_transform(f, t, s)
L =
  Python tuple with no properties.
    ((a + s)/(omega**2 + (a + s)**2), -a, Eq(2*Abs(arg(omega)), 0))

>> latex = py.importlib.import_module('sympy.printing.latex');
>> latex.print_latex(L{1})
\frac{a + s}{\omega^{2} + \left(a + s\right)^{2}}
```

The LaTex output renders as

$$\frac{a+s}{\omega^2 + (a+s)^2}$$

11.17 Unit Systems

The Python module pint allows one to assign units to numeric scalars and arrays, much like the similar capability in MATLAB's Symbolic Toolbox. Once units are assigned to variables, attempts to mix terms with incompatible dimensions in a computation—for example, adding an area to a temperature-raise a DimensionalityError. Mixing terms with compatible dimensions but different unit systems—adding a length in meters to a length in inches—works correctly because the appropriate scale factors are applied first.

In both pint and the Symbolic Toolbox, one must first initialize the units object (u in the following examples for both languages). Subsequent variables can receive units by multiplying a numeric value or variable by one of the units object's many attributes. Here, we show how one can convert metric values for aluminum 6061's[14] modulus of elasticity and density from the metric system to the US customary system.

---

[14] https://en.wikipedia.org/wiki/6061_aluminium_alloy

Python:

```
In : from pint import UnitRegistry
In : u = UnitRegistry()
In : E = 68.9 * u.GPa
In : rho = 2.70 * u.g/u.cm**3
In : E_us = E.to(u.psi)
In : rho_us = rho.to(u.lb/u.inch**3)
In : E_us
Out: 9993100.129611416 <Unit('pound_force_per_square_inch')>
In : rho_us
Out: 0.09754368840022593 <Unit('pound / inch ** 3')>
```

Both pint and the Symbolic Toolbox support hundreds of base and derived units; complete lists can be found at https://github.com/hgrecco/pint/blob/master/pint/default_en.txt and www.mathworks.com/help/symbolic/units-list.html.

Units can be assigned to a NumPy array; operations on individual terms or slices from that array will work only with unitless or other consistent unit variables. It is not possible to create a NumPy array with mixed units, though. This precludes the use of pint in applications that employ arrays whose rows or columns have different unit types. One such example is finite element matrices that contain both linear and rotational stiffnesses.

11.17.1 Defining Units in pint

Arbitrary units can be defined easily. In the next example, currency units of "dollar" and "euro" are defined. From these, prices per unit area are defined and then applied to a collection of real estate lots with four properties per lot. Finally, the price of each collection is given in dollars and euros. Note that pint does not automatically simplify the compound units when the cost vector is computed; we have to explicitly convert to dollars or euros:

Python:

```
In : from pint import UnitRegistry
In : u = UnitRegistry()
In : u.define('dollar = 1 = USD')
In : u.define('euro = 1.31 * dollar = EU')
```

```
In : USD_per_ft2 = 2.1 * u.USD/u.foot**2
In : EU_per_m2 = USD_per_ft2.to(u.EU/u.meter**2)
In : EU_per_m2
Out: 17.2551 <Unit('euro / meter ** 2')>

In : a = np.arange(20).reshape(5,4) * u.acre
In : a
array([[ 0,  1,  2,  3],
       [ 4,  5,  6,  7],
       [ 8,  9, 10, 11],
       [12, 13, 14, 15],
       [16, 17, 18, 19]]) <Unit('acre')>

In : P = np.ones(4) * USD_per_ft2
In : P
Out: array([2.1, 2.1, 2.1, 2.1]) <Unit('dollar / foot ** 2')>

In : cost = a@P
In : cost
Out: array([ 12.6,  46.2,  79.8, 113.4, 147. ])
          <Unit('acre * dollar / foot ** 2')>

In : cost.to(u.USD)
array([ 548858.19543059, 2012480.04991215, 3476101.90439371,
       4939723.75887528, 6403345.61335684]) <Unit('dollar')>

In : cost.to(u.euro)
array([ 418975.72170274, 1536244.31291004, 2653512.90411734,
       3770781.49532464, 4888050.08653194]) <Unit('euro')>
```

The pint documentation says adding units to variables causes a performance hit when performing computations with those variables. That's true each time pint has to check units. If the variable is a NumPy array, though, this units check is done only once for the entire array, not for each term in the array. By and large, programs whose performance is dominated by numeric array computations run as quickly with units as without.

11.18 Recipe 11-7: Using `pint` in MATLAB

The units example of Section 11.17 requires some modification for use in MATLAB. The primary difference is that units cannot be accessed from the registry variable using dot notation. Instead, we have to use the .Units() accessor function. The "meter" unit, for example, must be referenced in MATLAB as u.Unit('meter') instead of just u.meter as it is in Python. Also note that the a matrix is defined as the transpose of a 4 × 5 to get the same row-major values as Python.

MATLAB:

```
>> u = py.pint.UnitRegistry;
>> u.define('dollar = 1 = USD');
>> u.define('euro = 1.31 * dollar = EU');
>> USD_per_ft2 = 2.1 * u.Unit('USD')/u.Unit('foot')^2;
>> EU_per_m2 = USD_per_ft2.to(u.Unit('EU')/u.Unit('meter')^2);
>> a = reshape(0:19, 4,5)';
>> b = py.numpy.array(a)*u.Unit('acre');
>> P = py.numpy.ones(int64(4)) * USD_per_ft2;
>> cost = b.dot(P)
cost =

  Python Quantity with properties:

                    T: [1×1 py.pint.quantity.Quantity]
                         :
                units: [1×1 py.pint.unit.Unit]

    [12.6 46.2 79.8 113.4 147.0] acre * dollar / foot ** 2


>> cost.to(u.Unit('USD'))
  Python Quantity with properties:

                    T: [1×1 py.pint.quantity.Quantity]
                         :
                units: [1×1 py.pint.unit.Unit]

    [548858.195 2012480.050 3476101.904 4939723.759 6403345.613] dollar
```

```
>> cost.to(u.Unit('EU'))
  Python Quantity with properties:

                    T: [1×1 py.pint.quantity.Quantity]
                                   :
                units: [1×1 py.pint.unit.Unit]

  [418975.722 1536244.313 2653512.904 3770781.495 4888050.087] euro
```

The numeric value of the Python units array can be converted to a MATLAB matrix like this:

MATLAB:

```
>> euros = cost.to(u.Unit('EU'));
>> matlab_euros = double(euros.m)

    4.1898e+05   1.5362e+06   2.6535e+06   3.7708e+06   4.8881e+06
```

11.19 References

[1]   John Hedengren. *Programming for Engineers: Regression Statistics with Python*. 2021. URL: https://apmonitor.com/che263/index.php/Mai/PythonRegressionStatistics

[2]   MathWorks Support Team. "How do I perform a binary search of a presorted array?" In: (June 2017). URL: www.mathworks.com/matlabcentral/answers/92533-how-do-i-perform-a-binary-search-of-a-presorted-array

[3]   Storn, R.; Price, K. (1997). "Differential evolution – a simple and efficient heuristic for global optimization over continuous spaces." *Journal of Global Optimization*. 11 (4): 341–359. doi:10.1023/A:1008202821328

Plotting

MATLAB is well known for the ease with which one can visualize numeric data. Similar capability is available for Python, but before starting one must choose which among many excellent plotting modules to use. Standouts are

- Altair
- Bokeh
- matplotlib
- Plotly
- Seaborn

Altair allows one to produce complex plots with relatively little code; Bokeh and Plotly excel at creating interactive, web-based plots; Seaborn is built on matplotlib and has a refined visual style and shortcut functions that create relatively complex plots, notably for statistics work. I chose the oldest among these, matplotlib, for several reasons: its commands and plotting paradigm most closely resemble MATLAB's; it is the underlying plotting package for Cartopy (Section 12.4) and Pandas (Chapter 13); and Seaborn enhancements can be added at any time.

12.1 Point and Line Plots

Aside from the additional imports, commands to plot a parabola in Python look similar to doing the same in MATLAB. The result looks about the same, too:

© Albert Danial 2022
A. Danial, *Python for MATLAB Development*, https://doi.org/10.1007/978-1-4842-7223-7_12

MATLAB:	Python:
| ```
x=-10:10;
y= x .^2 - 36;
plot(x,y)
``` | ```
import numpy as np
import matplotlib.pyplot as plt
x = np.arange(-10,11)
y = x**2 - 36
plt.plot(x,y)
plt.show()
``` |

A notable difference between the two is that, by default, MATLAB automatically opens a display window to show the plot being created, while Python shows nothing unless an explicit `plt.show()` is invoked. MATLAB's behavior is convenient when working interactively. However, if you run a MATLAB m-file with long computations, the plot window that does eventually appear may "click-jack" your mouse if you are actively working in another window. This is especially onerous when your code creates plots in a loop causing a long stream of windows to keep popping up. A Python program, on the other hand, will not show the plot if you forget the final `plt.show()` (or `plt.savefig()` if you write an image file rather than display it). The same is true when working interactively with ipython. However, IDEs and other graphical Python work environments like PyCharm, Spyder, and Jupyter notebooks work like the MATLAB IDE and will show plots immediately.

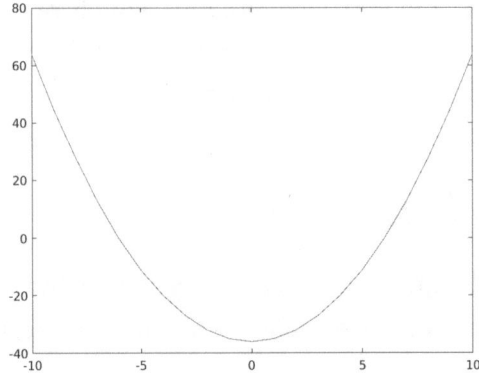

Figure 12-1. *MATLAB*

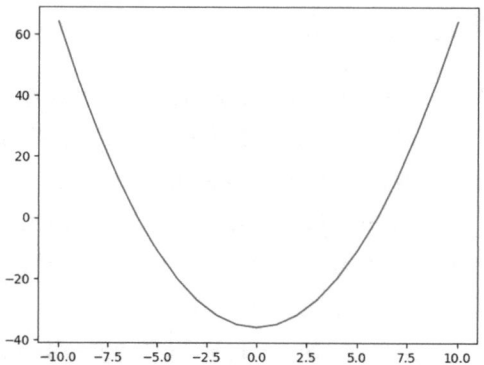

Figure 12-2. *Python*

matplotlib commands to add titles, axis labels, and legends closely resemble their MATLAB counterparts. Additionally, for simple plots, one need only reference matplotlib.pyplot, usually imported as plt, commands directly:

MATLAB:	Python:
t=linspace(0,10*pi,300);	import numpy as np
decay = exp(-t/10);	import matplotlib.pyplot as plt
osc = decay .* sin(t);	t = np.linspace(0,10*np.pi,num=300)
pts = -decay(1:10:end);	decay = np.exp(-t/10)
plot(t,osc,'g')	osc = decay*np.sin(t)
hold on	pts = -decay[::10]
plot(t,decay,'r')	plt.plot(t,osc,'g')
scatter(t(1:10:end),pts)	plt.plot(t,decay,'r')
grid on	plt.scatter(t[::10],pts)
hold off	plt.grid()
title('Decaying sinusoid')	plt.title('Decaying sinusoid')
xlabel('Time [seconds]')	plt.xlabel('Time [seconds]')
ylabel('exp(-t/10)*sin(t)')	plt.ylabel('exp(-t/10)*sin(t)')
saveas(1,"decay.png")	plt.savefig('decay.png')
	plt.show() # optional

495

12.1.1 Saving Plots to Files

Matplotlib's function to save plots to PNG, JPEG, and other formats is `plt.savefig()`. It resembles MATLAB's `saveas()`, `print()`, and `exportgraphics()` functions but has an advantage in that it supports transparent backgrounds for PNG files—a desirable property for inclusion in PowerPoint presentations, Word documents, websites, ebooks, and PDF. MATLAB only supports transparency for plots saved as PDF files, a much slower process than writing PNG or JPEG files.

The image file formats supported by matplotlib can be displayed with `plt.gcf().canvas.get_supported_filetypes()`:

```
In : plt.gcf().canvas.get_supported_filetypes()
Out:
```

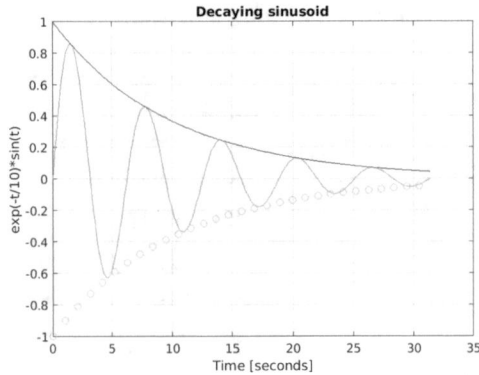

Figure 12-3. *MATLAB*

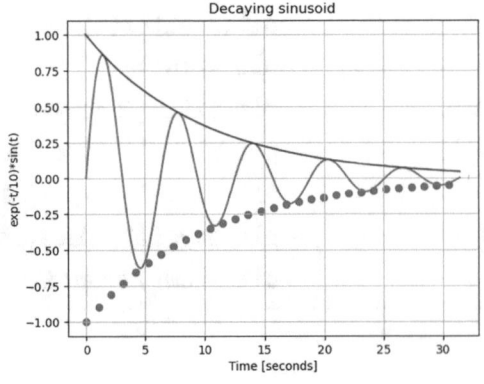

Figure 12-4. *Python*

```
{'ps': 'Postscript',
 'eps': 'Encapsulated Postscript',
 'pdf': 'Portable Document Format',
 'pgf': 'PGF code for LaTeX',
 'png': 'Portable Network Graphics',
 'raw': 'Raw RGBA bitmap',
 'rgba': 'Raw RGBA bitmap',
 'svg': 'Scalable Vector Graphics',
 'svgz': 'Scalable Vector Graphics',
 'jpg': 'Joint Photographic Experts Group',
 'jpeg': 'Joint Photographic Experts Group',
 'tif': 'Tagged Image File Format',
 'tiff': 'Tagged Image File Format'}
```

Most of the images in this book were saved with a command such as

```
plt.savefig('plot.png', dpi=200, bbox_inches='tight',
            pad_inches=0.1, transparent=True)
```

Tip   If you want your Python program to display a plot to the screen *and* save it to a file, call `plt.savefig()` before `plt.show()`; otherwise, the image file will be empty.

12.1.2 Multiple Plots per Figure

Matplotlib's `subplots()` function is similar to MATLAB's `subplot()` since both take the desired number of rows and columns of smaller plots as the first two arguments. The MATLAB function's third argument is the row-major offset to the plot being drawn, while matplotlib's function returns an array of axis handles:

MATLAB:	Python:

```
t = -10*pi:0.1:10*pi;
C = {{'blue' , 'red',}, ...
    {'green', 'black'}};
figure
i = 1;
for r = 0:1
  for c = 0:1
    subplot(2, 2, i)
    i = i+1;
    k = 1 + (1.1*r + 1.5*c)/10;
    y = sin(t) + sin(k*t);
    plot(t,y,C{r+1}{c+1})
    xlabel('t')
    ylabel('y')
    title(sprintf(...
              'r=%d, c=%d',r,c))
    grid on
  end
end
```

```
import numpy as np
import matplotlib.pyplot as plt
t = np.arange(-10*np.pi, 10*np.pi, 0.1)
C = [['blue' , 'red',],
     ['green', 'black']]
fig, ax = plt.subplots(nrows=2,
    ncols=2, constrained_layout=True)
for r in [0, 1]:
  for c in [0, 1]:
    k = 1 + (1.1*r + 1.5*c)/10
    y = np.sin(t) + np.sin(k*t)
    ax[r,c].plot(t,y,color=C[r][c])
    ax[r,c].set_xlabel('t')
    ax[r,c].set_ylabel('y')
    ax[r,c].set_title(
       f'r={r}, c={c}', fontsize=14)
    ax[r,c].grid(True)
plt.show()
```

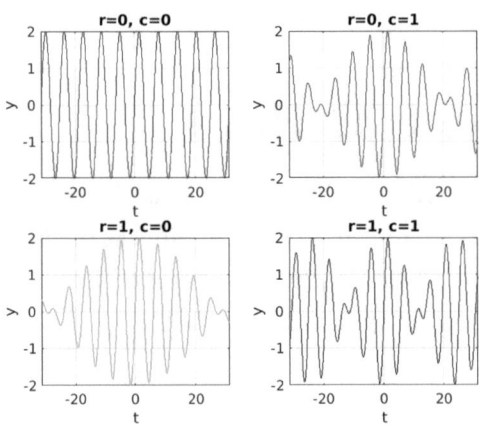

Figure 12-5. *MATLAB*

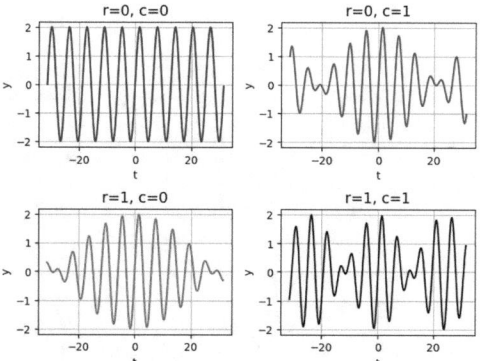

Figure 12-6. *Python*

12.1.3 Date and Time on the X Axis

Date and time annotations on the x axis can be tricky because they take so much space. MATLAB and matplotlib in Python allow fine control over the date string formatting as well as rotated axis labels to prevent overlaps. MATLAB's time markers are aligned to noon, while matplotlib's are aligned to midnight.

MATLAB:	Python:

```
MATLAB:
t = .1:.01:.8;
y = sin(3./t).*sin(5./(1-t));
S = 30*24*60*60*t + 1620000000;
dates = arrayfun(@(x) datetime(...
    x,'ConvertFrom','posix'), S);
scatter(dates,y,'v','filled')
grid()
xtickformat('yyyy-MM-dd hh:mm')
xtickangle(30)
```

```
Python:
import numpy as np
import matplotlib.pyplot as plt
import matplotlib.dates as mdates
from datetime import datetime
t = np.arange(.1, .8, .01)
y = np.sin(3/t)*np.sin(5/(1-t))
S = 30*24*60*60*t + 1620000000
dates = [datetime.fromtimestamp(_)
                for _ in S]
fig, ax = plt.subplots()
ax.scatter(dates,y,marker=11)
plt.grid()
ax.xaxis.set_major_formatter(
  mdates.DateFormatter('%Y-%m-%d %H:%S'))
fig.autofmt_xdate()
```

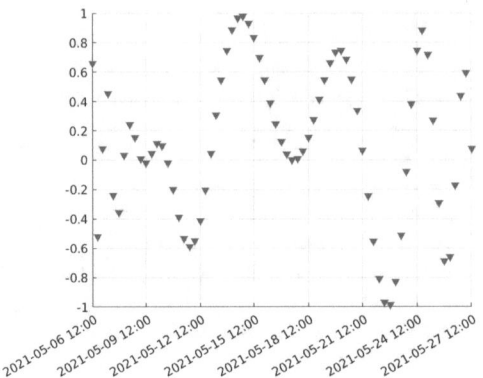

Figure 12-7. *MATLAB*

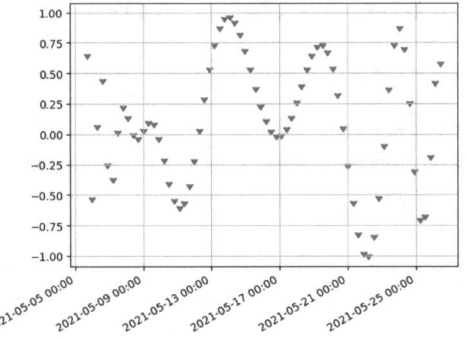

Figure 12-8. *Python*

12.1.4 Double Y Axes

Competing unit systems, for example, metric vs. US customary, can be shown simultaneously by labeling the left and right vertical axes with the different units. This example shows the modulus of elasticity, commonly known as Young's modulus, for several metals[1] in gigapascals (GPa) on the left and megapounds per square inch (Mpsi) on the right. This is somewhat easier in MATLAB with yyaxis left and yyaxis right commands which define the vertical axis on which subsequent commands operate. In matplotlib, we create a new vertical axis object by making a copy of the first one, then modify the copy with properties of the second unit system.

---

[1] https://en.wikipedia.org/wiki/Young%27s_modulus

MATLAB:	Python:

```
% file: code/plots/double_y_axis.m
yL = [68    108 112 116 193 200];
yR = [9.86 15.7 16.2 16.8 28 29];
yLmax = max(yL) * 1.1;
materials = {'aluminum',...
  'zinc', 'bronze', 'titanium',...
  'iron', 'steel'};
bar(yL)
yyaxis left
ylabel('GPa')
ylim([0 yLmax])
yyaxis right
ylabel('Mpsi')
ylim([0 yLmax/6.8965])
xticklabels(materials)
grid()
title("Young's Modulus")
```

```
# file: code/plots/double_y_axis.py
import numpy as np
import matplotlib.pyplot as plt
fig, ax = plt.subplots()
yL = [68,    108, 112, 116, 193, 200]
yR = [9.86, 15.7, 16.2, 16.8, 28, 29]
yLmax = np.max(yL) * 1.1
materials = ['aluminum', 'zinc',
  'bronze', 'titanium',
  'iron', 'steel']
P = ax.bar(materials, yL)
ax.set_ylabel('GPa')
ax2 = ax.twinx()
ax2.set_ylabel('Mpsi')
ax.set_ylim(ymax=yLmax)
ax2.set_ylim(ymax=yLmax/6.8965)
ax.grid(True)
ax.set_axisbelow(True)
plt.title("Young's Modulus")
plt.show()
```

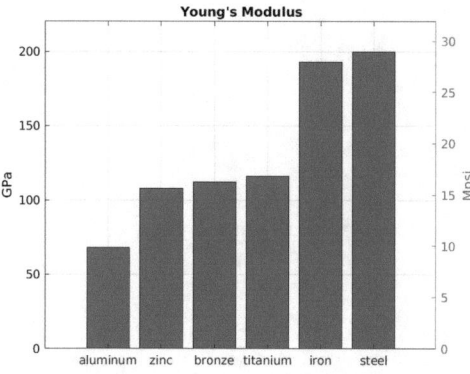

Figure 12-9. *MATLAB*

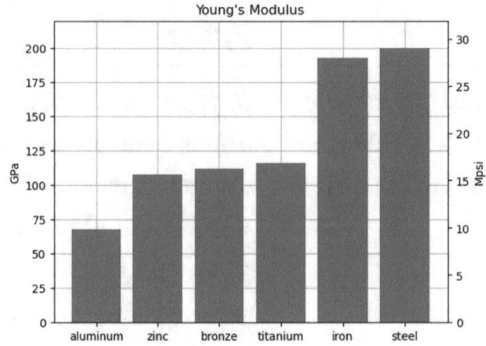

Figure 12-10. *Python*

12.1.5 Histograms

The following examples display histograms of normal and Rayleigh distributions. The MATLAB functions to produce these, normrnd() and raylrnd(), are in the Statistics and Machine Learning Toolbox. I don't have access to that, so instead in MATLAB I'll call the equivalent functions from NumPy. By using the same source of random numbers in MATLAB and Python, I can also initialize the same seed to produce identical distributions in both languages.

MATLAB:	Python:

```matlab
% file: code/plots/hist_demo.m
Im = @py.importlib.import_module;
rnd = Im('numpy.random');
N = int64(10000);
rnd.seed(int64(123));
w1 = rnd.rayleigh(int64(3), N);
w1 = py2mat(w1);
w2 = rnd.normal(int64(8),...
               int64(3), N);
w2 = py2mat(w2);
bins = linspace(-5, 20, 80);
h1 = histogram(w1,bins);
set(h1,'FaceAlpha',0.5,...
      'EdgeAlpha',0.0);
hold on
h2 = histogram(w2,bins);
set(h2,'FaceAlpha',0.5,...
      'EdgeAlpha',0.0);
legend('Rayleigh','Normal');
grid on
```

```python
# file: code/plots/hist_demo.py
import numpy as np
import matplotlib.pyplot as plt
N = 10000
np.random.seed(123)
w1 = np.random.rayleigh(3, N)
w2 = np.random.normal(8, 3, N)
bins = np.linspace(-5, 20, 80)
plt.hist(w1, bins, alpha=0.5,
         label="Rayleigh")
plt.hist(w2, bins, alpha=0.5,
         label="Normal")
plt.legend(loc='upper right')
plt.ylim([0, 700])
plt.grid(True)
plt.show()
```

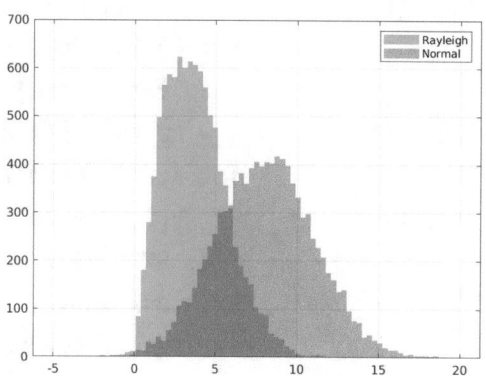

Figure 12-11. *MATLAB*

503

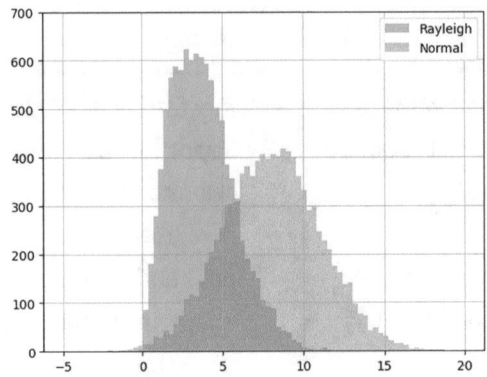

Figure 12-12. *Python*

12.1.6 Stack Plots

Stack (or sand) plots can be created with area() in MATLAB and stackplot() in matplotlib. (MATLAB has a stackedplot() function, but its purpose is to create multiple vertically aligned plots that share one x axis.)

MATLAB:	Python:

```
% file: code/plots/stack_demo.m
t = linspace(0, 20, 100);
w = [0.11, 0.25, 0.17, 0.32];
L = {};
y = zeros(length(t),length(w));
for i = 1:length(w)
    F = w(i);
    y(:,i) = cos(F*t).^2 + F;
    L{i} = sprintf(...
        '\\omega = %.2f', F);
end
area(t, y)
legend(L);
xlabel('\omega')
grid on
```

```
# file: code/plots/stack_demo.py
import numpy as np
import matplotlib.pyplot as plt
t = np.linspace(0, 20, 100)
w = [0.11, 0.25, 0.17, 0.32]
L = [f'$\omega$ = {_:.2f}'
        for _ in w]
y = np.zeros((len(w),len(t)))
for i,F in enumerate(w):
    y[i,:] = np.cos(F*t)**2 + F
fig, ax = plt.subplots()
ax.stackplot(t, y, labels=L)
ax.legend(loc='upper right')
ax.set_xlabel('$\omega$')
plt.grid()
ax.set_axisbelow(True)
plt.show()
```

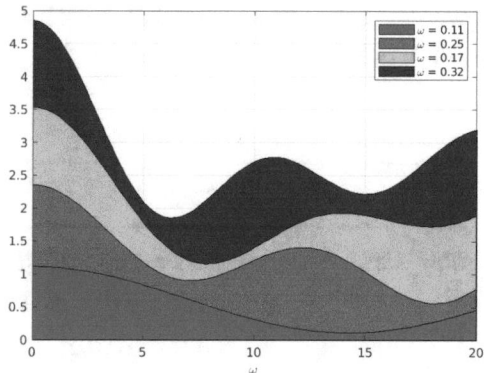

Figure 12-13. *MATLAB*

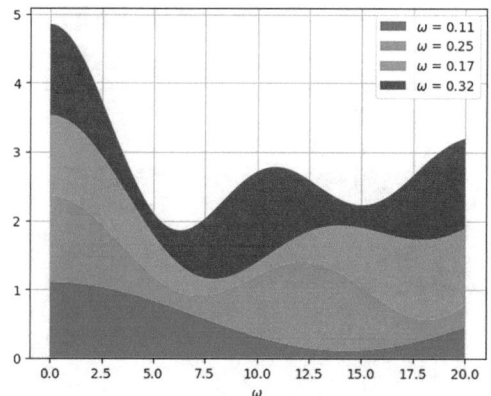

Figure 12-14. *Python*

12.2 Area Plots

12.2.1 `imshow()`

The simplest two-dimensional plot is a direct rendering of a two-dimensional numeric array using a colormap to color individual array elements. Both MATLAB and matplotlib can display 2D arrays as images using a function named `imshow()`. MATLAB's `imshow()`, however, displays the array so that each array element maps to one screen pixel; a 5 × 5 array appears microscopically small on most screens. The optional argument pair `'InitialMagnification','fit'` is needed to scale small arrays to reasonably sized images. MATLAB's `imagesc()` will scale the array to a comfortable size, but it doesn't offer different interpolation methods as `imshow()`.

This first example shows imagesc() in MATLAB and imshow() in matplotlib for a 16 × 16 array. (See Section 11.1.13 for a review of np.newaxis.) matplotlib conveniently sets a 1:1 aspect ratio:

MATLAB:	Python:

`% file: code/plots/imshow_demo.m`
`x = 0:0.2:pi;`
`S = sin(x);`
`z = S .* S';`
`imagesc(z)`
`colorbar`
	`# file: code/plots/imshow1_demo.py`
	`import numpy as np`
	`import matplotlib.pyplot as plt`
	`x = np.arange(0,np.pi,0.2)`
	`S = np.sin(x)`
	`z = S[:,np.newaxis] * S[np.newaxis,:]`
	`hz = plt.imshow(z)`
	`plt.colorbar(hz)`

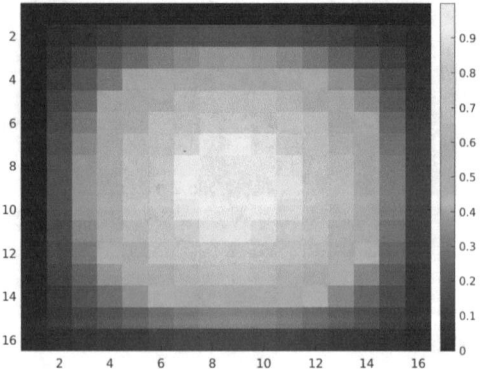

Figure 12-15. *MATLAB*

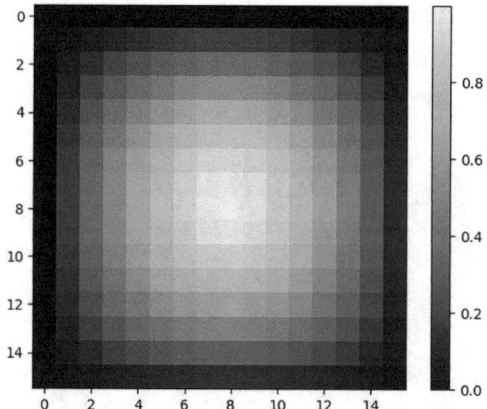

Figure 12-16. *Python*

The next example uses imshow() with bilinear interpolation in both MATLAB and matplotlib. The MATLAB image would appear in grayscale without the explicit colorbar argument.

MATLAB:	Python:
```% file: code/plots/imshow_demo.m```	```# file: code/plots/imshow2_demo.py```

```
% file: code/plots/imshow_demo.m
x = 0:0.2:pi;
S = sin(x);
z = S .* S';
imshow(z, 'Interpolation', ...
 'bilinear','Colormap',    ...
 parula,                   ...
 'InitialMagnification','fit')
colorbar
```

```
# file: code/plots/imshow2_demo.py
import numpy as np
import matplotlib.pyplot as plt
x = np.arange(0,np.pi,0.2)
S = np.sin(x)
z = S[:,np.newaxis] * S[np.newaxis,:]
hz = plt.imshow(z,
        interpolation="bilinear")
plt.colorbar(hz)
```

More specialized plots in Python require the user to obtain handles to separate figure and axis objects, however. Note the different prefixes `plt.`, `ax.`, and `fig.` before function names in the following contour example:

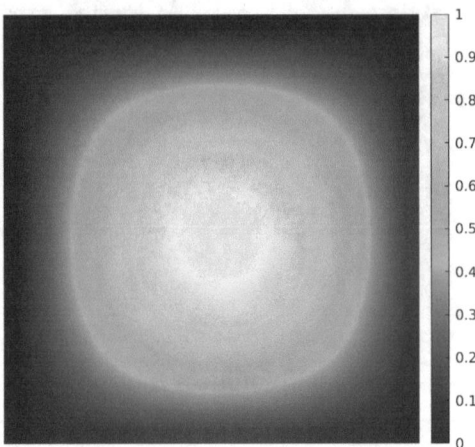

Figure 12-17. *MATLAB*

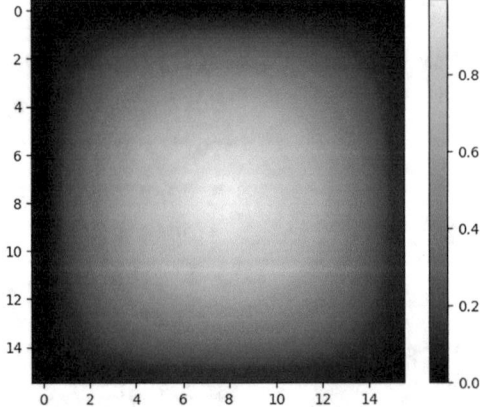

Figure 12-18. *Python*

MATLAB:	Python:
``N = 500;
rN = 1:N;
[J, I] = meshgrid(rN, rN);
x = -10 + 20*J/N;
y = -10 + 20*I/N;
z = cos(2*x/3).*sin(y/3)./ ...
(100 + x.^2+y.^2);
contourf(z)
daspect([1 1 1])
colorbar()
title('Filled Contour')
saveas(1,"m_contourf.png")```	```import numpy as np
import matplotlib.pyplot as plt
N = 500; rN = range(N)
J, I = np.meshgrid(rN, rN)
x = -10 + 20*J/N
y = -10 + 20*I/N
fig, ax = plt.subplots()
ax.set_aspect('equal')
z = np.cos(2*x/3)*np.sin(y/3)/(
100 + x**2+y**2)
cf = ax.contourf(z)
fig.colorbar(cf)
ax.set_title('Filled Contour')
plt.savefig('contourf.png')```

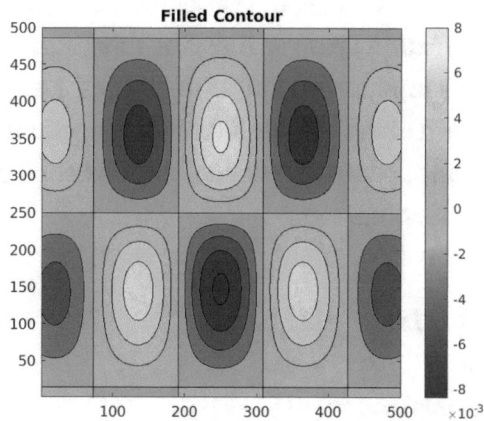

Figure 12-19. MATLAB

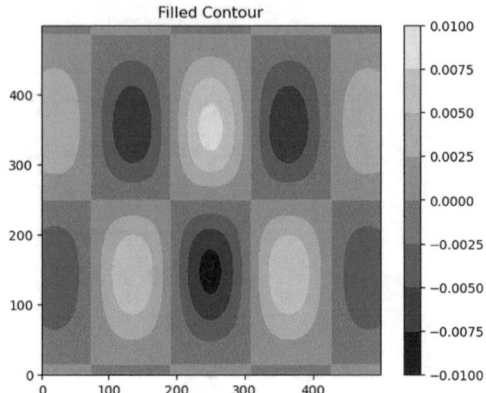

Figure 12-20. *Python*

12.3 Animations

Matplotlib can animate plots similarly to MATLAB. Unless the animations are simple though, it can be a challenge to avoid using global variables. We'll begin with a simple program that draws an ellipse whose width changes with every frame. All the action is encapsulated in one function, and no global variables are required.

Key elements of the animation are A_values, the third argument to FuncAnimation() on line 23, and the update() function on line 18. A_values is a vector of coefficients that will be used to scale the width of the ellipse; its values range from 0.9 down to 0.1 and then back up to 0.9. Each time update() is called, the next coefficient from A_values is taken, and the ellipse's image is redrawn.

Python:

```
1    # file: code/plots/circle_ellipse.py
2    import numpy as np
3    import matplotlib.pyplot as plt
4    from matplotlib.animation import FuncAnimation
5    def circle_to_ellipse():
6        fig, ax = plt.subplots()
7        T = np.linspace(0, 2*np.pi, 200)
8        x = np.cos(T)
9        y = np.sin(T)
10       curve, = plt.plot(x,y,'b')
11       A_values = np.hstack([np.linspace(0.1, 0.9, 100),
```

```
12                          np.linspace(0.9, 0.1, 100)])
13      def init():
14          ax.set_xlim(-1, 1)
15          ax.set_ylim(-1, 1)
16          ax.set_aspect('equal')
17          return curve,
18      def update(A):
19          x = A*np.cos(T)
20          y = np.sin(T)
21          curve, = plt.plot(x,y,'b')
22          return curve,
23      ani = FuncAnimation(fig, update, A_values,
24                          interval=20, # milliseconds
25                          init_func=init, blit=True)
26      plt.show()
27
28   circle_to_ellipse()
```

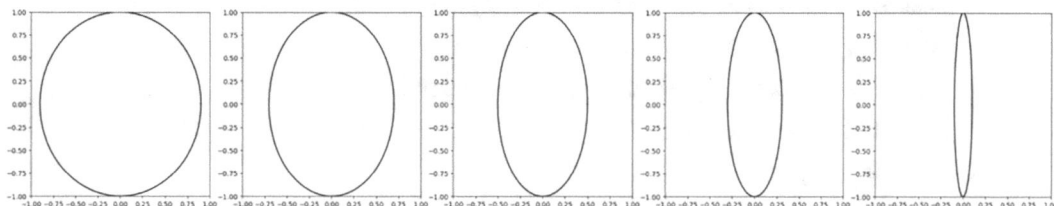

The second animation example shows a ball bouncing in a parabolic bowl. It is considerably more complex and uses global variables to store the ball's evolving trajectory.

Python:

```
# file: code/plots/bouncing_ball.py
import numpy as np
import matplotlib.pyplot as plt
import matplotlib.animation as animation
from copy import copy
A  = 0.08 # bowl shape: y = A*x^2
dt = 1.0/500 # time step, seconds
```

```
T  = np.arange(0, 20, dt)
n_iter = len(T)
damping = 0.9997
restitution = 0.995
ball_radius = 0.3
history_x, history_y = [], []
point, trace = None, None

def timestep(pos,vel):
    new_pos = copy(pos)
    new_vel = copy(vel)
    new_vel[1] += -9.8*dt
    new_vel *= damping
    new_pos[0] += new_vel[0]*dt
    new_pos[1] += new_vel[1]*dt
    bowl_y = A*new_pos[0]**2
    if new_pos[1] < bowl_y:
        # hit the bowl, bounce back
        normal = np.array([-2*A*new_pos[0],1])
        normal /= np.linalg.norm(normal)
        new_vel += -2*new_vel.dot(normal)*normal
        new_pos[1] = bowl_y
    return new_pos, new_vel

def run_simulation():
    nX = 21
    pos = np.zeros((n_iter,2))
    pos[0,:] = np.array([-3., 3.]) # initial position, m
    vel = np.array([0.5, 0])        # initial velocity, m/s
    bowl = np.zeros((nX,2))
    bowl[:,0] = np.linspace(-3.5, 3.5, num=nX)
    X = bowl[:,0]
    bowl[:,1] = A*X**2
    # centerline is the curve offset from the parabolic
    # bowl by the radius of the ball; it is where the
    # ball's center appears to bounce
```

```
    den = 1/np.sqrt(1 + (2*A*X)**2)
    centerline = np.zeros((nX,2))
    centerline[:,0] = X + 2*A*ball_radius*X*den
    centerline[:,1] = A*X**2 - ball_radius*den
    for i in range(1,n_iter):
        pos[i], vel = timestep(pos[i-1],vel)
    return bowl, centerline, pos, vel

def init(bowl, centerline):
    global point, trace
    fig, ax = plt.subplots()
    plt.plot(bowl[:,0],bowl[:,1],':')
    plt.plot(centerline[:,0],centerline[:,1])
    plt.ylim([-1,4])
    ax.set_aspect('equal')
    point, = ax.plot([], [], 'o', markersize=25)
    trace, = ax.plot([], [], ',-', lw=1)
    return fig

def animate(i):
    global history_x, history_y
    if i == 0:
        history_x.clear()
        history_y.clear()
    history_x.append(pos[i,0])
    history_y.append(pos[i,1])
    point.set_data(pos[i,0], pos[i,1])
    trace.set_data(history_x, history_y)
    return point, trace

bowl, centerline, pos, vel = run_simulation()
fig = init(bowl, centerline)
ani = animation.FuncAnimation(
    fig, animate, n_iter, interval=dt*1000, blit=True)
plt.show()
```

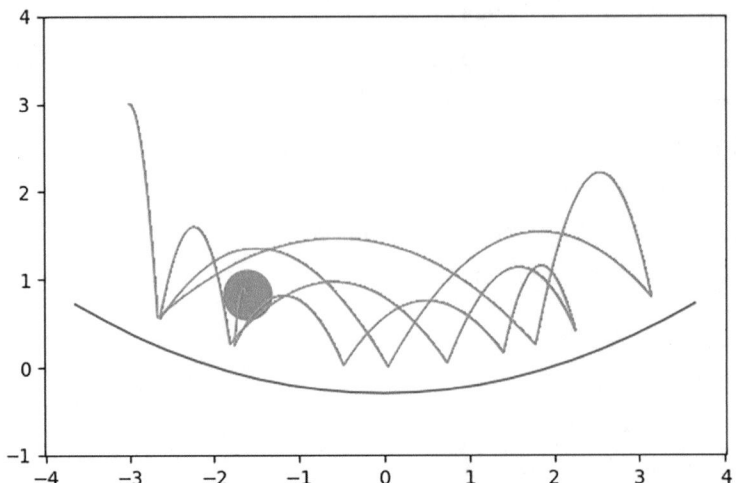

12.4 Plotting on Maps with Cartopy

Python's Cartopy module, developed by the UK's Meteorological Office, provides a vast collection of cartographic transformation and projection functions that work with matplotlib. It is as feature-rich as the Mapping Toolbox for MATLAB. Several Cartopy submodules make use of web-based map tile services, so a connection to the Internet is desirable for making imagery-enhanced plots.

As with all plotting packages, the easiest way to start using Cartopy is to view its gallery[2] and modify working examples.

We'll begin our exploration of plotting on maps with point and line data in Cartopy and with MATLAB's family of geo* functions. More complex geographical overlay plots in MATLAB need the Mapping Toolbox though. Alternatively, we can call Cartopy from MATLAB; this will be demonstrated with recipes to overlay sea surface temperature on a globe (Section 12.6) and draw a map of South America with countries shaded in proportion to their wheat production (Section 12.7).

12.4.1 Points

MATLAB's geo* functions work with tables, covered in the next chapter, as well as regular matrix variables. This example shows two dots are overlaid on a high-resolution Paris city map, using a table in MATLAB and scalar variables in Python. The red dot is over the Notre Dame cathedral and the blue dot over the Pantheon.

---

[2] https://scitools.org.uk/cartopy/docs/latest/gallery/index.html

Tip   Use Google Earth[3] to find latitude and longitude bounds for your maps (calls to ax.set_extent()).

MATLAB:	Python:

```
% code/plots/paris_pt.m
T = table([48.853;48.846], ...
        [2.3497;2.3464],...
    'VariableNames', ...
    {'Lat','Lon'}, ...
    'RowNames', {'Notre Dame',
                'Pantheon'});
C = [1 0 0; 0 0 1];
geoscatter(T.Lat, T.Lon,124,...
        C, 'Filled')
geolimits([48.8425 48.8625], ...
        [2.3283 2.3722])
geobasemap streets
title("Notre Dame (red) and " +...
    "the Pantheon (blue)")
```

```
#!/usr/bin/env python3
# code/plots/cartopy_pt.py
import matplotlib.pyplot as plt
import numpy as np
import cartopy.crs as ccrs
from cartopy.io.img_tiles import OSM
imagery = OSM()
PC = ccrs.PlateCarree()
fig = plt.figure()
ax = fig.add_subplot(1, 1, 1,
        projection=imagery.crs)
ax.set_extent([2.3283, 2.3722,
            48.8425, 48.8625],
            crs=PC)
ax.add_image(imagery, 14)
ax.plot(2.3497, 48.853, transform=PC,
        marker="o", color="red",
        markersize=6)
ax.plot(2.3464, 48.846, transform=PC,
        marker="o", color="blue",
        markersize=6)
ax.set_title('Notre Dame (red) and '
            'the Pantheon (blue)')
plt.savefig('Paris.png')
plt.show()
```

---

[3] https://earth.google.com/web/

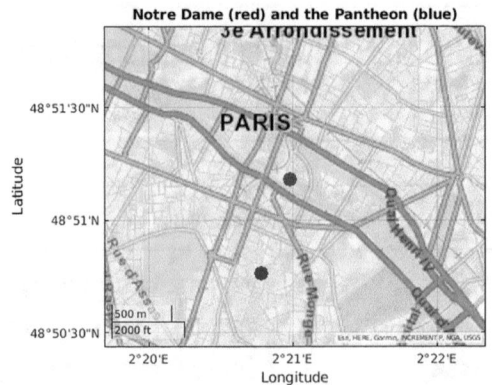

Figure 12-21. *MATLAB*

Figure 12-22. *Python*

A commonly seen error relates to downloading map tiles from the Internet:

```
<urlopen error [SSL: CERTIFICATE_VERIFY_FAILED] certificate verify failed:
    unable to get local issuer certificate (_ssl.c:1125)>
```

Numerous explanations and workarounds can be found on the Internet, but for the specific case of getting map tiles for Cartopy, I've found the most reliable solution to be modifying Cartopy's source code directly to use the requests module instead of urllib. Details appear in Section 12.4.4.

12.4.2 Lines

In this example, we plot the path of a whale known as "Blue Whale 158390" between September 21, 2018, and November 18, 2018. The location data[4] must have a significant error margin because one of the data points, 48.64328° N, 66.47227° W, is in a field in New Brunswick, Canada, about 60 km inland. This corresponds to roughly 0.5° of latitude or longitude at the equator. In Python, we'll use this information to overlay in blue a region 0.5° wide indicating the error bound on the whale's path. The MATLAB code, while elegant in its extreme simplicity, has no mechanism to control the width of lines drawn with geoplot() so its figure lacks this feature.

This example also shows how additional detail—latitude and longitude grid lines, country borders, rivers—is added to Cartopy maps.

The numeric values for latitude and longitude returned by whale_data() are in data/plots/whale_path.txt.

---

[4] http://www2.whalenet.org/whalenet-stuff/StopBm2016/data_2018.html

MATLAB:	Python:

```matlab
% code/plots/whale.m
P = importdata
('whale_path.txt');
geoplot(P(:,2),
P(:,1),'r')
geolimits([30 55],
[-80 -50])
geobasemap colorterrain
title("Blue Whale
        158390, " + ...
    "Fall 2018")
```

```python
#!/usr/bin/env python3
# code/plots/cartopy_whale.py
import numpy as np
import shapely.geometry as sgeom
import cartopy.crs as ccrs
import cartopy.feature as cfeature
import matplotlib.pyplot as plt

fig = plt.figure()
PC = ccrs.PlateCarree()
ax = fig.add_subplot(1, 1, 1, projection=PC)
ax.coastlines(resolution='50m')
ax.set_extent([-80, -50, 30, 55], crs=PC)

ax.add_feature(cfeature.LAND)
ax.add_feature(cfeature.OCEAN)
ax.add_feature(cfeature.COASTLINE)
ax.add_feature(cfeature.BORDERS, linestyle='-')
ax.add_feature(cfeature.LAKES.with_scale('50m'),
                alpha=0.5)
ax.add_feature(cfeature.RIVERS.with_scale('50m'))

plt.title('Blue Whale 158390, Fall 2018')
path = np.loadtxt('whale_path.txt')
track = sgeom.LineString(path)
error = track.buffer(.5) # degrees
ax.gridlines(draw_labels=True)
ax.add_geometries([error], ccrs.PlateCarree(),
        facecolor='#1F18F4', alpha=.5)
ax.add_geometries([track], ccrs.PlateCarree(),
        facecolor="none", edgecolor="r")
plt.savefig('whale.png', bbox_inches="tight",
        pad_inches=0, transparent=True)
plt.show()
```

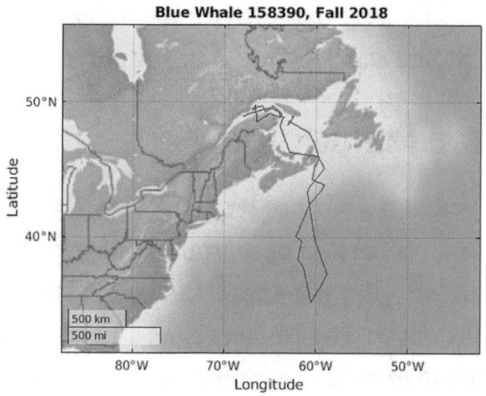

Figure 12-23. *MATLAB*

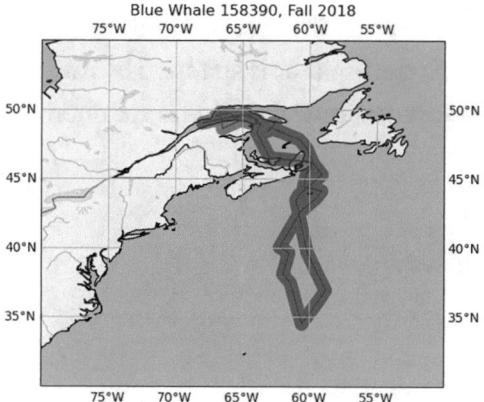

Figure 12-24. *Python*

If you need the fine control over geographic lines in your MATLAB plots that geoplot() can't give you, see Recipe 12.5, which shows how to reproduce the Cartopy plot on the right from MATLAB.

12.4.3 Area

The majority of data overlaid on maps spans areas rather than points or lines. There's an endless list of these: earth science data such as land and sea surface temperatures, land surface type, vegetation index, and rainfall; commercial data such as agricultural production and gross domestic production; political data such as voting results, party affiliation, and conflict zones.

Native MATLAB options for overlaying area data on maps are the Mapping Toolbox and the freely available Climate Data Toolbox.[5] In Python, we'll continue with Cartopy.

12.4.3.1 Sea Surface Temperature

Our first example shows global sea surface temperature using a pair of projections. The plot is enhanced by using a custom background image of the earth from NASA's Earth Observations[6] collection—the vegetation index in this case. To do this, save the vegetation index image file, earth_veg_index.jpeg, and accompanying JSON metadata to a directory, then set the environment variable CARTOPY_USER_BACKGROUNDS to this directory.[7]

The sea surface temperature (SST) data comes from NOAA's collection of daily AVHRR satellite data.[8] Each day's data is in a NetCDF file (Section 7.10) containing SST on a 0.5° latitude and longitude grid. The first row and column correspond to latitude –89.875° and longitude 0.125°; the equator is spanned by rows 359 and 360 (using zero-based indexing), while the international date line is spanned by columns 719 and 720.

Python:

```python
#!/usr/bin/env python3
# code/plots/cartopy_sst.py
import os
import numpy as np
import matplotlib.pyplot as plt
from netCDF4 import Dataset
import cartopy.crs as ccrs
from mpl_toolkits.axes_grid1 import make_axes_locatable

os.environ["CARTOPY_USER_BACKGROUNDS"] = "cartopy/background"
File = 'oisst-avhrr-v02r01.20190101.nc'
rg = Dataset(File, 'r')
lat = rg["lat"][:]
```

---

[5] www.mathworks.com/matlabcentral/fileexchange/70338-climate-data-toolbox-for-matlab

[6] https://neo.sci.gsfc.nasa.gov

[7] http://earthpy.org/tag/cartopy.html

[8] https://www.ncei.noaa.gov/data/sea-surface-temperature-optimum-interpolation/v2.1/access/avhrr/201901/oisstavhrr-v02r01.20190101.nc

```
lon = rg["lon"][:]
sst_ds = rg["sst"][0][0]
sst = sst_ds.data
mask = sst_ds.mask
sst[mask] = np.NaN
fig = plt.figure()
Ortho = ccrs.Orthographic(-10, 15)
PC = ccrs.PlateCarree()
ax = fig.add_subplot(1, 1, 1, projection=Ortho)
#          - or -
# ax = fig.add_subplot(1, 1, 1, projection=PC)
ax.coastlines()
ax.set_global()
ax.gridlines()
h = ax.contourf(lon, lat, sst, levels=20,
    vmin=-2, vmax=35, transform=PC, cmap='jet')
divider = make_axes_locatable(ax)
ax_cb = divider.new_horizontal(size="5%", pad=0.1,
    axes_class=plt.Axes)
fig.add_axes(ax_cb)
plt.colorbar(h, cax=ax_cb)
ax.background_img(name='VI', resolution='low')
ax.set_title('SST 2020-01-02 [Celcius]')
plt.savefig('sst_globe.png', bbox_inches='tight',
    pad_inches=0, transparent=True)
plt.show()
```

SST 2020-01-02 [Celcius]

Many projections are available. An orthographic projection over –10° longitude and 15° latitude can be produced by replacing the PlateCarree projection with

Python:

```
Ortho = ccrs.Orthographic(-10, 15)
ax = fig.add_subplot(1, 1, 1, projection=Ortho)
```

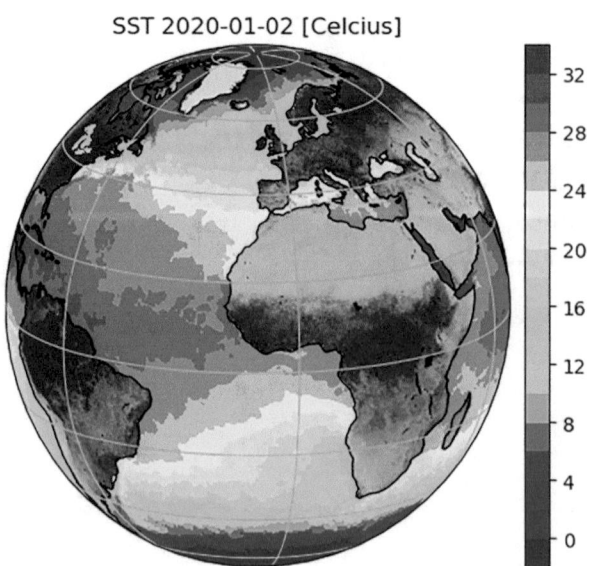

SST 2020-01-02 [Celcius]

Create this plot in MATLAB with the recipe in Section 12.6.

12.4.3.2 South American Wheat Production, 2014

Our second example shows data bounded by country borders. Our dataset will be South American wheat production from 2014.[9] The goal is to shade each country in proportion to its production values.

While Cartopy comes with a database of shore lines, it does not include country or state borders. Ideally, we would like to say something like `plot(region(country='Canada'), 'grey')` or `plot(region(zipcode=90210), 'orange')`, but such a capability does not exist. (Spoiler: GeoPandas, covered in Section 13.12, can do this.)

Instead, we will create our own database of country borders by downloading shape files and associated metadata from the Natural Earth project. The "low resolution" file[10] contains Cartopy-readable files that contain country borders, country names in a dozen languages, name of the containing continent, economic status, and population and GDP estimates, among other pieces of information. However, the burden is on us to acquire the data, read it, and store it in a convenient form.

The following Python code expects the file `ne_110m_admin_0_countries.zip` to have been expanded into a subdirectory called `nat_earth`. We'll use Cartopy's shape reader to load both the country shapes and metadata and from these construct a dictionary, `shp`, storing the English country names in keys and border geometry as the associated values. For fun, we'll populate a second dictionary, `rec`, storing each country's metadata.

Python:

```
In : from cartopy.io.shapereader import Reader
In : shp = {} # country shape indexed by name
In : rec = {} # country metadata indexed by name
In : Countries = Reader('nat_earth/ne_110m_admin_0_countries')
In : for geom, meta in zip(Countries.geometries(), Countries.records()):
...:     name = meta.attributes['NAME_EN']
...:     shp[name] = geom
...:     rec[name] = meta
```

---

[9] https://en.actualitix.com/country/amsu/south-america-wheat-production.php
[10] www.naturalearthdata.com/downloads/110m-cultural-vectors/ne_110m_admin_0_countries.zip

Exploring these dictionaries reveals interesting information:

Python:

```
In : sorted( shp.keys() )
Out: shp.keys()
['Afghanistan',
 'Albania',
 'Algeria',
 'Angola',
 'Antarctica',
 'Argentina',
 ...
 'Vietnam',
 'Western Sahara',
 'Yemen',
 'Zambia',
 'Zimbabwe',
 'eSwatini']

In : rec['Vietnam']
Out[9]: <Record: <shapely.geometry.polygon.Polygon object at
0x7fe5f7055220>,
{'featurecla': 'Admin-0 country', 'scalerank': 1, 'LABELRANK': 2,
'SOVEREIGNT': 'Vietnam', 'POSTAL': 'VN', 'MAPCOLOR7': 5, 'MAPCOLOR8': 6,
 'POP_EST': 96160163, 'POP_RANK': 16, 'GDP_MD_EST': 594900.0,
 'POP_YEAR': 2017, 'LASTCENSUS': 2009, 'GDP_YEAR': 2016,
 ...

[ins] In [12]: rec['Vietnam'].attributes['POP_EST']
Out[12]: 96160163
```

More importantly, the matplotlib + Cartopy combination understands polygonal regions created from shape files and thus allows countries to be shaded with desired colors. There is one subtlety with polygons made from geopolitical borders: some borders are individual polygons, while others (e.g., the islands of Indonesia) have multiple disjointed polygons. The matplotlib add_geometries() function, used to add regions defined by polygonal borders, expects a list of polygons as the first argument.

Therefore, we must first check to see if a country's shape is a single polygon or a list of polygons; if it is a single, the calling argument to add_geometries() must be extended to a one-item list. Line 42 in the following listing shows how to handle these cases appropriately:

Python:

```
1    #!/usr/local/anaconda3/2020.07/bin/python
2    # code/plots/cartopy_wheat.py
3    import numpy as np
4    import cartopy.crs as ccrs
5    import cartopy.feature as cfeature
6    from cartopy.io.shapereader import Reader
7    from shapely.geometry.polygon import Polygon
8    import matplotlib.pyplot as plt
9    from matplotlib.colors import from_levels_and_colors
10   from mpl_toolkits.axes_grid1 import make_axes_locatable
11
12   wheat_tons = {
13       'Argentina' : 13_930_078 ,
14       'Brazil' : 6_261_895 ,
15       'Chile' : 1_358_128 ,
16       'Uruguay' : 1_076_000 ,
17       'Paraguay' : 840_000 ,
18       'Bolivia' : 263_076 ,
19       'Peru' : 214_533 ,
20       'Colombia' : 9_718 ,
21       'Ecuador' : 6_584 ,
22       'Venezuela' : 161 , }
23
24   Countries = Reader('nat_earth/ne_110m_admin_0_countries')
25   shp = {} # country shape indexed by name
26   for geom, meta in zip(Countries.geometries(),
27                         Countries.records()):
28       name = meta.attributes['NAME_EN']
29       shp[name] = geom
30
```

```
31   PC = ccrs.PlateCarree()
32   fig, ax = plt.subplots(1, 1, subplot_kw=dict(projection=PC))
33   ax.set_extent([-85, -33, # lon
34                   -55, 14]) # lat
35
36   ton_intervals = np.array([0, 10_000, 100_000, 1_000_000, 10_000_000,
     15_000_000,])
37   fraction_interval = np.linspace(0.12, 1, num=len(ton_intervals))
38   colors = plt.cm.BuPu(fraction_interval[:-1])
39
40   for ctry in wheat_tons:
41       color = colors[np.searchsorted(ton_intervals, wheat_
         tons[ctry]) - 1]
42       shape = [shp[ctry]] if isinstance(shp[ctry], Polygon) else
         shp[ctry]
43       ax.add_geometries(shape, crs=PC, facecolor=color)
44
45   ax.add_feature(cfeature.BORDERS)
46   ax.add_feature(cfeature.COASTLINE)
47   ax.set_title('Wheat Production, 2014 [10$^6$ tons]')
48
49   # colorbar
50   divider = make_axes_locatable(ax)
51   ax_cb = divider.new_horizontal(size="5%", pad=0.1,
     axes_class=plt.Axes)
52   fig.add_axes(ax_cb)
53   cmap, norm = from_levels_and_colors(ton_intervals/1.0e+6, colors)
54   sm = plt.cm.ScalarMappable(cmap=cmap, norm=norm)
55   plt.colorbar(sm, cax=ax_cb)
56
57   plt.show()
58   #plt.savefig('SA_wheat_2014.png', dpi=200,
59   # bbox_inches='tight', pad_inches=0, transparent=True)
```

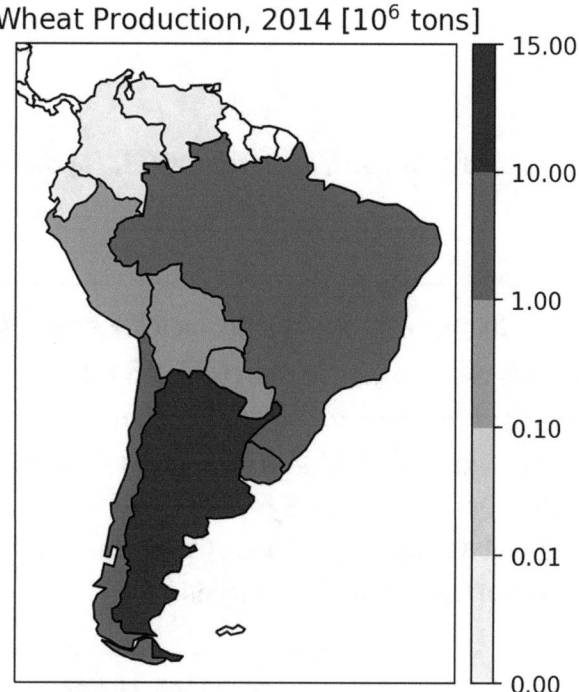
Wheat Production, 2014 [10^6 tons]

Create this plot in MATLAB with the recipe in Section 12.7.

12.4.4 MATLAB and Cartopy

There is a substantial challenge to using Cartopy from MATLAB though. Cartopy version 0.18.0 (current as of July 2021) exhibits an unusual interaction with MATLAB when it attempts to download imagery tiles from map services. One of two things can happen: either this error appears

```
<urlopen error [SSL: CERTIFICATE_VERIFY_FAILED] certificate verify
failed: unable
to get local issuer certificate (_ssl.c:1124)>
```

or the resulting plots simply lack background images.

There is a workaround, but it involves modifying the Cartopy's file cartopy/io/img_ tiles.py to use the requests module to download tiles instead of urllib.request from the Python standard library. The first step is to find the directory or folder containing img_tiles.py. That can be done within ipython by importing cartopy.io and then examining its __path__ attribute. On my Linux computer, this directory is ipython:

```
In : import cartopy.io
In : cartopy.io.__path__
Out: ['/usr/local/anaconda3/2020.07/envs/matpy/lib/python3.8/site-packages/
cartopy/io']
```

Note   If you installed Cartopy in multiple virtual environments, you'll need to edit img tiles.py in each one you plan to start MATLAB from.

Next, edit img_tiles.py so that it includes an import to requests (line 41 on the right) and replaces calls to urlopen(), six.BytesIO(), and fh.close() (lines 190–193 on the left) with the highlighted lines on the right. (The actual line numbers will vary depending on the version of Cartopy you've installed.)

---

img_tiles.py **original:**	img_tiles.py **fixed:**
39 import numpy as np	39 import numpy as np
40 import six	40 import six
41	41 import requests
42 import cartopy	42
43 import cartopy.crs as ccrs	43 import cartopy
188 url = self._image_url(tile)	44 import cartopy.crs as ccrs
189 try:	189 url = self._image_url(tile)
190 request = Request(url, headers={	190 try:
"User-Agent": self.user_agent})	191 request = requests.get(url, stream=True)
191 fh = urlopen(request)	192 request.raw.decode content =
192 im_data = six.BytesIO(fh. read())	True
193 fh.close()	193 img = Image.open(request.raw)
194 img = Image.open(im_data)	

The source listing for a utility that automates this patch, patch_cartopy.py, appears in Appendix E.

12.4.5 Avoid matplotlib's Qt Backend in MATLAB!

MATLAB uses the Qt library to render graphics. While matplotlib can use a half dozen different graphics libraries, it defaults to Qt. This is a problem! The Qt libraries that come with an Anaconda distribution are unlikely to match those shipped with MATLAB. As a result, if you use matplotlib's `plt.show()` command in MATLAB, you'll cause MATLAB to crash.

There's an easy workaround though: simply configure matplotlib to use a different backend. First, we'll query the Python installation to see what backend it currently uses:

Python:

```
In : import matplotlib
In : matplotlib.get_backend()
Out: 'Qt5Agg'
```

"Qt5Agg" will definitely be a problem in MATLAB. A good alternative is the `TkAgg` backend on Linux and macOS and `WXAgg` on Windows. Switching to the `TkAgg` backend, for example, is done like this in Python:

Python:

```
import matplotlib
matplotlib.use('TkAgg')
```

and like this in MATLAB:

MATLAB 2020b:

```
Im  = @py.importlib.import_module;
mpl = Im('matplotlib');
mpl.use('TkAgg')
```

12.5 Recipe 12-1: Drawing Lines on Maps with Cartopy

The MATLAB equivalent of the whale's track shown in Section 12.4.2 looks like this:

MATLAB 2020b:

```
% file: code/matlab_py/cartopy_whale.m
Im = @py.importlib.import_module;
np     = Im('numpy');
```

```
sgeom  = Im('shapely.geometry');
ccrs   = Im('cartopy.crs');
cfeat  = Im('cartopy.feature');
plt    = Im('matplotlib.pyplot');
mpl    = Im('matplotlib');
if ispc
    mpl.use('WXAgg')
else
    mpl.use('TkAgg')
end

PC = ccrs.PlateCarree();
fig = plt.figure();
i1 = int64(1);
ax = fig.add_subplot(i1, i1, i1, pyargs('projection',PC));
ax.coastlines(pyargs('resolution','50m'));
ax.set_extent([-80 -50 30 55], pyargs('crs',PC));
ax.add_feature(cfeat.LAND);
ax.add_feature(cfeat.OCEAN);
ax.add_feature(cfeat.COASTLINE);
ax.add_feature(cfeat.BORDERS, pyargs('linestyle','-'));
ax.add_feature(cfeat.LAKES.with_scale('50m'), pyargs('alpha', 0.5));
ax.add_feature(cfeat.RIVERS.with_scale('50m'));
plt.title('Blue Whale 158390, Fall 2018');
path = load('whale_path.txt');
track = sgeom.LineString(np.array(path));
error = track.buffer(.5); % degrees
ax.gridlines(pyargs('draw_labels','True'));
ax.add_geometries({error}, PC, pyargs('facecolor','#1F18F4','alpha',.5));
ax.add_geometries({track}, PC, pyargs('facecolor','none','edgecolor','r'));
plt.savefig('whale.png', pyargs('bbox_inches','tight','pad_inches',0, ...
    'transparent','True'));
plt.show()
```

12.6 Recipe 12-2: Overlay Contours on Globe with Cartopy

The sea surface temperature overlay made in Section 12.4.3.1 can be made in MATLAB with Cartopy.

MATLAB 2020b:

```
% code/matlab_py/cartopy_sst.m
Im = @py.importlib.import_module;
OS    = Im('os');
np    = Im('numpy');
plt   = Im('matplotlib.pyplot');
ccrs  = Im('cartopy.crs');
axes  = Im('mpl_toolkits.axes_grid1');
mpl   = Im('matplotlib');
if ispc
    netcdf.inqLibVers; % avoid DLL conflict
    mpl.use('WXAgg')
else
    mpl.use('TkAgg')
end
nc    = Im('netCDF4');
i1 = int64(1);
OS.environ{'CARTOPY_USER_BACKGROUNDS'} = ...
       '../plots/cartopy/background';
File = '../plots/oisst-avhrr-v02r01.20201001_preliminary.nc';
lat = ncread(File, 'lat');
lon = ncread(File, 'lon');
sst = ncread(File, 'sst')';
mask = isnan(sst);
fig = plt.figure();
Ortho = ccrs.Orthographic(-10, 15);
PC    = ccrs.PlateCarree();
ax = fig.add_subplot(i1, i1, i1,pyargs('projection',Ortho));
%             - or -
%ax = fig.add_subplot(i1, i1, i1, pyargs('projection',PC));
```

```
ax.coastlines();
ax.set_global();
ax.gridlines();
h = ax.contourf(lon, lat, sst,...
    pyargs('levels',int64(20), 'vmin',-2,'vmax',35,...
        'transform',PC,'cmap','jet'));
divider = axes.make_axes_locatable(ax);
ax_cb = divider.new_horizontal(...
    pyargs('size','5%','pad',0.1,'axes_class',plt.Axes));
fig.add_axes(ax_cb);
plt.colorbar(h, pyargs('cax',ax_cb));
ax.background_img(pyargs('name',"VI",'resolution',"low"));
ax.set_title('SST 2020-01-02 [Celcius]');
plt.savefig('sst_globe.png', pyargs('bbox_inches','tight',...
            'pad_inches',0,'transparent','True'));
plt.show()
```

12.7 Recipe 12-3: Shade Map Regions by Value with Cartopy

The map of South American wheat production made in Section 12.4.3.2 can be made in MATLAB with Cartopy.

MATLAB 2020b:

```
Im = @py.importlib.import_module;
np      = Im('numpy');
ccrs    = Im('cartopy.crs');
cfeat   = Im('cartopy.feature');
shape   = Im('cartopy.io.shapereader');
poly    = Im('shapely.geometry.polygon');
plt     = Im('matplotlib.pyplot');
col     = Im('matplotlib.colors'); % from_levels_and_colors
axes    = Im('mpl_toolkits.axes_grid1'); % make_axes_locatable
mpl     = Im('matplotlib');
```

```
if ispc
    mpl.use('WXAgg')
else
    mpl.use('TkAgg')
end
i1 = int64(1);

wheat_tons.Argentina = 13930078;
wheat_tons.Brazil    = 6261895;
wheat_tons.Chile     = 1358128;
wheat_tons.Uruguay   = 1076000;
wheat_tons.Paraguay  = 840000;
wheat_tons.Bolivia   = 263076;
wheat_tons.Peru      = 214533;
wheat_tons.Colombia  = 9718;
wheat_tons.Ecuador   = 6584;
wheat_tons.Venezuela = 161;

Countries = shape.Reader('nat_earth/ne_110m_admin_0_countries.shp');
shp = py.dict(); % country shape indexed by name
for geom_meta = py.list(py.zip(...
        Countries.geometries(), Countries.records()))
    name = geom_meta{1}{2}.attributes.get('NAME_EN'); % {1}{2} = meta
    shp.update(pyargs(name, geom_meta{1}{1})); % {1}{1} = geom
end
PC = ccrs.PlateCarree();
fig_ax = plt.subplots(i1, i1, pyargs('subplot_kw',...
                    py.dict(pyargs('projection',PC))));
fig = fig_ax{1};
ax  = fig_ax{2};
ax.set_extent([-85, -33, ... % lon
               -55, 14]) % lat

ton_intervals = [0, 10000, 100000, 1000000, 10000000, 15000000];
fraction_interval = linspace(0.12, 1, length(ton_intervals));
colors = plt.cm.BuPu(fraction_interval(1:end-1));
col_ind = np.arange(4, pyargs('dtype',np.int64));
```

```
country_names = fieldnames(wheat_tons);
for i = 1:numel(country_names)
   ctry = country_names{i};
   w_tons = wheat_tons.(ctry);
   color_row = np.searchsorted(ton_intervals, w_tons) - 1;
   fprintf('%20s %10d tons, color=%d\n', ctry, w_tons, int32(color_row))
   color = colors.take(col_ind + int64(4)*color_row);
   if py.isinstance(shp.get(ctry), poly.Polygon)
      shape = py.list({shp.get(ctry)});
   else
      shape = shp.get(ctry);
   end
   ax.add_geometries(shape, pyargs('crs',PC,'facecolor',color));
end

ax.add_feature(cfeat.BORDERS);
ax.add_feature(cfeat.COASTLINE);
ax.set_title('Wheat Production, 2014 [10$^6$ tons]');

% colorbar
divider = axes.make_axes_locatable(ax);
ax_cb = divider.new_horizontal(pyargs('size',"5%",'pad',0.1,...
                                      'axes_class',plt.Axes));
fig.add_axes(ax_cb);
cmap_norm = col.from_levels_and_colors(ton_intervals/1.0e+6, colors);
cmap = cmap_norm{1};
norm = cmap_norm{2};
sm = plt.cm.ScalarMappable(pyargs('cmap',cmap,'norm',norm));
plt.colorbar(sm, pyargs('cax',ax_cb));
plt.savefig('SA_wheat_2014.png', pyargs('bbox_inches','tight',...
            'pad_inches',0,'transparent','True'));
plt.show()
```

12.8 Plotting on Maps with GeoPandas

The next chapter covers MATLAB tables and Pandas dataframes. GeoPandas, an extension to Pandas, combines Cartopy, Pandas, and Shapely (among other Python modules) and makes it possible to plot geographical data quite easily. Section 13.12 shows how to make a map of Los Angeles County home prices by zip code. It takes considerably less effort than calling Cartopy functions directly.

12.9 Making Plots in Batch Mode

Plot generation is mostly an interactive experience where a user views plots on a display as they are drawn. A fully automated workflow on the other hand eliminates displays entirely; plots can be written directly to PNG or other image formats for direct inclusion in websites or documents. Both MATLAB and Python support "headless" plot generation albeit with different methods.

MATLAB's batch plot method relies on command-line arguments to the `matlab` command. This line runs the `hist_demo.m` script of Section 12.1.5:

MATLAB:

```
> matlab -nodesktop -nodisplay -nosplash -r "hist_demo;saveas(1,'hist.
png');exit"
```

matplotlib's batch plot method requires the use of the "Agg" backend as shown on lines 4 and 5:

Python:

```
1   #!/usr/bin/env python3
2   # file: code/plots/hist_demo_Agg.py
3   import numpy as np
4   import matplotlib as mpl
5   mpl.use('Agg')
6   import matplotlib.pyplot as plt
7   N = 10000
8   np.random.seed(123)
9   w1 = np.random.rayleigh(3, N)
10  w2 = np.random.normal(8, 3, N)
11  bins = np.linspace(-5, 20, 80)
```

```
12    plt.hist(w1, bins, alpha=0.5, label='Rayleigh')
13    plt.hist(w2, bins, alpha=0.5, label='Normal')
14    plt.legend(loc='upper right')
15    plt.ylim([0, 700])
16    plt.grid(True)
17    plt.savefig('hist.png', bbox_inches='tight', pad_inches=0,
      transparent=True)
```

Tip   From an ipython session, you can get a list of all available backends with

```
In :    import matplotlib
```

```
In :    matplotlib.rcsetup.interactive_bk
```

12.10 Interactive Plot Editing

Fine-tuning matplotlib plots for publication can become a maddening exercise of font, color, glyph, and coordinate selection. MATLAB enjoys an advantage here in that its plot editor allows one to modify plot elements interactively.

Matplotlib's Qt5Agg backend allows some interactive plot capability which can be accessed through the indicated icons in the display tool:

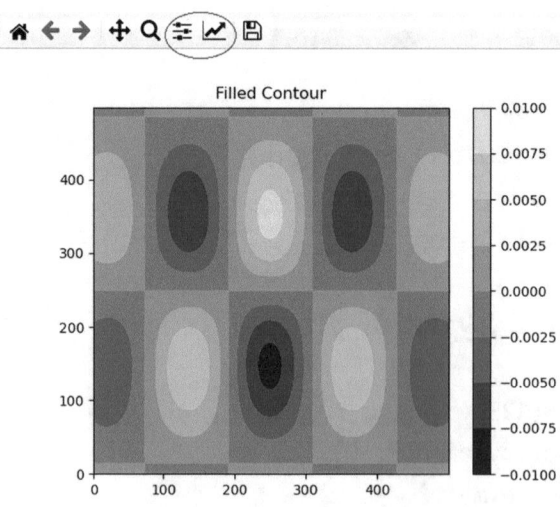

The Qt5Agg backend, however, is not included in the matpy conda environment because it conflicts with MATLAB's own Qt5 libraries. You'll need to leave that conda environment (`conda deactivate`) and return to the "base" environment to make such edits.

pylustrator[11] is a more advanced tool for interactive editing of matplotlib plots. Its capabilities are best appreciated by viewing the YouTube videos at its documentation site, `https://pylustrator.readthedocs.io/`.

---

[11] `https://github.com/rgerum/pylustrator`

CHAPTER 13

Tables and Dataframes

The Pandas module for Python [2] came out in 2008, five years before the MathWorks added tables to MATLAB in the R2013b release. Since its release, Pandas has become a core tool for data scientists, financial analysts, statisticians, and machine learning specialists. A comprehensive discussion of Pandas is far beyond the scope of this book; instead, here we show the functional similarities and notational differences between Pandas dataframes and MATLAB tables.

Comma-separated value files are a frequent source of inputs for tables and dataframes, so we begin with a pair of CSV files, pets.csv and pets_ns.csv ("ns" for "no spaces"), containing information on a few animals. The files have 11 lines—1 line of column names followed by 10 lines of data—and differ only in whitespace:

```
pets_ns.csv                        pets.csv

type,MF,weight,birthday            type  , MF, weight, birthday
dog,M,9.82,2023-11-26              dog   , M,  9.82 , 2023-11-26
cat,F,4.31,2023-11-18              cat   , F,  4.31 , 2023-11-18
bunny,F,8.40,2023-11-23            bunny , F,  8.40 , 2023-11-23
bunny,M,4.65,2023-11-24            bunny , M,  4.65 , 2023-11-24
dog,F,9.82,2023-11-25              dog   , F,  9.82 , 2023-11-25
cat,M,5.57,2023-11-24              cat   , M,  5.57 , 2023-11-24
bunny,M,1.12,2023-11-17            bunny , M,  1.12 , 2023-11-17
cat,M,2.96,2023-11-21              cat   , M,  2.96 , 2023-11-21
cat,M,5.08,2023-11-21              cat   , M,  5.08 , 2023-11-21
bunny,F,1.53,2023-11-15            bunny , F,  1.53 , 2023-11-15
```

© Albert Danial 2022
A. Danial, *Python for MATLAB Development*, https://doi.org/10.1007/978-1-4842-7223-7_13

Although the two files contain identical information, the file readers' default behaviors differ:

- Pandas ignores leading and trailing whitespace for row data but preserves whitespace for the column titles.

- MATLAB preserves whitespace throughout.

- Pandas does not automatically recognize date fields and so populates the fourth column with string literals.

- MATLAB recognizes dates and times in a variety of formats and correctly sets the type of the fourth column to `datetime`.

Additional data manipulation and cleaning is often necessary after loading a file. An aphorism in data science is that data cleaning typically takes four times as much effort as the actual data analysis. Frequently performed data cleaning tasks are covered in Section 13.3.

13.1 Loading Tables from Files

MATLAB and Pandas can load tables and dataframes from CSV, Excel, and text files. Pandas can additionally read HDF5, HTML, JSON, and Python pickle files and pull data from websites or database connections through SQLAlchemy. These commands show how to create a MATLAB table and Pandas dataframe from our `pets.csv` file:

MATLAB:	Python:

```
>> tb = readtable('pets.csv');
>> tb
tb =
  10×6 table
  Var1    Var2   Var3 Var4 Var5    Var6
  _____  _____  ____ ____ ____  _____
{'dog'  }{','}{'M,'}9.82{','}2023-11-26
{'cat'  }{','}{'F,'}4.31{','}2023-11-18
{'bunny'}{','}{'F,'} 8.4{','}2023-11-23
{'bunny'}{','}{'M,'}4.65{','}2023-11-24
{'dog'  }{','}{'F,'}9.82{','}2023-11-25
{'cat'  }{','}{'M,'}5.57{','}2023-11-24
{'bunny'}{','}{'M,'}1.12{','}2023-11-17
{'cat'  }{','}{'M,'}2.96{','}2023-11-21
{'cat'  }{','}{'M,'}5.08{','}2023-11-21
{'bunny'}{','}{'F,'}1.53{','}2023-11-15
```

```
In : import pandas as pd
In : df = pd.read_csv('pets.csv')
In : df
Out:
     type   MF weight    birthday
0    dog    M    9.82 2023-11-26
1    cat    F    4.31 2023-11-18
2    bunny  F    8.40 2023-11-23
3    bunny  M    4.65 2023-11-24
4    dog    F    9.82 2023-11-25
5    cat    M    5.57 2023-11-24
6    bunny  M    1.12 2023-11-17
7    cat    M    2.96 2023-11-21
8    cat    M    5.08 2023-11-21
9    bunny  F    1.53 2023-11-15
```

MATLAB's table is unexpected; instead of four columns, it returned six and also failed to recognize column names. There are two alternatives: either work with a file like pets_ns.csv whose entries have been trimmed of whitespace or use explicit column-specific format options via detectImportOptions followed by setvaropts. Here, we'll use the CSV file trimmed of whitespace:

MATLAB:	Python:
`>> tb = readtable('pets_ns.csv');`	`In : import pandas as pd`
`>> tb`	`In : import numpy as np`
`tb =`	`In : df = pd.read_csv('pets_ns.csv')`
` 10×4 table`	`In : df`
	`Out:`

```
  10x4 table
  type      MF  weight birthday

{'dog'  } {'M'}  9.82  2023-11-26
{'cat'  } {'F'}  4.31  2023-11-18
{'bunny'} {'F'}   8.4  2023-11-23
{'bunny'} {'M'}  4.65  2023-11-24
{'dog'  } {'F'}  9.82  2023-11-25
{'cat'  } {'M'}  5.57  2023-11-24
{'bunny'} {'M'}  1.12  2023-11-17
{'cat'  } {'M'}  2.96  2023-11-21
{'cat'  } {'M'}  5.08  2023-11-21
{'bunny'} {'F'}  1.53  2023-11-15
```

```
      type  MF  weight    birthday
0      dog   M    9.82  2023-11-26
1      cat   F    4.31  2023-11-18
2    bunny   F    8.40  2023-11-23
3    bunny   M    4.65  2023-11-24
4      dog   F    9.82  2023-11-25
5      cat   M    5.57  2023-11-24
6    bunny   M    1.12  2023-11-17
7      cat   M    2.96  2023-11-21
8      cat   M    5.08  2023-11-21
9    bunny   F    1.53  2023-11-15
```

String and floating-point types are obvious, but the birthday column type is not. Let's investigate by checking the data type of the first row in birthday (table and dataframe indexing is covered in Section 13.6.3). The .iloc() dataframe attribute, covered in more detail in Section 13.6, allows us to select one or more rows based on their (zero-based) indices.

MATLAB:	Python:
`>> tb{1,'birthday'}`	`In : df.iloc[0]['birthday']`
	`Out: '2023-11-26'`
` datetime`	
	`In : type(df.iloc[0]['birthday'])`
` 2023-11-26`	`Out: str`

MATLAB's birthday column is recognized as a datetime, but Python's is just a string—not ideal. The Pandas read_csv() function has 48 (!) optional keyword arguments, two of which govern date handling: parse_dates takes a list of column indices to interpret as dates, and infer_datetime_format=True enables the automatic date parser. This invocation of read_csv() will give us a time-aware type for birthday:

Python:

```
In : df = pd.read_csv('pets_ns.csv',parse_dates=[3],
...:                      infer_datetime_format=True)

In : type(df['birthday'].loc[0])
Out: pandas._libs.tslibs.timestamps.Timestamp
```

For now, we'll load the dataframe df using only default arguments to read_csv() and keep the birthday entries as strings. We show how to convert the strings to time-aware objects in the data cleaning section, Section 13.3.4.

13.2 Table Summaries

Most real-world tables have far more rows than can fit on a page. MATLAB and Pandas have summary functions that give rapid glimpses into the table contents.

13.2.1 Table Size, Column Names, Column Types

Table dimensions can be found the same way as with numeric arrays:

MATLAB:	Python:
`>> height(tb)` 10	`In : len(df)` `Out: 10`
`>> width(tb)` 4	`In : df.shape` `Out: (10, 4)`
`>> size(tb)` 10 4	

Column names are stored in a cell array in MATLAB and an index array in Pandas:

MATLAB:	Python:

`>> tb.Properties.VariableNames`
  `1x4 cell array`
 	
`{'type'} {'MF'} {'weight'}`
    `{'birthday'}`
	`In : df.columns`
	`Out: Index(['type', 'MF', 'weight',`
	                      `'birthday'], dtype="object")`

Column type information is a bit more obscured; the clearest method is to iterate over columns and explicitly print the type. MATLAB's column types are revealed by invoking `class()` on each column. Pandas dataframes have a type attribute, `.dtypes`, which contains column information, but the types often come back as just `object`, not at all helpful. In Pandas, too, we therefore explicitly loop over columns and report the type of the entry in the first row:

MATLAB:	Python:

`cols=tb.Properties.VariableNames;`
`for C = cols`
  `fprintf('%-8s %s\n', ...`
    `C{1}, class(tb.(C{1})))`
`end`
 	
`type      cell`
`MF        cell`
`weight    double`
`birthday datetime`
	`In : df.dtypes`
	`Out:`
	`type          object`
	`MF            object`
	`weight        float64`
	`birthday      object`
	`dtype: object`
	
	`In : for C in df.columns:`
	`...:     tp = type(df.iloc[0][C])`
	`...:     print(f'{C:<8s} {tp}')`
	
	`type     <class 'str'>`
	`MF       <class 'str'>`
	`weight   <class 'numpy.float64'>`
	`birthday <class 'str'>`

13.2.2 summary() and .info()/.describe()

MATLAB's summary() function and Pandas's .info() method for dataframes give information on each column:

MATLAB:	Python:
>> summary(tb)	In : df.info()
Variables:	<class 'pandas.core.frame.DataFrame'>
type: 10×1 cell array	RangeIndex: 10 entries, 0 to 9
of character vectors	Data columns (total 4 columns):
MF: 10×1 cell array of	# Column Non-Null Count Dtype
character vectors	- ------ -------------- -----
weight: 10×1 double	0 type 10 non-null object
Values:	1 MF 10 non-null object
Min 1.12	2 weight 10 non-null float64
Median 4.865	3 birthday 10 non-null object
Max 9.82	dtypes: float64(1), object(3)
birthday: 10×1 datetime	memory usage: 448.0+ bytes
Values:	
Min 2023-11-15	
Median 2023-11-22	
Max 2023-11-26	

Pandas dataframes also have a .describe() method that gives value distributions for columns holding numeric values:

Python:

```
In : df.describe()
Out:
        weight
count  10.000000
mean    5.326000
std     3.147289
min     1.120000
```

25%	3.297500
50%	4.865000
75%	7.692500
max	9.820000

The MATLAB summary information is more comprehensive as it gives extremal values for dates as well as numeric columns.

13.2.3 groupsummary() and .value_counts()

Another typical summary operation is obtaining unique counts of entries in desired columns. This can be done with groupsummary() in MATLAB and a column's .value_counts() method in Pandas. Counts of each type of animal are obtained as follows:

MATLAB:	Python:
```>> groupsummary(tb,'type') type GroupCount _____ _____ {'bunny'} 4 {'cat' } 4 {'dog' } 2```	```In : df['type'].value_counts() Out: cat 4 bunny 4 dog 2```

13.2.4 head() and tail()

Head and tail functions print the desired number of rows at the beginning and end of the table:

MATLAB:	Python:

```
>> head(tb,3)
   type      MF    weight  birthday

 {'dog'  } {'M'}   9.82   2023-11-26
 {'cat'  } {'F'}   4.31   2023-11-18
 {'bunny'} {'F'}    8.4   2023-11-23

>> tail(tb,2)
   type      MF    weight  birthday

 {'cat'  } {'M'}   5.08   2023-11-21
 {'bunny'} {'F'}   1.53   2023-11-15
```

```
In : df.head(3)
Out:
     type   MF weight   birthday
 0   dog    M    9.82 2023-11-26
 1   cat    F    4.31 2023-11-18
 2   bunny  F    8.40 2023-11-23

In : df.tail(2)
Out:
     type   MF weight   birthday
 8   cat    M    5.08 2023-11-21
 9   bunny  F    1.53 2023-11-15
```

13.3 Cleaning Data

Cleaning data refers to operations like renaming, adding, and deleting columns; editing strings to remove spurious whitespace and normalize spelling, hyphenation, and case; changing data types; and deleting duplicate rows or those with missing values.

13.3.1 Renaming Columns

Data sources may not have suitable or convenient column names. Renaming columns is simple, though. A dataframe's .rename() method takes a map of *before:after* names for keyword columns. In MATLAB, one simply updates the table's Properties. This example renames type to species and weight to kg:

MATLAB:	Python:

`>> head(tb,1)`
   type   MF   weight birthday
  ‾‾‾‾ ‾‾‾ ‾‾‾‾‾ ‾‾‾‾‾‾‾‾
`{'dog'} {'M'}  9.82   2023-11-26`
	`In : df.head(1)`
	`Out:`
	    type MF weight birthday
	`0   dog   M     9.82   2023-11-26`

`>> tb.Properties.VariableNames(...`
      `[1 3]) = {'species' 'kg'};`
`>> head(tb,1)`
species MF   kg   birthday
  ‾‾‾‾‾‾ ‾‾‾ ‾‾‾ ‾‾‾‾‾‾‾‾‾
`{'dog'} {'M'} 9.82 2023-11-26`
	`In : df.rename(columns={`
	        `'type':'species',`
	        `'weight':'kg'}).head(1)`
	`Out:`
	    species MF kg birthday
	`0     dog   M   9.82   2023-11-26`

Modifying `tb.Properties.VariableNames` causes MATLAB to change the table in-place. This differs from the `.rename()` method in Pandas which returns a new dataframe unless the option `inplace=True` is also given.

13.3.2 Changing Column Data Types

Operations involving multiple columns can typically only be performed if the columns have consistent data types. For example, if you have home prices for one year stored as strings in one column and floats in another year, you won't be able to compute differences between the years until the strings are converted to floats or integers.

Joins between multiple tables, covered in Section 13.11, also require matching data types in addition to common column names.

Column types can be changed with the `.astype()` method in Pandas and by conventional typecasting in MATLAB. Here, we change the "male/female" column `MF` from cells to strings in MATLAB and from the vague "object" type to a character array in Pandas.

MATLAB:	Python:

```
>> head(tb,2)                              In : df.head(2)
    type    MF  weight  birthday           Out:
    ____    __  _____  _____               type MF weight    birthday
   {'dog'  } {M}  9.82  2023-11-26          0   dog   M   9.82 2023-11-26
   {'cat'  } {F}  4.31  2023-11-18          1   cat   F   4.31 2023-11-18
>> tb.MF = string(tb.MF);                  In : df.MF = df.MF.astype(bytes)
>> head(tb,2)                              In : df.head(2)
    type    MF  weight  birthday           Out:
    ____    __  _____  _____               type    MF weight    birthday
   {'dog'  } "M"  9.82  2023-11-26          0   dog b'M'   9.82 2023-11-26
   {'cat'  } "F"  4.31  2023-11-18          1   cat b'F'   4.31 2023-11-18
```

13.3.3 Changing Column Data

Dataframe columns have an `.apply()` method which invokes a user-supplied function on each value in the column. This example defines a function `caps()` which makes the first letter of a string uppercase, then applies this function to the `type` column:

Python:

```
In : df['type'].head(5)
Out:
0       dog
1       cat
2     bunny
3     bunny
4       dog
Name: type, dtype: object

In : def caps(x):
...:     return x.capitalize()

In : df['type'].apply(caps).head(5)
Out:
```

```
0        Dog
1        Cat
2      Bunny
3      Bunny
4        Dog
Name: type, dtype: object
```

The type column is not modified unless it is reassigned to the output of the .apply() with

Python:

```
df['type'] = df['type'].apply(caps)
```

13.3.4 Making Timestamps from Strings

String-to-time conversions are handled directly with the Pandas to_datetime() function, provided the string follows conventional time formats.

Python:

```
In : df.iloc[0]['birthday']
Out: '2023-11-26'

In : type(df.iloc[0]['birthday'])
Out: str

In : df['birthday'] = pd.to_datetime(df['birthday'])
In : df.iloc[0]['birthday']
Out: Timestamp('2023-11-26 00:00:00')

In : type(df.iloc[0]['birthday'])
Out: pandas._libs.tslibs.timestamps.Timestamp
```

13.4 Creating Tables Programmatically

Tables and dataframes need not come solely from files; they can also be created programmatically. MATLAB has a collection of *X*2table() functions—array2table(), cell2table(), struct2table()—that perform the expected conversions. The Pandas DataFrame() function accepts lists and dictionaries and returns a dataframe.

`struct2table()` and `DataFrame()` with a dictionary argument are convenient because the structure attributes and dictionary keys become column names:

MATLAB:	Python:
`>> x.year = [1867 1776 1810]';`	`In : x = {`
`>> x.n_prov  = [9 50 31]';`	`...:    'year' : [1867,1776,1810],`
`>> x.country = [{'Canada'},...`	`...:    'nprov' : [9,50,31],`
`        {'USA'}, {'Mexico'}]';`	`...:    'country' : ['Canada',`
`>> tb = struct2table(x)`	`...:       'USA', 'Mexico'] }`
`  3×3 table`	`In : df = pd.DataFrame(x)`
`year n_prov   country`	`In : df`
	`Out:`
`____  _____  _____`	`    year  nprov country`
`1867    9    {'Canada'}`	`0   1867      9  Canada`
`1776   50    {'USA'  }`	`1   1776     50     USA`
`1810   31    {'Mexico'}`	`2   1810     31  Mexico`

13.5 Sorting Rows

Head and tail results of a sorted table reveal extremal values. Here, we find the lightest and heaviest animals by sorting on weight—and where weights are equal, we do a secondary sort on birthday.

A side note on sorting dates and times: Ideally, the column stores these with a time-aware data type. However, proper chronological sorting is possible with strings if the date is formatted from most significant to least significant time entries. This is the case with our year-month-day string; a lexical sort is equivalent to a chronological sort.

MATLAB:	Python:

```
>> head(sortrows(tb,{'weight',...
          'birthday'}),2)
   type     MF   weight  birthday
  _____ _____ _____ _____

  {'bunny'} {'M'}  1.12   2023-11-17
  {'bunny'} {'F'}  1.53   2023-11-15

>> tail(sortrows(tb,{'weight',...
          'birthday'}),2)
   type     MF   weight  birthday
  _____ _____ _____ _____

  {'dog'} {'F'}   9.82   2023-11-25
  {'dog'} {'M'}   9.82   2023-11-26
```

```
In : df.sort_values(by=['weight',
...:           'birthday']).head(2)
Out:
     type MF  weight     birthday
  6  bunny  M    1.12   2023-11-17
  9  bunny  F    1.53   2023-11-15

In : df.sort_values(by=['weight',
...:           'birthday']).tail(2)
Out:
     type MF  weight     birthday
  4  dog    F    9.82   2023-11-25
  0  dog    M    9.82   2023-11-26
```

13.6 Table Subsets

Portions of tables can be referenced through row and column slices using indexing techniques similar to those for MATLAB matrices and NumPy ndarrays. As with numeric arrays (Section 11.1.15), table indexing in MATLAB is a bit more convenient than in Python. MATLAB accepts any integer array as a table index, but Pandas needs special attributes .loc[] for label and logical indexing and .iloc[] for arbitrary numeric indexing.

The biggest differences between .loc[] and .iloc[] are that .loc[] permits Boolean expressions to filter on rows (in contrast, .iloc[] only accepts numeric indices), and .iloc[] enables one to select row and column subsets (.loc[] only works on rows).

13.6.1 All Rows, Selected Columns

New tables containing only weight and type can be created by specifying these column names in the indexing notation shown as follows:

MATLAB:	Python:

```
>> tb(:,{'weight','type'})
     weight        type
```

```
In : df[['weight','type']]
Out:
```

weight	type		weight	type
9.82	{'dog' }	0	9.82	dog
4.31	{'cat' }	1	4.31	cat
8.4	{'bunny'}	2	8.40	bunny
4.65	{'bunny'}	3	4.65	bunny
9.82	{'dog' }	4	9.82	dog
5.57	{'cat' }	5	5.57	cat
1.12	{'bunny'}	6	1.12	bunny
2.96	{'cat' }	7	2.96	cat
5.08	{'cat' }	8	5.08	cat
1.53	{'bunny'}	9	1.53	bunny

13.6.2 All Columns, Selected Rows

New tables containing all columns but only selected rows are produced using the
following indexing:

MATLAB:	Python:

```
>> tb([2,3],:)
    type     MF    weight   birthday
```

```
In : df.loc[[1,2]]
Out:
```

type	MF	weight	birthday		type	MF	weight	birthday
{'cat' }	{'F'}	4.31	2023-11-18	1	cat	F	4.31	2023-11-18
{'bunny'}	{'F'}	8.4	2023-11-23	2	bunny	F	8.40	2023-11-23

13.6.3 Selected Rows, Selected Columns

A subset of rows can be similarly targeted using a row slice with either a strided range or
an arbitrary list of integers. These select every third row starting with the first:

MATLAB:	Python:
`>> tb(1:3:end,{'weight','type'})`	`In : df[::3][['weight', 'type']]`

MATLAB:
```
>> tb(1:3:end,{'weight','type'})
  weight    type

  _____  _____

  9.82   {'dog'  }
  4.65   {'bunny'}
  1.12   {'bunny'}
  1.53   {'bunny'}
```

Python:
```
In : df[::3][['weight', 'type']]
Out:
     weight   type
0      9.82    dog
3      4.65  bunny
6      1.12  bunny
9      1.53  bunny
```

Selecting arbitrary rows of a dataframe requires the `.iloc[]` attribute:

MATLAB:
```
> tb([1,6,2],{'weight','type'})
  weight   type

  _____  _____

  9.82   {'dog'}
  5.57   {'cat'}
  4.31   {'cat'}
```

Python:
```
In : df[['weight','type']].iloc[[0,5,1]]
Out:
     weight type
0      9.82  dog
5      5.57  cat
1      4.31  cat
```

A unique feature of dataframes is that row and column indexing can be given in any order:

Python:
```
In : df.iloc[[0,5,1]][
        ['weight','type']]
Out:
    weight type
0     9.82  dog
5     5.57  cat
1     4.31  cat
```

Python:
```
In : df[['weight','type']
        ].iloc[[0,5,1]]
Out:
    weight type
0     9.82  dog
5     5.57  cat
1     4.31  cat
```

This is possible because each indexing component returns a new table which can subsequently be indexed independently. `df.iloc[[0,5,1]]` returns the first, sixth, and second rows, and df.iloc[[0,5,1]][['weight','type']] returns the weight and size columns from the three specified rows. Similarly, df[['weight','type']] is a table containing all rows of weight and type columns, and df[['weight','type']].iloc[[0,5,1]] returns the first, sixth, and second rows from those two columns.

MATLAB tables are indexed via *{columns}* or *{rows, columns}*.

13.6.4 Filter Rows by Conditional Operations

In addition to numeric indexing, rows of MATLAB tables and Pandas dataframes can be indexed with Boolean expressions on columns. This example returns males weighing more than four units:

MATLAB:

```
>> tb((tb.weight > 4) & (...
      cell2mat(tb.MF) == 'M'),:)
4×4 table
    type      MF    weight  birthday

  {'dog'  } {'M'}   9.82   2023-11-26
  {'bunny'} {'M'}   4.65   2023-11-24
  {'cat'  } {'M'}   5.57   2023-11-24
  {'cat'  } {'M'}   5.08   2023-11-21
```

Python:

```
In : df[(df.weight > 4) &
...:     (df.MF == 'M')]
Out:
    type MF  weight    birthday
0    dog  M    9.82  2023-11-26
3  bunny  M    4.65  2023-11-24
5    cat  M    5.57  2023-11-24
8    cat  M    5.08  2023-11-21
```

Note that in MATLAB, string values (as in column MF) must be converted to a matrix to allow a string equivalence test.

13.7 Iterating over Rows

Interaction with tables generally happens with entire columns of data. Occasionally though, access to individual rows is necessary. Rows of MATLAB tables are indexed using brace subscripts. Pandas rows may be indexed numerically using the .iloc[] accessor (Section 13.6.3), but when iterating over an entire table, the dataframe's .iterrows() generator invoked in a for loop is more convenient. Column values within a row may be indexed numerically or with column names:

MATLAB:	Python:
| ```matlab
>> for i = 1:height(tb)
    fprintf("%d %s %s\n",i,string(...
        tb{i,1}),string(tb{i,'MF'}))
end
1  dog M
2  cat F
3  bunny F
4  bunny M
5  dog F
6  cat M
7  bunny M
8  cat M
9  cat M
10 bunny F
``` | ```python
In : for i,row in df.iterrows():
...:     print(i,row[0],row['MF'])
0  dog M
1  cat F
2  bunny F
3  bunny M
4  dog F
5  cat M
6  bunny M
7  cat M
8  cat M
9  bunny F
``` |

13.8 Pivot Tables

Pivot tables allow one to aggregate data sharing common values. They help answer questions such as "what were sales by region?" or "how many points did home teams score compared to visiting teams?" Pandas has explicit functions for these—pd.pivot_table() and pd.groupby()—while MATLAB relies on different techniques depending on the complexity of the desired aggregation.

13.8.1 Single-Level Aggregation

MATLAB can produce a pivot table grouped by a single variable through its generic varfun() function with "GroupingVariables" as the third argument and the column name to group by as the fourth argument. The Pandas pd.pivot_table() function, which can also be invoked as a dataframe method, takes a list of column names to group by with the keyword argument index. This example returns a new table or dataframe with a count of animals based on type. It duplicates the result of .value_counts() from Section 13.2.3:

MATLAB:	Python:

```
>> varfun(@length,tb,...
    "GroupingVariables","type",...
    "InputVariables","type")
  type     GroupCount length_type

  _____  _____ _____

  {'bunny'}     4           4
  {'cat'  }     4           4
  {'dog'  }     2           2
```

```
In : pd.pivot_table(df,
        index=['type'], aggfunc="count")
Out:
          MF  birthday  weight
  type
  bunny   4      4         4
  cat     4      4         4
  dog     2      2         2
```

The aggregation function is provided in MATLAB as a function handle and in Pandas with the optional keyword argument aggfunc. Pandas uses mean() if this argument is not supplied.

varfun() and pd.pivot_table() return a new table and dataframe which can be sliced, sorted, and so on. The next example sums the weight of males and females using the method form of pivot_table():

MATLAB:	Python:

```
>> varfun(@sum,tb,...
    "GroupingVariables","MF",...
    "InputVariables","weight")
MF   GroupCount sum_weight

____  _____ _____

{'F'}    4        24.06
{'M'}    6        29.2
```

```
In : df.pivot_table(index=['MF'],
...:   values=['weight'],aggfunc='sum')
Out:
      weight
MF
F     24.06
M     29.20
```

The Pandas .groupby() function returns the same result, but only because weight is the only numeric column in df. Had there been others, sums would be returned for those too.

Python:

```
In : df.groupby(['MF']).sum()
Out:
    weight
MF
F     24.06
M     29.20
```

13.8.2 Multilevel Aggregation

Aggregation may be nested to multiple levels in Pandas simply by adding more columns to the index= keyword argument. Despite the plural form of "GroupingVariables", the same is not true for MATLAB's varfun(); it only allows grouping by one column. Multilevel pivot tables in MATLAB require the three-step "split-apply-combine" method involving several intermediate variables. Here, we'll get a more detailed view into animal weights by separating the aggregation by animal type in addition to gender:

MATLAB:	Python:

```matlab
>> [Idx, MF, Type] = ...
      findgroups(tb.MF, tb.type);
>> sum_weight = splitapply(...
      @sum, tb.weight, Idx);
>> table(MF, Type, sum_weight)
  6×3 table
  MF      Type      sum_weight

  _____   _____   _____

  {'F'} {'bunny'}      9.93
  {'F'} {'cat'  }      4.31
  {'F'} {'dog'  }      9.82
  {'M'} {'bunny'}      5.77
  {'M'} {'cat'  }     13.61
  {'M'} {'dog'  }      9.82
```

```python
In : pd.pivot_table(df,
         index=['MF','type'],
         values=['weight'],
         aggfunc='sum')
Out:
              weight
MF type
F  bunny       9.93
   cat         4.31
   dog         9.82
M  bunny       5.77
   cat        13.61
   dog         9.82
```

13.9 Adding Columns

New columns derived from data in existing columns can be helpful in subsequent aggregation and join operations. They can be added simply by indexing the table or dataframe with a new column name in an assignment statement. For example, tb. New = 4 and df['New' = 4] create column "New" with a value of 4 for all rows in table tb and dataframe df. In the following, we'll add a new column, wd, containing the integer weekday of each animal's birthday. The Pandas birthday column needs to be a timestamp rather than string (Section 13.3.4).

One complication is that MATLAB weekday values are Sunday = 1 to Saturday = 7, while Python's are Monday = 0 to Sunday = 6. We'll map the Python values to match MATLAB's with mod $(i + 1, 7) + 1$ where i is Python's weekday value.

MATLAB:

```
>> tb.wd = weekday(tb{:,'birthday'})

  type      MF  weight  birthday   wd
  _____   ____ _____  _____  __
{'dog'   } {'M'} 9.82  2023-11-26  1
{'cat'   } {'F'} 4.31  2023-11-18  7
{'bunny'} {'F'}  8.4   2023-11-23  5
{'bunny'} {'M'} 4.65  2023-11-24  6
{'dog'   } {'F'} 9.82  2023-11-25  7
{'cat'   } {'M'} 5.57  2023-11-24  6
{'bunny'} {'M'} 1.12  2023-11-17  6
{'cat'   } {'M'} 2.96  2023-11-21  3
{'cat'   } {'M'} 5.08  2023-11-21  3
{'bunny'} {'F'} 1.53  2023-11-15  4
```

Python:

```
In : i = df['birthday'].dt.weekday
In : df['wd'] = ((i+1) % 7) + 1
In : df
    type MF  weight    birthday  wd
0    dog  M    9.82  2023-11-26   1
1    cat  F    4.31  2023-11-18   7
2  bunny  F    8.40  2023-11-23   5
3  bunny  M    4.65  2023-11-24   6
4    dog  F    9.82  2023-11-25   7
5    cat  M    5.57  2023-11-24   6
6  bunny  M    1.12  2023-11-17   6
7    cat  M    2.96  2023-11-21   3
8    cat  M    5.08  2023-11-21   3
9  bunny  F    1.53  2023-11-15   4
```

If we count the number of animals born by weekday using a pivot table, sort the result by counts, then tail that, we'll see the weekday on which most animals were born. The selection of MF as the "value" column to sum over is arbitrary; the row count is the same regardless of the column chosen to count:

MATLAB:

```
>> tail(sortrows(varfun(@length,...
    tb,"GroupingVariables","wd",...
    "InputVariables","MF"),...
    "GroupCount"),1)
wd GroupCount length_MF

__ _____ _____

6      3          3
```

Python:

```
In : pd.pivot_table(df,index=['wd'],
      values=['MF'],aggfunc='count'
      ).sort_values(by=['MF']).tail(1)
Out:
        MF
wd
6       3
```

We find that three of the animals were born on wd = 6, that is, Friday.

13.10 Deleting Columns

Columns can be deleted as easily as they are added. A column can be removed from a MATLAB table by reassigning it to an empty array. In Pandas, a column is deleted the same way as a dictionary entry. Here, we remove the weekday column added in the previous section:

MATLAB:

```
>> head(tb,2)
  type     MF    weight  birthday    wd
  _____   ____   _____  _____  __
{'dog'} {'M'}  9.82    2023-11-26  1
{'cat'} {'F'}  4.31    2023-11-18  7

>> tb.wd = []; % remove wd column

>> head(tb,2)
  type     MF    weight  birthday
  _____   ____   _____  _____
{'dog'} {'M'}  9.82    2023-11-26
{'cat'} {'F'}  4.31    2023-11-18
```

Python:

```
In : df.head(2)
Out:
     type MF   weight   birthday   wd
0    dog  M     9.82  2023-11-26    1
1    cat  F     4.31  2023-11-18    7

In : del df['wd'] # remove wd column

In : df.head(2)
Out:
     type MF   weight   birthday
0    dog  M     9.82  2023-11-26
1    cat  F     4.31  2023-11-18
```

Multiple columns can be deleted from a dataframe with the .drop() method and removevars() in MATLAB:

MATLAB:	Python:

```
>> head(tb,2)                          In : df.head(2)
  type    MF    weight  birthday       Out:
  ____    ____  _____  _____          type MF   weight    birthday

{'dog'} {'M'}  9.82  2023-11-26      0   dog  M     9.82 2023-11-26
{'cat'} {'F'}  4.31  2023-11-18      1   cat  F     4.31 2023-11-18

>> head(removevars(tb,...             In df.drop(columns=['MF','weight']).head(2)
      {'MF','weight'}),2)             Out:
  type       birthday                    type    birthday
  ____       _____               0   dog    2023-11-26

{'dog'}    2023-11-26               1   cat    2023-11-18
{'cat'}    2023-11-18
```

In both cases, a new table is returned; the original tb and df remain unchanged.

13.11 Joins Across Tables

Complex datasets may span multiple tables. MATLAB and Pandas support join operations that yield results from data related by indices common to the tables. Joins come in four flavors—inner, full, left, right—that are the Boolean equivalents of intersection, union, and subtraction operations between two sets. Inner joins are seen frequently because they return results only where both tables have common indices.

As a simple example, say we have to feed our animals. We'll introduce a second table that has the cost of a unit of food for each animal type:

MATLAB:	Python:
| ```
>> food.type = {'dog','cat',...
            'bunny'}';
>> food.price = [1.2 3.5 0.7]';
>> cost_tb = struct2table(food)
  3x2 table
    type        price

  _____      _____

  {'dog'  }      1.2
  {'cat'  }      3.5
  {'bunny'}      0.7
``` | ```
In : food = {
...:   'type' : ['dog','cat','bunny'],
...:   'price' : [ 1.2, 3.5, 0.7]}
In : cost_df = pd.DataFrame(food)
In : cost_df
Out:
        type   price
   0     dog    1.2
   1     cat    3.5
   2   bunny    0.7
``` |

We can create a new table containing all the animal entries plus the type-specific price by joining the two tables on type. Joins are done in MATLAB with join(), innerjoin(), or outerjoin() and in Pandas with pd.merge(). pd.merge()'s default join type, "inner," can be changed with the how= keyword option.

MATLAB:	Python:
| ```
>> J = innerjoin(tb,cost_tb, 'Keys',...
                {'type'})
type       MF    weight  birthday   price

_____  _____  _____  _____  _____

{'bunny'} {'F'}   8.4    2023-11-23   0.7
{'bunny'} {'M'}   4.65   2023-11-24   0.7
{'bunny'} {'M'}   1.12   2023-11-17   0.7
{'bunny'} {'F'}   1.53   2023-11-15   0.7
{'cat'  } {'F'}   4.31   2023-11-18   3.5
{'cat'  } {'M'}   5.57   2023-11-24   3.5
{'cat'  } {'M'}   2.96   2023-11-21   3.5
{'cat'  } {'M'}   5.08   2023-11-21   3.5
{'dog'  } {'M'}   9.82   2023-11-26   1.2
{'dog'  } {'F'}   9.82   2023-11-25   1.2
``` | ```
In : J = pd.merge(df,cost_df,on='type')
In : J
Out:
     type MF weight    birthday price
0     dog  M   9.82  2023-11-26   1.2
1     dog  F   9.82  2023-11-25   1.2
2     cat  F   4.31  2023-11-18   3.5
3     cat  M   5.57  2023-11-24   3.5
4     cat  M   2.96  2023-11-21   3.5
5     cat  M   5.08  2023-11-21   3.5
6   bunny  F   8.40  2023-11-23   0.7
7   bunny  M   4.65  2023-11-24   0.7
8   bunny  M   1.12  2023-11-17   0.7
9   bunny  F   1.53  2023-11-15   0.7
``` |

The tables match although rows appear in different orders. The joined table J lets us compute the cost to feed each animal. If each animal eats its weight in food, the costs are

MATLAB:	Python:
`>> J.weight .* J.price`	`In : J.weight*J.price`
`ans=`	`Out:`
5.8800	0 11.784
3.2550	1 11.784
0.7840	2 15.085
1.0710	3 19.495
15.0850	4 10.360
19.4950	5 17.780
10.3600	6 5.880
17.7800	7 3.255
11.7840	8 0.784
11.7840	9 1.071
	`dtype: float64`
`>> sum(J.weight .* J.price)`	`In : sum(J.weight*J.price)`
`ans=`	`Out: 97.27799999999999`
97.2780	

What's the cost breakdown by animal type? A pivot table gives the answer, but first we'll need another temporary column storing the cost per animal computed earlier. We'll call this new column wxp for "weight times price":

MATLAB:	Python:

```
>> J.wxp = J.weight .* J.price;       In : J['wxp'] = J.weight*J.price
varfun(@sum,J,"GroupingVariables",... In : pd.pivot_
     "type","InputVariables","wxp")   table(J,index=['type'],
3×3 table                             ...:      values=['wxp'],aggfunc=sum)
    type    GroupCt   sum_wxp          Out:
                                                   wxp
  _____   _____   _____
  {'bunny'} 4.e+00  1.0990e+01        type
  {'cat'  } 4.e+00  6.2720e+01        bunny  10.990
  {'dog'  } 2.e+00  2.3568e+01        cat    62.720
                                      dog    23.568
```

13.12 GeoPandas

GeoPandas [1] adds spatial data types and operations to Pandas. It allows one to query and aggregate information from Pandas dataframes spatially ("how do home prices vary by postal code and time?"), perform geographic set operations ("over which countries did the airplane fly?"), and create maps with data overlays. Here, we'll explore that last capability.

GeoPandas needs geographic data in the form of GeoJSON files or shapefiles. In Section 12.4.3.2, we used shapefiles downloaded from the Natural Earth project. The US government's data.gov website is another source of shapefiles; among others, it contains a 500 MB compressed file with high-resolution outlines of every zip code in the United States.[1]

My goal is to make a map of Los Angeles County with zip codes colored by home prices. Zillow Research[2] generously makes available real estate price data grouped by zip code. From their portal, I downloaded the "ZVHI All Homes (SFR/Condo/Coop)" dataset, a 70 MB CSV file.

---

[1]https://catalog.data.gov/dataset/tiger-line-shapefile-2019-2010-nation-u-s-2010-census-5-digit-zip-code-tabulation-area-zcta5-na

[2]www.zillow.com/research/data/

Loading a CSV file into Pandas is easy (Section 13.1). The novel part here is making a dataframe with geographic data of zip code boundaries. Fortunately, GeoPandas makes loading a shapefile as easy as loading a CSV file. The US postal code file, tl_2019_us_zcta510.zip, expands to seven files, the largest of which is the shapefile tl_2019_us_zcta510.shp. All we need to do is read it with the GeoPandas read_file() function. These commands

```
In : import pandas as pd
In : import geopandas as gp
In : home_prices  = pd.read_csv('Zip_zhvi_uc_sfrcondo_tier_0.33_0.67_sm_sa_
mon.csv')
In : zipcode_geom = gp.read_file('tl_2019_us_zcta510.shp')
```

create two Pandas dataframes, home_prices, containing Zillow's home prices by zip code, and zipcode_geom, containing shapes of all zip codes. Their contents look like this:

```
In : home_prices
Out:
        RegionID  SizeRank  RegionName  ...  2021-03-31  2021-04-30  2021-05-31
0         61639         0       10025   ...   1053436.0   1071606.0   1089141.0
1         84654         1       60657   ...    514068.0    515876.0    517752.0
2         61637         2       10023   ...   1096338.0   1100727.0   1104368.0
3         91982         3       77494   ...    370188.0    376591.0    383493.0
4         84616         4       60614   ...    656960.0    659558.0    661174.0
...         ...       ...         ...   ...         ...         ...         ...
30832     62532     34430       12345   ...    167810.0    170959.0    174757.0
30833     87060     34430       66045   ...    219054.0    224651.0    233820.0
30834     58379     34430        1470   ...    398219.0    402924.0    407785.0
30835     58117     35187         822   ...    168439.0    169986.0    173515.0
30836     58110     35187         801   ...     37344.0     36687.0     36030.0
[30837 rows x 314 columns]

In : zipcode_geom
Out:
     ZCTA5CE10  ...                                      geometry
0        43451  ...  POLYGON ((-83.70873 41.32733, -83.70815 41.327...
1        43452  ...  POLYGON ((-83.08698 41.53780, -83.08256 41.537...
```

```
2            43456  ...  MULTIPOLYGON (((-82.83558 41.71082, -82.83515 ...
3            43457  ...  POLYGON ((-83.49650 41.25371, -83.48382 41.253...
4            43458  ...  POLYGON ((-83.22229 41.53102, -83.22228 41.532...
...            ...  ...                                                ...
33139        84044  ...  POLYGON ((-112.26022 40.76909, -112.25333 40.7...
33140        84045  ...  MULTIPOLYGON (((-111.92421 40.17034, -111.9240...
33141        84046  ...  POLYGON ((-110.00072 40.99745, -110.00036 40.9...
33142        84047  ...  POLYGON ((-111.92141 40.62772, -111.92134 40.6...
33143        84049  ...  POLYGON ((-111.59394 40.57707, -111.59386 40.5...
[33144 rows x 10 columns]
```

All we need to do is join the two dataframes on zip code and then invoke the
.plot() method on the result to see a map. Some data cleaning is needed to prepare the
dataframes for a join though; the two dataframes must use the same name and data type
for the join column.

```
In : zipcode_geom.rename(columns={'ZCTA5CE10':'ZipCode'}, inplace=True)
In : home_prices.rename(columns={'RegionName':'ZipCode'}, inplace=True)
In : zipcode_geom['ZipCode'] = zipcode_geom['ZipCode'].astype(int)
```

How did I know to change the data type of zipcode_geom['ZipCode'] to integer?
Initially, I didn't. I attempted the join with only renamed columns and then got a Pandas
error saying the join failed because of a type mismatch, "ValueError: You are trying to
merge an object and int64 columns."

After renaming and fixing the data type, I can do the join, but the resulting dataframe
includes every zip code in the United States—too much for my needs. I'll first subset the
data to just LA County, and only for May 2020 and 2021:

```
In : LA_prices = home_prices[
...:                 home_prices['CountyName'] == 'Los Angeles County'][
...:                 ['ZipCode','2020-05-31','2021-05-31']]
```

Finally, I'll do the join and create the plot:

```
In : LA_price_map = zipcode_geom.merge(LA_prices,on='ZipCode')  # join
In : LA_price_map['2020-05-31'] /= 1.0e6  # change units to million dollars
In : LA_price_map.plot(column='2020-05-31',cmap='plasma',legend=True)
In : plt.show()
```

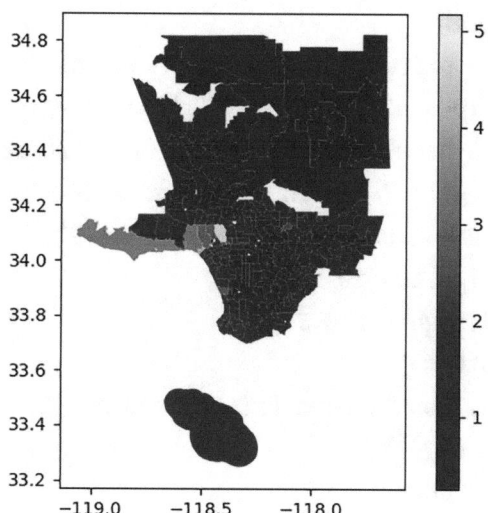

Not bad for just a dozen lines of code. There's room for improvement, though. The following program adds a title, axis labels, and identifiers for every zip code and zooms in to the South Bay region:

Python:

```
#!/usr/bin/env python3
# file: code/geopandas/LA_home_prices.py
import numpy as np
import matplotlib.pyplot as plt
from matplotlib.transforms import Bbox
import geopandas as gp
import pandas as pd

zipcode_geom = gp.read_file('usa_zip/tl_2019_us_zcta510.shp')
home_prices  = pd.read_csv('Zip_zhvi_uc_sfrcondo_tier_0.33_0.67_sm_sa_mon.csv')
# rename zip code columns to enable join
zipcode_geom.rename(columns={'ZCTA5CE10':'ZipCode'}, inplace=True)
home_prices.rename(columns={'RegionName':'ZipCode'}, inplace=True)
# change type from 'object' to 'int64'
zipcode_geom['ZipCode'] = zipcode_geom['ZipCode'].astype(int)
# subset to just LA County
```

```
LA_prices = home_prices[
                home_prices['CountyName'] == 'Los Angeles County'][
                ['ZipCode','2020-05-31','2021-05-31']]
LA_price_map = zipcode_geom.merge(LA_prices,on='ZipCode')
LA_price_map['2020-05-31'] /= 1.0e6  # change units to million dollars
LA_price_map.plot(column='2020-05-31',cmap='plasma',
        legend=True,figsize=(10,14))
plt.xlim(left=-118.55,right=-118.17)
plt.ylim(top=34.14,bottom=33.7)
plt.title('Los Angeles County Home Prices 2020-05-31, $M')
plt.ylabel('Latitude [deg]')
plt.xlabel('Longitude [deg]')
# label each zip code
for i,row in LA_price_map.iterrows():
    center = row['geometry'].centroid.xy
    xy = center[0][0], center[1][0]
    plt.annotate(text=row['ZipCode'], xy=xy,
                horizontalalignment='center')
plt.savefig('LA_home_prices.png', bbox_inches=Bbox([[0.9,0.9],[9,13]]),
            transparent=True)
plt.show()
```

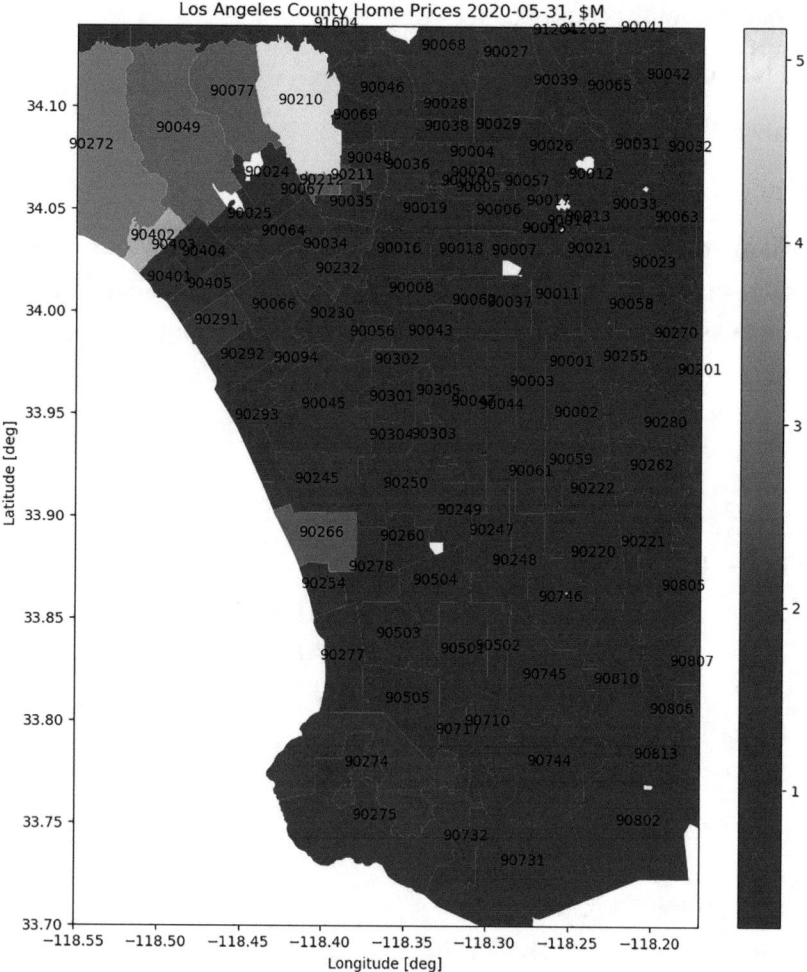

13.13 Recipe 13-1: Maps with GeoPandas

The map of Los Angeles County home prices created in Section 13.12 can also be made in MATLAB with GeoPandas. The Pandas idioms of filtering dataframe rows and columns with brackets (Section 13.6) and calling a dataframe's .iterrows() method to traverse rows are not available to MATLAB though. We'll need a bridge module to supply the following capabilities:

- Filter rows based on Boolean operations

- Extract selected columns

- Rename columns

- Change column data type

- Scale column values

- Iterate over rows

The last item, row iteration, is surprisingly challenging. An obvious solution is to create a Python generator that returns a new row each time it is called, but MATLAB doesn't seem to work with Python generators. Instead, I implemented iterrows() in the bridge module as a closure.[3]

Python:

```python
# file: code/matlab_py/bridge_geopandas.py
def row_filter(dframe, A, op, B):
    operation = {
            '==' : lambda DF, A, B : DF[DF[A] == B],
            '!=' : lambda DF, A, B : DF[DF[A] != B],
            '<=' : lambda DF, A, B : DF[DF[A] <= B],
            '>=' : lambda DF, A, B : DF[DF[A] >= B],
            '<'  : lambda DF, A, B : DF[DF[A] <  B],
            '>'  : lambda DF, A, B : DF[DF[A] >  B],
            }
    if op not in operation:
        print(f'bridge_geopandas.row_filter: "{op}" not recognized')
        return None
    return operation[op](dframe, A, B)
def col_filter(dframe, cols):
    return dframe[[*cols]]
def rename_col(dframe, A, B):
    dframe.rename(columns={A:B}, inplace=True)
def astype(dframe, col, new_type):
    if new_type == 'int':
        dframe[col] = dframe[col].astype(int)
    elif new_type == 'float':
```

---

[3] https://towardsdatascience.com/closures-and-decorators-in-python-2551abbc6eb6

```
        dframe[col] = dframe[col].astype(float)
    elif new_type == 'str':
        dframe[col] = dframe[col].astype(str)
    else:
        print(f'bridge_geopandas.astype: "{new_type}" not recognized')
def mult_by(dframe, col, scale):
    dframe[col] *= scale
def iterrows(dframe):
    i = -1
    n_rows = len(dframe)
    def increment():
        nonlocal i
        i += 1
        if i < n_rows:
            return dframe.iloc[i]
        else:
            return None
    return increment
```

Calls to bridge functions in the following MATLAB program are preceded by commented Python code which implement the Pandas operation. Additionally, the sequence of commands differs a bit from the pure Python program of Section 13.12 to reduce the memory footprint. Rows of the two dataframes are filtered immediately after they are read.

MATLAB 2020b:

```
% file: code/geopandas/LA_home_prices.m
Im  = @py.importlib.import_module;
pd  = Im('pandas');
gp  = Im('geopandas');
BG  = Im('bridge_geopandas');
plt = Im('matplotlib.pyplot');
trx = Im('matplotlib.transforms');
mpl = Im('matplotlib');
if ispc
    mpl.use('WXAgg')
```

```
else
    mpl.use('TkAgg')
end

zipcode_geom = gp.read_file('usa_zip/tl_2019_us_zcta510.shp');

% zipcode_geom.rename(columns={'ZCTA5CE10':'ZipCode'}, inplace=True)
BG.rename_col(zipcode_geom, 'ZCTA5CE10','ZipCode');

% zipcode_geom['ZipCode'] = zipcode_geom['ZipCode'].astype(int)
BG.astype(zipcode_geom, 'ZipCode', 'int');

% zipcode_geom = zipcode_geom[ zipcode_geom['ZipCode'] > 90000]
BG.row_filter(zipcode_geom, 'ZipCode', '>', 90000);

home_prices = pd.read_csv('Zip_zhvi_uc_sfrcondo_tier_0.33_0.67_sm_sa_
mon.csv');

% home_prices.rename(columns={'RegionName':'ZipCode'}, inplace=True)
BG.rename_col(home_prices, 'RegionName', 'ZipCode');

% home_prices = home_prices[['ZipCode','2020-05-31','2021-05-31']]
home_prices = BG.col_filter(home_prices, py.list({'ZipCode',...
                            'CountyName','2020-05-31','2021-05-31'}));

% LA_prices = home_prices[home_prices['CountyName'] == 'Los Angeles
County']]
LA_prices = BG.row_filter(home_prices, 'CountyName', '==', 'Los Angeles
County');

LA_price_map = zipcode_geom.merge(LA_prices,pyargs('on','ZipCode'));

% LA_price_map['2020-05-31'] /= 1.0e6  # change units to million dollars
BG.mult_by(LA_price_map, '2020-05-31', 1.0/1.0e6);

size_10_14 = py.tuple([10,14]);
LA_price_map.plot(pyargs('column','2020-05-31','cmap','plasma',...
        'legend',py.True,'figsize',size_10_14));

plt.xlim(pyargs('left',-118.55,'right',-118.17));
plt.ylim(pyargs('top',34.14,'bottom',33.7));
```

```matlab
plt.title('Los Angeles County Home Prices 2020-05-31, $M');
plt.ylabel('Latitude [deg]');
plt.xlabel('Longitude [deg]');
% label each zip code
next_row = BG.iterrows(LA_price_map);
while 1
    row = next_row();
    if strcmp(class(row), 'py.NoneType')
        break
    end
    geo = row.get('geometry');
    xy = py.tuple([geo.centroid.x, geo.centroid.y]);
    plt.annotate(pyargs('text',row.get('ZipCode'),'xy',xy,...
                'horizontalalignment','center'));
end
bbox = trx.Bbox([0.9 0.9; 9 13]);
plt.savefig('LA_m.png', pyargs('bbox_inches',bbox,'transparent',py.True));
plt.show()
```

Unfortunately, as of November 2021, attempting to use geopandas through MATLAB on Windows is problematic due to DLL load issues. Visit this book's GitHub repository[4] for updates.

13.14 References

[1]   Kelsey Jordahl et al. *geopandas/geopandas: v0.8.1.* Version v0.8.1. July 2020. DOI: 10.5281/zenodo. 3946761. URL: `https://doi.org/10.5281/zenodo.3946761`

[2]   Wes McKinney.*Python for Data Analysis, 2nd ed.* O'Reilly Media, 2017.

---

[4]`https://github.com/Apress/python-for-matlab-development`

CHAPTER 14

High Performance Computing

Engineers, scientists, and data analysts who perform large-scale or long duration numeric work crave ever faster and more cores, memory, bandwidth, and storage. By their nature, numerical models can always be improved with higher resolution, finer discretizations, and an abundance of everything—degrees of freedom, time steps, frequency intervals, neurons, layers, iterations, pixels, rays, cases.

A large subset of MATLAB users falls in this power-hungry group. The MathWorks invests considerable effort to make MATLAB as performant as possible for this core segment of its customer base. Accordingly, performance will interest many MATLAB users investigating Python.

In this chapter, we'll examine ways to make Python code run faster. By extension, faster Python code could mean faster MATLAB code since MATLAB can call Python. The steps to writing faster code will be familiar to practitioners of high performance computing (HPC):

1. Profile the program to learn where time is being spent.

2. Eliminate redundant I/O and batch I/O operations where possible.

3. Study the complexity of algorithms in the expensive sections of code. Are there, for example, $O(N^2)$ steps that could be replaced by $O(N \log N)$ algorithms?

4. Enable compiler or interpreter optimization features.

5. Organize the data into contiguous memory blocks.

© Albert Danial 2022
A. Danial, *Python for MATLAB Development*, https://doi.org/10.1007/978-1-4842-7223-7_14

6. Implement vector-capable portions of the algorithm as vector operations.

7. Call functions in optimized libraries (likely written in compiled languages).

8. Distribute work across cores on the same machine.

9. Use hardware with more cores (specifically GPUs).

10. Distribute the work across multiple machines.

A fundamental challenge in HPC is that steps 3–10 often conflict and their relative benefits vary with problem type, size, and available computer hardware. An $O(N^2)$ algorithm running on a GPU may run faster than an $O(N \log(N))$ algorithm on a conventional CPU, and a communication-intensive parallel program running on a single multicore computer can be faster than the same program running on many such computers tied by a slow network.

Finding a suitable balance in the performance tradespace comes down to deciding how much effort you're willing to expend to achieve a satisfactory speed boost.

14.1 Paths to Faster Python Code

Of the ten steps outlined earlier, we will focus on four that have Python-specific aspects:

1. Improve single CPU performance with Python-specific tools such as Cython, Numba, and Pythran.

2. Parallelize code over multiple cores with `multiprocessing`, Pythran, Numba, or Dask.

3. Rewrite critical segments in C, C++, or Fortran and create Python interface modules to them.

4. Parallelize code over multiple computers with Dask.

As we'll see in the recipes at the end of this chapter (Sections 14.12 and 14.14), MATLAB programs may also run much faster by calling accelerated Python code.

14.2 Reference Problems

Two programs will be used to demonstrate HPC techniques in Python. The first, computing terms of the Mandelbrot set, appears straightforward but has load balancing aspects that complicate vectorization. The second, a finite element solver, more closely resembles a real-world problem. It involves loading data from tens of megabytes of text data, assembling sparse mass and stiffness matrices with a million degrees of freedom, and solving the generalized eigenvalue problem with them. Code is spread across multiple files and classes.

The reference programs are also implemented in MATLAB to allow performance comparison with the Python versions.

A final remark about these problems is that their absolute performance numbers are not especially interesting. The reference problems are presented as proxies for computationally intensive work you want to do. The goal is to show the detailed steps to find slow sections of code, options to speed it up, and compare the techniques and their effectiveness.

14.2.1 The Mandelbrot Set

"The Mandelbrot set is the set of complex numbers c having magnitude ≤ 2 for which the function $f_c(z) = z^2 + c$ does not diverge when iterated from $z = 0$, i.e., for which the sequence $f_c(0), f_c(f_c(0))$, etc., remains bounded in absolute value."[1] In other words, if we pick a random complex number c with magnitude ≤ 2 and initialize the complex number z to zero, at what iteration i will the recurrence $z_{i+1} = z_i^2 + c$ exceed magnitude 2? The set is often visualized as a contour plot of iteration count, i, as a function of the real and imaginary components of z.

While a "toy" problem, several aspects make computing terms of the Mandelbrot set useful in illustrating HPC problems: the algorithm is easy to describe, can be implemented with little code, can be vectorized and readily implemented in parallel yet has nontrivial load balancing aspects, and can be made arbitrarily large. The fascinating images that arise are a nice side benefit.

---

[1] Paraphrasing https://en.wikipedia.org/wiki/Mandelbrot_set

Here are our reference sequential implementations:

MATLAB:	**Python:**

```
% file: code/hpc/MB_main.m


main()


function [i]=nIter(c, imax)
  z = complex(0,0);
  for i = 0:imax-1
    z = z*z + c;
    if abs(z) > 2
        break
    end
  end
end
end
function [img]=MB(Re,Im,imax)
  nR = size(Im,2);
  nC = size(Re,2);
  img = zeros(nR, nC, ...
            'uint8');
  for i = 1:nR
    for j = 1:nC
      c = complex(Re(j),Im(i));
      img(i,j) = nIter(c,imax);
    end
  end
end
```

```
#!/usr/bin/env python3
# file: code/hpc/MB.py
import numpy as np
import time
def nIter(c, imax):
  z = complex(0, 0)
  for i in range(imax):
    z = z*z + c
    if abs(z) > 2:
      break
  return np.uint8(i)



def MB(Re, Im, imax):
  nR = len(Im)
  nC = len(Re)
  img = np.zeros((nR, nC),
            dtype=np.uint8)
  for i in range(nR):
    for j in range(nC):
      c = complex(Re[j],Im[i])
      img[i,j] = nIter(c,imax)
  return img
```

(continued)

MATLAB:	Python:

```matlab
function [] = main()
  imax = 255;
  for N = [500 1000 2000 5000]
   tic
   nR = N; nC = N;
   Re = linspace(-0.7440,...
              -0.7433, nC);
   Im = linspace( 0.1315,...
              0.1322, nR);
   img = MB(Re, Im, imax);
   fprintf('%5d %.3f\n',N,toc);
  end
end
```

```python
def main():
  imax = 255
  for N in [500,1000,2000,5000]:
   T_s = time.time()
   nR, nC = N, N
   Re = np.linspace(-0.7440,
                 -0.7433, nC)
   Im = np.linspace( 0.1315,
                 0.1322, nR)
   img = MB(Re, Im, imax)
   print(N, time.time() - T_s)
if __name__ == '__main__': main()
```

14.2.2 A 2D Finite Element Solver

Many excellent finite element (FE) packages are available for Python. Industrial-strength applications include deal.II[2], FEniCS[3], SfePy[4], and Code-Aster.[5] These are substantial projects with hundreds of thousands of lines of source code developed by many domain experts.

Needless to say, our second representative program is a mere glimmer of these advanced programs. Although our FE solver implements only two-dimensional rod elements—linear springs, basically—the operations it performs are representative of many FE codes. Our program

1.   Reads text files of triangular element and 2D nodal coordinate data created by the triangle [4] program

2.   Creates rod elements from the triangle edges

---

[2] www.dealii.org/

[3] https://fenicsproject.org/

[4] http://sfepy.org/doc-devel/index.html

[5] www.code-aster.de/

3. Computes stiffness and mass matrices for each rod element, then inserts these into sparse global stiffness and mass matrices, K and M

4. Computes modes of vibration of the unconstrained model by solving the generalized eigenvalue problem $K_x = \lambda M_x$

The K produced in step 3 is exceptionally sparse; a typical mesh of rod elements derived from triangle's output leaves on average of just 14 non-zero terms per row or column. M is a diagonal matrix. As a result, a million degree of freedom models can be processed quite easily with 8 GB of memory. The names of the Python and MATLAB finite element source files appear in Appendix C; the source files themselves are available on the book's Github repository.[6]

The finite element solver accepts any 2D mesh created by triangle. The triangle program itself reads a text file defining the exterior (and interior, if there are holes) boundaries of the shape to be meshed. This input file, saved as

beam.poly

```
# file:  beam.poly
# A rectangle with dimensions 10 x 1.
4 2 0 0    # four vertices, 2D
# node ID   X    Y
      1      0    0
      2     10    0
      3     10    1
      4      0    1
4 0 # four boundary segments, no markers
# boundary ID    node A    node B
      1             1        2
      2             2        3
      3             3        4
      4             4        1
# no holes
0
```

---

[6] https://github.com/Apress/python-for-matlab-development

defines a 10 x 1 rectangle. The following are command-line invocations of the `triangle` executable with `beam.poly` to create five pairs of `beam.*.ele` and `beam.*.node` files with increasingly finer resolutions:

```
> triangle -pq34a.2 beam       # -> beam.1.ele, beam.1.node
> triangle -rpq34a.02 beam.1    # -> beam.2.ele, beam.2.node
> triangle -rpq34a.002 beam.2   # -> beam.3.ele, beam.3.node
> triangle -rpq34a.0002 beam.3  # -> beam.4.ele, beam.4.node
> triangle -rpq34a.00002 beam.4 # -> beam.5.ele, beam.5.node
```

The mesh from `beam.2.ele` and `beam.2.node`, for example, looks like this:

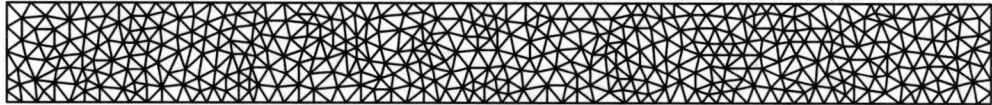

The last pair of files, `beam.5.ele` and `beam.5.node`, are 32 MB and 28 MB and define a mesh with more than a million degrees of freedom.

14.3 Reference Hardware and OS

The hardware, operating system, and MATLAB and Python versions used for the benchmarks in the remainder of this chapter are

- 2015 Dell XPS13 laptop

- 4 cores of i5-5200U CPU @ 2.2 GHz

- 8 GB memory

- Ubuntu 20.04

- MATLAB 2020b

- Anaconda Python 2020.07

While the Python code can easily run on faster cloud-hosted hardware, the MATLAB code, being license-locked to this machine, cannot.

14.4 Baseline Performance

Performance for the reference programs shown in Section 14.5.2 and Appendix C appears in the following for a variety of problem sizes.

14.4.1 Mandelbrot Set Performance

MATLAB does well on this problem as it runs three times faster than the Python version. Table 14-1 shows elapsed times for a variety of $N \times N$ image sizes.

The larger values of N may seem excessive, but their inclusion will be apparent once we begin applying optimization techniques.

14.4.2 FE Solver Performance

The four stages of the finite element solver described in Section 14.2.2 perform starkly different operations. The first, loading model data from files, is I/O intensive. The second stage, creating rod element connectivity data from triangle connectivity, is purely index manipulation.

Table 14-1. *Execution time in seconds for original Mandelbrot programs*

N	MATLAB	Python
500	1.3	4.2
1000	4.4	17.1
2000	17.7	67.4
5000	112.5	420.0

The third stage combines floating-point computations for element matrix generation and sparse matrix creation. The final stage, computing the smallest six eigenvalues and corresponding eigenvectors of the sparse matrices, is dominated by floating-point computation.

Table 14-2 shows timing and peak memory results for each stage. Peak memory use over the entire run is captured with GNU Time on Linux using the command /usr/bin/time -v followed either by the Python program or the matlab[7] command, then taking the value from its results for Maximum resident set size (kbytes) after the Python program ends or the MATLAB session is closed.

Table 14-2. *CPU time and memory use for baseline finite element solver*

Model	Degrees of Freedom	Stage	MATLAB Seconds	Peak GB	Python Seconds	Peak GB
beam.4	99,324	Read files	5.0		0.4	
		Triangle → rod	8.2		2.1	
		Assemble **K**, **M**	6.8		6.5	
		Eigensolution	2.9		2.5	
		Total	22.9	1.0	11.9	0.5
beam.5	1,025,250	Read files	48.4		4.1	
		Triangle → rod	84.6		26.5	
		Assemble **K**, **M**	70.0		68.9	
		Eigensolution	43.9		55.4	
		Total	240.2	7.1	157.1	5.4

Python code outperforms MATLAB on the first three stages—and the total solution time—but MATLAB's eigensolution is notably faster. Reading model data from text files in particular is ten times faster in Python than MATLAB. Python also uses considerably less memory than MATLAB.

14.5 Profiling Python Code

The first step to any performance boosting attempt is measuring where code is slow. Sometimes, such spots are obvious and one can wrap simple timing statements, as done for the preceding FE solver, at strategic locations to assess the effectiveness of subsequent code refinements. For fine-grained results though, we need additional profiling tools.

---

[7] MATLAB was run from a text console using matlab -nojvm to give the solver as much memory as possible.

The standard Python library includes two modules, cProfile and profile, that deterministically (as opposed to statistically, which is less accurate) measure the number of calls to, and time spent in, individual Python functions. Results are presented as tabular text. There are three drawbacks to the standard profilers:

1. Results are coarse; resolution is at the level of functions. This obscures individual performance-killing lines.

2. The text table can be difficult to interpret for large programs.

3. Only CPU use is profiled; there are no options to profile memory use.

Python IDEs such as Spyder and PyCharm, like MATLAB's IDE, have integrated profiling features, but the Python versions are based on cProfile and thus only give function-level resolution. MATLAB's IDE can show profiling results for individual lines. Per-line results are indispensable for performance tuning, so we turn to tools that do not come with Anaconda and must be installed separately.

14.5.1 Scalene

Scalene [1] is a low overhead sampling profiler that additionally reports GPU use (if a GPU is detected), memory copy metrics, and memory consumption—all at a per-line level.

Scalene is unique among Python code profilers for several reasons. Its primary killer feature is stratifying CPU results on each line to time spent in pure Python, time spent in underlying compiled libraries (referred to as "native" time), and system time (for I/O and operations not related to the code). This separation helps answer the implied question of what to do about a slow line of code. If the bulk of time is in pure Python, there might be a way to rewrite the code to call a faster library function. On the other hand, if most of the time is taken by an underlying library or the system, there may be less opportunity for improvement. Scalene also works with multiple threads and processes.

This command profiles the Mandelbrot program:

```
> scalene ./MB.py
```

which produces

```
     Memory usage: ======######====== (max: 117.00MB)
./MB.py: % of time = 99.58% out of 27.70s.
```

Line	Time % Python	Time % native	Sys %	Mem % Python	Net Python (MB)	Memory usage over time / %	Copy (MB/s)	./MB.py
1								#!/usr/bin/env python3
2								# code/hpc/MB.py
3								import numpy as np
4								import time
5				100%	3	|- -		def nIter(c, imax):
6		1%		100%	47	|-----		z = complex(0, 0)
7		6%		99%	46	|----		for i in range(imax):
8		43%	1%	100%	3609	|===== 95%		z = z*z + c
9		44%	1%	100%	-3608	|-------		if abs(z) > 2:
10					-57			break
11								return i

```
        [... lines truncated...]
```

Lines 8 and 9 are shown to be the hot spots, consuming nearly 90% of the solution time. The memory results on the other hand are counterintuitive because peak use is shown to happen on a line that simply multiplies and adds complex scalars.

By default, scalene prints every line in every source file whether or not it contributes significantly. This is clearly excessive for large programs; in such cases, output can be trimmed with `--reduced-profile`. Results can also be sent to an HTML file to simplify browsing results:

```
> scalene --html --outfile profile.html --reduced-profile make_mesh.py
```

The portion of `profile.html` showing the single most expensive line of code—12% overall CPU time spent returning an element stiffness matrix—looks like this in a browser:

Line	Time % Python	Time % native	Sys %	Mem % Python	Net (MB)	Memory usage over time / %	Copy (MB/s)	/home/al/MPC/code/rod_fem/pure_python/rod.py
...								
6				100%	-1	▃		`class Node:`
...								
34				86%	7			`        self.dX = self.node_b.x - self.node_a.x`
35				100%	3			`        self.dY = self.node_b.y - self.node_a.y`
36	3%			100%	-5		1	`        self.length = np.sqrt( self.dX**2 + self.dY**`
37				100%	4			`        self.cross_sect_area = np.pi * self.radius**2`
38				100%	-2			`        self.mass = self.rho * self.length * self.crc`
...								
44				51%	2			`        K     = self.E * self.cross_sect_area / self`
45				100%	1			`        cos   = self.dX/self.length`
46				100%	4			`        sin   = self.dY/self.length`
47	1%			100%	14			`        cos2  = cos**2`
48				100%	8			`        sin2  = sin**2`
49				100%	5			`        sincos = sin*cos`
50	12%		2%	98%	-68		12	`        return K*np.array([[ cos2  ,  sincos, -cos2`
51				99%	19			`                            [ sincos,  sin2 , -sincos`
52				100%	7			`                            [-cos2  , -sincos,  cos2`
53				100%	10			`                            [-sincos, -sin2 ,  sincos`
...								
60	6%		1%	98%	23		7	`        return 0.5 * self.mass * np.array([1.0, 1.0,`

Interestingly, the scalene results suggest the time was spent copying memory rather than performing computations.

14.5.2 Austin and FlameGraph

Austin[8] is another sampling profiler. Like scalene, it adds little overhead, requires no change to the code being profiled, and can send results to other metrics tools such as FlameGraph[9] for graphical display. (MATLAB's profiler also displays timing results as FlameGraphs, although with a slate gray color scheme instead of red/orange/yellow.)

---

[8] https://github.com/P403n1x87/austin
[9] https://github.com/brendangregg/FlameGraph

FlameGraphs represent the call stack vertically, with the main program at the bottom. The width of each bar represents the amount of time spent at a particular function in MATLAB or line of code with austin; hot spots in the code appear as the widest bars. The left-to-right arrangement of bars is arbitrary and does not indicate chronological execution sequence. Bar colors also are arbitrary. Vertical arrangement is significant: code represented by a bar calls the code in the bars immediately above it. The lowest bar is, naturally, the widest as it represents the program's main function entry point. Recognizable function names generally appear at the third or fourth bars from the bottom.

Like scalene, austin is invoked from the command line. The primary arguments are the sampling interval in microseconds and the Python program (and arguments) to run. Output can be directed to a file or to FlameGraph through a pipe. FlameGraph itself is a command-line program that takes arguments such as the minimum resolution to display results for and the units the timing results are given in. This command profiles the Mandelbrot program for $N = 1000$, collecting samples every 50 μs:

```
> austin -a -i 50 ./MB.py | flamegraph.pl --minwidth 10 --countname=us >
flame.svg
```

The `--minwidth 10` switch to FlameGraph excludes entries that would leave a bar fewer than 10 pixels wide. Without it, the graph would be cluttered with entries having inconsequential contributions that make it harder to interpret. Raise or lower this pixel width value to produce the level of resolution that interests you. FlameGraph's output is an SVG file which can be viewed with a web browser. The image

shows the bulk of compute time is spent in function `nIter()` at lines 8 and 9. Recall from Section 14.2.1 that `nIter()`'s implementation is

Python:

```
 5   def nIter(c, imax):
 6       z = complex(0, 0)
 7       for i in range(imax):
 8           z = z*z + c
 9           if abs(z) > 2:
10               break
11       return i
```

The computational effort at lines 8 and 9 happens with the statements z = z*z + c and if abs(z) > 2.

The same profiling command run against the finite element solver for the beam.4 case produces a more complex plot.

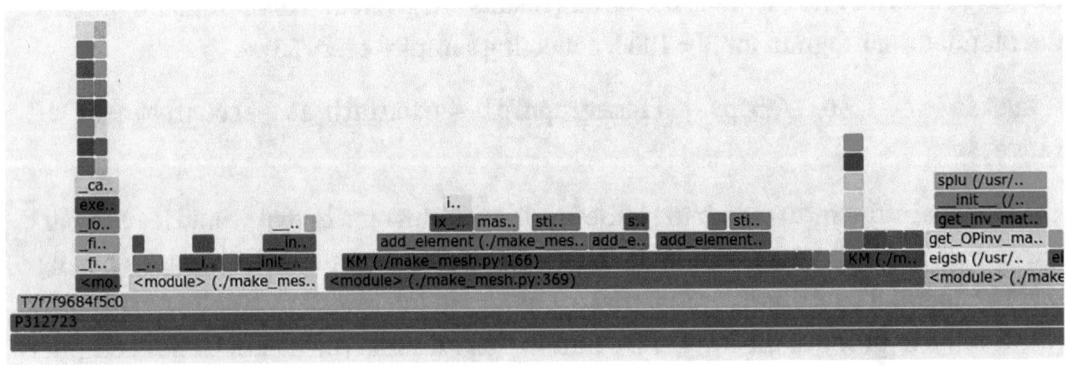

Unlike the Mandelbrot results, there are no obvious smoking guns here. The FlameGraph shows the bulk of execution time happens at line 369 of make_model.py where the global mass and stiffness matrices are created:

```
368 T_s = default_timer()
369 K,M = m.KM()
370 T_e = default_timer()
371 print(f'[K], [M] creation {m.nDof} dof : {T_e-T_s:.6f} s')
```

Going one level deeper in the stack, line 166 within the `.KM()` method is a time consumer:

```
163      # sparse K in COO (coordinate) form
164      I, J, kV = [], [], []
165      for eid in self.elem:
166          self.add_element(eid, kV, I, J, M)
```

14.6 Multicore Computation with `multiprocessing`

Python has a `threading` module which leads one to believe it can fork work off to multiple threads. It can, but is only effective for I/O events waiting to proceed. Generic computations submitted this way are blocked so that only one thread runs at a time, which renders it pointless for non-I/O tasks. To run arbitrary code simultaneously on a computer's multiple cores, you'll need to use another of Python's standard modules, `multiprocessing`.

The most common way to use `multiprocessing` is to set up a pool of workers—generally the number of cores you want to run on—then submit functions that are to run in parallel to the pool.

The following code shows one way to run the Mandelbrot computations on three cores with `multiprocessing`. Work is subdivided across cores by stepping through rows of the Im array in strides equal to the number of cores we'll employ. In our case, we'll set `n_workers` = 3 so process 0 gets rows 0, 3, 6, ...; process 1 gets 1, 4, 7, ...; and so on; this is done with the line `Im_subset = Im[i::n_workers]`.

The highlighted code shows the code modifications applied to use the `multiprocessing` module:

Python:

```
1    #!/usr/bin/env python3
2    # code/hpc/MB_multi.py
3    import numpy as np
4    import time
5    from multiprocessing import Pool
6    def nIter(c, imax):
7      z = complex(0, 0)
```

```
8      for i in range(imax):
9        z = z*z + c
10       if abs(z) > 2:
11         break
12     return np.uint8(i)

13

14   def MB(Re, Im, imax):
15     nR = len(Im)
16     nC = len(Re)
17     img = np.zeros((nR, nC), dtype=np.uint8)
18     for i,I in enumerate(Im):
19       for j,R in enumerate(Re):
20         c = complex(R, I)
21         img[i, j] = nIter(c, imax)
22     return img

23

24   def main():
25     imax = 255
26     for N in [500, 1000, 2000, 5000 ]:
27       T_s = time.time()
28       nR, nC = N, N
29       Re = np.linspace(-0.7440, -0.7433, nC)
30       Im = np.linspace( 0.1315,  0.1322, nR)
31       n_workers = 3
32       img = np.zeros((nR, nC), dtype=np.uint8)
33       with Pool(n_workers) as pool:
34           results = []
35           for i in range(n_workers):
36               Im_subset = Im[i::n_workers]
37               results.append( pool.apply_async(
38                       MB, (Re, Im_subset, imax,)) )
39           for i,R in enumerate(results):
40               img[i::n_workers, :] = R.get()
41       print(N, time.time() - T_s)
42   if __name__ == '__main__': main()
```

The loop at lines 35–38 finishes quickly because the functions are submitted to the worker pool asynchronously. Computations don't begin on the multiple cores until the .get() method is invoked for each submitted function on line 40.

Although multiprocessing dutifully keeps three cores busy, each with one-third of the overall task, Table 14-3 shows that performance is uninspiring for this problem.

Table 14-3. *Execution time in seconds for scalar vs.*
vector Mandelbrot implementations

N	MATLAB 1 Core	Python 1 Core	Python multiprocessing + 3 Cores
500	1.6	4.2	3.0
1000	5.8	17.1	11.4
2000	23.2	67.4	41.6
5000	145.1	420.0	250.0

Better options lie ahead, so for the sake of space I'll omit multiprocessing results from future benchmark results.

14.7 Vectorization

A well-known optimization technique for both MATLAB and NumPy is to write vectorized code—code that performs operations on entire matrices rather than on indexed terms within them. When all terms in the matrices require the same set of operations, vectorization can often yield a performance boost ranging between 10x and 60x over scalar code using explicit loops.

An interesting characteristic of the Mandelbrot set is the amount of computation varies widely across the solution domain. It isn't clear that vectorization will help performance because the slowest-converging terms govern the speed for the entire region. The only way to know for sure is to implement the solution in vector form and then compare performance.

The following vector solutions make heavy use of Boolean index masks (Section 11.1.14). Idx identifies terms which are still actively being updated, and New is the collection of terms which have converged at the current iteration. Each iteration ends with an update to Idx so that the newly converged terms are removed from further refinement. The solution is complete only if there are no new terms to update.

MATLAB:	Python:

```matlab
% file: code/hpc/MB_vectorized.m

main()

function [img]=nIter(c, imax)
 [nR,nC]= size(c);
 z = complex(zeros(nR,nC), ...
           zeros(nR,nC));
 img = zeros(nR,nC,'uint8');
 Idx = ones(nR,nC,'logical');

 for i = 0:imax-1
    z(Idx) = z(Idx).*z(Idx)+ ...
           + c(Idx);
    New = (real(z).^2+ ...
          imag(z).^2 <= 4);
    if ~any(New,'all')
       break
    end
    img(New) = i;
    Idx = Idx & New;
 end
end
function [] = main()
  imax = 255;
  for N = [500 1000 2000 5000]
    tic
    nR = N; nC = N;
    Re = linspace(-0.7440,...
             -0.7433, nC);
    Im = linspace( 0.1315,...
             0.1322, nR);
    [zR, zI] = meshgrid(Re,Im);
    z_init = complex(zR,zI);
    img = nIter(z_init, imax);
    fprintf('%5d %.3f\n',N,toc);
  end
end
```

```python
#!/usr/bin/env python3
# file: code/hpc/MB_vectorized.py
import numpy as np
import time
def nIter(c, imax):
  nR,nC = c.shape
  z = np.zeros_like(c)
  img = np.zeros(z.shape,
            dtype=np.uint8)
  Idx = np.ones(z.shape,
            dtype=np.bool )
  for i in range(imax):
    z[Idx] = z[Idx]*z[Idx] + \
            c[Idx]
    New = (z.real**2 +
           z.imag**2 <= 4)
          .reshape(nR,nC)
    if not np.any(New):
      break
    img[New] = i
    Idx *= New
  return img

def main():
  imax = 255
  for N in [500,1000,2000,5000]:
    T_s = time.time()
    nR, nC = N, N
    Re = np.linspace(-0.7440,
             -0.7433, nC)
    Im = np.linspace( 0.1315,
             0.1322, nR)
    zR,zI = np.meshgrid(Re,Im)
    z_init = zR + zI*(1j)
    img = nIter(z_init, imax)
    print(N, time.time() - T_s)
if __name__ == '__main__': main()
```

The performance results (Table 14-4) are interesting; vectorization made no difference in MATLAB, but gave a 3× speed increase in Python. Disappointingly, MATLAB 2020b on Linux crashes while computing the solution for $N = 5000$.

Table 14-4. *Execution time in seconds for scalar vs. vector Mandelbrot implementations*

N	MATLAB Scalar	MATLAB Vector	Python Scalar	Python Vector
500	1.6	1.7	4.2	1.3
1000	5.8	5.7	17.1	4.7
2000	23.2	24.6	67.4	19.3
5000	145.1	*crashes*	420.0	184.4

14.8 Cython

Cython[10] is a Python-to-C compiler. Although it doesn't implement the complete Python language, features which are not implemented are interpreted conventionally, just not compiled.

Cython has two powerful capabilities for making Python code run faster. It:

- Translates portions of your Python to C and then compiles the C into an optimized shared object that can be loaded as a Python module

- Provides an interface layer that makes it straightforward to call native C and C++ libraries

---

[10] https://cython.org/

14.8.1 Python Compiled with Cython

Four steps are needed to produce a compiled Python module with Cython:

1. Copy functions from existing Python source files you wish to compile to new files that end with `.pyx` instead of `.py`. The file containing `main()` is not compiled and must remain in a `.py` file.

2. Add C language type annotations to Python variables in the `.pyx` files where speed improvements are desired. If your code uses NumPy, also add a `cimport` line that mirrors the NumPy `import`.

3. Create a setup file—a small Python program—that tells Cython which `.pyx` files to compile and optionally identify the compiler and compile and link flags to use.

4. Run the setup file to compile your code.

The first two steps for the Mandelbrot program are illustrated with a side-by-side comparison of the original code on the left (excluding `main()`) and the Cython enhancements, in gray, on the right.

Python, Baseline:	Python, with Cython Annotations:

```
1   #!/usr/bin/env python3
2   # cython/mb/MB_orig.py
3
4   import numpy as np
5   import time
6   def nIter(c, imax):
7
8
9
10      z = complex(0, 0)
11      for i in range(imax):
12          z = z*z + c
13          if abs(z) > 2:
14              break
15      return i
16
17  def MB(Re, Im, imax):
18
19
20
21      nR = len(Im)
22      nC = len(Re)
23      img = np.zeros((nR, nC))
24      for i,I in enumerate(Im):
25          for j,R in enumerate(Re):
26              c = complex(R, I)
27              img[i, j] = nIter(c, imax)
28      return img
```

```
1   #  cython/mb/MB_cython.pyx
2   cimport numpy as np
3   import numpy as np
4   import time
5   def nIter(double complex c,
6               long imax):
7       cdef int i
8       cdef double complex z
9       z = complex(0, 0)
10      for i in range(imax):
11          z = z*z + c
12          if z.real*z.real +
                z.imag*z.imag > 4:
13              break
14      return i
15
16  def MB(Re, Im, imax):
17      cdef int i,j
18      cdef double I, R
19      cdef double complex c
20      nR = len(Im)
21      nC = len(Re)
22      img = np.zeros((nR, nC),
            dtype=np.uint8)
23      for i,I in enumerate(Im):
24          for j,R in enumerate(Re):
25              c = complex(R, I)
26              img[i, j] = nIter(c,
                              imax)
27      return img
```

A setup file that works for the third step looks like this:

Python:

```
1   # file: cython/mb/cython_setup.py
2   import os
3   from setuptools import setup
4   from Cython.Build import cythonize
5   import numpy
6   os.environ['CFLAGS'] = '-Ofast'
7   setup(
8       ext_modules=cythonize("MB_cython.pyx"),
9       include_dirs=[numpy.get_include()]
10  )
```

Finally, run this setup file to compile the code:

```
> python cython_setup.py build_ext --inplace
```

A typical invocation produces warnings, then new C source files, and, hopefully, a shared object named after the .pyx file. On my Linux machine, the shared object is MB_cython.cpython-38-x86_64-linux-gnu.so. Despite the long name, it is imported into Python with import MB_cython.

What have we gained for our efforts? A small driver program loads the compiled module and runs the cases:

Python:

```
#!/usr/bin/env python3
# cython/mb/main2.py
from MB_cython import MB
import numpy as np
import time

max_iter = 255
nR, nC = 1000, 1000
Re = np.linspace(-0.7440, -0.7433, nC)
Im = np.linspace( 0.1315,  0.1322, nR)
```

```
T_s = time.time()
image = MB(Re, Im, max_iter)
print(f'Cython time = {time.time() - T_s:.3f} sec')
```

For $N = 1000$, runtime drops from 17.1 seconds to just 1.85 seconds. The original Python code is 3x slower than MATLAB, but Cython enhancements have made Python 3x faster.

We can do even better. Recall our profiling work in Sections 14.5.1 and 14.5.2 pointed to if abs(z) > 2: as being a hot spot. The abs() of a complex number computes its magnitude, in other words, the square root of the sum of squares of the real and imaginary components. Since this line consumes a lot of time, we should bypass the square root operation by testing just the sum of squares. That can be done by changing line 13 from the original on the left to the accelerated one on the right:

Python:	Python:
13 if abs(z) > 2:	13 if z.real**2 + z.imag**2 > 4:

This single line refinement cuts the $N = 1000$ Python+Cython time from 1.85 to 1.01 seconds, and the MATLAB time, with an equivalent change, from 5.8 to 4.4 seconds.

14.8.2 Parallel for Loops with Cython

The core MATLAB product does not include the parfor parallel for loop command—that can only be found in MATLAB Coder or the Parallel Computing Toolbox. MATLAB implementations in this book are therefore limited to sequential for loops.

Cython has a prange() function that allows one to write parallel for loops. Under the hood, this prange() function is implemented via OpenMP and therefore inherits OpenMP restrictions. The Cython documentation shows trivial parallel for loop examples,[11] but in practice, nontrivial loops require an inordinate amount of code tweaks to overcome compile error such as "Indexing Python object not allowed without gil," "Constructing Python tuple not allowed without gil," and "Coercion from Python not allowed without the GIL."

---

[11] https://cython.readthedocs.io/en/latest/src/userguide/parallelism.html

Unless your code sections have elementary for loops, you will either need to spend a lot of time with the Cython documentation or avoid its prange(). The Pythran and Numba options for parallel for loops, described in Sections 14.9 and 14.10.1, are much easier to use.

14.8.3 Cython Performance

Our updated performance, after replacing abs(z) with z.real**2+z.imag**2 in the MATLAB and Python+Cython implementations, is shown in Table 14-5..

Table 14-5. *Execution time in seconds for Mandelbrot programs*

N	MATLAB	Python Baseline	Python+ Cython
500	1.3	4.2	0.25
1000	4.4	17.1	1.01
2000	17.7	67.4	4.03
5000	112.5	420.0	25.18

14.9 Pythran

Pythran [3] resembles Cython in that it creates a compiled binary module from a file of lightly annotated Python functions. Its primary advantage over Cython is that the required code modifications are implemented entirely as source code comments. This means Pythran-enhanced code is pure Python; the code will run identically, albeit slower, on a system that lacks the Pythran compiler. Another advantage is that for loop parallelization with OpenMP is implemented easily.

Pythran has disadvantages compared to Cython: Pythran supports a smaller subset of Python and then Cython. Some statements like with are not supported at all, and others, like f-strings, have limited support. Another drawback (as of late 2021) is the project's documentation website[12] lacks sufficient examples. To get a comprehensive sense of the different forms the #pythran directives can take, the best option is to download the project's source code and then study the many examples in pythran/tests/cases.

---

[12] https://pythran.readthedocs.io/en/latest/MANUAL.html

14.9.1 Examples of Signature Comments

The Pythran #pythran export Fn directive to declare arguments to the following function Fn() understands data types listed in the following table. In cases where the left column includes "or," the Pythran compiler will infer the necessary type. Similarly, "string or int" means the function will accept either a string or integer argument at the given position.

Table 14-6. *Pythran function signature types*

Scalar Type or Data Container	Pythran Type Designation
String	str
Boolean	bool
Unsigned 8-bit integer	uint8
Unsigned 16-bit integer	uint16
Unsigned 32-bit integer	uint32
Unsigned 64-bit integer	uint64
32- or 64-bit integer	int
String *or* integer	str or int
8-bit integer	int8
16-bit integer	int16
32-bit integer	int32
64-bit integer	int64
32- or 64-bit float	float
32-bit float	float32
64- or 128-bit complex	complex
128-bit complex	complex128
List of integers	int list
List of lists of integers	int list list

(continued)

Table 14-6. (*continued*)

Scalar Type or Data Container	Pythran Type Designation
List of floats	`float list`
1D array integers	`int[]` *or* `int[:]`
1D array floats	`float[]` *or* `float[:]`
2D array integers	`int[][]` *or* `int[:,:]`
2D array floats	`float[][]` *or* `float[:,:]`
Dict of strings to integers	`str : int dict`
Tuple of two integers	`(int, int)`

The comment line preceding the definition of a function `Fn()` which takes a string, a list of integers, and a 2D array of 32-bit floats would therefore be

Python:

```
#pythran export Fn(str, int list, float32[])
```

14.9.2 Python Compiled with Pythran; Parallel for Loops

As with Cython, the Mandelbrot functions `nIter()` and `MB()` are separated to their own file for compilation. Only three comment lines are needed to enable Pythran to compile our code:

Python:

```
1   # pythran/mb/MB_pythran.py
2   import numpy as np
3   #pythran export nIter(complex, int)
4   def nIter(c, imax):
5     z = complex(0, 0)
6     for i in range(imax):
7       z = z*z + c
8       if abs(z) > 2:
```

```
 9          break
10     return np.uint8(i)
11
12   #pythran export MB(float [], float [], int)
13   def MB(Re, Im, imax):
14     nR = Im.shape[0]
15     nC = Re.shape[0]
16     img = np.zeros((nR,nC),dtype=np.uint8)
17     #omp parallel for
18     for i,I in enumerate(Im):
19       for j,R in enumerate(Re):
20         c = complex(R, I)
21         img[i,j] = nIter(c, imax)
22     return img
```

The first two comments define signatures (excluding return type, which Pythran figures out on its own) of the functions on the following lines, and the third comment designates the for i,I loop to be parallel.

Compile the functions with

```
> pythran -Ofast -fopenmp MB_pythran.py
```

Among other things, Pythran needs the C header file to the basic linear algebra subroutines (BLAS). If your compile command shows

```
fatal error: cblas.h: No such file or directory
```

and does not create a shared object file, you'll need to download and install development headers for BLAS suitable to your OS. On Ubuntu, for example, this is resolved with apt install libopenblas-dev. Even after installing the headers, you may still see the "fatal error" even though the shared object file is created successfully.

To suppress OpenMP parallelism of the for loop, either remove the #omp parallel for comment from the source or remove the -fopenmp switch from the compile command.

The pythran command produces a compiled shared object file named after the input source file (MB_pythran.cpython-38-x86_64-linux-gnu.so on my computer). The driver program to run the Pythran-compiled module is identical to the driver used for the Cython-compiled module. The only difference is the name of the module being loaded—import MB_pythran instead of import MB_cython:

Python:

```python
#!/usr/bin/env python3
# pythran/mb/MB_pythran_main.py
import numpy as np
from MB_pythran import MB
import time

def main():
    imax = 255
    for N in [500, 1000, 2000, 5000]:
        T_s = time.time()
        nR, nC = N, N
        Re = np.linspace(-0.7440,
                         -0.7433, nC)
        Im = np.linspace( 0.1315,
                          0.1322, nR)
        img = MB(Re, Im, imax)
        print(N, time.time() - T_s)
if __name__ == '__main__': main()
```

14.9.3 Pythran Performance

Single-core Pythran performance gives more than a 2.5x speed over single-core Cython, and the four-core version is 2.5x faster than a single core (Table 14-7). Noteworthy is the order of magnitude performance increase over the baseline Python version, achieved merely by adding three comment lines and invoking the Pythran compiler on the file of functions.

Table 14-7. *Execution time in seconds for Mandelbrot programs*

N	MATLAB 1 Core	Python Baseline 1 Core	Python+ Cython 1 Core	Python+ Pythran 1 Core	Python+ Pythran 4 Cores
500	1.3	4.2	0.25	0.10	0.05
1000	4.4	17.1	1.01	0.40	0.15
2000	17.7	67.4	4.03	1.59	0.62
5000	112.5	420.0	25.18	9.93	3.88

14.10 Numba

Numba[13] is a just-in-time (JIT) compiler for Python with emphasis on accelerating numeric calculations. Like Cython and Pythran, Numba also allows one to write parallel for loops.

Also like Cython and Pythran, code modifications needed to use Numba mostly deal with type definitions. These changes are pure Python. Moreover, there are no externally generated source files, languages, or compilers to deal with. Another benefit is that the functions to be accelerated may coexist with unaltered functions—including the main program—they need not be sequestered to a separate file. For these reasons, Numba-enhanced code is more convenient to use and deploy than Cython- or Pythran-enhanced code.

Numba enhancements are added to Python by doing the following:

1. Include an import to the numba module, pulling in the jit decorator, numeric data types to be used, and optionally the prange function to write parallel for loops.

2. Apply the @jit() decorator to each function that is to be sped up. The arguments to this decorator are the function's signature, that is, its return type, and the types of each input argument. The decorator also takes additional keyword arguments such as nopython and fastmath.

3. Optionally, rewrite for loops using the Numba parallel range function prange().

---

[13] https://numba.pydata.org/

The Mandelbrot program enhanced with Numba looks like this:

Python:

```python
#!/usr/bin/env python3
# file: numba/mb/MB_numba.py
import numpy as np
from numba import jit, prange, uint8, int64, float64, complex128
import time
@jit(uint8(complex128,int64),nopython=True, fastmath=True)
def nIter(c, imax):
  z = complex(0, 0)
  for i in range(imax):
    z = z*z + c
    if z.real*z.real + z.imag*z.imag > 4:
      break
  return i

@jit(uint8[:,:](float64[:],float64[:],int64),
     nopython=True, fastmath=True, parallel=True)
def MB(Re, Im, imax):
  nR = len(Im)
  nC = len(Re)
  img = np.zeros((nR, nC),
                 dtype=np.uint8)
  for i in prange(len(Im)):
    I = Im[i]
    for j,R in enumerate(Re):
      c = complex(R, I)
      img[i, j] = nIter(c, imax)
  return img

def main():
  imax = 255
  for N in [500, 1000, 2000, 5000]:
    T_s = time.time()
    nR, nC = N, N
```

```
34        Re = np.linspace(-0.7440,
35                              -0.7433, nC)
36        Im = np.linspace( 0.1315,
37                              0.1322, nR)
38        img = MB(Re, Im, imax)
39        T_e = time.time()
40        print(f'{T_e - T_s:.3f}  {N:5d}')
41   if __name__ == '__main__': main()
```

The @jit() decorators to nIter() and MB() may look daunting, but their components are straightforward. nIter() returns a scalar uint8. Inputs are a double-precision complex scalar—a complex128—and a conventional Python integer scalar, an int64. Thus, nIter()'s signature is uint8(complex128, int64). The keyword arguments nopython and fastmath are explained in Section 14.10.2.

The MB() function returns a 2D array of uint8 which is expressed in Numba as uint8[:,:]. Inputs are a pair of 1D double-precision floating-point arrays and an integer scalar. Therefore, MB()'s signature is uint8[:,:](float64[:],float64[:], int64). MB()'s decorator has an additional keyword argument, parallel=True, to denote the use of the parallel range function prange().

14.10.1 Parallel for Loops with Numba

Numba's prange() function resembles Cython's. Writing a parallel for loop amounts to replacing the existing for i in ... construct with for i in prange(N) where N is an integer scalar. The requirement that the loop iterate over a range of integers may mean the loop needs small modifications if the existing loop iterates over other objects.

In our case, we have to replace the construct on the left, which populates both the index i and the i-th imaginary scalar value, with the one on the right which merely iterates over the index. The scalar value has to be extracted on a subsequent line:

Python, Baseline:	Python, Numba Parallel for:
`for i,I in enumerate(Im):`	`for i in prange(len(Im)):` `I=Im[i]`

Numba handles the distribution of work in the body of the loop to different cores as well as aggregation of results for variables shared between simultaneous computations.

606

14.10.2 Numba Keyword Arguments nopython, fastmath

The @jit() keyword argument nopython, most often seen set to True, instructs the JIT compiler to skip the Python interpreter completely and use only compiled code. This is the recommended setting and even has its dedicated decorator: @njit() is the same as @jit(...,nopython=True). This keyword should only be set to False if the compilation fails.

The keyword argument fastmath enables unsafe operations[14] such as assuming inputs are never NaNs or Infs and allows the compiler to reorder floating-point instructions. Naturally, compare output of your code with and without fastmath=True to ensure your results are not compromised.

14.10.3 Numba Performance

Performance of the Numba-enhanced Mandelbrot program, shown in Table 14-8, is nothing less than astonishing. With Numba, pure Python code exceeds the speed of Cython- and Pythran-compiled modules.

14.10.4 Numba Limitations

While Numba's performance boosts are impressive, they come with strings attached. Functions that are to be accelerated by Numba need to be relatively low level and computationally expensive.

---

[14] https://llvm.org/docs/LangRef.html#fast-math-flags

Table 14-8. *Execution time in seconds for Mandelbrot programs*

N	MATLAB 1 Core	Python Baseline 1 Core	Python+ Cython 1 Core	Python+ Pythran 1 Core	Python+ Pythran 4 Cores	Python+ Numba 1 Core	Python+ Numba 4 Cores
500	1.3	4.2	0.25	0.10	0.05	0.09	0.04
1000	4.4	17.1	1.01	0.40	0.15	0.36	0.15
2000	17.7	67.4	4.03	1.59	0.62	1.44	0.62
5000	112.5	420.0	25.18	9.93	3.88	8.95	3.71

Unless one employs Numba's Wrapper Address Protocol,[15] functions decorated by @jit may call only a subset of NumPy and standard library functions.

Before undertaking an optimization attempt with Numba, write a test program with functions that contains the language constructs and calls to other functions needed to perform the calculations you want to accelerate. Decorate these trial functions with @jit and see if the program runs. If you see an error like

```
NameError: global name 'XYZ' is not defined
```

and a call to XYZ() exists in a function decorated by @jit, it means Numba cannot compile this function. In this case, your options are to simplify the function until it can be compiled, revert to the multiprocessing module (Section 14.6), or use dask, to be covered in Section 14.13.

14.11 f2py

f2py is a command-line utility that comes with NumPy. It allows one to create compiled Python modules from specially annotated Fortran code far more easily than with any other binary interface tool. f2py brings two important benefits: it can create Python interface modules to legacy Fortran code, and it can give a substantial computational boost to Python functions that are rewritten in Fortran.

---

[15] https://numba.readthedocs.io/en/stable/reference/types.html?highlight=wrapper #wrapper-address-protocol-wap

The following Fortran code implements the nIter() and MB() functions seen early in the Mandelbrot implementations. The five cf2py lines defining the input and output arguments are all f2py needs to create the Python interface, including documentation.

Fortran:

```
1    c file: code/f2py/mb.f
2          integer function nIter(c, imax)
3    cf2py intent(in)    :: c, imax
4    cf2py intent(out)   :: nIter
5          implicit none
6          complex*16 z, c
7          integer i, imax
8          nIter = imax
9          z = 0
10         do i = 0,imax - 1
11           z = z*z + c
12           if (zabs(z) .gt. 2.0) then
13             nIter = i
14             return
15           endif
16         enddo
17         nIter = imax
18         end
19
20         subroutine MB(nR, nC, Re, Im, img, imax)
21   cf2py intent(in)    :: Re, Im, imax
22   cf2py intent(out)   :: img
23   cf2py intent(hide)  :: nR, nC
24         implicit none
25         integer nR, nC, nIter, imax, i, j, ij
26         integer(kind=2) img(nR*nC)
27         real*8 Re(nR), Im(nC)
28         complex*16 c
29         do i = 1,nR
30           do j = 1,nC
31             c = cmplx(Re(i), Im(j))
```

```
32              ij = (i-1)*nC+j
33              img(ij) = nIter(c,imax)
34          enddo
35        enddo
36        end
```

The command

```
> f2py -c --opt="-Ofast" -m MB_fortran mb.f
```

generates Python/Fortran interface code, compiles it and mb.f listed earlier with the
system's Fortran compiler, then links these into a compiled Python module, MB_fortran
(the full name of this module is MB_fortran.cpython-38-x86_64-linux-gnu.so on my
computer).

In addition to writing the interface code, f2py also generates documentation for each
function:

Python:

```
In : import MB_fortran
In : MB_fortran.mb?
Call signature: MB_fortran.mb(*args, **kwargs)
Type:           fortran
String form:    <fortran object>
Docstring:
img = mb(re,im,imax)

Wrapper for ``mb``.

Parameters
----------
re : input rank-1 array('d') with bounds (nr)
im : input rank-1 array('d') with bounds (nc)
imax : input int

Returns
-------
img : rank-1 array('h') with bounds (nr*nc)
```

This driver program loads the Fortran-compiled module and then runs our benchmark cases:

Python:

```python
#!/usr/bin/env python3
# file: code/f2py/MB_main.py
import numpy as np
import time
from MB_fortran import mb

def main():
    imax = 255
    for N in [500,1000,2000,5000]:
        T_s = time.time()
        nR, nC = N, N
        Re = np.linspace(-0.7440, -0.7433, nC)
        Im = np.linspace( 0.1315, 0.1322, nR)
        img = np.zeros((nR*nC,), dtype=np.int16)
        img = mb(Re, Im, imax).reshape(nR,nC)
        print(N, time.time() - T_s)
if __name__ == '__main__': main()
```

Table 14-9 shows how the f2py-compiled module stacks up with other single CPU results.

Table 14-9. *Execution time in seconds for Mandelbrot programs*

N	MATLAB 1 Core	Python Baseline 1 Core	Python+ Cython 1 Core	Python+ Pythran 1 Core	Python+ Numba 1 Core	Python+ f2py 1 Core
500	1.3	4.2	0.25	0.10	0.09	0.10
1000	4.4	17.1	1.01	0.40	0.36	0.40
2000	17.7	67.4	4.03	1.59	1.44	1.60
5000	112.5	420.0	25.18	9.93	8.95	10.05

14.12 Recipe 14-1: Accelerating MATLAB with Python on a Single Computer

Single CPU MATLAB performance on the Mandelbrot problem looks great compared to the vanilla single CPU Python implementation (Table 14-8). It pales next to the performance-enhanced Python versions though. Like Python, MATLAB's performance can also be enhanced several ways:

- Use parallel for loops (needs the Parallel Computing Toolbox or the MATLAB Coder).

- Write `MB()` and `nIter()` in C, C++, or Fortran, add headers and call `mex` API functions, then create a compiled MATLAB extension with the `mex` command.

- Call performance-enhanced Python modules.

Here, we'll explore the last option by calling the Python-based Cython, Pythran, Numba, and f2py accelerated solutions from MATLAB. In all cases, the solution includes the overhead of converting MATLAB inputs to Python variables and converting the Python return value to a MATLAB variable. Timing results, shown in Table 14-10, do not include Python module load times within MATLAB when the MATLAB programs start.

14.12.1 Compile Python Modules in a MATLAB-Friendly Virtual Environment

Three of the next four sections, Sections 14.12.2, 14.12.3, and 14.12.5, use your computer's C, C++, or Fortran compiler to build binary Python modules. On macOS, this means the Xcode development library must be installed. On all operating systems, it is important to work in a conda environment like `matpy` (Section 2.5.1) whose shared libraries are consistent with MATLAB's. The compiled modules won't load in MATLAB otherwise.

14.12.2 MATLAB + Cython

This driver loads the `MB_cython` module compiled in Section 14.11.

MATLAB 2020b:

```
% file: cython/mb/MB_main.m
np = py.importlib.import_module('numpy');
MB_cython = py.importlib.import_module('MB_cython');
imax = int64(255);
for N = [500 1000 2000 5000]
    tic
    nR = N; nC = N;
    Re = np.array(linspace(-0.7440, -0.7433, nC));
    Im = np.array(linspace( 0.1315,  0.1322, nR));
    img = py2mat(MB_cython.MB(Re, Im, imax));
    fprintf('%5d %.3f\n',N,toc);
end
```

14.12.3 MATLAB + Pythran

This driver loads the MB_pythran module compiled in Section 14.9.

MATLAB 2020b:

```
% file: pythran/mb/MB_main.m
np = py.importlib.import_module('numpy');
MB_pythran = py.importlib.import_module('MB_pythran');
imax = int64(255);
for N = [500 1000 2000 5000]
    tic
    nR = N; nC = N;
    Re = np.array(linspace(-0.7440, -0.7433, nC));
    Im = np.array(linspace( 0.1315,  0.1322, nR));
    img = py2mat(MB_pythran.MB(Re, Im, imax));
    fprintf('%5d %.3f\n',N,toc);
end
```

14.12.4 MATLAB + Numba

This driver loads the parallel for loop MB_numba_prange module of Section 14.10.

MATLAB 2020b:

```
% file: numba/mb/MB_main.m
np = py.importlib.import_module('numpy');
MB_numba = py.importlib.import_module('MB_numba_prange');
imax = int64(255);
for N = [500 1000 2000 5000]
    tic
    nR = N; nC = N;
    Re = np.array(linspace(-0.7440, -0.7433, nC));
    Im = np.array(linspace( 0.1315,  0.1322, nR));
    img = py2mat(MB_numba.MB(Re, Im, imax));
    fprintf('%5d %.3f\n',N,toc);
end
```

14.12.5 MATLAB + f2py

This driver loads the MB_fortran module compiled in Section 14.11.

MATLAB 2020b:

```
% file: code/f2py/MB_main.m
np = py.importlib.import_module('numpy');
MB_fortran = py.importlib.import_module('MB_fortran');
imax = int64(255);
for N = [500 1000 2000 5000]
    tic
    nR = N; nC = N;
    Re = np.array(linspace(-0.7440, -0.7433, nC));
    Im = np.array(linspace( 0.1315,  0.1322, nR));
    img = py2mat(MB_fortran.mb(Re, Im, imax));
    fprintf('%5d %.3f\n',N,toc);
end
```

14.12.6 MATLAB + Python Performance Results

Table 14-10 shows that, for our benchmark problem, performance increases seen in Python benefit MATLAB equally well.

Table 14-10. *Execution time in seconds for MATLAB-based Mandelbrot programs enhanced by Python*

N	MATLAB 1 Core	MATLAB+ Cython 1 Core	MATLAB+ Pythran 4 Cores	MATLAB+ Numba 4 Cores	MATLAB+ f2py 1 Core
500	1.3	0.29	0.05	0.05	0.11
1000	4.4	1.02	0.21	0.19	0.41
2000	17.7	4.21	0.69	0.58	1.59
5000	112.5	26.02	4.10	3.93	10.13

While the single-core f2py performance is modest compared to multicore Numba performance, f2py offers a secondary benefit the other accelerants lack: with f2py you can create a Fortran interface to MATLAB much more easily than you can with MATLAB's own mex utility.

14.13 Distributed Memory Parallel Processing with Dask

Previous sections showed that distributing work across a computer's multiple cores can give significant performance increases. We can do even better—much better—by distributing work across multiple computers. Several Python modules, among them Ray,[16] dispy,[17] and dask,[18] make it easy to run a Python program that farms work out to many computers.

Dask has advantages over the other modules because it also provides an out-of-core data container, the dask array, which enables computation with arrays too large to fit in a computer's memory, similar to MATLAB's "tall arrays." Additionally, dask is backed by Coiled[19] which offers commercial support and cloud computing for dask jobs. Coiled offers 1000 hours of free CPU hours on up to 100 cores each month for dask jobs, an attractive proposition for individuals who lack access to high-end compute clusters.

---

[16] https://ray.io/

[17] https://dispy.org/

[18] https://dask.org/

[19] https://coiled.io/

Dask will be used to demonstrate distributed memory parallel processing in the following sections. The main dask concepts are covered in Section 14.13.2, but they likely won't mean much without a detailed example. Such an example follows in Section 14.13.3 where we tackle an embarrassingly parallel and computationally intensive problem—summing prime factors of many numbers. For starters, we'll just use multiple cores of a single computer.

The real fun doesn't begin until we use multiple computers. Before we can run dask on multiple computers, we have to launch background scheduler and worker jobs on those computers; the details of that are explained in Section 14.13.4. Once the background machinery is in place, in Section 14.13.5 we'll rerun the prime factor summation problem on a collection of computers and see some nice speed-ups.

Memory-intensive jobs introduce additional complications. In Section 14.13.6, we'll generate a gigapixel image of the Mandelbrot set we computed earlier in Section 14.2 using a collection of computers with only 1 GB of memory. Needless to say, we have to take precautions to avoid crashes.

Finally, in Section 14.13.7, we'll combine our accumulated experience with dask to solve a problem closely resembling a real-world application. We'll solve a transient dynamic finite element problem with a half million degree of freedom model using a frequency domain solution spanning thousands of frequencies. Such problems can take days on individual computers, but we'll get solutions—from either Python or MATLAB— in less than 15 minutes using Coiled's cloud.

14.13.1 Parallel MATLAB

Like Python, MATLAB can run on distributed memory clusters and on clusters in the cloud. The most direct way to do so is to use the Parallel Computing Toolbox. Other options include using MATLAB Coder or the MATLAB Compiler to create a stand-alone executable that can be sent to remote computers.

The MathWorks also offers MATLAB Online, and through it, MATLAB in the Cloud, but its capabilities are limited to those enabled in your MATLAB license. In other words, if you don't have a license for the Parallel Computing Toolbox or for cloud use, you won't be able to run your m-files on multiple computers in the cloud.

As mentioned earlier (Section 1.3), this book's scope is limited to the core MATLAB product which precludes comparisons of pure MATLAB cloud solutions to their Python equivalents. Nonetheless, we'll see in Section 14.14 that hybrid MATLAB/Python code runs quite effectively on private clusters as well as Coiled's cloud.

14.13.2 Dask Execution Paradigm and Performance Expectations

The dask execution paradigm covers four main concepts:

- A **cluster** is a collection of computers the job owner can access. The computers in the cluster must have a consistent Python installation with the dask and distributed modules. The cluster can actually be as small as just the single computer you are currently working on, in which case dask jobs are distributed across the computer's cores, or it can be a large HPC compute cluster, optionally with its own job scheduler like LSF, Slurm, or PBS. In the latter case, the user must have the same account on all computers, be able to ssh between computers without a password, or be able to submit jobs to the computers through a separate job scheduler.

- **dask-scheduler** and **dask-worker** are background jobs that run on the computers of the cluster. An instance of the scheduler runs on one of the computers, while a worker instance runs on each computer. These processes have to be started manually with the dask-ssh command or will be started and managed by a job scheduler–specific configuration file.

- A **client** is a Python variable created by connecting to the dask scheduler process.

- A **delayed** task is a Python function plus its calling arguments that is not evaluated immediately but instead added to a list of tasks that will be executed later.

A dask-enabled Python program populates a list with delayed tasks and then passes this list to dask.compute(). This function hands tasks off to the dask scheduler which in turn sends each task to the next idle worker (likely running on a different computer). After a worker receives a task, the worker calls the user-provided function defined for the task with the user's arguments, then sends its return values back to the scheduler. dask.compute() gets the task return values from the scheduler and appends these to its list of results.

Our program sets up the function calls to be made in parallel, and dask handles everything else—assigning these calls to processors, serializing and then sending input arguments over the network, invoking the calls on remote computers, and finally serializing and sending the return arguments back to the computer which launched the jobs.

The convenience dask brings comes with a performance cost that varies with factors that you may have only limited control over:

- Load balancing strategy

- Volume of data passed to or received from remotely executed functions

- Network speed

- Uniformity of computer resources

Most importantly, dask decides how and when to transmit data. Code developers are generally happy to offload this burden even if the interleaving of compute/transmit steps isn't ideal, yet may be disappointed by the ensuing parallel efficiency. The adage "your mileage may vary" is ever true in parallel processing.

This all sounds complicated (and under the hood, it is!). How exactly do we set up and run a distributed memory parallel program? What can be done to make the code run faster? The only way to make sense of this is to work through examples.

14.13.3 Example 1: Sum of Prime Factors on One Computer

Our first example is a program that computes the sum of unique prime factors of all numbers in a given range. The hard part, computing the prime factors themselves, is done with SymPy's `primefactors()` function, comparable to MATLAB's `factor()`.[20] The sequential versions look like this:

---

[20] `primefactors()` returns unique factors, while `factor()` returns repeated factors as well. Also, `primefactors(1)` returns an empty set, while `factor(1)` returns 1.

MATLAB:	Python:
| ```
% code/dask/prime_seq.m
A = 2;
B = 10000000;
incr = 1;
[S, dT] = my_fn(A, B, incr);
fprintf('A=%d B=%d, %.3f sec\n',...
        A, B, dT);
fprintf('S=%ld\n', S);
function [S, dT]=my_fn(A, B, incr)
  tic;
  S = 0;
  for i = A:incr:B-1
    S = S + sum(unique(factor(i)));
  end
  dT = toc;
end
``` | ```
#!/usr/bin/env python3
# code/dask/prime_seq.py
from sympy import primefactors
import time
def my_fn(a, b, incr):
  Ts = time.time()
  s = 0
  for x in range(a,b,incr):
    s += sum(primefactors(x))
  return s, time.time() - Ts
def main():
  A = 2
  B = 10_000_000
  incr = 1
  S, dT = my_fn(A, B, incr)
  print(f'A={A} B={B}, '
        f'{dT:.4f} sec')
  print(f'S={S}')
if __name__ == "__main__": main()
``` |

and produce this on my Linux laptop:

MATLAB:	Python:
| ```
>> prime_seq
A=2 B=10000000, 682.681 sec
S=5495501355056
``` | ```
> ./prime_seq.py
A=1 B=10000000, 519.531 sec
S=5495501355056
``` |

Calls to the compute-intensive function my_fn() are independent and can be called in any order, or even simultaneously. We'll do exactly that with dask, using three cores of the local machine. To spread the load evenly, we merely need to offset the starting counter by the job number and let the call to range(a,b,incr) in my fn() scatter the numbers to factor across processors. For example, if we compute prime factors for numbers between 2 and 20 and want to spread the work evenly over three jobs, the assignments will be

Python:

```
In : list(range(2,21))          # original set
Out: [2, 3, 4, 5, 6, 7, 8, 9, 10, 11, 12, 13, 14, 15, 16, 17, 18, 19, 20]

In : list(range(2+0,21,3))
Out: [2, 5, 8, 11, 14, 17, 20]

In : list(range(2+1,21,3))
Out: [3, 6, 9, 12, 15, 18]

In : list(range(2+2,21,3))
Out: [4, 7, 10, 13, 16, 19]
```

or equivalently in MATLAB

MATLAB:

```
>> 2:3:20
     2     5     8    11    14    17    20

>> 2+1:3:20
     3     6     9    12    15    18

>> 2+2:3:20
     4     7    10    13    16    19
```

The dask-enabled version of the prime factor summation program on the local computer, splitting up the work to three tasks that are to run simultaneously, looks like this:

Python:

```
1   #!/usr/bin/env python3
2   # code/dask/prime_dask.py
```

```
3    from sympy import primefactors
4    import time
5    import dask
6    from dask.distributed import Client
7
8    def my_fn(a, b, incr):
9        Ts = time.time()
10       s = 0
11       for x in range(a,b,incr):
12           s += sum(primefactors(x))
13       return s, time.time() - Ts
14
15   def main():
16       client = Client('127.0.0.1:8786')
17   #   client = Client('143.198.155.245:8786')
18       tasks  = []
19       main_T_start = time.time()
20   #   n_jobs = 11*18
21       n_jobs = 3
22       A = 2
23       B = 10_000 # _000
24       incr = n_jobs
25       for i in range(n_jobs):
26           job = dask.delayed(my_fn)(A+i, B, incr)
27           tasks.append(job)
28       results = dask.compute(*tasks)
29       client.close()
30       total_sum = 0
31       for i in range(len(results)):
32           partial_sum, T_el = results[i]
33           print(f'job {i}:  sum= {partial_sum}  T= {T_el:.3f}')
34           total_sum += partial_sum
35       print(f'total sum={total_sum}')
36       elapsed = time.time() - main_T_start
37       print(f'main took {elapsed:.3f} sec')
38   if __name__ == "__main__": main()
```

When the program runs, the call to Client('127.0.0.1:8786') at line 16 attempts to connect to a dask scheduler running on the localhost and listening on port 8786. (Line 17, currently commented out, will be discussed in Section 14.13.5.) If such a scheduler isn't running, the program fails after 30 seconds with

Python:

```
OSError: Timed out trying to connect to tcp://127.0.0.1:8786 after 30 s
```

Line 21 defines n_jobs, our counter for the number of tasks to create. At a minimum, to take full advantage of your hardware, this should equal or exceed the number of cores available in your cluster. If tasks vary in duration and you have many of them, setting n_jobs to a value much greater than the number of cores will help balance the load across cores more equitably.

Lines 24–26 add delayed tasks to the list tasks which was initialized at line 18. Each task is a call to my_fn() with arguments A+i, B, incr.

The computations are performed at line 27 when dask hands the list of delayed tasks to the scheduler to farm out to workers. Return values from each call appear in the list results which will have n_jobs entries.

Finally, lines 29–32 aggregate the partial sums of primes into a total value.

Details on setting up dask scheduler and worker processes on multiple computers appear in the next section. For now, we'll avoid many complications by just working on the local computer. Background scheduler and worker jobs can be started most easily by creating a text file containing three copies of the loop-back IP address:

```
hostfile.txt
127.0.0.1
127.0.0.1
127.0.0.1
```

then passing this file name as an argument to the dask-ssh command:
console

```
> dask-ssh --hostfile hostfile.txt
```

This starts a worker process on each computer defined in the file, plus a scheduler process on the computer defined on the first line. Of course, in this case, all these background processes run on the local computer.

With the scheduler and workers running in the background, we can now run the dask-enabled prime factor summation program `prime_dask.py`. It runs faster than the sequential version, but not by much:

3 worker processes, 3 dask jobs:

```
job 0:  sum= 2418248946959  T= 327.969
job 1:  sum= 659400211060  T= 206.228
job 2:  sum= 2417852197037  T= 327.709
total sum=5495501355056
main took 328.852 sec
```

Performance disappoints for two reasons. First, the workload is clearly imbalanced since one job took around 200 seconds, while the other two took more than 320. Evidently, terms of the sequence 3, 6, 9 ... can be factored much more rapidly than terms in 2, 5, 8 ... and 4, 7, 10 ...—who knew? The second reason is less obvious. It is that the sum of individual core times, 328.0 + 206.2 + 327.7 = 861.9 seconds, is 66% higher than the single-core time of 519.5 seconds. Dask seems to impose a severe overhead.

Three experiments shed light on the source of dask's overhead. First, we'll repeat the single-core runtime using the dask infrastructure with only one worker process, meaning only one CPU core will receive work. A scheduler is always needed so that must also run in the background. Performance in this case is reasonable since dask added less than 7% overhead (555.0 seconds vs. 519.5 seconds):

1 worker process, 1 dask job:

```
job 0:  sum= 5495501355056  T= 554.426
total sum=5495501355056
main took 555.002 sec
```

Next, we'll spin up two more dask worker processes, but still only submit one job:

3 worker processes, 1 dask job:

```
job 0:  sum= 5495501355056  T= 587.976
total sum=5495501355056
main took 588.105 sec
```

This time, overhead doubled to 13% even though the additional two workers are merely standing by, waiting for work that never comes.

Finally, we'll again use just one worker but give it three tasks where the ranges are separated by strides of three, just as when these ranges are given to three workers.

1 worker process, 3 dask jobs:

```
job 0:  sum= 2418248946959  T= 725.613
job 1:  sum= 659400211060  T= 481.670
job 2:  sum= 2417852197037  T= 725.893
total sum=5495501355056
main took 726.482 sec
```

The cause of the overhead must be related to how the work is split up. While there's no obvious remedy to improve this situation, dask does have nice performance monitoring and reporting tools to help diagnose performance issues. One of these tools is the web-based real-time cluster statistics seen on the scheduler host's port 8787, http://127.0.0.1:8787 in our case. Another is a report generator that can be invoked directly from our program. We merely need to import the performance_report function from dask.distributed and then wrap the dask-specific code in a context manager that calls performance_report to get a rich HTML file graphically showing many different aspects of the parallel job.

Python:

```python
1   #!/usr/bin/env python3
2   # code/dask/prime_dask.py
3   from sympy import primefactors
4   import time
5   import dask
6   from dask.distributed import Client, performance_report
7
8   def my_fn(a, b, incr):
9       Ts = time.time()
10      s = 0
11      for x in range(a,b,incr):
12          s += sum(primefactors(x))
13      return s, time.time() - Ts
14
15  def main():
16      client = Client('127.0.0.1:8786')
17      tasks = []
18      main_T_start = time.time()
```

```
19      n_jobs = 30
20      A = 2
21      B = 1_000_000
22      incr = n_jobs
23      with performance_report(filename="prime-perf.html"):
24          for i in range(n_jobs):
25              job = dask.delayed(my_fn)(A+i, B, incr)
26              tasks.append(job)
27          results = dask.compute(*tasks)
28      total_sum = 0
29      for i in range(len(results)):
30          partial_sum, T_el = results[i]
31          print(f'job {i}:  sum= {partial_sum}  T= {T_el:.3f}')
32          total_sum += partial_sum
33      print(f'total sum={total_sum}')
34      elapsed = time.time() - main_T_start
35      print(f'main took {elapsed:.3f} sec')
36  if __name__ == "__main__": main()
```

While the reporting tool is easy to use, comprehending the output is less so.

14.13.4 Setting Up a Dask Cluster on Multiple Computers

Running dask on a single computer is a useful first step during code development and initial troubleshooting. It fails to satisfy on the performance front, however. To really benefit from dask's power, we'll need to run it on many computers.

A dask cluster can be set up several ways: manually, with ssh; with Kubernetes; with Helm; or with dask-specific configurations for job schedulers like LSF, MOAB, Slurm, and PBS. This section describes how a dask cluster can be implemented with ssh, perhaps the most approachable method for regular users. Kubernetes, Helm, LSF, and the others may require assistance from coworkers, DevOps specialists, or cluster administrators to set up. The ssh method implies two things: a uniform Python installation and seamless ssh access across all computers. Specifically, all computers should have

- Compatible (preferably identical) Python installations
- The same path to the Python executable

- The same account name for the user setting up and using the cluster

- Uniform bidirectional, key-based ssh access across all computers for the user account

- Same ssh port

- Firewall rules open to allow ssh and the dask scheduler and metrics ports (8786 and 8787 by default)

Once these conditions are met, add IP addresses (or hostnames, if name resolution works) of each computer in the cluster in a host file (my_hosts.txt represents this file as follows). The computer listed first in the host file will run the background scheduler process, and all computers will run background worker processes. Then invoke dask-ssh from a console to start the scheduler and workers:

```
dask-ssh --hostfile my_hosts.txt
```

Warning!   Setting up a distributed dask cluster with dask-ssh is extremely insecure! Any user who knows the scheduler's IP address and port can connect to your cluster and run arbitrary Python code under the account—namely, yours— that launched the workers.

The correct way to set up a secure, multi-user dask cluster is to configure a dask gateway[21] which implements an authentication layer.

14.13.5 Example 2: Sum of Prime Factors on Multiple Computers

Once the computers in the dask cluster are running a scheduler and workers, we can begin to enjoy significant performance increases. This section uses a collection of 18 virtual machines running on DigitalOcean's[22] cloud infrastructure. Each VM runs their lowest tier "droplet" which has 1 GB of memory, 1 CPU core @ 2.5 GHz, and 25 GB of storage. The VMs run Ubuntu 20.04.3 LTS, have Anaconda 2021.05 installed, and use the matpy conda environment (Section 2.5.1).

---

[21] https://gateway.dask.org/install-user.html

[22] www.digitalocean.com/

The first step is to log in to one of the 18 VMs and issue the dask-ssh command to start a scheduler and worker:

```
dask-ssh --hostfile DigitalOcean_VMs.txt
```

where DigitalOcean_VMs.txt has the IP addresses of all 18 computers. The only change needed to prime_dask.py (code listing in Section 14.13.3) is replacing the call to Client(127.0.0.1:8786) with the IP address of the VM running the scheduler, in other words, the first entry in DigitalOcean_VMs.txt. Line 17 shows what this might look like.

Finally, we can run prime_dask.py from any computer which is able to connect to the scheduler; the program does not need to be invoked from a VM on the dask cluster itself. In my case, I'll run the program on my home computer. I chose the number of tasks to be a multiple of the number of workers: 11 x 18 = 198. The result is

```
/usr/../client.py:1105: VersionMismatchWarning: Mismatched versions found
+---------+--------+-----------+---------+
| Package | client | scheduler | workers |
+---------+--------+-----------+---------+
| numpy   | 1.19.4 | 1.20.3    | 1.20.3  |
| pandas  | 1.2.4  | 1.3.2     | 1.3.2   |
+---------+--------+-----------+---------+
warnings.warn(version_module.VersionMismatchWarning(msg[0]["warning"]))
job 0:   sum= 58821526361  T= 4.812
job 1:   sum= 20950602326  T= 2.896
job 2:   sum= 21058399941  T= 5.235
job 3:   sum= 20835967514  T= 2.718
job 4:   sum= 58744527113  T= 5.268
                  :
job 192:  sum= 58671468728  T= 4.242
job 193:  sum= 21006229047  T= 2.808
job 194:  sum= 21149296400  T= 3.376
job 195:  sum= 20947903441  T= 3.108
job 196:  sum= 58678967783  T= 3.779
job 197:  sum= 217715273  T= 0.847
total sum=5495501355056
main took 43.393 sec
```

The sequential version of the program takes 718.057 seconds on a single VM, so the 18 cores gave a 16.5 × speed-up.

14.13.6 Example 3: A Gigapixel Mandelbrot Image

In Section 14.10.3, we used Numba to reduce the time needed to compute a 5000 x 5000 Mandelbrot image from 420 seconds to about 9 seconds on one core. Let's up the stakes and use our dask cluster of 18 single-core VMs to compute an image with 35,000 x 35,000—1.2 billion—pixels. Each pixel will be represented by a single byte which is the number of iterations needed for the z equation to converge. Both MATLAB and Python running on a computer with at least 8 GB of memory can easily store such an image; MATLAB can even display it with `imshow()` (matplotlib's `imshow()` crashes with an image this size).

Our gigapixel image will be 7^2, or about 50x larger than our 5k image so a single Numba-powered core should take about 440 seconds to generate it. Then, again, our dask cluster has 18 computers, so if we can load balance the jobs well, that time will come down by a lot. Let's give it a shot.

One strategy for load balancing the Mandelbrot set is to assign rows or columns to workers in a round-robin fashion. Here's what the dask + Numba solution looks like with that strategy:

Python:

```python
#!/usr/bin/env python3
# code/dask/MB_numba_dask.py
import numpy as np
from numba import jit, uint8, int64, float64, complex128
import dask
from dask.distributed import Client
import time
import matplotlib.pyplot as plt
@jit(uint8(complex128,int64), nopython=True, fastmath=True)

def nIter(c, imax):
    z = complex(0, 0)
    for i in range(imax):
        z = z*z + c
```

```
15      if z.real*z.real + z.imag*z.imag > 4:
16        break
17    return i
18
19  @jit(uint8[:,:](float64[:],float64[:],int64,int64,int64),
20                 nopython=True)
21  def MB(Re, Im, imax, job_id, n_jobs):
22    nR = len(Im)
23    nC = len(Re)
24    my_rows = range(job_id, len(Im), n_jobs)
25    n_rows_here = len(my_rows)
26    img = np.zeros((n_rows_here, nC), dtype=np.uint8)
27    row_counter = 0
28    for i in my_rows:
29      I = Im[i]
30      for j,R in enumerate(Re):
31        c = complex(R, I)
32        img[row_counter, j] = nIter(c, imax)
33      row_counter += 1
34    return img
35
36  def main():
37    imax = 255
38    N = 35_000
39    T_s = time.time()
40    nR, nC = N, N
41    Re = np.linspace(-0.7440, -0.7433, nC)
42    Im = np.linspace( 0.1315,  0.1322, nR)
43    n_jobs = 18
44    #client = Client('127.0.0.1:8786')
45    client = Client('413.198.155.245:8786')
46    tasks  = []
47    for i in range(n_jobs):
48      job = dask.delayed(MB)(Re, Im, 255, i, n_jobs)
49      tasks.append(job)
```

```
50      results = dask.compute(*tasks)
51      client.close()
52
53      # reassemble the image
54      img = np.empty((N,N), dtype=np.uint8)
55      for i in range(n_jobs):
56        my_rows = range(i, len(Im), n_jobs)
57        img[my_rows,:] = results[i][:]
58
59      print(f'{time.time() - T_s:.3f}  {N:5d}')
60      plt.imshow(img)
61      plt.show()
62  if __name__ == '__main__': main()
```

Values of $N < 15,000$ work and give quite satisfactory speed-ups, but larger sizes introduce new problems. The dask workers crash with

```
[ worker 127.0.0.1 ] : distributed.core - INFO - Event loop was unresponsive
in Worker for 4.89s.  This is often caused by long-running GIL-holding
functions or moving large chunks of data. This can cause timeouts and
instability.
```

causing the main program to end with

```
distributed.comm.core.CommClosedError: in <TCP (closed)
ConnectionPool.gather
local=tcp://u.v.x.y:55364 remote=tcp://a.b.c.d:8786>: Stream is closed
```

In other words, the workers crashed because they ran out of memory. While the computer submitting the job has 8 GB of memory, the workers only have 1 GB, some of which is taken by the operating system and the dask worker processes.

Rather than have each remote computer accumulate all results for the jobs it was assigned, we'll need to harvest results from the remote computers as the run progresses. One way to do that is to split the jobs into groups and then call the .compute() method after each group is submitted. The revised version of the following Mandelbrot program does just that. An additional modification is implemented to improve parallel efficiency: instead of sending the real and imaginary arrays to the remote workers, we'll just send the starting and ending values and let the workers figure out the array terms on their own. Finally, to simplify reassembly of the final image, we'll have each worker tell us the row indices it worked on in addition to its image slices.

Python:

```
1    #!/usr/bin/env python
2    # code/dask/MB_numba_dask2.py
3    import numpy as np
4    from numba import jit, uint8, int64, float64, complex128
5    from numba.types import Tuple as nb_tuple
6    import dask
7    from dask.distributed import Client
8    import time
9    import matplotlib.pyplot as plt
10
11   @jit(uint8(complex128,int64), nopython=True, fastmath=True)
12   def nIter(c, imax):
13     z = complex(0, 0)
14     for i in range(imax):
15       z = z*z + c
16       if z.real*z.real + z.imag*z.imag > 4:
17         break
18     return i
19
20   @jit(nb_tuple((int64[:],uint8[:,:]))(int64,float64[:],int64,float64[:],
21          int64,int64,int64), nopython=True)
22   def MB(nC, Re_limits, nR, Im_limits, imax, job_id, n_jobs):
23     Re = np.linspace(Re_limits[0], Re_limits[1], nC)
24     Im = np.linspace(Im_limits[0], Im_limits[1], nR)
25     my_rows = np.arange(job_id, len(Im), n_jobs, dtype=np.int64)
26     n_rows_here = len(my_rows)
27     img = np.zeros((n_rows_here, nC), dtype=np.uint8)
28     row_counter = 0
29     for i in my_rows:
30       I = Im[i]
31       for j,R in enumerate(Re):
```

```
32              c = complex(R, I)
33              img[row_counter, j] = nIter(c, imax)
34          row_counter += 1
35      return my_rows, img
36
37  def main():
38      imax = 255
39      N = 35_000
40      T_s = time.time()
41      nR, nC = N, N
42      Re_limits = np.array([-0.7440, -0.7433])
43      Im_limits = np.array([ 0.1315,   0.1322])
44      n_groups = 16
45      n_jobs_per_group = 18
46      n_jobs = n_jobs_per_group*n_groups
47      #client = Client('127.0.0.1:8786')
48      client = Client('143.198.155.245:8786')
49      results = []
50      for c in range(n_groups):
51          tasks  = []
52          Tcs = time.time()
53          for i in range(n_jobs_per_group):
54              job = dask.delayed(MB)(nC, Re_limits, nR, Im_limits, 255,
55                        c*n_jobs_per_group+i, n_jobs)
56              tasks.append(job)
57          results.extend( dask.compute(*tasks) )
58          Tce = time.time() - Tcs
59          print(f'group {c:2d} took {Tce:.3f} sec')
60      client.close()
61
62      # reassemble the image
63      img = np.empty((N,N), dtype=np.uint8)
64      for i in range(len(results)):
65          my_rows, img_rows = results[i]
66          img[my_rows,:] = img_rows
```

```
67
68      print(f'{time.time() - T_s:.3f}  {N:5d}')
69      return
70      plt.imshow(img)
71      plt.show()
72   if __name__ == '__main__': main()
```

Our 35,000 x 35,000 array of uint8's means our cluster will generate, then transmit more than 1 GB of data. Clearly, network speed will affect performance. Two runs demonstrate this quite vividly. The job on the left was launched from my home computer and executed on my cluster of 18 VMs on DigitalOcean's cloud. The job on the right was launched from one of the VMs directly, so all traffic stayed on DigitalOcean's network. Of course, since these VMs only have 1 GB of memory, I had to skip the final assembly of the img matrix.

Launched on Home Computer:	Launched on DigitalOcean Computer:
chunk 0 took 7.500 sec	chunk 0 took 7.929 sec
chunk 1 took 5.564 sec	chunk 1 took 2.427 sec
chunk 2 took 4.944 sec	chunk 2 took 1.955 sec
chunk 3 took 4.873 sec	chunk 3 took 1.851 sec
chunk 4 took 4.978 sec	chunk 4 took 1.808 sec
chunk 5 took 5.834 sec	chunk 5 took 1.806 sec
chunk 6 took 5.280 sec	chunk 6 took 1.812 sec
chunk 7 took 4.559 sec	chunk 7 took 1.817 sec
chunk 8 took 4.531 sec	chunk 8 took 1.805 sec
chunk 9 took 5.989 sec	chunk 9 took 3.032 sec
chunk 10 took 4.997 sec	chunk 10 took 3.456 sec
chunk 11 took 4.574 sec	chunk 11 took 2.697 sec
chunk 12 took 4.459 sec	chunk 12 took 2.612 sec
chunk 13 took 4.799 sec	chunk 13 took 2.114 sec
chunk 14 took 5.020 sec	chunk 14 took 1.842 sec
chunk 15 took 4.785 sec	chunk 15 took 1.777 sec
83.715 35000	40.819 35000

My original estimate for solving the Numba-accelerated Mandelbrot set of this size on a single core of my home computer was 440 seconds, so the 83 seconds using 18 cloud-based computers represents a speed-up of 5.3. Disappointing, perhaps, but a clear demonstration that performance for problems involving substantial data transfers depends heavily on the network.

14.13.7 Example 4: Finite Element Frequency Domain Response

As in the multicore sections earlier, I'll use a finite element model subject to a dynamic load to represent a more real-world distributed memory computing problem. Toy problems for summing prime numbers and computing the Mandelbrot set are instructional but don't deal with complications that arise with large input sets.

Simulating the behavior of structures subject to a sudden acceleration, for example, an impact, or the firing of explosive bolts (common in spacecraft that release articulating members) is tricky. A finite element model suited to such work needs small elements to capture the short wavelengths of the resulting structural waves. The spectral content of impacts and explosions is high, so if a modal analysis were undertaken, many eigensolutions—often an impractical number—would be needed. Alternatively, one could attempt a direct time integration (e.g., with the Newmark-beta method) of the equilibrium equation of motion:

$$M\frac{d^2u}{dt^2} + C\frac{du}{dt} + Ku(t) = P(t)$$

$u(t)$ and $P(t)$ are the time-varying response and applied load. A third possibility is where M, C, and K are finite element mass, damping, and stiffness matrices, and perfect for large parallel computers: transform the equilibrium equation to the frequency domain where each of the many frequencies can be worked on independently. Such a transformation can be done with the substitution:

$$u(t) = \sum_{n=1}^{N} \hat{u} e^{i\omega_n t}$$

which leaves a series of N linear equations

$$-\omega_n^2 M\hat{u}_n + i\omega_n C\hat{u}_n + K\hat{u}_n = P(\omega_n)$$

Or

$$\left[K + i\omega_n C - \omega_n^2 M\right]\hat{u}_n = P(\omega_n)$$

where $P(\omega)$ is the Fourier transform of the load time history $P(t)$. Our time domain second-order differential equation now becomes a collection of linear equations which are independent at each of the N frequencies ω_n. The frequency band must be sufficiently wide to capture the full spectral content of the applied load, and the frequency interval small enough that all motion has been dampened to a quiescent state in the equivalent time domain.

In theory, if we had N processors, we could give each processor one frequency and get our solution $\hat{u}$ in the amount of time it takes to solve the system of equations just once. The time domain solution $u(t)$ can then be recovered with an inverse Fourier transform of $\hat{u}$ [2]. In reality, thousands of frequencies are needed for accurate solutions, and a few of us have access to that many processors. Also, the data volumes are substantial; the overhead of transmitting matrices to a processor so it can solve a system of linear equations just once is unlikely to be worthwhile.

For our final example, we'll use dask to solve a direct frequency response problem. This example is more representative of real workloads because, unlike the earlier problems, this one requires large amounts of input data to be sent to the workers.

14.13.7.1 A Notional Satellite Model

As a sample problem, we'll model a satellite whose solar panel extension mechanism is to be released by an explosive bolt. The satellite has a delicate sensor in the middle. Our objective is to measure the deformation of the sensor's mount as a result of the detonation.

Once again, we'll use `triangle` to tessellate a boundary file, `satellite/satellite.poly`, to a series of increasingly finer finite element meshes:

```
triangle -pa0.8        satellite.poly
triangle -rpq34a0.2    satellite.1
triangle -rpq34a0.1    satellite.2
triangle -rpq34a0.05   satellite.3
triangle -rpq34a0.02   satellite.4
triangle -rpq34a0.015  satellite.5
triangle -rpq34a0.005  satellite.6
```

After the last command, we'll have a pair of files `satellite.7.ele` and `satellite.7.node`, that define a model with about 600,000 degrees of freedom that we'll use for the analysis. The model will be fully constrained at the base of the adapter ring (the lowest horizontal edge) and loaded (meaning the location of the explosive bolt) at the elbow joint on the left. We'll only save deformation at the few nodes that represent the sensor's mount which is the small stem supporting the central cutout. The following figure is of the second refinement of the model, `satellite.2`, which has about 7600 degrees of freedom (roughly 1% of our 600k DOF model).

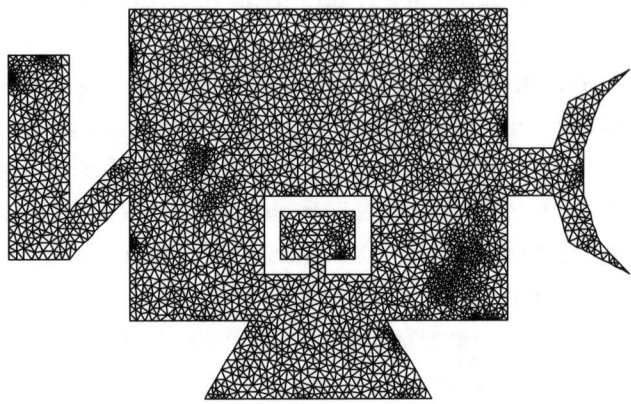

Time and frequency domain plots of the explosive bolt's load history look like this:

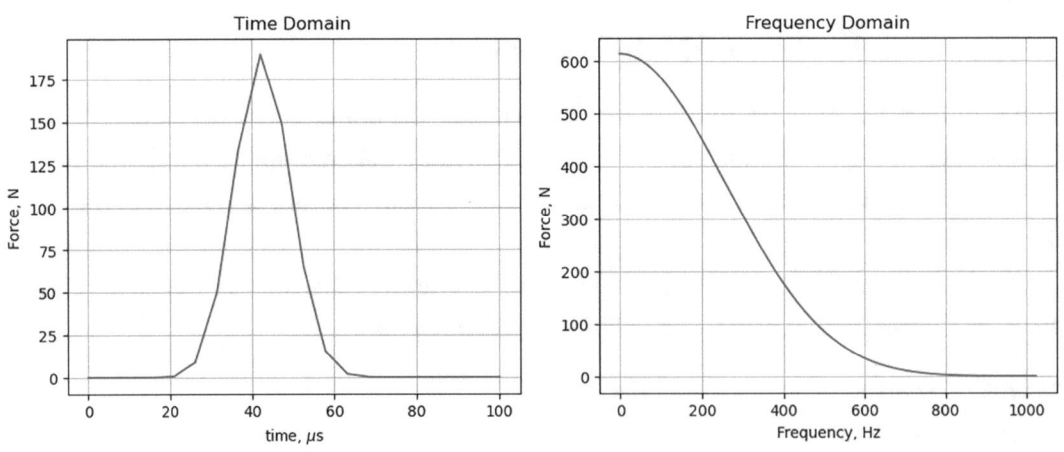

14.13.7.2 An Outline of the Problem

Here's the pseudocode for the direct frequency response problem:

```
load model data from file
load force time history from file
compute FFT of force history
determine suitable frequency interval and range
assemble K, C, M matrices
loop over frequencies:
    KCM = K - i*omega*C + omega^2*M
    solve x = KCM\b
    store subset of x
```

Which part should be done sequentially on the parent (also referred to as the client, or driver) program and which should be sent to the remote workers? A couple of strategies come to mind: (1) send the model data and force history files to the remote computers and have them solve the entire problem from beginning to end but only portions of the frequency loop, or (2) do everything before the frequency loop on the client, then send the matrices and load history to the remote computers to run their portions of the frequency loop.

Both approaches are feasible, especially since the steps before the frequency loop can be done relatively quickly on a single computer.

Say you're tackling this problem in MATLAB where you already have the entire solution coded in m-files, but it runs too slowly on your computer. You can use Python and dask to distribute the work to a cluster, but the remote computing part has to be written in Python. Now the decision boils down to (1) translate the entire application to Python or (2) write a linear equation wrapper in Python. While I like Python, I like to avoid extra work even more. In this situation, I'd definitely leave the majority of the direct frequency response program in MATLAB and only do the linear algebra part in Python.

14.13.7.3 Sending Large Inputs to Remote Computers

Our solution strategy will be to send each remote computer a subset of frequencies, ω_n; the three finite element matrices K, C, and M; load vector b; the load spectrum $\hat{P}_n$; and the list of degrees of freedom at which we want the response. Unlike the examples for prime number summation and Mandelbrot set, for this problem we have to send huge arrays totalling hundreds of megabytes or more to each worker. (A .mat file of K, C, M, and b for satellite.7 is 224 MB.) Fortunately, dask has a data distribution mechanism—a client's .scatter() method followed by a client_submit()—to handle this situation. The following code fragments show the conventional method to send data to remote workers on the left and the data distribution method on the right:

Python; Dask Without Scatter:	Python; Dask with Scatter:
| ```
client = Client(cluster)
for i in range(n_jobs):
  job = dask.delayed(solve)(
    K, C, M, b, omega_subset[i])
  tasks.append(job)
results = dask.compute(*tasks)
``` | ```
client = Client(cluster)
client.wait_for_workers(n_jobs)
KCMb_dist = client.scatter(
  [K, C, M, b], broadcast=True)
for i in range(n_jobs):
  job = client.submit(solve2,
    KCMb_dist, omega_subset[i])
  tasks.append(job)
results = client.gather(tasks)
``` |

The regular dask code on the left lets the scheduler serialize the calling arguments to solve() and send them to the workers. If the arguments take a lot of memory, as ours do, you'll see dask warnings and the code may hang. The code on the right does a few extra steps. First, after creating the client, it waits until the requested workers are ready. It then passes a list of our large variables to the scatter method for distribution to all workers before the solver is invoked. The solver function itself differs slightly in that the arrays are packed into a single list which has to be unpacked by the remotely executing function. Instead of receiving the matrices as on the left, the solver working with the previously scattered data would take arguments as shown on the right:

Python:	Python, Using Prescattered Data:
`def solve(K, C, M, b, omega):`	`def solve2(KCMb, omega):` `    K, C, M, b = KCMb`

14.13.7.4 Subdividing Work to Minimize Data Movement

We've taken care to predistribute our matrices to each remote computer. The last thing we want is to have the dask scheduler make more calls to the solver, and therefore possibly transfer more data, than are strictly necessary. To achieve this goal, we'll submit exactly one dask job for each computer in our cluster and have that job run a subset of the frequencies.

We'll spread frequencies across processors the same way we distributed rows of the Mandelbrot domain, namely, by creating subsets that stride by the number of computers involved. If `Hertz` is the array of frequencies and we have `n_jobs` processors, then processor `i` will get the slice of terms shown here:

MATLAB:	Python:
`Hz_subset = Hertz(i:n_jobs:end);`	`Hz_subset = Hertz[i::n_jobs]`

14.13.7.5 Subsetting Results from the Remote Computers

Finite element direct frequency response solutions can be enormous, even for modestly sized models. The complex double-precision frequency domain displacement vector $\hat{u}$ takes $N_{dof} \times N_{freq} \times 16$ bytes. Our 600k degree of freedom model at 4092 frequencies would take 40 GB.

Both dask and MATLAB can store and work with arrays larger than memory, but there's rarely a need to store everything in a direct frequency response analysis. There the goal is to measure displacement (and from it, derived quantities like velocity, acceleration, strain) over time at critical locations rather than at every node. In our case, we just want the response at the sensor mount. We'll therefore subset our solution $\hat{u}$ after computing results to just a critical list of user-provided degrees of freedom. This will be done by passing the solver routine an extra list of indices, `keep_dof`, which identify the rows of $\hat{u}$ to return.

The center of the stem holding the sensor in our finite element model is at (23.5, 10.5). We can get the degree of freedom list by first getting the indices of nodes around that point, say within ±0.5 units, then inflating the node list to a degree of freedom list with the simple rule that horizontal DOF IDs are twice the node ID and vertical DOF are twice the node ID plus 1. The DOFs found this way correspond to the unconstrained model. The solution DOF set is smaller because the constrained DOF, those belonging to the base of the adapter ring, have been removed. The dictionary u_to_c maps unconstrained DOF to constrained DOF, so we can use that to get the correct DOF in our solution set:

MATLAB:

```
keep_nodes = np.argwhere((np.abs(23.5 - node_xy[:,0]) < 1.5) *
                         (np.abs(10.5 - node_xy[:,1]) < 1.5)).ravel()
keep_dof_full = sorted(np.hstack([keep_nodes*2, keep_nodes*2+1]))
keep_dof = sorted([u_to_c[_] for _ in keep_dof_full]) # constrained DOF
```

Python:

```
keep_nodes = np.argwhere((np.abs(23.5 - node_xy[:,0]) < 0.5) *
                         (np.abs(10.5 - node_xy[:,1]) < 0.5)).ravel()
keep_dof    = sorted(np.hstack([keep_nodes*2, keep_nodes*2+1]))
```

np.argwhere() always returns a two-dimensional array of indices even if, as in our case, the input array has only one dimension. The .ravel() method strips the extraneous dimension. After that, we can subset the results by keeping only the terms we want from the solver. The Python solution array could have been indexed the same way as MATLAB, but index chaining (Section 3.4.5) saves an intermediate step.

MATLAB:	Python, Subsetted Ax=b:

`KCM = K+1j*omega*C-omega**2*M;`
 `xfull = KCM\(b*P);`
 `x   = xfull(keep_dof);`
	`from scikits import umfpack`
	 `KCM = K+1j*omega*C-omega**2*M`
	 `LU = umfpack.splu(KCM)`
	 `x   = LU.solve(b*P)[keep_dof]`

Regarding the solver: I picked UMFPACK's linear equation solver over than the one from SciPy since the UMFPACK solver is faster with complex matrices. It can be found in the `scikit-umfpack` package.

14.13.7.6 A Parallel Solver Module

The pseudocode of Section 14.13.7.2 presents a simple algorithm: loop over a collection of frequencies and at each one sum matrices together and then solve the resulting sparse complex system of equations.

For the sake of flexibility—and an eye out for later use in MATLAB—I organized the solver code in a Python module, `pysolve.py`, that has three functions:

- **remote_solve()** takes the user's top-level inputs (matrices K, C, M, load vector b, frequency-dependent load magnitude P, the list of frequencies at which to solve, and the degrees of freedom at which to report results), configures a dask cluster for n_jobs workers, waits until all workers are ready, distributes the large inputs to those workers, then calls submit_solve_jobs(). One instance of remote_ solve() runs on the computer submitting the job.

- **Submit_solve_jobs()** subdivides the frequency domain into n_jobs pieces, then submits a dask job to run solve_subset() on each piece. It waits for all workers to produce their solutions and then returns them to remote_solve(). One instance of submit_solve_jobs() runs on the computer submitting the job.

- **Solve_subset()** implements the for loop described in the pseudocode. It solves the system of equations on its given frequencies and returns the subsetted solution. When invoked from submit_solve_jobs(), one instance runs on each of n_jobs remote workers. Solve_subset() can also be invoked directly from a conventional, non-dask sequential program in which case only one instance runs.

Here's the code:

Python:

```python
1   # code/dask/pysolve.py
2   import numpy as np
3   from scikits import umfpack
4   from dask.distributed import Client, LocalCluster
5   def solve_subset(K,C,M,b, P_subset, Hertz_subset, keep_dof):
6       results_subset = np.zeros((len(keep_dof),len(P_subset)), dtype=np.complex128)
7       for i,(w,P) in enumerate(zip(Hertz_subset,P_subset)):
8           omega = 2*np.pi*w
9           KCM = K + 1j*omega*C - omega**2 * M
10          LU = umfpack.splu(KCM)
11          x   = np.squeeze( LU.solve(b*P)[keep_dof] )
12          results_subset[:,i] = x
13      return results_subset
14  def submit_solve_jobs(client, KCMb, P, Hertz, keep_dof, n_jobs):
15      K, C, M, b = KCMb
16      results = []
17      n_keep = len(keep_dof)
18      n_freq = len(Hertz)
19      x = np.zeros( (n_keep, n_freq), dtype=np.complex128)
20      results = []
21      for i in range(n_jobs):
22          Hertz_subset = Hertz[i::n_jobs]
23          P_subset     = P[i::n_jobs]
24          job = client.submit(solve_subset,
25                              K,C,M,b, P_subset, Hertz_subset, keep_dof)
26          results.append( job )
27      for i,x_subset in enumerate(client.gather(results)):
28          x[:,i::n_jobs] = x_subset
29      return x
30  def remote_solve(solve_with, n_jobs, K, C, M, b, P, Hertz, keep_dof):
31      if solve_with == 'localhost':
32          cluster = LocalCluster('127.0.0.1:8786')
```

```
33        elif solve_with == 'digitalocean':
34            cluster = LocalCluster('143.198.155.245:8786')
35        elif solve_with == 'coiled':
36            import coiled
37            #coiled.create_software_environment(
38            #    name="and-fe-env",
39            #      conda={ "channels": ["conda-forge", "defaults"],
40            #                 "dependencies": ["dask", "numba",
41            #                 "scikit-umfpack", "requests" ], },)
42            cluster = coiled.Cluster(n_workers=n_jobs,
                 software="and-fe-env")
43        client = Client(cluster)
44        client.wait_for_workers(n_jobs)
45        client.upload_file('pysolve.py')
46        KCMb = client.scatter([K, C, M, b], broadcast=True)
47        solnx = submit_solve_jobs(client, KCMb, P, Hertz,
              keep_dof, n_jobs)
48        client.close()
49        cluster.close()
50        return solnx
```

Organizing the code this way lets us use the same module for both sequential processing, where solve_subset() is called directly, and parallel processing—including parallel processing invoked from MATLAB, as we'll see in Section 14.14.

The compound if statement on lines 31–42 is part of a "walk before you run" strategy. Sending an untested parallel program to 1000 processors is seldom a good idea. Success comes incrementally: first, get the sequential algorithm working, then verify a parallel run on two or three cores of your local machine, then on a small cluster, and finally pull the trigger on a massive run after the smaller runs check out. The variable solve_with lets me choose the target dask cluster for the run I have in mind—a shakeout of new features or bug fixes on the local machine, an initial performance test on my DigitalOcean virtual machine cluster, or a production run on Coiled's cloud.

The Python driver which loads the satellite.7 node and element data, assembles the finite element model, applies constraints, then calls pycode.remote_solve() can be found in code/dask/run_fr_dask.py.

14.13.7.7 Running on Coiled's Cloud

Coiled, the company behind dask, offers a cloud service specifically for dask jobs. This is ideal for individuals or companies that lack access to a private cluster and want to avoid the complications of creating a dask-capable cluster on commercial clouds such as Amazon's AWS, Microsoft Azure, or Google Cloud. Better still, as of late 2021, Coiled offers its users 1000 CPU hours per month at no cost.

Using Coiled's cloud requires initial setup. First, create an account at their website.[23] Next, install the `coiled` Python module following instructions you'll receive by email on all the computers from which you plan to launch dask jobs.

The last setup step involves creating a custom software configuration that includes Python modules you need but are not included in Coiled's default configuration. The default includes NumPy, SciPy, Pandas, and many others but lacks Numba and UMFPACK. The commented lines 37–41 of the `pysolve.py` module listing show how I created my own custom environment, called `and-fe-env`, with extra modules. (An earlier experiment used the `requests` module but that didn't pan out.) The custom environment is created on Coiled's cloud the first time these lines run. This is a one-time step so the call to `coiled.create_software_environment()` can be commented out or deleted in later runs; your custom setup will be remembered and used in future runs when referenced by name with the `software = ` keyword to `coiled.Cluster()`. Perhaps it goes without saying, but when you submit your initial setup run, there's no need to use more than one or two workers.

14.13.7.8 Performance and Cost on Coiled's Cloud

When you submit a dask job to Coiled's cloud, you'll see this in your terminal:

```
: Creating Cluster. This might take a few minutes...
```

followed by a delay, possibly a long one. What's going on?

Your job runs after two conditions are met: (1) your job's container is created, and (2) the number of workers you requested is available. Upon receiving your job, Coiled creates a Docker image containing Python, your extra modules, and the code you submitted. This can take up to five minutes. Next, your job has to wait until the requested

---

[23] https://cloud.coiled.io/

number of workers is available. If you're running during prime time hours in the United States or requesting a huge number of workers, this delay could be substantial. If the delay exceeds 20 minutes, the dask job times out, and you'll need to resubmit.

The state of your job can be found by logging in to your Coiled account and visiting the Dashboard page. The "Num Workers" column shows the number of workers running your job. Additional details appear in log files which can be seen by hitting the "Logs" button on the right side of the job.

Another source of delay is the data distribution step. In our case, the call Python:

```
KCMb = client.scatter([K, C, M, b], broadcast=True)
```

in `pysolve.remote_solve()` takes about 200 seconds to send our 600k matrices to 100 workers, which works out to about 1 MB per second per 100 workers.

With this much overhead—creating a Docker image, waiting for workers, distributing large datasets—it is pretty clear there's no point in using Coiled's cloud for small problems.

Table 14-11 shows elapsed time for runs of the 600k `satellite.7` model for a range of frequencies and workers. The elapsed time measurement begins when the job is submitted and includes Coiled-related overhead of creating the Docker image and waiting for workers. The cost values are copied from Coiled's web-based Dashboard.

Table 14-11. *Elapsed time and cost for direct frequency response on Coiled's cloud*

Number of Workers	Number of Frequencies	Time [Seconds]	Cost [US$]
2	2	388.6	0.01
3	16	413.1	0.02
16	16	348.9	0.08
32	32	388.4	0.19
64	64	445.6	0.31
100	100	523.7	0.58
100	1024	740.1	1.21
100	2048	918.3	1.55

Some observations:

- The "price of admission" to run just a single frequency on 32 workers or less on the Coiled cloud is around 400 seconds.

- The time to solve the 600k system of equations on my Linux laptop is about 12 seconds per frequency using UMFPACK in Python and 15 seconds using MATLAB's sparse solver. 2048 frequencies would take about 7 hours on a single computer in Python and 8.5 hours in MATLAB. The 100 Coiled workers give us a speed-up of 26× over sequential Python and 33× over sequential MATLAB.

- Elapsed time to solve 2048 frequencies with 100 workers is only 1.75 greater than solving 100 frequencies. The baseline overhead still amounts to one-third of the overall time.

Bottom line: The Coiled cloud excels at solving large computational problems. Keep small problems on your local computer.

14.14 Recipe 14-2: Accelerating MATLAB with Python on Multiple Computers

MATLAB can send work to a dask cluster—and gain the same performance increases— as easily as Python can. The "work" sent by MATLAB must be implemented in Python though. In this recipe, we'll write MATLAB programs that submit the Python functions from the three example problems of Section 14.13 (sum prime factors, create a gigapixel Mandelbrot image, and solve a direct frequency response problem) to a dask cluster, then collect the solutions as MATLAB variables.

The first two examples, prime sums and the Mandelbrot set, will use this small bridge module from MATLAB to submit the jobs to dask and then to start the computations:

Python:

```python
# code/dask/bridge_dask.py
import dask
def delayed(Fn, *args):
    return dask.delayed(Fn)(*args);
def compute(delayed_tasks):
    return dask.compute(*delayed_tasks)
```

The third example, direct frequency response, requires a different strategy and does not use the bridge module.

14.14.1 Parallel Prime Sums with MATLAB

The following MATLAB program uploads the file my_fn.py to the dask cluster and then calls the same-named function within it, my_fn.my_fn(), to sum prime factors in the given interval.

Python:

```python
# code/dask/my_fn.py
from sympy import primefactors
import time
def my_fn(a, b, incr):
    Ts = time.time()
    s = 0
    for x in range(a,b,incr):
        s += sum(primefactors(x))
    return s, time.time() - Ts
```

MATLAB:

```matlab
% code/dask/prime_dask.m
Im = @py.importlib.import_module;
ddist = Im('dask.distributed');
my_fn = Im('my_fn');
br_dask = Im('bridge_dask');
```

```
A = int64(2);
B = int64(1000000);
n_jobs = int64(11*18);

[S, elapsed] = do_parallel(A, B, n_jobs);

tic;
%client = ddist.Client('127.0.0.1:8786');
client = ddist.Client('143.198.155.245:8786');
client.upload_file('my_fn.py');

% submit the jobs to the cluster
output = py.list({});
incr = n_jobs;
for i = 0:n_jobs-1
    task = br_dask.delayed(my_fn.my_fn, A+i, B, incr);
    output.append(task);
end
output = br_dask.compute(output);
client.close()

% post-processing:   aggregate the partial solutions
S = 0;
mat_output = py2mat(output);
for i = 1:length(mat_output)
    partial_sum = mat_output{i}{1};
    S = S + partial_sum;
end
dT = toc;
fprintf('A=%d B=%d, %.3f sec\n', A, B, dT);
fprintf('S=%ld\n', S);
```

14.14.2 Parallel Gigapixel Mandelbrot with MATLAB

Here's a MATLAB program that sends the Numba-enhanced MB() function in MB_numba_
dask2.py shown in Section 14.13.6 to a dask cluster:

MATLAB:

```matlab
% code/dask/MB_numba_dask.m
Im = @py.importlib.import_module;
ddist = Im('dask.distributed');
np     = Im('numpy');
br_dask = Im('bridge_dask');
MB_py = Im('MB_numba_dask2');

N = int64( 35000 );
Tc = tic;
nR = N; nC = N;
Re_limits = np.array({-0.7440, -0.7433});
Im_limits = np.array({ 0.1315,  0.1322});
n_groups = 16;
n_jobs_per_group = 18;
n_jobs = n_jobs_per_group*n_groups;
%client = ddist.Client('127.0.0.1:8786');
client = ddist.Client('143.198.155.245:8786');
results = py.list({});
for c = 1:n_groups
  tasks  = py.list({});
  Tcs = tic;
  for i = 1:n_jobs_per_group
    job = br_dask.delayed(MB_py.MB, nC, Re_limits, ...
        nR, Im_limits, 255, (c-1)*n_jobs_per_group+i-1, n_jobs);
    tasks.append(job);
  end
  results.extend( br_dask.compute(tasks) )
  Tce = toc(Tcs);
  fprintf('group %2d took %.3f sec\n', c-1, Tce)
end
client.close();

% reassemble the image
img = zeros(N,N, 'uint8');
```

```
Tps = tic;
for i = 1:length(results)
  my_rows  = py2mat(results{i}{1}) + 1; % 0-indexing to 1
  img_rows = py2mat(results{i}{2});
  img(my_rows,:) = img_rows;
end
Tpe = toc(Tps);
fprintf('py2mat conversion took %.3f\n', Tpe);
Te = toc(Tc);
fprintf('%.3f  %5d\n', Te, N);
imshow(img)
```

Performance is worse than the pure Python solution (which took 84 seconds) because MATLAB has to convert the 1.1 GB img array from a Python-native to MATLAB-native variable. Without this conversion time, performance would be the same:

```
>> MB_numba_dask
group   0 took 5.658 sec
group   1 took 6.278 sec
group   2 took 4.812 sec
group   3 took 5.495 sec
group   4 took 4.746 sec
group   5 took 5.028 sec
group   6 took 4.982 sec
group   7 took 5.098 sec
group   8 took 4.911 sec
group   9 took 5.036 sec
group  10 took 4.923 sec
group  11 took 4.790 sec
group  12 took 4.946 sec
group  13 took 4.530 sec
group  14 took 4.528 sec
group  15 took 5.192 sec
py2mat conversion took 30.253
111.463   35000
```

Recall the 5k x 5k performance time of 112 seconds for MATLAB from Table 14-1. Here, with the help of Python and an 18-node cluster, MATLAB can solve a problem 49x larger in the same amount of time. Much of the performance boost comes from Numba running the MB() function much faster, while the rest from the number of computer themselves.

One advantage MATLAB has over Python for this problem is that MATLAB is able to render the gigapixel image. matplotlib in Python fails with an obscure error.

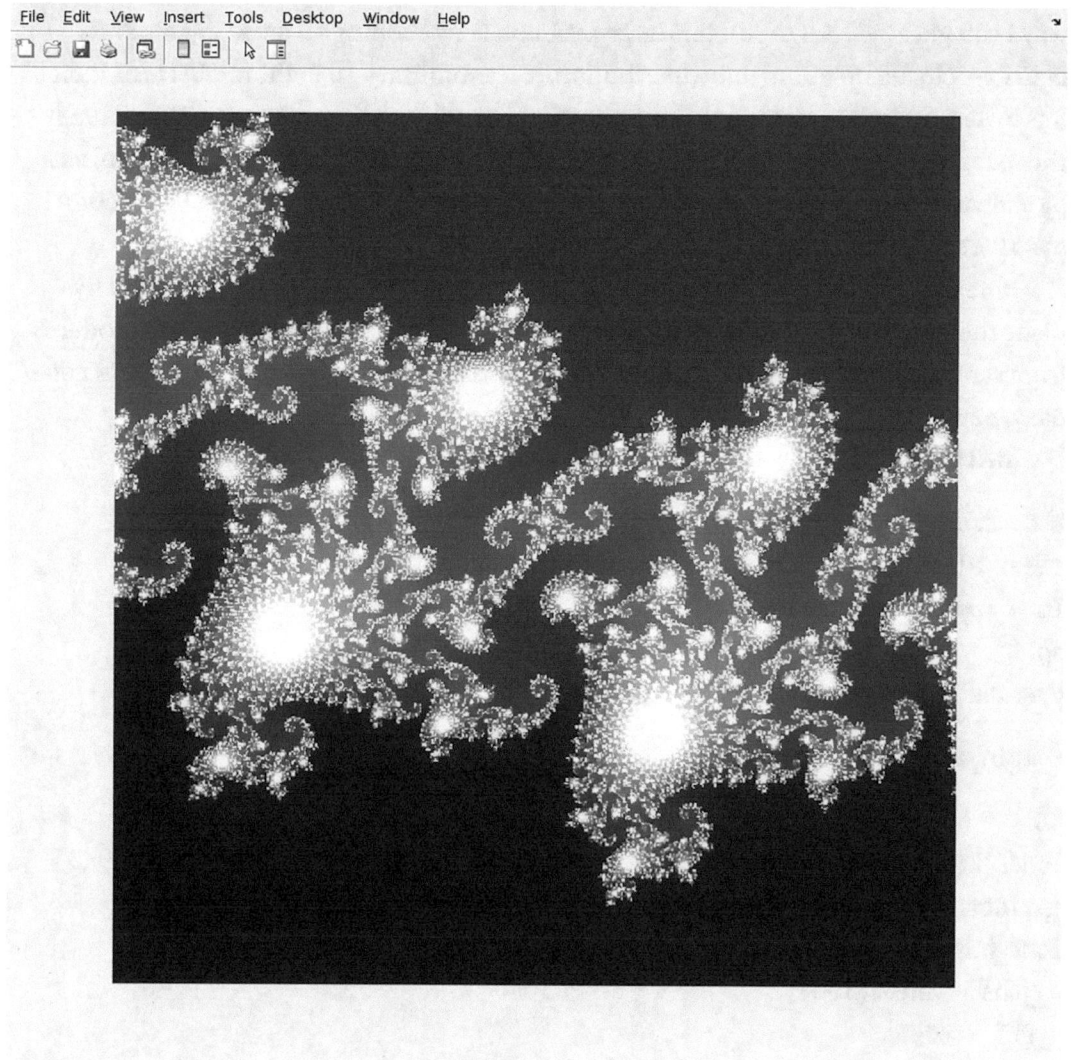

14.14.3 Parallel Direct Frequency Response with MATLAB

The previous two MATLAB-with-dask examples imported the Python dask module directly into MATLAB and from there submitted jobs to, and collected results from, the dask cluster.

That does not work with the much more substantial direct frequency response problem. For unknown reasons, the Python-based workers for this problem lose connection with the MATLAB-based dask `cluster` variable, and the job fails. The only way I can get MATLAB to run this large problem is by keeping all dask objects and activity—cluster creation, data distribution, job submittal—in Python. MATLAB then has to access the dask-based solver indirectly through a Python wrapper. This actually the main reason for organizing the direct frequency response solver code of `pysolve.py` shown in Section 14.13.7.6 into the three functions. The `remote_solve()` function in `pysolve.py` is the wrapper MATLAB needs.

Here is the MATLAB code that solves the direct frequency response problem by using the Python-based dask solver. Rather than recreating the finite element model from scratch, we'll load matrices from `.mat` files created with the Python program `code/dask/save_KCMb.py`.

MATLAB:

```
% code/dask/run_fr_dask.m
clear all
Im = @py.importlib.import_module;
np      = Im('numpy');
pysolve = Im('pysolve');

T_main_s = tic;

%%
load('KCMb_7.mat') % K, C, M, b, keep_dof
fprintf('Keeping response at %d DOF\n', length(keep_dof))
load_history = load('load_hist_smoothed.txt');
n_jobs = int64(100);
n_FFT = 4096;
solve_with = "coiled";
% solve_with = "localhost";
% solve_with = "digitalocean";
```

```
%%
n_freq = int64(floor(n_FFT/2));
dT     = 5.0e-4;    % time between each load_history point
Time   = 0:dT:dT*n_FFT;
Fs     = 1/dT;      % sampling frequency Hz
Hertz = linspace(0, Fs/2, n_freq); % only to Nyquist
dHz    = Hertz(2);
P = fft(load_history);
P_Nyq = P(1:n_freq);
n_dof = size(M,1);
fprintf('Time: %d times, 0.0 to %.6f sec steps of %.6f sec\n', n_FFT,
Time(end), dT)
fprintf('Freq: %d freq, 0.0 to %.1f Hz steps of %.1f Hz\n', n_freq,
Hertz(end), dHz)

% convert MATLAB-native arrays to Python-native
b = rand(n_dof,1);
K = mat2py(K);
C = K * 0.004; % proportional damping
M = mat2py(M);
b = np.array(b);
P_Nyq = mat2py(P_Nyq);
Hertz = np.array(Hertz);
keep_dof = np.array(keep_dof).astype(np.int64);

x = pysolve.remote_solve(solve_with, n_jobs, K, C, M, b, P_Nyq, Hertz,
keep_dof);
x = py2mat(x);

fprintf('%d frequencies took %.3f s\n', n_freq, toc(T_main_s))
```

Performance and cost resemble the values in Table 14-11. The load on Coiled's cloud causes time and cost variations that are beyond our control.

As mentioned in Section 14.13.7.8, the time to run 2048 frequencies on a single computer in MATLAB is about 8.5 hours. With help from Python and 100 workers on Coiled's cloud, the time drops tois about 15 minutes, a 33 × speed increase.

Table 14-12. *Elapsed time and cost for MATLAB-based direct frequency response on Coiled's cloud*

Number of Workers	Number of Frequencies	Time [Seconds]	Cost [US$]
3	16	402.1	0.02
64	64	472.1	0.50
100	100	628.0	0.88
100	1024	743.0	0.95
100	2048	940.2	1.60

14.15 References

[1]   Emery D. Berger. *Scalene: Scripting-Language Aware Profiling for Python.* 2020. arXiv: `2006 . 03879 [cs.PL]`. URL: `https://github.com/plasma-umass/scalene`

[2]   James F. Doyle. *Wave Propagation in Structures.* Springer-Verlag, 1989.

[3]   Serge Guelton et al. "Pythran: Enabling static optimization of scientific python programs." In: *Computational Science & Discovery* 8.1 (2015), p. 014001.

[4]   Jonathan Richard Shewchuk. "Triangle: Engineering a 2D Quality Mesh Generator and Delaunay Triangulator." In: *Applied Computational Geometry: Towards Geometric Engineering.* Ed. by Ming C. Lin and Dinesh Manocha. Vol. 1148. Lecture Notes in Computer Science. From the First ACM Workshop on Applied Computational Geometry. Springer-Verlag, May 1996, pp. 203–222. URL: `www.cs.cmu.edu/˜quake/triangle.html`

CHAPTER 15

Language Pitfalls

15.1 Troublesome Language Features

Neither MATLAB nor Python are ideal languages. Both have annoying and downright dangerous aspects—at least for novice programmers unfamiliar with more subtle aspects of the languages' designs. Detractors of one or the other language are keen to point out the other's flaws while brushing off criticism of their preferred language.

15.2 MATLAB

- Dangerous: Mixed-type mathematical expressions are typecast *downward* instead of upward.

```
>> a = uint8(1) - 0.6
a =

    uint8

    0
```

The result of 0 instead of 0.4 is astonishing (or, more plainly put, flat-out wrong). MATLAB stands alone in this design choice. C, C++, Fortran, Go, Java, JavaScript, Julia, Mathematica, OCaml, Python+NumPy, R, Rust, and Scala all typecast upward and yield the expected result of a floating-point value of 0.4 for the preceding calculation. It goes without saying that MATLAB's downcasting can lead unsuspecting developers to incorrect results.

© Albert Danial 2022
A. Danial, *Python for MATLAB Development*, https://doi.org/10.1007/978-1-4842-7223-7_15

- Dangerous: MATLAB's "every conceivable function exists in the namespace" can cause unexpected behavior when running the same m-file on computers with the same version of MATLAB but different toolboxes.

- Annoying: While an .m file may contain multiple functions, none of these may be called from other .m files unless the file with these functions is converted into a class. Code in large projects that don't embrace object-oriented programming ends up spread over hundreds of .m files. This adds logistical hassle to code editing, debugging, and project file management.

- Annoying: Matrix slices inherit the dimensions of the original matrix rather than the dimension of the slice itself. For example, if we create a 4D matrix and then extract a 1D slice along each dimension, the result has either two, three, or four dimensions:

```
>> a = rand(3,4,5,6);
>> size(a)
     3     4     5     6

>> size(a(:,1,1,1))
     3     1

>> size(a(1,:,1,1))
     1     4

>> size(a(1,1,:,1))
     1     1     5

>> size(a(1,1,1,:))
     1     1     1     6
```

This causes problems for functions such as plot() that cannot handle more than two dimensions:

```
>> plot(a(:,1,1,1))    % plot appears
>> plot(a(1,:,1,1))    % plot appears
>> plot(a(1,1,:,1))
Error using plot
Data cannot have more than 2 dimensions.
```

To get the desired behavior—a slice with just one dimension in this example—one must explicitly call `squeeze()` on the slice.

- Annoying: The default emacs keybindings (*control*-w and *control*-y to cut and paste; *control*-x *control*-s to save, and so on) irritate new MATLAB users. The rest of the world has adopted Windows keybindings (*control*-c and *control*-v to cut and paste; *control*-s to save, etc.) for GUI applications. Although the MATLAB IDE allows one to change the keybinding to Windows style (Home/Environment/ Preferences/Keyboard/Shortcuts/Active Settings/Windows Default Set), a few users seem to be aware of this and continue with the default.

- Annoying: One cannot cut and paste function definitions to the MATLAB prompt—"Error: Function definition not supported in this context. Create functions in code file." This impedes rapid sandbox testing of simple functions.

- Annoying: One cannot control whether arguments passed to MATLAB functions are pass-by-value or pass-by-reference.[1] Technically, all arguments are pass-by-reference, but MATLAB's just-in-time (JIT) compiler employs copy-on-write logic that may or may not honor the code's repeated use of input and output arguments. The performance penalty can be severe if the JIT compiler decides to copy rather than use a variable in-place.

- Annoying: It is not possible to determine which toolboxes a MATLAB program needs unless the toolboxes are already installed. In other words, if one receives a MATLAB program from an external source, the `matlab.codetools.requiredFilesAndProducts()` function only reports toolbox dependencies in the program for toolboxes found on the computer running the function.

- Annoying: The keyword end closes index ranges, classes, functions, if blocks, for loops, while loops, switch/case statements, try/catch blocks, and possibly other language constructs. While the MATLAB IDE makes it easy to see what construct an end closes, viewing an m-file with a less sophisticated editor or on paper, a web page, a PDF or Word document can make this pairing quite challenging.

---

[1] `https://blogs.mathworks.com/loren/2007/03/22/in-place-operations-on-data/`

- Annoying: Is it a function or a data structure? MATLAB's use of parentheses to pass arguments to a function *and* to index matrices and cell arrays makes it impossible to look at code, for example, grF(x), and tell whether the symbol grF is a function or a data container. In Python, one can immediately identify grF(x) as a function call and grF[x] as an indexed data container.

- Annoying: The MATLAB File Exchange hosted by The MathWorks is a helpful repository of m-files contributed by users. Unlike other code sharing sites such as GitHub or SourceForge, downloads from the File Exchange require an authenticated login. This nuisance inhibits MATLAB code sharing.

15.3 Python

- Dangerous: Lists and NumPy arrays are bounds-checked when indexed by scalar indices, but not index ranges. This can allow errors to propagate silently through a program (Section 4.3.6).

- Dangerous: When the right-hand side of an equals sign is a data structure, the variable on the left-hand side becomes a *reference* to the right-hand side, not a copy of it (Section 4.8). Thus, if A is a list, dictionary, NumPy array, and so on, the assignment $B = A$ leaves one with two variables that point to the data. Changes to A become changes to B and *vice versa*. To have B contain a copy of A's data, one must import the copy module and use its copy() or deepcopy() functions. Developers unaware of Python's reference copy behavior are likely to see corrupted data and incorrect results from their code.

- Annoying: Index slices M:N and calls to range(N) and np.arange(N) are maddening to MATLAB programmers who expect N to appear. The "don't use the end value" behavior of these constructions takes a long time to get used to.

- Annoying: NumPy and SciPy both have linear algebra submodules called linalg with common functions but different capabilities. For example, scipy.linalg.eig() can solve both standard ($Ax = \lambda x$) and general ($Ax = \lambda Bx$) eigenvalue problems, while numpy.linalg.eig() only solves the standard problem. At a minimum, the built-in documentation for both functions should have a "See also" entry that refers to its companion in the other module.

- Annoying: Compared to MATLAB's comprehensive implementation of sparse matrices, Python's sparse matrices feel like second-class citizens.

- Annoying: Typecasting NumPy arrays requires a different notation than typecasting scalars. These examples demonstrate the syntax for converting scalars and arrays from integers to doubles:

```
In : I_scalar = 4  # 64 bit integer
In : I_array  = np.array(([5, 6]), dtype=np.int64)

In : D_scalar = np.double(I_scalar)        # <- type cast scalar
In : D_array = I_array.astype(np.double)   # <- type cast array
```

The I.astype(np.double) notation is not intuitive. It would be clearer if one could just write np.float(I) to typecast a NumPy array as well as a scalar to a float.

- Annoying: Virtual environments are a drag. They add unwelcome complexity by forcing one to fragment collections of modules among multiple environments and then having to remember which environment is capable doing.

- Annoying: Compared to the uniformly high quality of built-in MATLAB documentation, documentation for the many Python modules one needs for science and engineering work varies widely in quality, style, and location. While a good Internet connection and web browser often yield answers to complex Python questions quickly, developers on isolated networks struggle in this regard.

APPENDIX A

MATLAB/Python Recipe Index

The following recipes show hybrid MATLAB/Python solutions to problems the core MATLAB product cannot solve on its own. Other solutions are, of course, possible using toolboxes, posts to the File Exchange,[1] projects on GitHub, and so on.

Several solutions use the py2mat.m Python-to-MATLAB variable converter (Appendix D), so this utility should be placed on the MATLAB search path.

Section	Title
7.2	Read YAML files
7.3	Write YAML files
7.4	Read an ini file
7.5	Write an ini file
7.8	Write an .xlsx file
7.12	CRUD with a SQLite database
7.18	TCP server
7.20	CRUD with a PostgreSQL database
7.21	CRUD with a MongoDB database
7.22	Interact with Redis

---

[1] www.mathworks.com/matlabcentral/fileexchange/

© Albert Danial 2022
A. Danial, *Python for MATLAB Development*, https://doi.org/10.1007/978-1-4842-7223-7

Section	Title
11.6	Curve fitting with `differential_evolution()`
11.8	Weighted least squares
11.11	Solving simultaneous nonlinear equations
11.15	Using SymPy in MATLAB
11.16	Compute Laplace transforms
11.18	Using `pint` in MATLAB
12.6	Overlay contours on globe with Cartopy
12.7	Shade map regions by value with Cartopy
13.13	Maps with GeoPandas
14.12	Accelerating MATLAB with Python on a single computer
14.14	Accelerating MATLAB with Python on multiple computers

APPENDIX B

Generating Sample Data with Faker

Data-intensive algorithms need data, and lots of it, to test algorithmic correctness, assess performance, track memory use, estimate scale limits, and so on. Some algorithms need nothing more than large random matrices (Section 11.1.6.14), while others require realistic structured data.

The Python module faker[1] is a great resource for creating structured data. It has functions that can generate endless streams of names, addresses, phone numbers, nonsensical text, and many others. Table B-1 lists many of these functions.

Table B-1. *A subset of data creation methods in faker*

address()	file_extension()	mac_processor()
am_pm()	file_name()	military_ship()
bank_country()	file_path()	mime_type()
bban()	first_name()	month()
boolean()	fixed_width()	month_name()
bs()	format()	msisdn()
building_number()	free_email()	name()
catch_phrase()	free_email_domain()	paragraph()
city()	future_date()	password()
color()	future_datetime()	past_date()

(continued)

---

[1] https://github.com/joke2k/faker

© Albert Danial 2022
A. Danial, *Python for MATLAB Development*, https://doi.org/10.1007/978-1-4842-7223-7

Table B-1. (*continued*)

company()	hex_color()	phone_number()
company_email()	hexify()	port_number()
coordinate()	hostname()	postalcode()
country()	http_method()	pricetag()
country_code()	image_ url()	provider()
credit_card_expire()	ios_platform_token()	sentence()
credit_card_full()	ipv4()	ssn()
credit_card_number()	ipv4_network_class()	state()
credit_card_provider()	ipv4_private()	street_address()
cryptocurrency()	ipv4_public()	street_name()
csv()	ipv6()	street_suffix()
currency()	isbn10()	suffix()
date()	isbn13()	swift()
date_between()	iso8601()	text()
date_of_birth()	items()	time()
date_this_century()	itin()	timezone()
date_this_decade()	job()	tld()
date_this_month()	language_name()	unix_device()
date_this_year()	last_name()	unix_partition()
day_of_month()	latitude()	unix_time()
day_of_week()	latlng()	uri()
dga()	lexify()	url()
domain_name()	license_plate()	user_name()
ean()	linux_processor()	uuid4()
ean13()	locale()	word()
ean8()	longitude()	year()
email()	mac_address()	zipcode()

This brief example shows how to create five names and phone numbers:

Python:

```
from faker import Faker
fake = Faker()
Faker.seed(123)
for i in range(5):
    name  = fake.name()
    phone = fake.phone_number()
    print(f'{name:30s} {phone}')

# output:

Brandon Russell                068-855-0225
Mia Martin                     001-196-105-7101x220
Jeffrey Woods                  (045)873-9895x068
Joshua Hogan                   786.580.2174x255
Stacey Sharp                   503-915-0536x8804
```

Setting the random generator seed to a fixed value with Faker.seed() enables repeatable values—although the same seed value used on different Python installations will not necessarily yield the same output.

Faker is used in the Python and MATLAB programs that demonstrate interaction with the MongoDB database engine in Sections 7.19.2 and 7.21.

APPENDIX C

Finite Element Source Listing

Code to run the finite element examples can be found at the book's Github repository, `https://github.com/Apress/python-formatlab-development`. The file names are:

```
code/mesh/FE_model.m
code/mesh/load_model.m
code/mesh/Node.m
code/mesh/Rod_Elem.m
code/mesh/run_fem.m (main)
```

Python:

```
code/rod_fem/pure_python/make_mesh.py
code/rod_fem/pure_python/rod.py
```

© Albert Danial 2022
A. Danial, *Python for MATLAB Development*, https://doi.org/10.1007/978-1-4842-7223-7

Python-to-MATLAB and MATLAB-to-Python Variable Converters

The MATLAB function py2mat() converts native Python variables returned by calls to Python functions via MATLAB's py module into native MATLAB variables. Such a conversion is necessary if you want to perform MATLAB operations on values returned from Python.

mat2py() does the opposite and can be useful for converting MATLAB variables into equivalents that can be understood by Python functions.

Conversions from Python native to MATLAB native are demonstrated with the Python file demo_py2mat.py which has two functions. simple_vars() returns an integer, a floating-point value, a string, a list, a dictionary, a tuple, and a 2D NumPy array. nested_var() returns a list containing scalars and a dictionary which itself has compound values such as a NumPy array and a tuple.

Python:

```python
# file: code/matlab_py/demo_py2mat.py
import numpy as np
def simple_vars():
    I = 42
    F = np.e
    S = 'Red'
    L = [1, 2.2, 'green']
    D = {'A' : 65, 'B' : 66, 'Z' : 90}
    T = (225, 'blue')
```

A. Danial, *Python for MATLAB Development*, https://doi.org/10.1007/978-1-4842-7223-7

```python
    N = F*np.arange(12).reshape(3,4)
    return I, F, S, L, D, T, N
def nested_var():
    N = np.arange(12).reshape(3,4)
    return [1, 2.2, 'green',
            {'A' : 65, 'B' : 66,
             'N' : N,
             'Z' : (225, 'blue')},
            27.8]
def arrays():
    arr_int8       = np.array([1, 2], dtype=np.int8)
    arr_uint8      = np.array([1, 2], dtype=np.uint8)
    arr_int16      = np.array([1, 2], dtype=np.int16)
    arr_uint16     = np.array([1, 2], dtype=np.uint16)
    arr_int32      = np.array([1, 2], dtype=np.int32)
    arr_uint32     = np.array([1, 2], dtype=np.uint32)
    arr_int64      = np.array([1, 2], dtype=np.int64)
    arr_uint64     = np.array([1, 2], dtype=np.uint64)
    arr_float16    = np.array([1, 2], dtype=np.float16)
    arr_float32    = np.array([1, 2], dtype=np.float32)
    arr_float64    = np.array([1, 2], dtype=np.float64)
    arr_complex64  = np.array([1-1j, 2-2j], dtype=np.complex64)
    arr_complex128 = np.array([1-1j, 2-2j], dtype=np.complex128)
    return arr_int8      , \
           arr_uint8     , \
           arr_int16     , \
           arr_uint16    , \
           arr_int32     , \
           arr_uint32    , \
           arr_int64     , \
           arr_uint64    , \
           arr_float16   , \
           arr_float32   , \
           arr_float64   , \
           arr_complex64, \
           arr_complex128
```

First, let's see what happens if we call these functions from MATLAB and then try to use the Python return values without conversion:

MATLAB 2020b:

```
>> x = py.demo_py_to_mat.simple_vars();
>> x

x =

  Python tuple with no properties.

    (42, 2.718281828459045, 'Red', [1, 2.2, 'green'],
        {'A': 65, 'B': 66, 'Z': 90}, (225, 'blue'),
        array([[ 0.        ,  2.71828183,  5.43656366,  8.15484549],
            [10.87312731, 13.59140914, 16.30969097, 19.0279728 ],
            [21.74625463, 24.46453646, 27.18281828, 29.90110011]]))

>> I = x{1}; F = x{2}; S = x{3}; L = x{4}; D = x{5}; T = x{6}; N = x{7};

>> whos
  Name      Size          Bytes  Class               Attributes

  D         1x1               8  py.dict
  F         1x1               8  double
  I         1x1               8  py.int
  L         1x3               8  py.list
  N         1x1               8  py.numpy.ndarray
  S         1x3               8  py.str
  T         1x2               8  py.tuple
  x         1x7               8  py.tuple
```

The double-precision floating-point variable F is the only returned value that comes over directly as a native MATLAB variable. The Python integer, string, and NumPy array mostly behave like normal MATLAB variables or can be easily coerced into MATLAB-native variables with calls to int64(), double(), and string().

MATLAB 2020b:

```
>> I
I =
  Python int with properties:
    denominator: [1×1 py.int]
           imag: [1×1 py.int]
      numerator: [1×1 py.int]
           real: [1×1 py.int]

    42

>> I3 = I * 3
I3 =
    126

>> S
S =
  Python str with no properties.
    Red

>> fprintf('S = %s\n', S)
S = R
S = e
S = d

>> fprintf('S = %s\n', string(S))
S = Red

>> N
N =
  Python ndarray:
         0     2.7183     5.4366     8.1548
   10.8731    13.5914    16.3097    19.0280
   21.7463    24.4645    27.1828    29.9011
    Use details function to view the properties of the Python object.
    Use double function to convert to a MATLAB array.
```

```
>> sin(N)
Check for missing argument or incorrect argument data type in call to
function 'sin'.

>> sin(double(N))
ans =
            0      0.4108     -0.7490      0.9551
      -0.9925      0.8547     -0.5661      0.1775
       0.2425     -0.6196      0.8873     -0.9984
```

The list and dictionary can be converted to a MATLAB cell array and struct via cell() and struct():

MATLAB 2020b:

```
>> C = cell(L)
C =
  1×3 cell array
    {1×1 py.int}    {[2.2000]}    {1×5 py.str}
>> Str = struct(D)
Str =
  struct with fields:
    A: [1×1 py.int]
    B: [1×1 py.int]
    Z: [1×1 py.int]
```

These conversions are problematic though; although the containers are MATLAB native, their contents are not. Another wrinkle is the restrictive set of rules governing field names in a MATLAB struct. A MATLAB struct's field name must be a valid MATLAB variable name which means it must begin with a letter followed by letters, digits, and/ or underscores. However, Python dictionary keys, which struct() function will try to use for MATLAB field names, have no such restrictions; dictionary keys may be numeric, strings with arbitrary contents, even tuples of other items.

Let's look at the more complex example:

MATLAB 2020b:

```
>> x
x =
  Python list with no properties.
    [1, 2.2, 'green', {'A': 65, 'B': 66, 'N': array([[ 0,  1,  2,  3],
           [ 4,  5,  6,  7],
           [ 8,  9, 10, 11]]), 'Z': (225, 'blue')}, 27.8]
```

Superficially, it looks like x comes across cleanly. Internally, though, these are all native Python entities. To access the numeric array, for example, we have to use a Python dictionary accessor: x4.get('N').

My solution to this problem is the function py2mat(). Within MATLAB, it recursively descends a Python-native variable until it reaches primitives (integers, floats, strings, datetimes) and then applies MATLAB's conversion functions to build up a corresponding MATLAB variable. Care is taken to map Python dictionary keys to valid MATLAB field names; key names that violate MATLAB variable name rules are replaced by the string K<i><name> where <i> is a six-digit, zero-padded index of key position and <name> is as much of the original key name as can be preserved.

The returned value from py2mat.m is a pure MATLAB variable, cell, or struct.

MATLAB 2020b:

```
% file code/matlab_py/py2mat.m
function [x_mat] = py2mat(x_py)
  Im = @py.importlib.import_module;
  np = Im('numpy');
  % Convert a native Python variable to an equivalent
  % native MATLAB variable.
  switch class(x_py)
      % Python dictionaries
      case 'py.dict'
      try
        % the obvious dict -> struct conversion only works
        % if the key string can be a MATLAB variable
        x_mat = struct(x_py);
```

```matlab
  catch EO
    % A failure most likely means a Python key is not
    % a proper MATLAB variable name. Go through them
    % individually
    key_index = int64(0);
    for key = cell(py.list(x_py.keys()))
      key_index = key_index + 1;
      v_name = string(key);
      if isvarname(v_name)
        x_mat.(v_name) = x_py.get(v_name);
      else
        % this key can't be used; replace it
        fixed = sprintf('K%06d_', key_index) + ...
                regexprep(string(key),'\W','_');
        x_mat.(fixed) = x_py.get(v_name);
      end
    end
  end
  fields = fieldnames(x_mat);
  for i = 1:length(fields)
    new_var = py2mat(x_mat.(fields{i}));
    x_mat = setfield(x_mat,fields{i}, new_var);
  end

% NumPy arrays and typed scalars
case 'py.numpy.ndarray'
  switch string(x_py.dtype.name)
    case "float64"
      x_mat = x_py.double;
    case "float32"
      x_mat = x_py.single;
    case "float16"
      % doesn't exist in matlab, upcast to float32
      x_mat = single(x_py.astype(np.float32));
    % only reals and logicals can be cast to arrays so
    % have to cast the rest to either single or double
```

```matlab
        case "uint8"
          x_mat = uint8(x_py.astype(np.float32));
        case "int8"
          x_mat = int8(x_py.astype(np.float32));
        case "uint16"
          x_mat = uint16(x_py.astype(np.float32));
        case "int16"
          x_mat = int16(x_py.astype(np.float32));
        case "uint32"
          x_mat = uint32(x_py.astype(np.float32));
        case "int32"
          x_mat = int32(x_py.astype(np.float32));
        case "uint64"
          x_mat = uint64(x_py.astype(np.float64));
        case "int64"
          x_mat = int64(x_py.astype(np.float64));
        % Complex types require a math operation to coerce the
        % real and imaginary components to contiguous arrays.
        % Use "+0" for minimal performance impact. Without this,
        % complex creation fails with
        %    Python Error: ValueError: ndarray is not contiguous
        case "complex64"
          x_mat = complex(single(x_py.real+0), single(x_py.imag+0));
        case "complex128"
          x_mat = complex(double(x_py.real+0), double(x_py.imag+0));
        case "complex256"
          fprintf('py2mat: MATLAB does not support quad precision
          complex\n')
          x_mat = [];
          return
        otherwise
          % gets here with np.float16, custom dtypes
          fprintf('py2mat: %s not recognized\n', ...
                  string(x_py.dtype.name));
          x_mat = [];
          return
    end
```

```matlab
% Scipy sparse matrices
case {'py.scipy.sparse.coo.coo_matrix', ...
      'py.scipy.sparse.csr.csr_matrix', ...
      'py.scipy.sparse.csc.csc_matrix', ...
      'py.scipy.sparse.dok.dok_matrix', ...
      'py.scipy.sparse.bsr.bsr_matrix', ...
      'py.scipy.sparse.dia.dia_matrix', ...
      'py.scipy.sparse.lil.lil_matrix', }
   ndims = x_py.get_shape();
   if length(ndims) ~= 2
       fprintf('py2mat: can only convert 2D sparse matrices\n')
       x_mat = [];
       return
   end
   nR = int64(ndims{1});
   nC = int64(ndims{2});
   x_py = x_py.tocoo();
   values = py2mat(x_py.data);
   if isempty(values)
       % gets here if trying to convert a complex256 sparse matrix
       return
   end
   % add 1 to row & col indices to go from 0-based to 1-based
   x_mat = sparse(single(x_py.row)+1, single(x_py.col)+1,
   values, nR, nC);

% Python sets, tuples, and lists
case {'cell', 'py.tuple', 'py.list'}
   [nR, nC] = size(x_py);
   x_mat = cell(nR,nC);
   for r = 1:nR
     for c = 1:nC
       x_mat{r,c} = py2mat(x_py{r,c});
     end
   end
```

```matlab
    % Python strings
    case 'py.str'
      x_mat = string(x_py);

    % Python integers
    case 'py.int'
      x_mat = x_py.int64;

    % Python floats (float64) -- same as matlab double
    case 'double'
      x_mat = x_py;

    case 'py.datetime.datetime'
      x_mat = datetime(int64(x_py.year), ...
                       int64(x_py.month), ...
                       int64(x_py.day), ...
                       int64(x_py.hour), ...
                       int64(x_py.minute),...
                       int64(x_py.second),...
                       int64(x_py.microsecond));
    % punt
    otherwise
      % return the original item? nothing?
      fprintf('py2mat: type "%s" not recognized\n', ...
              string(x_py.dtype.name));
      x_mat = [];
    % x_mat = x_py;
  end
end
```

The MATLAB-to-Python converter, mat2py.m, is as follows:

MATLAB 2020b:

```matlab
% code/matlab_py/mat2py.m
% Convert a MATLAB variable to an equivalent Python-native variable.
function [x_py] = mat2py(x_mat)
    Im = @py.importlib.import_module;
    np = Im('numpy');
```

```matlab
sp = Im('scipy.sparse');
dt = Im('datetime');
tz = Im('dateutil.tz');
x_py = np.array({});
switch class(x_mat)
    case 'char'
        x_py = py.bytes(x_mat,'ASCII');
    case 'string'
        x_py = py.str(x_mat);
    case 'datetime'
        int_sec = int64(floor(x_mat.Second));
        frac_sec = x_mat.Second - double(int_sec);
        micro_sec = int64(round(1e6 * frac_sec));
        if length(x_mat.TimeZone)
            tzinfo = tz.gettz(x_mat.TimeZone);
        else
            tzinfo = py.None;
        end
        x_py = dt.datetime(int64(x_mat.Year), int64(x_mat.Month), ...
                           int64(x_mat.Day) , int64(x_mat.Hour) , ...
                           int64(x_mat.Minute), int64(x_mat.
                           Second), ...
                           micro_sec, tzinfo)
    case {'double', 'single'}
        if issparse(x_mat)
            if ndims(x_mat) ~= 2
                fprintf('mat2py: can only convert 2D sparse
                matrices\n')
                return
        end
        [nR,nC] = size(x_mat);
        [i,j,vals] = find(x_mat);
        % subtract 1 to go from 1-based to 0-based indices
        py_I    = np.array(int64(i)-1);
        py_J    = np.array(int64(j)-1);
```

```matlab
        py_vals = mat2py(vals);
        py_dims = py.tuple({int64(nR), int64(nC)});
        py_IJ   = py.tuple({py_I, py_J});
        V_IJ    = py.tuple({py_vals, py_IJ});
        x_py = sp.coo_matrix(V_IJ,py_dims);
    elseif ismatrix(x_mat)
        if isreal(x_mat)
            x_py = np.array(x_mat);
        else
            x_py = np.array(real(x_mat)) + 1j*np.array(imag(x_mat));
        end
    end
    otherwise
        fprintf('mat2py: %s conversion is not implemented\n', ...
        class(x_mat))
    end % switch
end
```

A Utility to Patch Cartopy to Use requests

Run the following program in a matpy conda environment to modify Cartopy's img_tiles.py file to use the requests module to download image tiles. This allows MATLAB calls to Cartopy to download map image tiles without errors. Additionally, on Windows it modifies geos.py to set a library path correctly and avoid a DLL error.

Python:

```python
#!/usr/bin/env python
# code/bin/patch_cartopy.py
#
# Change the active cartopy installation so that:
#   1. Replace urllib with requests to download image tiles in
#      cartopy/io/img_tiles.py
#   2. [Windows only] Replace variable sys.prefix with expanded
#      string in shapely/geos.py when searching for geos_c.dll
#      so it can be found by MATLAB.

import sys
import pathlib
import shutil
import re
import cartopy.io
import shapely
```

A. Danial, *Python for MATLAB Development*, https://doi.org/10.1007/978-1-4842-7223-7

```python
def fix_geos():                                            # {{{
    """

    On Windows, modify shapely/geos.py when the CONDA_PREFIX
    string is empty so that
        sys.prefix
    is hardcoded to the correct virtual environment path
    to load the geos_c.dll.
    """
    if sys.platform != 'win32':
        print('fix_geos() exit since this is not Windows')
        return

    shapely_dir = shapely.__path__

    if not shapely_dir:
        print(f"Unable to determine shapely's location, exit")
        return

    P = pathlib.Path(shapely_dir[0]) / 'geos.py'
    if not P.exists():
        print(f"{str(P)} doesn't exist, exit")
        return

    lines_in = P.read_text().split('\n')
    found_win = False
    for L in lines_in:
        if re.search(r'_lgeos\s*=.*?sys\.prefix,.*?geos_c\.dll', L):
            found_win = True
    if not found_win:
        print(f"{str(P)} does not use sys.prefix to determine "
                f"geos_c.dll path, nothing done.")
        return

    shutil.copy(str(P), f'{str(P)}.bak') # backup the original version
    print(f'Wrote backup {str(P)}.bak')
```

```
        lines_out = []
        found_win = False
        did_fix = False
        for L in lines_in:
            if did_fix:
                lines_out.append( L )
                continue
            if re.search(r"\s*==\s*'win32':", L):
                found_win = True
                lines_out.append( L )
            elif found_win and L.endswith("'geos_c.dll'))"):
                did_fix = True
                lines_out.append( f'#{L}' )
                lines_out.append( L.replace('sys.prefix', f"r'{sys.prefix}'") )
            else:
                lines_out.append(L)

    P.write_text('\n'.join(lines_out))
    print(f'Wrote updated {str(P)}')
# }}}
def fix_img_tiles():                                    # {{{
    """

    Modify cartopy/io/img_tiles.py to use
        requests.get()
    instead of
        urllib.request.Request()
    to download an image tile.
    """

    cartopy_io_dir = cartopy.io.__path__

    if not cartopy_io_dir:
        print(f"Unable to determine cartopy.io's location, exit")
        return
```

```python
    P = pathlib.Path(cartopy_io_dir[0]) / 'img_tiles.py'
    if not P.exists():
        print(f"{str(P)} doesn't exist, exit")
        return

    lines_in = P.read_text().split('\n')
    if 'import requests' in lines_in:
        print(f'{str(P)} already uses requests module, nothing done')
        return

    shutil.copy(str(P), f'{str(P)}.bak') # backup the original version
    print(f'Wrote backup {str(P)}.bak')

    New = [
        'request = requests.get(url, stream=True)',
        'request.raw.decode_content = True',
        'img = Image.open(request.raw)',
        ]

    lines_out = []
    request_start = 0
    for L in lines_in:
        if re.search(r'^import\s+cartopy\s*$', L):
            lines_out.append('import requests')
            lines_out.append(L)
        elif re.search(r'^\s+request\s+=\s*', L):
            request_start = 1
            lines_out.append(f'#{L}')
            spaces = ' ' * L.find('r') # 12
            lines_out.append(f'{spaces}{New[0]}')
            lines_out.append(f'{spaces}{New[1]}')
            lines_out.append(f'{spaces}{New[2]}')
        elif 0 < request_start < 5:
            request_start += 1
            lines_out.append(f'#{L}')
```

```python
        else:
            lines_out.append(L)
    P.write_text('\n'.join(lines_out))
    print(f'Wrote updated {str(P)}')
# }}}
def main():
    fix_geos()
    fix_img_tiles()
    pass

if __name__ == "__main__": main()
```

Index

A

Altair, 493
Anaconda, 203
Animations
    ball bouncing, 511–513
    key elements, 510, 511
    matplotlib, 510
Application program interface (API), 276
arange() function, 52
Area plots
    imagesc(), 506
    imshow(), 506, 507
        bilinear interpolation, 507, 508
        prefixes, 508, 509
astimezone() method, 150
Austin, 586–589

B

Basic linear algebra subroutines
    (BLAS), 602
Block compressed row (BSR), 411
Bokeh, 493
Bridge modules, 177
built-in scope, 52

C

Cartopy
    cartographic transformation, 514
    drawing lines, map, 529, 530
    MATLAB, 527, 528
    overlay contours, globe, 531, 532
    projection functions, 514
    shade map regions, value, 532–534
Cell arrays, 163, 165
Class
    circle, 327
    constructor method, 329
    custom exceptions, 331, 333
    custom printers, 330
    __init__() function, 328
    instances, 329
    private *vs.* public, 329, 330
    variables, 327
Cloud service, 644
Coiled's cloud
    performance, 644, 645
    running, 644
Command-line input
    argparse, 271, 273
    function arguments, 270
    sys module, 269, 270
Comma-separated value (CSV), 199, 539
Comments
    block comment, 54
    definition, 54
    docstrings, 54
Communication-intensive parallel
    program, 576
Compressed Sparse Column (CSC), 406
Compressed Sparse Row (CSR), 406
Computer Algebra System (CAS), 481
conda package manager, 62

© Albert Danial 2022
A. Danial, *Python for MATLAB Development*, https://doi.org/10.1007/978-1-4842-7223-7

T

Printed in the United States
by Baker & Taylor Publisher Services